THE ANGLO-DUTCH MOMENT

Much new research and writing on the Glorious Revolution of 1688–91 in England, Scotland, Ireland, and North America, and on the Dutch role in the Revolution, has materialized in the last few years in connection with the tercentenary celebrations of 1988 and 1989 and the various accompanying conferences, symposia, and exhibitions in Britain, the Netherlands, and the United States. There has also been a spate of associated publications. This is, however, the first large-scale work to emerge from the tercentenary commemoration, and the first to attempt to bring together the main strands of the new research and writing for the general reader and for the student, placing the English Revolution of 1688–9 for the first time in its full British, European, and American setting, and showing how fundamentally our picture of the Revolution itself, as well as the Revolutionary process of 1688–91 as a whole, is now being transformed.

Contributors: Harm Den Boer, K. N. Chaudhuri, Ian B. Cowan, D. W. Hayton, Jonathan I. Israel, Richard R. Johnson, D. W. Jones, J. R. Jones, E. H. Kossmann, John Morrill, Robert Oresko, Geoffrey Parker, P. J. A. N. Rietbergen, Hugh Trevor-Roper, Wouter Troost, Blair Worden.

THE ANGLO-DUTCH MOMENT

Essays on the Glorious Revolution and its world impact

Edited by
JONATHAN I. ISRAEL
Professor of Dutch History and Institutions, University of London

The right of the University of Cambridge to print and sell all manner of books was granted by Henry VIII in 1534. The University has printed and published continuously since 1584.

CAMBRIDGE UNIVERSITY PRESS
Cambridge
New York Port Chester
Melbourne Sydney

Published by the Press Syndicate of the University of Cambridge
The Pitt Building, Trumpington Street, Cambridge CB2 1RP
40 West 20th Street, New York, NY 10011, USA
10 Stamford Road, Oakleigh, Melbourne 3166, Australia

First published 1991

Printed in Great Britain by The Bath Press, Avon

British Library cataloguing in publication data

The Anglo-Dutch moment: essays on the Glorious Revolution
and its world impact.
1. Great Britain. Political events, 1685–1702
I. Israel, Jonathan I. (Jonathan Irvine)
941.067

Library of Congress cataloguing in publication data

The Anglo-Dutch moment: essays on the Glorious Revolution and its
world impact/edited by Jonathan I. Israel.
p. cm.
Includes index.
ISBN 0 521 39075 3
1. Great Britain – History – Revolution of 1688. 2. Great Britain –
History – Revolution of 1688 – Influence. 3. Great Britain – History –
William and Mary, 1689–1702. 4. Civilization, Occidental – Dutch
influences. 5. Dutch – Great Britain – History – 17th century.
6. Revolutions – History – 17th century. 7. Netherlands –
History – 1648–1714. I. Israel, Jonathan Irvine.
DA452.A54 1991
941.06′7 – dc20 90-36082 CIP

ISBN 0 521 39075 3 hardback

BS

Contents

Plates

Illustrations

MAPS

GENEALOGICAL TABLE

TABLES

Abbreviations

These are general abbreviations applicable throughout the volume. Other abbreviations, the use of which is confined to particular contributions, are explained in the relevant footnotes.

AGS Estado	Archivo General de Simancas, archives of the Consejo de Estado
ARH	Algemeen Rijksarchief, The Hague
SG	archives of the States General
SH	archives of the States of Holland
BIHR	*Bulletin of the Institute of Historical Research*, University of London
BL	British Library
BL MS Add.	British Library, Department of Manuscripts, section Additional Manuscripts
CJ	*Journals of the House of Commons* (London, 1803–)
CSP Col.	*Calendar of State Papers, Colonial Series*
CSP Dom.	*Calendar of State Papers, Domestic*
DNB	*Dictionary of National Biography*
GA Amsterdam PJG	Amsterdam City Archive, archives of the Portuguese Jewish Community
GA Amsterdam vroed.	Amsterdam City Archive, resolutions of the *vroedschap*
GA Haarlem	Haarlem City Archive
GA Leiden Sec. Arch	Leiden City Archive, archives of the secrétairerie
HMC	*Historical Manuscripts Commission*
IOR EIC	India Office Records, London, archives of the English East India Company
LJ	*Journals of the House of Lords* (London, 1803–)
PRO SP	Public Record Office, London, State Papers
Prov. Res.	Provisional Resolution

res.	resolution
Res. Holl.	resolution of the States of Holland in *Resolutien van de Staten van Holland* (289 vols., Amsterdam, 1789–1814)
SH	States of Holland
St.	States of
VOC	Verenigde Oost-Indische Compagnie (The United Dutch East India Company)

Editor's preface

This present collection of essays on the Glorious Revolution began life at the all-day gathering of historians at the British Academy on 10 April 1989, held to mark the tercentenary of the Revolution of 1688–9 and the Dutch involvement in it. But while it is thus a product of a temporary wave of public and media interest in the subject, and part of the small torrent of publications which have followed, in the wake of the tercentenary celebrations, it does, I believe, differ from the other tercentenary volumes of essays not only in exploring in detail the crucial Anglo-Dutch connection but in placing the English Revolution of 1688–9 in the full context of British revolutions of the years 1688–91 and their international impact, that is, alongside the offshoot revolutions in Scotland, Ireland, and the American colonies, and against the backcloth of the continental European response. The basic aim of the volume is to present the Glorious Revolution as an event in world history rather than solely an English event and, in so doing, to open up new perspectives on the English Revolution of 1688–9 itself.

I am enormously in the debt of a number of colleagues for advice and assistance in building the structure and selecting the themes of this volume. In particular I wish to thank John Morrill, Graham Gibbs, Dale Hoak, and A. G. H. Bachrach for their extremely valuable and much appreciated help in giving shape to the project as a whole. For assistance with specific themes and issues, I would like to thank John Miller, Nicholas Tyacke, John Carswell, Blair Worden, Mark Goldie, Mia Rodríguez-Salgado, and Robert Oresko. With regard to the illustrations, I would particularly like to thank Professor Bachrach for his generous help in supplying me with photographs of a number of those included and Barry Price and the William and Mary Tercentenary Trust for helping with the cost of those obtained from the various institutions mentioned below. Photographs of contemporary prints and engravings were supplied promptly and efficiently by the British Library, the Royal Library in The Hague, the Print Collection of the University of Leiden, the Jewish Historical Museum in Amsterdam, the Museum Atlas van Stolk in Rotterdam, and the Massachusetts Historical Society, and to all these I am most grateful for permission to reproduce them in this volume. Yet other illustrations were provided by Professors Chaudhuri and Johnson and of their kindness too I am most appreciative. Finally, I am also extremely grateful to Professor R. W. Davis, director of the Center for the History of Freedom of Washington University, St Louis, Missouri, for his kindness in allowing me to see, and cite ahead of publication, the volume of essays on the Glorious Revolution compiled under the auspices of the Center and the editorship of Professor J. R. Jones.

A particular problem which besets any discussion of the Glorious Revolution in its international setting is the ten-day gap in dates between those given Old Style, as was usual at the time in Britain, and those given New Style as was the case in Holland and Zeeland (but not in all the Dutch provinces) and in most of continental Europe. My solution, though it will assuredly not please everyone, has been to employ Old Style for British events, New Style when referring to events on the continent, and both styles where there is overlap or room for confusion. Thus, for example, William III is stated as having effected his landing at Torbay on 5/15 November 1688, the earlier date being Old Style.

Foreword
BY THE PRESIDENT OF THE BRITISH ACADEMY

During 1988 and 1989, the British Academy joined enthusiastically with the Royal Society and the Royal Netherlands Academy, in Amsterdam, in reflecting upon the events of 300 years earlier and upon the impact they had both at the time and in succeeding generations. As well as lecture meetings and colloquia in London and in Amsterdam during the latter part of 1988, there was a memorable full-day meeting at the British Academy on Monday 10 April 1989 when there was another opportunity to engage in discussion with some of the scholars who had played a leading role in the other events, including Professor Kossmann and Professor Israel.

Indeed, it was Jonathan Israel who organized the programme of lectures on the Glorious Revolution, on 10 April 1989, and he too who has gathered and edited the present volume of papers which have emerged, some directly, some indirectly from that event. At a point in our history when Britain becomes more and more decisively involved as a part of Europe, the collection makes a notable and timely contribution in reviewing the role that our continental neighbours – notably the Dutch – came to play in shaping our political lives and private aspirations three centuries ago.

Sir Randolph Quirk, The British Academy
May 1989

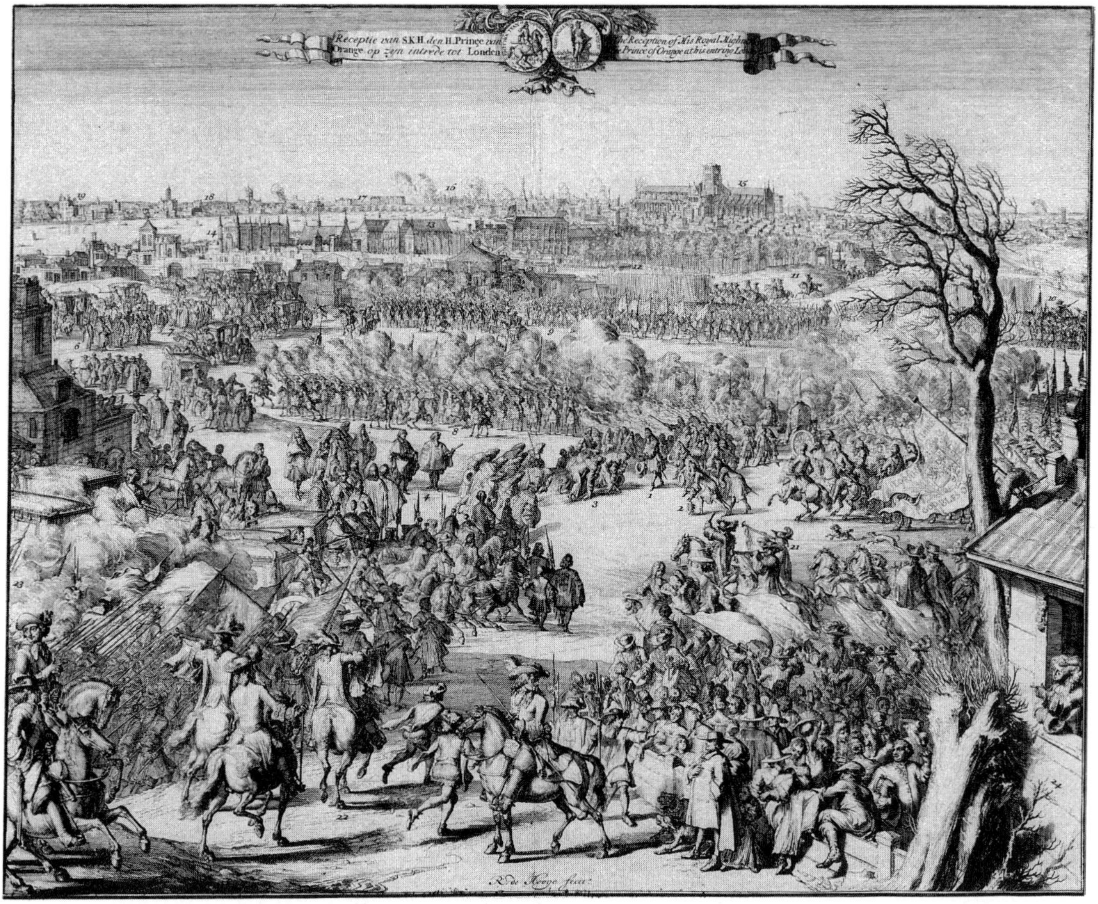

1 *The Reception of His Highness the Prince of Orange in London (18 December 1688)*. Signed 'R. de Hooge fecit'.
The Prince is the standing figure marked '1'. Westminster Abbey, the Houses of Parliament and the Thames are in the background.

General introduction

JONATHAN I. ISRAEL

'That stupendous revolution in England', as Edmund Bohun, a contemporary Tory pro-Revolution writer, called the Revolution of 1688–9, reached its astounding climax on 18 December 1688, the day the king of England, James II, left London under duress (for the second and last time) and William III, Prince of Orange and Dutch Stadholder, entered the city in triumph. It made a grand spectacle which was afterwards recorded in a magnificent engraving by the great Dutch political artist of the time, Romeyn de Hooghe, several of whose illustrations of the Glorious Revolution are included in this volume. William entered in a carriage 'attended by a great number of persons of quality in coaches and on horseback' including numerous peers of the realm and dignitaries of the city of London, the famous German general, Marshal Friedrich Hermann von Schomberg by his side, 'to the loud acclamations of a vast number of people of all sorts and ranks, the bells everywhere ringing', repeated salutes of guns being fired off, and the 'people putting oranges on the ends of their sticks to shew they were for him'. Despite persistent rain, London, after weeks of tension, turmoil, and rioting, erupted with relief and enthusiasm for the Prince, his entourage and army, the evening concluding with 'vast bonfires and such a general joy', as one eager Williamite put it, 'as can scarce be parallel'd'.[1]

The mood was euphoric. Yet there was also, unmistakably, a good deal of unease in the air. Why was the Prince of Orange entering London in this fashion? James II in private conversation at his palace two months previously, before

[1] On the Prince of Orange's triumphal entry into London, on 18 December 1688 and James II's second 'flight', see BL MS Add. 25377, fos. 204, 213v, 218–20, Terriesi to Bassetti, London, 14/24 and 17/27 Dec. 1688; *The London Courant*, no. 4 (18–22 Dec. 1688), pp. 1–2; *A True Account of His Highness the Prince of Orange's Coming to St. James, on Tuesday the 18th of December 1688* (London, 1688); [J. Whittle], *An Exact Diary of the Late Expedition of His Illustrious Highness The Prince of Orange* (London, 1689), pp. 71–2; Giovanni Gerolamo Arconati Lamberti, *Mémoires de la dernière révolution d'Angleterre* (2 vols., The Hague, 1702), I, pp. 680–7; *The Diary and Autobiography of Edmund Bohun* (London, 1853), p. 82; Robert Beddard, *A Kingdom without a King. The Journal of the Provisional Government in the Revolution of 1688* (Oxford, 1988), pp. 57–61, 180; apparently it 'rained all that day'; whilst the Prince cut across the park 'so that he came not into the city at all', the British troops of the States army, and some German regiments, marched down Fleet Street to the City and the Tower; most of the Dutch regiments remained in the western suburbs of the city; ARH SG 5916–1, fo. 3, Van Citters to SG, London, 18/28 Dec. 1688.

the great Dutch fleet had set out from Hellevoetsluis for England, had admonished a group of his courtiers: 'you will all find the Prince of Orange a worse man than Cromwell'.[2] Few of the king's subjects were yet prepared to believe that. But many were perplexed and some were anxious. After weeks of military movements and spreading disturbance in the country, the king of England, Scotland, and Ireland had been 'escorted' (as it was put) out of his own palace and capital and removed to Rochester under Dutch guard. Nor could there be the slightest doubt as to who was responsible for expelling him. Clearly it was not the people of London who, only two days before, on James' return from his abortive attempted flight, had given him an astonishingly friendly, even enthusiastic, reception: however much Englishmen might loathe the king's religion, there was a deep residual loyalty to the person of the king and respect for the sanctity of kingship which should not be underestimated. Nor had James been ejected by any representative body of the peerage or any other section of the privileged elite of English society. The plain fact was that it was the Prince of Orange acting in collusion with a tiny group of lords, some of whom were political exiles who had accompanied the invasion from Holland, who had made the king leave.

The Prince of Orange entered London through Knightsbridge, along a two-mile route lined with Dutch Blue Guards, the same troops who now stood guard at all the posts around St James's and Whitehall, and at Somerset House. Characteristically, William, who disliked crowds, took a short cut from Knightsbridge to Whitehall across St James's Park, thereby avoiding most of the popular throng and orange-waving. Furthermore, he entered, crossed the park, and installed himself in the very palace from which King James had been ejected, only hours before, accompanied not by any regiments of the English army but at the head of a formidable foreign army, that of the States General of the United Provinces. Tactfully, the Prince had placed the English and Scots regiments of the States' army, under the command of Major-General Hugh Mackay, at the head of his triumphal procession. But this could not hide the fact that before entering London, the Prince had taken it upon himself to order all the English regiments in, and around, London, including the palace guards, to vacate the city and its environs. The fact – already unpalatable to some – was that the Prince, with the full acquiescence of the peerage and the city of London, had manoeuvred himself into an almost impregnable position of strength. Not surprisingly, a good deal of muttering was to be heard even during the Prince's grand entry. Edmund Bohun who was amongst the London crowds on 18 December, hearing talk that was contrary as well as favourable, already began 'to fear we might

[2] For this, and the following references to Lord Clarendon's observations, see the *Correspondence of Henry Hyde, Earl of Clarendon, and of His Brother Laurence Hyde, Earl of Rochester, with the Diary of Lord Clarendon from 1687 to 1690* (2 vols., London, 1828), II, pp. 194, 229, 231.

divide'. The next day the signs of anxiety were still more evident: 'it is not to be imagined', noted a deeply uneasy Lord Clarendon 'what a damp there was upon all sorts of men throughout the town. The treatment the King met with from the Prince of Orange, and the manner of his being driven, as it were, from Whitehall ... moved compassion even in those who were not very fond of him'.

Many were apprehensive. But Clarendon took a gloomier view than most and failed to note the profound sense of relief felt by many, as well as the fervour felt by some. After seeing London in the hands of mobs of apprentices and other *canaille*, as Aernout van Citters, the Dutch ambassador, called them, roaming the streets of the capital, subjecting the Catholic population to a reign of terror, and sacking Catholic chapels, eminent Londoners of all sorts had become seriously alarmed during the last month at the possibility of a complete breakdown of order and government. Indeed, many Englishmen, not without reason, were fearful of a new civil war. Fear of disorder and the chronic instability likely to result from the collapse of James II's government had contributed in no small way to the alacrity with which – once James' authority was broken – the lord mayor, Corporation, and militia leaders of London, together with sundry peers, had fallen both figuratively and literally at the feet of the invading Prince.[3] They had dispatched messages to him during the latter stages of his slow march from the west country, urging him to hasten his advance on London and take over the reins of government on an interim basis, thanking him profusely for 'appearing in arms to rescue these kingdoms from slavery and popery' and promising to 'venture all that was dear to them to attain the glorious Ends of the [Prince's] Declaration', the manifesto to the English nation which William had published in Holland before setting out.

But there was more than just relief. There was every reason to hope that the country had been definitively saved from the style of royal government practised by James II – which contemporaries called 'absolute power' – and that a new political era, based on respect for constitutional procedures and proprieties, as well as privileges and charters, was about to begin. Many Englishmen were convinced that the 'late, wonderful revolution' was, constitutionally speaking, 'our deliverance', a rescue as miraculous in its virtual bloodlessness as in its astounding speed, less than fifty days having elapsed between the Dutch landings at Torbay and James' removal from London.

But even those who were most elated could not deny that the situation in the country, and most of all in London, was bizarre and totally unprecedented.

[3] BL MS Add. 25377, fos. 204, 212v, Terriesi to Bassetti, 14/24 Dec. 1688; *The Revolution Vindicated*, in *A Collection of State Tracts Publish'd on Occasion of the Late Revolution in 1688, and during the Reign of King William III* (3 vols., London, 1705), III, pp. 711–12; the Court of Aldermen of London, at its meeting on the afternoon of 16 December, narrowly rejected a Tory motion to congratulate the king on his 'gracious returne' to Whitehall, Beddard, *A Kingdom without a King*, p. 53.

Nor could King James' final admonitions to the people be ignored for, until the beginning of December, the king had continued to control the London press, including *The London Gazette*, then the only regular, licensed newspaper in the country, and had filled Britain with his complaint that the Prince and his army had 'invaded' the country, intent on an 'absolute conquest of these our kingdoms and the utter subduing and subjecting Us and all our people to a foreign power'.[4] These were challenging words that had to be answered: thus, on 20 December, when the Corporation of London 'waited on the Prince' at the Palace, to congratulate him on his triumph, their spokesman, the Whig lawyer–politician Sir George Treby replied to the talk of 'invasion' by insisting that James' ministers and advisers were 'our *true* invaders, that brake the sacred fences of our laws (and which was worst) the very constitution of our Legislature'.[5]

Treby's speech was designed to be acceptable to both moderate Tories and Whigs. For James' absolutism was detested by both Tories and Whigs and, so far, the 'Glorious Revolution' as it became known to posterity, had been based on an unprecedentedly broad consensus. At the decisive moment Whigs and Tories had joined hands to break James' power, or at least allow it to be broken. The various local risings which had taken place in the north and midlands in the wake of the Prince's invasion, and then throughout the rest of the country, had been jointly instigated by combinations of Whigs and Tories and whilst

[4] *London Gazette*, no. 2397 (5/8 Nov. 1688); *A True Copy of His Majesties Proclamation for England upon the Occasion of the Designed Invasion* (28 Sept. 1688); BL G 5302: James II's printed proclamations of 28 Sept. and 2 Nov. 1688, condemning the 'Prince of Orange and his adherents who design forthwith to invade our kingdoms'; for James' proclaiming the pending invasion of Britain to his subjects in North America, see illustration no. 15; see also the tract *Seasonable and Honest Advice to the Nobility, Clergy, Gentry, Souldiery, and other the King's Subjects, upon the Invasion of His Highness the Prince of Orange* (London, 1688) pp. 3, 8, deploring 'those who had rather see their just and merciful King dethroned and murthered, and the Dutch establish their Hogen Mogenship here, than that a Papist should live amongst them' and insisting that 'this is a Dutch Invasion for Conquest'.

[5] *The Speech of Sir George Treby Kt. Recorder of the Honourable City of London to His Highness the Prince of Orange, December the 20th 1688* (London, 1688); *The London Courant*, no. 4 (18/22 Dec. 1688), p. 2; most Tories agreed with the Whigs that James' rule was illegal,'unconstitutional', and 'arbitrary' and deeply resented what the king had done, indeed, from mid-December onwards, as Robert Beddard has shown, Tories were generally keener than Whigs on promoting the main Revolutionary manifesto, the Prince of Orange's *Declaration* being just as willing to condemn the unconstitutionality of James' rule, and the need for a 'free Parliament' to settle the nation, while hoping to use its protestations that William did not seek the throne to retain James as king, see Robert Beddard, 'The Guildhall Declaration of 11 December 1688 and the Counter-Revolution of the Loyalists', *Historical Journal*, 11 (1968), p. 409; at the opening of the Convention Parliament it was the leaders of the Tories, such as Sir Robert Seymour and Sir Thomas Clarges, who were keenest to proceed according to the Prince's *Declaration*, as was Clarendon in the Lords, see L. G. Schwoerer, 'A Jornall of the Convention at Westminster begun the 22 of January 1688/89', *BIHR*, 49 (1976), pp. 253, 256; see also John Kenyon, *Revolution Principles* (Cambridge, 1977), pp. 5–7; John Miller, 'Proto-Jacobitism? The Tories and the Revolution of 1688–9', in E. Cruickshanks and J. Black (eds.), *The Jacobite Challenge* (Edinburgh, 1988), pp. 11–12; W. A. Speck's contention that James II's style of government was not necessarily 'unconstitutional' was not one which most Tories shared at the time, see W. A. Speck, *Reluctant Revolutionaries* (Oxford, 1988), pp. 141, 153.

the Whigs were arguably the more prominent in giving a lead, the defection of most Tories had been even more crucial in engineering the rapid collapse of the king's authority. The leaders and main participants in these risings were, whether Whig or Tory, generally nobles and gentry, though much of the rest of the population had also participated in the Revolution by attending the many public meetings and readings of declarations, if not the demonstrations and anti-Catholic rioting which had quickly spread from London all over the country.

The Revolution in the north and midlands had found expression in various local declarations, such as those issued at Nottingham, Stafford, and Hull, denouncing 'arbitrary, tyrannical government' and 'popery', albeit in rather vague general terms, acceptable to both Whigs and Tories. Some of the northern declarations had been accompanied by strong protestations of loyalty to the king. Yet, for all its being broadly based, this the most thoroughly English part of the English Revolution had been remarkably slow to start and had possessed little momentum until it became clear that the Prince had gained the upper hand militarily in the south. Most of England's nobility and gentry evinced so healthy a respect for James' standing army, and the practical side of his authority, that they had preferred to sit on the fence, declining to commit themselves, for as long as they decently could without prejudicing their interests and standing. Consequently, the Revolution in the north and midlands was merely a by-product. Whether one spoke of 'rescue' or 'invasion' in the England of December 1688 no one supposed that there would, or could, have been a Revolution, or anything remotely like one, without the armed intervention of the Prince of Orange. It was the Prince who had shattered James' power and destroyed his previously considerable military might and the Prince who had now restored order and government, quelling the popular riots and turmoil. Nor, indeed, was there anyone else who could have done these things. Consequently, Sir George Treby did not exaggerate when he declared in his speech that the 'only person under Heaven that could apply this remedy was Your Highness'.

But it soon emerged that the central role of the Prince was by no means to be confined to setting the Revolution in motion, restoring law and order, and discharging the functions of regent, at the head of the national administration, on an interim basis for a month or two until the Convention Parliament (for which everyone had been calling) settled the future form of government in the country. For the consensus on which the first stage of the Glorious Revolution was based broke down even more quickly than it had arisen. For Whigs and Tories had agreed merely momentarily and with very different ends in mind. Very soon, the profound differences dividing Englishmen, of which Bohun and Lord Clarendon were aware even at the time of the Prince's entry into London, had split Parliament and surged to the fore of the nation's political consciousness.

Many Tories, it turned out, had no intention of dethroning James, or altering the form of the monarchy, and still less of tampering with the Church of England and its dominance over the religious life of the nation. Whigs, on the other hand, both moderate and radical, did wish to remodel the monarchy and weaken the ascendancy of the Church of England and many either desired, or for the sake of the rest were willing to acquiesce in, the deposition of James. Consequently, while the initial stage of the Revolution was carried through painlessly amidst a high degree of national consensus, very shortly the Glorious Revolution turned into something remarkably different – becoming one of the most deeply divisive, bitterly disputed, and passionately argued over episodes in English – not to mention the rest of British – history. In a few weeks the Revolution changed from one of consensus, a feeling of 'deliverance' shared by Whigs and Tories, into one of profound, almost hopeless division. Not the least of the oddities of the Glorious Revolution is that it has so often been praised, by 'revisionists' as well as adherents of the Whig historiographical tradition, as a triumph of English common sense, the pragmatic Revolution *par excellence*, when in fact, far from banishing ideology and philosophizing from the scene, the English Revolution of 1688–9 was arguably the most intensely ideological and philosophical of all major episodes in English history. Almost everything that happened involved bitter arguments over principles. Every step was saturated in ideology. Not only did real philosophers such as John Locke, Pierre Bayle, Gottfried Leibniz, and Samuel Pufendorf deeply ponder the Revolution but so did the great artistic and literary minds of the day, including John Dryden whose poetic outlook was rooted in Divine Right, anti-Revolution principles, and Daniel Defoe who emerged as one of the most eloquent advocates of Whig Revolution principles. But it was by no means only the great talents who endlessly preoccupied themselves with the clashes of principle generated by the Revolution. A large part of the public did too as we see from the fact that in 1689 over 2,000 political and politico-ecclesiastical tracts and pamphlets were published in England, most of them dealing with the disputed points of political, constitutional, and theological doctrine ensuing from the Revolution settlement.[6] Before the middle of the eighteenth century, only four other years were comparable to 1689 in terms of the number of English political tracts published – 1642, 1648, 1660, and 1710. But none of these compared with 1689 in terms of pamphlets arguing doctrine, principle, and ideology and 1689 was only the

[6] Mark Goldie, 'The Revolution of 1689 and the Structure of Political Argument', *Bulletin of Research in the Humanities*, 83 (1980), p. 478; on the highly complex and varied impact of the Glorious Revolution on political discourse and ideology in eighteenth-century England, see Kathleen Wilson, 'A Dissident Legacy: Eighteenth Century Popular Politics and the Glorious Revolution', in J. R. Jones (ed.) *Liberty Secured? Britain before and after 1688* (to be published as Volume II of the series 'The Making of Modern Freedom', by the Center for the History of Freedom of Washington University, St. Louis). (I am most grateful to Professor R. W. Davis for allowing me to see the text of this ahead of publication).

first of a series of years, indeed decades, characterized by a deep ideological rift permeating almost every aspect of English life and culture.

But as the political and ideological factions proliferated, from late December 1688 onwards, there remained one crucial point on which all the factions – in contrast to most modern historians – agreed: that the Prince of Orange was the central, decisive figure. Jacobite propagandists attributed the Revolution mainly to William III's intrigues and 'debauching' of the people of England with his insidious propaganda. Those moderate Tories who supported the Revolution initially but became disillusioned with it during the late winter and the spring of 1689 did so essentially because of William's elevation to (or, as some put it, acquisition of) the throne and his attitude to the Church of England. Moderate Whigs, during the early years of the new reign, regarded the new king as indispensable to their precarious position of influence. Even radical Whigs (if only for tactical reasons) felt obliged to praise William to the skies as 'our great and glorious deliverer' and constantly reminded the public that it was he 'who hath rescued us from a captivity equal to what Moses redeemed the People of Israel from'.[7] In 1698, the Scots writer Andrew Fletcher pointedly reminded both the Scots and the English that King James had 'provoked these nations to the last degree, and made his own game as hard as possible, not only by invading our civil liberties, but likewise by endeavouring to change the established religion for another ... yet notwithstanding all his mismanagement, Britain stood in need of a foreign force to save it'.[8]

By the time of the coronation of William and Mary, in April 1689, there were six major factions – which were at the same time ideological blocks – in English public life. First, there were the loyalists, the Jacobites, those who had either adhered all along to the interests of the departed monarch and his infant heir, James, the Prince of Wales, or did so now. Secondly, there were those moderate Tories who had initially supported the Revolution but who became subsequently so alienated by the dethroning of James and William's church and toleration policies that, without being open Jacobites, they were as ready to defect from the new regime as they had been from the last. Thirdly, there were those moderate Tories who, while alienated by William and his policies, nevertheless preferred to retain William and Mary as *de facto* king and queen than have back the monarch that many, or most, still regarded as *de jure* the true king. Fourthly, there were the moderate Whigs, the only group which can be described as strongly committed to the new political arrangements. Fifthly, there were the Whig radicals who were profoundly disappointed by what they regarded as the limited nature of the constitutional changes introduced

[7] John Trenchard, *An Argument Shewing that a Standing Army is Inconsistant with a Free Government, and absolutely destructive to the Constitution of the English Monarchy* (London, 1698), pp. 9, 31.

[8] Andrew Fletcher, *The Political Works* (London, 1737), p. 27.

by the Revolution and had seen this disappointment coming from the moment it had seemed likely that William would be made king in place of James: one Whig radical had urged William to refuse the Crown and 'be the glorious author of Britannique liberty as his great grandfather was of the Belgique'.[9] Finally, there was the dissenting interest, pressing for a firm toleration in religion, education, and publishing.

The public was no less deeply divided than Parliament and the Church of England, the latter now split into three ideological factions – Nonjurors who refused, on principle, to accept William and Mary as king and queen, the High Church conservatives, or 'high flyers' who opposed William's far-reaching church policies and deliberate favouring of Latitudinarian bishops, and finally the Latitudinarians who favoured a more accommodating and flexible approach on questions of dogma and ritual. Parliament, Church of England, and public alike were deeply perplexed by the intricacies and paradoxical character of the Revolution. Indeed, there was much that was baffling. Had James voluntarily deserted England, as the 'Revolution party' claimed, or, as James himself insisted, in the statement which he drew up at Rochester and subsequently published, been forcibly driven from London and compelled to leave to avoid becoming the prisoner of the Prince of Orange?[10] Was, as James maintained, the Prince of Wales his legitimate heir or, as the Revolution party claimed, was the young Prince 'suppositious'? Had the English monarchy now been made elective? If not, and if it was not for Parliament to choose England's monarch, how could Parliament declare that James had 'abdicated' when the latter insisted that he had done no such thing and put William and Mary in his place? Moreover, as the Glorious Revolution spread to the rest of Britain, and Ireland, the layers of paradox thickened. Even if James had voluntarily left England, he had not left Scotland; yet while the English Parliament opted for the obvious fiction that James had 'abdicated' as a way of cutting free of the ideological tangle in which it found itself, the Scots Parliament formally 'deposed' James from the throne of Scotland. When most of Ireland rallied to James in the spring of 1689, English and Scots as well as Irish Jacobites called it a display of loyalty to the legitimate monarch, while the Williamites dubbed it 'the Irish rebellion'.

Parliament's role in the Glorious Revolution, for all the reverence with which it has usually been treated, was, in reality, hesitant, hindered by deep division, and, at times, downright confused. 'Revolution principles' as expounded in, and by, the Convention Parliament were indeed a pragmatic mix of makeshift

[9] *Now is the Time* (London, 1689), p. 1.

[10] BL MS Add. 25377, fo. 220, Terriesi to Bassetti, London, 17/27 Dec. 1688; [Edmund Bohun], *The History of the Desertion* (London, 1689), pp. 105–6; [Jeremy Collier], *The Desertion Discuss'd* (London, 1689), pp. 2–3; and *Reflections on a Paper Intituled His Majesty's Reasons for Withdrawing Himself from Rochester* (London 1689), p. 4; Arconati Lamberti, *Mémoires* I, p. 681.

expedients, but expedients produced less by practical wisdom than ideological deadlock. Only a minority of Parliament believed that kings were accountable to the people or that tyrannical kings who subvert the rule of law might justly be resisted. A narrow majority, it is true, eventually settled for what has been called the 'unreal fiction' that King James had 'abdicated', but many of those induced to vote for 'abdication' silently objected even to this much, let alone to proposals that Parliament could lawfully depose the king. As for notions that Parliament could, or should, settle the succession to the throne in case both the new royal pair, and Mary's younger sister, Anne, should die without legitimate issue, these precipitated a deep split in the summer of 1689 and continuing dissension through the 1690s.[11] There were moderate Tories willing to accept William and Mary as *de facto* king and queen who were by no means willing to set aside the claims of James' heir, James, Prince of Wales. There were those willing to reject the Prince of Wales who were by no means willing to overlook the claims of the Catholic House of Savoy. The proposition that Parliament should, as King William himself at times seemed to desire, name Sophia of Hanover next in line, after Anne, in the event that she should die childless had, as early as the summer of 1689, caused uproar in Parliament as well as intense excitement among the princely courts of Germany, not least in the mind of the great Leibniz who, as a secretary and adviser at the Hanoverian court, was one of Germany's closest observers of the Glorious Revolution. Historians have generally praised Parliament's undoubted penchant for unreal fictions and side-stepping ideological pitfalls during the Glorious Revolution as highly impressive. But there is another way of looking at the phenomenon. According to Don Pedro Ronquillo, the Spanish ambassador in London during the Glorious Revolution, the rifts and animosities in Parliament were deep, innumerable, and implacable, for the time being a source only of chronic instability which could be offset only by the strength and dexterity of the Prince of Orange.[12]

Parts of what eventually became the modern Whig interpretation of the Glorious Revolution are nowadays rightly dismissed as incorrect, misleading, and even, here and there, absurd.[13] The idea that the people of England were united, or almost so, in dethroning James II, putting William and Mary on the throne, introducing religious toleration on the basis of parliamentary statute, or leaving

[11] Gabriel Maura Gamazo (ed.), *Correspondencia entre dos embajadores. Don Pedro Ronquillo y el Marqués de Cogolludo, 1689–1691* (2 vols., Madrid, 1951), I, pp. 274–5, 287; W. Fricke, *Leibniz und die englische Sukzession des Hauses Hannover* (Hildesheim, 1957), pp. 9–11.

[12] Maura Gamazo (ed.), *Correspondencia entre dos embajadores*, I, pp. 275–7, 333.

[13] J. P. Kenyon, *The Nobility in the Revolution of 1688*, University of Hull Inaugural lecture (Hull, 1963), pp. 1–5, 9; J. R. Jones, *The Revolution of 1688 in England* (London, 1972); J. R. Western, *Monarchy and Revolution: The English State in the 1680s* (London, 1972); Kenyon, *Revolution Principles*, pp. 6–17; E. Cruickshanks, 'Introduction' to E. Cruickshanks (ed.), *Ideology and Conspiracy: Aspects of Jacobitism, 1689–1759* (Edinburgh, 1982), pp. 4–8; J. C. D. Clark, *English Society, 1688–1832* (Cambridge, 1985), pp. 46, 144–6.

the matter of constitutional checks as it was left, is, as 'revisionists' have argued since the 1960s, seriously misleading. These things were, on the contrary, thoroughly divisive. James II's quest for 'absolute power' – that is (as the term was conventionally used in this period in all European languages) monarchial rule without effective constitutional checks – was not only perfectly feasible but close to being attained and, in a nation where Divine Right principles were widely adhered to, much more broadly acceptable than was once supposed. As it was, Jacobitism undoubtedly remained a much more powerful force in English life and sentiment at least down to the middle of the eighteenth century than the Whig historiography of the Revolution would have us believe.[14]

Yet, in the final analysis, it is arguable that it was not the Whig historians, such as Thomas Babington Macaulay and G. M. Trevelyan, but the 'revisionists' who were the more mistaken in their overall assessment of the Revolution. For all the errors in the Whig view, a great deal remains, as several contributions in this volume, especially that of John Morrill, demonstrate, which is still sound and valid. What in the end mattered most in the Whig view of the Revolution was the contention that it was *the* crucial turning-point in England's constitutional development, the moment when the strong possibility of England being turned into an absolute monarchy, as had Denmark and Sweden but a few years before, was finally removed and the decisive shift to limited, parliamentary monarchy achieved. The Revolution did make Parliament supreme; and it did transform England into a religiously and intellectually pluralistic society. 'Revisionists' have tried to argue that the major constitutional developments of the twelve years following the Revolution, culminating in the Act of Settlement of 1701, were due to a variety of circumstances and did not grow directly out of the Revolution as such. But it is evident, once the British revolutions of 1688–91 are placed in their full international context, that here the 'revisionists' were mistaken and that the great changes of the 1690s which transformed England into a 'crowned republic' in which Parliament was supreme arose directly out of, and were inherent in, the Glorious Revolution.

A central theme of this collection of essays is that there can be no adequate grasp of the English Revolution of 1688–9 without seeing it as part of a wider revolutionary process closely linked to its offshoot revolutions in Ireland, Scotland and the American colonies. The contributions by David Hayton, Ian B. Cowan, and Richard R. Johnson on the Irish, Scottish, and American revolutions of 1688–91 should thus be regarded as integrally related to those essays in the volume dealing specifically with the Revolution in England. Such an approach to British history has, as J. G. A. Pocock pointed out in a notable article published

[14] Cruickshanks, 'Introduction', pp. 4–8; Clark, *English Society, 1688–1832*, pp. 144–6; J. C. D. Clark 'On Moving the Middle Ground: The Significance of Jacobitism in Historical Studies', in Cruickshanks and Black (eds.), *The Jacobite Challenge*, pp. 177–82.

in 1975, in the past been somewhat unusual.[15] To isolate English developments from the rest of British history, as is still customary in England, is not only, as Professor Pocock urged, parochial and narrow-minded but can obscure and make nonsensical some of the deepest processes of English history itself. Setting the English Revolution in its wider British context is not just a matter of placing developments in Ireland, Scotland, and English-speaking America alongside those in England but of learning to view developments in the whole group of English-speaking nations as belonging together, closely connected parts of a single complex.

J. G. A. Pocock's plea for a new kind of British history has a special relevance to the study of the Glorious Revolution and shows up one of the main shortcomings of the discussion hitherto. The divorcing of the English Revolution of 1688–9 from the other revolutions precipitated by the events of 1688 turns out to be not just misleading but wholly inadmissible, resulting in a severely truncated view of the English Revolution itself. Yet Pocock's plea, wide-ranging and innovative in one way, is itself curiously parochial in another. If the study of English history has long suffered from the mistaken but deeply entrenched habit of separating English from the rest of British history, what of the equally unwarranted and entrenched practice of viewing English history apart from that of continental Europe, the tradition based on the premise that everything of significance which happens in England must be due to English causes? This state of mind, common to both the Whig and the 'revisionist' approaches to the Glorious Revolution has, arguably, even more seriously cramped our understanding of this great event in world history than the separating of English from the rest of British history. If it is generally true that discussing English history apart from that of Europe, a tendency built in to history teaching in English schools and universities, is deplorable and produces major distortion, this is nowhere more the case than with the Revolution of 1688–9 where outside intervention set the ball rolling and decisively shaped much of what subsequently ensued. This 'outside involvement' was, in the first place, of course, that of the Dutch Stadholder – soon to be king of England – and the States General; but, as we shall see, it included also the intervention of the Emperor Leopold, and of Brandenburg, Brunswick, Hanover, Denmark, Spain, Savoy, and other European powers, not to mention France which backed James II's efforts to recover his three crowns of England, Scotland, and Ireland.

Outside intervention played a crucial role from beginning to end in the English Revolution, and those in the rest of Britain, in the years of 1688–91, and this could not have been otherwise; for there was an insufficient basis within Britain

[15] J. G. A. Pocock, 'British History: A Plea for a New Subject', *Journal of Modern History*, 48 (1975), pp. 604–28.

itself for the kind of revolution which occurred. It is now some considerable time ago that Professor J. P. Kenyon set the wheels of 'revisionism' in motion with his demonstration that the degree of active support for the Glorious Revolution in England in 1688 had in the past been vastly exaggerated. In 1688, most of the nobles and gentry of England either remained neutral, playing no part in James II's overthrow, or else only jumped on William III's bandwagon at a late stage, out of opportunism, once it was clear that he was likely to succeed in breaking the power of his father-in-law. Kenyon pointed out that the seven supposedly leading men who signed the so-called 'Invitation' of 30 June 1688 were 'neither considerable nor representative'.[16] Sir John Dalrymple called them the 'Immortal Seven whose memories Britain can never sufficiently revere'; from the outset both the Whig party and historiographical tradition made much of this 'Invitation', for it was the indispensable fig-leaf with which to cover the embarrassing fact of the Whigs having collaborated with a foreign invasion. But it is not just the insignificance of the seven signatories which makes this the weakest and most bizarre strand in the entire Whig historiographical canon. For William had already been actively planning his invasion since April and the 'Invitation', slow in coming, was not only something he repeatedly requested but emphatically stipulated.[17] The final irony is that several of the seven, including Bishop Compton – who was not at all sympathetic to the ideals of religious toleration and liberty of conscience which today we celebrate as one of the main achievements of the Glorious Revolution – turned against the Revolution once they saw what it actually entailed.[18]

The seven were neither important in setting the Revolution in motion nor had any notion what kind of Revolution was being set in motion. It is doubtful whether anyone in England at the time had. For outside intervention not only imparted to the English Revolution of 1688–9 much of its essential impetus but also played a vital part in determining its agenda and ideology. The revolutionary programme was drawn up by Whig opposition politicians in exile in consultation with the Prince of Orange and his advisers and with the Pensionary of the States of Holland, Caspar Fagel. The programme of the Revolution was set out in a series of key documents drawn up in the weeks preceding the landing at Torbay. The most important of these were the Prince of Orange's *Declaration* to the English people of 30 September/10 October 1688, the States General's published resolution, explaining the participation of the Dutch state, of 28

[16] Kenyon, *The Nobility in the Revolution of 1688*, p. 9; see also Speck, *Reluctant Revolutionaries*, p. 220.

[17] Jones, *The Revolution of 1688*, p. 250; see also N. Japikse, *Prins Willem III, de Stadhouder-koning* (2 vols., Amsterdam, 1930–3), II, pp. 236–9; John Carswell, *The Descent on England* (London, 1969), pp. 145, 150.

[18] The case of Danby is well known; on Compton, see E. F. Carpenter, *The Protestant Bishop, being the Life of Henry Compton, 1632–1713, Bishop of London* (London, 1956), pp. 121, 161–2, 169.

October 1688, and the secret resolution of the States of Holland on English affairs of 29 September 1688. The Whig opposition politicians in exile were by no means at one with the Prince and Pensionary on all points. But there was full agreement on the most essential point: James II had subverted the 'lawes, liberties and customs established by the lawfull authority' in England, 'lawfull authority' being defined as the 'joint concurrence of King and Parliament'. The purpose of the planned invasion, the architects of the Revolution assured both the English people and continental Europe, was to crush the 'absolute power' (*absolute macht*) of James II and restore the rule of law through the convening, and under the supervision, of a free and lawful Parliament.

Much the most widely circulated (and also arguably the most crucial) single political document of the English Revolution of 1688–9 was the Prince of Orange's *Declaration*,[19] the full significance of which is almost always missed by historians. According to some scholars, this key text was compiled on the basis of drafts and advice submitted to William and his advisers at The Hague by members of the Whig opposition to James. But it is wrong to regard the Prince's *Declaration* as merely a compendium of Whig views.[20] In fact, it was written by Caspar Fagel, the leading figure in the States of Holland and William's right-hand man in the Dutch government, and was translated into English by Gilbert Burnet.[21] Furthermore, the text was deliberately withheld from the Whig leadership in exile in Holland, until the last possible moment before the invasion and with good reason, since the Prince, Fagel, and Hans Willem Bentinck (in whose rooms the stocks of copies were kept sealed up) knew perfectly well that many Whigs would not like its contents.[22] Of course, the fact that the *Declaration* was a translation, and had a good deal of Dutch calculation behind it, was not revealed either at the time or subsequently. To print the manifesto quickly and in unprecedented quantity, the Dutch government employed several different presses simultaneously, at The Hague, Amsterdam, and Rotterdam, while imposing conditions of strict secrecy. The pamphlet's subsequent distribution was a masterpiece of co-ordinated propaganda which ensured that the *Declaration* had an exceptional, indeed enormous, impact not only in England and the United Provinces but generally. There were altogether some twenty-one different editions of the Prince's *Declaration* in 1688 and over the next few years

[19] *The Declaration of His Highness William Henry, By the Grace of God Prince of Orange, etc. Of the Reasons Inducing him to appear in Armes in the Kingdome of England* (The Hague, 1688).

[20] L. G. Schwoerer, 'Propaganda in the Revolution of 1688–89', *American Historical Review*, 82 (1977), p. 852.

[21] Burnet states that the *Declaration* 'was brought to me to be put in English', Gilbert Burnet, *History of His Own Time* (6 vols., Oxford, 1833), III, p. 300; Japikse, *Prins Willem III*, II, p. 251; see also Th. B. Macaulay, *The History of England from the Accession of James the Second*, ed. C. H. Firth (6 vols., London, 1913–15), II, p. 1103.

[22] BL MS Add. 41816, fo. 251, d'Albeville to Middleton, The Hague, 21 Oct. 1688; the text was withheld also in England, until the last possible moment; see [Bohun], *History of the Desertion*, p. 38.

there were to be numerous reprints in a variety of topical works.[23] Eight of the editions of 1688 were in English, the rest in French, German, and Dutch. The text was subsequently rendered into still more languages including a Latin version made at Berlin by Samuel Pufendorf.

The Prince of Orange's *Declaration* was one of the greatest and most decisive propaganda coups of early modern times. Through his agents, Bentinck, who master-minded its distribution, arranged for stocks of copies to be transported to, and concealed, in key locations all over England and Scotland and then released on the eve of the Prince's invasion.[24] Distribution was preceded by a campaign of rumour and reports 'with so much art and cunning spread ... that nothing could be more eagerly desired, than a sight of the Prince of Orange's Declaration'.[25] James' ministers were aware of the crucial importance of the manifesto even before they managed to get hold of a copy. On its release, the government first reacted by trying to suppress it, proclaiming that members of the public were not to 'publish, disperse, repeat or hand about the said treasonable Declaration'.[26] Finding this to be useless, the government next tried to discredit its 'specious and plausible pretences', claiming that the *Declaration* proved that the Prince's

> designs in the bottom do tend to nothing less than an absolute usurping of our crown and royal authority as may fully appear by his assuming to himselfe in the said Declaration the regal style, requiring the peers of the realm, spiritual and temporal, and all other persons of all degrees, to obey and assist him in the execution of his Designs.[27]

Here James made a highly pertinent point. The Prince of Orange claimed to have come to restore lawful government, constitutional procedures, charters, and privileges but insisted at the same time that everyone from the peerage downward in Britain was required to assist him (and his Dutch army) in effecting this imposed restoration.

Finally, in desperation, the king authorized his propagandists to reprint the Prince's *Declaration* under challenging titles and prefaces replete with what the Williamites dismissed as 'frivolous animadversions upon it'.[28] The impact of the manifesto in other words was so great that ultimately the only way that

[23] Schwoerer, 'Propaganda in the Revolution', p. 854; L. G. Schwoerer, *The Declaration of Rights, 1689* (Baltimore, 1981), pp. 115–16.

[24] [Bohun], *History of the Desertion*, pp. 35, 73, 106, 127–9; Abel Boyer, *The History of King William the Third* (3 vols., London 1702), I, pp. 229–30.

[25] *The Prince of Orange His Declaration: shewing the Reasons why he Invades England with a short Preface, and some modest remarks on it* (London, 1688), p. 3.

[26] BL G 5302 (Proclamations). Proclamation of James II, Whitehall, 2 Nov. 1688; Boyer, *History*, I, p. 23.

[27] *The London Gazette*, no. 2397 (5–8 Nov. 1688); *Some Reflections upon His Highness the Prince of Orange's Declaration* (Edinburgh, 1688), pp. 2–4.

[28] Boyer, *History*, I, p. 23; *Some Reflections*, pp. 1–13; *The Prince of Orange His Declaration*, pp. 1–3.

the royal government could respond was to escalate discussion of its contentions still further. Soon the text was circulating also in Ireland, the West Indies, and the English colonies in North America, despite the success of James' governor of New England in seizing the first batch of copies to reach Boston. In England, even at court and amongst the royal family, the excitement caused by the Prince's *Declaration* was intense. Clarendon mentions that he read a copy which he borrowed from Princess Anne who had borrowed it from the king! In London, reportedly, one of Bentinck's most effective distributors was the Spanish ambassador.[29]

In England outside London there is an important sense in which the distribution and reading of the Prince of Orange's *Declaration* was the very essence of the Glorious Revolution. On the Prince's entry into Exeter, the first town secured by the invading army, the canons and clergy were 'commanded' by Gilbert Burnet in the Prince's name to assemble at the cathedral, sing a *Te Deum* and listen whilst Burnet 'read aloud the Prince's Declaration and reasons for this his expedition'.[30] On 6 December, following the seizure of Durham by the Williamite gentry of the north-east, Lord Lumley read out the Prince's *Declaration* at Durham Castle in the presence of most of the gentry in the county.[31] At Leeds, the Revolution consisted in the 'reading in the Moot-hall of the Prince of Orange's Declaration'. When the governor of Plymouth, the earl of Bath, having held the town against the invaders for five weeks, decided to defect, he justified himself by having the Prince's *Declaration* read out to the assembled town's people.[32] The Glorious Revolution in Cornwall consisted of the justices and gentry of the county being summoned by the earl of Bath to Saltash, near Plymouth, 'where he read the Prince's Declaration to them and they subscrib'd to the Association'. Chester was seized by the Williamite county militia on 14 December: they disarmed James' military governor and the regular regiment stationed there, along with two troops of Irish dragoons, 'then they read the Prince's *Declaration* and declared for him'.[33] The next day Lord Delamere seized Manchester and ordered the Prince's manifesto to be read out publicly there. At Oxford the Glorious Revolution consisted of a trumpet being blown at Carfax and the Prince's *Declaration* 'being read openly to the multitude by Lord Lovelace'; that night the scholars and inhabitants of Oxford, in a state of great agitation,

29 [Bohun], *History of the Desertion*, p. 35.

30 *The Expedition of His Highness the Prince of Orange for England* (1688), in *Harleian Miscellany*, 1 (London, 1744), p. 438.

31 For the details about Durham, see W. A. Speck, 'The Revolution of 1688 in the North of England', *Northern History*, 25 (1989), p. 194; on Leeds, see *The Diary of Ralph Thoresby* (2 vols., London, 1830), I, p. 188.

32 For Plymouth, see Arconati Lamberti, *Mémoires*, I, p. 624; for Cornwall, see N. Luttrell, *A Brief Historical Relation of State Affairs from September 1678 to April 1714* (6 vols., Oxford, 1857), I, p. 474.

33 For Chester, see *The London Courant*, no. 4 (18/22 Dec. 1688), p. 1; for Manchester, see Arconati Lamberti, *Mémoires*, I, p. 596.

pulled down Magdalen College Bridge lest James' dragoons should try to break into the city.[34] At King's Lynn, Henry Howard, seventh duke of Norfolk, sent in the county militia in support of James but then, like many other noblemen (and despite his family's well-known Catholic traditions and connections), seeing how things were going, changed sides, declaring to the assembled gentry of the vicinity that he was acting 'in concurrence with the lords and gentlemen in the North, and pursuant to the Declaration of the Prince of Orange'. At his first meeting with the peers, after entering London, on 21 December, Van Citters reported to the States General, the Prince 'exhibited' a copy of his *Declaration*, asking them how its aims should be achieved.

When the mayor and aldermen of Bristol came to London to pay court to the Prince of Orange at St James's Palace, early in January 1689, they promised in their speech to 'stand by His Highness in maintaining His Declaration'.[35] At the opening of the Convention Parliament, Tory MPs were particularly conspicuous in promoting the Prince's *Declaration* and the entire text was set down in the *House of Commons Journal.* So great was the impact of the Prince's *Declaration* that it became central to both Jacobite and French propaganda to argue that the people of England had been loyal to their king until their minds were corrupted by reading the Dutch Stadholder's pernicious manifesto.[36] Pro-Revolution Tory writers, such as Edmund Bohun (1645–99) agreed that 'wherever the Prince's Declaration was read, it conquered all that saw or heard it; and it was to no purpose to excite men to fight against their own interest, and to destroy what was more dear to them than their lives'.[37] Right through the 1690s this document continued to attract enormous attention, vastly more than Parliament's Declaration of Rights, and it remained at the heart of the bitter ideological and propaganda struggle which continued through the decade. Dozens of tracts and pamphlets cited and debated it and several reprinted the complete text. According to Defoe, Dissenters generally deeply revered the *Declaration*.[38] Those people disillusioned with the Revolution complained that its promises had not been lived up to. Jacobite writers ceaselessly attacked the manifesto as a well of hypocrisy and 'parcel of sham pretences', insisting that its high-sounding phrases were nothing but a cover for the Prince's diabolical

[34] For Oxford, see A. Clark (ed.), *The Life and Times of Anthony Wood, Antiquary of Oxford, 1632–1695* (5 vols., Oxford, 1891–1900), III, pp. 286–7; for King's Lynn, see J. M. Robinson, *The Dukes of Norfolk* (Oxford, 1982), pp. 144–5.

[35] *The London Mercury or, The Orange Intelligence*, no. 9 (7–10 Jan. 1689).

[36] *The Dutch Design Anatomized, or A Discovery of the Wickedness and Unjustice [sic] of the Intended Invasion* (London, 1688), p. 26; *Esprit politique ou l'histoire en abrégé de la vie et des actions de Guillaume III de Nassau, Roi de la Grande Bretagne* (Amsterdam, 1695), p. 137; *The Late King James's Manifesto answer'd Paragraph by Paragraph* (London, 1697), p. 10.

[37] [Bohun], *History of the Desertion*, p. 72; see also N. Chevalier, *Histoire de Guillaume III* (Amsterdam, 1692), p. 77.

[38] Daniel Defoe, *A New Test of the Church of England's Honesty* (London, 1704), p. 8.

ambition, and ridiculing its claims that he had come to defend the Church of England, claiming that William had done more to weaken the Church of England, with his concessions to Catholics and Dissenters, than had King James.[39] Williamites cited the text in the Stadholder-king's defence, maintaining that his pro-Catholic policy was consistent with the principles set out in the *Declaration* which, in turn, were consistent with the principles of toleration set out in Caspar Fagel's exposition of the Prince of Orange's views on religion in England contained in his famous open letter of 1687 on the Test Acts.[40]

It has been suggested that, through his *Declaration*, William boxed himself in in such a way that he was unable to avoid acquiescence in Parliament's Declaration of Rights, a formal statement of the previous regime's invasion of Englishmen's liberties for which the Prince himself had called in his so-called *Second Declaration*, the addendum to the first also published at The Hague.[41] But this is not quite exact. It is true that once he had brought Parliament to the point of offering him the Crown, the Prince was anxious to retain as much monarchical power as possible, that he had a hand in the process of weakening earlier drafts of the Declaration of Rights, and that he refused to have it put to him as a set of conditions upon which he was being offered the Crown.[42] There is indeed truth in the view that William was a prince of 'authoritarian stamp'. But in William's case authoritarian tendencies were the result of long practice in the art of bending representative assemblies to do his bidding. For he was a prince who perfectly understood the value, wherever large resources and revenues were needed, of close collaboration with parliaments. Admittedly, it is unlikely (whatever he asserted in his *Declaration*) that the Prince had any particular reverence for constitutional monarchy as such. But as long as its terms were moderate, he had no interest in seeking to prevent or avoid the Declaration of Rights for which he himself had called. On the contrary, during the opening weeks of 1689, the Prince was anxious to clinch the Crown of England with all haste, preserve unity in Parliament and the country as far as was feasible and, above all, coax England into coming promptly to the aid of the United Provinces. And, if he was to achieve all this, in a matter of weeks, all the time retaining the confidence of the Dutch regents, he had no alternative but

39 [Sir James Montgomery], *Great Britain's Just Complaint for Her Late Measures Present Sufferings, and the Future Miseries she is expos'd to* (n.p., 1692), pp. 16–18; [William Anderton], *Remarks upon the Present Confederacy and Late Revolution in England* (London, 1693), pp. 18–20; *The Late King James's Manifesto answer'd*, pp. 40–2.

40 *The Late King James's Manifesto answer'd*, pp. 42–3.

41 Schwoerer, *Declaration of Rights*, pp. 17–18.

42 BL MS Add. 25377, fo. 326v, Terriesi to Panciatichi, London, 11/21 Feb. 1689; Nicholaas Witsen, 'Uittreksels uit het bijzonder verbaal nopens de deputatie en ambassade daarop gevolgd, in Engeland (1688)', in Jacobus Scheltema, *Geschied- en Letterkundig Mengelwerk* (6 vols., Amsterdam and Utrecht, 1817–36), III, p. 141; R. J. Frankle, 'The Formulation of the Declaration of Rights', *Historical Journal*, 17 (1974), pp. 276–7; see also J. P. Kenyon, *Robert Spencer, Earl of Sunderland, 1641–1702* (London, 1958), p. 244.

continually to emphasize his willingness to submit to broad constitutional limitations and parliamentary control of his finances. In theory he might have ignored the undertakings given in his *Declaration*, but he could not discard his own (and the States General's) promise to 'restore' constitutional monarchy in England, making Parliament the final arbiter, without undermining his position in the United Provinces, depriving the Republic of English assistance (which, from the Dutch point of view, was the point of the whole exercise) and simultaneously generating a great deal more opposition in Britain than he faced already. Consequently, on approaching London in December 1688, and once ensconced in St James's Palace, and formally entrusted with the interim administration of the country by the peers, the Prince made a point of continually reminding everyone of the constitutional priorities set out in his *Declaration*. During the Convention Parliament's debate over how to settle the Crown, the Prince's supporters deliberately spread the notion that 'his unchangeable adherence to what he promised in his *Declaration* shews with what sacredness he will observe his oath as a king'.[43]

William set about obtaining what he needed from England by giving in exchange the parliamentary form of monarchy which some Englishmen had been pressing for. A week after entering London, the Prince convened a meeting of former members of Charles II's Parliaments, together with aldermen and the common council of London, so that they should 'advise the best manner how to pursue the Ends of my Declaration'.[44] He readily accepted their advice that he should summon a Convention Parliament to settle the affairs of the nation. When the Prince opened the Convention Parliament on 22 January, he urged Parliament to move with all possible haste so that the 'Ends of my Declaration will be attained'.[45] William adopted the same approach in setting the Scots Revolution of 1689 in motion. On 7 January he summoned such Scots lords and gentlemen as were at hand, in London, to ask 'what is to be done for the securing the Protestant religion and restoring your laws and liberties, according to my Declaration',[46] a reference to his separate manifesto for Scotland which was, however, a direct offshoot from, and repeats many of the points in, his English *Declaration*.

43 [R. Ferguson], *A Brief Justification of the Prince of Orange's Descent into England and of the Kingdoms Late Recourse to Arms* (London, 1689), p. 36.

44 *Divers of the Members of the Parliaments in the Reign of the Late Charles the Second ... pursuant to His Highness the Prince of Orange's desire, meeting at St James the 26 December 1688* (London, 1688), p. 1; Abraham van Poot, *Engelands Gods-dienst en vryheid hersteldt door syn Hoogheyt den Heere Prince van Oranje* (2 vols., Amsterdam, 1689), I, p. 167; *CJ*, X, p. 5.

45 *An Historical Account of the Memorable Actions of the most Glorious Monarch William III king of England* (London, 1689), p. 143; the letters sent out to the localities over the Prince's name calling the elections for the Convention explain that he was doing so 'heartily desiring the Performance of what we have in our said Declaration expressed', see *CJ*, X, p. 8.

46 *His Highness the Prince of Orange His Speech to the Scots Lords and Gentlemen* (London, 1689), p. 1; Van Poot, *Engelands Gods-dienst en vryheid hersteldt*, I, p. 205.

The Declaration of Rights drawn up by the Convention and read to William and Mary at the ceremony at which they were offered the Crown, at the Banqueting House, on 13 February 1689, was thus not a set of conditions but a fulfilling of what the Prince himself had previously stipulated was needed. The Declaration of Rights was not a law but a method of legitimating the revolutionary content of the Prince's *Declaration*.[47] It is scarcely surprising, therefore, that, in part, the Declaration of Rights is merely a reiteration of the content of the Prince's manifesto insofar as it applied to England. It set the seal on William's promise, proclaimed from The Hague, that English government would henceforth be by the 'joint concurrence of King and Parliament' and that he would 'concurr in everything that may procure the peace and happiness of the nation which a free and lawfull Parliament shall determine'.[48]

Like the Prince's *Declaration*, Parliament's Declaration of Rights condemned James' use of the suspending and dispensing powers as illegal and laid down that the 'levying of money for, or to the use of the crowne by pretence of the prerogative without grant of Parliament for longer time or in other manner than the same is or shall be granted is illegal'.[49] On the need for 'free' elections, the Prince's *Declaration* is the more specific, stating that 'all elections of Parliament men ought to be made with an entire liberty without any sort of force or the requiring the electors to choose such persons as shall be named to them'.[50] To demonstrate his adherence to this part of his *Declaration*, the Prince issued orders from St James's Palace on 5 January that army officers were to remove their troops from localities where elections for the Convention were in progress, 'so that elections may be carried on with greater freedom and without any colour of force or restraint'.[51]

It is true that the Declaration of Rights goes further than the Prince's *Declaration* on one or two points, notably the stipulation that 'raising or keeping a standing army within the kingdome in time of peace unlesse it be with the consent of Parliament is against the law'.[52] Nevertheless, in most respects the Prince's *Declaration* is a better guide to the actual content of the English Revolution, and the way that it was perceived abroad, than Parliament's Declaration of Rights – as well as being, until the beginning of the eighteenth century, much the better known document. In the first place, the Prince's *Declaration* roundly maintained, as Parliament's did not, that England had an 'ancient constitution'

[47] *The Declaration of His Highness William Henry . . . England*, p. 8, the addendum or 'Second Declaration'; *CJ*, X, p. 23; see also John Morrill, 'The Sensible Revolution', *infra*, pp. 89–91.
[48] *The Declaration of His Highness William Henry . . . England*, pp. 3–4.
[49] Jones, *The Revolution of 1688*, p. 318; J. P. Kenyon, *Stuart England* (London, 1985), pp. 276–7; Schwoerer, *Declaration of Rights*, p. 296.
[50] *The Declaration of His Highness William Henry . . . England*, p. 6.
[51] *The London Gazette*, no. 2416 (3–7 Jan. 1689), p. 1.
[52] Jones, *The Revolution of 1688*, p. 318.

which James II had subverted.[53] Secondly, whilst the Prince's *Declaration* does not speak of a contract between king and people, or mention the accountability of kings to their subjects, it does justify, as Parliament's Declaration did not, the use of force against tyrannical monarchs, albeit in a rather round-about way, maintaining that the 'publicke peace and happiness of any state or kingdome can not be preserved, where the Lawes, Liberties and Customs established by the lawfull authority in it, are openly transgressed and annulled'.[54] On the continent (not surprisingly), the essence of the English Revolution (though Parliament never indicated any such thing) was its justification of armed resistance to tyrannical kings. Then, the Prince's *Declaration* indicates, as Parliament's does not, that the liberty of conscience and freedom of worship which the Revolution was to establish was to apply to Catholics as well as to Dissenters.[55] Accordingly, during the toleration debate of the spring of 1689, proponents of toleration were able to point to the Prince's *Declaration* as a means of exerting additional pressure on Parliament.[56] Parliament undoubtedly opposed toleration for Catholics and the Toleration Bill assuredly makes no provision for Catholic worship. But in the sense in which the English Revolution is being defined here, as partly shaped by outside intervention, there can be no doubt that toleration for Catholics and Catholic worship was an integral part of it. The Prince's *Declaration* states that there would be toleration for Catholics; both the Prince and the States General gave repeated assurances – both before and after their invasion of Britain – to the emperor, pope, king of Spain, and the Catholic princes of Germany that they would ensure that Catholic worship in England was placed on the same tolerated basis as in the United Provinces.[57] And, as we shall see, that is precisely what the Revolution achieved.

In addition, the Prince's *Declaration* is more emphatic than Parliament's that all charters and privileges 'illegally' suspended or cancelled by King James would be restored. For this reason, it was the Prince's *Declaration* which was the more relevant document to the New Englanders in their subsequent struggle to obtain the restoration of their former colonial charters, abolished by the late Stuart monarchy.[58] Then, the Prince's *Declaration* has more to say than does Parliament's about the independence of the judiciary and the need for the latter to

[53] *The Declaration of His Highness William Henry . . . England*, pp. 1–3.

[54] Ibid., p. 3.

[55] Ibid., p. 7; Defoe, *A New Test of the Church of England's Honesty*, p. 8; *The Late King James's Manifesto answer'd*, pp. 40–3; see also the *Vertoog inhoudende dat d'expeditie van sijn Hoogheyt den Heer Prince van Oranjen in Engelant geensints op een oorlog van religie tegen de Rooms-Catholycken is aengesien* (Amsterdam, 1689), p. 5.

[56] [J. Humfrey], *King William's Toleration: being an Explanation of that Liberty of Religion which may be Expected from His Majesty's Declaration* (London, 1689), p. 15.

[57] *Vertoog inhoudende dat d'expeditie van sijn Hoogheyt*, pp. 3–5; Gregorio Leti, *Teatro Belgico o vero ritratti historici, chronologici, politici, e geografici delle Sette Provincie Unite* (2 vols., Amsterdam, 1690), I, p. 363; *The Late King James's Manifesto answer'd*, pp. 32, 40–3.

[58] D. S. Lovejoy, *The Glorious Revolution in America* (Middleton, Conn., 1972), pp. 279–80.

be free from interference by the Crown, a principle which William was later at some pains to uphold. Finally, given that the Parliament of England could not legislate for Scotland and that its powers in Ireland were a matter of dispute, the Prince's *Declaration* proclaims in a way that the Declaration of Rights could not the intimate connection between the Revolution in England and the offshoot revolutions in Scotland and Ireland.

The Prince of Orange's manifesto was the most important statement of the programme of the Glorious Revolution. But it was not the only one compiled outside of England which has a claim on our attention. The resolutions of the States of Holland and States General of the United Netherlands relating to English affairs of September and October 1688 are of great relevance also. This is not only because these documents give the reasons – the real reasons in the case of the secret resolutions and the ostensible ones in the published States General resolution of 18/28 October 1688 – why the Dutch Republic was carrying out an invasion of England. The significance of these statements for a correct understanding of the Glorious Revolution stems also from the fact that behind the scenes the Dutch regents continued to exert a good deal more influence over what was happening in Britain (and also in Ireland) after the early stages of the Revolution were completed, and the Convention Parliament had settled the throne, than has hitherto been realized. This continuing Dutch leverage in Britain arose in the first place from the States' links with their Stadholder who was now king of England, Scotland, and Ireland. This was more than just a matter of allegiance and sentiment. William III's entire military and diplomatic stance on the continent was crucially dependent on a continuing close collaboration with the States of Holland, including Amsterdam, and this alone accorded the regents a far from negligible weight in British affairs down to the end of the Nine Years War, in 1697. But there was an additional reason why the Dutch government continued to wield an appreciable influence in England for several years after 1688: the pro-Revolution 'party', as it was called, in Parliament and the country, like William and his advisers, were acutely aware that the Revolution in Britain and Ireland at any rate down to late 1691 was fragile and insecure, especially in 1689. For several years the English army was not considered altogether reliable. The threat of a Jacobite counter-Revolution was, or seemed, very real. Consequently, for several years a substantial Dutch army was kept in Britain at the expense of the English tax-payer and at the wish of Parliament as well as of the new king and his advisers. The States General was more than willing to bolster and protect the new regimes in England, Scotland, and Ireland in the years 1689–91 but only under certain conditions.

The Dutch secret resolutions on Britain are discussed in detail below (see pp. 118–20). But it is pertinent here to include a few words about the States General's important published resolution drawn up in The Hague on 28 October

1688,[59] a text translated into French, German, and English and disseminated by the, at this time, extremely energetic Dutch diplomatic service, in a matter of days, in Vienna, Madrid, Rome, Brussels, and other European capitals.[60] This document was intended to persuade European courts that the Dutch had no objectives of their own in Britain but were merely making their army and navy available to the Prince of Orange so that he might overthrow James' arbitrary government and establish 'un Parlement libre et légitime' which would end England's political difficulties and give 'au peuple une entière assurance que les loix, droits et privilèges de leur royaume, ne seront plus violez ny revoquez à l'avenir'. The purpose of this text was to reassure the Republic's potential Catholic allies on the continent that the aim of the invasion was not to dethrone England's legitimate monarch, or alter the legitimate succession, 'et moins encore pour exterminer la religion catholique, ou pour la persécuter'.[61]

When the States General drew up this resolution, the armies of France and the emperor were already engaging in hostilities on the Rhine and the French declaration of war on the United Provinces was less than one month away. In effect, the Nine Years War had already begun, though England was not to enter the struggle until the following May. The connections between the Glorious Revolution and the Nine Years War – or War of the League of Augsburg – are indeed very close and have also been the ground for a good deal of confusion particularly amongst 'revisionist' historians. During the 1690s the balance between king and Parliament in England was fundamentally and irrevocably altered in favour of the latter. Parliament and the various parliamentary committees which were now established became a regular partner in the routine government and administration of the country. Parliament's role in national life now became constant rather than, as before, occasional. Where Charles II and James II had effectively ruled England without Parliament between 1681 and 1688, from 1689 Parliament met every year, the longest gap between parliamentary sessions during William III's reign being ten months. The immediate reasons for the change are not in dispute. In May 1689 England entered the Nine Years War, engaging in a major way in a great European conflict for the first time since the fifteenth century. The financial implications of this were immense. Almost overnight England was transformed from being one of the

[59] *Resolution contenant les raisons qui ont meues leurs Hauts Puissants Seigneurs d'assister son Altesse allant en personne en Angelterre avec de vaissaux et de la milice* (28 Oct. 1688) (The Hague, 1688); *Engeland Beroerd onder de regering van Iacobus de II en hersteldt door Willem en Maria, Prins en Princesse van Orangie* (Amsterdam, 1689), pp. 245–6; Gregorio Leti, *La Monarchie Universelle de Louys XIV* (2 Vols., Amsterdam, 1689), II, pp. 609–15.

[60] ARH SG 7084, Hulst to SG, Brussels, 3 Nov. 1688; ibid., Battier to SG, Madrid, 2 Dec. 1688; *The Late King James's Manifesto answer'd*, p. 32.

[61] *Resolution contenant les raisons*, p. 5; J. Tronchin de Breul, *Lettres sur les matières du temps* (3 vols., Amsterdam, 1688–90), I, pp. 130–3; Samuel Pufendorf, *De Rebus gestis Friderici Tertii Electoris Brandenbvrgici* (1688–1690) (Berlin, 1784), pp. 88–9.

most lightly taxed countries in Europe to being the second most heavily taxed after the Dutch Republic. Before 1689, royal revenue during the 1680s amounted to less than £2m per year and was raised largely without reference to Parliament. Between 1689 and 1702, the figure fluctuated between £5m and £6m mostly voted by Parliament.[62] Furthermore, public accounts and expenditure were now closely scrutinized by parliamentary committee. In addition, an array of new public credit facilities and mechanisms, including the now established Bank of England, evolved – all guaranteed by Parliament. During the 1690s, this so-called 'Financial Revolution' made a considerable contribution to the emergence of England as a major European power. None of this is controversial. But the fact that these developments grew out of England's new role as a continental power, committed to a large-scale war effort, has been cited by 'revisionist' historians to suggest that they were therefore merely a by-product of the Glorious Revolution and not integral to it.[63] It is a mistake that stems from viewing Parliament as the main, or sole, author of the Revolution. For if, as here, the Revolution is seen as having been shaped in part by outside forces the distinction between the Revolution and the ensuing war totally ceases to apply. The principal reason propounded by the States of Holland and States General for the invasion of England in 1688, in the secret resolutions, was that by this means the Republic would be able to turn England round against France and obtain large-scale English support in the European struggle which was now commencing. English involvement in the Nine Years War, against France, in other words, was not incidental to but inherent in the Glorious Revolution which has rightly been seen as in some respects a 'War of the English Succession'.

The Glorious Revolution in England, then, was profoundly divisive but was also a pivotal constitutional and ideological turning-point. Whether one viewed the event from a Divine Right perspective, adhered to by many moderate Tories who accepted William and Mary as *de facto* monarchs, as well as Jacobites, from a Catholic, dissenting, or moderate Whig view-point, or in terms of the republican notions of mixed government with a minimum of kingship, favoured by the Whig radical intellectuals, analysed in Blair Worden's contribution, everyone in England in the 1690s – and for most of the next century – agreed that the events of 1688–9 constituted, as Sir James Montgomery put it, 'a great revolution' which exercised the hearts and minds of all the inhabitants of the country. But the English Revolution was also important as an impulse, a potentially liberating upheaval, for Scotland, Ireland, the American colonies, and

[62] P. G. M. Dickson, *The Financial Revolution in England, 1688–1756* (London, 1967), p. 46.

[63] Jones, *The Revolution of 1688*, p. 190; Geoffrey Holmes, 'Introduction', in Geoffrey S. Holmes (ed.), *Britain after the Glorious Revolution, 1689–1714* (London, 1969), p. 8; Jennifer Carter, 'The Revolution and the Constitution', in Holmes (ed.), *Britain after the Glorious Revolution*, pp. 39–40, 55; Kenyon, *Stuart England*, pp. 278–9.

indeed for others including French Protestants and Caribbean colonists. Some of the wider ramifications of the English Revolution were already evident, before the landing at Torbay, from the barrage of Williamite and Dutch government propaganda pouring out of the United Provinces. In his *Declaration* to the English nation, the Prince of Orange also discussed the affairs of Scotland and Ireland and, at the same time that he issued his *Declaration* to the English, issued a separate *Declaration* addressed to the Scots.[64] In the latter the Prince offered not only a Scotland free in the future 'from all hazard of Popery and arbitrary power' but a separate settling of Scotland's affairs under the supervision of the Scots Parliament, implying a revival of the Scots Parliament and of Scotland's separate constitutional life. It was a change to take place without the English or English Parliament having any role. The Prince (and his army) were the only outside factors which were to play any part in this promised Scots Revolution. The reality of the Revolution in Scotland, for many Scots, proved profoundly disappointing. But it was not the English who were blamed for this – at least not until the late 1690s. Earlier, the complaint was that William had 'failed to fulfil what he had promised in his *Declaration*'.[65]

In his *Declaration*, the Prince promised the Scots an autonomous constitutional monarchy; in the case of Ireland, however, what he promised was to settle the country on the basis of the 'Protestant and British interest' and strive to 'procure such an establishment in all Three Kingdoms, that they may all live in a happy union and correspondence together'.[66] He said nothing about the Irish Parliament but was clearly hinting to the Irish Protestants (and, in a sense, also the Catholics) that the new Ireland need not be subjected to England and the English Parliament. In view of the Prince's promises to the Scots there was room to interpret his remarks on Ireland as an undertaking that the Prince would also revive the autonomy and institutions of Ireland. Certainly the Irish were being offered dignity and equality with the English and Scots. It was therefore with some justification that William Molyneux, in his *The Case of Ireland* (1698), complained that the increasingly blatant subordination of Ireland and Irish interests to England in the later 1690s, under relentless pressure from the English Parliament, following a Revolution which had secured the 'rights and liberties of the Parliament of England', and also the 'rights of Scotland', violated the 'Design of His Majesty's Expedition into these Kingdoms, that we are told by

[64] *The Declaration of His Highness William Henry ... England*, p. 8; *The Declaration of His Highness William Henry By the Grace of God Prince of Orange etc. Of the Reasons inducing him to appear in Arms for the Preserving of the Protestant Religion, and Restoring the Laws and Liberties of the Ancient Kingdom of Scotland* (The Hague, 1688); *The Prince of Orange His Declaration*, pp. 8–10; Pufendorf, *De rebus gestis Friderici Tertii*, p. 93.

[65] Maura Gamazo (ed.), *Correspondencia entre dos embajadores*, I, p. 126: Ronquillo to Cogolludo, London, 18 Mar. 1689 'que muchos hablan en que William III ha faltado a lo que prometio por su declaracion'.

[66] *The Declaration of His Highness William Henry ... England*, p. 8.

Himself (whom we cannot possibly mistrust) was to assert the rights and liberties of these nations'.[67]

The Glorious Revolution in England imparted a revolutionary impulse to Scotland and Ireland and also to the American colonies and West Indies. But in North America as in the British Isles and Ireland the impetus emanating from the English Revolution, the liberating effect, was towards greater autonomy from, not closer links with, England and the English Parliament. The English Revolution, as projected in the Prince of Orange's *Declaration*, had major ramifications for America because, however, circuitously, it justified armed resistance to tyrannical government, as did the example of the armed risings in northern England, and because it offered a restoration of cancelled charters and privileges. For Americans, the Glorious Revolution offered an opportunity to recover the autonomy of which the governmental reforms of Charles II and James II had threatened to deprive them. The New Englanders resorted to arms, and overthrew James' administration in New England, claiming that 'no man does really approve of the Revolution in England but must justifie that in New-England also'.[68] The Americans argued that the people's right of armed resistance to arbitrary kings, and their right to live under the rule of law maintained by their own legislative and representative assemblies, was divisible, exportable, and federal in character.[69] The Glorious Revolution, they argued, obliged the English Crown and Parliament to accord Englishmen living in the New World the same constitutional rights and benefits that it accorded to those within the kingdom.

The Glorious Revolution was a shared experience of the community of English-speaking nations also in its divisiveness. It split the Irish, Scots, Americans, and Caribbean planters just as it did the English. In all the realms and colonies linked to England society was divided, factionalized, and energized. Moreover in the New World the splits amongst the British and Irish were carried over, further complicating the turmoil resulting from the overthrow of James II's monarchy. In the Caribbean there was considerable enthusiasm for the Glorious Revolution but also widespread disapproval and opposition.[70] The ceremony at which William and Mary were proclaimed king and queen of England in Barbados was boycotted by all the Anglican clergy on the island except for one.[71] As in England many of the clergy of the established Church in Barbados

[67] William Molyneaux, *The Case of Ireland's Being Bound by Acts of Parliament in England Stated* (Dublin, 1698), p. 115.

[68] William H. Whitmore (ed.), *The Andros Tracts* (3 vols., Boston, 1868–74), I, p. 71.

[69] J. R. Pole, *Political Representation in England and the Origins of the American Republic* (London, 1966), pp. 55, 89; Bernard Bailyn, *The Ideological Origins of the American Revolution* (Cambridge, Mass., 1967), pp. 122–3; J. G. A. Pocock, '1776: The Revolution against Parliament', in J. G. A. Pocock (ed.), *Three British Revolutions: 1641, 1688, 1776* (Princeton, 1980), pp. 266, 280.

[70] On this topic see Nuala Zahedieh, 'The Glorious Revolution in Jamaica', in *The Glorious Revolution in America – Three Hundred Years After. A Conference at the University of Maryland, College Park* (April, 1988).

[71] *CSP Col. America and the West Indies, 1689–92*, pp. 48, 56.

continued long after the Revolution reciting prayers for the king and queen, refusing to specify which king and queen they intended. In the Leeward Islands, one of the main foci of Anglo-French tension in the New World at this time, the governor, Sir Nathaniel Johnson, on hearing the news of James II's overthrow, decided to resign his governorship: 'I have no liking for the Romish faith', he explained, 'it is from the doctrines of the Church of England that I have learned the scruples which oblige me to ask my demission'.[72]

Three distinct elements may be discerned amongst the anti-Revolution party in Barbados, Jamaica, and the Leewards. First there were the Anglican clergy and those scrupulous Anglicans unable to accept, on Divine Right principles, that the English Parliament could set aside one king and choose another. Next, there was a group of disaffected gentry such as Sir Thomas Montgomery, the Jacobite leader in Barbados, an opportunist who had converted to Catholicism during James' reign, had contacts with the French, and proclaimed that 'if the Dutch maintain their ascendancy in England' the whole West Indies would be lost to the Crown.[73] Finally, there was a substantial body of Irish Catholic settlers, noticeable in Jamaica, numerous enough on Barbados to be considered a military threat, and in the Leewards, especially Montserrat, Antigua, Nevis, and St Christopher, constituting a high proportion of the white population. Indeed, on St Christopher, an island divided between the English and French, the 'bloody, popish, Irish rebels' did in fact rise in rebellion in 1689, declare for James, join forces with the French, and assist in the capture of the English fort.[74]

The English governors in the Caribbean had some trouble with the anti-Revolution party; but they were also worried by signs of what they considered excessive enthusiasm *for* the Revolution. For the Revolution in the Caribbean was not just an anti-Catholic reaction, purging of the island militias, and resurgence of tension between English and French and English and Irish. It was also a reaction against the packing of the island assemblies and manipulation of the judiciary by the royal governors. There were calls for the island assemblies and judiciaries to enjoy greater independence. The new governor sent out to the Leewards reported to London in November 1689 that there was an urgent need to subject the islands more closely to the English Crown, remarking that some of the planters 'fancy these colonies independent states and attribute to their little assemblies the power and authority of the Parliament of England'.[75]

In North America the Glorious Revolution was essentially a reaction to the far-reaching innovations in government, administration, and justice introduced under James II. Like the Glorious Revolution in England, the revolutions in the North American colonies ensued from what Professor J. R. Jones in this

72 Ibid., p. 43.
73 Ibid., p. 55.
74 Ibid., pp. 48, 53, 65, 73, 111.
75 Ibid., p. 177.

volume terms 'James II's Revolution'. In England James had sought to strengthen royal government by weakening the legislature and established Church, and undermining the independence of the judiciary. In America the story was not dissimilar. There too what the opposition called the 'invading of our civil liberties' had begun under Charles II but then gone further under James.

There were four principal motives, or impulses, behind James II's innovations in North America. The first was mercantilist and anti-Dutch, a desire to subject especially New England more strictly than had been the case in the past to the commercial, maritime, and industrial interests of the mother country. One of the main grounds for impeaching the charters of Massachusetts and Rhode Island during the mid-1680s had been the charge that, under cover of their constitutional autonomy, the New Englanders had been systematically flouting the 'Acts of Trade and Navigation', maintaining direct links with the Dutch and shipping goods to and from non-English Caribbean islands.[76] The second main impulse was strategic: the 1680s were a decade of rapid growth in French power around the Great Lakes and in the Mississippi Valley as well as in Canada, and this, and the growing incidence of armed clashes with French-backed Indians along the northern part of the inland frontier, persuaded James' ministers that the New England colonies and New York should be formed 'into one government' in part for their more effective protection.[77] The third main impulse was James' commitment to a policy of religious toleration: Massachusetts and Connecticut especially were regarded in London as unacceptably intolerant in matters of religion, suppressing the 'exercise of the Anglican religion, arbitrarily fining those who refuse to come to their congregational assemblies'.[78] Finally, there was a growing desire to end, or diminish, the great variety of practice in matters of ordinary administration in America and achieve a more standardized and centrally controlled pattern of justice, taxation, and regulation of coinage.

James II's 'Revolution' in America commenced with the 'impeaching' and suspending of the charters of Connecticut, Rhode Island, New Jersey, Delaware, and Maryland, the Massachusetts charter having already been 'impeached' and cancelled at the end of Charles II's reign. Next, the New England and Middle Colonies (except for Maryland) were formed into a single strategic and administrative entity, Sir Edmund Andros being named governor of this new wider 'dominion of New England'. Although there was a delay, until 1688, in adding New York and New Jersey to the main entity, Andros made rapid progress.[79] The system of frontier forts facing the French and Indians, and with it the English

[76] *CSP Col. America and the West Indies, 1685–8*, pp. 65, 77, 270.
[77] Ibid., pp. 77, 270; *CSP Col. America and the West Indies, 1689–92*, p. 47.
[78] *CSP Col. America and the West Indies, 1685–8*, p. 65.
[79] Th. J. Archdeacon, *New York City, 1664–1710: Conquest and Change* (Ithaca, N.Y., 1976), pp. 100–1; Lovejoy, *The Glorious Revolution in America*, pp. 179–81, 235; D. S. Lovejoy, 'Two American Revolutions, 1689 and 1776', in Pocock (ed.), *Three British Revolutions*, pp. 244–51.

military presence, was strengthened. The Navigation Laws were enforced more stringently than in the past. Religious toleration was imposed, one of Andros' achievements being the establishment of the first Anglican church in Boston. A motley of legal systems was replaced with English procedure and in the city of New York, English replaced Dutch as the language of justice.

Two of the main revolutionary movements in North America in the years 1689–91 – in Massachusetts and New York – were essentially a reaction against these innovations. The third main revolution, in Maryland, was a more straightforward affair being basically aimed against the Catholic policies of the colony's proprietor, Lord Baltimore, and the growth of Catholic influence in the area. In both New England and New York, therefore, the Glorious Revolution showed a strong tendency to be backward-looking. 'The greater part of Massachusetts, Plymouth and Connecticut', were, by May 1689, according to a Boston merchant, controlled by people who 'call themselves the true Israel', intent on restoring the 'old charters' and designing the 'fall of false worship and idolatry among us'.[80] But by no means all New Englanders in 1689 preferred the Massachusetts Revolution to 'King James' Revolution'. There was, especially in Rhode Island and Maine, strong support for religious toleration and 'a general governor under the laws of England'.[81] There was also, especially in frontier areas of New York and Maine, support for a strong royal military presence. Consequently, the eventual response of the new regime in England to the revolutionary turmoil in America was an ambiguous one. Up to a point William III and the Parliament of England sanctioned the reaction against James II's policies. A form of charter government was restored in Massachusetts in 1691 and it would be true to say that the position of legislative assemblies in the colonies generally was strengthened. It was also difficult for the new regime in England not to sanction the colonists' use of force against the 'arbitrary' and illegal actions of James II's ministers and officials. On the other hand, in New York the Crown resorted to a policy of military repression while Massachusetts was not permitted to regain the full autonomy that colony had enjoyed until the 1680s.[82] In respect of religion, military matters, and some other aspects of policy there was indeed much in common between the new regime and that of James II, a continuity assisted by the fact that William Blathwayt, one of those who had chiefly inspired James' colonial policy, was retained by William as his secretary for the colonies as well as for war, and eventually gained an even tighter grip over royal policy in North America than he had had before the Revolution.[83]

In North America, as in Britain, the Glorious Revolution was divisive and

[80] *CSP Col. America and the West Indies, 1689–92*, p. 40.
[81] Ibid.
[82] Archdeacon, *New York City*, pp. 115–18, 123, 132; Lovejoy, 'Two American Revolutions', pp. 256–60.
[83] S. S. Webb, 'William Blathwayt, Imperial Fixer: Muddling through to Empire, 1689–1717', *William and Mary Quarterly*, 3rd ser. 26 (1969), pp. 377–8, 399.

replete with paradox. On the one hand, the Revolution was a liberating, emancipating impulse; on the other, it simultaneously displayed unmistakably repressive tendencies. The Revolution instilled new life into all the parliaments and assemblies of the English-speaking lands; but, at the same time, accorded the Parliament of England an unprecedented supremacy and authority. Nor was the repressive side of the Revolution manifested only in the subjection of Ireland, the rapid strengthening, from the early 1690s onwards, of the English grip over Scotland and North America. The population of England itself also now felt something of the pressure of government in ways they had not previously.

In Scotland the contradictions inherent in the Glorious Revolution became fully evident at a particularly early stage. Many of those who most fervently supported the Williamite cause in Scotland, and applauded the convening of the Scots Convention, were soon bitterly disillusioned by 'K. William's delay to redress those grievances which in his Declaration were mentioned to be the principal end of his Expedition' and his retaining in Scotland many of those ministers most closely identified with the policies of James II.[84] This proceeded not from Machiavellian calculation, or sinister proceedings, but plain neglect. The sad reality was that William's only real interest in Scotland was that the country should be quiet and submissive and not obstruct his wider, European, concerns.[85] Sir James Montgomery, the eloquent Scots Whig-Jacobite politician and pamphleteer, may have been untypical in the lengths to which he took his personal disillusionment but was nevertheless profoundly representative of Scottish sentiment in his exasperation that in Scotland the Glorious Revolution 'had only chang'd masters and not measures', that it was all a sham.[86] But while Montgomery's anger was grounded in what he saw as the betrayal of the Scots, he had no less relentless an eye for what he regarded as the shortcomings of the Revolution in England. In his view both Scots and English had been cheated by the removal of James from the scene, bamboozled into wrong courses by 'self-designing and ambitious men', and, the core of the disaster, deprived of 'a most infallible way of securing liberty and property to all future ages, which the ambition of the Prince of Orange and the hard circumstances of our king [i.e. James] had put into our hands'.[87]

In England the rising frustration and resentment among the people which fed the Jacobite and High Church reaction of the 1690s, and first decade of the eighteenth century, was suffused with reactionary sentiment and religious intolerance. It fed on the estrangement of the bulk of the Anglican clergy,

84 George Ridpath, *The Reducing of Scotland by Arms, and Annexing it to England, as a Province, Considered* (London, 1704), pp. 34–5.

85 P. W. J. Riley, *King William and the Scottish Politicians* (Edinburgh, 1979), pp. 161–3.

86 Ridpath, *The Reducing of Scotland*, p. 35; Goldie, 'The Revolution of 1689 and the Structure of Political Argument', pp. 498–500.

87 [Montgomery], *Great Britain's Just Complaint*, p. 2.

infuriated by the effects of 'the Toleration', the vast upsurge of dissenting churches and schools, of Catholic worship, of deism and Socinianism, and the impotence of the established Church to stem its loss of influence.[88] But much of the intensity of the English Jacobite reaction against the Revolution derived less from ideological and religious considerations than from the effects of the mounting burdens imposed on the country by its involvement in a vast European war. As we see from the pamphlets,[89] English Jacobitism systematically played on, and drew strength from, the huge escalation in taxation, the greatly increased burdens of recruiting and billeting and from what, as D. W. Jones demonstrates in his contribution, was the highly disruptive effect of the war on shipping and trade. English Jacobites also shared with Whig radicals a profound unease over the sheer efficiency of the newly forged collaboration of Crown and Parliament. While diverging sharply in their aims, Jacobites and radicals agreed that the people were 'sadly sensible how wretchedly they have fallen short of their expected happiness' and that their present frustration and misery stemmed from the new practices and demands of government.[90] Like the Dutch republican opposition to William III in the United Provinces, English radicals and 'republicans' were particularly dismayed by the unedifying methods used by William and his political managers to obtain the co-operation of the representatives of the people. 'The true spring and fountain from whence all the people's misfortunes flow', wrote one English radical writer, 'is indeed no other than that barefac'd and openly avow'd corruption which, like a universal leprosy, has so notoriously infected and overspread both our Court and Parliament.'[91]

The Glorious Revolution of 1688–91 in England, Scotland, Ireland, and the American colonies had a profound and far-reaching effect on the entire English-speaking community of peoples. But, at the same time, it also exerted an immense impact on Europe as a whole and the rest of the world. This vast effect flowed in the first place from the ensuing transformation of the European balance of power. All of Europe, including states which remained on the fringes of the Nine Years War such as Sweden, Portugal, and the Ottoman Empire, were dir-

[88] Geoffrey Holmes, *The Trial of Doctor Sacheverell* (London, 1973), pp. 26, 30–1, 36; Clark, *English Society, 1688–1832*, pp. 279–81.

[89] [Montgomery], *Great Britain's Just Complaint*, pp. 34–5, 38, 60; [Nathaniel Johnston], *The Dear Bargain, or, A True Representation of the State of the English Nation under the Dutch* (1690), in *A Third Collection of Scarce and Valuable Tracts* (Lord Somers) (3 vols., London, 1751), III, pp. 230–4; [Anderton], *Remarks upon the Present Confederacy*, pp. 8–10, 17; Samuel Grascombe, *An Appeal to all True English-men (If there be any left) Or, A Cry for Bread* (n.p. [London?], n.d. 1695?), p. 3: 'for we are now under Dutch comptrollers, and as nothing must be done, so nothing must be said, that may be offensive to the Hogen Mogens'.

[90] [John Toland?], *The Danger of Mercenary Parliaments* (London, 1695?), p. 3; [Montgomery], *Great Britain's Just Complaint*, pp. 2–3; Grascombe, *An Appeal to all True English-men*, pp. 5–6; Robert Price, *Gloria Cambriae: Or, the Speech of a Bold Britain in Parliament, against a Dutch Prince of Wales*, in *A First Collection of Scarce and Valuable Tracts* (Lord Somers) (4 vols., London, 1748), I, pp. 101–3.

[91] [Toland?], *The Danger of Mercenary Parliaments*, p. 3.

ectly affected by the downfall of the Stuart monarchy in Britain and the sudden emergence during the mid-1690s (from 1692) of England as a European great power ranged against France. But it was not just a matter of power, profound and enduring though the change in Europe's power politics was. A good deal more was involved. We see this from the fact that whilst European Protestant states such as Brandenburg, the Brunswicks, and Denmark–Norway were prompt to recognize William III as king of England, Scotland, and Ireland,[92] and collaborate with him diplomatically, Catholic courts, even those locked in conflict with France, understandably showed much more concern about the dynastic and religious implications of the Revolution and its effect on the principle of monarchical legitimacy. Needless to say, all states showed avid interest in the question of the English succession and most of all those with a close dynastic involvement in the matter such as the courts of Hanover and, as Robert Oresko shows in his contribution, Savoy. Nor was this preoccupation only one way. During the 1690s English Parliamentarians showed a great deal of interest in the Savoy connection and, after the birth of a son to Vittoreo Amedeo and his Stuart wife, the Duchess Anna Maria, in the idea of his being sent to be educated as an Anglican Protestant in England and groomed to succeed to the English throne after Princess Anne, assuming that she, like her elder sister, should die without issue.[93]

The Glorious Revolution created a real balance of power in Europe where, before 1688, the continent had been virtually prostrate before the political and military supremacy of France. Nor was the effect of this confined solely to the sphere of diplomacy, the battle-ground, and the European courts. Militarily, the effect of the English Revolution was to replace French dominance with general deadlock. The Nine Years War, one of the great struggles of European history, ended inconclusively. But, politically, there was a world of difference between this deadlock and the European situation prevailing before 1688. Europe now lived in a whole new climate as if a gigantic cloud of intimidation and insecurity had been lifted from the skies above the Low Countries, Germany, and Italy. In Germany, even Catholic Germany – though there was some support for the French and for James II – the triumphant success of the Dutch intervention in Britain elicited not just approval but a deep sigh of relief.[94] Well before England actually went to war with France, in May 1689, the breaking of James II had eased the pressure on the Empire. 'Tous les gens de bons sens non prévenus',

[92] PRO SP 75–22, fo. 14, Christian V of Denmark to William III, Copenhagen, 9 Apr. 1689; Pufendorf, *De rebus gestis Friderici Tertii*, p. 177.

[93] Fricke, *Leibniz und die englische Sukzession*, p. 11.

[94] Leti, *Monarchie Universelle de Louys XIX*, II, pp. 527, 559–60; Georg Schnath, *Geschichte Hannovers im Zeitalter der neunten Kur und der englischen Sukzession, 1674–1714* (4 vols., Hildesheim, 1938), I, pp. 358, 492–3; P. Havelaar, *Der deutsche Libertätsgedanke und die Politik Wilhelms III von Oranien* (Berlin, 1935), pp. 145–9.

urged the Italian Protestant writer Gregorio Leti, 'avoueront sans doute, que les Hollandois, par cette entreprise ont beaucoup contribué au bien publique, à la liberté de l'Europe, et sur tout à celle de l'Allemagne.'[95] Right down to the end of the Jacobite wars in Scotland and Ireland, late in 1691, the Glorious Revolution in Britain was seen by Europeans as being not just insecure but highly precarious while at the same time the long-term security of the Low Countries, Germany, and Italy, and therefore of all Europe, depended on the outcome of the Glorious Revolution. Hence the great emphasis placed during these years by European writers such as Gregorio Leti and Pierre Jurieu, the Huguenot leader, on the vital role of the Dutch Republic: the Dutch state was the prop of Britain, the 'rampart of Germany', and still more – 'la clef de la liberté commune'.[96]

It is remarkable that European Catholic opinion, though divided, came predominantly to see matters in the same light as Protestant writers such as Leti and Jurieu.[97] Even the papacy, at any rate during the early stages of the Glorious Revolution, under Pope Innocent XI, agreed with the view that the success of the Dutch invasion of Britain was not just a momentous turning-point but an enormous gain for Europe as a whole. In early December, while William III was still in the west country, advancing slowly towards London, Louis XIV unleashed a tremendous, co-ordinated propaganda and diplomatic campaign throughout Italy as well as in Germany and at Vienna, Madrid, and Brussels,[98] portraying the Dutch intervention in Britain (he did not yet know that it would topple James II) as the onset of a general *guerre de religion* in Europe fomented by the Dutch in collusion with the Elector of Brandenburg who, as Wouter Troost shows in his essay, now, after years of uneasy relations with the United Provinces, threw his whole weight behind the Dutch strategy, and other German Protestant rulers. Throughout Catholic Europe, not least at Rome, Louis' diplomats insisted that the Dutch were endeavouring to overthrow a legitimate Catholic monarch out of Protestant motives and to destroy the Catholic cause in Britain and Ireland as a prelude to further assaults on the Catholic world. Consequently, the role of the papacy at this point became of critical importance. For Louis' contention that Catholic rulers who backed William III were the dupes of an international Protestant conspiracy was hardly likely to carry conviction if the

[95] Leti, *Monarchie Universelle de Louys XIV*, II, p. 525.

[96] Ibid., II, pp. 558–60, 598, 615; Pierre Jurieu, *Examen d'un libelle contre le religion, contre l'état et contre la révolution d'Angleterre* (2 parts, The Hague, 1691), I, p. 123; see also Gregorio Leti, *Ragguagli historici, e politici, o vero compendio delle virtù heroiche sopra la fedeltà de' suditi, e amore verso la patria* (2 vols., Amsterdam, 1700), ragguaglio III, pp. 250–2, 271–2.

[97] Tronchin de Breul, *Lettres sur les matières du temps*, II, pp. 104–5, 110–12; Ch. Gerin, 'Le Pape Innocent XI et la Révolution anglaise de 1688', *Revue des Questions Historiques*, 20 (1876), pp. 472–80.

[98] ARH SG 7084, Battier to SG, Madrid, 2 Dec., 30 Dec. 1688, and 13 and 27 Jan. 1689; Tronchin de Breul, *Lettres sur les matières du temps*, II, pp. 92, 104–5, 161, 43–4; N. J. den Tex, *Jacob Hop, gezant der Vereenigde Nederlanden* (Amsterdam, 1861), pp. 272–3.

pope himself refused to sanction it. On the other hand, if the pope did denounce William III's expedition and call on the Catholic rulers of Europe to support James II, it would be much harder for the emperor and Spain to persist in their pro-Dutch, anti-French policy. For these reasons the papal court at Rome now came under ferocious international pressure and in the following months everything that happened at Rome in any way concerning Britain came to be minutely scrutinized by the international community. In fact, throughout December 1688, public prayers were recited in the churches of Rome for the preservation and success of James II,[99] but, to the exasperation of the French, behind the scenes the pope's advisers made little secret of their desire for William III to succeed. The pope refused to publish a word in support of James. Louis threatened and blustered but the Emperor Leopold and king of Spain were no less relentless in asserting contrary pressure, urging the pope that 'dès qu'il donnerait aux affaires d'Angeleterre une apparence de guerre de religion, il deshonnerait leur conduite, et rendrait les liaisons qu'ils ont et veulent conserver avec le Prince d'Orange trop odieuses dans le monde'.[100] The pope knew what he had to do. James II's emissaries were received coldly in Rome and subsequently the exiled monarch was refused the pope's moral and financial support. It is true that Pope Innocent, like the emperor and Spanish monarch, long hesitated to accord formal recognition to William III as king of England – no European ruler concerned himself much with Mary – but by May 1689 it was obvious that on a *de facto* basis the pope willingly accepted William as England's king and that 'l'on ne nomme plus au palais le Prince d'Orange que le Roi d'Angleterre et le vrai roi', as the French ambassador in Rome put it, 'que Jacques II'.[101] Louis made no attempt to hide his anger with the pope. Even before the landing at Torbay, Louis had been insinuating through the French press that His Holiness was surreptitiously aiding and abetting a 'Protestant' invasion of Britain launched in the name of the Protestant cause and had very little compunction about doing so more abrasively now.[102]

The Glorious Revolution plunged Europe in controversy about how far religion should be allowed to determine the contours of international politics.[103] At the same time the Revolution posed the issues of monarchical legitimacy and the relationship between monarchical authority and the rule of law in new,

[99] E. Michaud, *Louis XIV et Innocent XI d'après les correspondences diplomatiques inédites* (4 vols., Paris, 1882), II, pp. 128–30.

[100] Ibid., II, pp. 135–40.

[101] Ibid., II, p. 137.

[102] Tronchin de Breul, *Lettres sur les matières du temps*, II, pp. 110–11; Gerin, 'Pape Innocent XI', pp. 427–8; Jean Orcibal, *Louis XIV contre Innocent XI* (Paris, 1949), pp. 39–43; Max Immich, *Papst Innocenz XI, 1676–1689* (Berlin, 1900), pp. 103–6.

[103] Henri Basnage de Beauval *et al.*, *Lettres Historiques concernant ce qui se passe de plus important en Europe*, I (The Hague, 1692), pp. 287–96; Schnath, *Geschichte Hannovers im Zeitalter der neunten Kur*, I, pp. 492–3, 500.

challenging, and dramatic ways. Thus, there is an important sense in which the English Revolution of 1688–9 was also a French Revolution. Since the fall of La Rochelle in 1628, French Protestants had had little alternative but to distance themselves from the revolutionary doctrines of justified resistance to royal authority expounded by François Hotman and Philippe Duplessis-Mornay in the aftermath of the St Bartholomew's Day massacres of 1572. Under Louis XIV, the Huguenots, deprived of all prospect of successful political or military action in support of their cause, had lapsed into an entirely passive attitude, falling back on the principles of resignation, obedience, and submission. The political response of the French Protestant leadership to the increasing intolerance of the king during the early 1680s was publicly to espouse and strongly affirm absolutist and Divine Right principles.[104] The Huguenots endeavoured, as it were, to stave off further royal displeasure, with profuse assurances of their loyalty to the king. Nor did the Revocation of the Edict of Nantes, in 1685, and the ensuing mass exodus of Huguenots from France in itself bring about a change in the political attitudes and doctrines of the French Protestant Church. It was the Glorious Revolution in Britain and Ireland in which more than 2,000 Huguenot officers and men participated which revolutionized political discourse amongst the Huguenot diaspora in western Europe. Leading Huguenot theologians and publicists, such as Pierre Jurieu and Jean Le Clerc, now forged a new Huguenot political outlook, taking the Glorious Revolution as their theoretical and practical model.[105] But the English Revolution which they espoused was not that of fictions, fudges, and compromises with Tory and Divine Right views proclaimed by Parliament but the revolution of armed resistance to illegal royal authority proclaimed by William III and the Whigs.

In his *Lettres Pastorales*, a series of open letters sent to the Huguenot population remaining in France, Jurieu denounced the political doctrines of the Church of England for their illogicality, on the one hand insisting on the 'constitution' and the need for constitutional restraints on the power of the king while simultaneously making it impossible to secure those constraints by preaching total submission to royal authority, that very 'obeissance passive sans bornes' from which French Protestants were now freeing themselves.[106] The English Revolution in the sense of armed rebellion against unconstitutional royal authority, was fully justified, Jurieu assured his flock, because 'l'authorité des souverains vient des

[104] [Jurieu], *Examen d'un libelle*, II, p. 99; *Avis Important aux Refugiez sur leur prochain retour en France* (Amsterdam, 1690), pp. 83–4.

[105] *Avis Important aux Refugiez*, pp. 83, 242; Jacques Abbadie, *Défense de la Nation Britannique ou les Droits de Dieu, de la Nature et de la societé clairement établis au sujet de la révolution d'Angleterre* (London, 1692), pp. 171–5, 412–13; F. R. J. Knetsch, *Pierre Jurieu. Theoloog en politikus der Refuge* (Kampen, 1967), pp. 289–90, 313.

[106] Pierre Jurieu, *Lettres Pastorales addressées aux fidèles de France, qui gémissent sous la captivité de Babylon*, 3e année (Rotterdam, 1688), pp. 137–9, 141; the *Avis Important aux Refugiez* countered by defending the doctrines of the Church of England, see the *Avis*, p. 219.

peuples'.[107] He vigorously defended the doctrine of an original contract between ruler and people which, if violated by the ruler, frees the people from the duty of obedience and justifies them in taking up arms against monarchical authority.[108] Both Scripture and political philosophy were harnessed in support of the new revolutionary doctrine.[109] Like the Dutch Calvinist clergy, those Huguenot preachers who fervently supported William III's invasion of Britain and acquisition of the three Crowns of England, Scotland, and Ireland, forcefully reminded their congregations of Ancient Israel's rejection of Saul, with the Almighty's blessing, in favour of David with whom William III, at least in the Dutch Republic, was frequently compared at this time.[110] In the sphere of political thought, Jurieu, like the English Tory writer Bohun, chiefly relied on the ideas of the early seventeenth-century Dutch jurist Hugo Grotius to buttress his doctrine that 'la souveraineté appartient radicalement et originalement au peuple'. But whether they shielded behind Grotius or Scripture, for French Protestants the English Revolution which mattered was the revolution which said that 'les roys peuvent être déposés'.

The revolutionary outlook propagated by Jurieu and Le Clerc in the wake of the Glorious Revolution led directly to the line of thought that what France needed to throw off the abominable tyranny of Louis XIV was a 'pareille révolution'.[111] What Jurieu, Le Clerc, and Elie Benoist, the French pastor at Delft (and another public advocate of the idea that there is a contract between king and subjects which, if broken by the former, justifies the latter in taking up arms to depose him)[112] had in mind was not the overthrow of monarchy in France as such, or the setting aside of the House of Bourbon, but a constitutional remodelling of France. They aspired to turn the French monarchy into the kind of parliamentary monarchy that England now was, hoping, with the assistance of the Prince of Orange and the League of Augsburg, to defeat Louis XIV, dethrone him, replace him with another king – preferably the Dauphin, and cleanse France of what Jurieu terms 'pouvoir arbitraire ... c'est à dire le pouvoir absolu'. The new French monarchy which they hoped to create would, of course, adhere to the principles of religious toleration and constitutional guarantees for a religious minority such as the Huguenots, enabling them to return from

[107] Jurieu, *Lettres Pastorales*, 3e année, p. 124; [Jurieu], *Examen d'un libelle*, II, pp. 94–9.
[108] Jurieu, *Lettres Pastorales*, 3e année, p. 138.
[109] Ibid., p. 139; [Jurieu], *Examen d'un libelle*, II, pp. 81, 94–5, 181; Kenyon, *Revolution Principles*, p. 31.
[110] Jurieu, *Lettres Pastorales*, 3e année, p. 139; *Sauls Boosheid en Davids Opregtigheid; of een vertoog van het quade Beleid van Jacobus de Twede gewesene koning van Engeland, Scotland, Vrankryk en Yrland* (Amsterdam, 1689), pp. 1, 9.
[111] [Jurieu], *Examen d'un libelle*, II, pp. 113–14; *Les Soupirs de la France esclave qui aspire après la liberté* (Amsterdam, 1690), pp. 3, 8, *et seq.*; Friedrich Kleyser, *Der Flugschriftenkampf gegen Ludwig XIV zur Zeit des pfälzischen Krieges* (Berlin, 1935), pp. 42–3, 45–6.
[112] F. van Dijk, 'Elie Benoist (1640–1728), Historiographer and Politician after the Revocation of the Edict of Nantes', *Nederlands Archief voor Kerkgeschiedenis*, 69 (1989), pp. 69–70.

exile to their homes and property and live tranquilly in France. Inspired by such notions many of the Huguenot ministers in the Dutch Republic, the intellectual centre of the Huguenot refugees, lent enthusiastic support to William III's enterprises both in their preaching and writing. Louis, for his part, was only too glad to link the Huguenots with the Glorious Revolution in his European propaganda, seeking to blacken the Huguenots in the eyes of all European rulers as 'insatiables de séditions' and 'ennemis naturels des souverains'.

Precisely because they were afraid of this, and other consequences of Louis' anger, a minority of the Huguenot intellectual leadership in the Netherlands not only refused to agree with the doctrines being propagated by Jurieu and his supporters but felt so strongly on this issue that they precipitated a deep and painful rift in the Huguenot camp. This ideological split over the Glorious Revolution among the French Protestants was especially acute at Rotterdam where both Jurieu and several of his most vehement critics resided.[113] The great 'philosopher of Rotterdam', Pierre Bayle, together with Jacques Basnage, Isaac Jacquelot, and a number of others, firmly rejected the doctrine that in consequence of Louis XIV's actions the Huguenots were now entitled to take up arms against him and support the Dutch Republic in its war against their own king. Bayle was closely associated with a sensational pamphlet, the *Avis Important aux Refugiez* which vitriolically attacked Jurieu's doctrine that 'L'authorité des rois vient des peuples', ridiculing the ideological somersault which Jurieu, Le Clerc, and Benoist, and their supporters, had performed since 1688. This pamphlet continued to cause bitter dissension in Huguenot circles throughout the 1690s and the War of the Spanish Succession (1702–13) which followed. Bayle feared that through their participation in the Glorious Revolution all Huguenots everywhere would now be labelled republicans, insurgents, and rebels against legitimate monarchs. If Huguenots persisted in denouncing their own king from the pulpit and in their writings, and openly supporting Dutch arms against France, this would prove only that Louis had been right to expel the Huguenots from France for their disloyalty. If the Huguenots were ever to return to their homeland they could achieve this only by patience, submission, and convincing Louis XIV of their unshakable loyalty.

But if the Glorious Revolution was a French as well as an English Revolution it was also in an important sense a key watershed for Germany. There were several reasons why the Glorious Revolution should have generated such extraordinary excitement at all the German courts, Protestant and Catholic alike. In the first place, there was the mounting French pressure on Cologne, the Palatinate, and other Rhineland states just at the moment when the Emperor Leopold was proving triumphantly successful in his war with the Turks in the east. Having

[113] [Isaac de Larrey], *Réponse à l'Avis aux Refugiez* (Rotterdam, 1709), pp. 17, 49; Knetsch, *Pierre Jurieu*, pp. 313–23; Elisabeth Labrousse, *Pierre Bayle* (2 vols., The Hague, 1963), I, pp. 219–22.

expelled the Turks from Hungary and advanced with impressive speed, the imperial armies in the east, on 6 September 1688, captured Belgrade. Not only did Islam appear to be beaten; the Ottoman Empire seemed on the point of collapse. Louis XIV, however, was determined to prevent a further fundamental shift in the balance of prestige, power, and territory in favour of the emperor – which could only be to the detriment of French power in Europe – by threatening to bring the entire Rhineland, by force, under French domination. On 26 September the French offensive on the middle Rhine began. The emperor was now caught on the horns of a painful and extraordinary dilemma: it was both difficult and humiliating to be compelled to give up his great offensive in the east, and he was urged by Venice and the Polish king not to do so; but, if he refused to take up the French challenge in conjunction with the Dutch, on the Rhine, his prestige and authority in the German Empire would suffer a devastating setback from which the very principle of the empire as a meaningful political and strategic concept might not survive.[114] In the end, Leopold had little alternative but to halt his eastern offensive and commit his forces to a major effort to contain the French advances on the Rhine.

Meanwhile, French propaganda in the empire, and not least in Vienna, was by no means wholly ineffective. In the weeks following William III's invasion of Britain, it became clear that Louis might succeed in driving such a wedge between Protestant and Catholic Germany as to impair fatally the cohesion of the empire to the permanent advantage of France. The news of the anti-Catholic disturbances in England, luridly related in the Dutch newspapers, caused such a sensation, and sense of revulsion, amongst the Catholic courts of Germany that the Dutch resident at the Imperial Diet, at Regensburg, became seriously alarmed and wrote to the States General complaining in particular about a report of English violence which had appeared in the *Haerlemsche Courant*.[115] The States General asked the States of Holland to admonish the *courantiers* to tone down their reportage of English events.

But for Germany as for France, the Revolution in England had important implications also for domestic politics. By the late seventeenth century, there had long been a struggle in progress, on both the practical and theoretical levels, in Germany between princely absolutism on the one hand and entrenched constitutional traditions and procedures on the other. In the past this contest had been expressed mainly in terms of local constitutional traditions and preoccupations with little reference to wider political ideas or trends and little reference to the evolution of the German Empire as a whole. But by the 1680s the whole process had reached a decisive phase which was now generating more tension,

[114] Lothar Höbelt,'Die Sackgasse aus dem Zweifrontenkrieg: Die Friedensverhandlungen mit den Osmanen 1689', *Mitteilungen des Instituts für österreichische Geschichtsforschung*, 97 (1989), pp. 336–40.
[115] ARH SG 4033, sec. res. SG, 11 Mar. 1689.

and giving rise to a broader political awareness than in the past. The rise in recent years of several new absolutist regimes which had begun to display strongly expansionist and militaristic ambitions, most notably in Brandenburg, Denmark (and the Danish territories in Germany), Sweden, and the Palatinate was generating deep apprehension amongst the large number of petty princes of the empire and those more substantial princes who lacked powerful armies and also felt vulnerable. In the Imperial Diet, and in constitutionalist circles in states such as electoral Saxony and Württemberg where local diets remained strong, there was real fear that absolutism based on the model of that of Louis XIV, but now firmly planted in Germany, was fast eroding the institutions, conventions, and traditions of the empire and undermining what was called the 'common cause of Germany'.

It is true that in Lutheran as in Catholic Germany there were strong inhibitions against the proposition that political authority emanates from the people and that rulers who place themselves above the law might justly be opposed. But this did not prevent either courtly or constitutionalist Germany from taking a keen interest in the spectacle of James II, the ruler who had sought to discard constitutional constraints, being removed from his throne. Several different German-language versions of the Prince of Orange's *Declaration* of 10 October circulated in the empire as did German translations of the States General's resolution of 28 October and a whole series of English libertarian pamphlets and books over the next years, including John Toland's *Anglia Libera*. Samuel Pufendorf, the foremost German jurist and political writer of the time, was intensely interested in the Glorious Revolution and devoted many pages to the subject both in his private correspondence and in his history of Frederick III of Brandenburg, a book in which he included Latin translations of a number of Glorious Revolution documents including even the Prince of Orange's separate *Declaration* to the people of Scotland.[116] As a Lutheran writer, Pufendorf had difficulty with the idea that a ruler might justifiably be overthrown. Nevertheless, he emphasized that James had flouted the laws and constitutional properties of his kingdom and implies, if he does not maintain, that the English were right to deprive James of his throne.

Meanwhile, in the United Provinces, the Glorious Revolution had a profound impact on both the political elite and the entire public. In 1688, the Republic was, or at any rate was generally perceived to be, caught in a situation of extreme danger from which the Dutch state and people could be extricated only by a drastic and grandiose undertaking. The expedition to England was seen by the Dutch public as well as by the regents as an enterprise of the state as well as of the Prince of Orange, an enterprise mainly designed to serve Dutch not

[116] Pufendorf, *De rebus gestis Friderici Tertii*, pp. 88–98, 169–77; Hans Rödding, *Pufendorf als Historiker und Politiker in den 'Commentarii de rebus gestis Friderici Tertii* (Halle, 1912), pp. 14–15.

British interests, or those of the Prince of Orange. The expedition was, moreover, seen as crucial to the Republic's survival as a major, independent European power. The passage of the States General's crack regiments from their garrisons to the places of embarkation produced scenes of intense emotion, crowds of Dutch men and women cheering, praying, and weeping as they went. Nor was it only the Reformed clergy who, at the bidding of the burgomasters, laid on rousing sermons and special services for the success of the invasion of England but also, as at Haarlem, the Mennonite, Lutheran, and Remonstrant churches.[117] At Leiden, during November and December 1688, both of the city's big churches were used for the special additional Monday and Friday evening services to implore the Almighty to extend his 'blessing and grace over the Fatherland and Reformed Church and, in particular, to grant success to the great and important design of the state and His Highness the Prince of Orange presently undertaken in England'.[118] At Amsterdam, the Portuguese Jewish community – whose lay leaders were closely involved in helping to organize the expedition – also laid on special services and prayers to implore the Almighty to grant favourable winds and ensure the success of the States General's 'armada'.[119]

Dutch reaction, it is true, varied considerably according to religious and political affiliation. The United Provinces was a land of religious minorities. If the Calvinist preachers and their flock were euphoric this was not necessarily the case with the rest of the public. The other Protestant churches in the Netherlands tended to identify themselves less closely with the doings of the Dutch state than did the so-called 'public church'. Catholics, moreover, had, in the past, been disinclined to sympathize with the Republic at all. According to the marquis d'Albeville, Dutch Catholics in 1688 prayed 'ardently' for the preservation of James II.[120] In Reformed circles, it was alleged that they also recited prayers for the success of Louis XIV. But such allegations must be treated with caution. Other evidence suggests that by the 1680s many Dutch Catholics had come to appreciate the considerable degree of religious freedom that they enjoyed in the Republic and it is striking that in 1685–6 the Catholic churches in Holland contributed significantly to the collections on behalf of the Huguenot refugees as a sign of their disapproval of Louis XIV's intolerance and their solidarity with the Dutch state. As for Dutch Protestant nonconformists, they had ample reason to support the momentous design on which the Republic had embarked. For it was clearly realized that a great deal in Europe's religious life, and the general prospects for toleration, depended on the outcome. As Philip van Limborch, a leading Remonstrant minister and champion of toleration, wrote

[117] GA Haarlem. Stad Haarlem 10 (Burgermeestersresoluties), no. 27, fo. 88, res. 13 Nov. 1688.
[118] GA Leiden Acta Kerkeraad VII res. 3 Dec. 1688.
[119] See p. 439 below.
[120] BL MS Add. 41816, fo. 231, D'Albeville to Middleton, The Hague, 10 Oct. 1688; BL MS Add. 38495, fo. 41; *Sauls Boosheid en Davids Opregtigheid*, pp. 9–10.

to his friend John Locke, in England, in May 1689, 'we are hoping for a happy outcome of affairs in your country being not unaware that the affairs of Europe depend in a great part on this'.[121]

The Glorious Revolution undoubtedly strengthened William III's standing in the United Provinces as well as enhancing his position as a European statesman. In general, his elevation to the throne of England, and his strengthened authority, elicited a remarkably muted response among traditionally anti-Orangist, 'States party' circles in the Republic. Of course, there were regents and others who disapproved and there was certainly widespread unease that the Stadholder's acquisition of the crowns of England, Scotland, and Ireland might serve to tilt the political balance also in the United Provinces further in his favour, an anxiety which French propaganda strove with some vigour to exploit. But those who criticized the Stadholder, and resented the corrupt methods employed by his political managers in handling the Dutch provincial and municipal assemblies, were unable to mount any effective opposition owing to the sheer extent of Dutch popular enthusiasm for the Prince's achievements. Aside from some half-hearted moves on the part of anti-Orangist regents at Amsterdam in 1690, Dutch republican opposition to William III in the years after the Glorious Revolution amounted to little more than a relatively weak stream of republican pamphlets and the occasional hostile printed caricature such as the cartoon *Hollands hollende koe* (see Plate 8). The ineffectiveness of the Dutch domestic opposition to William III in the 1690s moved one French writer to enquire sarcastically whether the Dutch regents, those *sages politiques*, had now totally forgotten all about their true interests.[122] Another asked rhetorically whether the regents by giving their Stadholder the means to acquire three kingdoms – England, Scotland, and Ireland – had not also supplied the means whereby he could acquire a fourth, meaning the United Provinces.[123] But all to no avail. A more effective Dutch political reaction against the in some respects repressive political legacy of William III was delayed until after his death, in 1702.

To conclude this general introduction let us cast a final glance at that deeply enigmatic figure who stood at the centre of the Glorious Revolution not only in England but also in Scotland, Ireland, and, in a sense, America. How paradoxical was William III's contemporary reputation and image! How inspiring and fascinating but at the same time offputting and disappointing a figure he appeared to the British, Dutch, and other Europeans of his day. Many revered him as the undisputed leader of the international Protestant cause and Europe's great

[121] E. S. de Beer (ed.), *The Correspondence of John Locke* (8 vols., Oxford, 1976–8), III, p. 607. Van Limborch to Locke, 26 April/6 May 1689.

[122] Denis de Sainte-Marthe, *Entretiens touchant l'entreprise du Prince d'Orange sur l'Angleterre* (Paris, 1689), p. 18.

[123] Ibid.; Eustache de le Noble de Tennelière, *La Pierre de touche politique* (28 parts, Paris, 1688–91), II, pp. 41–2, VI, p. 23, VII, pp. 4–44.

2 *William III, King of England, Scotland, France, and Ireland.* Print based on a portrait by Sir Godfrey Kneller.

struggle to thwart and defeat the despotism, expansionism, and Catholic militancy of Louis XIV. Others revered him as the unchallenged champion of the cause of constitutional rights and toleration. But still others, very many others, saw him as the great deceiver and usurper, a monster of ambition, the new 'Absalom' rather than 'David', the supreme *politique*. While he claimed to be the great upholder of constitutional rights, republicans and radicals both in the United Provinces and England deplored his efforts to bend constitutional bodies to his will and extend his influence in the body politic, and the corrupt practices of his political managers, even while, in England at least, republicans, for tactical reasons, felt bound to applaud him outwardly as the chief architect of what John Toland called the 'inestimable blessings of the Revolution'. Here is a striking paradox which was highlighted by Jacobite propaganda as early as November 1688 when the pro-government London press strove to prevent the people of Britain lending their support to a 'prince who having well nigh enslaved his own States, is come to fight us into liberty'.[124] Yet while republicans disapproved of him more openly perhaps in the United Provinces than in England, the Stadholder-king retained more support amongst the public at large in the United Provinces than in Britain. Indeed, in England William III became, quite soon after the Revolution, highly unpopular, possibly even more so than James II had been in 1688. Certainly, the national detestation of William III was an intense and remarkable historical phenomenon. For it was not simply dislike for the man and his aloof, almost contemptuous manner. Rather, English antipathy to the Stadholder-king was a highly complex, social and political phenomenon which is one of the keys to a correct understanding of the Glorious Revolution itself. The reaction against him was so strong that it remained a feature of the English scene for many decades. Dr Johnson's view that William III was one of the greatest scoundrels who had ever lived was a far from uncommon sentiment in eighteenth-century England. Toland commented at one point that the ferocious xenophobia exuded by the English against the Dutch during the 1690s should to some extent be understood as coded talk intended to convey detestation of the king, remarking that Englishmen 'us'd formerly to damn all the Dutch when they durst not expressly curse King William'.[125] But it would perhaps be even truer to say that the fierce antipathy which developed towards King William was a means of embodying the deeply felt hostility of the Tory gentry, the Church of England, and large sections of the common populace to those aspects of the Revolution legacy which came to be widely detested, in particular the heavy taxation, the weakening of the Church of England, the effect of 'the toleration' in terms of increased dissenter and Catholic freedom,

[124] *Seasonable and Honest Advice*, p. 2.

[125] Quoted in J. I. Israel, 'William III and Toleration', in O. Grell, J. I. Israel, and N. Tyacke (eds.), *From Toleration to Persecution* (Oxford, 1991), p. 165.

and the post-1688 influx into England of a much-noticed wave of fortune-seeking Dutchmen, Huguenots, and Jews. Daniel Defoe penned his famous satire *The True-Born English-Man* (1702) as a send-up of this powerful xenophobic reaction and what he regarded as the appalling ingratitude of the gentry and Church of England clergy towards the man they had once called 'their deliverer', accusing them of having turned against him when they saw that 'their persecuting days were done', out of violent prejudice against nonconformists. By contrast, Jacobite writers made full use of the antipathy against the Stadholder-king, recognizing it as a crucial factor in the struggle to unseat the 'usurper' and restore England's legitimate king. They also did their best to exploit William's well-known negative feelings towards his English subjects, exaggerating his lack of sympathy for them in order to intensify further their dislike of him. One Williamite pamphleteer derided the Jacobite press for depicting the Stadholder-king as a 'Dutch Nero, a Dutch Monster, nay a Dutch devil ... who has so great an antipathy to the English that he could be willing they were all knockt o'th head and our country repeopled with foreigners'.[126]

The striking paradoxes which make up the figure of William III emerge clearly also from contemporary French propaganda. Louis XIV's propagandists, like the Jacobite press, depicted the Prince of Orange as the great usurper, hypocrite, corrupter, and tyrant, the new Nero who twisted legality and 'enslaved' representative bodies to advance his own relentless ambition. He is portrayed as the debaucher of the formerly loyal subjects of James II who at the same time deceived them. Yet French writers, again like the Jacobite press, also portray the Prince of Orange as the archfoe of monarchs, the champion of parliaments and 'republican' sentiments. One French writer simultaneously vilified him as the 'enslaver' of the Dutch and the enemy of all sovereigns, the architect of a new form of monarchy in England so entirely subordinate to Parliament that future English kings 'ne seroit tout au plus ce que le Doge à Venise'.[127] The apparent contradiction was neatly resolved by styling William 'le nouveau Cromwell', the destroyer of thrones who simultaneously subverts parliaments. The comparison with Cromwell continually recurs: 'que l'on dise ce que l'on voudra du fameux Olivier Cromwell', as one writer put it, 'il n'a rien de comparable à sa Majesté Britannique'.[128]

[126] *The Spirit of Jacobitism: or, Remarks upon a Dialogue between K. W. and Benting* (London, 1695), p. 23.
[127] Sainte-Marthe, *Entretiens*, p. 22.
[128] *Esprit politique ou l'histoire en abrégé de la vie et des actions de Guillaume III de Nassau*, p. 241; see also Antoine Arnauld, *Le véritable portrait de Guillaume-Henri de Nassau, Nouvel Absalom, Nouvel Hérode, Nouveau Cromwell, Nouveau Néron* ('Brussels', but Paris?, 1689), pp. 42–4, 48–9; Le Noble de Tennelière, *Pierre de touche politique*, III, pp. 4–5, and VI, pp. 26–7, 31.

PART I

The Glorious Revolution

Chapter 1

James II's Revolution: royal policies, 1686–92

J. R. JONES

There cannot be a clearer example of the axiom that history is the propaganda of the victors than the fate of James II. During the tercentenary commemorations of the Revolution of 1688 he and his policies have simply been ignored. This is nothing new. When Edmund Burke made his often cited comment that 1688 did not see a revolution, in the sense of an alteration of the constitution, he did so for contemporary polemical reasons, but he did not attempt to examine the statement on which his whole argument depended, that what happened in 1688 was 'a revolution not made, but prevented'.[1]

In this essay I will argue that an understanding of the developments of 1688–9 depends on a serious examination of the startlingly innovative policies that James adopted and systematically attempted to implement in 1686–8. In examining the reasons for their adoption and analysing the methods used to enforce the king's directives a clear and logical process of development and extension can be discerned. Secondly, it becomes apparent that James was as concerned to strengthen the authority of the monarchy as to promote the interests of the Roman Catholic Church and its adherents, indeed that the two objectives were inseparably linked.

In attempting to implement the two centrally important policies, the establishment of universal freedom of conscience and the campaign to pack a pre-engaged Parliament, James not only employed former Whigs as agents and propagandists, but also appropriated Whig concepts and principles.[2] This was because he was consciously addressing and attempting to enlist the support of interests and sections of opinion that had formerly adhered to the first Whigs. The arguments which were deployed on his behalf go a long way to explain what most historians have regarded as James' surprising, or even suicidal, behaviour in abandoning the Stuart monarchy's traditional reliance on the Divine Right princi-

[1] Edmund Burke, *Works*, 6 vols., London (1906), III, p. 284.

[2] J. R. Jones, 'James II's Whig Collaborators', *Historical Journal*, 3 (1960), pp. 65–73. I am analysing James' appropriation of Whig principles and concepts in an introductory chapter in the volume of essays entitled *Liberty Secured? Britain before and after 1688*, ed. J. R. Jones, due to appear in 'The Making of Modern Freedom' series, published by the Center for the History of Freedom at Washington University, St Louis.

ples and teaching of the Church of England and its clergy, and in discarding the Tories who had rallied to him in 1679–81, in favour of a new alliance with Dissenters and former Whigs. James' apologists developed as a substitute a theory of political obligation in which an appeal to interest, and specifically the prospect of fostering economic prosperity, was advanced as the surest way of securing domestic peace and unity.

With the advantage of historical hindsight one can see that James inherited from his brother a significantly strengthened royal authority. However, in the first weeks of his reign James felt extremely vulnerable, and made vigorous appeals for the renewal of subsidies from Louis XIV.[3] His primary reason for wanting French aid was not to enable him to suppress the rebellions which he knew that the earl of Argyll and the duke of Monmouth were preparing from their exile in the Dutch Republic, but rather to make it possible for him to adopt a firm and confident attitude towards Parliament from the moment of its first meeting.[4] James had been consistently critical of Charles for deferring to Parliament, and for authorizing his ministers to manage the Lords and Commons by the use of patronage, and by making concessions in order to obtain votes of supply.[5] He was determined not to employ such demeaning and weakening practices. Even when the election returns showed that the composition of the 1685 Commons would be totally different from the Whig dominated Houses that had pressed for the Exclusion Bill in 1679, 1680, and 1681, James explicitly warned the self-proclaimed 'loyal' majority against attaching conditions to the settlement of the revenue which they were about to vote to him. He also gave them notice that he expected them to serve him from motives of loyalty, and that consequently they should not expect to be offered inducements or rewards for service.[6] In private James told the French ambassador, shortly before the session began, that he would immediately dissolve Parliament if his warnings were ignored, even though a settlement of the revenue had not been passed.[7] Clearly he was anticipating some kind of remonstrance about his religion, and in authorizing the payment of subsidies Louis specified that their purpose was to strengthen James' authority in relation to Parliament, so that he would not be prevented from promoting the interests of Catholicism.[8] James had made it clear to him that Tory or 'loyal' peers and MPs regarded themselves as guarantors of the established Church of England. But despite this

[3] Sir John Dalrymple, *Memoirs of Great Britain and Ireland* (3 vols., London, 1771–8), II, appendix, part the first, pp. 141–2, Barrillon to Louis, 26 Mar. 1685 (NS); p. 153, Barrillon, 9 Apr.
[4] Ibid., pp. 141–2.
[5] Ibid., appendix, pp. 219, 227.
[6] Ibid., appendix, part the first, p. 153, Barrillon, 30 Apr. 1685; p. 154, 13 Dec.
[7] Ibid., p. 142, Barrillon, 26 Mar. 1685.
[8] Ibid., pp. 145–6, Barrillon to Louis, 26 Mar. 1685. F. Puaux and A. Sabatier, *Etudes sur la Révocation de l'Édit de Nantes* (1886), p. 99, citing Louis to Barrillon, 6 Apr. 1685.

James was from the beginning determined to give his co-religionists equality, civil as well as religious, with Anglicans.

In the first part of its single session, the Commons voted James an adequate revenue for life, together with what proved to be an over-generous amount of extraordinary supply to suppress Monmouth's rebellion.[9] This made the Crown financially solvent until the eve of the Revolution, when the extensive naval preparations to repel William's invasion used up reserves, and mounting political uncertainties undermined royal credit. But in the second part of the session, in November, James abruptly prorogued Parliament and it was never to meet again, although it was kept in suspended animation by four further prorogations until it was finally dissolved in June 1687.[10] James had two main reasons for asserting his authority by this totally unexpected prorogation. First, the Commons remonstrated against his continued employment of Catholic officers in the army, despite his candid statement that he was determined to keep them in his service. Insisting that Catholics required statutory immunity if they were to continue in their commissions, an immunity bill was introduced by independent or 'Country' MPs acting on their own initiative.[11] Such men had far more parliamentary experience and procedural skill than the king's own official representatives, so that the possibility of the latter losing the capacity to influence or control proceedings began to emerge. Specifically it became apparent that the Country leaders intended to make progress on the indemnity bill in close parallel with an additional supply bill that would have strengthened royal finances still further.[12] At most times this would have been a delicate operation. When the two bills went to the Lords it would be open to peers to reject, obstruct, amend, or ignore the indemnity bill, but by constitutional convention they could not touch a money bill but were obliged to pass it. In fact, as James knew, the royal position in the Lords was weaker than that in the Commons, partly because of the inexperience and mistakes of the Speaker, the recently ennobled Jeffreys.[13] Collusion between Country elements in the Lords and Commons totally contravened James' interpretation of the proper role of Parliament. The likelihood of an explicit or implicit connection being established between the provision of additional supply, which he could do without, and the passing of an indemnity bill, represented for him a retrograde move. If James allowed the two measures to pass together it could be seen as tantamount to recognizing as legitimate the practice of attaching conditions to legislative support for the sovereign, the practice which had weakened Charles' authority

[9] C. D. Chandaman, *The English Public Revenue 1660–1688* (Oxford, 1975), pp. 256–61.
[10] *CJ*, IX, pp. 761–2; 10 Feb. 1686, 10 May 1686, 22 Nov. 1686, 15 Feb. 1687, 28 Apr. 1687.
[11] Ibid., IX, p. 757.
[12] Ibid., IX, pp. 756, 759, 760–1.
[13] G. W. Keeton, *Lord Chancellor Jeffreys and the Stuart Cause* (London, 1965), pp. 332–4, 338. J. R. Jones, *The Revolution of 1688 in England* (London, 1984), pp. 63–4.

during the life of the Cavalier Parliament, a similarly self-proclaimed 'loyal' body.

James believed that peers and MPs were bound to his service by their oaths. Consequently they had a duty to legislate in accordance with the directions which the king gave them at the start of a session, and to follow the lead given them by royal officers and spokesmen. Parliament had behaved in this way during the first part of the session, but primarily because the danger of Argyll and Monmouth igniting a new and general civil war had created a complete but, as it proved, temporary identity of interests between king, peers, and MPs. But James consistently believed, and repeatedly acted on the belief, that he could properly demand unconditional co-operation from MPs; this was to be seen especially in 1687–8, when he demanded from intending parliamentary candidates pledges or pre-engagements to legislate in accordance with royal instructions. This campaign of 1687–8, however, represented his second and more sophisticated attempt to obtain co-operation from Parliament on his own terms. In the second half of 1686 he carried out a process known to contemporaries as 'closeting'.[14] James personally approached peers and MPs to extract from them undertakings to vote to repeal the Test Acts, when he allowed Parliament to sit again. There was little resemblance between these approaches and the kind of managerial practices that had been developed by the earl of Danby in the 1670s. James did not delegate the work to subordinates or offer inducements to purchase collaboration. Usually an outright rejection of his approach led to the dismissal of MPs holding offices, but James persisted in cases where he thought that agreement could eventually be obtained. In the campaign of 1687–8 a far more extensive canvass was involved and James had to employ lords lieutenant and itinerant professional agents. Those who agreed to his demands were frequently given offices in corporations or the commission of the peace. Yet they did not receive offices as rewards, but for functional purposes to enable them to act in James' interests, either as MPs committed to repealing the Tests and penal laws, or by using local office to procure the election of such MPs.

After the Revolution such conduct was vigorously denounced as constitutionally subversive. Danby's pensioners in the Cavalier Parliament had been charged with selling their votes in parliamentary divisions, but James' collaborators were accused of undermining the essential principle of representative institutions, by binding themselves in advance to the election of a Commons composed of royal collaborators.[15] If successful James' attempt to pack Parliament would put all

[14] PRO 31/3, Baschet transcripts, Barrillon to Louis, 20 Jan., 6, 10, 13, 17, 24 Feb., 10 Mar., 1687. BL MS Add. 34510, fo. 17.

[15] *Important Questions of State, Law, Justice and Prudence* (London, 1689), p. 3. *A Discourse concerning the Nature, Power and Proper Effects of the present Conventions in both Kingdoms* (London, 1689), pp. 9, 19. *CJ*, X, p. 110.

the liberties of the nation at his mercy, and this led to the inclusion in the Bill of Rights of the seemingly bland clause, that elections to Parliament ought to be free. In 1689 Whigs and especially radical Whigs denounced James' practices as an attempt 'to destroy that share in the Government that every Commoner hath, who has the vote', of attacking the most fundamental of all rights, that of 'having a share in the Legislation, and of being governed by such laws as we ourselves shall choose'.[16] However, past Whig conduct had not been irreproachable, but had provided the model which James imitated. The Whig party machine had organized 'instructions' in many constituencies during the 1681 elections, committing newly returned members to pre-engage themselves to support a new Exclusion Bill and to reject any alternative measure.[17] Furthermore, many of the men who assisted Shaftesbury organize the campaign for James' exclusion took on the job of agents for James in his packing of corporations.[18] On the other side, many Tories had earlier acquiesced in the attempts by their chiefs to restrict freedom of action and discussion within Parliament. The proposed Tests of 1665 and 1675 would have imposed an oath on all peers and MPs not to endeavour any alteration of the existing forms of government established in both church and state. James' attempts to pre-determine the proceedings of Parliament were not unique, then, but they were seen as exceptionally dangerous because they were pressed so systematically and energetically.[19]

The main purpose of the proposed Tests of 1665 and 1675 had been to make it impossible to initiate legislation in favour of religious toleration or comprehension. On James' accession most Tories and Anglican clergy do not seem to have anticipated even his first moves in favour of his co-religionists. They were ready to accept that James should practice his religion within the court, and that the penal laws should not be enforced generally against Catholics, but they were, perhaps naively, taken by surprise by the king's undisguised belief that of all his subjects the Catholics were the most truly loyal. James acknowledged that the Church of England was committed to the Crown by its past pronouncements, and its clergy by the oaths which they had to subscribe, but contrary to the almost universal belief of his subjects he thought that his Catholic subjects were truly loyal to the Crown, and not just to himself because he had become a Catholic. In his view the principles of their religion inculcated loyalty to rulers whose authority was derived from God. Consequently their loyalty was based on principles, not on a coincidence of interests. It could be relied on; as James

[16] 'Good Advice before it be too late', *An Eighth Collection of Papers* (London, 1689), p. 22.
[17] J. R. Jones, *The First Whigs* (London, 1970), pp. 167–73.
[18] Jones, 'James II's Whig Collaborators', pp. 65–70.
[19] D. T. Witcombe, *Charles II and the Cavalier House of Commons 1663–1674* (Manchester, 1966), pp. 36–7, 92, 167.

said to Parliament in November 1685, 'they have approved the Loyalty of their Principles by their practice'.[20]

Therefore James thought it eminently reasonable for him to demand from Anglicans acquiescence in his plans to grant Catholics equality of both civil and religious rights with themselves. He spurned as unprincipled, insecure, and inadequate the concession which was as much as most Tories and Anglicans were, if reluctantly, prepared to recognize, that of 'connivance', that is the non-enforcement of the penal laws. The hostility of Anglicans to the grant of legal rights to Catholics, and the everyday continuation of polemical preaching and publishing against Catholic claims and practices led James to combine exerting pressure on the clergy with demonstrations of direct royal support and encouragement for Catholic missionary activities. The process of exerting pressure became self-perpetuating; it had to be intensified as it became apparent that the missionary campaign was producing unexpectedly meagre results. In the first place James issued Directions to Preachers, defining or limiting the subjects which could be expounded in sermons.[21] When these restrictions were widely disregarded, often by clergy who conscientiously believed that it was their duty to defend their faith and protect their parishioners against Catholic assaults, the king established the Ecclesiastical Commission to enforce his orders. It derived its jurisdiction from his ecclesiastical prerogative, and was universally (if perhaps wrongly) seen as a revival of the execrated Court of High Commission, which had been abolished by statute in 1641, with a clause against its re-establishment.[22] James was intent on extracting unconditional obedience from the clergy, making it clear that he would not accept what he and his apologists described as 'partial obedience', but which Anglicans excused as 'non-compliance' with orders detrimental to their rights.[23]

By suspending Henry Compton, bishop of London, from his episcopal functions, the Ecclesiastical Commission provoked acute fears that James intended to undermine the established Church by disabling it from defending the Protestant religion. Compton had certain demerits. He was blatantly careerist and too involved in secular politics to have the confidence of his fellow bishops.[24] But he was one of the very few seventeenth-century Anglican leaders who took any

[20] *CJ*, IX, pp. 756, 758.

[21] *CSP Dom. James II*, II (Jan. 1686–May 1687), pp. 56–8. *King James' Letter to the Archbishops*, in *A First Collection of Scarce and Valuable Tracts* (Lord Somers) (4 vols., London, 1748), II, pp. 355–6.

[22] Edward Stillingfleet, *A Discourse concerning the Legality of the late Ecclesiastical Commission* (London, 1689), pp. 5–6, 8. *The History of King James' Ecclesiastical Commission* (1711). *A First Collection of Scarce and Valuable Tracts* (Lord Somers), II, p. 355. *CSP Dom., James II*, II, p. 202.

[23] T. B. Howell (ed.), *A complete collection of State Trials and Proceedings for High Treason* (34 vols., London, 1809–28), XII, p. 44. R. Granville, *The Life of . . . Denis Granville* (Exeter, 1902), pp. 376, 380.

[24] Howell (ed.), *State Trials*, XI, pp. 1123–66. PRO 31/3, Baschet transcripts, Barrillon, 29 Aug. 1686. See also Edward F. Carpenter, *The Protestant Bishop, being the Life of Henry Compton, 1632–1713, Bishop of London* (London, 1956).

interest in the Protestant churches of Europe. This interest was not confined to matters of theology. Compton achieved an outstanding reputation by taking the lead in organizing hospitality and charitable relief for the waves of Huguenot refugees who flooded into the country from persecution in France, especially after Louis XIVs formal Revocation of the Edict of Nantes in October 1685. The prosecution of the champion and protector of the Huguenots, for failing to take action against a distinguished Anglican cleric – John Sharp, a future archbishop – planted suspicions in the public mind, which every subsequent move to bring pressure on the Church confirmed, that James was imitating the techniques used in France to undermine Huguenot rights for years before the actual Revocation.[25] Probably most Englishmen and women, brought up in a political and religious culture impregnated with anti-popery, needed little evidence to jump to the conclusion that James intended to destroy the Protestant religion and, like Mary, force his subjects to submit to Rome.

What in reality were James' religious objectives? How practicable were his expectations of achieving them? He had to take into account two major impediments to the expansion of Catholic numbers and influence and to the realization of his ambition to secure for Catholics a secure future. The first was the minuscule size of the existing Catholic minority in England.[26] It provided a much smaller base than that in European countries and regions – such as Bohemia and south-western France – which had been re-converted to Catholicism during the century. Furthermore, the Catholic clergy who were available to staff the missionary campaign in England were inadequate in numbers. By training and experience they were better suited to their previous and largely defensive role of preventing further erosion of the scattered Catholic communities; most were ill-prepared to take advantage of the new opportunities which James gave them, to preach and work openly in an effort to proselytize widely, and to do so without provoking undue hostility and alarm.[27] By contrast, in Ireland the Catholic hierarchy and clergy were already well organized and able to take full advantage of the opportunity which James gave them. The (Anglican) Church of Ireland was forced on to the defensive and found its strength ebbing away, not because of religious persecution (which did not occur) or conversions, but because of the emigration to England of Protestants who had lost their privileged positions (particularly in the corporations) and had no confidence that they would regain them. In Scotland, James' toleration policies were handicapped by the fierce hostility of most Presbyterians to any toleration for Catholics.

[25] A. Tindal Hart, *The Life and Times of John Sharp* (London, 1949), pp. 90–5.

[26] Most contemporaries followed the estimate given in Bishop Compton's 1676 religious census, that Catholics constituted well under 1 per cent of the population: Andrew Browning (ed.), *English Historical Documents, 1600–1714*, VIII (London, 1966), pp. 411–16.

[27] Jones, *The Revolution of 1688*, pp. 86–91. H. C. Foxcroft, *The Life and Letters of Sir George Savile, Bart., first Marquis of Halifax* (2 vols., London 1898), I, p. 466.

James could do little to make up for the deficiencies of the English Catholic clergy, but he made a determined if unsuccessful effort to eliminate the second obstacle to the implementation of his religious policies. In the summer of 1686 he sent his Quaker confidant, William Penn, to the Hague, in an attempt to persuade his daughter and heir presumptive Mary to give advance approval to his planned intention to have the penal laws repealed. Mary (and William) would concede no more than a private assurance that, when she came to the throne, the penal laws would not be enforced – but this was the 'connivance' alternative that James had already rejected.[28] Moreover, Mary's promise could prove to be worthless: she might find herself in the same position as Charles in 1673, when pressure by an aggressively Anglican Parliament had forced him to retract his promises of toleration and acquiesce in the resumption by his ministers of prosecutions against Catholics. James made further attempts to persuade Mary to change her mind, or even to become a Catholic, but she was out of his reach. He also made repeated but clumsy attempts to convert his other daughter, Anne, which she vigorously rejected.[29] In the light of these failures what could James hope to achieve for the Catholics, when it might seem that the policies which he was following were certain to be abandoned, and would probably be reversed, after his death? How far did this apparent difficulty, which could be seen as insuperable until the birth of the Prince of Wales in June 1688, affect his decisions and policies?

James appreciated the difficulties, but he categorically rejected one suggested solution, put forward by some Catholic extremists, of altering the succession and cutting out Mary and Anne, on the pretexts that either they were heretics or the children of what in most European ruling houses would have been a morganatic marriage. Given James' triumph over the attempts to exclude him from the succession, because of his religion, and his strong dynastic feeling, James could not accept any arbitrary interference with his daughters' rights. As he told Paul de Barrillon, the French Ambassador: 'it is God that gives Crowns, and my intention is to do nothing against God and Right'.[30] It was also to Barrillon that James most fully explained his religious objectives. These were to 'establish' the Catholic religion in England, by which he did not mean imposing it on the nation, or substituting the Catholic Church for the Church of England as the officially established Church – although in the fullness of time and with

[28] Gilbert Burnet, *History of His Own Time* (6 vols., Oxford, 1833), III, pp. 139–40. François A. J. Mazure, *Histoire de la Révolution de 1688 en Angleterre* (2 vols., Paris and Brussels, 1825), II, p. 184. PRO 31/3, Baschet transcripts, Barrillon, 26 June 1687. E. Mallet (ed.), *Négociations de Monsieur le Comte d'Avaux en Hollande depuis 1679* (6 vols., Paris, 1752–3), VI, pp. 53, 66.

[29] PRO 31/3, Baschet transcripts, Barrillon, 27 June 1686, 3 Apr., 23 Sept. 1687: Bonrépos to Seignelay, 28 Mar. 1686. See also PRO Barrillon, 26 Jan. 1688, for a feeble attempt to procure Mary's conversion.

[30] Mallett (ed.), *Négociations*, VI, p. 63. Mazure, *Histoire de la Révolution de 1688*, II, p. 188. PRO 31/3, Baschet transcripts, Barrillon, 30 Jan., 12 June 1687: Bonrépos to Seignelay, 21 July 1687.

God's help and blessing this could be expected to come about. The 'entire establishment' of the Catholic Church was the phrase he used to describe that ultimate eventuality.[31] But for practical reasons he could not expect to go further than the more limited objective, which he stated often in private, but never publicly, of giving Catholics full religious rights to put them on terms of full equality with Anglicans, and then by giving them full civil rights (together with the Dissenters) put a coalition of non-Anglicans in a position of permanent security. By this he meant that they would be able to retain their rights, and liberties in the reigns of Mary and Anne, and by their strength and influence in Parliament and the country resist any attempt at a Protestant reaction.[32]

Even so, with the advantages of historical hindsight we tend to see these expectations, and the policies based on them, as completely futile. Looking at the situation up to confirmation of the queen's pregnancy (towards the end of 1687) and before the birth of a healthy male heir in June 1688, it is easy to conclude that James' reign was fated to amount to no more than a Catholic interlude, with a high probability that all his policies would be reversed by his successors. Yet it was during this period, well before the queen became pregnant, that James made his two major and irrevocable policy decisions: the publication of a Declaration of Indulgence (4 April 1687), and the dissolution of Parliament on 2 July, which from the outset was intended to be followed by the campaign to pack a new and pre-engaged Parliament.

In order to make sense of these crucial moves it is necessary to try to view matters as they seemed in March 1687, to make the attempt to see how the future looked to James at that point in time. What such an exercise shows is that there was a strong and increasing possibility that it was not James' reign that would turn out to be a Catholic interlude, but that Mary and Anne (and possibly William) would do no more than provide a Protestant interlude, before they were succeeded by a Catholic dynasty. Mary was childless, after suffering a miscarriage, and as William's health deteriorated the chances of her bearing a child receded.[33] Anne had given birth to two daughters, but both died in February 1687, when she also miscarried. Anne had earlier had a still-born child, and was to miscarry twice again in the next fifteen months.[34] Should James' two daughters have no living children the next in line were two Catholics, the daughters of Henrietta, first duchess of Orleans, Charles I's youngest child, and the only one to be brought up as a Catholic. One could be ignored because

[31] PRO 31/3, Baschet transcripts, Barrillon, 5 May, 12 June, 9 Oct. 1687. *HMC Downshire* I, appendix, part 1, p. 243.

[32] PRO 31/3, Baschet transcripts, Barrillon, 9 Oct. 1687: Bonrépos to Seignelay, 21 July 1687.

[33] S. B. Baxter, *William III* (London, 1966), p. 217. An early miscarriage is documented, but there may have been at least one other. I am indebted for this information to Professor Lois G. Schwoerer, who is researching Mary's life, including her medical history.

[34] David Green, *Queen Anne* (London, 1970), p. 335.

she was married to Carlos II and so was inevitably childless, but the other (Anna Maria) married Vittorio Amedeo (see pp. 365–6, 368 below). Had it not been for the disqualifications imposed later by the Bill of Rights, and the provisions of the 1701 Act of Settlement, the succession would have gone, through her, to the House of Savoy in 1714.[35]

It is this possibility, which in James' mind would obviously serve God's purposes by facilitating a long-term return of the English nation to the True Church, that provides the context for his two central policies with which he was to persist right up to the eve of the Revolution, the establishment of universal religious toleration, and the preparation of a Parliament pre-engaged to legislate according to his directives.

James' Declaration of Indulgence, issued on 4 April 1687, differed in almost every important respect from the Declaration which Charles II had issued in 1672.[36] Unlike the earlier Declaration, which came out of the blue in an abrupt reversal of policy only two years after the passage of the stringent Conventicle Act against Dissenters, it was the culmination of a gradual and selective process of granting effective immunity from the penal laws. Catholics had been the first beneficiaries, then Quakers, and finally through stays on prosecutions and discharges of fines other Dissenters on whose behalf representations were made.[37] James' Declaration followed Charles' in suspending all 'penal laws in matters ecclesiastical', but it gave complete freedom of public worship, whereas in 1672 meeting houses for Dissenters had to be licensed, and Catholics were authorized only to worship in private houses. Now all sects were free to build or adapt places for public worship. Catholic clergy walked the streets in ecclesiastical garb, publicly celebrated mass and taught in newly founded schools – developments that would have been utterly inconceivable a few years earlier. Catholics and Dissenters were given equality with Anglicans in terms of civil rights; this was an area not covered by the 1672 Declaration, which had preceded the enactment of the Tests by the statutes of 1673 and 1678.[38]

The most significant difference can be seen in the markedly inferior guarantees which James gave to the Church of England. In 1672 Charles had been absolutely explicit in giving secure guarantees to the Church as an institution. He promised

[35] For the Savoy line see below, pp. 368–9, and genealogical table 4 in Browning (ed.), *English Historical Documents*, VIII, p. 133. If that line had ended the succession would go to the senior (and Catholic) branches of the Palatine family, who took precedence over the House of Hanover; see table 5, ibid., p. 135. For an explicit reference at the time to the prospect of a Savoyard succession see *A Letter to a Friend, advising in this Extraordinary Juncture how to free the Nation from Slavery for ever* (London, 1689).

[36] For the texts of the 1672 and 1687 Declarations: J. P. Kenyon, *The Stuart Constitution* (Cambridge, 1966), pp. 407–8, 410–13; or, Browning (ed.), *English Historical Documents*, VIII, pp. 387, 395–7.

[37] *HMC Downshire*, I, appendix, part 1, pp. 95, 138–9. *CSP Dom. James II*, II, p. 71. BL MS Add. 34508, fos. 102, 103, 110, 136.

[38] Kenyon, *Stuart Constitution*, pp. 461–2, 465–6. Browning (ed.), *English Historical Documents*, VIII, pp. 389–91, 391–4.

'that the Church of England be preserved and remain entire in its doctrine, discipline and government, as now it stands established by law ... and that no person shall be capable of holding any benefice or preferment of any kind ... who is not exactly conformable'.[39] In contrast James did not grant any institutional guarantees or safeguards. His promises were directed only to individual persons: 'we will protect and maintain our archbishops, bishops and clergy, and all other our subjects of the Church of England in the free exercise of their religion as by law established, in the quiet and full enjoyment of all their possessions'. This can be said to have given the clergy no more than a life-interest: the omission of the 1672 clause that only conformists could hold benefices added to existing fears that vacancies were being prolonged so that they could be filled with Catholics – although there is no evidence that James intended to do this.[40] His reasons for using a different formula of words from Charles' were ideological, and in the long term ominously threatening. Although in his speech to the Council immediately after his accession, repeated to Parliament on 22 May 1685, James went very close to doing so, he was sincerely inhibited in fully guaranteeing the position of the Church of England by his belief, the reason for his conversion to Catholicism, that it was not a true church but an heretical and schismatic body.[41]

The statement of the authority on which the Declaration was based also had perturbing implications. In 1672 Charles based his action on 'that supreme power in ecclesiastical matters' which he claimed to be inherent in the Crown. James did not place a similar limit on his freedom of action. He cited as his authority 'our royal prerogative'. This opened up the possibility that he intended to use his suspending power in secular matters also, outside the sphere of religion covered by the Declaration, and for this reason he thought it advisable to end with an assurance that he intended to preserve subjects in their properties.[42] In addition the arguments which he advanced to justify the cessation of all attempts to impose religious uniformity by coercive methods also contained extremely wide and very ominous implications. In 1672 Charles argued in a pragmatic fashion that coercive legislation had not achieved its objective of reducing the nation to uniformity in the twelve years since the Restoration. James adopted a much wider perspective. He contended that all attempts to impose uniformity in 'the four last reigns' had failed. That meant all attempts since the establishment

[39] Kenyon, *Stuart Constitution*, p. 407. Browning (ed.), *English Historical Documents*, VIII, p. 387.

[40] Two cases gave rise to these suspicions: at Putney a convert was permitted to retain his stipend, provided that a curate was put in to do duty (BL MS Add., 34508, fo. 115); more seriously the archbishopric of York, left vacant by Gilbert Dolben's death in April 1686, was not filled until November 1688.

[41] John Miller, *James II: A Study in Kingship* (Hove, 1978), p. 120. *CJ*, IX, p. 714. The speech to the Council was published.

[42] Kenyon, *Stuart Constitution*, p. 413. Browning (ed.), *English Historical Documents*, VIII, p. 397.

of the Church of England by Elizabeth in 1559, that is over the whole period during which the Church had existed in its present forms.[43]

This pronouncement contained a sincere, personal note. One of the principal reasons for James' defection from the Church was his belief that it was essentially a political creation and entity. Its clergy had always shown themselves particularly concerned to defend and perpetuate their own exclusive privileges, and the Church as a false body had always been insistent on persecution, and always would be. The failure of its persecuting efforts could not be explained in purely pragmatic terms. They could never succeed. As he said in the Declaration, the obstructions to their success were 'invincible', they could never be overcome because the Church of England was not a true church of God.[44]

The conviction of this belief had led James to defect from the Anglican communion, and to reject all arguments and attempts to persuade him to return – although such a reconciliation would have been enormously beneficial, in political terms, as Charles had pointed out. James' tenacious adherence to his new faith, and his dismissal of the Church of England as spurious and its clergy as having no validity, explains his abandonment of the Tory and Anglican alliance forged (insincerely and expedientially but very effectively) by Charles in order to defeat Exclusion. More generally it explains his decision to discard the reliance which his four predecessors had placed on the inculcation of Divine Right principles by the Anglican clergy and universities.[45]

James was nothing if not consistent. The first indications of his conversion to Catholicism had appeared in the early 1670s, when he abstained from Easter communion, because he had come to believe that the Anglican sacraments lacked validity.[46] Similarly he came to believe that the political teachings of those whose ecclesiastical orders were invalid could not be effective. Nor had they been in practice, as the Whig campaign for Exclusion, and the Monmouth rebellion, demonstrated. In practice the clergy had shown themselves loyal, but this was because their interests happened to coincide with those of the Crown.[47] Moreover, the Church had proved to be a political liability. Like many of the Dissenters who associated themselves with James' toleration policies, he

[43] Kenyon, *Stuart Constitution*, pp. 407, 411. Browning (ed.), *English Historical Documents*, VIII, pp. 387, 396.

[44] Kenyon, *Stuart Constitution*, p. 411. Browning (ed.), *English Historical Documents*, VIII, p. 396. *A Letter in Answer to two main Questions of the first Letter to a Dissenter* (London, 1687), pp. 18, 23–4.

[45] The July 1683 decrees of Oxford University were perhaps the most polemical expression of Divine Right theses: Kenyon, *Stuart Constitution*, pp. 471–4. James' apologists made frequent use of itemized pronouncements by Anglican clergy on the duty of unconditional submission to authority: Sir Roger L'Estrange, *An Answer to a Letter to a Dissenter* (London, 1687). *The Rights of the Imperial Soveraignty of the Crown of England Vindicated* (n.p., n.d.). *Vox Cleri pro Rege* (London, 1687).

[46] *CSP Dom. 1673–5*, p. 131. F. C. Turner, *James II* (London, 1950), pp. 125–6. J. S. Clarke, *The Life of James the Second*... (2 vols., London, 1816), I, pp. 482–3, 537–41.

[47] *Animadversions on a late paper entituled a Letter to a Dissenter* (London, 1687), pp. 14–16.

over-estimated the degree of its unpopularity, the extent to which its commitment to coercion had made it hated. He exaggerated both the strength and attractiveness of the dissenting churches, calculating that toleration would lead large numbers of lay men and women to desert the established Church to become either Catholics or Dissenters, and so provide him with a broadly based and less demanding set of associates.[48]

James' propagandists developed the economic arguments contained in the Declaration. Prosperity would be fostered by allowing the free exercise of whatever religion people chose to follow. They would no longer suffer disturbance in the pursuit of their trades and occupations by fines and distraints or imprisonment. Toleration would ensure that the interests of government would coincide with those of the subjects. James made this point explicit when he described the free exercise of religion and the sanctity of private forms of property as 'the two things men value most', and measures to secure them as the 'truest methods' for the achievement of domestic peace. Subjects would be united to their rulers by inclination as well as by duty.[49]

William Penn was one of those who had a hand in the composition of the Declaration, and after its publication he was the most active and prominent among the group of propagandists and pamphleteers who explicated and expanded James' arguments. Penn developed and deployed the most sophisticated proposals for the implementation of James' toleration policies. With the king's express approval, he advanced the idea or project that the religious freedom which James granted in the Declaration on the basis of his prerogative powers, but which was to be put into a statutory form when the next, pre-engaged, Parliament met, should be enshrined as a fundamental and perpetual liberty. This was to be accomplished by what he called a new 'Magna Carta of Religion'.[50] A statute making religious liberty perpetual and irreversible was to be enforced by an ingenious constitutional mechanism, making it impossible for it to be diminished or terminated by any statutes of subsequent Parliaments. As justification Penn argued that religious liberty belonged to the same category of rights as civil liberties and property. Consequently, any statute purporting to deprive subjects of these rights must in constitutional theory be null and void. Therefore like the original Magna Carta the new charter of religious liberty

[48] Ibid., p. 34. PRO 31/3, Baschet transcripts, Barrillon, 31 Mar., 19 May 1687.

[49] *Animadversions on a late paper*, pp. 14–15, 19. Henry Care, *The Legality of the Court held by his Majesty's Ecclesiastical Commissioners Defended* (London, 1688), pp. 32–3.

[50] *The Humble Address of the Presbyterians ... with his Majesty's Gracious Answer* (1687), in *A First collection of Scarce and Valuable Tracts* (Lord Somers), II, p. 360. *A Discourse for Taking Off the Tests and Penal Laws* (London, 1687), preface. Giles Shute, *A New Naked Truth* (London, 1688), pp. 24–5. Burnet, *History of His Own Time*, III, p. 141. *Three Letters tending to demonstrate how the Security of this Nation against all future Persecution for Religion lies in the abolishment of the Present Penal Laws and Tests and the establishment of A new Law for Universal Liberty of Conscience* (London, 1688), pp. II–III.

would be declaratory, stating that such liberty was 'the Natural Right of All Men'.[51]

Penn proposed to ensure the irreversibility of the charter of religious liberty by requiring all office holders, peers, and MPs to take an oath that they would respect it and not attempt to make any alteration in its provisions. Ironically, Penn was thereby appropriating the device which Danby and the bishops had tried to employ in the 1675 Test bill, which had been intended for exactly the opposite purpose, to prevent any legislation being introduced for religious toleration.

Religious liberty was also seen as contributing to the effective authority of government by depriving demagogues of one of their most dangerously effective methods of creating and exploiting distrust – the calculating and cynical encouragement of religious, and especially anti-papist, fears and prejudices. James never credited with sincerity any of those politicians who expressed fears of Catholic influences, or who connected Catholicism with absolutist forms of government. Naturally he detested Shaftesbury, the author of the policy of Exclusion, but he had also profoundly distrusted Danby who had adopted an Anglican line of policy, which involved renewing the prosecution of Catholics, purely in order to develop an independent power base.[52] Bishop Compton could be seen as continuing that line. But James had hopes of winning over a third standard bearer (self-appointed) of the Anglican cause, his own brother-in-law, the earl of Rochester. Rochester had played the decisive role in ensuring the defeat of Exclusion and represented James at Whitehall during Charles' last years. James made him lord treasurer, and pinned his hopes of persuading a significant section of the Anglican clergy and Tories to become Catholics on getting Rochester to take the lead. It was Rochester's final refusal to become a convert which led to his dismissal at the end of 1686, and subsequently to the issuing of the Declaration of Indulgence and James' switch to seek the Dissenters as political and religious allies.[53]

In establishing his sincerity as the sponsor of toleration, James had to distance himself from Louis XIV and the Revocation of the Edict of Nantes. It was in the effort to gain credibility for James' policies that his apologists proposed an unalterable Magna Carta and emphasized the economic benefits of religious toleration. Indeed, they cited the adverse economic effects of the emigration of Huguenots from France after the Revocation as an argument for trusting James.[54] Developments in France showed him what would happen, in terms of economic depression, if toleration was withdrawn, and they hinted that

[51] Ibid., p. II.
[52] PRO 31/3, Baschet transcripts, Barrillon, 12 June 1687.
[53] Ibid., Barrillon, 9 Dec. 1686, 2 Jan. 1687.
[54] *Animadversions on a late paper*, pp. 16–17. *An answer to the Letter to a Dissenter, detecting the many unjust insinuations which highly reflect on his Majesty* (London, 1687), pp. 9–10.

William and the Dutch would be only too pleased with the resulting loss of English economic competitiveness. One former Whig, now writing as a royalist apologist, advanced the thesis that while toleration would bind all subjects in voluntary and economically beneficial obedience to the Crown, it would bring particular advantages to the most useful members of society, the prime creators of wealth. Using arguments that the physiocrats were to be concerned a generation later to refute, he identified these useful elements as those engaged in foreign trade and industrial production, and depreciated the relative importance of others who were employed in agriculture and retailing – occupational groups who were predominantly Tory in their political affiliations. Those whom he favoured – artisans, merchants, and entrepreneurs – were often the backbone of dissenting congregations, and they were concentrated in the urban centres on which James concentrated in his campaign to pack a pre-engaged Parliament.[55]

The campaign to pack Parliament had already been decided on when James finally dissolved Parliament on 2 July 1687, an action that amounted to an admission that closeting had not worked, and that James could no longer expect Tories and the Anglican clergy to concede his demands. Active preparations for the election of a new Parliament began at the end of September, with a purge of the London livery companies. In November purges were extended to the counties and provincial corporations, with an initial estimate that these preparations would have to be continued for about six months. But the sheer magnitude of the work soon resulted in a new target for completion being set; Parliament would be convened in the late autumn of 1688.[56]

This process of electoral preparation involved canvassing, and in practice bringing direct personal pressure on, a high proportion of members of the political nation – that is, several thousand individuals. In the counties the work was done by the lords lieutenant, who put questions to the gentry and substantial freeholders, in the corporations by dispatching former Whig party organizers who now acted as itinerant electoral agents. The action in the counties proved to be relatively unproductive, but significantly it was not repeated despite the evidence that many of the lords lieutenant had done their work incompetently.[57] There was no alternative machinery available, and to use professional agents to bring pressure to bear on their social superiors, the gentry, would have been counter-productive. In the towns these agents worked systematically and intensively, in some cases executing as many as four purges. In April 1688 they began a general review, which led to a final set of dismissals and replacements of men whom they judged to be unreliable.[58] On 24 August James at least was

[55] *A Third Letter from a Gentleman in the Country* (London, 1687), p. 5. Shute, *A New Naked Truth* pp. 24–5.

[56] Jones, *The Revolution of 1688*, pp. 128–75. PRO 31/3, Baschet transcripts, Barrillon, 6 Oct. 1687.

[57] Jones, *The Revolution of 1688*, p. 136. PRO 31/3, Baschet transcripts, Barrillon, 17 Nov. 1687.

[58] Jones, *The Revolution of 1688*, pp. 149–50.

sufficiently satisfied with the results to set 27 November as the date on which the new Parliament should assemble. Letters went out to royal candidates on 15 September, and six days later writs for elections followed – only to be recalled on 28 September.[59]

Since James' campaign of electoral preparations was never put to the test, it is now impossible to judge how much success he would have achieved in the constituencies. However, the evidence does not support the old view that the campaign was a muddle that ended in confusion, and that it could not possibly have succeeded. Not only did James persist with the campaign, but his opponents feared that the chances of success were considerable. It was not just that he threatened to remove or destroy the privileges and influence of many members of the political nation, James also infringed some of their most deeply entrenched and valued principles.[60] The campaign constituted the most blatant royal invasion of, or intrusion into, the affairs of the localities. Although the extent of the autonomy possessed by the county communities should not be exaggerated, many people and especially those just below the social elite of the aristocracy and greater gentry still regarded their county as their 'country', the area in which most matters important to their lives took place. James' interference in the affairs of the counties was as greatly resented as had been the Long Parliament's subordination of the counties. That had at least been at first necessitated by the demands of a civil war, but even so it eventually provoked the risings of 1648 in counties previously loyal to its cause.[61] Similarly James' interventions resulted in the provincial risings of November and December 1688 which completed the collapse of his authority.[62]

The activity of James' electoral agents had the effect of displacing local interest groups in constituencies, and would have made it impossible to continue with the kind of arrangements that had been informally concerted by the county gentry, the so-called 'selectorate'.[63] Shaftesbury had overriden locally acceptable conventions in mobilizing support for Exclusion, particularly in the elections of 1681. He had had no option but to rely increasingly on organization – employing many of the same agents whom James used in 1687–8 – because spontaneous support for Exclusion was waning. Fearing that some Whigs would be ready to compromise, he had also committed successful Whig candidates in 1681 by having 'instructions' imposed on them, to insist on Exclusion, and these were

[59] PRO SP, James II Entry Book 56, fos. 425, 428–9, 431–5, 436–40.

[60] *Important Questions of State*, p. 3. *HMC 12th Report*, appendix, part VI, pp. 422, 429. *CJ*, X, p. 110; charges against Robert Brent 'for endeavouring the subversion of the Government by new modelling several Corporations of England'.

[61] Alan Everitt, *The Community of Kent and the Great Rebellion* (Leicester, 1966), pp. 218–30.

[62] David H. Hosford, *Nottingham, Nobles and the North* (Hamden, Conn., 1976), especially pp. 78–99, 103–18.

[63] Mark A. Kishlansky, *Parliamentary Selection: Social and Political Choice in Early Modern England* (Cambridge, 1986).

organized by the party.[64] This pinning down of newly elected MPs provided James with a model on which he based his strategy of obtaining pre-engagements from intending candidates.

In opting for the techniques which Shaftesbury had used, James was departing from the strategy that had produced the overwhelming Tory majority of 1685, and for the very good reason that most of the 'loyal' members had subsequently proved their personal independence, and their respect for the gentry consensus of their localities, by rejecting his approaches. Only a minority of the 'loyal' members of 1685 had been nominated or supported by the Crown. Most owed their usually unopposed returns to agreements worked out by meetings of the county gentry. Those attending such meetings reached agreements on fit candidates, and often asked the patrons of closed boroughs to reserve a place for men who agreed to stand down in other constituencies, so as to avoid electoral contests. The avoidance of local conflict, rather than a reduction in election expenses, provided them with their main motive.[65] By polarizing the political nation into Whigs and Tories Shaftesbury had revived feuds and factional divisions going back to the 1640s. Similarly by purging the commission of the peace and the corporations, by his wholesale ejections of Tories and his appeal to Dissenters, James revived the bitter divisions of 1679–83.

A principal attraction of the Dissenters as political allies for James was their dependence upon him for religious toleration and local offices. In another area of government James sought to free himself from any dependence upon obtaining the voluntary (and therefore potentially conditional) co-operation of subjects. As a matter of considered policy, ostensibly because of their indifferent or unreliable performance during Monmouth's rebellion, James allowed most county militias to run down in organization and training, so that by 1688 most of them were moribund and unfit for any kind of duties.[66] James placed his entire confidence in the considerably expanded standing, or professional, army. He had no wish for citizen militias to co-exist with the army, to which they might act as a counter-weight. The stationing of his professional forces, in 'inland garrisons' and annual camps near to London, indicated his principal purpose in retaining the new regiments that had been raised during the emergency of Monmouth's rebellion. James' army was intended, like the New Model in the 1650s, primarily as a police force, almost as an army of occupation.[67] Moreover the New Model had acted as the prop of a regime that most people regarded

[64] Jones, *First Whigs*, pp. 167–73.

[65] *HMC, 11th Report*, appendix, part VII, pp. 105–7; *12th Report*, appendix, part V, pp. 85–6; *14th Report*, appendix, part IV, p. 178. Andrew Browning (ed.), *The Memoirs of Sir John Reresby* (Glasgow, 1936), pp. 354–6.

[66] PRO SP 31/4, part 1, fos. 79, 81, 82, part 2, fo. 158. BL Ms Add. 41805, fos. 72, 85. PRO 31/3, Baschet transcripts, Barrillon, 30 July, 6 Aug. 1685.

[67] See John Childs, *The Army, James II and the Glorious Revolution* (Manchester, 1980).

as based on usurpation: James' reliance on a standing army to uphold a legitimate monarchy revealed an ominous distrust of his subjects. His preference for professional or mercenary soldiers flew in the face of the connection which, in the view of many contemporaries, existed between participation in militia duties and the concept of active citizenship.[68]

Of all sections of the nation it was the Anglican clergy who were subjected to the closest and most apparent pressure. Starting with the Directions to Preachers and the creation of the Ecclesiastical Commission it mounted to a climax in 1688. The intensification of pressure in that year was directly connected with James' preparations for parliamentary elections: the second Declaration of Indulgence, issued in April, concluded with an explicit reference to the meeting of Parliament planned for November.[69] Its text was almost entirely a repetition of the 1687 Declaration: the crucial addition consisted of the order that it should be read from the pulpit by the Anglican clergy on two successive Sundays.[70] This reading of Declarations by the Clergy was a device used sparingly by Charles II, but (ominously) more frequently by Louis XIV.[71] Like all James' moves at this time it was related to his electoral preparations. By obeying and reading the Declaration clergy would be seen by their congregations as giving it their 'interpretative consent'.[72] This would separate them from most of the gentry, who had rejected James' approaches, and make it more difficult for them to endorse candidates against James' nominees in elections that would be directly and primarily concerned with the king's objectives, as stated in the Declaration. It had to be expected that some clergy would refuse to read the Declaration, but the Ecclesiastical Commission could be used to discipline them.

Of course, the celebrated petition of the seven bishops upset all James' calculations and comparatively few clergy read the Declaration.[73] Once challenged so successfully, James could not have ignored clerical defiance – unless he also called off his intention to hold elections as planned. The acquittal of the bishops at their trial for seditious libel actually led him to order an intensification, not an abandonment, of his exertion of pressure on the clergy. James ordered diocesan chancellors to make returns of clergy who had failed to read the Declaration.[74] In August he directed that lists of pluralists should be compiled; they were likely

[68] Anchitell Grey, *Debates of the House of Commons from the year 1667 to the year 1694* (10 vols., London, 1769), VI, p. 214 (in 1678). *The Severall Debates of the House of Commons in the Reign of the Late King James II* (London, 1697), pp. 8–9, 19–20.

[69] Browning (ed.), *English Historical Documents*, VIII, pp. 399–400.

[70] PRO PC 2/72, p. 661.

[71] Simon Schama, *Citizens* (New York and London, 1989), p. 489.

[72] *A Letter from a Clergyman in the City to his Friend in the Country containing his Reasons for not reading the Declaration* (London, 1688), pp. 45–6.

[73] Narcissus Luttrell, *A Brief Historical Relation of State Affairs from September 1678 to April 1714* (6 vols., Oxford, 1857), I, pp. 440, 442.

[74] BL MS Add. 34487, fos. 11, 15, 21. Marquise E. Campana de Cavelli, *Les Derniers Stuarts à Saint-Germain en Laye* (2 vols., Paris, 1871), I, p. 241.

to be the wealthier and better connected clergy.[75] This information would in theory make it possible to launch prosecutions before the Ecclesiastical Commission, but the numbers involved and the shortness of time available would have made effective action operationally impracticable before the elections were due. The details suggest that the intention was intimidatory; returns did not have to be made until 6 December, that is after the elections had taken place.[76] The threat of being singled out for prosecution could deter clergymen from making themselves conspicuous by working on behalf of candidates opposed to royal policies. James employed two further forms of pressure. He had already established a commission to investigate prosecutions of Catholics and Dissenters, since 1677, and to report irregularities and specifically what had happened to money levied in fines and goods distrained.[77] Abuses and cases of cruelty uncovered by the commission would also make good electoral propaganda. James was also known to be considering a project put up by one of his advisers for a revaluation of first-fruits, a charge paid by the clergy to the Crown.[78]

However, James uncharacteristically had second thoughts about his policies towards the Anglican clergy. Before he rather belatedly realized that William was preparing to invade, in his Declaration of 21 September announcing that writs were about to be issued for parliamentary elections, James publicized two decisions which show that he seems to have realized that his intimidatory methods might have counter-productive effects. He stated that Catholics would not be eligible for election as MPs; however, this did not extend to Catholic peers, barred by the 1678 Test Act, whom he needed to make up a working majority in the Lords. Furthermore when, as he planned, Parliament repealed the Test Acts, Catholics would become capable of sitting as MPs. Even more significantly, because it constituted an implicit recognition of the alarm he had been provoking about the integrity and security of the Church of England, James expressed his intention of demonstrating his 'resolution inviolably to preserve' the Church. That is, he recognized it as an institution, and proposed to secure it by obtaining from the new Parliament a statute to confirm the Act of Uniformity.[79]

Despite this last minute concession, and others which followed in October, James' earlier behaviour towards the clergy made it inconceivable that they would respond to his appeals in October and November to help rally the nation against William's invasion.[80] The spate of concessions made on the eve of the invasion

[75] BL MS Add. 34487, fo. 25.
[76] Howell (ed.), *State Trials*, XII, p. 432.
[77] *HMC. Downshire*, I, appendix, part 1, p. 298; *9th Report*, appendix, part II (Pole-Gell), p. 398. Burnett, *History of His Own Time*, III, p. 186.
[78] Grey, *Debates*, IX, p. 329.
[79] PRO PC 2/71, p. 736.
[80] *An Account of the late Proposals of the Archbishop of Canterbury to his Majesty*, in *A First Collection of Scarce and Valuable Tracts* (Lord Somers), I, pp. 289–91.

made little impact because they were so obviously enforced and were out of character. However, the effects of having to make concessions on James himself were little short of crippling. Up to the beginning of October he took all the initiatives; others reacted to them. But he became confused and irresolute once he had to react to decisions and moves of his opponents. It is no exaggeration to describe James as becoming increasingly disorientated during the actual period of the Revolution.[81] Beset by a succession of unexpected developments – above all the defection of his daughter Anne and key officers from the field army – James found himself increasingly at the mercy of events and unable to reassess his own lines of policy. In the turmoil and flux of a rapidly deteriorating situation his conduct was governed by three very basic lines of thought. First, only Catholics were truly and unconditionally loyal:[82] he saw virtually no one else after the failure of his first attempt to flee the country. Secondly, he felt that he must at all costs regain personal freedom of action and decision: this necessitated removing himself from the turmoil. He must not allow himself to fall into the position of his father who, after his flight from Oxford in 1646, had no choice but to negotiate with his own subjects under duress, while virtually a prisoner in their hands.[83] Thirdly, he believed that only by seeking asylum in France could he regain his personal freedom, and of all his mistakes this proved to be the most fatal and irrevocable. As soon as his position began to crumble, James' concern for the safety or survival of his wife and infant son led him to dispatch them to France, without understanding that Louis would be able to use them as hostages. This decision was consistent with previous attitudes of James. In 1679, when ordered into exile by Charles as part of his strategy to reduce the hysteria caused by the so-called Popish Plot, James' first instinct was to go to France. This did not just reflect his life-long francophile sympathies. It was also because he feared that pressure from Parliament would lead Charles to abandon his rights to the succession, and that the only support on which he could rely absolutely was that of Louis. However, in the event James accepted Charles' order to leave for Brussels instead.[84]

Not surprisingly Louis treated James as a useful pawn, packing him off without delay to Ireland to act as a diversion under the guidance of the comte d'Avaux.[85] Once established in Dublin James was able at last to convene a Parliament entirely committed to his right, the Jacobite or Patriot Parliament that met in May

[81] W. A. Speck, *Reluctant Revolutionaries* (Oxford, 1988), pp. 117–38.

[82] John Sheffield, earl of Mulgrave and duke of Buckingham, *Works* (4th edn., London, 1753), II, p. 70.

[83] *HMC, 12th Report*, appendix, part VI, p. 21. Campana de Cavelli, *Les Derniers Stuarts*, I, pp. 451, 453–4.

[84] PRO 31/3, Baschet transcripts, Barrillon, 13 Mar. 1679. James had earlier, in 1673, threatened to withdraw to France with his daughters; *CSP Col. Venetian, 1673–5*, p. 37.

[85] J. Hogan (ed.), *Négociations de M. Le Comte d'Avaux en Irlande 1689–90* (Dublin, 1934).

1689.[86] Its Act of Recognition represented a classic statement of Divine Right ideology. It denounced the constitutional settlement being enacted in England as 'a horrid usurpation', and its provisions as contrary to 'the law of God, nature and nations'. It charged William with throwing down all 'the bulwarks and fences of law', and of subverting the 'very being and constitution of Parliaments' in a revival of the 'desperate anti-monarchic principles' of the regicides who had established the Commonwealth. The Act formally acknowledged that

> your Majesty's right to your Imperial Crown is originally, by nature and descent of blood, from God alone, by whom kings reign, and not from your people, not by virtue or pretext of any contract made with them or any Act of your estates on that behalf ... and do hereby further publish and declare that by the undoubted fundamental laws of this kingdom and of England neither the peers ... nor the people collectively or representatively, nor any other persons whatsoever, ever had, have or ought to have any coercive power over the persons of the kings of this realm, and that our allegiance to your Majesty ... is indissoluble, and cannot be renounced by us or our posterities.[87]

In the years after his defeat in Ireland James had to recognize that such principles possessed only a limited appeal in England. In order to attract support he varied the provisions for a permanent settlement which he promulgated in the Declarations which he issued before attempts at invasion by the French. These variations, which obviously had tactical purposes, were generally interpreted as evidence of his insincerity and falseness, and made little impact.[88] For James' private and considered views about the forms that the future government of England should take, after a Stuart Restoration, there is evidence in the personal memorandum he composed in 1692 for the guidance of his infant son.[89]

The emphasis in the memorandum on a monarch's personal and exclusive accountability to God for his performance of royal duties testifies to James' sincere belief in the principles of Divine Right monarchy. But its advice on how the government of England was to be organized underlines the contrast between James' ideological conservatism and his readiness – so apparent in 1687–8 – to innovate and experiment in matters of governmental method. Understandably, they were also designed specifically to prevent any repetition of the Revolution of 1688, and they also reflect the influence on James of French methods of administration, which he had seen in his two periods of exile.

[86] Clarke, *Life of James the Second*, II, pp. 355–61. J. G. Simms, 'The Jacobite Parliament of 1689', in D. W. Hayton and G. O'Brien (eds.), *War and Politics In Ireland, 1649–1730* (London, 1986), pp. 65–90.

[87] Browning (ed.), *English Historical Documents*, VIII, pp. 747–9.

[88] Clarke, *Life of James the Second*, II, pp. 286–91 (Feb. 1689); 362–5 (May 1689); 479–88 (1692); 507–10 (1693); 532–6 (1696, not published). For reactions see *Reflections upon the late King James's Declaration* (London, 1692). *The Pretences of the French Invasion Examined* (London, 1692).

[89] Clarke, *Life of James the Second*, II, pp. 619–42.

3 *Les Monarches Tombants (1689).*
A complex political caricature by Romeyn de Hooghe, depicting a blindfolded James II being thrown from a bucking unicorn representing England. Falling with

him are the queen, Mary of Modena, and the infant James, Prince of Wales. James calls for help to Louis XIV who sits unsteadily on a globe with the sign of the sun on his hat and a Jesuit whispering in his ear while a Dutch sailor applies a huge enema to his posterior. In the centre Father Edward Petre flees, grasping a banner on which are inscribed the names of the great Catholic assassins – Balthasar Gerards, Ravaillac, etc. In the background William III is proclaimed king of England whilst, to the left, Heidelberg lies in flames. See F. Muller, *De Nederlandsche Geschiedenis in platen* (2 vols., Amsterdam, 1863–70), I, p. 429.

French influences were most apparent in James' recommendation that no chief minister should be employed again (the Treasury being kept in commission as a matter of policy) and that the size of the Cabinet Council should not exceed seven.[90] On the other hand, in complete contrast to French practice, all sale and purchase of governmental offices were to be abolished in order to increase the personal authority of the king, who was to make all appointments directly. James' proposals amounted to a complete reorganization of the principal governmental structures. Two new secretaryships of state were to be created, one for the army, the other for the navy. The duties of the two existing secretaries were to be differentiated; in future one was to deal exclusively with foreign affairs, the other with domestic. The four secretaries would constitute an *ex officio* majority in the Cabinet Council; the other members were to be the first commissioner of the Treasury and two non-officials.

These key officials were to be served, and obviously their performance would be monitored, by professional bureaucrats – chief clerks to the secretaries, the secretary to the Treasury, who would be permanent and salaried.[91] Two other important bureaucratic innovations were also proposed. The attorney-general and solicitor-general were to serve the Crown exclusively, while the provision that the lord chancellor should not be a lawyer, but a bishop or a peer, meant that he would only be titular head of the legal profession. A major element of professionalism was to be introduced in local government with two innovations that reflected French practice. Lords lieutenant were to become salaried officials, like the French lieutenant governors.[92] A corps of royal lawyers comparable to *intendants* was to be established, men educated by the Crown in

[90] This proposal was obviously based on Louis XIV's practice, since 1661, of keeping membership of the *conseil en haut* to between four and seven members. John B. Wolf, *Louis XIV* (New York, 1970), pp. 216–18.

[91] Clarke, *Life of James the Second*, II, p. 641. The effectiveness of such a provision had been proved, within James' own personal experience, by the career of Samuel Pepys.

[92] Ibid., p. 642.

the study of the prerogative and its powers before being employed to exercise them.

All James' policies in 1687–8 had been based on the assumption that his strong professional army gave him impregnable security, so that he was free to impose policies that were unacceptable to the politically and socially most influential sections of society. In his memorandum James drew appropriate conclusions from the collapse of the army during the Revolution and the defections of courtiers that had broken his power. Since the standing army was to continue to serve as the power base of the restored monarchy it was essential to ensure its loyalty. The only way of doing this was to make the army Catholic in personnel, as far as this was practicable, and to stipulate that the holder of the key post of secretary of war must also be a Catholic. So too should the holders of all household posts in the court. Catholics would also enjoy a share of other high offices. Two of the four secretaries of state, one commissioner (out of five) at the Treasury would be Catholics; only at the Treasury would Anglicans be in a majority.[93]

The picture given in this essay of James' policies and objectives differs drastically from that given in the Declaration and Bill of Rights. James did not intend, and lacked the capability, to destroy the established Church of England. But he undoubtedly believed that by inaugurating universal religious liberty – the first ruler of England to do so – he would be creating conditions that would be advantageous for the advance of Catholicism. Similarly, by attempting to pack a pre-engaged Parliament he did not plan to create a tyranny by means of statutes, and deprive his subjects of their constitutional rights and properties. Nevertheless, there is a revealing contrast between the amount of attention he gave to preparing for parliamentary elections in 1687–8 and his silence about Parliament in the 1692 memorandum, which contains only an incidental reference to Parliament. James' organization of parliamentary elections was intended to be a one-off; there is no evidence that it would have been repeated, or that he saw Parliament as a permanent partner in government.

The state of England which James foresaw in his 1692 memorandum had earlier been implicit in the policies which he followed in 1687–8. The king would live in a Catholic (and insulated) royal court, with his authority safeguarded against subversion by a predominantly Catholic army. But the obedience of the people would be secured by considerations of interest: they would be thankful for religious liberty and absorbed in the pursuit of their daily professions and occupations. In time the Catholic religion would advance, and the balance between Catholic and Protestant would alter to the benefit of the former. But the strength of royal authority, buttressed by an entirely loyal army, would

[93] Ibid., p. 641.

ensure that such a transformation would be accomplished without rebellion. Whether such a system could have survived without constant support from France must be a matter of speculation, but it would have been a very different England from the one that developed after the Revolution of 1688.

Chapter 2

The Sensible Revolution

JOHN MORRILL

I

Back in 1938, on the 250th anniversary of the Glorious Revolution, it all seemed very straightforward. The English had opted for compromise, common sense, the abandonment of extremism and of enthusiasm:

> The element of 'moderation' which the Revolution enthroned ... was, in its essence, the chaining up of fanaticism alike in politics and in religion. Religion in those days was the chief motive of politics, and after the Revolution a movement towards Latitudinarianism in religion enveloped first England and then for a while all Europe.[1]

These were the confident words of G. M. Trevelyan, concluding his commemorative volume, *The English Revolution, 1688–1689*. His book is unhesitating in its judgment that the Revolution was a good thing, that the institutions and values which emerged from it were those that lay at the foundations of England's greatness as a world power and as a liberal state in the succeeding decades and centuries. It is written with such a transparent insouciance, such a lightness of touch in its laying out of evidence, and with such a fluency of style, that as I struggled through the confusing and hesitant writings of recent years, reading Trevelyan felt like a glass of glycerine and honey slipping down a sore throat. It momentarily eased the inflammation; but was it a cure?

Trevelyan was Whiggish in his approval of the Revolution as a progressive event that contributed much to the advance of modern and advanced values. This is perhaps at its most exposed in his peroration:

> The great emollient of the common ills of life, the humanitarian movement in all its aspects, began in the eighteenth century before the issue of democracy was aroused ... This great humanitarian movement to whose sphere of operations there is no limit, was a new birth of time. It arose in the milder atmosphere of

I am grateful to Julian Hoppit, Jonathan Israel, David Smith, and Bill Speck for some deservedly heavy criticism of drafts of this article.

1 G. M. Trevelyan, *The English Revolution, 1688–1689* (Oxford, 1938), pp. 240–1.

> the great religious and party truce which the Revolution settlement had ushered in. It could not have arisen if the feuds of the Stuart era had been carried on in their full intensity into later generations.[2]

But Trevelyan saw this effect of the Revolution as neither willed nor inevitable. The outcome was, for him, a classic example of the law of unintended consequences: 'in the affair of the Revolution, the element of chance, of sheer good luck, was dominant'.[3] Much of his book is concerned with might-have-beens. Furthermore (as his very choice of title makes clear), Trevelyan was not concerned to endorse the events of 1688–9 as a 'Glorious Revolution'. In his view '"the Sensible Revolution" would have been a more appropriate title'.[4] Thus: 'the true glory of the Revolution lies not in the minimum of violence which was necessary for its success, but in the way of escape from violence which the Revolution Settlement found for future generations of Englishmen'.[5] The elements of his argument were straightforward: England had an intrinsically unstable form of government, and had oscillated dangerously between royal absolutism and the growing power of Parliaments, 'chary of supply to governments whose policy they could not continuously control'.[6] James II's grotesque despotism constituted 'the accident ... that gave our ancestors the opportunity to right themselves'.[7] By his overt popery and clumsy tyranny, he did what even Charles I had avoided doing: he united his subjects in a desire to be rid of him. As a result,

> wise compromise ... staunched for ever the bloodfeud of Roundhead and Cavalier, of Anglican and Puritan, which had broken out first at Edgehill and Naseby, and bled afresh four years back at Sedgemoor. Whig and Tory, having risen together in rebellion against James, seized the fleeting moment of their union to fix a new-old form of government, known in History as the Revolution Settlement.[8]

The outcome was a firm subordination of monarchy to the law, an 'agreement between parties and churches to live and let live', a supple but durable balancing of the interests of the three estates, 'an ordered and legal freedom [which gave England] her power'.[9]

> She often abused her power, as in the matters of Ireland and the Slave Trade, till she reversed her engines; but the whole of mankind would have breathed a harsher air if England had not grown strong. For her power was based not only on her free constitution, but on the maritime and commercial enterprize of her

2 Ibid., pp. 243–4.
3 Ibid., p. 240.
4 Ibid., p. 7.
5 Ibid., p. 9.
6 Ibid., pp. 17–18.
7 Ibid., p. 240.
8 Ibid., p. 10.
9 Ibid., pp. 11, 62–3, 175, 240.

sons, a kind of power naturally akin to freedom, as the power of great armies in its nature is not.[10]

This essay will explore just how much of Trevelyan's confident celebration of the 'Sensible Revolution' has stood up to the corrosive effects of empirical research and, more recently, of 'revisionist' method. I certainly do not wish to deny that Trevelyan's lightness of touch overlays a thinness of research that would forbid publication nowadays. But I find judgments such as Jonathan Clark's to be too harsh (he is writing of the work of both Trevelyan and Basil Williams): 'Whatever their professional gifts it is now impossible to examine their narratives without a mounting sense of frustration at their shallowness, the superficiality and glibness of much of their writing, their willingness to skate over ignorance with a commonly received form of words, and to evade important problems with well-turned generalizations.'[11] What struck me on re-reading it after many years was its startling quality, not its pleasantries and platitudes. Trevelyan is concerned to show that *despite* the confusions and fudges, the Revolution came to have unanticipated and unsought-after consequences. The book as a whole lacks the apparatus, the thorough immersion in the sources, to command scholarly reverence. I am not trying to rehabilitate it as a standard textbook. In deciding to write this essay around a series of quotations from *The English Revolution*, I was doing no more than seeking a framework (I originally intended a series of Aunt Sallies) within which to meet my brief from the editor: to summarize recent historiographical trends in relation to the Revolution of 1688. I came to the view that in his counterpointing of the confusions of the actors with the unintended consequences of their actings, Trevelyan had set up a number of challenging and shrewd assertions which have been subsequently not so much demolished as ducked.

The tactical decision to structure a review of recent literature around passages of Trevelyan has, it is hoped, advantages. It creates a natural agenda and allows for greater clarity of argument. It has the drawback that certain major new approaches are hard to accommodate within that agenda. Trevelyan was concerned with two things: with the short-term causes and immediate nature of the Revolution; and with its long-term consequences. He was not concerned with explicating the medium-term effects and developments – and he ignores or glosses over the rage of party, the nature and extent of Jacobitism, the constitutional and ecclesiological debates over the twenty-five years after 1689, indeed the whole question of how sustaining myths about the Revolution emerged from the ideological tongue-biting of 1689. Something will be said about these issues

[10] Ibid., p. 240.
[11] J. C. D. Clark, *Revolution and Rebellion: State and Society in England in the Seventeenth and Eighteenth Centuries* (Cambridge, 1986), pp. 18–19.

towards the end of the essay. But first we will pursue Trevelyan through the agenda he created.

In turn we will review recent work concerning the nature of James' government and the political context of his downfall; the circumstances of his flight; the significance of the dynastic change; the political aims of William himself; the significance of the Declaration of Rights and the relationship between the Declaration and the offer of the Crown; the significance of the Toleration Act; the impact of the Revolution on Scotland and Ireland; the political and constitutional impact of the wars of the decades after 1689; and the long-term consequences of the Revolution settlement.

II

> Since Parliament would not alter the laws, James could only attain his ends by regarding the law as a restriction on the royal will. The prerogative of the kings of England, their ancient claims to an undefined residuary power, had sometimes in the course of our history swelled to monstrous proportions, and sometimes shrunk back to little, but never quite to nothing. Prerogative was now to be conjured up once more and fashioned into the one substantial reality of a new constitution. This vital change in the royal authority must be effected by pronouncements from the judicial Bench ... James, in short, in his desire to restore Romanism in England, found it necessary to become an absolute monarch like the Princes of Europe. The absurd medieval shackles on the royal power, peculiar to our retrograde island, must be removed ... James, though he was most imprudent in making such an attempt, had at least some reason to hope for success. He had complete control of the executive power, he could dismiss and nominate every servant of the State, and the higher Church patronage was in his hand. Above all he had a large army ... James proceeded to break law on law. Prerogative was to be everything, statutes nothing, if they were not to the liking of the King.[12]

This passage raises a whole series of points which have been much debated since 1938. Was the crisis of 1688 the crisis of a system of government or of a particular man? Is it correct to describe James' government as a despotism or an absolutism or neither? Could James have succeeded in his aims (whatever those were)? Was James seeking to 'restore Romanism'?

Trevelyan's discussion of the origins of the Revolution focuses on the misdeeds of James II. The crisis of 1688–9 was a crisis of confidence in a particular king more than with a system of government.[13] There was an inherent instability in the system of government, a lack of precision in the locus of sovereignty which gave the people of England little protection against a man like James II. But it was the particular way in which power was abused, and the particular

[12] Trevelyan, *The English Revolution*, pp. 62–4.

[13] This is, of course, precisely parallelled by recent concentration by historians of the English Civil War on the iniquities of Charles I, who, it is said, inherited and threw away an essentially strong position.

circumstances of James' rule that determined the nature and outcome of the crisis. Trevelyan began his account with a discussion of 'the provisional compromise between kingly and parliamentary power',[14] but the pre-1685 section is by way of preamble only, to explain how it was that James was able to erect such a despotism. Most of the writing on the Revolution in recent years has followed Trevelyan's lead. J. R. Jones and W. A. Speck in the two most thorough and comprehensive surveys[15] both adopt the same approach as he did – a survey chapter of the Restoration settlement and then an account of the destabilization of politics once James was on the throne. J. R. Western, who was concerned to see 1688 as a counter-revolution, treated the crisis as dating from the early 1680s, and both the Tory reaction of 1681–5 and James' reign as part of a process with a unifying underlying theme – a bid to establish the autonomy and pre-eminence of royal prerogative.[16] The different ends of Charles and James were seen by Western as subordinate to a common purpose as to means – the establishment of royal absolutism. There never has been any serious attempt, however, to see the crisis of 1688 as the culmination of a gradual process of disintegration, in the sense that many scholars from the 1950s to the 1970s saw the collapse of Charles I's government in 1640–9 as the culmination of a century of decline and atrophy.

There are no serious adherents to the view that the settlement of 1660–2 was so inherently unstable that the further collapse of royal authority was only a matter of time. There is no reason to disturb the central claims of Trevelyan that what happened in the Revolution resulted from the actions of a particular king following particular policies.

Trevelyan clearly believed that James could have succeeded – especially once he had a son and (presumably Catholic) heir to succeed him. The above passage describes James' promotion of 'Romanism' as 'imprudent', but the drift of the book as a whole is to see James as all too likely to succeed. This view has been sharply contested. John Miller, for example, has argued that such freedom of action as the Crown possessed was quite inadequate to the task of establishing an authoritarian state. There was no alternative to a reliance upon Parliament for taxation and for the creation (rather than the modification or abrogation) of law, and neither Charles II nor James II believed otherwise; the ubiquity of jury trial was a major safeguard against royal diktat; the Crown continued to rely upon unpaid local elites to supervise tax-collection, enforce law, regulate much social and economic activity, and any attempt to bypass

[14] Trevelyan, *The English Revolution*, p. 22. The difference between this shallow compromise of 1660 and the sensible compromise of 1688 was, of course, that in 1688 the location of sovereignty was not fudged, although everything else was.

[15] J. R. Jones, *The Revolution of 1688 in England* (London, 1972); W. A. Speck, *Reluctant Revolutionaries* (Oxford, 1988).

[16] J. R. Western, *Monarchy and Revolution: The English State in the 1680s* (London, 1972).

that elite would lead to a rapid decline of efficiency and an eventual collapse of royal authority. Many historians have agreed with Miller that both Charles and James were well aware of these constraints, and that neither had any intention of erecting a royal absolutism.[17] It is now widely accepted that Charles was too lazy, too easy-going, too unsystematic to be a threat to liberties. He might turn a blind eye to the assassination of some, and the continuing harassment of many other former republicans, he might for short-term political advantage seek to bend his prerogative to help or strain due process to disrupt the lives of Protestant Dissenters, but the anxieties genuinely felt and exaggeratedly expressed in the 1670s about popery *now* and arbitrary government *now* were a chimera.[18] It has been pointed out that for much of his reign, James expected to be succeeded by his Protestant daughter and her Dutch husband. Why should he seek to establish an absolutism for their benefit? Rather, he was a man in a hurry, trying to secure full civil and religious equality and liberty for his co-religionists. He was sufficiently bigoted to believe that once those rights were established, the self-evident truth and majesty of the Roman Catholic faith would impress itself upon a people who had never had a chance to study or experience it. There would be widespread conversions and no future monarch would be able to suppress the devotion of a largely convert nation. Thus, the emphasis in much recent writing has been on James' genuine commitment to religious toleration; and his single-minded determination to create the conditions within which this counter-reformation would develop the necessary free momentum was political folly but not a despotic design.[19] In that sense at least Trevelyan now appears to be the victim of the seventeenth-century conviction that popery and absolutism were indissolubly linked.

Yet, somehow a lot of recent writing has missed the point. James may not have been absolutist in the technical sense that he imitated the methods of continental absolutisms. He may have misused agreed powers more than he claimed novel ones. But there is no denying his natural authoritarianism. He was like his father only more so. He examined his conscience, he satisfied himself that what he was doing lay within the discretionary area allowed to the king under the law, and he acted. He could not accept that criticism of his policies was principled or sincere. Any protest was of its nature seditious, the questioning of the superior (in every sense) wisdom of the king. And W. A. Speck reminds

[17] This is a theme which can be found in much of John Miller's extensive writing, but perhaps most succinctly in 'The Potential for Absolutism in Later Stuart England', *History*, 69 (1984), pp. 187–207.

[18] The best recent biography of Charles II is by J. R. Jones, *Charles II: Royal Politician* (London, 1987); others by Ronald Hutton and John Miller are imminent. From the papers deriving from these biographies which I have heard, neither is likely to challenge the view expressed here.

[19] This is the view of J. Miller, *James II: A Study in Kingship* (Hove, 1978); M. Ashley, *James II* (London, 1977); and Jones, *The Revolution of 1688*, ch. 5; and more recently of J. Miller, 'James II and Toleration', in E. Cruickshanks (ed.), *By Force or by Default: The Revolution of 1688–89* (Edinburgh, 1989), ch. 2.

us that 'the exercise of absolutism across the Atlantic was not merely the means to an end of religious toleration; it was an end in itself'.[20] It should be said, furthermore, that perhaps not enough attention has been paid to the fact that, in English conditions, royal absolutism would have to be erected not outside and at the expense of Parliament as an institution, but *through* a packed and managed Parliament. What made the period of Danby's rule in the mid-1670s so much more threatening than the extra-parliamentary tinkerings of 1670–3 to many both within and without the elite, and what made the whole of the manipulation of borough charters in the 1680s more menacing still, was this apparent attempt to subvert the independence of Parliament. The buying of MPs' votes or the rigging of elections could be seen as an effort to transform the Houses into a rubber-stamp of the royal will. Given the omnicompetence of statute, and the absence of all checks against legislative tyranny, this was a palpable danger. Professor Jones has suggested that James could have brought this off in 1688, and gained a House of Commons willing to repeal the Test Acts and penal laws. If this is so, then it has to be admitted that the Revolution settlement did little to prevent further gerrymandering. The pious and vacuous hope of the Bill of Rights 'that elections ought to be free' did nothing in itself to protect the realm from executive subversion of the independence of Parliament. Pragmatism and not prescription ensured that nothing like the methods employed by Sunderland and Brent were attempted again; but it must be remembered that opportunities were created and ruthlessly exploited from the 1690s onwards to secure the return of 150 placemen to the House of Commons which were largely responsible for the effectiveness of ministerial control of Parliament in the succeeding decades.[21]

James may well have been genuinely tolerant, but it was surely for complacent, cynical, and shallow reasons and it was not the product of precocious Enlightenment. Toleration would unleash the fissiparous tendencies within Protestantism; there would be a reversion to the chaos of the 1650s and a consequent demoraliza-

[20] Speck, *Reluctant Revolutionaries*, p. 12. James suppressed representative assemblies throughout New England, and created a highly authoritarian viceroyalty. For Trevelyan's awareness of the implications of James' New England policies, see *The English Revolution*, pp. 204–5. The fullest recent accounts are D. S. Lovejoy, *The Glorious Revolution in America* (Middleton, Conn., 1972), and J. Sosin, *English America and the Revolution of 1688* (Lincoln, Nebr., 1982). See also James' policies in Ireland, as discussed in J. Miller, 'The Earl of Tyrconnel and James II's Irish Policy, 1685–1688', *Historical Journal*, 20 (1977), pp. 803–23.

[21] Jones, *The Revolution of 1688*, pp. 127–75. Several historians have doubted that James could have persuaded even a packed Parliament to do his bidding (see the comments of Speck, *Reluctant Revolutionaries*, pp. 131–2). Two things are worth noting about James' obsession with the repeal of these laws. One is the recognition that he had to secure repeal. Suspension would make Catholics dependent upon his prerogative for protection and that protection would die with him. Full equality for Catholics rested upon full statutory protection. More importantly, James believed/recognized that he could only secure the repeal of those Acts in a Parliament made up of Protestants. He acknowledged that he could not suspend the second Test Act and thereby pack the Commons with Catholics. It is a telling illustration that he was a constitutionalist, albeit a warped one.

tion amongst Anglican leaders; the scandal of Protestant disunion would itself turn men and women to the order, cohesion, and authority of the Catholic religion. One does not have to agree with Halifax's dictum that James was hugging the Dissenters now the better to squeeze them thereafter to see that his alliance with them was a patronizing expedient.

More problematic is quite what James meant when he called for the establishment of full civil and religious rights for Catholics.[22] It is true, as has been often pointed out, that in 1688 still less than one quarter of the army and naval officers and of the JPs were Catholic. But in a nation in which rather less than one in twenty overall were Catholic, James' appointments since 1685 still represented an affirmative action programme with a vengeance! And what of James' plans for the full establishment of the Catholic Church on an equality with the Church of England? He had made no progress by 1688 in his plans to appoint diocesan bishops for the Catholic Church in England, and his willingness in 1688 to establish four vicars-apostolic with authority over the Catholics in the four quarters of England indicates at least a medium-term abandonment of the hope of having diocesan bishops appointed.[23] Yet there are suggestions that he had previously been thinking much more in terms of diocesan bishops and the delay in introducing even the compromise of vicars-apostolic was the result not of James' concern for Anglican scruples as of the refusal of the pope to accept James' first nominees. He would not, for example, appoint Fr Petre because of an objection to the consecration of Jesuits to the episcopate.[24] It can hardly be imagined that James would want to see England in a subordinate 'missionary' status for more than a limited time. The establishment of equality for Anglicans and Roman Catholics would involve the establishment of diocesan bishops, who would necessarily have their own courts (it is unthinkable that James would long continue to allow Catholics to be subject to Anglican church courts in such matters as marriage litigation, defamation, or the transmission of property by will). The envisaged wholesale conversions would lead to a massive demand for priests. Where were they to be trained? Surely a full equality for Catholics would entail a sharing of the resources of the universities. Indeed, had not many of the colleges been founded centuries before to train up the administrative elite of the Catholic Church and to combat heresy? Is this not

[22] There are clear and consistent accounts of James' aims in each of the following: Miller, *James II*, pp. 125-8; Western, *Monarchy and Revolution*, pp. 185–210; Jones, *The Revolution of 1688*, pp. 80–6.

[23] For the appointment of vicars-apostolic, see R. Beddard, *A Kingdom without a King. The Journal of the Provisional Government in the Revolution of 1688* (Oxford, 1988), p. 15. The four appointees were, of course, all bishops *in partibus infidelium*.

[24] For the general question of James II's poor relations with Innocent XI, see J. Miller, *Popery and Politics in England 1660–1688* (Cambridge, 1973), ch. 12, and B. Neveu, 'Jacques II, médiateur entre Louis XIV et Innocent XI', *Mélanges d'Archéologie et d'histoire de L'Ecole Française à Rome*, 79 (1967), pp. 699–764.

what ultimately lay behind the Catholic takeover of Magdalen College, Oxford,[25] and the proposed takeover of other colleges at both universities? Particularly sinister was the launching of an enquiry into the management of college property, especially of charitable funds. This raised the spectre of the security of the former monastic lands.[26] Would they not be needed for the re-endowment of Catholic churches? And would not the tithes of the Catholics need to be appropriated for the maintenance of a Catholic clergy? Little of this had materialized by 1688, but it fuelled Anglican fears for the future. If these speculations are right, then James' aim of achieving a full civil and religious equality for Catholics was *not* a moderate programme. James was an authoritarian bigot utterly determined to destroy not only the Anglican control of evangelism but the structures of its material and jurisdictional pre-eminence. Furthermore, the intimidation of the judiciary, the unprecedented reliance upon a supposed suspending power, dubious redefinitions of the dispensing power and the host of other misuses of prerogative power complained against in the Declaration of Rights did happen, and even as means to other ends in James' mind are frightening enough in themselves for his unbigoted or differently bigoted subjects. Trevelyan's harsh view still has something to commend it.

III

> If James had remained in England and submitted to be King under the tutelage of Parliament, it is probable that the change made by the Revolution in the forms of our Constitution would have been greater than it actually was. James would not have been trusted again, without defined limitations on his power. But since William was put on the throne, it was not thought necessary to tie his hands by quasi-republican restrictions on his free action ... We were saved by James' flight to France from the necessity of making such formal change in the law of the constitution, which would have proved in practice a very clumsy and possibly a disastrous experiment.[27]

There are many layers of irony in this passage. First, the appropriation by some scholars of the Bill of Rights as a dummy run for the American Revolution is challenged by Trevelyan's almost contemptuous dismissal of paper-constitutionalism with its built-in rigidities. Secondly, the flight of James, the offer of the Crown to William and Mary, and the legislation of 1689–90 are seen as leading to a minimalist settlement. Since the problem was more with a particular king than with a system of government, the departure of the particular king lessened

[25] G. V. Bennett, 'Loyalist Oxford and the Revolution', in L. S. Sutherland and L. G. Mitchell (eds.), *History of the University of Oxford*, V (Oxford, 1986), pp. 16–19.

[26] Western, *Monarchy and Revolution*, p. 202. Speck, *Reluctant Revolutionaries*, pp. 144–5, has an important discussion of the perceived threat of James seeking the wholesale recovery of monastic lands.

[27] Trevelyan, *The English Revolution*, pp. 129–30.

the need to change the system. In re-examining the claims of historians like Lois Schwoerer that those 'men who endorsed the Declaration of Rights did ... want to change the kingship as well as the king',[28] we should bear Trevelyan's counter-factual speculation in mind: the way in 1688 to change kingship was *not* to change the king.

But there is another layer of irony too. Much recent work has suggested that William was soon seen as anything but the deliverer hailed in 1689. Although Angus MacInnes has characterized him as 'the betrayer of English absolutism', a man 'far less tenacious of the Crown's prerogatives than any of his predecessors had been',[29] much recent work has emphasized the ruthlessness with which William subordinated the scruples of his English subjects to his drive to mobilize resources against Louis XIV. The standing army controversy of 1697–1700 is but the most prominent example of this. We must never forget that what we now call the Act of Settlement of 1701 was officially entitled 'An act for the further limitation of the Crown and better securing the rights and liberties of the subject' – the better securing of them, that is, against the practices of William III. Only the securing of the tenure of judges was present in that Act as a hangover from 1689. The bulk of the clauses relate to the perceived malpractices of the new king.[30] Trevelyan's sense of the complaisance of the political elite at having a Protestant king clearly smoothed over a rather more unsettling tale.

IV

The dynastic change ... coloured everything.[31]

Coloured, Trevelyan writes, not determined. At the heart of the resolution of the political crisis of 1688–9 are two ineluctable facts: an *Interregnum* and the curious arrangements made for the dual monarchy of William and Mary.

The fact of an Interregnum was probably more important than the breach in the line of succession. The legitimate line had been broken at almost half

[28] L. G. Schwoerer, 'The Glorious Revolution as Spectacle: A New Perspective', in S. B. Baxter (ed.), *England's Rise to Greatness, 1660–1783* (Berkeley, Calif., 1983), pp. 127–8.

[29] A. MacInnes, 'When was the English Revolution?', *History*, 66 (1982), p. 376.

[30] R. J. Frankle, 'The Formulation of the Declaration of Rights', *Historical Journal*, 17 (1974), pp. 275–9; J. Childs, '1688', *History*, 73 (1988), pp. 415–24; S. B. Baxter, *William III* (London, 1966), chs. 18–22; J. Carter, 'The Revolution and the Constitution', in G. S. Holmes (ed.), *Britain after the Glorious Revolution 1689–1714* (London, 1969), pp. 39–58; Edmund Ludlow, *A Voice from the Watch Tower*, ed. A. B. Worden (Royal Historical Society, Camden, fourth series 21, London, 1978), pp. 38–55 (Worden rightly commends us to look still at the 23rd chapter of Macaulay's *History*); H. Horwitz, *Parliament, Policy and Politics in the Reign of William III* (Manchester, 1977), chs. 4, 9, 13; L. G. Schwoerer, *'No Standing Armies!' : The Anti-Army Ideology in Seventeenth-Century England* (Baltimore, 1971), ch. 6; P. Hopkins, 'Aspects of Jacobite Conspiracy in England in the Reign of William III', Univ. of Cambridge PhD thesis (1981), esp. pp. 244–64.

[31] Trevelyan, *The English Revolution*, p. 133.

the accessions between 1066 and 1685, and several 'usurpers' were further removed from the natural line of succession than was William III from James II. Neither was there anything in the fact that a living monarch was superseded by a rival following a military coup. The period 1327–1485 saw more irregular than regular transmissions of the kingly office, with kings regnant being deposed on no less than seven occasions. Parliament had more than once been called upon to arbitrate the right to the Crown, most notably in 1460 when, by the Act of Accord, Richard of York was granted the reversion of the Crown ahead of Henry VI's own son Edward. Some historians have seen the titles of both Henry IV and Richard III as being as fully 'parliamentary' and 'constitutionalist' as those of William and Mary.[32] More importantly, Henry VIII had used statute to alter and determine the line of succession, incorporating his bastards at law (Mary and Elizabeth) and excluding and barring a legitimate line (the heirs of his sister Margaret).[33] In the mid-1580s, no less a personage than William Cecil had seriously canvassed the proposal that an act be passed whereby when Elizabeth died, there should be a thirty-day Interregnum during which anyone who asserted his or her title would be debarred, and at the end of which the members of the last sitting Parliament should meet together with a Great Council of dignitaries, to consider the claims to the throne submitted to them, and to determine the succession. Here indeed are pre-echoes of 1689.[34]

Yet the events we are considering were 'coloured' by the dynastic change. The period between 11 December 1688[35] and 13 February 1689 was deemed to be legally and actually an Interregnum. Although from the eleventh to the fourteenth century, kings dated their reigns from their coronations and not from the date of the death of their predecessors, it had become fully established since the accession of Richard II that the throne was never vacant. The regnal years

[32] G. T. Lapsley, 'The Parliamentary Title of Henry IV', *English Historical Review*, 44 (1934), pp. 423–49, 577–606; W. H. Dunham and C. T. Wood, 'The Right to Rule in England: Depositions and the Kingdom's Authority', *American History Review*, 81 (1976), pp. 738–61; cf. J. W. McKenna, 'The Myth of Parliamentary Sovereignty in Late-Medieval England', *English Historical Review*, 99 (1979), pp. 481–506, which argues against any of the parliamentary acts being more than declaratory or confirmatory in nature. It seems to me by extrapolation, that if Dunham and Wood are right, William and Mary's title derived from the same principles as these fourteenth and fifteenth-century precedents; if (as is more likely) McKenna is right, then his arguments reduce the 1689 settlement to the last in a long sequence of *confirmatory* acts.

[33] G. R. Elton, *The Tudor Constitution* (2nd edn, Cambridge, 1984), pp. 2–3.

[34] P. Collinson, 'The Monarchical Republic of Elizabeth I', *Bulletin of the John Rylands Library of Manchester*, 69 (1987), pp. 419–23.

[35] None of the constitutional documents of 1689 specify the date of his presumed abdication. *DNB*; E. B. Fryde *et al.* (eds.), *Handbook of British Chronology* (Royal Historical Society Handbook, 3rd edn, London, 1986), pp. 44–5; and C. Cheney (ed.), *A Handbook of Dates* (RHS Handbook, London, 1978), p. 27, all give 11 December as the effective date for his abdication. I have not had an opportunity to confirm this date although various commissions and patents would need renewal from the end of the reign and James' grants made during his brief return to London from 16 to 22 December might well have been subject to judicial investigation. If the reign was deemed to have ended with his formation of the intention to desert his charge and not from when he actually did so, it could be argued that Whig views had prevailed over Tory ones.

for all legal purposes began at the very moment when the previous reign ended.[36] Thus Charles II was proclaimed by his Convention in 1660 to have been king since 30 January 1649. The Cromwellian Interregnum was deemed not to have been an Interregnum. Although the historical situation was not straightforward, therefore, it is clear that the transition of authority in 1689 did constitute a discontinuity. England could be, in the full legal sense, a monarchy without a monarch.

Various options were logically open to those for whom the flight of James II required a transfer of title: some form of regency, Mary alone, William alone, or some form of joint or dual monarchy of William and Mary. The decision was effectively William's. He would settle for nothing less than full executive power; but recognized the value of keeping wavering Tories in line by granting Mary a share in the title. The result was a unique and purely parliamentary creature: a dual monarchy totally unlike anything that had preceded it. The offer of the crown, the acceptance of it and the formal investiture of William and Mary in Westminster Abbey in April all represented an equal share in the dignity of the title. In that sense, there are real differences between their situation and that of Philip and Mary.[37] For example, it was made clear that when one of them died, the other would become sole ruler. This had been excluded by the Act making Philip King of England in 1554. Yet – in the words of the Declaration of Rights – 'the sole and full exercise of regal power'[38] resided, during his lifetime, with William alone. Only on his death did Mary have the right to issue writs, assent to acts, grant pardons by her own authority. This was an intellectually confused but practical solution to the need to keep very different groups happy in 1689. It did not of itself guarantee that a parliamentary title would thereafter govern the succession. Acts of the Convention declared that once William was dead the hereditary order of succession would be resumed. It was a major victory for Tory scruples that William's heirs by any marriage he might make after Mary's death should take their place in the order of succession *after* Anne and her heirs.[39] Setting aside James' right and that of the son he presented to the world in June 1688 (on the grounds that there were sufficient doubts as to the Prince's actually being James' son to make his accession unsafe), Parliament was in fact seeking to reinstate the hereditary principle. It is unlikely, had Anne left a son or daughter to succeed her, that the dynastic hiccup of 1689 would of itself be now proclaimed as of fundamental importance.

[36] Fryde *et al.* (eds.), *Handbook*, pp. 30-1, 34–45. Henry VII, in order to convict of treason those opposed to his conquest of treason, dated his reign from the day *before* the death of Richard III at the battle of Bosworth. Mary I dated her reign from the moment of her brother's death, not from the moment she was proclaimed against Jane Grey.

[37] D. Loades, *The Reign of Mary Tudor* (London, 1979), pp. 121–2, 219, 223–6.

[38] The phrase was an amendment proposed in the Lords at the last minute, replacing the words 'administration of the government' which had appeared in the Commons draft (*CJ*, X, pp. 24, 25, 29).

[39] 1 William and Mary 1, s. 2, c. 2 (the Bill of Rights).

4 *Allegory on William III's Crossing to England in 1688.*
By Romeyn de Hooghe. William III stands flanked by Marshal Schomberg on one side and a figure symbolizing the unity of the United Provinces on the other. To the left, sits England holding a portrait of Princess Mary on her lap and the fetters of oppression and slavery. Behind her stand the English nobility and clergy calling on the Prince of Orange for help. In the background are the Dutch invasion fleet and army. See Muller, *Nederlandsche Geschiedenis in platen*, I, p. 414.

The replacement of James II by William and Mary is itself of far less constitutional significance than the enforcement of the 1701 Act of Settlement and the bringing in of the Hanoverians. Trevelyan was right: the dynastic change coloured but did not dominate everything.

V

> William did not come over for love of England or for pity of her misfortunes. Neither the country nor its inhabitants made any appeal to his affections, which were all centred in Holland ... In his cold judgment, Holland could only be saved from ultimate conquest by France if England was brought in as an active partner of the anti-French alliance which he had painfully built up in Europe. If he could himself become King of England that object could certainly be secured. Failing that, the object might still be attained if the policy of James were subjected to the will of a freely elected Parliament.[40]

This generally harsh view of William has been endorsed by most recent scholars. Far from being the champion of English liberties, he is now generally por-

[40] Trevelyan, *The English Revolution*, pp. 101–2.

5 *Allegory on William III's Coronation as King of England.*
By Romeyn de Hooghe. A female figure representing England receives the crowned portrait of William III from another figure, with seven spears, behind her, representing the United Provinces, whilst the Dutch Lion looks on.

trayed as a cold, ruthless politician who used the resources of the English state as an arsenal for his continental ventures. As we have already seen, by the mid-1690s many leading Whigs and Tories regretted placing William on the throne. Many of them even opened secret negotiations with James to find out the terms on which he would come back.[41] Certainly a majority of recent scholars would concur with Geoffrey Holmes that:

> too often a convenient blanket [is] thrown over a whole series of changes affecting government, finance, the judiciary and the Church between 1689 and 1701 ... [which] consequently conveys an entirely false idea of the grievances and aspirations of those who chased James II from the throne ... The Act of Settlement provides a perfect illustration of this confusion. Its celebrated restrictive clauses ... reflected dissatisfaction not with James but with William.[42]

In other words, if the Bill of Rights 'gave the throne to William and Mary on condition that they did not behave like James II',[43] then the Act of Settlement

[41] Hopkins, 'Jacobite Conspiracy', esp. ch. 5. See also above, pp. 7, 82.
[42] Holmes, 'Introduction', in Holmes (ed.), *Britain after the Glorious Revolution*, pp. 7–8.
[43] Carter, 'The Revolution and the Constitution', p. 42.

promised it to the Hanoverians on condition that they did not behave like William III.

The above extract also reveals the conundrum of William's initial purpose. Like Monck in his invasion of England in 1660, it is impossible to penetrate the mask to see whether there was a set purpose beyond the remedying of a great evil. Was he expecting to have to settle for less than the Crown? His purposes down to James' flight from Salisbury surely remain as inscrutable in 1988 as they did in 1938. But his purposes thereafter can now be read much more clearly, as a result of the brilliant reconstruction of his reactions to the unfolding of events on a day-by-day basis recently offered by Robert Beddard. He has shown that by early December at the latest, William would settle for nothing less than the Crown, but that he had the patience of Job in working and waiting for it to fall into his lap.[44]

If Trevelyan had a suitably tart view of William, he also had a sense of William's priorities: continental war. He does not develop this at any length in *The English Revolution*, however. Books like John Carswell's *The Descent on England* and Stephen Baxter's *William III*[45] have fleshed out what Trevelyan alluded to, but only recently – and especially elsewhere in this volume (see above, pp. 11–13, 21–3, and below, pp. 105–24) – has the co-equal responsibility of the States of Holland and the States General of the United Provinces with William become clear. This was less a dynastic adventure on William's part than a Dutch invasion intended to appropriate English resources for a live-or-die struggle against Louis XIV. If Trevelyan had read Jonathan Israel's essay, there would surely have been some entries in his index under 'Netherlands', which in 1938 there were not. In view of that piece, too, we should see the events of 1689 less as the imposition of terms upon invited rulers than as the granting of concessions to a conquered people by a new William the Conqueror.

VI

> Here then lay the revolutionary and extra-legal basis of all that was done in 1689. It was impossible to avoid a flaw in the legal title of a Parliament summoned and chosen during an Interregnum, for the English constitution cannot function legally without a King. None the less, the Revolution settlement was first and foremost the establishment of the rule of law ... Apart from the dynastic change, which coloured everything in the new era, there were only two new principles of any importance introduced in 1689. One was that the Crown could not remove Judges, and the other was that Protestant dissenters were to enjoy toleration for their religious worship. Almost everything else was, nominally at least, only resto-

[44] Beddard, *A Kingdom without a King*, pp. 25–41.

[45] J. Carswell, *The Descent on England* (London, 1969); Baxter, *William III*; and more generally, see W. A. Speck, 'The Orangist Conspiracy against James II', *Historical Journal*, 30 (1987), pp. 453–62.

> ration, to repair the breaches in the constitutional fabric made by the illegalities of James II.[46]

> William and Mary were not made King and Queen without conditions. The instrument by which the Convention raised them to the throne was the famous Declaration of Right ... It required the acceptance of these limitations [in the Declaration] as a condition of their elevation to the throne ... The Declaration of Right was, in form at least, purely conservative. It introduced no new principle of law ... for the Convention had wisely decided that alterations in existing laws would require time for debate, and that not another day could be spared before the throne was filled, without great risk to the public safety.[47]

> The settlement of 1689 was not ... a mere party or sectarian triumph, but an agreement between parties and Churches to live and let live.[48]

We have already considered the dynastic points. Here we must ponder the following arguments of Trevelyan: that in its conception and execution the settlement of 1689 was conservative; that William and Mary were made King and Queen upon conditions but that those conditions were that they did not behave like their predecessor; that what mattered was that the parties sank their differences and agreed not to ram their beliefs and philosophies down one another's throats. Let us take each of these propositions in turn.

Trevelyan's cool assessment of the Convention of 1689 seems just about right. By comparison Lois Schwoerer's description of it as 'a revolutionary tribunal' seems inapposite.[49] It differed in hardly any significant way from that of 1660. If anything it was less of an aberration, because the Convention of 1660 was elected on writs issued by a body at least as irregular as that which summoned the Convention of 1689, and writs which placed political constraints on those allowed to be elected. The nervousness of the 1689 Convention at its own legitimacy is seen in the Act which it passed once William and Mary were safely on the throne retroactively confirming the propriety of its summons, and, more importantly, by the Act passed by the Parliament summoned upon royal writs in 1690 which again confirmed everything done by the Convention. The meetings of Caroline MPs and of the Great Council of Peers were indeed irregular, but James' flight created a situation which was wholly without precedent, and for which there was no provision. Nothing was done to give bodies of that kind any standing in any foreseeable future crisis. They were part of the constitutional

[46] Trevelyan, *The English Revolution*, pp. 133–4.
[47] Ibid., pp. 149–50.
[48] Ibid., p. 175.
[49] Schwoerer, 'Revolution as Spectacle', p. 111. But see also her important discussion of 'The Transformation of the 1689 Convention into a Parliament', *Parliamentary History*, 3 (1984), pp. 57–76.

black hole that separated the 'flight(s)' of James from the proclamation of William and Mary.

The nub of the claim that 1689 created constitutional monarchy is, of course, the status of the Declaration of Rights and the Bill of Rights. Here two points need to be more starkly distinguished than they usually are: first, whether the Declaration actually placed any effective constraints upon William's freedom of action; and secondly, whether it was, as Trevelyan unambiguously argued, a condition of the offer of the Crown, a form of contract between king and people.

In relation to the former, the weight of modern opinion is with Trevelyan: the Declaration looked at those actions of James II (and, to a much lesser extent, those of Charles II in the years 1681–5)[50] which were in breach of existing law, and confirmed the illegality of those royal acts. More importantly, it has been argued that the major constraints on the Crown in the eighteenth century, the effective parliamentary power of the purse, the consequent necessity for annual sessions of Parliament, the accountability of the executive to the legislature, and the ending of the Crown's ability to remove judges at will and hence to secure an intimidated (or at any rate compliant) judiciary,[51] were all the consequences of the wars that followed the Revolution and not of the Revolution itself.[52] To this, Jonathan Israel's essay below powerfully retorts that war was the purpose of the invasion and conquest of England and was not an optional or unnecessary extra.[53] But it is no longer sensible to predicate whatever new form of monarchy one wants to see in the eighteenth century upon the *content* of the Declaration of Rights. Fourteenth-century kings had been bound in tighter swaddling bands than bound William in 1689 but had escaped from them soon enough.

The best argument against what I take to be this majority view is that of Lois Schwoerer and Howard Nenner, who concur that 'it was a time-honored tactic in seventeenth-century England for parliamentmen to win new rights by claiming to recover old ones'. Lois Schwoerer's careful study of the text and context are the best and most persuasive account we have for any seventeenth century document of the methodological and evidential problems of sorting out

[50] Most prominently in the clauses against abuses in treason trials (which looked back to the trials of the Rye House plotters) and the levying of excessive fines (principally referring to the 1682 fine on Sir Thomas Pilkington and the 1684 fine on Sir Samuel Barnardiston). See Speck, *Reluctant Revolutionaries*, pp. 147–8, 162.

[51] This in turn disallows Trevelyan's assertion that the loss of the right to remove judges was one of 'the two new principles of any importance introduced in 1689'. It was introduced – and only partially as an afterthought from 1689 – in 1701. See D. Rubini, 'The Precarious Independence of the Judiciary', *Law Quarterly Review*, 83 (1967), pp. 1–19.

[52] The classic statement of this case is Carter, 'The Revolution and the Constitution', pp. 39–58; see also C. Roberts, 'The Constitutional Significance of the Financial Settlement of 1690', *Historical Journal*, 20 (1977), pp. 59–76.

[53] See below, pp. 119–21, 134–5.

whether we can determine what politicians meant from what they said.[54] This raises fundamental problems of hermeneutic and exegesis which have bedevilled historical discussion of the 1620s, 1640s, and 1670s as well as the years around 1688 – and for none of these periods can it be said that historians have really come to grips with this question.[55] I would here try to side-step the issue by saying that – as Trevelyan realized – it did not matter what those who drew up and passed the Declaration intended. The historian of 1689 needs to know who was responsible for the draft finally agreed, but the historian of the consequences of the Revolution is concerned more with the crucial ambiguities which everyone acknowledges to have been left in the text. There was enough of a fudge for everyone to believe what they wanted. Furthermore – and more crucially – the Declaration of Rights could not and did not have the power or the authority to bind kings, however much a majority of those who proferred it on 13 February may have believed that William and Mary were bound to observe it. It did not compel anyone else to accept that there was now a contract between king and people, and it did not help those who believed that there had been and should be a contract to make such contracts easier to enforce.

Many historians, like contemporaries of the Declaration, can and do argue whether the offer of the throne was conditional upon the acceptance of the Declaration.[56] Trevelyan certainly argues too readily that it was. But even if it had been a condition, how could it be enforced? Unlike the Petition of Right of 1628 it was not assented to by the king using a formula of assent known to the law. It was not a statute, and its engrossment on parchment and enrolment in Chancery could not and did not give it any status as a statutory instrument that could be pleaded in court. It did not bind the judges. It was not even in any tangible form incorporated into the new coronation oath. What redress did the subject have if he or she believed a future monarch had violated it? That subject could not plead protection under it in court, but would have to

[54] This is a principle theme of L. G. Schwoerer, *The Declaration of Rights, 1689* (Baltimore, 1981), and more specifically in L. G. Schwoerer, 'The Role of the Lawyers in the Revolution of 1688–9', in R. Schnur (ed.), *Die Rolle der Juristen bei der Entstehung des modernen Staates* (Berlin, 1986), p. 484. Howard Nenner's important discussion of this point (which has important implications for early Stuart historians) is in *By Colour of Law: Legal Culture and Constitutional Politics in England, 1660–1689* (Chicago, 1976), pp. 63–70.

[55] I have attempted some discussion of these questions with relation to the early 1640s in an article 'Charles I, Tyranny and the Origins of the English Revolution', in W. Lamont (ed.), *Religion, Resistance and the English Civil War* (Washington D.C., Folger Institute Publications, 1990), pp. 91–114.

[56] For four attempts to show it *was* a condition, see L. Pinkham, *William III and the Respectable Revolution* (Cambridge, Mass., 1954), pp. 234–5; Frankle, 'The Formulation of the Declaration of Rights', p. 270; H. Nenner, 'The Convention of 1689: A Triumph of Constitutional Form', *American Journal of Legal History*, 10 (1966), p. 295, and 'Constitutional Uncertainty and the Declaration of Right', in B. Malament (ed.), *After the Reformation* (Philadelphia, 1980), pp. 291–308; Schwoerer, *Declaration of Rights*, esp. pp. 281–91. For a more convincing denial, see Carter, 'The Revolution and the Constitution', pp. 40–4; Horwitz, *Parliament*, pp. 10–14. Most of these are discussed by Schwoerer in 'Revolution as Spectacle', pp. 127–31. A close consideration of the meaning to those engaged in the debates of the crucial words 'abdicate' and 'contract' is to be found in a sequence of articles by Thomas Slaughter and John Miller in *Historical Journal*, 24 (1981), 25 (1982), and 28 (1985).

cite the statutes and precedents which the Declaration itself claimed to have been violated. The Declaration laid down no new procedure for investigating violations of those laws and precedents. There was no attempt to revive constitutional forms that could call the king to account. The subjects had no way to remove an arbitrary king in the aftermath of 1688 other than the ways they had to remove an arbitrary king before 1688: by parliamentary pressure, by passive disobedience or by rebellion.[57]

The Bill of Rights was a diluted version of the Declaration. It was indeed an Act which had received royal approval, it was enrolled in Chancery, it was pleadable. But it was a statute only in the normal sense, revocable by the simple act of any future Parliament. It was a part of the fabric of the law, not a yardstick by which other laws could be judged. And it is certainly not part of a contract between king and people. By the time William assented to it, he and Mary had been crowned.[58]

The final point Trevelyan makes about the settlement of 1689 is that it was 'an agreement between parties ... to live and let live'. He was well aware that this truce of the parties was of short duration. I doubt whether he would have quibbled with the phrase 'the rage of party' so favoured by more recent historians of the period 1694–1715. But in his keenness to see the Revolution as ending the sectarianism of Roundhead and Cavalier, Anglican and Puritan, and so on,[59] he certainly smoothes out the bitterness of the following decades. If Toryism is equated too much with the temporizings of the likes of Nottingham and Danby, then Whiggism is also assumed too readily to be reborn in 1688 fully formed in the shape of the Venetian oligarchs of the eighteenth century.

Trevelyan's account can be faulted on all sorts of levels. We are by no means as sure as we were that we can speak of Whig and Tory parties with a continuous history from the 1670s to the 1700s and beyond. The coherence of the Whigs in the great crisis of the Restoration is coming in for attack.[60] The continuities from the 1670s to the 1690s are looking increasingly hard to find. Certainly

[57] L. G. Schwoerer makes a further important claim when she draws attention to the wording of the proclamation issued following the offer of the Crown to William and Mary and their acceptance of it. She writes: 'the text they finally agreed upon is significantly different from that of the documents proclaiming earlier Stuart kings. The Privy Council is not named, but the House of Commons and "others of the commons of the realm" are specifically mentioned along with the Lords Spiritual and Temporal and the Lord Mayor and Citizens of London as persons proclaiming the new monarchs' (Schwoerer, 'Revolution as Spectacle', pp. 113–14). There was no Privy Council capable of proclaiming William and Mary in February, and the Londoners and Commoners are pointedly not mentioned in the first half of the proclamation which describes how the Crown came to be offered and accepted; they are simply mentioned as those who sought to broadcast news of an accomplished fact (*CJ*, X, p. 28).

[58] The date of the coronation was 11 April 1689 (Baxter, *William III*, p. 248) and of the royal assent to the Bill of Rights was 16 December 1689. For an admirable discussion of the *content* of the Bill of Rights, see L. G. Schwoerer, 'The Bill of Rights: Epitome of the Revolution of 1688–9', in J. G. A. Pocock (ed.), *Three British Revolutions: 1641, 1688, 1776* (Princeton, 1980), pp. 224–43.

[59] See above, pp. 73–4.

[60] See J. Scott, *Algernon Sidney and the Restoration Crisis* (Cambridge, forthcoming).

once one has read Geoffrey Holmes' masterpiece *British Politics in the Age of Anne*,[61] one is in no doubt that the structure of 'party' and the existence of party organization is neither present in nor a necessary consequence of, the events of 1688–9. The 1690s remain the most difficult and incoherent of all decades to narrate precisely because of the lack of strong party identities.[62] It is not just that Whig and Tory groupings are political invertebrates in the 1690s; fundamental shifts were to occur in the way most groups conceptualized and articulated their view on the nature of the state and the polity. Most Whigs had to decide whether to abandon their roots as a natural 'Country' party, suspicious of, even hostile to, the pretensions of the executive; and the Tories, upholders of strong but responsible government, had, through a politics of regret, and for some a politics of nostalgia, to adjust to perpetual exile from power and disdain, even contempt, for the burgeoning apparatus of an expanding state.[63] Particularly important on the Whig side is the way in which initially dangerous, subversive, destabilizing political philosophies which played minimal part in the making of the Revolution itself were appropriated by later Whigs but reinterpreted so as to draw their sting. Above all the eighteenth century was to lionize the thought of Locke and Sidney but only after emasculating the one and sanitizing the other.[64]

What Trevelyan's account even more fatally obscures is the fissiparous tendencies of the Revolution settlement. Because Jacobites and Nonjurors died out eventually, there is no reason to discount their anguish and the threat they constituted, or were believed to constitute, to those who, however frigidly, embraced the Revolution.[65] I doubt whether there is any livelier debate at present over

[61] G. Holmes, *British Politics in the Age of Anne* (rev. edn, London 1987).

[62] Horwitz, *Parliament*, has three excellent analytical chapters (4, 9, and 13), but the narrative is impossible to follow. B. W. Hill, *The Growth of Parliamentary Parties, 1689–1742* (London, 1976), comes into its own after 1700 and especially after 1715, while D. Rubini, *Court and Country 1688–1702* (London, 1968), flounders completely. Two articles provide the best context for understanding what was happening: H. Horwitz, 'The Structure of Parliamentary Politics', in Holmes (ed.), *Britain after the Glorious Revolution*, pp. 96–114, and D. Hayton, 'The "Country" Interest and the Party System', in C. Jones (ed.), *Party and Management in Parliament, 1660–1784* (Leicester, 1984), pp. 37–86. J. C. D. Clark, 'A General Theory of Party, Opposition and Government', *Historical Journal*, 23 (1980), pp. 295–325, is one of that author's most thought-provoking pieces.

[63] The best discussion of the tergiversations and transmutations of party ideology in the years after 1689 is J. P. Kenyon, *Revolution Principles* (Cambridge, 1977), but there is a great deal of value (and which has not appeared in his stream of influential articles) in Mark Goldie's unpublished 1978 Cambridge PhD thesis, 'Tory Political Thought in England, 1688–1714'.

[64] R. Ashcraft, *Revolutionary Politics and Locke's Two Treatises of Government* (Princeton, 1986); J. Scott, *Algernon Sidney and the English Republic 1623–1677* (Cambridge, 1988), esp. ch. 1; Kenyon, *Revolution Principles*, pp. 17–19, 63–4; J. Dunn, 'The Politics of Locke in Eighteenth-Century England and America', in J. W. Yolton (ed.), *John Locke: Problems and Perspectives* (Cambridge, 1969), pp. 45–80.

[65] For a cross-section of the large-scale recent rediscovery of Jacobitism, see B. Lenman, *The Jacobite Risings in Britain, 1689–1746* (London, 1980); E. Cruickshanks (ed.), *Ideology and Conspiracy: Aspects of Jacobitism, 1689–1759* (Edinburgh, 1982); Hopkins, 'Jacobite Conspiracy'. Clark, *Revolution and Rebellion*, appendix 2, is a bibliography of recent Jacobite writings. M. Goldie, 'The Nonjurors, Episcopacy and the Origins of the Convention Parliament', in Cruickshanks (ed.), *Ideology and Conspiracy*, pp. 15–35, is an important study of the 'clerical counterpart of Jacobitism'.

the political aftermath of the Revolution than that over the nature and significance of Jacobitism. Both as a real threat to the survival of the 1689 settlement, let alone the settlement of 1701/14, and as a tantalizing option which in the 1710s bankrupted politically if not intellectually the lives of many of those Tories who had gone along with William and (with a sigh of relief) with Anne, it certainly disturbs the irenic atmosphere conjured up by Trevelyan.

Curiously while the radicals of the 1640s and 1650s enjoyed a heyday in the historiography of the 1960s and 1970s, the radicals of the period around and after 1689 received little attention. We certainly know less about them than about the Jacobites. Their religious ideas are finally receiving the attention they deserve.[66] But the importance of republican thinking at the heart of the Revolution has been glanced at more often than confronted head-on. Recently, however, Mark Goldie has – better than anyone else – retrieved for us the 'roots of true Whiggism', the frustrated republican hopes of a broad, radical grouping in 1689 who had to be rudely shoved aside.[67] Goldie's article makes ever greater sense as a far more complex picture is being painted of politics of the 1670s, and as intellectually much tougher and more ruthless republican strands of thought and activist groups are identified.[68] What seems to have happened is that in 1688–9 the more moderate of the Tories made common cause, albeit very briefly, with the more moderate of the Whigs to produce a centrist compromise and constitutional blur to the frustration of significant numbers of principled men on both wings, a centrist compromise more enduring than the alliance of moderates. It is as though neutralism had triumphed in 1642 to the rage, discomfiture, and frustration of Cavaliers and of Puritan bigots.

All this admitted, the absence of any pogroms, the informal oblivion if not a formal indemnity for all indiscretions up to the moment of William's landing, the willingness by the parties to the Declaration, especially the Whigs, not to make others devour their own vomit, all suggest that Trevelyan is right in essence. And his transcription of the crucial words with a running gloss that sums up the spirit of compromise clinches it.[69]

[66] The classical texts on post-1688 republicanism are C. Robbins, *The Eighteenth-Century Commonwealth men* (Cambridge, Mass., 1959), and J. G. A. Pocock, *The Machiavellian Moment* (Princeton, 1977), esp. ch. 13. An important recent contribution is M. Goldie, 'The Roots of True Whiggism', *History of Political Thought*, 1 (1980), pp. 195–236. On the religious radicalism of the 1690s, all previous accounts are supplanted by J. Champion, 'The Ancient Constitution of the Christian Church: The Church of England and its Enemies, 1660–1730', Univ. of Cambridge PhD thesis (1989), chs. 4–6.

[67] Goldie, 'True Whiggism', pp. 195–236. This point is powerfully reinforced by the essay by Blair Worden (see below, pp. 255–67).

[68] Scott, *Sidney and the English Republic*; Scott, *Sidney and the Restoration Crisis*; Ashcraft, *Revolutionary Politics*; Ludlow, *Voyce from the Watch Tower*, ed. Worden, introduction.

[69] Trevelyan, *The English Revolution*, p. 146: 'That King James the Second, having endeavoured to subvert the constitution of the Kingdom, by breaking the *original contract* between the King and people [a Whig remark], and by the advice of Jesuits and other wicked persons having violated the fundamental laws and withdrawn himself out of the kingdom, hath *abdicated* the government [a concession to the Tories] and that *the throne is thereby vacant* [a Whig conclusion]'.

As a coda to this section, I will just add a few further observations about Trevelyan's view of the constitutional harmony engendered by 1689. The first is a paradox in relation to the Catholic community. The right of free assembly conferred upon Protestant Dissenters under the Toleration Act was not, of course, extended to Roman Catholics, but this was just part of a general reinforcement of anti-papal legislation – most notably by the extension of the Oath contained in the Second Test Act to the monarch in the Act Settling the Succession of the Crown and by the clauses of the Act of Settlement debarring Catholics from the throne. It was – a point often missed – the former Act, not the latter, that produced a contract limiting the throne to non-Catholics.[70] At least as significant, however, is the fact that while the settlement did not overnight destroy the anti-popery of the mass of Englishmen, it transformed it. Before 1603 and after 1688 fear of popery was a fear of an external threat, of foreign rulers (Philip II and Mary Queen of Scots, Louis XIV and the Stuarts) working with a fifth column in the English provinces and, of course, in Ireland. The nation sought to rally around a Protestant ruler against this double threat. Between 1603 and 1688 the threat was very different: the threat of an insidious conspiracy at the heart of government, the poisoning of the king's mind, the weakening of the state's defences against the international popish conspiracy.[71]

A final comment upon the constitutional settlement: it was clearly intended to prevent any further attempt at executive tyranny, at least in the form which, it was believed, James had practised it. But it did nothing to prevent any further legislative tyranny. For the Dissenters in particular, measures like the Second Conventicle Act of 1670 (which subjected them to invasions of their property and to severe penalties without trial by jury) demonstrated that Parliament could as readily set aside natural rights as could a popish king. The readiness of the Convention, almost as soon as it had proffered the Declaration of Rights to William and Mary, to suspend rights of *habeas corpus* and to allow William, upon his request, 'in this conjuncture of affairs, and for the public safety, [to] secure some persons as dangerous to the government and [if] it might be convenient to secure more',[72] did not augur well. Given the ease with which Charles II and James II had sought to subvert the independence of the Houses, and the absence of safeguards in 1689 to prevent a return by the Crown to that

[70] 1 William and Mary 1 s. 2, c. 2. This was a *quid pro quo* for the Tory concern, expressed in the bill, that the natural line of inheritance should reassert itself no later than at the death of William: the succession was to lie with Mary's heirs, then Anne and her heirs, then William's heirs by any second or further wife.

[71] Compare C. Wiener, 'The Beleaguered Isle: A Study of Elizabethan and Early Jacobean Anti-Catholicism', *Past and Present*, 51 (1973); P. Lake, 'Anti-Popery: The Structure of a Prejudice', in R. Cust and A. Hughes (eds.), *Conflict in Early Stuart England* (Harlow, 1989); and J. Scott, 'England's Troubles: Exhuming the Popish Plot', in T. Harris, P. Seaward, and M. Goldie (eds.), *Liberty and authority: The Politics of Religion in Restoration England* (Oxford, 1990).

[72] *LJ*, XIV, p. 135. It is, however, a point not missed by Henry Horwitz, '1689 (and All That)', *Parliamentary History*, 6 (1987), pp. 25–31.

policy at a later date, this is a glaring omission.[73] Here, above all, it was not the bloodlessness of the Sensible Revolution so much as the bloodiness of the wars against Louis XIV which reduced the risk of legislative tyranny. The risk was reduced but never (down to this day) removed.

VII

> The Ecclesiastical Settlement of 1689 was a compromise inclining to the Church and Tory side of things, whereas the Dynastic Settlement had inclined to the Whig side ... The success of the Toleration Act was in part due to its limitations. It had been drawn up with great practical skill and prudence, so as to win the consent of all parties, to relieve the timid and to placate the prejudiced. Its limitations, its illogicality, its want of theoretical principle which made it acceptable in a bygone age, amuse or irritate the modern student ... No general principle of Toleration is announced. Indeed the suspected word 'Toleration' is nowhere to be found in the measure ... The Clarendon code of persecuting laws is not repealed but certain classes of people on certain conditions are allowed to claim exemption ... In fact, by this careful picking of steps along a slippery path, England advanced further towards Toleration in practice than any other European country except Holland.[74]

Trevelyan's discussion of the Toleration Act and of its consequences is one of the most remarkable and most perceptive sections of his book. To show why I think this is so, it is necessary to digress a little.

Patrick Collinson once drew an exceptionally helpful distinction between two types of ecclesiastical history; but the distinction holds for all kinds of history. It is between the vertical approach, which he associated with 'denominationally committed historians' isolating and tracing the developments of those characteristic values, beliefs, structures which came to characterize their sect; and the horizontal approach, which seeks to recreate the particularity of the subject studied in time and place. William Lamont, in developing this distinction, describes the vertical approach as an attempt to discard the 'dross, the prejudices and contentiousness of the age ... and to extract the residual gold'.[75] Horizontal history, by comparison, gives the contingent, the idea which withered and perished, the dross, equal importance in recapturing the particularity of the past. In many ways the search for a fuller *horizontal* history is the story of 'revisionism'. 'Revisionists' refuse to use the historical filter, to highlight or emphasize those events, values, structures which were to persist, endure, *win out*. The hazard with 'revisionism' is a kind of nominalism. Every event, every idea is over-contex-

[73] For fuller comments on this, see J. S. Morrill, 'The Later Stuarts: A Glorious Restoration?', *History Today*, 38 (July 1988), pp. 8–16.

[74] Trevelyan, *The English Revolution*, pp. 173–5.

[75] P. Collinson, 'Towards a Broader Understanding of the Early Dissenting Tradition', in C. R. Cole and M. E. Moody (eds.), *The Dissenting Tradition* (Ohio, 1975), pp. 1-38; W. M. Lamont, *Richard Baxter and the Millennium* (Brighton, 1979), pp. 19–22.

tualized and over-particularized. By looking at the short-term and often muddled or unprincipled actions of those involved, particular Acts, actions, judgments, can be stripped of their role in changing things. It has led to the not wholly unjustified complaint that early Stuart historians have demonstrated that there was no need for a civil war; that there was no deepening crisis in the hearts and minds of those living through the reign of a man whose notion of his own powers and of their liberties was fundamentally different from their own. A lesser quantity of less critical ink has been devoted to showing that the offer of the Crown to William and Mary along with the Declaration of Rights, the later Bill of Rights, and the Toleration Act were all muddled compromises, most things to most men, and were not, could not be, the foundation of a new order. The immense value and importance of Trevelyan's book was that it accepted all the contingency, all the dross, all the unsatisfying and irritating compromise of the settlement, and then shows how despite that (even because of it) English history took a new course.

Modern scholarship has amply demonstrated the niggardly aspects of the Toleration Act, how narrowly it was conceived, how limited were the rights conferred.[76] But modern scholarship has also shown what a body-blow it came to be to the Church of England. The limited rights accorded to the few who set up in competition with the Church created a space to be taken advantage of by the many who chose to ignore all organized religion. The collapse of ecclesiastical discipline and the ability of the church courts to enforce moral and spiritual norms was far steeper in the decades after 1688 than in the previous period. What modern scholarship would modify in Trevelyan's account would be the way he underestimates the bitter feuding over the next thirty years occasioned by the ambiguities in the Act, feuds which reached a height in the years 1702–5 and 1709–13 and which culminated in the passage of the Occasional Conformity and Schism Bills. In the search for long-term benefits, he smooths over medium-term perturbations.

Yet the Toleration Act *was* a bi-partisan measure, introduced by the Tory earl of Nottingham. It satisfied no one, but that was its merit. It caused the corrosion of Anglican triumphalism; it recognized, and in the decades that followed it inculcated the recognition, that it was no longer possible for English governors to seek to recreate a confessional state. Thus, like the Tories after the Great Reform Act of 1832, the Tories of the eighteenth century continued to regret that fundamental changes had taken place, but they could not seek

[76] It is difficult to think of a reliable and full account of the making of the 'Toleration Act' (or *An Act for exempting their Majestyes Protestant Subjects dissenting from the Church of England from the penalties of certain laws* as it was properly called) – 1 William and Mary c. 18. H. Horwitz, *Revolution Politicks* (Cambridge, 1968), pp. 87–94, and G. Holmes, *The Trial of Doctor Sacheverell* (London, 1973), pp. 23–36, are as clear and straightforward as any. But see the important article by John Spurr, 'The Church of England, Comprehension and the 1689 Toleration Act', forthcoming.

to reverse them. They could seek to interpret the Toleration Act as narrowly as possible; but they could not think of repealing it, even with the majorities of 1710 or 1713. On the other hand, the Act's meanness and pettiness meant that membership of dissenting churches remained unattractive, inducing most respectable Dissenters into the dreary compromise of occasional conformity, a blow to self-esteem and to the holier-than-thou side of the Puritan tradition. The effect again was to accelerate change. Trevelyan was able to discern the link between these changes and the death of Enthusiasm, of Zeal – 'the chaining up of fanaticism', as he put it.[77]

It could be argued that the experience of defeat in 1660, the shattering experience of abandonment by God of the people He had led and caused to overthrow both monarchy and idolatry in the 1640s, had already transformed English Puritanism. The persecution of the 1660s completed what the catastrophe of 1660–2 had not achieved. William Lamont, amongst others, has suggested that it was not as straightforward as that.[78] Self-confidence, self-assurance (I use the latter term conscious of its theological ambiguity) drained after 1660; but it is not clear that the belief in a New Jerusalem, the perfection of human institutions under divine guidance so that all men could be brought to an understanding of and disciplined obedience to the revealed Will of God, vanished so quickly. Equally, it is not at all clear that the bishops and their apologists would agree that their version of a godly symmetry of church and state working together to bring imperfect men and women to a perfect obedience was unrealizable, however much in practice it seemed further from realization than before the civil wars. The Toleration Act, by its humbling of everyone's pretensions, by being 'a compromise inclining to the Church and Tory side of things',[79] but only just, completed the disillusionment with using perfected institutions to perfect Man. Instead, those forms of pietism came to predominate which accepted the world as a broken and fallen place and sought only to use religious institutions as forms within which individuals could find the means to build Temples of Grace within themselves. Of course, this is only part of the picture: one cannot see the Toleration Act as achieving this of itself. Deeper intellectual currents were flowing and creating new imperatives. The late seventeenth century saw the rise of more optimistic accounts of human nature and above all human reason. In these new accounts all men and women – not just a clerical elite

[77] See above, pp. 73–4. For Anglican triumphalism in the period 1660–1714 see especially the work of Mark Goldie, as in 'John Locke and Anglican Royalism', *Political Studies*, 31 (1983), pp. 65–85, and 'The Political Thought of the Anglican Revolution', forthcoming, a marvellous reconstruction of the foiled 'Anglican' coup against James in the second half of 1688. For the shriller Anglicanism of the twenty-five years after 1688, see G. V. Bennett, *The Tory Crisis in Church and State 1688–1730* (Oxford, 1975).

[78] Lamont, *Baxter*, ch. 4, 'Baxter and the Non-Emancipation of Restoration Dissent'.

[79] Trevelyan, *The English Revolution*, p. 153.

or a cosy coterie of intellectuals gathered at Great Tew[80] – were invested with reason enough to make sense of the Christian message and of its moral demands, with the final dethronement of Calvinism as one outcome. But Trevelyan's point that the Toleration Act made fanaticism and persecution *impracticable* remains one of his most important insights.

VIII

> The Revolution had its consequences in the other lands ruled by James, on the English colonies, on Scotland and on Ireland.[81]
>
> Ireland had to be reconquered before she would submit to the change of sovereigns. To the Roman Catholic majority of her inhabitants the Revolution meant not political and religious freedom but foreign domination and religious persecution.[82]
>
> The new spirit of independence that the Revolution had breathed into the Scottish Parliament made it impossible to preserve the system of Dual Monarchy. Either England and Scotland must again have separate kings, or else they must cease to have separate Parliaments.[83]

Trevelyan devoted almost one fifth of his book to the differing patterns of Revolution in the three kingdoms and casts a sideways glance across the Atlantic as penetrating as any general study since of the English Revolution of 1688. While the historiography of early modern Scotland and Ireland has been transformed in the past two decades, scholars have generally failed to reach 1688. Whereas the major convulsions in Scotland around 1560 and 1637 have received several extensive treatments, and whereas the historiography of Tudor Ireland and of mid-seventeenth-century Ireland is in uproar,[84] not one major study of the events of 1688–9 in either has been published since 1938.[85]

The situation could not be more grave. In his standard textbook *The Stuart Age*, Barry Coward does not deal with the settlements in either Scotland or

[80] As captured in the splendid essay on 'The Great Tew Circle' by Hugh Trevor-Roper, in *Catholics, Anglicans and Puritans* (London, 1987), pp. 166–230.
[81] Trevelyan, *The English Revolution*, p. 203.
[82] Ibid., p. 205.
[83] Ibid., p. 220.
[84] For Scotland, one only has to look at the catalogue of the splendid Edinburgh publisher John Donald or the bibliographies in J. Wormald, *Court, Kirk and Community 1461–1625* (London, 1981), and R. Mitchison, *Lordship to Patronage* (London, 1983); for Ireland the many works of Brendan Bradshaw, Ciaran Brady, Nicholas Canny, Aidan Clarke, Steven Ellis, and others.
[85] The best introduction (which covers 1680–1750) now is by Daniel Szechi and David Hayton, 'John Bull's Other Kingdoms: The English Government of Scotland and Ireland', in Clyve Jones (ed.), *Britain in the First Age of Party 1680–1750: Essays Presented to Geoffrey Holmes* (London, 1987), pp. 241–80. There is much of importance on Scottish politics in the aftermath of the Revolution in P. W. J. Riley, *King William and the Scottish Politicians* (Edinburgh, 1979), and P. Hopkins, *Glencoe and the End of the Highland War* (Edinburgh, 1986), but neither offers an analysis of the nature and consequences of the settlement. The same can be said of J. G. Simms, *Jacobite Ireland 1685–91* (London, 1969).

Ireland.[86] In J. R. Jones' more advanced survey *Country and Court*, covering the period 1658–1714, there is no entry in the index under 'Scotland', 'Covenanters', 'Parliament, the Scottish', or any other clue to a Scottish dimension, despite a preface which speaks of the author having 'inhabited the strange world of late-Stuart *Britain*'.[87] The index entry in J. R. Western's *Monarchy and Revolution* rather promisingly offers us 'Scotland, Revolution of 1688 in, 376ff' but this leads us merely to a one and a half page coda to a fifty-five page chapter on the aftermath of the settlement in England.[88] In his recent book *Reluctant Revolutionaries*, Bill Speck has one index entry to Scotland, which explains why he has not been able to write about it.[89] No major biography of James II offers a serious consideration of his government of Scotland; there is no researched study of the Argyll rebellion to set alongside the many serious studies of the Monmouth rebellion. I will not labour the point. Yet in evaluating the nature of the English settlement, the kind of comparisons Trevelyan attempted are invaluable. In Scotland, there was an explicit forfeiture of the Crown, predicated not upon James' flight and desertion of his realms but upon his 'subversione of the protestant religione, and the violation of the lawes and liberties of the Kingdome, inverting all the Ends of Government'.[90] There was a totally different religious settlement, the substitution of a Presbyterian for an episcopal Church, a purge of those held responsible for past persecutions, and the creation of two religious groups on either wing – Jacobite episcopalians and Cameronian Covenanters who were denied religious freedom as well as civil rights. Even in books unashamedly concerned with *English* affairs, it is surely essential to look at the destabilizing effects of the Scottish settlement on Scotland and hence on England, just as in calculating how the English settlement changed attitudes in the long term, the Scottish settlement acts as an important control.

The state of Irish historiography is even less satisfactory. Basic questions about the transfer of sovereignty, and how it was perceived by different groups in England and in Ireland, have not been addressed. That the Irish gained little of what the historians of England see as the benefits the world derived from the placing of government under law needs constant reiteration.

There are broader points which could be made about the *British* dimension of the Revolution of 1688. In a sense it marks a fundamental shift in the relationship between Britain and Europe. Recorded British history can be divided essentially into four periods. In the first all parts of Britain, but especially England, were repeatedly invaded, colonized, conquered. This phase culminated in the

86 B. Coward, *The Stuart Age: A History of England, 1603–1714* (London, 1980).
87 J. R. Jones, *Country and Court* (London, 1978), p. x.
88 Western, *Monarchy and Revolution*, index.
89 Speck, *Reluctant Revolutionaries*, pp. 14–16.
90 From 'The Claim of Right', printed in *Acts of the Parliament of Scotland* (11 vols., Edinburgh, 1844–75), IX, pp. 37–40.

Norman Conquest of and after 1066. The second phase, from 1066 to 1453, saw the creation of an Anglo-Norman state in the south and east of England straddling the Channel and extending through much of south and western France. There was a subsidiary Anglo-Norman kingdom in the Lowlands of Scotland, but broadly speaking the Gaelic/Celtic Highland regions of northern and western England, Wales, Scotland, and Ireland were only periodically and incompletely the central concern of Norman and Plantagenet kings. This phase abruptly ended with the loss of France by Henry VI and the treaties of 1453. From 1453 to 1688, English monarchs were less active in European wars, less important certainly in the calculations of continental rulers, for the most part reacting to, and on the defensive about, events abroad. But the period saw sustained attempts to subordinate the outlying parts of England, the principality of Wales and the kingdoms of Ireland and (to a lesser extent) Scotland to the bureaucratic-centralist concerns of a London-based government. This activity created the greatest strains on the resources of the state from the 1530s to the 1630s, was in large part responsible for the War in Three Kingdoms which lasted from 1637 to 1651, and certainly had important consequences for the shape and outcome of the three-nation civil war of 1688–91. But thereafter, the central preoccupation of Crown and ministers reverted to the continent and to Britain's role within it. The uneasy compromises of British and federalist structures which were the product of Tudor and Stuart aggrandizement were firmed up by the Treaty of Limerick and its betrayals and by the 1707 Act of Union. With the major exception of the events leading up to the 1801 Act of Union, the dynamic elements in the geopolitics of the eighteenth and the first half of the nineteenth centuries relate to England-in-Europe rather than England-in-Britain.[91]

IX

> William and Anne, because they were trusted and supported by Parliament, were able to fight a long and ultimately successful war against the great strength of France. England's efficiency was doubled by the Revolution, without that loss of our domestic liberty which had been the price of Cromwell's power in the counsels of Europe ... The financial system that arose after the Revolution was the key to the power of England in the eighteenth and nineteenth centuries ... It was also the chief sanction of the revolution ... With all its disadvantages and dangers, party spirit at least served to mitigate corruption. Whigs and Tories, each with their one-sided idealism and factious loyalty preserved an incorruptible core of zealots ready to bribe but not to be bribed.[92]

[91] This paragraph draws heavily on conversations with Dr Steven Ellis. See also on neglected aspects of the first and final forms of the Treaty of Limerick, W. Troost, *William III and the Treaty of Limerick (1691–1697): A Study of his Irish Policy* (Leiden, 1983).

[92] Trevelyan, *The English Revolution*, p. 179.

Stripped of its unfashionable value judgments, this could almost be a blurb for John Brewer's book *The Sinews of Power*, published in 1989. He too sees the growth of the state, especially its ability to tax and to borrow, its increased efficiency of operation, and its imperviousness to the more crippling forms of corruption, as 'the direct consequence of the political and diplomatic crisis which surrounded the Glorious Revolution'.[93] It was war which was the engine of change, but it was the political settlement of 1689 which gave the political nation the confidence to entrust itself and its resources to governments which were more accountable and more securely Protestant. Brewer's work is important as a synthesis of much preceding work. It is original principally in its study of the working of the Excise, and in its suggestion (not quite a demonstration) that it is the ability to tax rather than the ability to sustain an immense burden of debt at controllable levels of interest that was crucial to the success of the extended military and naval operations.[94] On the growth of the civil service,[95] on the rise of permanent standing armies, on the politics of 'big government', he draws together a mass of work that in fine confirms the general judgment that Trevelyan more by intuition than research summed up in the above. Insofar as it is possible to criticize Trevelyan, it would have to be for the reasons that one might criticize Brewer: that while they are not unaware of the prehistory of much of the administrative revolution in the decades before 1688, they yet understate it. A series of studies of the army and navy, and the administrative departments behind both, and recent work on taxation, show that the mechanics of achieving higher tax yields without provoking serious popular resistance, and the increasing role of government contractors and others involved in generating credit for the state, owed much to the Interregnum and the period following the Restoration.[96] The sheer scale of warfare and the financial and bureaucratic efforts needed to sustain that warfare after 1689 did see an irreversible shift of resources from the nation to the state: but almost all the techniques were tried and tested. Let me give one little known example. The state's reliance upon the assistance of major gentry families for the enforce-

93 J. Brewer, *The Sinews of Power: War, Money and the English State* (London, 1989), dust jacket.

94 The latter was the major and important conclusion of P. G. M. Dickson, *The Financial Revolution in England 1688–1756* (London, 1967); and is powerfully reinforced by D. W. Jones, *War and Economy in the Age of William III and Marlborough* (Oxford, 1988), essentially a study of the logistics of paying armies, the formidable task of maintaining the flow of bullion to the armies, navies, and their suppliers.

95 The work which itself subsumes and transcends a whole literature on this subject is G. Holmes, *Augustan England: Professions, State and Society, 1680–1730* (London, 1982) which has a particularly helpful bibliography.

96 On the army, see the three volumes of John Childs: *The Army of Charles II* (London, 1976); *The Army, James II and the Glorious Revolution* (Manchester, 1980); *The British Army of William III, 1689–1702* (Manchester, 1987). See, too, H. Tomlinson, *Guns and Government: The Ordnance Office under the Later Stuarts* (London, 1981). On the navy, all previous work has been supplanted by D. Davies, 'The Seagoing Personnel of the Navy, 1660–1689', Univ. of Oxford D Phil. thesis (1986). Much of the groundwork for efficient tax collection was laid between 1640 and 1689: see M. J. Braddick, 'Parliamentary Lay Taxation, c. 1590–1670: Local Problems of Assessment and Collection with Special Reference to Norfolk', Univ. of Cambridge PhD thesis (1987).

ment of government policy in the localities is well known.[97] Equally well known is how before 1640 the Privy Council, through a complex application of sticks and carrots, persuaded and cajoled often reluctant elites into co-operation in the collection of taxes and non-statutory rates, in the regulation of society and of the economy, in maintaining order, and so on. It is widely recognized that the collapse of the prerogative and conciliar courts and the demise of the Council as a manageable administrative overseer in 1660 reduced the Crown's (and ministers') ability to monitor, let alone to control, the work of local governors. The complaisance of the gentry at the Restoration, the real reason why they did not need to place firm statutory controls on the king's freedom to hire and fire members of the executive was that the gentry were immune from central diktat.[98] This is what I used to argue myself. But Norma Landau pointed out to me[99] – and I hope she will publish more on this – that the Crown had far less need to exercise personal, administrative oversight of the work of JPs and other local commissioners. A study of King's Bench records reveals that lazy, negligent or obstructive commissioners were proceeded against in increasing numbers by judicial process, the Assize judges hauling them up to London to answer charges under writs of *mandamus* and *certiorari*. Just as personal royal surveillance of justice in the late fifteenth century gave way to an impersonal supervision by conciliar and the central law courts, so the supervision of local government became a routine judicial matter in the late seventeenth century. A major development in administrative law preceded the Revolution of 1688 and made much possible after it.[100]

In a more general sense, however, Trevelyan's account, like most recent accounts, finds little evidence of a *social* revolution in 1688–9. The most interesting challenge to this view has been that of J. R. Jones, who sees James as abandoning the Crown's natural alliance with the gentry and making a deliberate bid for the support of new and prosperous social groups – business and professional men. An attempted alliance of James and the bourgeoisie led to a feudal reaction in 1689.[101] But Jones does not make too much of this point. It is more of a suggestion than a principal plank in his argument. Other historians have been quick to describe the events of the winter of 1688–9 as an aristocratic coup.[102]

[97] A. Fletcher, *Reform in the Provinces: The Government of Stuart England* (New Haven, 1986), esp. chs. 1 and 10, subsumes a mass of earlier works.

[98] I will defend this proposition in a forthcoming study. It is rather at odds with the attractive thesis of Andrew Coleby, *Government in the Localities: Hampshire 1649–89* (Cambridge, 1987); but see P. J. Norrey, 'The Restoration Regime in Action: The Relationship between Central and Local Government in Dorset, Somerset and Wiltshire', *Historical Journal*, 31 (1988), pp. 789–812.

[99] When she was a considerate commentator on a paper entitled 'A Glorious Resolution?', which I gave to the Joseph Cassassa Conference on the theme of 'John Locke and the Glorious Revolution' at Loyola Marymount University, Los Angeles in April 1988.

[100] E. G. Henderson, *The Foundations of English Administrative Law* (Cambridge, Mass., 1963).

[101] Jones, *The Revolution of 1688*, pp. 13–15, 130–75.

[102] See the discussion in Speck, *Reluctant Revolutionaries*, pp. 6–7.

Like the similar claims made for an aristocratic coup of 1640–2, this is an important dimension long played down too much. Yet most nobles in 1688–9 were paralysed by a commitment to passive obedience or by sheer fright,[103] and it took the willing and free actions of men of all social groups to see the crisis resolved.

X

The Sensible Revolution of 1688–9 was a conservative Revolution. It did not create damaging new rifts in the English nation, although it did sharpen and to some extent extend divisions in Scotland and Ireland that were of lasting consequence. The constitutional settlement and the ecclesiastical settlements were both fudges. It was possible in 1689 for all kinds of people to continue to believe all sorts of contradictory things.[104] I will give just two examples. First, that James had been lawfully resisted by his subjects because he had violated their civil rights and threatened the true religion; or that there had been no resistance in 1688, only passive disobedience, and that William's expedition had been intended merely to remonstrate with his uncle about the violations of Englishmen's rights and to secure his wife's rights to the succession in the face of a possible dynastic fraud. Second, that England had an elected king contractually bound to his subjects; or that it had a caretaker ruler – to whom no allegiance was due other than as to one who maintained a bare order – because the rightful, anointed king had abandoned his responsibilities by desertion, but that the true succession would in due course be restored. Such ambiguities kept the peace (more or less) in 1688, were productive of much political disagreement in the decades to come, and gradually hardened into alternative myths of the Revolution that became normative in the eighteenth century. Trevelyan's argument was that it was this triumph of particular myths that contained glorious benefits for the British people. There has been some vigorous 'revisionism' that shows (and to my mind conclusively) that more than one myth survived and prospered in the eighteenth century.[105] But one myth, the Whig myth, legitimated the possession and retention of power by one group and one politico-religious vision predicated upon a particular view of liberty. It is possible for historians to recognize that this is what happened without saying that it was a good thing. What makes Trevelyan read oddly now is not his subtle distinctions between what

[103] J. P. Kenyon, *The Nobility in the Revolution of 1688*, University of Hull Inaugural lecture (Hull, 1963); cf. D. H. Hosford, *Nottingham, the Nobles and the North* (Hamden, Conn., 1976).

[104] J. G. A. Pocock, 'The Fourth British Civil War', *Government and Opposition*, 23 (1988), pp. 151–66.

[105] J. C. D. Clark, *English Society 1688–1832* (Cambridge, 1985). I have no argument with Jonathan Clark's recovery of the survival and resilience of both patriarchalism and Divine Right ideas well into the eighteenth century. But why do we have to wait until the fourth of the six sections, over halfway through, to reach 'the self-image of the state: the case for the establishment' and then for the period 1760–1815? Did not the state have a self-image before that?

was intended in 1689 and what eventuated; not his uncomplicated application of the law of unintended consequences; but his approval of particular forms of development. Revisionist historians – like many intellectuals in many fields – have tended to confuse *actus rea* and *mens rea*. Intention is all. If the actors in 1689 were confused, largely unprincipled, living from day-to-day and scrambling for solutions, then there can be no turning-point, no great divide. The 'revisionist' question precludes the Whig answer. In establishing a new pattern of constitutional relationships (many of them unanticipated); in creating a new context within which men and women had to make sense of spiritual and moral imperatives; in crystallizing out the two great parties which, in constant evolution, would dominate English politics for the next 200 years; in forcing a redefinition of England's relationship to Europe and the world, thereby bringing on administrative and institutional change already slowly gestating, and (just as importantly) in reformulating the relationship between the constituent kingdoms of the British Isles, the events of 1688–9 quickened and nurtured a distinctive phase in British historical development. Whether this process is called Glorious, Respectable, or just plain Sensible, it is certainly a Revolution.

Chapter 3

The Dutch role in the Glorious Revolution

JONATHAN I. ISRAEL

One of the most important aspects of the Glorious Revolution in Britain – and hitherto the most consistently neglected – is the part played by the Dutch state, that is the States General, the States of Holland, and the Prince of Orange in his capacity as Stadholder. Neither Whig historiography, nor the 'revisionists', nor indeed Dutch scholars, have in the past had a great deal to say about the fundamental role played by the Dutch in the British revolutions of 1688–91 and it is arguable that it is here that the existing historiography of the Glorious Revolution is at its weakest.[1] For the Dutch intervention in Britain not only set the Glorious Revolution in motion, making possible the landing at Torbay and William III's subsequent triumphant entry into London, in December 1688, but continued to be an essential factor in all the main developments in England, Scotland, and Ireland at least down to the final suppression of armed Jacobite resistance to the Williamite regime towards the end of 1691.

One certainly cannot explain the continual neglect of the Dutch role in terms of its having been in any way inconspicuous. For the Dutch invasion of Britain in November 1688 was regarded at the time, and for years after, by Dutch, British, and other European commentators as not just remarkable but nothing less than sensational and certainly the boldest and riskiest strategic venture attempted by the Dutch Republic since its birth amid the struggle against the might of Spain, more than a century before.[2] The invasion was universally

[1] The two most relevant contributions on the British side are J. Carswell, *The Descent on England* (London, 1969), and W. A. Speck, 'The Orangist Conspiracy against James II', *Historical Journal*, 30 (1987), pp. 453–62; both retain much validity but focus only on the early stages of the Revolution and neither makes any attempt to distinguish the role of the Dutch state as such from that of William; on the Dutch side, N. Japikse, *Prins Willem III, de Stadhouder-koning* (2 vols., Amsterdam, 1930–3), again focuses only on William's role while G. van Alphen, *De stemming van de Engelschen tegen de Hollanders in Engeland tijdens de regeering van den koning-stadhouder Willem III, 1688–1702* (Assen, 1938), in many ways a useful work, does not analyse the strategic decisions of the Republic.

[2] Constantijn Huygens, William's secretary, vividly describes the feeling amongst his entourage in October 1688 that they were participating in 'une grande et glorieuse entreprise', *Journaal van Constantijn Huygens, den zoon, van 21 Oktober 1688 tot 2 September 1696* (2 vols., Utrecht, 1876–7), I, p. 2; as early as 12 October, the Polish resident at The Hague wrote 'Nous voici à la veille de voir un événement aussi considérable qu'aucun de ceux qui ayent été marqués dans l'histoire du siècle ou nous vivons quoiqu'il en ait produit de bien singuliers et de fort extraordinaires', BL MS Add. 38495, fo. 28v. Moreau to king of Poland, The Hague, 12 Oct. 1688; see also Gregorio Leti, *La Monarchie Universelle de Louys XIV* (2 vols., Amsterdam, 1689), I, pp. 187–8, 243–5.

regarded as one of the most amazing and dramatic events of the age. The landings of November 1688 in south-west England were also a vast and immensely complex and costly enterprise. The army which the States General sent into Britain was actually a good deal larger and more powerful than Williamites subsequently cared to admit or than modern historians have generally realized.[3] Nearly all modern accounts compute only the 14,352 regular infantry and cavalry which formed the core of the invading army and some accounts give a total figure as low as 11,212. But such figures are arrived at by omitting substantial sections of the army from the count. In fact the prevailing notion that William III landed in England with 'a fairly modest force' heavily outnumbered by the army of James II is a misconception which results from historians being misled by the later Williamite and Whig desire to play down the military involvement of the Dutch. If we include the Huguenots, the English, Dutch, and Scots volunteers, and the men of the (very substantial) Dutch artillery train in the reckoning, it emerges that the invasion army totalled at least 21,000 men and in my own view – because of the deliberate swelling of the Dutch regiments beyond their nominal strength – slightly more. Furthermore, the States General sent *only* their best regiments – all the crack regiments of the Dutch army – so that it was an army of exceptionally high quality and experience, for its size, as well as being massively supplied and equipped in a way that was unusual with seventeenth-century armies. To match James II's strength in cavalry, the invasion army also included some 5,000 horses. To transport the troops, horses, and supplies an immense fleet of specially hired vessels was required. To protect the transports and support the army, there came also a powerful war fleet. Together the war fleet and transports numbered some 500 vessels, approximately four times as many as participated in the Spanish Armada of 1588.[4] Nothing like so vast a seaborne expedition had been attempted in northern European waters before.

Not only the foreign diplomats at The Hague but all Europe was astounded by the unprecedented speed and efficiency with which the Dutch state – which historians generally like to describe as one of the less efficient states of seventeenth-century Europe – assembled so great and so enormously complicated an expedition. They were amazed by the huge quantities of shipping involved and by the profusion of supplies and every imaginable kind of specialized equipment. Yet the invasion armada, however grand and audacious, was merely the hub of a much vaster Dutch strategic design. While they prepared their invasion fleet at Amsterdam, Rotterdam, Hellevoetsluis (the final assembly point) and in Zeeland, the regents at the same time assembled a second field army, under Prince Waldeck, on the Lower Rhine, to guard against the French army now

[3] See pp. 337–8 below.
[4] Ibid.

6 *The Landing of William III and his Army at Torbay (5/15 November 1688).* Engraving by Romeyn de Hooghe.
Note the lines of horses which had been lowered (or pushed) overboard from the ships swimming ashore tied by ropes to the backs of the troop-landing boats.

operating in the Rhineland, and replenished the troop strength of the Dutch garrison towns and strongholds vacated by the regiments being drawn off for the invasion armada with forces specially hired for the occasion. Under a series of secret agreements finalized in September 1688, the States General hired from the German Protestant Princes 14,000 veteran troops in complete regiments – 6,000 from Brandenburg, 4,000 from the two Brunswicks, 2,400 from Hesse-Cassel and over 1,000 from Württemberg.[5] As the best regiments of the Dutch army were transported in flotillas of flat-bottomed boats down the Rhine, Waal,

[5] ARH SG 4029, secret res. 20 Sept. 1688 gives the number of troops hired from Germany as 5,900 (Brandenburg), 3,951 (Brunswick-Celle and Wolfenbüttel), 2,400 (Hesse-Cassel) and 1,000 (Württemberg); see also Renate Wiebe, *Untersuchungen über die Hilfeleistung der deutschen Staaten für Wilhelm III von Oranien im Jahre 1688* (Göttingen, 1939), pp. 4–5, 6–7, 21.

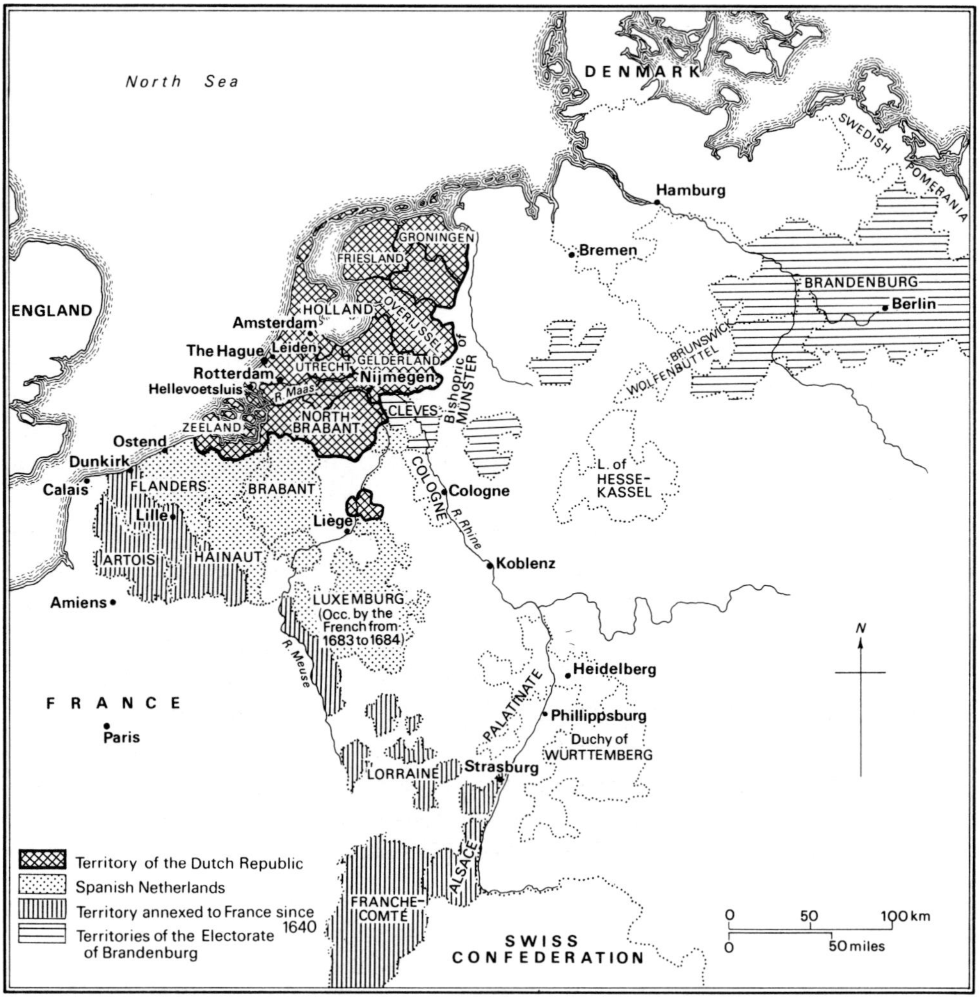

Map 1 The Low Countries and Lower Germany in 1688.

and Maas to Rotterdam and Hellevoetsluis, the German regiments marched in to take their place in the great fortified strongholds protecting the eastern and southern borders of the Republic. They served under oath to the States General, under the flag of the United Provinces, and at Dutch rates of pay. But even this was deemed insufficient. In October, the States of Holland approved their Stadholder's view that their vast strategic design would require still larger forces.[6] A month before invading England, the States hired a further 6,000 veterans from the Swedish Crown, 4,500 of these troops being sent, via Bremen,

[6] GA Leiden Sec. Arch. 488, p. 391, res. 11 Oct. 1688.

from the Swedish enclaves in Germany, and 1,500 troops from Sweden itself.[7] As with the German regiments, the States General remitted their transportation costs and the first instalments of their pay in advance. All considered, the military, including the naval, manpower on the States' payroll escalated between June and October 1688 in a dramatic fashion: the Dutch navy virtually doubled its manpower to around 20,000 men while the troop strength at the Republic's disposal rose from 40,000 in July, equivalent to James II's standing army in England, to about double this strength if we include the German and Swedish veterans, 80,000 men by October.[8]

The Holland regents committed the cream of their forces to a full-scale invasion of Britain, incurring vast expenditure of money, effort, and resources, and did so, furthermore, on the eve of an almost certain outbreak of war with France. In doing so, the Dutch leadership, utterly uncharacteristically in the view of diplomatic onlookers, took a stupendous gamble. Nor could even the most unperceptive member of the Dutch government possibly be in the slightest doubt as to the immensity of the risk the Republic was taking. For, in June 1688, when the preparations for the invasion began, relations between the Republic and Europe's mightiest ruler, Louis XIV, were already worse than at any point since the end of the Franco-Dutch war of 1672–8. As the invasion armada took shape, Franco-Dutch relations inexorably deteriorated. More than two months before the landing at Torbay, on 9 September New Style, the French ambassador at The Hague, the comte d'Avaux, appeared before the States General and delivered a clear warning from Louis: the French king knew what the Dutch preparations were for, and his close ties with James II, he warned, 'would oblige him not only to come to James' assistance, but to regard the first hostile act committed by your troops, or your ships, against His Britannic Majesty as an open infraction of the peace and act of war against his own crown'.[9] In other words, the moment the Dutch moved against the king of England, Louis XIV would declare war on the Republic. Consequently, in invading Britain in November, the Dutch Republic not only took the unheard of risk of mounting a major seaborne operation on the threshold of winter but were precipitating certain war with both James II and Louis XIV. The States General, in fact, staked everything on crushing James II's power quickly. For if the Dutch regiments were lost at sea, or defeated in England, or even just seriously depleted

[7] BL MS Add. 41831, fos. 240–1, Poley to Middleton, Stockholm, 10 Oct. 1688; BL MS Add. 41828, fo. 94, Wyche to Middleton, Hamburg, 5 Oct. 1688; *The London Gazette*, no. 2403 (1688); the Swedish troops arrived in the Republic, via Bremen and Münster, in December 1688.

[8] BL MS Add. 41816, fo. 186; Moreau gives 84,000 without counting the Swedes, BL MS Add. 38495, fo. 25v.

[9] ARH SG 3318, fos. 229–30, res. 9 Sept. 1688; *Res. Holl.* 15 Sept. 1688; the States General sent copies of d'Avaux's memorial to the provincial assemblies; the States of Zeeland then sent copies to the Zeeland town councils, *Notulen der Staten van Zeelandt* (118 vols., Middleburg, 1595–1713), vol. for 1688, p. 164.

in the midst of a new English civil war, the Republic was likely to be overwhelmed by the combined might of Louis and James. On 25 August 1688, the dealers of the Amsterdam stock exchange (always attentive to what was happening on the international political scene) suddenly realized – at the same moment that d'Avaux realized – what the Dutch state was intending.[10] They were horrified. At first they panicked, throwing the Amsterdam exchange into the second most disastrous financial crash of the entire seventeenth century after that of 1672, many millions of guilders being wiped off the value of government stocks and East and West India Company shares in a few days. This, in turn, set off a series of major bankruptcies. But during September, leading Amsterdam financiers, including, we may assume, those with close connections with the Stadholder, and the financing and provisioning of the invasion armada, engineered a partial recovery in share prices and the markets steadied. Diplomatic onlookers noted that the initial panic in financial circles gave way to that same mysterious confidence that seemed to have taken hold of the Dutch public as a whole: despite all the risks, the expedition 'against England' was going to succeed.

But what moved the Holland regents to take such breath-taking risks? Even if they succeeded in destroying James II's 'absolute power' – as the States of Holland called it – would they not merely be replacing this with a new, stronger form of regime in England which would then pose a more powerful challenge to Dutch interests in commerce and the Indies as well as in international power politics? The English ambassador at The Hague, the marquis d'Albeville, was continually amazed at the seeming recklessness of what the Dutch were planning. Once convinced that they really were going to invade England, by mid-September, he was inclined to explain it, in his despatches to London, as an act of collective madness totally inconsistent with the prudence and caution universally regarded as the hallmarks of Dutch statecraft and one which would cost the Republic dearly. In his view the only result of Dutch success would be a new English commonwealth, or limited monarchy, either of which would prove to be as relentless a foe to Dutch interests as had been the commonwealth fashioned by Cromwell. Commenting on the prolonged deception practised in London by the States General's ambassador there, Aernout van Citters, who continued to assure James and his ministers that the States intended no hostile act against the English Crown – at a time when the entire diplomatic community at The Hague could see from the large number of troop and horse transports being hired and fitted out that the only conceivable purpose of such an armada was to invade Britain – d'Albeville concluded that the Dutch 'are fallen ... into treacherous proceedings beyond any they accuse the French of, *in fine* to run

[10] See J. I. Israel, 'The Amsterdam Stock Exchange and the English Revolution of 1688', *Tijdschrift voor Gescheidenis*, 103 (1990), pp. 428–30.

headlong into dependence and slavery, like to be subject to England for the future'.[11] He continued: 'their sea and land forces will soon be there, and detain'd there, if the Prince succeeds, destroy'd if he fails.'

Insofar as the question of why the Dutch invaded Britain in 1688 at such enormous risk to themselves has been discussed at all, historians have tended to place the main emphasis on the religious factor.[12] It is perfectly true that in the United Provinces, as in much of the rest of Europe, there had been a marked escalation of Catholic–Protestant tension in the wake of the Revocation of the Edict of Nantes (1685) and the onset of the mass exodus of Huguenots from France. In the years 1685–8, the United Provinces, and above all Holland, took in larger numbers of Huguenot refugees than any other European country. Moreover, the Huguenots who settled in Amsterdam, The Hague, Rotterdam, Leiden, and other Dutch towns during those years included most of the Huguenot theologians and publicists who went into exile, which had the effect of powerfully reinforcing Calvinist orthodoxy in the Republic and the rising chorus of Dutch indignation against Louis XIV. Nevertheless, it is most unlikely that religious considerations were anything more than a marginal factor in shaping the States' decision to collaborate with William in invading Britain. In the past the Dutch regents had never been known to embark on a major undertaking in the international arena, especially any kind of military operation, on grounds of religion. The general perception abroad that the statecraft of the Holland regents was totally impervious to religious considerations may have been exaggerated but was essentially true. The Jacobite pamphleteer who wrote, on the eve of the Dutch invasion of England, that 'none that know the religion of an Hollander would judge the Prince or States would be at the charge of a dozen fly-boats or herring-busses to propagate it, or especially the Church of England' was not far off the mark.[13] In any case, no prominent Dutch political figure in 1688, or any diplomatic observer of the Dutch scene – in contrast to modern historians – claimed that the invasion was primarily motivated, or influenced, by religious factors. On the contrary, Burgomaster Nicolaas Witsen who was the pre-eminent burgomaster at Amsterdam in 1688 told William's confidant, Dijkvelt, that in his view far from there being religious grounds why the Dutch Republic should invade Britain, considerations of religion dictated that the United

[11] BL MS Add. 41816, fo. 226, d'Albeville to Middleton, The Hague, 9 Oct. 1688.

[12] Carswell seems to have thought that the Dutch provinces hardly contributed to the costs of the armada; according to Renier, 'the hostility previously shown to William by the Holland regents had completely vanished since the persecution of the Protestants in France', G. J. Renier, *William of Orange* (London, 1932), p. 106; though closer to the mark than Renier, more recent accounts still see the religious factors as important, or more important, than the renewed *guerre de commerce*, see S. B. Baxter, *William III* (London, 1966), pp. 207–11, and J. R. Jones, *The Revolution of 1688 in England* (London, 1972), pp. 194–5.

[13] *The Dutch Design Anatomized, or, A Discovery of the Wickedness and Unjustice [sic] of the Intended Invasion* (London, 1688), p. 8.

Provinces should do no such thing.[14] For it was plain that the Republic was in a situation of worsening conflict with France while the main potential allies on the continent, the Emperor Leopold and the king of Spain, rulers upon whom the Republic's security, and conceivably its very survival, depended, were avowedly Catholic powers sympathetic to James II's papist statecraft and extremely unlikely to come to the aid of a Dutch state intervening in Britain out of Protestant motives. The Italian Protestant city historiographer of Amsterdam writing at this time, Gregorio Leti, was undoubtedly correct in maintaining, as he did repeatedly and in several of his works, that the decision of the Dutch state to invade Britain in 1688 was almost exclusively motivated by non-religious considerations of *raison d'état*.[15]

There were two main factors behind the Dutch decision to invade the realms of His Britannic Majesty James II in 1688 – one economic, the other strategic. The economic factor is of crucial significance and, although largely ignored by modern historians, was very heavily emphasized at the time by the French ambassador at The Hague and other diplomats.[16] Major decisions based on concern for commerce were, assuredly, more usual in seventeenth-century Dutch statecraft than that of other European states. In a sense, there was nothing new about this in 1688. But where in the past the regents' zeal for the advancement of trade and shipping had generally inspired cautious policies, a preoccupation with peace and stability rather than confrontation, in 1688 commercial concerns caused the Dutch state to adopt a radically different, and unprecedented, posture.

The enigma posed by the drastic and exceedingly risky course of action which the regents resolved on in the summer and autumn of 1688 was all the more perplexing in that, earlier in the 1680s, the Republic had seemed to be growing more rather than less cautious. The key episode of the early 1680s in Dutch domestic politics was the furious quarrel which developed in 1682–4 between the Prince (backed by four of the six lesser provinces), on one side, and the Holland 'States party', headed by the Amsterdam city council, on the other. This was a rift which had deep roots and which seemingly paralysed all attempts to improve the Republic's military and naval preparedness during the early and mid-1680s. This latest stage in an old rift originated in the way that peace was made with Louis XIV in 1677–8. At that time Louis had divided the Dutch

[14] Jan Wagenaar, *Vaderlandsche Historie verattende de geschiedenissen der nu Vereenigde Nederlanden* (21 vols., Amsterdam, 1749–59), XV, p. 427; J. Gebhard, *Het leven van Mr Nicolaas Cornelisz Witsen (1641–1717)* (2 vols., Utrecht, 1881–2), II, pp. 321, 327.

[15] Leti, *Monarchie Universelle de Louis XIV*, I, pp. 68–9, 418, 433; Gregorio Leti, *Teatro Belgico o vero ritratti historici, chronologici, politici e geografici delle Sette Provincie Unite* (2 vols., Amsterdam, 1690), I, pp. 363, 394.

[16] Besides d'Avaux who frequently states that the *guerre de commerce* was the major factor which swayed the Holland regents to co-operate with William's war strategy in 1688, Moreau too recognized that 'le commerce est ce qui touche de plus près la nation hollandoise et que la France l'a entièrement rompu', and that the Prince's swaying Holland depended chiefly on this, see BL MS Add. 38495, fo. 28, Moreau to king of Poland, The Hague, 5 Oct. 1688.

body politic by offering Holland wide-ranging economic concessions, including cancellation of Colbert's 1667 tariff list which, as he knew, was bitterly resented by the Dutch and which had greatly damaged their trade.[17] Not surprisingly, Holland, and especially Amsterdam, had jumped at Louis' offer. William III had been entirely thwarted in his efforts to prevent the Republic breaking ranks with her allies and making a separate peace with France. Indeed, it was clear that the Stadholder, when opposed by Holland's leading city, Amsterdam, was largely powerless. The resulting Treaty of Nijmegen secured economic gains for the Dutch, and political and territorial gains for France, at the expense of the Republic's allies, particularly Spain and Brandenburg.

The Prince of Orange and the 'States party' in Holland and Zeeland therefore nurtured diametrically opposed views of the Treaty of Nijmegen, the one regarding it as a disaster and the other as a triumph. They also differed profoundly over whether there was a continuing need to co-ordinate a Europe-wide coalition to oppose the further political and territorial ambitions of Louis. This basic clash of views lay at the root of the major Dutch domestic political crisis which erupted in the years 1682–4. The immediate cause of the crisis was Louis' renewed encroachments into the Spanish Netherlands and Spain's request to the United Provinces for assistance. The Stadholder did despatch Dutch troops to Flanders. But when he urged the regents to increase the Dutch army by 16,000 men and join with the emperor and Spain in forming a coalition to block further French expansion, Amsterdam, supported by several other Holland and Zeeland towns, and the provinces of Friesland and Groningen, refused to agree. The clash in the States General, States of Holland, and States of Zeeland became extremely bitter.[18] The general public became greatly aroused, intensifying the traditional rivalry between Orangists and 'States party' supporters. A fierce pamphlet war broke out, further aggravating the quarrel between the Prince and the Republic's greatest city. Neither side gave any ground. Amsterdam refused to jeopardize the Nijmegen agreement with the French king, or sacrifice the tranquillity of the Republic, for the sake of defending other people's territory. The Prince conceded that 'commerce is the pillar of the state', but insisted that the Republic would eventually lose her commerce too if she failed to safeguard her security.[19]

The lesson which Louis XIV drew from the Dutch domestic crisis of 1682–4 was that the Dutch regents were afraid of him and that the Republic, under the leadership of William III, was incapable of concerted action. But William drew a different lesson. He had already learnt to speak in the States of Holland

[17] BL MS Add. 37981, fo. 12, Carr to Blathwayt, Amsterdam, 21 Mar. 1681; J. I. Israel, *Dutch Primacy in World Trade, 1585–1740* (Oxford, 1989), pp. 339–40.

[18] E. Mallet (ed.), *Négociations de Monsieur le Comte d'Avaux en Hollande depuis 1679* (6 vols., Paris, 1752–3), I, pp. 2–3, 36, 40, 104; G. H. Kurtz, *Willem III en Amsterdam, 1683–1685* (Utrecht, 1928), pp. 16–22.

[19] Kurtz, *Willem III*, pp. 67–8.

in terms of commerce and commercial interest. But that was pure rhetoric. What he now realized was that the United Provinces would be capable of effective action against France only if he could find some means of bringing together, and harmonizing, the economic and strategic interests of the state. It was Louis XIV who was to provide him with the opportunity.

Until 1685 the rift between Amsterdam and the Stadholder appeared unbridgeable. From 1685, there was a slight thaw in relations but nothing of a sort to suggest that Louis XIV's perception of the situation was wrong. Never had the power of France in Europe seemed more overwhelming and Europe less capable of checking it. Not a few of the German princes, the Elector of Brandenburg among them, despaired of finding any way to block the further growth of French power either on the Rhine, and among the ecclesiastical principalities of Germany, or in the Spanish Netherlands.

But if the Treaty of Nijmegen (1678) secured political rewards for France these were obtained at considerable economic cost. Reverting to the 1664 tariff list meant large reductions across the whole range of Dutch and other foreign manufactures and commodities entering France. The 1680s was a decade in which a steadily swelling stream of Dutch pepper, spices, fine cloth, camlets, Indian textiles, Delftware, Gouda pipes, fish and whale products, and naval stores poured into France. At the same time the Dutch merchant fleet fully regained the dominance over the carrying of France's wine, brandy, and salt exports which it had enjoyed before 1672. Then, on top of all this, from 1685, came the massive transfer of Huguenot cash and skills from France to Holland, further depressing the French textile, paper, and canvas industries while enhancing those of the Dutch. As the economic balance tilted further against France, the temptation to use the power of the French state to hit back, heightened by the rising chorus of complaint within France, became too great to resist.

The new Franco-Dutch *guerre de commerce* began just over a year before the Dutch invasion of Britain, in August 1687. Louis commenced with a ban on the importing of Dutch herring into France except where certified as having been salted with French salt.[20] Next, in September, Louis re-introduced the tariff list of 1667, at a stroke doubling imposts on imported Dutch fine cloth and drastically raising those on many other products.[21] Further measures, including additional rises in selected tariffs, were taken subsequently, especially against Dutch textile and fish products.[22] By December, Dutch factors at Paris, Metz, Lyons, and Lille were reporting that it was now virtually impossible to sell

[20] GA Amsterdam vroed. XXXIX, p. 18, res. 13 Jan. 1688; Ch. W. Cole, *French Mercantilism, 1683–1700* (New York, 1943), p. 294.

[21] Mallet (ed.), *Négociations*, VI, pp. 110–16; M. Arnould, *De la balance du commerce et des relations commerciales exterieures de la France dans toutes les parties du globe* (2 vols., Paris, 1791), I, p. 188; Israel, *Dutch Primacy*, p. 341.

[22] Cole, *French Mercantilism*, p. 308; ARH SG 6790, Starrenburg to SG, Paris, 27 Sept. 1688.

Dutch textiles in France.[23] Since France was the largest market for Dutch herring and whale products, one of the largest for Dutch textiles, and the French market was generally very much more important to the Dutch than was the British market, the effect of all this was extremely serious. The South Holland herring fishery reckoned that exports from its area dropped by a third during the year following the introduction of the French ban.[24] Leiden's deputies to the States of Holland complained bitterly that Louis' 'heavy impost in effect means an absolute ban on the sale of our *lakens* [fine cloth] in France'.[25] Nor was it only the losses which were deeply resented. Regents and public alike were infuriated by Louis' bad faith in going back on his undertakings made at Nijmegen. Louis' new commercial measures, noted d'Avaux, 'ont achevé d'aigrir les esprits du peuple et des regents et les ont portés à un point de furie, que les bourgemestres comme la canaille, ne parloient d'autre chose que de périr les armes à la main plutôt que de demeurer en l'état ou ils étoient'.[26]

The Prince of Orange was quick to grasp the implications of the resumed Franco-Dutch *guerre de commerce* for himself, the Republic, and internationally. From being a virtual prisoner of Dutch domestic political forces, he now had his opportunity to mobilize the Dutch state for war and put himself at the head of a European coalition of powers aimed at curbing the might of France. But his chances of succeeding depended – as was constantly in his mind during the momentous months preceding the invasion of England – on the continuing escalation of the Franco-Dutch economic conflict; for this, as William III, at least, understood with perfect clarity was the motor on which the whole of his astounding enterprise depended. No economic war with France, then no invasion of England – and no overthrowing of James II; it was as simple as that.

During the spring of 1688 it became clear that the diplomatic efforts to persuade Louis XIV to cancel his aggressive economic measures were of no avail and that the Dutch would either have to acquiesce or resort to stronger methods, with all the attendant dangers of antagonizing Louis further.[27] Several Holland towns, led by Leiden and spurred by Caspar Fagel, Pensionary of the States of Holland, and William's right-hand man among the regents, began to press for a Dutch ban on the importing of French products. The Prince, who had not forgotten that Leiden had supported Amsterdam against him in 1682–3, no doubt savoured the irony of the fact that Leiden was now the most forward of the Holland towns in clamouring for retaliation against France.[28] D'Avaux,

[23] GA Leiden Sec. Arch. 2402. 'Extracten uyt brieven raekende belastinge vande manufacturen' (Dec. 1688).
[24] *Res. Holl.*, 21 July 1688.
[25] Ibid., 18 Mar. 1688.
[26] Mallet (ed.), *Négociations*, VI, p. 288.
[27] GA Leiden Sec. Arch. 488, p. 359, res. 11 May 1688.
[28] N. Japikse (ed.), *Correspondentie van Willem III en Hans Willem Bentinck, eersten Graf van Portland* (5 vols., The Hague, 1927–37), I, p. 44.

for his part, was filled with dismay as he saw the ground slipping beneath the feet of those regents who preferred to seek a deal with France rather than proceed to confrontation with all the incalculable consequences that would follow. For the time being, a majority of the Amsterdam city council preferred to block the proposed ban on French goods. But d'Avaux was aware by August that Amsterdam was now completely isolated in the States of Holland in urging a moderate course.[29] Even Delft, traditionally anti-Orangist and pro-French, and Rotterdam, the chief depot for the French wine trade – with the most to lose from the disruption of Franco-Dutch trade – were supporting the moves for a ban.

By June 1688 matters had developed to the point where William could confidently urge the States of Holland that they must expand their forces, strengthen their fortifications, look to their alliances, and prepare for war. He could also now begin discussing secret contingency plans, as to the most effective strategy the Dutch could adopt, with the inner circle of leading regents of the States of Holland. Through his two most trusted personal advisers, Hans Willem Bentinck and Everard van Weede van Dijkvelt, both nobles, the Prince opened a secret strategic dialogue with Witsen and two others of the four Amsterdam burgomasters, Johannes Hudde and Joan Geelvinck – the fourth, Appelman, he judged excessively pro-French and excluded from the consultations.[30] Witsen and Hudde were appalled by the risks implied by an autumn invasion of England; but they could see that war with France might well now be unavoidable and understood the fearful consequences for the Republic should Louis combine with James II against the Dutch. Consequently, they agreed to co-operate with the build-up of the invasion armada for the time being.[31] However, from June right through to September most of the Amsterdam *vroedschap* (city council) continued to hope that some new accommodation with France could be reached and regarded the Republic's warlike preparations chiefly as a means of exerting psychological pressure on Louis.[32] Their hope was that talk of economic retaliation and war would suffice to persuade Louis XIV to back down. If he had done so, neither the invasion of England, nor the Glorious Revolution, would have taken place; but doing so was the only available way of blocking William's plans. Again and again d'Avaux warned his master that the sole means of mobilizing the regents to stop the sending of the invasion armada to England was 'en rétablissant le commerce sur le pied du traité de Nimègue'.[33]

[29] Mallet (ed.), *Négociations*, VI, pp. 176, 190, 200.
[30] Wagenaar, *Vaderlandsche Historie*, XV, pp. 426–7, 431; Gebhard, *Het leven*, I, pp. 320–7.
[31] Gebhard, *Het leven*, I, pp. 320, 331–2; Mallet (ed.), *Négociations*, VI, p. 175.
[32] GA Amsterdam vroed. XXXIX, pp. 139–40, res. 21 and 24 Sept. 1688.
[33] Mallet (ed.), *Negociations*, VI, pp. 175, 208, 229, 255; during August, d'Avaux advised Louis 'que le commerce de Hollande étoit diminué de plus du quart et que les peuples en étoient extrêmement touchés et fort airgris contre la France', ibid., VI, p. 198.

Thus, during the summer of 1688, the Amsterdam city council followed a middle course, collaborating with the build-up of the invasion armada but at the same time holding up the ban on French commodities in the States of Holland, and repeatedly urging d'Avaux to make Louis understand that there would be war if his hostile economic measures were not withdrawn. By August Amsterdam's middle-of-the-road stance was beginning to exasperate the Prince, for he was aware that without Amsterdam's full collaboration he would be unable to invade England. Amsterdam's role was indeed of overwhelming importance, for a majority of the warships for the armada were being fitted out at Amsterdam, the bulk of the hiring of transports and provisioning was going on there, and much of the financial side of the invasion was being handled there. Early in September, the Prince wrote 'from Minden to the magistrates of Amsterdam assuring them to have perfected the alliances with the Princes of Germany, that therefore they should come to the assembly of Holland ... with a unanimous resolution for the prohibition of the French commodities'.[34] But at the meeting of the Amsterdam *vroedschap* on 14 September on which the Prince had set his hopes, the council remained split. The anti-Orangist faction were still strong enough to prevent the retaliatory ban on French products from going through. William was now seriously alarmed: 'je crains extrèmement', he confided to Bentinck, 'la timidité de quelques uns d'Amsterdam et la méchanceté des autres, car, si cette affaire ne se fait avec vigueur et résolution l'on ne peut attendre un bon succès, et la manière que les bourgemaistres ont parlé à M. de Dijkveld me donne une terrible fraieur'.[35]

But if the Prince was worried by Amsterdam's stance, the French and English ambassadors were still more so. D'Avaux, realizing that his proud master would not give way, was close to despair: 'il n'y avoit rien à attendre', he wrote, 'même des mieux intentionnés à moins qu'ils n'eussent satisfaction sur le fait du commerce'.[36] D'Albeville too was now desperate about the situation in the Amsterdam city council. On 17 September, he met Amsterdam's deputies at The Hague and strove to shake them out of their persisting in the pretence that the preparations in progress in their city were a routine matter intended for a punitive expedition against the Algerian corsairs. Losing patience with their 'weak pretext', d'Albeville insisted on the

> impossibility that the town of Amsterdam which gave the peace to Christendom in 1683 and was the soule of the States should not know to what design so great preparations, and such vast expense were made; such proceedings were never heard of before now in these States, that it was neglect not only blameable but also dangerous as to give the ear to the suggestions of the English rebels and discontented men who languished for invasion and insurrection to change the government [in

[34] BL MS Add. 41816, fo. 179, d'Albeville to Middleton, The Hague, 14 Sept. 1688.
[35] Japikse (ed.), *Correspondentie*, I, p. 57.
[36] Mallet (ed.), *Négociations*, VI, p. 229

England] into a Commonwealth which, once established, would soon prove the ruine and overthrow of this.[37]

The Prince still lacked Amsterdam's full co-operation. But with time pressing, war clouds gathering over Germany, and the German troop-hire agreements awaiting ratification, William could wait no longer in seeking the States of Holland's backing for his overall strategy. By mid-September, nobody in Holland any longer doubted what all the preparations and the vast armada were for. The Stadholder and Pensionary now proposed in a formal secret session of the States of Holland that France had gravely damaged Dutch commerce and navigation, and the Republic's fisheries, that Louis maintained close links with James II, that the Dutch forces should now be fully mobilized for war, and that the troop-hire agreements with the German Protestant Princes should be ratified.[38]

Approval of the Prince's overall assessment and of the troop-hire agreements was secured from the town councils and provincial assemblies at breakneck speed. With Amsterdam's assent, Holland approved the German troop agreements on 22 September, the States of Zeeland following suit eight days later.[39] These were the provinces with major commercial and shipping interests. In the rest the Stadholder's prestige and his deliberate fanning of fears of the alleged secret collusion of Louis and James against the Republic were sufficient. At a specially called emergency meeting of the States of Gelderland, at Zutphen, on 24 September, the Prince of Orange's representative made much both of the French attack on Dutch commerce and the supposed collusion between France and England, and secured prompt approval for the Stadholder's plans.[40] The States of Overijssel proceeded equally promptly.[41] On 4 October, the Stadholder of Friesland addressed a special secret session of the States of Friesland, laying heavy stress on the 'conspiracy which the two kings of France and England have formed against this state' and swayed that province.[42] Clearly William III did not scruple to make the most of the fear and trauma evoked by memories of 1672.

But still the Prince lacked the full backing of Amsterdam. At the meetings of the *vroedschap* on 21 and 24 September, the city council was still split and still failed to approve the ban on French imports.[43] Some of the Amsterdam regents did not yet accept that there was no possibility of doing a deal with

[37] BL MS Add. 41816, fo. 183, d'Albeville to Middleton, The Hague, 17 Sept. 1688.

[38] ARH SG 4029, secret res. 19 Sept. 1688; *Secreete Resolutien van de Ed. Groot Mog. Heeren Staaten van Hollandt en West-Vrieslandt* (16 vols., The Hague, 1791), IV, pp. 226–7, res. 19 Sept. 1688.

[39] *Secreete Resolutien ... Hollandt*, IV, p. 229, res. 22 Sept. 1688; *Notulen Zeelandt*, vol. for 1688, p. 170, res. 30 Sept. 1688.

[40] ARH Prov. Res. XX. res. St Gelderland, 15/25 Sept. 1688.

[41] ARH SG 4029, res. St Overijssel 15/25 Sept. 1688.

[42] Rijksarchief in Friesland, Archives of the States of Friesland S4/1. 'Secreet Resolutie-boeck, 1671–1699', res. 25 Sept./5 Oct. 1688.

[43] GA Amsterdam vroed. XXXIX, pp. 139–41, res. 21 and 24 Sept. 1688.

France and wanted to resume contacts with Louis through d'Avaux. The Prince was filled with anxiety. But he need not have worried. At the critical moment the French monarch played right into his hands. Angered by the presumptuousness of the Dutch regents in threatening to retaliate against French commodities, Louis decided to teach the Dutch a lesson and slapped a general arrest on all Dutch ships in French ports.[44] Bordeaux, Nantes, and other west coast French ports were then just beginning to fill with Dutch vessels sent to carry off that part of that autumn's wine harvest earmarked for export. According to reports circulating in the Republic and among the diplomatic community at The Hague (which the Dutch government did nothing to discourage) some 300 Dutch ships were seized, though, in fact, the lists drawn up over the next few weeks show that the real total was only slightly over one hundred, including fifty-four at Bordeaux, thirty-two at La Rochelle, and thirteen at Nantes. But this did nothing to lessen the impact of the news of the arrests on Dutch opinion or the fury that it aroused. Even those regents with no enthusiasm for the Prince's plans now had no choice but to acquiesce: 'l'arrêt des vaisseaux', d'Avaux summed it up, 'a fermé la bouche à tous les honnets gens et obligé Messieurs d'Amsterdam à consentir à l'interdiction du commerce de France'.[45]

The die was now cast. 'The Dutch believe a war with France unavoidable', noted the English consul at Amsterdam, little realizing the full implications of this, 'and the arrest laid upon their ships as a certain forerunner'. He was right.[46] Within days, the Amsterdam city council agreed to the ban on French commodities – the threat of which (according to what French ministers told the Dutch ambassador in Paris) was the reason for the arrests – approved the seizure of French ships in Dutch ports and, most crucial of all, gave the green light for the invasion of England.[47] Amsterdam along with Haarlem and the other main Holland towns now sent a number of very senior extra deputies to The Hague so that the momentous decision to invade England, and other related secret decisions, could be taken by this inner circle working with Fagel and William, without further reference back to the city councils. At the special order of the Stadholder, Fagel laid the full plan, and the strategic logic behind it, before the States of Holland, in secret session, on 29 September: France had grievously damaged Dutch trade, shipping, and fisheries; war with France was now unavoidable; if the Republic remained in a defensive posture, France, in alliance with England, whose king, with his large standing army, might soon overcome his

[44] ARH SG 6790, Starrenburg to SG, Paris, 27 Sept. 1688, and Fontainebleau, 28 Oct. 1688; ibid., 'Lyste vande scheepen ... tot Bordeaux in arrest genomen'; BL MS Add. 38495, fo. 36, Moreau to king of Poland, The Hague, 19 Oct. 1688; *Res. Holl.* 30 Sept. 1688; Baxter, *William III*, p. 211.

[45] Mallet (ed.), *Négociations*, VI, p. 321.

[46] BL MS Add. 41816, fo. 214, Petit to Middleton, Amsterdam, 5 Oct. 1688.

[47] GA Amsterdam vroed. XXXIX, pp. 145–6, 153, res. 3 and 15 Oct. 1688; GA Haarlem vroedschapsresoluties XXVI, fos. 217–18, 220, res. 28 Sept. and 11 Oct. 1688; Gebhard, *Het leven*, I, pp. 331–2; *Res. Holl.* 2 Oct. 1688.

domestic opposition, would overwhelm the Republic; the only way, in these circumstances, in which the Dutch state could be made secure was to break the 'absolute power' of James II quickly, suppress the Catholic, pro-French influence in England, convene Parliament and restore its authority, and turn England round against France. The essential purpose of the Dutch invasion of Britain was quite specific and was spelt out clearly: it was to make the English Crown and nation 'useful to their friends and allies, and especially to this state', as it was expressed in the secret resolution of 29 September of the States of Holland, and, as the Haarlem deputies put it in their report home, 'make this state secure against all external danger'.[48] Safeguarding the Protestant religion, and securing the dynastic interests of the Prince and Princess of Orange in England were, admittedly, tagged on as additional reasons; but both of these were given far less emphasis than the strategic factor. In the light of the resolutions of the States General and States of Holland there can be no doubt whatever that the Dutch state invaded Britain not to support religion, or the dynastic objectives of William and Mary, or to dethrone James, but to crush late Stuart absolutism thoroughly, turn England into a parliamentary monarchy and, by so doing, transform Britain into an effective counter-weight to the then overmighty power of France.

This was the objective and a breathtakingly grand and ambitious one it was too. It could not conceivably have succeeded without the concerted, unified, support of all sections of the Dutch state – something exceedingly rare in seventeenth-century Dutch history – but this was now assured thanks to the actions of Louis XIV. The outrage aroused by the Sun King's measures against Dutch trade and shipping in the United Provinces was, by the end of September 1688, so intense that there was no longer any possibility of any of the regents trying to oppose William's daring plan. The Holland towns backed the invasion of England with all the force and resources at their disposal, to the very hilt. The secret resolution of 29 September was approved, as the Haarlem deputies reported home, by all the Holland towns unanimously. On 2 October, the States of Holland took the unheard of step of authorizing the burgomasters, should there be any likelihood of a shortage of transports for the invasion armada, to use force to requisition vessels at imposed rates of hire.

Neither, of course, could the invasion have succeeded had not many or most Englishmen believed that the Prince of Orange (and not the Dutch state) was 'appearing in arms' in England on behalf of the Church and 'ancient constitution' of England. Up to a point the English public was deliberately misled. But the great advantage of the Dutch scheme was that while neither Prince nor States

[48] *Secreete Resolutien ... Hollandt*, IV, pp. 230–4, res. 29 Sept. 1688; GA Haarlem vroedschapsresoluties XXVI, fo. 220, res. 11 Oct. 1688.

felt any great zeal for the Church of England, the whole of the Dutch government – Stadholder, States of Holland, and States General – was genuinely set (albeit for reasons which had nothing to do with English concerns and interests) on the overthrow of what they called James II's 'absolute power' and on replacing his absolutism with a fundamentally different, that is, parliamentary, form of monarchy. This was enough to lead many Englishmen to overlook the means by which all this was to be achieved. But neither Prince nor States regarded the English opposition to James II as very reliable and both were determined to invade Britain with an army powerful enough to destroy James even without any military help from the English. The Dutch were intent on breaking James' authority and destroying his army – as far as possible by demoralizing it first – for it was from this that Parliament's supremacy and the turning of England round against France would follow. By mid-October d'Albeville grasped perfectly what the Dutch were doing; but still could not get over his amazement at the audacity of it all: 'they speak of nothing new more than of having England joine in a warre against France'.[49] 'An absolute conquest is intended', he summed it up on 15 October, 'under the specious and ordinary pretences of religion, liberty, property and a free parliament and a religious, exact, observation of the laws; this and a warr against France, they make account, will be but a work of a month's time'.[50]

Immense care went into the propaganda campaign. Even if the English were as unreliable as was commonly claimed at The Hague, people 'qui peuvent se resoudre subitement à prendre un parti tout contraire à celui qu'ils s'étoient mis dans la tête un moment auparavant', it was essential that the Dutch state, through a massive propaganda effort, generate at least an initial surge of enthusiasm in Britain for the Prince and his invasion.[51] The key propaganda piece, as we have seen in the Introduction, was the Prince of Orange's *Declaration* to the English people of 10 October 1688, a manifesto which both Jacobites and Williamites later acknowledged did have a major impact at the crucial moment. The Dutch state put great effort into the production and deployment of this pamphlet. Around 60,000 copies were printed in English amid great secrecy by specially commissioned printers working simultaneously at The Hague, Amsterdam, and Rotterdam.[52] This was a stupendous quantity for an age in which even the best-selling political pamphlets were rarely printed in more than 2,000 or 3,000 copies. Although the existence of this manifesto was widely known about, and there was much feverish speculation as to its contents for weeks before the landings at Torbay, both in Britain and in the United

[49] BL MS Add. 41816, fo. 232, d'Albeville to Middleton, The Hague, 12 Oct. 1688.
[50] BL MS Add. 41816, fo. 238, d'Albeville to Middleton, The Hague, 15 Oct. 1688.
[51] BL MS Add. 38495, fo. 32v, Moreau to King of Poland, The Hague, 12 Oct. 1688.
[52] BL MS Add. 41816, fo. 237, Petit to Middleton, Amsterdam, 15 Oct. 1688.

Provinces, it proved almost impossible to get hold of copies until the Prince and Bentinck ordered its release.[53] D'Albeville was quite baffled as to how to obtain a copy to send to London, finding the printers and their employees under strict oath of secrecy and 'not to be corrupted'.[54]

When at length the manifesto was released political observers were not a little amazed at what its critics considered the surpassing cynicism of its contents.[55] The Prince had persuaded the Dutch to help him invade England by making much of the alleged secret conspiracy of France and England against the Republic; but his *Declaration* said not a word about this conspiracy. The Prince was invading England with an army containing a substantial number of Whig volunteers either in exile in Holland or recently come over to join him, and in collusion with various Whig politicians in England: but the wording of the *Declaration* contained no Whig slogans or terminology and was clearly intended, as Macaulay put it, to 'please the cavaliers and parsons'. The Whig volunteers on the invasion armada at Hellevoetsluis were furious, the Earl of Macclesfield, Lord Mordaunt, and other Whig leaders demanding to know why they should take up arms on such grounds. No less cynical, indeed outrageous in James II's eyes, was William's declaring James, Prince of Wales, to be 'supposititious' and insisting on the need for Parliament to make an official enquiry into the matter, when both he and Princess Mary knew perfectly well that her brother was the king's legitimate heir.

A key feature of the Dutch propaganda drive was to play down and conceal as much as possible the involvement of the Dutch state and Stadholder – as distinct from the Prince of Orange in his capacity as husband of Princess Mary – in the invasion. Any suggestion that the Dutch had their own reasons for invading England was bound to be counter-productive. Consequently, much stress was placed on the claim that the Dutch state was not directly involved. 'Some of the States have already declared to some ministers who reside here, and to some others in discourse', reported d'Albeville on 16 October, 'that the States have nothing to do, nor have no hand in these preparations, and that they are at no expense at all; that the Prince of Orange hath something to say, and is call'd by the [English] nation, but they do but lend their ships not

[53] Ibid., fo. 251, d'Albeville to Middleton, The Hague, 21 Oct. 1688; Japikse (ed.), *Correspondentie*, II, pp. 618–19; the States General resolved to send copies to Dutch diplomats abroad only on 5 November, see the *Resolutien van de Hoogh Mog. Heeren Staten Generael der Vereinighde Nederlantsche Provincien genomen in den jare 1688* (The Hague, n.d.), pp. 662–3, res. 5 Nov. (25 Oct.) 1688.

[54] BL MS Add. 41816, fos. 232v, 238v, d'Albeville to Middleton, The Hague, 12 and 15 Oct. 1688.

[55] Ibid., fos. 238v, 249, d'Albeville to Middleton, The Hague, 20 Oct. 1688; *Some Reflections upon His Highness the Prince of Orange's Declaration* (Edinburgh, 1688), pp. 3, 6–7, 8, 13; *The Prince of Orange His Declaration: shewing the Reasons why he Invades England with a short Preface, and some modest remarks on it* (London, 1688), pp. 3–4; *Seasonable and Honest Advice to the Nobility, Clergy, gentry, Souldiery, and other the King's Subjects, upon the Invasion of His Highness the Prince of Orange* (London, 1688).

themselves'.[56] The States General's published statement of the reasons why they had resolved to 'assist His Highness crossing in person to England with ships and troops' of 28 October was instantly circulated among foreign diplomats in Holland, relayed to the courts of Europe – except for London and Paris, and published in several languages. The States professed to have no intention of dethroning James, altering the succession in England, subjecting England, or oppressing Catholic worship in the country. The Dutch state was 'assisting' the invasion only to prevent the overwhelming Anglo-French joint attack on the Republic which would surely ensue 'should the king of Great Britain succeed in his aim of achieving absolute power over his people'.[57]

It was especially important for the Dutch regents to reassure Catholic powers such as the emperor and Spain and gain their co-operation. At Vienna, Jacob Hop, an Amsterdam regent and one of the Republic's ablest diplomats, delivered personal letters to the emperor from the Prince and copies of the States General's resolution of 28 October, assuring ministers that the Prince and the States would see to it that Catholic worship in England was tolerated in the future on a similar basis to that in the United Provinces.[58] At Brussels, the Dutch resident used the resolution of 28 October to counter those who denounced the Dutch expedition as a Protestant bid to overthrow a legitimate Catholic monarch; and with considerable success.[59] At Madrid, the Dutch resident did likewise, assuring Carlos II's ministers that the Dutch were invading Britain only out of fear of France and in no way out of Protestant motives.[60]

Both the regents and the Prince were at great pains to claim that the invasion had been 'called by the English nation' and was essentially a British affair. In Britain many people believed this, though to more sophisticated minds the proposition that the Dutch Republic was merely 'assisting', and not actually responsible for, the invasion seemed inherently implausible even before Torbay, especially when it emerged that the States General – while pretending not to be paying for the invasion, and avoiding making official allocations for the armada – had all along been shouldering most of the cost. Even the Prince's *Declaration*, for all its stress on Englishmen's rights and liberties, and scrupulous omission of

[56] BL MS Add. 41816, fo. 243, d'Albeville to Middleton, The Hague, 16 Oct. 1688; in a concerted fashion the regents met by foreign diplomats at The Hague assured them that 'cette affaire n'est point celle de l'état et qu'elle se fait sans sa participation', BL MS Add. 38495, fo. 27, Moreau to king of Poland, The Hague, 5 Oct. 1688.

[57] *Hollandse Mercurius verhalende de voornaemste saken van staet en andere voorvallen die in en omtrent de Vereenigde Nederlanden en elders in Europa in het jaar 1688 zijn geschiet* (Haarlem, 1689), p. 273; *Engeland Beroerd onder de regering van Iacobus de II en hersteldt door Willem en Maria, Prins en Princesse van Orangie* (Amsterdam, 1689), pp. 245–6.

[58] N. J. den Tex, *Jacob Hop, gezant der Vereenigde Nederlanden* (Amsterdam, 1861), pp. 138, 268–9; Onno Klopp, *Der Fall des Hauses Stuart und die Succession des Hauses Hannover in Gross-Britannien und Irland im Zusammenhange der europäischen Angelegenheiten von 1660 bis 1714* (14 vols., Vienna, 1875–87), IV, p. 418.

[59] ARH SG 7084, Hulst to SG, Brussels, 3 Nov. 1688.

[60] Ibid., Battier to SG, Madrid, 2 Dec. 1688.

any mention of the Dutch state and its armed forces, gave the game away to the attentive reader.[61] In the first place, not only was the task of restoring England's ancient constitution reserved to the Prince and his army, but the manifesto required Englishmen and Scots to assist the Prince in the 'execution of his designs'.[62] The text of the *Declaration*, as James' propagandists were quick to point out, is full of 'We and Us, commanding, preferring, advancing, rewarding, punishing, having of parliaments, and settling the [English, Scots, and Irish] nations'.[63] Still more revealing was the Prince's promise 'as soon as the state of the Nation will admit of it... to send back all those forraigne forces that we have brought along with us', with its obvious implication that the Dutch army would remain in England until, in the Prince's estimation, the state of the country *was* satisfactory.[64] But James' counter-propaganda, the efforts to make the English public aware of these implications and undertones, had no effect. The Dutch won the propaganda war hands down.

The Dutch invasion fleet successfully landed the Prince and his army of 21,000 men on 5/15 November, at Torbay, in Devon. It has been suggested that by landing in the south-west, when most of the potential military support for the invasion was concentrated in the northern counties, William displayed an attitude almost of contempt towards the English nobility. In fact, it is now clear that the Prince had no particular design to land in the south-west rather than in the north-east but had simply followed the logic of the prevailing winds at the time.[65] It is also clear, despite his scepticism as to the reliability of the promises he had received from the English opposition, that he was deeply shaken by the lack of any support during the first ten days or so and complained of the 'timidity' of the English.[66] When the gentry of the south-west did begin to come over, the Prince characteristically ticked them off for being so slow to support him while reminding them that he had no need of their 'military assistance' but only of their 'countenance and presence' to justify his expedition and actions.[67]

On paper James II had a standing army of some 40,000 men, but his forces were scattered in strongholds and garrisons all over the country and he had to retain substantial forces in London and major strongholds such as Plymouth, Portsmouth, and Hull. Clearly, the king would be unable to muster much more

[61] *The London Gazette*, no. 2397 (5–8 Nov. 1688), p. 1.
[62] Ibid.
[63] Ibid.; *Seasonable and Honest Advice*, p. 6.
[64] *A True Copy of His Majesties Proclamation for England upon the Occasion of the Designed Invasion* (28 Sept. 1688), p. 1.
[65] See pp. 339–41 below.
[66] ARH Collectie Fagel 507, William III to Fagel, Exeter, 16/26 Nov. 1688.
[67] BL C122 L5/14: *The Speech of the Prince of Orange to some Principal Gentlemen of Somersetshire and Dorsetshire, on their coming to join His Highness at Exeter the 15th of November 1688*, p. 1.

than half the nominal strength of his army in the field, for a decisive battle. Given that William now had an army of over 21,000 men, mostly of higher quality, and much greater military experience, than James' troops, as well as better morale, more modern muskets, and a far more formidable artillery train than the king possessed, it is plain that in fact William, not James, was militarily the stronger. Surprise has often been expressed that in the end there was no battle on Salisbury Plain, James having in the past been a brave and resolute commander. But it is perhaps not so surprising that James decided to retreat, if it became evident to him that, were he to fight, he would almost certainly be beaten. In any case, the Prince had every reason to display confidence as he began his slow, inexorable advance towards London.

During the weeks of his cautious advance, the Prince was able to concentrate his thoughts on confusing, neutralizing, and scattering all pockets of power in Britain other than his own. He wrote to Fagel from Exeter, that he was worried that Lord Dartmouth, having failed to prevent the landing, might bring the English war fleet back from the south coast to the Thames Estuary to reinforce James' grip on the London area. Should this happen he would send the Dutch warships round to the Thames to force the English captains to declare either 'for or against him'; those English warships that refused to desert the king were (if possible) to be 'chased up the river' and disposed of.[68] As it turned out there was no need for this as Dartmouth's fleet, demoralized and racked by divided councils, remained inactive at Portsmouth until it capitulated to the Prince on 12 December.

The Prince was scarcely any less relentless in his attitude to his Whig and Tory noble supporters in the north with their bands of armed gentry and county militia. William deliberately made only a minimum of acknowledgment of the risings in his favour in the north and stubbornly ignored Danby's repeated requests to be given major military responsibilities.[69] The Prince wanted no rival focus of power in the north or south. On approaching London, he revealed his determination to bring the capital firmly under his own control. His Whig advisers had warned the Prince not to arouse the notorious xenophobia of the English by making too conspicuous a use of his Dutch troops.[70] Typically, William took no notice of such advice, being more concerned with how to maximize his political leverage. All the English army regiments in and around London were ordered to move out to towns and billets scattered over a wide area stretching from Sussex round to the northern home counties so that the army should be thoroughly dispersed and all its regiments placed at least 20 miles from

[68] ARH Collectie Fagel 507, William III to Fagel, Exeter, 16/26 Nov. 1688.

[69] J. P. Kenyon, *The Nobility in the Revolution of 1688*, University of Hull Inaugural lecture (Hull, 1963), pp. 13–16; A. Browning, *Thomas Osborne, Earl of Danby* (3 vols., Glasgow, 1944–51), I, pp. 424–5.

[70] Van Alphen, *De stemming van de Engelschen*, pp. 8, 22.

London.[71] The Life Guards were packed off to St Albans and Chelmsford. 'The English souldiers sent out of towne to distant quarters', notes John Evelyn, were 'not well pleased.'[72] This accomplished, the Prince then brought almost the entire Dutch army into London and its outskirts.

The Prince had several reasons for disposing matters in this way. First, he wished to preclude any possibility of the English army being used as a factor in the making of the new English regime or being used against his own forces. Secondly, he desired to secure London, the seat of power. Thirdly, by militarily occupying London, he reduced James to a virtual pawn. On the king's return to London, on 16 December, the London crowd had given him an unmistakably favourable reception. William could not be sure that he could count on popular support for long. 'So slight and unstable a thing is a multitude and so soon altered',[73] complained Burnet, but, in reality, relatively few Englishmen had, at any stage, entertained ideas of discarding James. Certainly Danby and most of the rebellious nobles in the north had not.[74] Consequently, the Prince of Orange's decision forcibly to remove the king from London was to be one of the most crucial steps of the entire Revolution. Before William's triumphant entry into London, Count Solms was sent ahead of the main army, with units of Dutch Blue Guards, to occupy Whitehall, St James's Park, and St James's Palace where the king had now resumed residence. The Coldstream Guards (who were still in place around the palace) refused to withdraw when Solms ordered them to do so and several accounts attest that the Dutch troops were about to open fire on them when the king ordered them to withdraw, to avoid useless bloodshed.[75] The king was then 'escorted' out of his palace by Dutch guards, 'under pretence to keep off the rabble',[76] and taken to Rochester. The Coldstream Guards were ordered by the Prince to withdraw to St Albans.

If William did not actually deport the king of England, his removal from the scene was not far short of forcible expulsion. It was thus with some justification that James, Jacobite apologists, and French propaganda subsequently

[71] *The London Gazette*, no. 2411; Abraham van Poot, *Engelands Gods-dienst en vryheid hersteldt door syn Hoogheyt den Heere Prince van Oranje* (2 vols., Amsterdam, 1689), I, p. 158; Sir John Dalrymple, *Memoirs of Great Britain and Ireland* (3 vols., London, 1790), II, pp. 221–2, 265; A. Browning (ed.), *The Memoirs of Sir John Reresby* (Glasgow, 1936), p. 553.

[72] E. S. de Beer (ed.), *The Diary of John Evelyn 1632–1695* (6 vols., Oxford, 1955), IV, p. 612.

[73] Quoted in W. A. Speck, *Reluctant Revolutionaries* (Oxford, 1988), p. 89; see also Robert Beddard, *A Kingdom without a King. The Journal of the Provisional Government in the Revolution of 1688* (Oxford, 1988), p. 51.

[74] Speck, *Reluctant Revolutionaries*, pp. 238–40; W. A. Speck, 'The Revolution of 1688 in the North of England', *Northern History*, 25 (1989), pp. 200–2.

[75] *Journaal van Constantijn Huygens*, I, p. 50; Isaac Dumont de Bostaquet, *Mémoires* (Paris, 1968), p. 201; Abel Boyer, *The History of King William the Third* (3 vols., London, 1702), I, pp. 296–7; James Macpherson, *The History of Great Britain, from the Restoration to the Accession of the House of Hannover* (2 vols., London, 1776), I, p. 544.

[76] A. Clarke (ed.), *The Life and Times of Anthony Wood, Antiquary of Oxford, 1632–1695* (5 vols., Oxford, 1891–1900), III, p. 290.

Seaborne troop landings
William III's march from Torbay to London (Nov.–Dec. 1688)
William III's march to the Boyne and Dublin (June–July 1690)
Ginkel's offensive from Athlone to Limerick (June–Sept. 1691)
Battle
Siege
Other incidents
N
Cromdale (1 May 1690)
Fort William (est. July 1690)
Ben Nevis
Killiecrankie (27 July 1689)
Glencoe massacre (13 Feb. 1692)
Dunkeld (21 Aug. 1689)
NORTH SEA
Leith
Edinburgh Castle (Apr.—June 1689)
Newcastle
Danish troop landings (Nov. 1689)
Londonderry (Apr.–28 July 1689)
Carrickfergus
Bangor
Enniskillen (Apr.–July 1689)
Newtonbutler (July 1689)
Dundalk (Schomberg, Sept. 1689)
William III (June 1690)
York
Hull (surrender of James II's garrison, Dec. 1688)
The Boyne (1 July 1690)
Athlone (Ginkel, June 1691)
Galway (Ginkel, Aug. 1691)
R. Boyne
Schomberg (1689)
Hoylake
Chester
Aughrim (12 July 1691)
Dublin (falls to William III in July 1690)
Limerick (1st siege: Aug. 1690) (2nd siege: Sept. 1691)
Waterford
Ipswich (mutiny Mar. 1689)
Oxford
London (William enters, 18 Dec. 1688)
Gunfleet
Bristol
Rochester
Dover
Salisbury (23 Nov. 1688)
Portsmouth (submission of James II's fleet to William, Dec. 1688)
Calais
William III
Exeter (8 Nov. 1688)
Beachy Head (30 June 1690)
Teignmouth (burnt by the French, July 1690)
Plymouth
Torbay
Dutch invasion armada (Nov. 1688)
La Hougue (29 May–1 June 1692)
0 150 km
0 100 miles
FRANCE

Map 2 Progressions, battles, and sieges of the British revolutions, 1688–91.

claimed that the Prince of Orange drove the king out of his kingdom using foreign troops, thereby creating a political situation which was not of the choosing of the English nation.[77] The Prince entered London at the head of a large and powerful Dutch army.[78] 'To the general disgust of the whole English army', Dutch Blue-Coats continued to guard Whitehall, St James's Palace, and Somerset House over the ensuing months which marked the formative phase of the Glorious Revolution.[79] Indeed, the whole of the London area remained under Dutch military occupation until the spring of 1690.[80] No English regiments were allowed within twenty miles of the city. The English and Scots regiments of the States' army were stationed at the Tower and Lambeth.[81] The Holsteiners were billeted at Woolwich. Other Dutch and German regiments encamped at Kensington, Chelsea, and Paddington while another crack regiment was positioned at Richmond and the Huguenots put up in various parts of London. As far as possible, the Prince avoided billeting his troops on private households. The troops were also under the strictest instructions to pay fully for everything they consumed and to be on their best behaviour. During the first week of January, the Prince received complaints that 'several of his soldiers took the freedome in their discourse to say they had conquered this nation'. Anxious to avoid jarring local sensibilities as far as possible, William 'made a severe order to punish any under his command that should utter any reproaches of this kind'.

Since the early eighteenth century, a thick wall of silence has descended over the Dutch occupation of London 1688–90. The whole business came to seem so improbable to later generations that by common consent, scholarly and popular, it was simply erased from record. But at the time, and through the 1690s, the occupation was one of the most fiercely debated aspects of the Glorious Revolution. Critics, by no means all Jacobites, blamed the Dutch soldiery for behaving in a heavy-handed manner. According to one writer, the Dutch soldiers 'take what they will and pay what they will, with oaths and blows into the

[77] [Jeremy Collier], *The Desertion Discuss'd* (London, 1689), pp. 2–3; *The Late King James's Manifesto answer'd Paragraph by Paragraph* (London, 1697), p. 10; *A Memorial drawn by King William's special Direction intended to be given at the Treaty of Reswick: Justifying the Revolution* (London, 1705), pp. 2–3; see also Clark (ed.), *The Life and Times of Anthony Wood*, III, pp. 289–90.

[78] BL C122 L 5/23: *A True Account of His Highness the Prince of Orange's Coming to St James's, on Tuesday the 18th of December 1688* (London, 1688), p. 1.

[79] Gilbert Burnet, *History of His Own Time* (6 vols., Oxford, 1833), III, pp. 357, 359; see also Van Poot, *Engelands Gods-dienst en vryheid hersteldt*, I, pp. 164–7.

[80] Van Poot, *Engelands Gods-dienst en vryheid hersteldt*, I, pp. 164–7; N. Luttrell, *A Brief Historical Relation of State Affairs from September 1678 to April 1714* (6 vols., Oxford, 1857), I, pp. 488–9; Eustache de le Noble de Tennelière, *La Pierre de touche politique* (28 parts, Paris, 1688–91), VI, pp. 23–32; Leopold von Ranke, *Englische Geschichte vornehmlich im sechszehnten und siebzehnten Jahrhundert* (7 vols., Leipzig, 1859–68), VI, pp. 13–14.

[81] Von Ranke, *Englische Geschichte*, VI, p. 13; ARH SG 5916/1, fo. 3.

bargain'.[82] On the other side, Burnet contended that never were the 'peace and order of the suburbs better upheld' than over the winter of 1688–9.[83] Other Williamites granted that the troops' behaviour was not always blameless but argued that on the whole they did behave 'civilly and respectfully', more so at any rate than James' soldiery had, and that in any case it was 'impossible that souldiers should be full out as civill as girls at a boarding-school'.[84] One apologist maintained that murders and robberies had appreciably diminished in the London area 'since our new friends have quartered about us'.[85]

But, for the historian, there is a more important question to consider than that of whether the occupying Dutch soldiery behaved civilly or not. Marching through London on 18 December 1688, and over the ensuing weeks, the States General's army had been cheered by the populace. But, by the spring of 1689, the mood was very different. Indeed the upsurge of anti-Dutch sentiment in London caused partly, if not mainly, by the presence of the Dutch soldiery, conspicuous by April, had, as Nicholas Witsen reported in a number of his dispatches from London, reached such a pitch of intensity by the summer as to have become a major political factor in its own right.[86] No doubt the Prince knew this perfectly well but never once wavered from his decision to keep the English regiments out, and a large proportion of the Dutch soldiery in, London. The question is, then, to what extent did the Dutch military occupation of London affect the course of the Glorious Revolution?

Whig historians have always treated the Convention Parliament with great reverence and all modern accounts of it, Whig and 'Revisionist' alike, assume, as a matter of course, that the Convention – which is usually seen as the guiding force behind the Revolution – was that 'free parliament' so insistently called for in Williamite propaganda. But was it a 'free parliament'? There is a considerable amount of evidence to set against such a view.[87] All sorts of pressure was brought to bear within a framework strictly controlled by William himself. Some members of the Convention themselves complained that it was not a 'free

82 *The State-Prodigal his Return; containing a true State of the Nation* (London, 1689), p. 4; *The Orange Gazette*, no. 4 (7/10 Jan. 1689).

83 Burnet, *History of His Own Time*, III, p. 359.

84 *An Answer to Two Papers Call'd, A Lords Speech Without-Doors, and a Commoners Speech* (London, 1689), p. 28.

85 Ibid.

86 GA Amsterdam Inv. no. 5027. Witsen to Amsterdam *vroedschap*, London, 21/31 May, 31 May, 10 June, 18/28 June and 25 June/5 July 1689; Nicolaas Witsen, 'Uittreksels uit het bijzonder verbaal nopens de deputatie en ambassade daarop gevolgd, in Engeland (1688)', in Jacobus Scheltema, *Geschied- en Letterkundig Mengelwerk* (6 vols., Amsterdam and Utrecht, 1817–36), III, part ii, pp. 135, 138.

87 ARH SG 5916/1, fo. 60, Van Citters to SG, London, 5/15 Feb. 1689; as early as 8 November 1688, James proclaimed in *The London Gazette*, no. 2397 (5–8 Nov. 1688), that 'nothing is more evident than that a Parliament cannot be free, so long as there is an army of forreigners in the heart of our kingdoms'; for subsequent attacks on the Convention as a tool of the Prince of Orange, see

parliament', particularly when, in London, popular Williamite agitation was organized by Lord Lovelace – until William, realizing that using the populace was alienating some members of Parliament, ordered Lovelace to desist. More effective was the behind-the-scenes pressure. Contemporary Jacobite and French critics contended that the Convention was in no sense a 'free parliament' because it convened at the bidding of a foreign prince who had already assumed control of the country's army, finances, and interim administration in a London occupied by a foreign army. No doubt one might object that such claims were biased and exaggerated; but one might also wonder whether the modern historian is being objective in ignoring these allegations.

It would, of course, be absurd to portray the Convention as the mere tool of a foreign prince and army. But it seems to me that one cannot reasonably deny that opinion in the Convention must have been profoundly influenced by the highly unusual political and military realities prevailing in the London area at the time. It is evident that many MPs, especially Tories, eventually consented to measures with which they were not in sympathy. We know that a good many, and probably most, participants in the Convention would have preferred not to depose James. But the Tory loyalist campaign to defend the latter's interests, and those of his infant heir, exploiting the Prince's own *Declaration* which expressly disclaimed any intention of dethroning the king, withered under the relentless pressure which was brought to bear.[88]

The Prince of Orange played his hand with consummate skill.[89] Princess Mary's total submissiveness to her husband in matters of state and the succession was made abundantly clear. At an informal meeting with the Lords (probably on the evening of 3 February), William showed that he desired the Crown in his own right with executive power, with or without Mary as nominal joint sovereign. Dijkvelt, on William's behalf, obtained from Princess Anne her under-

Remonstrance and Protestation of All the Good Protestants of This Kingdom against Deposing Their Lawful Soveraign, K. James II (London, 1689), pp. 1–3; *The State-Prodigal*, p. 4; Le Noble de Tennelière, *Pierre de touche politique*, VI, pp. 26–7; Antoine Arnauld, *Le véritable portrait de Guillaume-Henri de Nassau, Nouvel Absalom, Nouvel Hérode, Nouveau Cromwell, Nouveau Néron* ('Brussels', Paris?, 1689), pp. 71–3; *Apologie pour leurs Sérénissimes Majestés Britanniques contre un infame libelle intitulé Le Vray Portrait de Guillaume-Henri de Nassau* (The Hague, 1694), p. 22.

[88] R. Beddard, 'The Loyalist Opposition in the Interregnum: A Letter of Dr. Francis Turner, Bishop of Ely, on the Revolution of 1688', *BIHR*, 40 (1967), p. 106; R. Beddard, 'The Guildhall Declaration of 11 December 1688 and the Counter-Revolution of the Loyalists', *Historical Journal*, II (1968), p. 409; L. G. Schwoerer, 'A Jornall of the Convention at Westminster begun the 22 of January 1688/9', *BIHR*, 49 (1976), pp. 253, 256.

[89] Witsen, 'Uittreksels', pp. 140–1; Gebhard, *Het leven*, I, p. 349; E. Cruickshanks, D. Hayton, and C. Jones, 'Divisions in the House of Lords on the Transfer of the Crown and Other Issues, 1689–94; Ten New Lists', *BIHR*, 53 (1980), p. 61; see also Arnauld, *Véritable portrait*, pp. 71–3.

taking to waive her right to succeed should Mary predecease the Prince. Dijkvelt, who was more palatable to the English than the haughty Bentinck, also worked assiduously on individual members of the Commons and Lords.[90] Parliament was made to realize that failure to depose James and set aside the Prince of Wales would mean not just chronic instability but, almost certainly, civil war. Even those Tories who, in other circumstances, would have been strongly attached to James' cause now realized, as the Spanish ambassador noted,[91] that even though they had had no hand in James' expulsion the fact that they had supported the Prince's invasion initially, or at any rate failed to assist the king, meant that they now had reason to fear retribution should he return. Another factor inhibiting what otherwise would have been stronger support for James was the realization that those subsequently revealed as having voted against 'abdication' would be remembered, should William nevertheless have his way, as having opposed 'King William's sovereignty'.

But real enthusiasm for making William king was so limited that the campaign in favour of James, inhibited and half-hearted though it was, might, were it not for the considerable amount of arm-twisting that went on, easily have blocked the Prince's path. Parliament may have made the Revolution settlement, but historians are seriously at fault if they overlook the external interference and the fear and opportunism, which helped shape the outcome. The eventual majorities in the Commons and Lords in favour of the king having 'abdicated' were much less convincing in reality than the numbers of votes might suggest.[92] Indeed, in the Lords it was the loyalists who commanded a substantial majority during a series of votes at the end of January and during the first few days of February. The seemingly substantial majority in favour of James' 'abdication' in the crucial vote on 6 February transpired only because a considerable number of Lords were afraid to persist in opposing the Prince. The vote was won by the Williamites by sixty-four to forty-six, but if one allows for the deliberate absence of six loyalists who had sided with the Jacobites in previous days, four new Williamite recruits, and no less than five Jacobite 'defectors', it is undeniable that the vote was won only because of the 'falling off of some and the absence of others'.[93] Particularly unedifying was the behaviour of Nathaniel Crew, bishop of Durham and hitherto a staunch supporter of James and of Divine Right principles. To the amazement of many, he joined Compton in being one of

[90] Gebhard, *Het leven*, I, p. 349; Witsen, 'Uittreksels', p. 151.
[91] Gabriel Maura Gamazo (ed.), *Correspondencia entre dos embajadores. Don Pedro Ronquillo y el Marqués de Cogolludo, 1689–1691* (2 vols, Madrid, 1951), I, pp. 64–5.
[92] E. Cruickshanks, J. Ferris, and D. Hayton, 'The House of Commons Vote on the Transfer of the Crown, 5 February 1689', *BIHR*, 52 (1979), pp. 38–9; Beddard, 'The Loyalist Opposition', p. 107.
[93] Cruickshanks, Hayton, and Jones, 'Divisions in the House of Lords', pp. 59, 62–5.

only two bishops to vote with the Williamites, as far as anyone could tell 'to cringe to the Prince of Orange in hopes to keep his bishoprick'.[94]

The votes to depose James and set aside the Prince of Wales were obtained under pressure and were but narrowly won. William and Mary, in other words, were made jointly king and queen of England reluctantly, by a deeply divided Parliament. Not surprisingly, a large part of the nation never regarded William as their legitimate monarch. As several contemporaries noted, the Prince's very acceptance of the Crown shocked many of his former Tory supporters including Danby, and intensified the growing reaction against the Revolution which, as early as February 1689, was clearly evident.[95] Radical Whig nobles such as Lord Mordaunt (said to have been the first English nobleman to have proposed to William that he should invade England) were similarly deeply alienated.[96] Enough of the initial support for the Revolution still lingered to make a success of the joint coronation of William and Mary, in April. Even so, it was noticeable that the coronation was 'not attended by soe many of the nobility as when the last two kings were crowned', that there were 'several ... greate ladys wanting', and that there were only five bishops present.[97] Privately, William derided the pomp and circumstance of the coronation ceremony in conversation with Witsen, making fun of the 'foolish, old papist ceremonies'.[98]

William acquired his Crown and, shortly, also that of Scotland. But the British crowns were by no means his only pressing requirements of the Convention. In his opening addresses to the Lords and Commons of the Convention, of 22 January, the Prince stated that the most urgent priority facing Parliament was to send immediate, large-scale assistance to the United Provinces.[99] William put his whole weight behind this demand, impelled not only by his own zeal for assembling an effective European coalition against Louis XIV but by insistent pressure emanating from Amsterdam and the States. The regents warned him that if English troops and money were not made available for service in the Low Countries promptly and in quantity, it would be difficult to check those

94 Ibid., p. 64; Clark (ed.), *The Life and Times of Anthony Wood*, III, p. 298; see also A. Simpson, 'Notes of a Noble Lord, 22 January to 12 February 1688/9', *English Historical Review*, 52 (1937), pp. 94–5.

95 Maura Gamazo (ed.), *Correspondencia entre dos embajadores*, I, p. 143; John Miller, 'Proto-Jacobitism? The Tories and the Revolution of 1688–9', in E. Cruickshanks and J. Black (eds.), *The Jacobite Challenge* (Edinburgh, 1988), p. 17.

96 G. D. Warburton (ed.), *A Memoir of Charles Mordaunt Earl of Peterborough and Monmouth* (2 vols., London, 1853), I, pp. 43, 57.

97 Browning (ed.), *Memoirs of Sir John Reresby*, p. 571; de Beer (ed.), *The Diary of John Evelyn*, IV, p. 633.

98 Witsen, 'Uittreksels', pp. 143–5.

99 *His Highness the Prince of Orange His Letter to the Lords Spiritual and Temporal Assembled at Westminster in the Present Convention on January 22nd 1688/9* (London, 1689), p. 1; see also the Prince's letter to the Commons, *CJ*, X, p. 9; N. Chevalier, *Histoire de Guillaume III* (Amsterdam, 1692), p. 89; A. Montanus, *Het Leven, Bedryf en Oorlogs-daaden van Wilhem de Derde, koning van Engeland, Schotland, Vrankryk en Ierland* (4 vols., Amsterdam, 1703), III, p. 159; Witsen, 'Uittreksels', pp. 143–4.

7 *The Coronation of William III and Mary as King and Queen of England in Westminster Abbey on 11 April 1689*. By Romeyn de Hooghe.

who preferred to seek accommodation with France rather than plunge into a long and gruelling war. Historians of the Revolution settlement invariably fail to point out William's heavy insistence on the need for Parliament to assist the Dutch because in the context of a Revolution viewed as a purely British affair this seems irrelevant. But the moment that we postulate that the Glorious Revolution, however central in British history, was not solely due to British factors and was partly imposed from outside, with London under Dutch military occupation, the Prince's demands of the Convention Parliament assume great significance. In his opening address the Prince called for promptness and unity in meeting the ends of 'my Declaration' and a speedy resolution on help for the Dutch. He warned that the 'States by whom I have been enabled to rescue this nation, may suddenly feel the ill effects of it both by being too long deprived of the service of their troops which are now here, and of your early assistance against a powerful enemy who hath declared war against them'. Here the Prince was referring to the French declaration of war on the United Provinces of 26 November 1688, Louis XIV having carried out his threat to go to war with the Dutch – should they defy him by intervening in England – eleven days after the landings at Torbay.[100] The Republic was now locked in conflict with Europe's mightiest monarch and although Parliament, as yet, did not know it, the Prince and the Dutch regents were already deeply engrossed in the question of how and when to bring England into the war. To the Convention, the Prince expressed his confidence that the States' 'cheerfull concurrence to preserve this kingdom with so much hazard to themselves, will meet with all the returns of friendship and assistance which may be expected from you as Protestants and Englishmen'.[101]

William had already decided, before the Convention met, that the Dutch troops in Britain should henceforth be paid for entirely by the English tax-payer as from 1 January 1689.[102] During the first week of January, he also announced in the London papers, his decision to send 8,000 English troops to the Netherlands 'to act against France' as, he claimed, England was obliged to do under the terms of the Treaty of Nijmegen 'according to mutual stipulation, against the violater of that treaty'.[103] However, the deteriorating situation in Ireland obliged him to send the troops there instead. Consequently, there had still been no dispatch of assistance to the Dutch by mid-February when William and Mary were proclaimed king and queen. In his speech of 18 February to the Convention, the Stadholder-king once again heavily emphasized the need for England to assist the Dutch, reminding the Lords and Commons of the Republic's 'zeal and affection to promote the Expedition' by which he had been able to 'rescue' England and again expressing his confidence that 'your generosity will have as little bounds towards them, as theirs had towards you'.[104]

Parliament, absorbed in the complexities of the Revolution at home, and still dazed by the rapidity of events since November, understandably felt no irresistible impulse to rush into a war with France, or repay an alleged immense debt to the Dutch. The situation was further complicated by the fact that while William

[100] *Res. Holl.* 7 Dec. 1688; Klopp, *Fall des Hauses Stuart*, IV, p. 227.
[101] *His Highness The Prince of Orange His Letter*, p. 1.
[102] ARH SG 4594, fos. 37v–8v, Dijkvelt, Odijk, and Witsen to SG, London, 3 Feb. 1689; Maura Gamazo (ed.), *Correspondencia entre dos embajadores*, I, pp. 68–9; *Res. Holl.* 3 Feb. 1689.
[103] Ibid.; *The Orange Gazette*, no. 2 (31 Dec. 1688/3 Jan. 1689), p. 2; *The London Courant*, no. 6 (1/5 Jan. 1689).
[104] *His Majesty's Most Gracious Speech in the House of Lords to the Lords and Commons assembled at Westminster, the Eighteenth Day of February 1688/9* (London, 1689), p. 5.

for the moment demanded only 'assistance' but not yet England's entry into the war on the side of the Dutch, the States were pressing William 'to assist' and to declare war. Indeed, by the spring, the regents, seeing the mounting difficulties which the Stadholder-king now faced in Ireland and Scotland as well as England became seriously alarmed lest he settle for assistance only, for the time being, and put off declaring war on France until he had consolidated his position in Britain and Ireland. The result was a triangular tug-of-war during February, March, and April with Holland pressing William to declare war, the new king urging Parliament to vote the Dutch large-scale 'assistance', and Parliament dragging its feet.[105]

It was indeed widely expected on the continent, not least in the Dutch assemblies, that the new king of England would delay declaring war on France until he had strengthened his – for the moment – precarious position in the British Isles. But observers were also inclined to think that in this situation it was not the Stadholder-king but the Dutch regents who exerted the greater leverage. The Spanish ambassador in London, Don Pedro Ronquillo, for example, advised his colleague in Rome that Parliament would not for long be able to prevent England's entry into war with France, or becoming massively involved in the Low Countries, for unless Parliament acquiesced, William would be unable to retain in England the 'fourteen to sixteen thousand high-quality, veteran [Dutch] troops who will, without difficulty, disperse the forces which King James may bring'.[106] Additional Dutch troops had been sent over after the main invasion in November 1688 so that although William had had to send 3,500 of his veterans back to the United Provinces, in March, he still had some 12,000 Dutch troops in Britain.[107] Parliament's resistance to declaring war on France collapsed in April when King James, accompanied by the comte d'Avaux, landed in Ireland and rapidly gained control of most of the country. Once England did declare war on France, at the beginning of May, the States General agreed to send additional help across and another 5,000 Dutch troops were sent over.[108] William, as king of England, Scotland, and Ireland, now faced the French, as well as the English, Scots, and Irish Jacobites, but, in support of his regime, he now had some 17,000 Dutch veterans supplemented by around 2,000 Huguenots.

[105] ARH SG 4594, fo. 74v, res. 2 Apr. 1689; BL MS Add. 38495, fo. 97, Moreau to king of Poland, The Hague, 19 Apr. 1689.

[106] Maura Gamazo (ed.), *Correspondencia entre dos embajadores*, I, p. 129. Ronquillo to Cogolludo, London, 25 Mar. 1689.

[107] Back in February, William had promised, circumstances permitting, to send back seven regiments of Dutch troops to the Republic, as well as nine English regiments, but in the event sent more English but only 3,500 of the Dutch, Van Alphen, *De stemming van de Engelschen*, p. 34; the States General not only required some of their troops from Britain, but the pontoon bridges and some of the trained artillerymen and engineers, see ARH SG 4594, fos. 14–15, res. 11 Jan. 1689.

[108] Lambert van den Bos, *Leven en Bedryf van Willem de Derde, koning van Groot Brittanien* (2 vols., Amsterdam, 1694), I, p. 338; Klopp, *Fall des Hauses Stuart*, IV, p. 386.

Besides demanding large-scale assistance for the Republic, William had another and scarcely less urgent requirement of Parliament and the English establishment. He needed an effective religious toleration in England and he needed it quickly. In his *Declaration* of 10 October 1688, William had announced that he would change the laws of England as far as the Dissenters were concerned;[109] and with the Revolution and James' departure – which automatically cancelled the latter's edicts of Indulgence – the Dissenters had been in an enthusiastic, expectant but also impatient mood.[110] The Dissenters, as Defoe describes, were the section of the population of England most strongly committed to the Revolution. But it was not only because he needed Dissenter support that William was in such a hurry to establish an effective toleration in England: in his eyes, it was still more urgent to satisfy the Republic's potential Catholic allies on the continent. Whatever Parliament's opinion might be, William was determined to transform England from being the country known as the most intolerant towards Catholics in all Europe into a country as tolerant of Catholicism as the United Provinces in the shortest possible space of time.

Admittedly, this was a tall order even for the man one French writer called the 'plus fin politique qui ait jamais été'.[111] But William had to succeed in performing this (astounding) feat. While exploiting James' pro-Catholic policy to overthrow him, and assuring the English that he had come as the champion of the Protestant cause, he had simultaneously been assuring the emperor and the king of Spain that there were no Protestant motives for his intervention in Britain and that he would see to it that English Catholics would now be even better off than they had been under James.[112] Fulfilling his commitment to secure an effective toleration for Catholics in England became an immensely urgent matter for William not only because he had made his promises on behalf of England's Catholics repeatedly, and with great emphasis, but because, as James' authority disintegrated, a powerful anti-Catholic backlash erupted first in London and then in towns all over England.[113]

As the Prince and his army had slowly approached London, in December

[109] *The Declaration of His Highness William Henry, by the Grace of God Prince of Orange, etc. Of the Reasons Inducing him to appear in Armes in the Kingdome of England* (The Hague, 1688), p. 8; [J. Humfrey], *King William's Toleration: being an Explanation of that Liberty of Religion which may be Expected from His Majesty's Declaration* (London, 1689), p. 15; Leti, *Teatro Belgico*, I, p. 363.

[110] [Humfrey], *King William's Toleration*, pp. 1, 15; *Les Soupirs de la France esclave qui aspire après la liberté* (Amsterdam, 1690), p. 222.

[111] *Esprit politique ou l'histoire en abrégé de la vie et des actions de Guillaume III de Nassau, Roi de la Grand Bretagne* (Amsterdam, 1695), p. 241.

[112] ARH SG 7084, Battier to SG, Madrid, 2 Dec. 1688; Arnauld, *Véritable portrait*, pp. 61–2; den Tex, *Jacob Hop*, p. 138.

[113] Van Poot, *Engelands Gods-dienst en vryheid hersteldt*, I, pp. 146–7, 154–6, 166, 252; W. L. Sachse, 'The Mob and the Revolution of 1688', *Journal of British Studies*, 4 (1964), pp. 28–31; Giovanni Gerolamo Arconati Lamberti, *Mémoires de la dernière révolution d'Angleterre* (2 vols., The Hague, 1702), I, pp. 660–2.

1688, the London mob had gone on the rampage, sacking Catholic chapels – including those of the Spanish and Tuscan ambassadors – hunting Catholic priests, and pillaging wealthy Catholic homes.[114] Still worse from William's point of view and that of the Holland regents, this upsurge of anti-Catholic feeling had caused a sensation throughout Europe and acute alarm in Vienna, Madrid, Catholic Germany, and Rome as well as at The Hague.[115] Louis XIV seized his opportunity to embarrass the emperor and Spanish king and undermine the moves to assemble a powerful European coalition against him. French propaganda portrayed what was happening in England as the start of a general European *guerre de religion*, precipitated by the Dutch, in collusion with Brandenburg and Sweden, and ultimately intended to destroy the Catholic cause everywhere. Catholic powers which abetted William's invasion of England were simply dupes of the Dutch. In spreading this message, French diplomats had the assistance of James' envoys at the Catholic courts and formidable *dévot* factions at Vienna and Madrid. Cardinal Kollonitsch, leader of the *dévot* faction at Vienna was, indeed, almost as eager as Louis and James to prevent the emperor allying with the Dutch.[116] The Holland regents had every reason to be horrified by the upsurge of anti-Catholic violence in Britain; for, if Louis did sway Vienna or Madrid, or prevail upon the pope to declare the invasion of England the start of a *guerre de religion*, he would largely have succeeded in isolating the United Provinces in Europe.

The States General lost no time in instructing their diplomats to go all out to contest Louis' and James' diplomacy and propaganda. At The Hague foreign diplomats were told that, as soon as the Prince had managed to restore order in England, the position of Catholics in that country would be even better than it had been before the Revolution.[117] William received a flood of letters from the Hague beseeching him to write without delay to the emperor, king of Spain, and other Catholic potentates repeating his assurances to establish an effective toleration for Catholics in England.[118] The Prince did so and, in a series of meetings with the Spanish ambassador and imperial envoy in London, he and

[114] Van Poot, *Engelands Gods-dienst en vryheid hersteldt*, I, pp. 146–7, 154–6, 166, 252. Klopp, *Fall des Hauses Stuart*, IV, p. 265.

[115] ARH SG 7085/1, Battier to SG, Madrid, 30 Dec. 1689; Hulst to SG, Brussels, 22 Jan. 1689; Leti, *Monarchie Universelle de Louys XIV*, I, pp. 418, 433, 520–1; Leti, *Teatro Belgico*, I, pp. 363, 394; Denis de Sainte-Marthe, *Entretiens touchant l'entreprise du Prince d'Orange sur l'Angleterre* (Paris, 1689), pp. 25–6; J. Tronchin de Breul, *Lettres sur les matières du temps* (3 vols., Amsterdam, 1688–90), II, pp. 43–4, 104–5, 112.

[116] G. van Antal and J. C. H. de Pater (eds.), *Weensche gezantschapsberichten van 1670 tot 1720* (2 vols., The Hague, 1929–34), I, pp. 400–1; den Tex, *Jacob Hop*, pp. 272–3.

[117] ARH SG 4030, res. 22 Nov. 1688; BL MS Add. 38495, fos. 68, 74, Moreau to king of Poland, The Hague, 4 and 18 Jan. 1689.

[118] Van Poot, *Engelands Gods-dienst en vryheid hersteldt*, I, pp. 176–8; Tronchin de Breul, *Lettres sur les matières du temps*, II, p. 21; Van Antal and de Pater (eds.), *Weensche gezantschapsberichten*, I, p. 402; P. L. Müller, *Wilhelm III von Oranien und Georg Friedrich von Waldeck* (2 vols., The Hague, 1873–80), II, p. 121.

Dijkvelt spared no effort to convince them of the sincerity of these promises and with evident success. The undertakings conveyed to the English Catholics, through the Spanish ambassador, may have had little effect on them, the English Catholics remaining stubbornly loyal to James.[119] But the Spanish ambassador himself was sufficiently impressed to write to his colleague in Rome that he should assure His Holiness that more might be expected on behalf of English Catholics from William than had been achieved by James.[120]

Princess Mary played her part in calming the Catholic courts. On taking her leave of the diplomatic community at The Hague, upon her return to England, early in February, she told the Catholic representatives present that

> elle étoit sensiblement touchée des insolences que le peuple avoit commises à Londres à l'égard des chapelles et l'imprisonnement de plusieurs seigneurs catholiques, que toutes ces choses étoient entièrement contraires aux sentiments de M. le Prince d'Orange et que enfin ils feroient connoître l'une et l'autre par la suite qu'ils n'avoient rien tant à coeur que d'établire solidement la liberté de conscience pour tous les catholiques dans les trois royaumes.[121]

William knew that anti-Catholicism was the main impulse behind the English popular involvement in the Revolution against James' absolutism. But he also knew that he had to give the Catholics their *de facto* toleration in England and without delay. In his letter of 4 March, the emperor warned him that he could check the impact of French diplomacy and propaganda for the moment, but unless there was concrete progress soon, Louis would succeed in driving a wedge between the imperial court and the Dutch Republic.[122] The Toleration Act of the spring of 1689 was a rushed job, watered down by Tories who succeeded even in having the very word 'toleration' deleted. But everyone informally called it 'the toleration' and what mattered from William's and the Dutch point of view was not the principles – if there were any – embodied in the Act but the destruction of the mechanisms whereby the Church of England and the judiciary could force the individual conscience and fine, and otherwise harass, those who attended non-Anglican religious services. If the Catholics were not included in the terms of the parliamentary Act, this was less important than the Act's removing all practical hindrances from church gatherings and conventicles of whatever kind. Through his directives to the circuit judges, William ordered the judiciary to cease interference with Catholic priests and their celeb-

[119] Maura Gamazo (ed.), *Correspondencia entre dos embajadores*, I, p. 236; Ronquillo blames the Jesuits for helping keep English Catholics solid for James and the French interest.

[120] Ibid., I, pp. 63, 67–9, 71, 86, 140. II, pp. 93, 130; William promised Ronquillo that 'los católicos quedesan con mas libertad que cuando murió Carlos II'; Ronquillo urged Cogolludo 'asegure a Su Santidad que mas sacaré del Príncipe para los católicos, que pudiera sacar del Rey'.

[121] BL MS Add. 38495, fo. 79, Moreau to king of Poland, The Hague, 8 Feb. 1689.

[122] Van Poot, *Engelands Gods-Dienst en vryheid hersteldt*, II, pp. 309–10; L. Sylvius, *Tweede vervolg van saken van staat en oorlog in en omtrent de Vereenigde Nederlanden ... beginnende met het jaar 1687* (3 vols., Amsterdam, 1698), III, pp. 104–5; den Tex, *Jacob Hop*, p. 273.

ration of the mass.[123] In this way it soon became evident that the 'papists have enjoyed the real effects of the Toleration', as Burnet put it, 'though they were not comprehended within the statute that enacted it'.[124] Jacobite propaganda had begun by attacking William as a champion of Protestantism and foe of toleration. But by the spring of 1689 this line of attack no longer made sense and Jacobites switched to attacking William for his hypocrisy, in claiming to champion the Protestant cause while in fact being as favourable to the Catholics as King James.[125]

Indeed, Jacobites came to claim that King William did more to weaken the Church of England than did James.[126] Modern 'revisionists', for their part, insist that the Toleration Act so-called was a much more grudging measure than James' Declarations of Indulgence. Both are right; for, indeed, the Act was more narrowly framed than James' edicts on religion. Nevertheless, the Toleration Act undoubtedly did more to weaken the Church of England; for it was much the more effective in curtailing the powers of the Anglican Church, and the judiciary, over the individual conscience and, consequently, had a very much wider and more positive impact on all aspects of Dissenter, Catholic, and anti-trinitarian Christian activity – meetings, preaching, chapel-building, fund-raising, education, and publishing. William had promised English Catholics, on reaching London, and suppressing the anti-Catholic disturbances in the capital, that they would 'live as much at ease and undisturb'd under the regency of William Henry, as under the reign of James II' and he proved as good as his word.[127] High Church Anglicans who recognized William as *de facto* king poured out their anger at William's ecclesiastical policies throughout the 1690s and for many years after his death. Ironically, it was harder for the out-and-out Jacobites to do so. They had to content themselves with the sneer that it was 'well known that the Prince's moderation, such as it is, had no other ground than the fear he was in to alarm the confederate Catholic princes'.[128]

A major challenge facing King William and the Dutch regents during a large part of 1689 was that of securing Europe's acceptance of the Glorious Revolution and the altering of the English line of succession. Protestant princes, such as the Elector of Brandenburg and Christian V of Denmark–Norway were less

[123] [Nathaniel Johnston], *The Dear Bargain, or A True Representation of the State of the English Nation under the Dutch* (1690), in *A Third Collection of Scarce and Valuable Tracts* (Lord Somers) (4 vols., London, 1751), III, p. 250.

[124] Burnet, *History of His Own Time*, IV, p. 21–2; Jones, *The Revolution of 1688*, p. 319.

[125] [Sir James Montgomery], *Great Britain's Just Complaint for Her Late Measures Present Sufferings and the Future Miseries she is expos'd to* (n.p., 1692), p. 17.

[126] *The Spirit of Jacobitism: or, Remarks upon a Dialogue between K. W. and Benting* (London, 1695), p. 18.

[127] R. W., *The Happy Union of England and Holland or, the Advantageous Consequences of the Alliances of the Crown of Great Britain with the States General of the United Provinces* (London, 1689), p. 7.

[128] *The Late King James's Manifesto answer'd*, p. 42.

inhibited about recognizing William's elevation than Catholic rulers, but the Protestant princes too had to be coaxed into providing material support. Meanwhile, the vital task of securing recognition, and with it alliances, from the emperor and king of Spain proved far from easy. The Emperor Leopold nurtured strong personal objections to recognizing Parliament's setting James and the Prince of Wales aside, and proclaiming William as king of England, and, according to Jacobite pamphleteers, eventually only brought himself to sign his formal letter of recognition with tears in his eyes. However that may be, there is no doubt that the emperor's ministers were divided over the desirability of recognizing William and signing formal alliances with the Republic and with England.[129] It was fortunate for both the Dutch and the new regime in England that, in the end, Leopold simply could not turn his back on the Rhine and concentrate on his war with the Turks, refusing to have anything to do with William, without demolishing his own standing and prestige, and making France supreme, in the empire. At Madrid too, the Consejo de Estado was initially split over the question of whether to recognize and sign an alliance with William.[130]

To the task of winning European powers over to support the English Revolution, and the elevation of William and Mary, English diplomacy could contribute very little. For the English diplomatic service had largely collapsed following William's invasion and most of James' envoys on the continent remained loyal to his cause. Consequently, the new king of England relied initially mainly on Dutch diplomacy. It was the States General's ambassadors and residents who countered the French and Jacobite diplomatic and propaganda onslaught in the courts of Europe during the early months of 1689 and Dutch diplomats who negotiated William's alliances and agreements with Denmark, the emperor, Spain and other powers. At Copenhagen, the first post-Revolution English diplomat, Robert Molesworth, arrived only in July, by which time the States General's envoy, Heemskerk, had already agreed the terms whereby the Danish Crown hired out an entire Danish army to support the new English regime in Britain and Ireland. William, through Molesworth – who had only to finalize the arrangement – signed this important troop-hire treaty in August.[131]

The hardest task, that of winning over the emperor, fell to Jacob Hop. There is no doubt that Leopold was responsive (in a way that the pope was not)

[129] Klopp, *Fall des Hauses Stuart*, IV, pp. 418–19, 424.

[130] *Cartas del Duque de Montalto a don Pedro Ronquillo, embajador . . . en Inglaterra* (1688), in *Colección de documentos inéditos para la historia de España* (113 vols., Madrid, 1842–95), LXXIX, pp. 456–7, 469–70, 475; in December 1688, Montalto wrote to Ronquillo that 'yo jamas creí ni creeré de éste hombre [William III] nada bueno, sino lo mas perniciosio a nuestros intereses'.

[131] PRO SP 75/22, fo. 77, Molesworth to Warre, Copenhagen, 16 Aug. 1689; Montanus, *Leven, Bedryf en Oorlogs-daaden*, III, p. 233.

to the pleas of James II and to Louis' admonition that the Dutch, by corrupting James II's subjects, had offended 'tous les souverains en la personne du Roy de Grande Bretagne'.[132] Clearly, the emperor's recognition would not come cheaply. Leopold wanted satisfaction regarding Catholic worship in England. But he was also anxious that William should declare war on France as soon as possible so as to relieve the pressure of the French armies on the Rhine. The emperor's reluctance to recognize William as king of England thus came to be used as an additional lever to hasten England's entry into the War of the League of Augsburg. In April, Hop passed a secret message to Witsen, in London intimating that the emperor would not recognize William as king of England until after he had declared war on France.[133] Whether this manoeuvre originated with Leopold or with the Holland regents is hard to say; but Witsen certainly lost no time in communicating Leopold's message to the Stadholder-king and, as he reported to the Amsterdam city council, was delighted to see that this stung him into redoubling his efforts to prod Parliament into declaring war.

Even after the English declaration of war on France both the emperor and Spain continued to prevaricate on the matter of recognition. Hop reported to London in mid-May that the emperor's ministers had assured him that they would recognize William but in this matter wished to move 'in concert ... with the Spanish court'.[134] A month later Hop reported that Leopold's letter of recognition had now been prepared but that it had not yet been signed.[135] When finally the letter arrived, a month later still, it turned out that the emperor's recognition was closely linked with, indeed virtually conditional on, the toleration of Catholic worship in England and military collaboration against France.[136] Spanish recognition followed soon after.[137]

During the months following the coronation of William and Mary the Revolution in Britain remained precarious and seemed to be becoming more so. Support for the Glorious Revolution, never anything like so universal or strong as the Whig historiographical tradition later assumed, was, by all contemporary

[132] Sainte-Marthe, *Entretiens*, pp. 25–6; the emperor never was entirely reconciled to William III's elevation to the English throne, see M. A. Thomson, 'Self-Determination and Collective Security as Factors in English and French Foreign Policy, 1689–1718', in R. Hatton and J. S. Bromley (eds.), *William III and Louis XIV. Essays 1680–1720 by and for Mark A. Thomson* (Liverpool, 1968), p. 273.

[133] GA Amsterdam Inv. no. 5027. Witsen to Amsterdam *vroedschap*, London, 16/26 Apr. 1689; the emperor formally declared war on France on 3 Apr. 1689, Klopp, *Fall des Hauses Stuart*, IV, p. 450.

[134] Van Antal and de Pater (eds.), *Weensche gezantschapsberichten*, I, p. 444.

[135] Ibid., I, pp. 445, 447.

[136] Tronchin de Breul, *Lettres sur les matières du temps*, II, pp. 242–3; [Johnston], *The Dear Bargain*, p. 249; Van den Bos, *Leven en Bedryf van Willem de Derde*, I, p. 382; Sylvius, *Tweede vervolg*, III, pp. 153–4.

[137] Tronchin de Breul, *Lettres sur les matières du temps*, II, p. 242.

accounts, ebbing away relentlessly during the spring and summer.[138] Even before the passing of the Toleration Act, High Church Anglicans were outraged by William's speech to the Convention of 16 March in which he had called for the holding of public office to be opened to Dissenters. Discontented Anglicans took to calling the Stadholder-king 'the Presbyterian messiah'. The king's English ministers, Whig and Tory, all of whom (except Halifax) were reportedly anti-Dutch, were infuriated by William's obvious distrust of the English and his habit of discussing his most important decisions only with his 'Dutch junto in London', particularly Bentinck and Dijkvelt. William evidently jarred on the sensibilities of the English courtly nobility both through his aloofness and the simplicity of his dress. Partly owing to his asthma, the king tended to isolate himself at Hampton Court. According to Witsen, court wits joked about the king doing all the thinking, the queen all the talking, the Prince of Denmark the drinking, and Princess Anne the eating, while Parliament did nothing!

In any case there was a general perception on all sides that support for the Revolution and for William amongst the English was becoming weaker. In his reports to Amsterdam and The Hague, Witsen constantly refers to what he calls 'the change of mind' among the English, the reaction against the Revolution, the increasing hostility of the Church of England clergy, and an upsurge of anti-Dutch sentiment which, according to him, had by July reached an unbelievable pitch of intensity. Don Pedro Ronquillo wrote to Rome, in April, that it was 'certain that King William has more opponents now than at the beginning', that the Anglican clergy were leading this reaction, and that many moderate Tories, those 'who previously were in favour of a regency but not for king James', had now changed their minds and wanted King James back.[139] Ronquillo also confirms that some Whigs also now wanted James back, being convinced that in the new circumstances James would have to submit to strong constitutional checks and to having the Prince of Wales educated under the care of the archbishop of Canterbury.[140] Meanwhile, d'Avaux reported to Paris, from Dublin, that the reports he was receiving from England confirmed that William's support was being seriously eroded.[141] Even William's own ministers entertained grave doubts as to whether the beleaguered regime could survive. In March,

[138] Maura Gamazo (ed.), *Correspondencia entre dos embajadores*, I, pp. 143–5; J. Hogan (ed.), *Négociations de M. le Comte d'Avaux en Irlande 1689–90* (Dublin, 1934), pp. 228–31, 504–6; see also Warburton (ed.), *A Memoir of Charles Mordaunt*, I, pp. 43, 57; E. Carpenter, *The Protestant Bishop, being the Life of Henry Compton, 1632–1713, Bishop of London* (London, 1956), pp. 107–8, 161–2, 169, 174; Miller, 'Proto-Jacobitism?', p. 17.

[139] 'Es cierto que el Rey Guillermo tiene ahora mas contrários que al principio, y que muchos de los que fueron por la regencia, y no por el Rey Jacobo, desean que vuelva', Maura Gamazo (ed.), *Correspondencia entre dos embajadores*, I, p. 143.

[140] Ibid., p. 270; further on Whig Jacobitism, see [Montgomery], *Great Britain's Just Complaint*, p. 60.

[141] Hogan (ed.), *Négociations*, p. 227–8, 231, 296, 423, 504.

Sir John Reresby heard 'my Lord Privy Seal say that as the nation now stood, if the king was a Protestant (viz James) he could not be kept out four months'.[142]

By the summer of 1689, with taxation becoming rapidly heavier and the burdens of war more evident, Jacobite propaganda had an abundance of material to work with, not least the almost hysterical national detestation of the Dutch.[143] In a few months William and the Convention had turned England from one of the lightest into one of the most heavily taxed countries in Europe, soon, indeed, the most heavily taxed after the Dutch Republic itself. But what, people were asking, was the purpose of the war with France, the taxation, and the heavy burdens of recruiting, empressment, and the disruption of overseas commerce? It was not easy to see that the conflict was being fought in England's interest. On the contrary, it seemed more plausible that the unprecedented commitment of English troops and resources in the Low Countries had been undertaken on behalf of the Dutch. It became increasingly common for Jacobite writers to represent the English since the Revolution as 'under the Dutch', the dupes of a Dutch design to obtain 'our money and troops'.[144] William was portrayed as an 'instrument more humble, obedient and active for emptying the English treasures into Dutch exchequers than ever they could expect from our native king'.[145] Englishmen, appalled that the 'kingdom is full of foreign forces', were said to 'curse the Dutch in the court and in the camp, in the city and in the country, by sea and land, both here and in Flanders'.[146] 'All the prodigious expence we have been at to carry on the war in Flanders and Piedmont', insisted another writer, 'was not in order to recover anything from France that we had any right to, but only to assist the rest of the confederates.'[147]

If the king was worried by the reaction against the Revolution amongst the Anglican clergy, he gave little sign of it. By May 1694, according to one report, 'four parts out of five of the Anglican clergy are disposed to declare for the King [i.e. James]'.[148] William persevered with church policies which were bound to alienate and infuriate them further. What did worry him was the lack of support for the Revolution in the English army and navy. Like 'the Toleration', the purging and reorganization of the army was an aspect of the Glorious Revolu-

[142] Browning (ed.), *Memoirs of Sir John Reresby*, pp. 564, 577.

[143] GA Amsterdam Inv. no. 5027. Witsen to Amsterdam *vroedschap*, London, 21/31 May, 31 May/10 June, 28 June/8 July1689; Hogan (ed.), *Négociations*, pp. 423, 504–6; *The State-Prodigal*, pp. 2–4; *The Spirit of Jacobitism*, pp. 4, 10, 18, 19, 23; Sir James Montgomery, *The People of England's Grievances offered to be Enquired into and redress'd by their Representation in Parliament*, in *A First Collection of Scarce and Valuable Tracts* (Lord Somers) (4 vols., London, 1748), I, pp. 519–24.

[144] [Johnston], *The Dear Bargain*, pp. 228–63; *The State-Prodigal*, p. 3; [Montgomery], *Great Britain's Just Complaint*, pp. 2, 35.

[145] [Montgomery], *Great Britain's Just Complaint*, p. 35; [William Anderton], *Remarks upon the Present Confederacy and Late Revolution in England* (London, 1693), pp. 8–10, 17.

[146] Montgomery, *The People of England's Grievances*, p. 520.

[147] [Anderton], *Remarks upon the Present Confederacy*, p. 10.

[148] James Macpherson, *Original Papers Containing the Secret History of Great Britain* (2 vols., London, 1776), I, p. 484.

tion for which the impetus derived largely from outside of Parliament. William began 'reforming' the English army well before Parliament decided to make him king, indeed before the Convention convened, in his capacity as interim regent, or head of the administration, in December 1688.[149] The War Office was directed by Dutch officials from St James's Palace over a period of several months. The most suspect regiments were disbanded, Catholic officers and known loyalists were dismissed, and the rest were placed mainly under leading Whig noblemen previously outside of the army. It is noticeable that where, in Parliament, William's strategy was to balance Whigs against Tories the better to manage both, in the army the Prince relied mainly on the Whigs who were more likely to remain loyal to himself than the Tories. William turned the army into a virtual Whig preserve.[150] The nobles that he entrusted with reorganizing the regiments were the dukes of Somerset, Grafton, and Ormonde (a leader of the Anglo-Irish nobility), the earls of Shrewsbury, Oxford, Devonshire, Danby, Macclesfield, Bath, and Derby, and the Lords Delamere, Mordaunt, Churchill, and Wiltshire. The purging of Catholics from the English army contrasted sharply with practice in the Dutch army where there were numerous Catholic officers and was seized on by French propaganda as yet one more example of the Prince's boundless hypocrisy.[151] But the one area to which the Stadholder-king could not afford to extend his pro-Catholic policy in England was the army; for, as Don Pedro Ronquillo confirms, English Catholics remained solidly loyal to James.

But the purges and reorganization failed to turn the army into a reliable instrument of the new regime. By and large neither officers nor men showed much zeal for the Revolution.[152] Relatively few ordinary soldiers had defected from King James, in November 1688, and their subsequently being sent out of London had done little to improve their mood, indeed in the guards regiments was regarded as nothing less than a humiliation.[153] With regard to the officers, it proved easier to remove known Jacobite loyalists than to find men loyal to the new king. An analysis of the officer corps over the first few years of the new reign suggests that only about one third of the officers that William inherited from James, in December 1688, showed willingness to serve for any length of time after the proclamation of William and Mary as king and queen.[154] Roughly another third, unwilling either to serve or join the Jacobites, retired from military life over the next few months. The remaining third were either purged or defected to join the Jacobite armies in Scotland, Ireland, or in France.

[149] GA Amsterdam Inv. no. 5027. Witsen to Amsterdam *vroedschap*, London, 4/14 Jan. 1689; ARH SG 5916/1, fo. 5, Van Citters to SG, 21/31 Dec. 1688.
[150] Ibid.; John Childs, *The British Army of William III, 1689–1702* (Manchester, 1987), p. 63.
[151] Arnauld, *Véritable portrait*, p. 84.
[152] John Childs, *The Army, James II and the Glorious Revolution* (Manchester, 1980), pp. 194–5; Arconati Lamberti, *Mémoires*, I, pp. 680–1; Witsen, 'Uittreksels', p. 138.
[153] Childs, *British Army of William III*, pp. 15, 19.
[154] Ibid., p. 13.

In any case even the most zealous of the English officers, such as John Churchill, were not greatly trusted by William or Bentinck who took the view that those who had so readily deserted King James might just as readily desert King William.[155] As far as military matters were concerned, the report which d'Avaux received from London, in May 1689, that the 'Prince d'Orange se defie non seulement des vieilles troupes que sa Majesté laissa en Angleterre, mais de presque tous les Anglois' was no exaggeration.[156] There was practically no English, or Scottish, officer whom William was prepared to trust in positions of high command with the exception only of Major-General Hugh Mackay whom he sent to command the Williamite forces in Scotland. The Stadholder-king trusted Mackay. But this commander had, since 1674, lived mainly in the Netherlands, was married to a Dutch wife from a prominent family, and had long been a loyal officer of the States General's army. Aside from Mackay, the military men upon whom William relied, from November 1688 until the end of the wars of the Revolution, in late 1691, were all either Dutchmen, such as Solms and the baron van Ginkel, or else other foreigners such as the duke of Schomberg, Ferdinand Wilhelm, the duke of Württemberg-Neustadt, who was to command the troops hired from Denmark, and the Huguenot commander Henri de Ruvigny, later earl of Galway. It was specifically stipulated in the agreement signed in Copenhagen, in August 1689, that the Danish forces hired for service in Britain and Ireland were not to serve under English officers.[157]

William's lack of trust in his English troops, evident from the outset, increased with the wave of unrest which swept the army, in March 1689, when orders were issued for the transfer of approximately a third of the army to the Low Countries. There was a series of minor incidents at Croydon, Abingdon, and elsewhere, and a more serious mutiny at Ipswich, where the earl of Dunbarton's Scottish regiment refused their orders, seized the regimental cannon and colours, and with shouts of 'Long Live King James!' marched off to join the Jacobite insurgents in Scotland. William and his entourage, and the Williamites in Parliament,were greatly alarmed.[158] It was understood, Witsen reported to Amsterdam, that it would look bad to use Dutch troops to suppress British soldiers on English soil, but the king felt that he had no alternative since English troops could not be trusted. Ginkel was sent in pursuit of the mutineers with 4,000 Dutch dragoons. The Dutch surrounded the main band in Lincolnshire: 'the officers would have had them to have fought', recorded Reresby, 'though the Dutch

155 Ibid., p. 14.
156 Hogan (ed.), *Négociations*, pp. 194–5; Maura Gamazo (ed.), *Correspondencia entre dos embajadores*, I, pp. 132, 145; *The State-Prodigal*, p. 4.
157 Montanus, *Leven, Bedryf en Oorlogs-daaden*, III, p. 233; see also Childs, *British Army of William III*, pp. 74–5.
158 GA Amsterdam Inv. no. 5027. Witsen to Amsterdam *vroedschap*, London, 21 Mar./1 Apr. 1689; Browning (ed.), *Memoirs of Sir John Reresby*, p. 567.

horse and dragoons were four times their number; but the common souldiers laid down their arms'. The mutineers, along with thousands of other British troops, were hastily bundled off to the continent.

With the arrival of the 5,000 additional Dutch troops, in May, the Dutch army in England now heavily outnumbered the English army in England.[159] At this point William had some 30,000 English troops on his payroll. But around one third of these were now in the Low Countries and another 10,000 had been sent to the enclaves holding out against James in Ireland. This left only 10,800 English troops in Britain itself. Meanwhile, the Dutch army in Britain had risen to some 17,000 men and, in addition, William disposed of around 2,000 Huguenots most of whom were also under oath of allegiance to the States General.[160] To maximize the effect of his foreign troops, William kept the English regiments dispersed while maintaining the Dutch and Huguenots in two compact blocks, one inside London and nearby, at Hounslow, Guildford, and Waltham, and the other in the north-west to guard against Jacobite incursions from Scotland or Ireland. William also advised the Spanish authorities in Flanders to differentiate in the deployment of the two sets of troops arriving from, and via, the Republic. The Dutch veterans were to be placed in key strongholds such as Ghent and Bruges. The English regiments, by contrast, should be placed in the least important locations 'pues los ingleses son tan malos y tan poco de fiar'.[161] Nor was this only William's opinion, since Spanish ministers too were soon complaining of the poor discipline of the English troops and their constant toasting and acclaiming of 'King James'.[162]

Meanwhile, in Scotland, as Mackay recognized from the outset, the Williamites faced a far from easy task. In Scotland, as in England, the Presbyterians were firmly behind the Revolution and this gave William a solid base of support in the western Lowlands. But the Scots episcopalians remained, like their clergy, mostly loyal to James and were either sullen or actively hostile as were both episcopalian and Catholic Highlanders.[163] On arriving from England, Mackay noted that most of the population of Edinburgh 'appeared not well pleased with the late ... so necessary a revolution'.[164] One of Mackay's problems was the defiance of Edinburgh Castle which held out against him, under the Catholic duke of Gordon, through the spring of 1689. Though its defenders were few,

[159] *CSP Dom. 1689–90*, p. 48, states that in April 1689 William had 10,972 English troops in the Low Countries, 9,030 in Ireland, and only 10,864 English troops in Britain; see also ibid., p. 265.

[160] Hogan (ed.), *Négociations*, p. 422; Dumont de Bostaquet, *Mémoires* p. 203.

[161] Maura Gamazo (ed.), *Correspondencia entre dos embajadores*, I, p. 182.

[162] David Salinas, 'Las relaciones de España con Holanda durante el reinado de Carlos II (1665–1700)', Univ. of Barcelona PhD thesis (1984), II, p. 293.

[163] Bruce Lenman, 'The Scottish Episcopal Clergy and the Ideology of Jacobitism', in E. Cruickshanks (ed.), *Ideology and Conspiracy: Aspects of Jacobitism, 1689–1759* (Edinburgh, 1982), pp. 36–7, 39–40.

[164] Hugh Mackay, *Memoirs of the War Carried on in Scotland and Ireland, 1689–1691* (Edinburgh, 1833), p. 7.

the fortress was all but impregnable. Reports of the castle's continued resistance were broadcast all over Europe, the siege of Edinburgh Castle being for several months as much of a morale-boosting emblem for the forces of counter-Revolution in Britain and Ireland, and on the continent, as was the siege of Londonderry for the supporters of King William.

But the securing of Edinburgh, in June 1689, proved to be the easy part. The brunt of the Jacobite opposition was in the Highlands. Mackay and the Scots Convention recruited large numbers of fresh troops in Scotland, but, like his master, the major-general took the view that the only really reliable troops at his disposal were the so-called 'Dutch brigade', that is the Scots regiments which he brought with him, via England, from the Netherlands.[165] Overconfidence in the efficiency of these troops was evidently one of the reasons for the unexpected (and serious) defeat of Mackay's army by the Jacobites, under Viscount Dundee, at the battle of Killiecrankie, in July.[166] Scotland, it seemed, would not easily be pacified.

But William's difficulties in Scotland were secondary by comparison with the threat posed by the French-backed, Jacobite counter-Revolution in Ireland. By March 1689, the earl of Tyrconnel, James' Lord Deputy of Ireland, already held Dublin and most of the country except for Ulster. In April, James arrived in person, from France, and within a few weeks almost all of Ireland except for the besieged towns of Londonderry and Eniskillen, were under his control. James understood, as did d'Avaux and Louis XIV, that if his wider plan to recover the thrones of Scotland and England, as well as that of Ireland, was to succeed, the Jacobite resurgence in Ireland would have to be projected in Britain as something other than essentially Irish and Catholic. If he was to use Ireland as a springboard for a counter-invasion of Britain, the ousted monarch could not afford to be too indulgent towards the grievances of his Irish Catholic supporters. On the contrary, at the risk of seriously offending them, James went out of his way to show favour to Irish Protestants who submitted to his authority and to appeal to the Anglican Church in Ireland to support him. On convening the Irish Parliament in Dublin, in May, James took care that it should be a joint Catholic–Protestant assembly, or at least have some appearance of being so, and issued a proclamation from Dublin Castle directed towards his potential supporters in Britain in which he reaffirmed his unshakeable commitment to religious toleration and insisted that his chief concern was to 'satisfy our Protestant subjects'.[167] Accordingly, the onset of counter-Revolution in Ireland preci-

[165] Ibid., pp. 3, 6; Paul Hopkins, *Glencoe and the End of the Highland War* (Edinburgh, 1986), pp. 125, 139, 144–6, 156–7.

[166] Hopkins, *Glencoe*, pp. 156–8.

[167] *A Declaration of His Most Sacred Majesty, King James II to All His Loving Subjects in the Kingdom of England* (8 May 1689) (Dublin, 1689), p. 1; [James Welwood], *An Answer to the Late King James's Declaration to all His Pretended Subjects in the Kingdom of England dated at Dublin Castle, 8 May 1689* (London, 1689), pp. 10–15.

pitated a contradictory double reaction in Britain. On the one hand, the spectacle of Irish Protestants fleeing Ireland, and stories of atrocities inflicted by Irish Catholics on Protestants, caused something of a backlash in England and Scotland which proved useful to the new regime. James' confiscation of the lands of Anglo-Irish gentry serving in William's army or serving him abroad, also gave men such as Robert Molesworth, the radical Whig writer, an added incentive to work for William's eventual triumph. James' return to Ireland with French backing also assisted William in prodding Parliament into war with France; and in persuading the Scottish Parliament, subsequently, to issue its own separate declaration of war on France.[168] But, at the same time, the Jacobite resurgence in Ireland imparted new impetus to the gathering forces of counter-Revolution in Britain. James' arrival in Dublin had been marked in Edinburgh by a tremendous thundering of guns and waving of banners from the castle. King James' Dublin proclamation was widely noted in England, coinciding as it did with the vehement reaction of the Anglican clergy to the Stadholder-king's interventions on behalf of Dissenters, toleration, and 'comprehension', and lent both encouragement and a rationale to the increasing numbers of English and Scots Anglicans rejecting the Revolution.[169]

Initially, James, d'Avaux, and Louis' minister of war, the marquis de Louvois, concerned themselves mainly with schemes for a crossing from Ireland to Scotland to join up with the Scottish Jacobites. But, by June 1689, an important change had occurred in James' strategic thinking and that of his French backers. So emphatic were the reports pouring in to Dublin and Paris that the English nation were turning against William and his Revolution that it now seemed to make more sense to bypass Scotland and invade England from Ireland directly.[170] It may be that the reports that support for the Glorious Revolution in England had now largely withered away were exaggerated. But it would be even more wrong to jump to the conclusion that James and Louis were labouring under a gigantic misconception. A very wide variety of sources insist that backing for the Glorious Revolution in England was now drastically diminished compared with the situation at the end of 1688 and that all that stood between James and regaining his Crowns were William's Dutch and Huguenot soldiery.[171] When the Spanish ambassador in London assured his colleague in Rome that the survival of the new regime depended specifically on the Dutch army in Britain he

[168] Proclaimed at Edinburgh nine days after the English declaration of war, giving as grounds Louis XIV's interference in Scotland, via Ireland, see Tronchin de Breul, *Lettres sur les matières du temps*, II, pp. 258–9.

[169] GA Amsterdam Inv. no. 5027. Witsen to Amsterdam *vroedschap*, London, 21/31 May 1689; [Welwood], *An Answer*, pp. 1–2; W. L. Mathieson, *Scotland and the Union. A History of Scotland from 1695 to 1747* (Glasgow, 1905), pp. 189–90.

[170] Hogan (ed.), *Négociations*, pp. 284, 296–7, 506, 552–3, 562, 568.

[171] Ibid., pp. 284, 296, 552–3; Le Noble de Tennelière, *Pierre de touche politique*, X, pp. 35, 39; Louis, Louvois, d'Avaux, and James all expressed this view.

was expressing what was now the general view.[172] No one supposed in Dublin or Paris that it would be possible to ship enough French and Irish troops across to England to deal with the forces at William's disposal on their own. Everything depended on the intensity of the reaction against the Revolution amongst all but the dissenting section of the English populace. James and Louis were aware that the Stadholder-king was now negotiating in Copenhagen to hire 7,000 crack Danish troops with which to bolster his military might in Britain and believed that they could succeed if they invaded England before the Danes arrived, relying on the strength of the estrangement from William amongst the majority of the English nation.[173] As the comte d'Avaux put it, James should strike before the 'Prince of Orange' filled England with so many foreign troops that the English, however tired of the upstart's rule, 'ne seroient en estat de rappeler leur roy légitime'.[174] English Jacobites in contact with Dublin enthusiastically beckoned, although somewhat worried about the likely effect of the appearance of French troops on English soil, recommending that, on landing, James should proclaim that he would send the French away as soon as the Dutch were 'chased out' of the country.[175]

In the event William struck first, even though, in the difficult circumstances of 1689 he could do so only in modest strength. The first Williamite invasion of Ireland, in the summer of 1689, was organized principally by Bentinck and led by Schomberg and (almost as important) Solms.[176] Not a single English minister or commander played a part of any significance in this major operation. But while the expedition secured Belfast, Carrickfergus, Londonderry – the siege of which had been raised earlier in the summer – and most of the rest of Ulster, it was otherwise a failure. Most of Ireland remained firmly under James' control. Schomberg's army, sapped by sickness, low morale, and desertions – especially amongst the English troops – soon lapsed into a purely defensive role and ceased to pose a threat to the Jacobite grip on Dublin. The Protestant army was also rent by chronic friction between the foreigners who were noticeably better fed and accommodated and the English. Solms, who seemed incapable of treating the English 'with any civility', was especially resented. Little effort was made to make the English officers feel themselves in a position of equality with their Dutch and Huguenot colleagues. Schomberg, apparently, had eight aides-de-camp, only one of whom could speak English![177]

With the threat from Schomberg neutralized, James, in the autumn of 1689, resumed his plans for a Jacobite–French invasion of England from Ireland. Louis

[172] Maura Gamazo (ed.), *Correspondencia entre dos embajadores*, I, pp. 129, 132, 145.
[173] Hogan (ed.), *Négociations . . . en Irlande*, pp. 296, 552–3.
[174] Ibid., p. 297.
[175] Ibid., p. 506.
[176] *CSP Dom. 1689–90*, pp. 193, 195, 201, 215.
[177] Ibid., p. 201.

XIV promised troops and naval backing and agreed with his unfortunate brother monarch that 'la pluspart de ses sujets ne sont pas satisfaits du gouvernement du Prince d'Orange'.[178] All reports reaching Dublin and Paris from England continued to stress, as d'Avaux expressed it in a letter to Louis, on 24 November 1689, that in both England and Scotland 'tout le monde est mécontent du Prince d'Orange'.[179] In d'Avaux's view James' autumn invasion of England was fully feasible. Again, he urged Louis that it was vital to strike before William's hired Danish army arrived to bolster his position. D'Avaux also recommended that the invasion of England be co-ordinated with a French push in Flanders to prevent the States General sending more of their troops across the Channel 'au secours du Prince'. In effect, all three kings agreed that all that stood between James and his regaining his lost thrones was the Dutch army in Britain.

By January 1690 it was clear to William that he would have to go in person to Ireland and stake all on a decisive encounter with James. Moreover, he was now in a great hurry to get it over with. For as long as James held most of Ireland it was impossible for the Stadholder-king to transfer troops, or think of going in person, to fight the French in Flanders. Consequently, William took his decision to invade Ireland in overwhelming strength. His stock of foreign soldiery was now at a peak. The Danish troops, 6,100 infantry and 1,000 cavalry, had had a frightful voyage from Jutland 'stowed closer than barill herrings', many sleeping on deck exposed to being 'swept away by half dozens' in the freezing November wind; but they had all arrived, via Leith, Newcastle, and Hull, in December, and they were troops of superlative quality, armed with the latest muskets, the 'flower of the [Danish] king's army'.[180] The Spanish ambassador in London, surveying the 36,000 strong army which William was assembling, to be shipped across to Ireland, or already there, was confident of his success not because William would have a larger army in Ireland than James but because only a relatively small part of the force William was transporting across the Irish sea, not much more than a third, consisted of English troops.[181] Ronquillo judged that William's strength lay in his having with him 22,000 'reliable' by which he meant foreign troops, no less than 13,000 Dutch veterans, 7,000 Danes whom he described as 'admirable', and four regi-

[178] Hogan (ed.), *Négociations ... en Irlande*, p. 577.

[179] Ibid., pp. 552–3.

[180] PRO SP 75/22, fo. 142, Fotherby to Molesworth, Jutland coast, 25 Oct. 1689; ibid., fo. 130, Molesworth to Warre, Copenhagen, 5 Oct. 1689; earlier, referring to the 'treachery and desertion of some Scotch troops' (a contributory factor in the Williamite defeat at Killiecrankie), Molesworth wrote: 'I hope those which I am now takeing care to send his Majesty, will by their fidelity and courage make amends for the baseness of his own subjects: for indeed these troops are extraordinary good', PRO SP 75/22, fo. 83, Molesworth to Warre, Copenhagen, 20 Aug. 1689.

[181] Maura Gamazo (ed.), *Correspondencia entre dos embajadores*, II, p. 86; Van den Bos, *Leven en Bedryf van Willem de Derde*, II, pp. 62–3; Knoop gives the number of Huguenot troops in William's army in Ireland in 1690 as 2,250, see W. J. Knoop, *Kriegs- en geschiedkundige beschouwingen over Willem den Derde* (3 vols., Schiedam, 1895), III, p. 66.

ments of Huguenots. In addition, a powerful artillery train, including some of the huge Dutch twenty-four and nineteen pounders and siege howitzers – until the 1690s England did not possess the larger types of artillery in use on the continent – together with 150 special transport vessels suitable for shipping horses (again a resource unavailable in England) were to be sent over from Holland (see Plate 9).[182] James II in Ireland had some excellent cavalry. But there was no way that he could counter William's artillery. The Dutch Sephardi Jewish contractor, Isaac Pereira, whose father had handled the provisioning of a large part of the invasion armada in Holland, in 1688, was entrusted with the provisioning and logistics, and the supply of 300 four-horse food wagons, for this new seaborne invasion.

For his major offensive in Ireland, William III needed Dutch artillery, wagons, transport vessels and other specialized equipment, including field ovens, as well as the 13,000 Dutch troops who were to be the spearhead of his army. Needless to say, he also required the continued support of the States General and the States of Holland without which none of these resources, or the opportunity to deploy them, would have been available. Thus, one of the most important aspects of the Williamite invasion of Ireland, in 1690, was the Stadholder-king's success in carrying most Dutch regent opinion, and most of the Dutch public with him. This was no small feat. Disruption of trade, heavy taxation, and the other burdens of war were now biting deep in the Republic as in England. Some of the regents were growing impatient with the situation in Britain which was threatening to become more of a drain on, than a boost to, Dutch resources in the struggle against France. On top of this, regent fears that their Stadholder, as king of England, would become too powerful in the Republic were enabling the anti-Orangist faction at Amsterdam to challenge the dominance of Witsen and Hudde. Yet, despite all this, the Dutch 'republican' challenge to William over the winter of 1689–90 turned out to be surprisingly weak.

The anti-Orangists at Amsterdam began testing the political water in December 1689 by disputing the Stadholder-king's right to select the city's eschevins (magistrates) from the customary double lists submitted by the *vroedschap* whilst residing outside the Republic, in London. William reacted indignantly. To head off trouble just when he needed maximum co-operation for his Irish campaign, he sent Bentinck across with secret instructions to rally Holland against the Amsterdam malcontents.[183] The latter countered by disputing Bentinck's right to take his seat amongst the nobility of the States of Holland being now a naturalized English subject. But the Amsterdam anti-Orangists were quickly out-

[182] Maura Gamazo (ed.), *Correspondencia entre dos embajadores*, II, pp. 117, 151–2; P. Berresford Ellis, *The Boyne Water, The Battle of the Boyne, 1690* (Belfast, 1989), pp. 25–6.

[183] *Archives ou correspondance inédite de la maison d'Orange-Nassau*, 3rd ser. (1689–1702), ed. F. J. L. Krämer (5 vols., Leiden, 1907–9), I, pp. 45–6. William to Heinsius, Kensington, 30 Dec./8 Jan. 1689/90; Montanus, *Leven, Bedryf en Oorlogs-daaden*, III, pp. 256–7.

8 *Hollands hollende koe (1690).*
A complex Dutch republican, anti-Orangist political caricature by G. Bouttats, attacking Hans Willem Bentinck, now earl of Portland, as the right-hand-man

of Williamite oppression. Bentinck is depicted wearing his earl's coronet, riding a crazed cow symbolizing Holland and her 'oppressed freedom', treading the people under hoof with the burdens of war and heavy taxation. In the foreground to the right is the Dutch lion chained to a wall, its claws being clipped by an Englishman. On the wall behind Bentinck's head is a representation of the Prince of Orange now also king of England with sycophantic courtiers kissing his posterior. In the centre foreground *Freedom* and *Commerce* lie weeping by a tomb upon which is inscribed *Hic iacet Edictum Perpetuum 1672. Vi et fraude*, a lament for the discarding of Johan de Witt's Perpetual Edict abolishing the Dutch Stadholderate. See Muller, *Nederlandsche Geschiedenis in platen*, I, p. 429.

manoeuvred and humiliated, having 'much prejudiced themselves in the opinion of the people of Holland by this unseasonable stiffnesse'.[184]

With the Amsterdam city council elections of February 1690 the previous ascendancy of Witsen and Hudde was fully restored.[185] The differences between Amsterdam and the Stadholder were settled. The somewhat weak stream of republican, anti-Orangist pamphlets emanating from opposition writers such as Nicolaas Muys van Holy subsided. The indisputable fact was that William III continued to enjoy the support not just of the traditional *prinsgezind* and orthodox Calvinist constituency but a large part also of the former constituency of the 'States party'. What was conspicuously lacking from the anti-Orangist effort of the winter of 1689–90 in the United Provinces was momentum, popular backing, and intellectual impetus.[186] Most Dutchmen were still more or less swayed by the rhetoric of the Glorious Revolution. They accepted that if the Republic was to maintain its freedom and independence the tyranny of Louis XIV had to be fought and that this could be done only hand in hand with England. They responded enthusiastically to the idea of law, liberty, religion, and constitutional forms having been restored in Britain. Men such as the elderly Arminian poet Joachim Oudaan, in the old days a supporter of Johan de Witt and enemy of the House of Orange, continued to applaud William's triumphs not least because he was now the undisputed standard bearer of religious toleration. By his insistence on widening religious toleration in the Republic as in England, the Stadholder had in effect split the former Dutch 'States party', winning to himself those who were chiefly motivated by their antipathy to the Dutch Reformed Church.

[184] PRO SP 84/221, fo. 21, Aglionby to Warre, The Hague, 27 Jan. 1690; A. Porta, *Joan en Gerrit Corver. De politieke macht van Amsterdam, 1702–1748* (Assen, 1975), pp. 10–11.

[185] Porta, *Joan en Gerrit Corver*, pp. 10–11; PRO SP 84/221, fo. 51. Aglionby to Warre, The Hague, 10 Mar. 1690.

[186] Le Noble de Tennelière, *Pierre de touche politique*, IX, p. 35.

But William had little cause for complacency. His position in Britain and Ireland was precarious and his position in the United Provinces potentially so. One defeat in Ireland might well mean the collapse of the entire shaky edifice, Glorious Revolution and all. The Stadholder-king was in constant apprehension that the regents might switch to the view that their military involvement in Britain and Ireland was more of a hindrance to them than a help. 'God send us some successe in Ireland and at sea', wrote the English resident at The Hague, on the eve of the great battles of that summer, 'for else we cannot hope for union between Holland and England and perseverance; there is something brewing here by the French faction which will give trouble in time'.[187]

On the eve of the decisive encounter in Ireland, William did, in fact, suffer a major defeat – at sea. It was a setback germinating since the commencement of the Revolution. For, according to d'Avaux's informants in England, the navy was as demoralized by the Glorious Revolution as the army.[188] There was a stream of reports of low morale, unprecedented difficulty in finding seamen to serve in King William's navy, and seething anti-Dutch sentiment, infinitely stronger than any dislike of the French. Parliament, like William, was keen that the States General should continue to mount a large-scale naval effort in support of the Revolution both in the Channel and, after April 1689, in the Irish Sea. But co-operation between the two navies was greatly impeded by the exceedingly fraught relationship between the English and Dutch admirals and officers.[189] Then, just a few days before the battle of the Boyne in Ireland, the French fleet, under Tourville, won a major victory over the two allied fleets together at the battle of Beachy Head. The disaster ensued mainly because the English backed off, leaving the Dutch to face the French broadsides on their own.[190] There was a terrible outcry in the Republic and, briefly, the prestige of the new English regime on the continent was seriously damaged. 'For a week ... neither I nor any Englishman here', reported Molesworth, from Copenhagen, 'has had the confidence to shew our faces, so deep is the stain and ignominy of the last sea fight', the English in the Danes' eyes being 'cover'd with shame'.[191]

This, one of the most inglorious moments of many during the Glorious Revolution, was, at the same time, one of the most dangerous. With the French victory at sea, and William and his army in Ireland, England itself now lay temptingly open to invasion from France. But William was, in any case, resolved to crush

[187] PRO SP 84/221, fo. 162v, Aglionby to Warre, The Hague, 14 July 1690.
[188] Hogan (ed.), *Négociations ... en Irlande*, pp. 229, 504.
[189] GA Amsterdam Inv. 5027, Witsen to Amsterdam *vroedschap*, London, 26 Apr., 6 May, 5 July, 22 July 1689.
[190] Japikse, *Prins Willem III*, II, p. 309; according to Grovestins, Beachy Head was a battle in which 'la France recueillit toute la gloire, la République toutes les pertes, et l'Angleterre toute la honte', Sirtema de Grovestins, *Histoire des luttes et rivalités politiques entre les puissances maritimes et la France durant la deuxième moitié du XVIIe siècle* (6 vols., Paris, 1851–5), VI, p. 210.
[191] PRO SP 75/22, fos. 260, 262, Molesworth to Warre, Copenhagen, 15 and 22 July 1690.

9 *The Big Guns at the Boyne: The Dutch Heavy Artillery Firing across the River at James II's Troops in Support of the Blue Guards and Danish Infantry Effecting the Crossing*. Print by Theodor Maas.

James in Ireland quickly. Advancing towards Dublin, the Williamite forces assembled across the Boyne water from the Jacobite army, which was reinforced by some 7,000 French infantry under the comte de Lauzun. William was in no mood to take any chances with his English soldiery.[192] They were kept in the rear and given the least important role in the battle. The thrust across the river was spearheaded by the Dutch Blue Guards. As James' army began to break, William threw in the Danes and then the Huguenots. James was beaten; and fled shortly afterwards back to France. Drogeda fell and the way to Dublin lay open.

Four days after the Boyne, William entered Dublin in triumph. Wexford and Waterford capitulated to Williamite forces during the next month and Cork in October. The Irish Protestants were jubilant. Irish Anglicans largely dispensed with the doubts and heart-searching which so troubled their English and Scots co-religionists. In Ireland, of course, there was no difficulty about swearing

[192] Montanus, *Leven, Bedryf en Oorlogs-daaden*, III, p. 283; Van den Bos, *Leven en Bedryf van Wilhem de Derde*, II, p. 108; Knoop, *Krijgs- en geschiedkundige beschouwingen*, III, pp. 69–70; Berresford Ellis, *The Boyne Water*, pp. 89–91, 96–7, 104, 107; in 1702, a pamphleteer rebutted Defoe's claim that, at The Boyne, Church of England men had shot at their own anointed king, James, by pointing out that nearly all the shooting was done 'by Dutch, Danes, Swiss, French, Irish Protestants and Scots Presbyterians', see *Some Necessary Considerations* (1702), in *A Fourth Collection of Scarce and Valuable Tracts* (Lord Somers) (4 vols., London, 1752), III, p. 19.

10 *The Towns of Drogeda and Wexford Capitulate to the Troops of William III in July 1690.*
Wexford fell after Protestant prisoners held in the town broke free after hearing the news of the battle and overpowered their Jacobite guards. Remembering the atrocities of the past, great care was taken by the Williamite officers, on the fall of Drogeda, to prevent any mistreatment or massacre of the inhabitants by the English soldiery.

11 *The Entry of the Troops of William III into Dublin and Cork in July and October 1690*. Cork was taken for William by John Churchill.

allegiance to William and Mary as rightful king and queen by right of conquest. For Irish Anglican writers such as Edward Wetenhall, William was simply the 'second William the Conqueror': 'I do averr us in Ireland conquered and bless

God for it'.[193] But the Boyne and William's subsequent operations in Ireland that summer failed to end the war in Ireland. Moreover, the campaign opened up a significant divergence between 'Dutch' and 'English' interests in that country. For William III – and the States – what mattered was to conclude the war in Ireland as soon as possible, conciliate the Irish as far as feasible, and transfer a large part of William's military strength to the Low Countries. But, for Parliament, the Church of England, and the Irish Protestants, what mattered most was to subjugate Ireland and subordinate that unfortunate country entirely to English interests. In February 1689, when the Convention in London had only just assembled and Parliament was still weak and hesitant, William had issued a proclamation offering the Irish Catholics who laid down their arms, and acknowledged their new king and queen, 'all the favour for the private exercise of their religion that the law allows'.[194] But by the time of the Boyne, the English Parliament was in a far stronger position and there was now a formidable pressure for retaliatory confiscations of land and the rigorous suppression of Catholic worship.

William's failure to take Limerick, in September, and his subsequent return to London meant that there would have to be another Irish campaign the following year. Command of the allied army in Ireland was assigned first to Solms (Schomberg having been killed at the Boyne) and then to Ginkel. During the spring of 1691, Ginkel received secret instructions from William and Bentinck that he must conclude the war in Ireland that year 'de quelle manière l'on pourra', even if, to do so, he had to concede the Irish Jacobites generous terms.[195] In June 1691, Ginkel took Athlone; advancing next on Galway, he inflicted a major defeat on the Jacobites at the battle of Aughrim which turned out to be the decisive battle of the Irish war. Some 7,000 Jacobite dead were left on the field. Ginkel took Galway and commenced the second siege of Limerick.

The Jacobites offered to negotiate an end to the war and Ginkel readily agreed. The Dutch general made three crucial concessions which he had William's (but not Parliament's) authority to make.[196] First, the Irish Jacobite army, of some 12,000 men, was to be allowed to withdraw with its weapons to France, with transportation arranged by Isaac Pereira. Secondly, Irish Catholics were to enjoy freedom of private exercise of the Catholic faith which William had already offered in February 1689. Thirdly, there were to be limitations on the confiscation of lands proclaimed after The Boyne.

[193] [Edward Wetenhall], *The Case of the Irish Protestants* (London, 1691), pp. 6, 24.

[194] *The Declaration of William and Mary King and Queen of England, France, and Ireland. To all their Loving Subjects in the Kingdom of Ireland 22 Feb. 1688* (London, 1689), p. 1.

[195] W. Troost, *William III and the Treaty of Limerick (1691–1697): A Study of his Irish Policy* (Leiden, 1983), p. 30.

[196] Ibid., pp. 33–6; J. G. Simms, *The Treaty of Limerick* (Irish History Series no. 2, Dundalk, 1961), pp. 6–19.

The Stadholder-king wished to approve the draft Treaty of Limerick without more ado and get on with the war in the Low Countries. But it proved no easy matter to settle Ireland. By the end of 1691 William's grip on British affairs was already slipping. There now commenced in London what was to be a long and, for William, frustrating battle over implementing the Limerick articles. For neither the Parliament of England nor the (now solidly Protestant) Irish Parliament took a favourable view of Ginkel's concessions to the Irish Catholics. As opposition to ratifying the draft treaty mounted the Emperor Leopold, who kept a close eye on the British scene, took alarm.[197] Several times William assured him that the terms negotiated with the Irish Jacobites would be honoured; but he proved unable to deliver on his promise. A formidable anti-treaty party arose in the two parliaments driven by Protestant zeal and the Parliament of England's increasing success, across the board, in clipping the monarch's power. It is striking that Whigs, including radicals, played a prominent part in establishing Parliament's supremacy over Irish affairs. One of the leaders of the opposition in the Irish Parliament was Robert Molesworth who had now returned from Denmark and won international acclaim as a critic of royal absolutism through publication of his *Account of Denmark*. During the critical half-decade from the end of 1691 the balance between king and Parliament tilted further towards the latter with every year that passed. The appointment of John Methuen as lord chancellor of Ireland in 1697, at the prompting of the earl of Shrewsbury, completed the process, opening the way for the final ditching of the Limerick terms.[198] In the end William had no choice but to swallow an Irish settlement shorn of its conciliatory content.

The momentous change in the balance between William and Parliament which we see in Irish affairs during the 1690s was, in turn, part of a wider and deeper shift of fundamental importance in the history of Britain. From the end of 1691 circumstances were peculiarly favourable to a rapid and unprecedentedly wide-ranging accretion of power to Parliament in London. With the suppression of the last armed Jacobite resistance in Scotland and Ireland, the transfer of much of the king's foreign soldiery, including the Danes, to the continent, and the Stadholder-king's own growing absorption in campaigns in the Low Countries, a political vacuum was created in Britain which Parliament was only too eager to fill. Yet this too, the final rise of Parliament to undisputed dominance in British and Irish affairs with all that that meant, was essentially an effect of the Revolution which William and the Dutch state had set in motion: for the diversion of the English Crown's effort, attention, and money to the continent had been entirely inherent in the Glorious Revolution from its very inception, indeed from the Dutch point of view was the essential purpose of the whole

[197] Troost, *William III and the Treaty of Limerick*, pp. 42–3, 119, 164, 168.
[198] Ibid., pp. 160, 182, 184.

exercise. It was William's and the States' success in largely taking charge of British affairs in 1688–91 which explains not only the tremendous momentum but also the virtual unanimity of the post-1691 reaction.

The relentless resolve, and the speed, with which Parliament moved to wrest real power from William and his 'Dutch junto' between 1691 and 1697 was due above all to the readiness of all groups and factions in English political life, however diverse their ultimate aims, to work together to subordinate the king to Parliament. The previous ascendancy of William and his favourites was thus an interlude of crucial significance in the longer term evolution of British institutions. Outside intervention played a main role in setting the Glorious Revolution in motion. Between November 1688 and the autumn of 1691 the course of the Glorious Revolution was to a great extent shaped by Dutch calculation and interests. But, ultimately, what is perhaps most important about the dominance of 'Dutch counsels and Dutch measures of acting' in Britain in the years 1688–91 is that it achieved, as nothing else possibly could have done, the mobilizing of every English political strand and faction behind the drive to subordinate king and court to Parliament.

This crucial transition in English history was powered by the extraction of resources from the English people on an unprecedented scale for continental war and the great wave of resentment and xenophobia which accompanied that process. As William, from 1691, took to spending long periods of the year away from Britain, campaigning in the Spanish Netherlands, or residing at The Hague, or his country retreat at Het Loo, in Gelderland, pressure built up for decisions to be made in London or, as one MP expressed it, for Queen Mary to dispatch more business herself, advised by English ministers, 'without sending abroad for orders'. Frustration mounted that 'though we were drawn into this war by the Dutch – they being the principals', as Sir Thomas Clarges put it, 'yet we must bear a greater share of the burden'.[199] While MPs were less likely than others to oppose the war as such, they were adamant that English interests should now predominate in the making of war strategy. Parliament also shared in the resentment at English regiments being placed under Dutch and other foreign officers.[200] What all groups in Parliament wanted, right across the board, was that English counsels, ministers, commanders, and strategies should no longer be subordinate but should predominate, and the way to achieve this was cross-party collaboration to master the king.

William fought a tenacious rear-guard action but little by little his authority

[199] H. Horwitz (ed.), *The Parliamentary Diary of Narcissus Luttrell 1691–93* (Oxford, 1972), p. 304 (9 Dec. 1692); the previous month Clarges remarked in the House that 'Holland and the Emperor were the principals in the war; that Spain was ... drawn in by the Emperor as we were by the Dutch; that though we were drawn in by them, yet we were higher charged in proportion than they', ibid., p. 250 (22 Nov. 1692).

[200] Ibid., pp. 252–4, 304–5.

was inexorably cut back. He was not shy about using his influence to thwart the obvious will of Parliament. The controversial bill which passed the Commons in December 1692 which was designed to curb the royal influence in Parliament by curtailing the participation of 'place', office holders under the Crown in Parliament, the king thwarted in the Lords (for the time being) literally only owing to the 'Dutch' votes of Bentinck and the younger Schomberg.[201] The relentless drive to master the Stadholder-king culminated in 1697–8 in the wake of the Peace of Rijswijk when, despite William's frantic efforts to prevent it, Parliament insisted on disbanding most of the English army and subjecting the king to tight restrictions in all matters military. The supreme humiliation was Parliament's refusing to keep on the

> Dutch Blue Guards, and my Lord Portland's regiment of Dutch horse, who attended His Majesty in all his Expeditions long before and after his accession to the throne of England. His Majesty was much dissatisfied at the proceedings, and made all the interest he possibly could in the House ... but all to no effect; he used intreaties to the Parliament, but to no purpose; and upon this occasion behaved himself much different from the haughty character he had all along maintained.[202]

In the crucial years 1692–7 the Whig radicals, so bitterly disappointed in 1689, had their chance at last to help turn England into a 'crowned republic' with Parliament supreme. Yet, the great transition in English institutions can not be said to have been chiefly the work of the Whigs. For Tories of all shades, including the most reactionary, were just as eager, even if their motives were in part different, to demolish William's power. William had his 'placemen' and used his influence to manipulate some MPs; but there was no longer any such thing as loyalist support for monarchical authority. The loyalists were all for James, or at least the Church of England, and were more resentful of William, and more xenophobic, than the Whigs.

Our conclusion, then, is that the Glorious Revolution was indeed a decisive turning-point in the constitutional history of England and that of the English-speaking nations generally but that, in some respects, it has been seriously misread. The view that 'Parliament was ... the focal point and the vital instrument of the Glorious Revolution'[203] is fundamentally mistaken. Robert Beddard was surely right in asserting that 'it is one of the myths of the Revolution of 1688 that it was a parliamentary revolution', and in adding that the doings of the Convention Parliament were in reality much less important than they have generally been taken to be: 'The decisions that mattered had been taken before it met'.[204] Nevertheless, it is true that the Parliament of England was the Revolu-

[201] Cruickshanks, Hayton, and Jones, 'Divisions in the House of Lords', pp. 69–70.
[202] *Political remarks on the Life and Reign of King William III*, in *A Fourth Collection of Scarce and Valuable Tracts* (Lord Somers), III, p. 185.
[203] H. Horwitz, 'Parliament and the Glorious Revolution', *BIHR*, 47 (1974), p. 36.
[204] Beddard, *A Kingdom without a King*, p. 65.

tion's ultimate heir and beneficiary and that many positive political and constitutional effects flowed from it. The Convention Parliament may not have subscribed to the view that there is a contract between king and people, or that power derives from the people. Nevertheless, the spectacle of the resort to arms to break James II, and the ideological justifications emanating from the pens of William's and the States General's apologists conveyed exactly that message, a message which echoed widely not least in America and Louis XIV's France. Anyone who reads the Convention's debates on religious toleration knows that there was little genuine support for toleration as such, on principle, discernible in Parliament. Yet, in the sense that the Glorious Revolution is being read here, as substantially imposed from outside by William and the States in collaboration with Whig politicians in exile, there is no doubt that toleration on principle, on the basis which prevailed in the United Provinces, including a broad freedom of the press, and including also *de facto* freedom of Catholic worship, was a key component from the very inception of the Revolution during the summer of 1688.

Yet we must also remember that much that was integral to the Glorious Revolution was repressive in character, both within England and beyond. A system of government was created which imposed heavy new burdens on the people, including far higher taxation than had prevailed before as well as intensive recruiting for the army and empressment for the navy. With Parliament's dominance, penal justice in England tended to become much harsher. But the most repressive tendencies of the Revolution manifested themselves outside England. Parliament may have emerged supreme in England in the 1690s but at the same time the Parliament of England became dominant also in Scotland and Ireland. As Irish Protestants, as well as Catholics, and Scots Presbyterians, as well as episcopalians, soon came to realize, this was not simply a matter of integrating Ireland and Scotland politically more closely with England. By the late 1690s the Parliament of England was systematically, even ruthlessly, subordinating the interests of the Irish and Scots to those of England.

Chapter 4

Church and state reformed? The Revolution of 1688–9 in Scotland*

IAN B. COWAN

The antecedents of the Glorious Revolution in Scotland were markedly different from those south of the Border, despite the similarity of the policies pursued by James II and VII in both his kingdoms.[1] The birth of his son on 10 June 1688 which precipitated the succession crisis in England and led to the so-called 'Invitation' to William of Orange to intervene by restraining, if not necessarily displacing, the king generated little interest north of the Border.[2] Even the news of the outbreak of the Revolution in England triggered by William's landing at Torbay on 5 November brought little initial reaction from the Scots. It was the flight of James on 23 December which set the Revolution in Scotland in motion.[3]

The Scottish reluctance to rebel stemmed from a variety of reasons, both political and ecclesiastical. In political terms James appeared to be impregnable and indeed enjoyed more widespread support than had his brother before him.[4] Ecclesiastically, established churchmen, despite their dislike of the toleration introduced by the Indulgences of 1687, were unwilling to stir up opposition lest their privileged position be put at risk and in the case of the Presbyterians until further concessions were on offer.[5] Like the Catholic faction they had much to lose and little to gain.[6] If the flight of the chancellor, the earl of

* It was with deep regret that the editor learnt, while this volume was in proof, that Professor Cowan died on 22 December 1990.

1 For the antecedents of the Revolution, see Ian B. Cowan, 'The Reluctant Revolutionaries: Scotland in 1688', in E. Cruickshanks (ed.), *By Force or by Default: The Revolution of 1688–89* (Edinburgh, 1989), pp. 65–81.

2 *The Register of the Privy Council of Scotland* (hereafter *Reg. Privy Council*), ed. J. H. Burton *et al*, (Edinburgh, 1877–) 3rd ser., XIII, p. xlvii; *Historical Notices of Scottish Affairs Selected from the manuscripts of Sir John Lauder of Fountainhall bart., one of the senators of the College of Justice* (hereafter *Fountainhall, Historical Notices*), ed. D. Laing (2 vols., Bannatyne Club, 1848), II, pp. 896–7.

3 R. Wodrow, *The History of the Sufferings of the Church of Scotland from the Restoration to the Revolution* (2 vols., Edinburgh, 1721–2, cited hereafter in the later edition, ed. R. Burns, 4 vols., Glasgow, 1828–30), IV, pp. 470–2.

4 W. Ferguson, *Scotland's Relations with England: A Survey to 1707* (Edinburgh, 1977), pp. 158–61; Paul Hopkins, *Glencoe and the End of the Highland War* (Edinburgh, 1986), pp. 68–71, 83–8.

5 Wodrow, *History*, II. Appendix, pp. cxxix, cxxxiv; ibid., IV, pp. 428, 431–3; Cowan, 'The Reluctant Revolutionaries', p. 72.

6 *The Acts of the Parliaments of Scotland* (hereafter *Acts Parl. Scot.*), ed. T. Thomson and C. Innes (12 vols., Edinburgh, 1814–75), VIII, pp. 579–81; Cowan, 'The Reluctant Revolutionaries', pp. 69–70.

Perth, on 10 December and mob riots in Edinburgh that evening indicated a change of attitudes, the turmoil might have been contained but for the king's flight.[7] This soon revealed the venality and self-interest of many of his former councillors who, as unrest swept the country, accepted a change of sovereign without any undue concern. The chaos which followed the departure of most of the councillors for London (where office under the new regime could alone be secured) reduced support for James even further.[8] His ill-judged policies, his flight to France, and the consequent declaration in the English Bill of Rights that he had 'abdicated' the throne allowed Presbyterian politicians such as John Cunningham, tenth earl of Glencairn, William, eighteenth earl of Crawford, and Sir James Montgomery of Skelmorlie an influence which they might otherwise have been denied.[9] A return to normality was not easily achieved, for although the Council as early as 24 December urged William to call a free Parliament, the plea had to be reiterated formally in early January 1689 when a meeting of Scots notables asked William to summon a Convention, but it was not until 14 March that a fairly representative meeting took place, with all Protestant freeholders and burgesses being allowed to vote.[10]

Although attempts had been made by the Presbyterians to influence the composition of the Convention, Jacobites were almost as numerous at the commencement as their opponents. However, whereas the opposition was single-minded in its resolve to dispose of James, his supporters were uncertain as to their best course of action. Waverers and place-seekers abounded, the initial narrowness of the gap between the contending parties being apparent in the relatively close contest for the presidency of the Assembly between William Douglas, third duke of Hamilton, representing the Williamites, and John Murray, second earl of Atholl, for the Jacobites, the former winning the day by a majority of 40 among 150 votes.[11] Although important, this result was not decisive, that moment being reserved for the reading on 16 March of letters from the rivals for the Crown. That of William was a model of diplomacy, safeguarding the Protestant faith, but making no firm pronouncement on the future form of church government. James' letter on the other hand threatened all who forsook their 'natural

[7] Wodrow, *History*, IV, pp. 472–4; D. Burnet, *Siege of Edinburgh Castle, MDCLXXXIX*, presented by R. Bell (Bannatyne Club, 1828), pp. 16–19; *Memoirs Touching the Revolution in Scotland, MDCLXXXVIII–MDCXC by Colin Earl of Balcarres* (hereafter Balcarres, *Memoirs*), ed. Lord Lindsay (Bannatyne Club, 1841, pp. 14–17.

[8] Fountainhall, *Historical Notices*, II, p. 884; M. Wood and Helen Armet (eds.), *Extracts from the Records of Edinburgh 1681 to 1689* (Edinburgh, 1954), pp. 156–8; Balcarres, *Memoirs*, p. 18.

[9] W. Ferguson, *Scotland, 1689 to the Present*, The Edinburgh History of Scotland (4 vols., Edinburgh, 1968), pp. 1–2.

[10] W. Fraser, *The Melvilles Earls of Melville and the Leslies Earls of Leven* (3 vols., Edinburgh, 1890), III, p. 193; E. W. M. Balfour-Melville (ed.), *An Account of the Proceedings of the Estates in Scotland* (2 vols., Scottish History Society, 1955), I, p. 1, II, pp. 193–7.

[11] Balfour-Melville (ed.), *Proceedings of the Estates*, I, p. 1; Balcarres, *Memoirs*, pp. 24–5; Sir John Dalrymple, *Memoirs of Great Britain and Ireland* (Edinburgh, 1721), I, pp. i, 218.

allegiance'.[12] Even James' most loyal supporters were disheartened and many left, leaving a relatively small body of committed Jacobites under the ineffectual leadership of Atholl, who took no meaningful part in further proceedings, and eventually withdrew to Bath, pleading ill-health.[13] Even before he did so, James Graham, Viscount Dundee, had likewise withdrawn to plan a rising on the king's behalf. Forced to translate words into deeds after being declared 'rebel' by the Convention on 30 March 1689, Dundee (a staunch Protestant) raised his standard on Dundee Law in early April, thus initiating a guerrilla campaign in the north of Scotland which – although he recruited some 2,000 men of the western clans – significantly failed to gain the necessary support from the episcopalian and Jacobite gentry of the north-east Lowlands. With only an additional 300 Irish recruits, lack of supplies and money, and a force as much motivated by a desire for plunders and hostility to Clan Campbell, as by religious and political principles, Dundee was eventually compelled to make a dramatic bid for military success. Although victorious against an ill-prepared government army at Killiecrankie on 27 July his death made it a Pyrrhic victory. The repulse of his remaining forces after an heroic defence of Dunkeld by a newly formed Cameronian regiment, on 21 August, marked the effective end of the 'rebellion', although a further skirmish at Cromdale in Strathspey on 1 May 1690 fuelled fears that continuing pockets of resistance would be reactivated if the expected invasion by an Irish Catholic army materialized. Such thoughts which were foremost in government thinking throughout the years 1690–1 were only allayed by the pacification of Ireland by the Treaty of Limerick in October 1691.[14]

The military campaign achieved little; but the consequent absence of Jacobite leadership in the Convention subsequently dominated by William's supporters achieved much. Various committees were appointed including one for securing the peace and another for settling the government. The former had the power to raise and deploy armed forces, the latter was to determine the conditions under which Scotland would accept William and Mary.[15] The first task was easily accomplished, for after protracted negotiations, Edinburgh Castle (which had been held by the Catholic duke of Gordon at the behest of Viscount Dundee) surrendered on 17 June.[16] The other remit was to be more demanding. Nevertheless, on 4 April it was resolved that James had not abdicated, but 'by doing

[12] Balcarres, *Memoirs*, pp. 26–8; Balfour-Melville (ed.), *Proceedings of the Estates*, I, pp. 4–5; *Acts Parl. Scot.*, IX, pp. 9–10.

[13] Balcarres, *Memoirs*, pp. 28–9; Ferguson, *Scotland, 1689 to the Present*, p. 4.

[14] Ferguson, *Scotland, 1689 to the Present*, pp. 10–11; Balcarres, *Memoirs*, pp. 33–4, 39–49; *Reg. Privy Council*, 3rd ser., XIII, pp. 565–6; ibid., XIV, pp. 82–4, 125–6; Balfour-Melville (ed.), *Proceedings of the Estates*, I, pp. 183, 185–7, 220–5.

[15] Balfour-Melville (ed.), *Proceedings of the Estates*, I, pp. 9, 16.

[16] W. L. Melville (ed.), *Leven and Melville Papers: Letters and State Papers Chiefly Addressed to George Earl of Melville, Secretary of State for Scotland, 1689–1691* (Bannatyne Club, 1843), no. 51; Balfour-Melville (ed.), *Proceedings of the Estates*, I, pp. 125–6.

acts contrary to law' had forfeited his right to the Crown for himself and his successors.[17] A Claim of Right, which enshrined this principle, condemned prelacy as 'a great and insupportable grievance and trouble to the nation'; and less convincingly argued that James had 'invaded the fundamental constitution of the Kingdom and altered it from a legal limited monarchy, to an arbitrary despotic power'. This was accepted by the Convention on 11 April and was followed by the proclamation of William and Mary as joint sovereigns.[18] Two days later the passage of the Articles of Grievances restated the ecclesiastical and constitutional ideals of the Revolution settlement by calling for the repeal of the Act of Supremacy of 1669 on the grounds that it was 'inconsistent with the establishment of the church government now desyred'; and specifically condemned the Committee of the Articles as 'a great grievance to the nation'.[19] On 11 May William and Mary accepted the Crown of Scotland, apparently on the principles laid down.[20] In the months which followed, this assumption was to be severely tested as attempts were made to turn a half-hearted revolution into a major turning-point in the political and ecclesiastical governance of Scotland.

As things stood in May 1689 the character of the Revolution had still to be determined. The Convention had outlined a programme for constitutional and ecclesiastical reform which if implemented implied a change in the nature of the monarchy. However, was William's acceptance of the Claim of Right and the Articles of Grievances binding upon him or would he try to retain the prerogative powers enjoyed by his predecessor?[21] The king's Scottish advisers clearly expected him to defend his privileges and tried to allay ministerial suspicions that he may have entered into a contractual relationship. Thus Lord Melville wrote of the Claim of Right and the Grievances: 'they are loosely drawn and may be helped in Parliament what dissatisfies'.[22] Sir John Dalrymple moreover wrote to Melville in alarm at his discovery that members of the Convention, which after a short recess had been reconvened as a Parliament on 5 June:

> plainly pretend that the King is obliged to redress all their grivances which som proposed as a quality in ther recognising him; and whatever they think a grivance he must redress, otherwys he fails, and they may do right to themselfs; whereas the King said only he would redress every thing that was justly grievous wherof they are not sol judges.[23]

Arguments such as these were unlikely to appeal to a Parliament of which the vast majority of members had suffered at the hands of the Stuarts and were

[17] Balcarres, *Memoirs*, pp. 35–6.
[18] Balfour-Melville (ed.), *Proceedings of the Estates*, I, pp. 25–6; *Acts Parl. Scot.*, IX, pp. 37–41.
[19] *Acts Parl. Scot.*, IX, p. 45.
[20] *Facsimiles of the National Manuscripts of Scotland* (London, 1867–71), III, no. cvii.
[21] Balcarres, *Memoirs*, pp. 59–60.
[22] *HMC, Buccleuch*, II, i, 44.
[23] *Leven and Melville Papers*, no. 60.

determined to ensure that no future king would have the power to enforce his arbitrary will upon his subjects. From the onset, however, William seemed determined to proceed on authoritarian lines. His Privy Council included known Jacobites and persecutors of Covenanters; particular resentment being reserved for the selection of Sir James Dalrymple of Stair and his son, Sir John.[24] Dislike of these appointments not only occasioned disappointment among those who had been passed over, but also raised doubts as to William's goodwill in other respects. Archibald Campbell, tenth earl of Argyll and Sir James Montgomery of Skelmorlie were prominent amongst those who had expected preferment, the latter as secretary of state. However, they failed to gain office as William Douglas, third duke of Hamilton, refused to support them and a combination of the Dalrymples and George Leslie, first earl of Melville, who opposed their interests gained influence over the King.[25] Montgomery, who 'was ambitious for power rather than the spoils of office', also faced the opposition of William Carstares, a Presbyterian minister, who was one of the royal chaplains and as such William's adviser on ecclesiastical affairs north of the Border.[26] He sought a moderate settlement and feared that Montgomery was an extremist in such matters.

If Argyll and Montgomery were unlikely allies, together they made formidable opponents. They both became prominent members of what became known as 'the club', so called from its meeting place – Penston's tavern in Edinburgh's High Street.[27] There the opposition concerted its campaign and developed a rudimentary party organization which decided policy, arranged speakers in debates and predetermined votes. By these means 'the club' dominated the 1689 session of Parliament in which they strove to secure a Presbyterian settlement for the Church and the supremacy of Parliament in the constitution. To this end they chose to withhold supply until their wishes were met and to follow each concession gained with a fresh demand.[28] Against such manoeuvres government ministers had few answers, other than adjournments, one of which effectively delayed the commencement of parliamentary business until 17 June 1689.[29] In the course of that day Montgomery proposed 'that the Act recognizing the King and Queen's right to the Crown should had [*sic*] that claws, because they had undertaken to rederess the grivances, and, at this rait, to vote what was meant, tho' not exprest in the grivances'.[30]

[24] Ibid., no. 23.
[25] Ferguson, *Scotland, 1689 to the Present*, pp. 6–7; *Leven and Melville Papers*, no. 23.
[26] Ferguson, *Scotland, 1689 to the Present*, p. 7; *State Papers and Letters addressed to William Carstares* (hereafter *State Papers and Letters addressed to William Carstares*), ed. J. McCormick (Edinburgh, 1774), pp. 32–5.
[27] *Leven and Melville Papers*, no. 111.
[28] James Halliday, 'The Club and the Revolution in Scotland, 1689–1690', *Scottish Historical Review*, 46 (1966), pp. 143–59; *Leven and Melville Papers*, no. 71.
[29] Balfour-Melville (ed.), *Proceedings of the Estates*, I, pp. 119–20.
[30] *Leven and Melville Papers*, no. 57.

Thereafter every effort was made to pursue this objective, constitutional issues being given priority as it was felt that if ecclesiastical issues were attained, loss of interest in curbing William's political power would follow. In consequence, although prelacy was abolished on 22 July 1689, nothing was placed in its stead and the opposition concentrated on three basic issues: the right of the Crown to nominate to judicial offices; the abolition of the Committee of the Articles, and an Incapacity Act.[31] Formulated to debar from public office all individuals 'who were grivous in the former Government, or who had bein opposit to this revolution, or who had bein opposers or retardes of the Stats desings' and aimed primarily at Stair and Dalrymple, the bill for exclusion of such figures from public office was couched in general terms.[32] Stair's former association with Lauderdale had alienated him from former Covenanters, while Dalrymple's service as lord advocate in the service of James VII had likewise aroused old enmities. A bill was introduced on 26 June and produced active debate on 28 June and 2 July when the Act was passed by seventy-four votes to twenty-four, thereby committing the House to the view that:

> no person ... who [was] in the said former evil Government [which] hath been Grievous to the Nation by acting in the Incroachments mentioned in the Articles of the Claim of Right ... [should be allowed] ... to possess or be admitted into any Public Trust, Place or Imployment of whatsoever kind under their Majesties in this Kingdom.[33]

If the objective had been attained, William was unlikely to concede the principle. As Dalrymple remarked, it was the 'Kings perogativ' that was in question – the constitutional right to select his own ministers.[34] With this in mind, William refused to give his assent to the Incapacity Act. By doing so he hoped not only to protect his own interests but also to placate former supporters of James VII.[35] In this he was following Viscount Mackenzie of Tarbat's advice that the act would: 'fix many in bad humours, who else would willingly be good subjects to the king'.[36]

It was not in William's interest, he added; 'to force persons to disaffection to his persone or authority. Indeed the narrower that the lines of good subjects be drawne the few within it may have the surer hopes of advancement in offices, and in so farr the politick may attaine som end'.[37] In suggesting that supporters of the Act were motivated by greed for office, Tarbat may have been less than

[31] Ibid., nos. 136–7.
[32] Ibid., nos. 74, 81; Balfour-Melville (ed.), *Proceedings of the Estates*, I, p. 141.
[33] *Leven and Melville Papers*, nos. 74, 80, 84, 98; Balfour-Melville (ed.), *Proceedings of the Estates*, I, pp. 152–3.
[34] *Leven and Melville Papers*, no. 81.
[35] Ibid., nos. 110–13.
[36] Ibid., no. 110.
[37] Ibid., no. 110.

fair as the constitutional issue was equally important to most of its promoters. Of this William was only too well aware and despite active lobbying, it was a point which he resolutely refused to concede.[38]

The controversy, nevertheless, continued with Parliament seeking a definitive ruling as to the basis for William's claim to the throne; an issue which called into question the conduct of the commissioners – Argyll, Montgomery, and Dalrymple – in offering William the Crown on 11 May 1689.[39] Suspicions were rife about Dalrymple's conduct, who it was suggested had offered William the throne before his acceptance of the Claim of Right.[40] On his own admission he certainly seems to have offered the Claim of Right, the Oath, and finally the Grievances – in that order – contrary to his original instructions.[41] Few were prepared to press this issue to a logical conclusion as the proposal to question the commissioners had only been carried by two votes on 12 July.[42] Nevertheless, Dalrymple's reputation had suffered and his standing was to be further threatened by a dispute over the use of royal appointments to the Court of Session, including that of his father, Lord Stair, as lord president.[43] Among the nominees the promotion of James Murray of Philiphaugh, 'a persone under bad characters, having had a chief hand in rwining manie families', caused particular consternation, but others equally were of doubtful allegiance.[44] Indeed, three of the prospective members declined their offer of appointment, much to the relief of the earl of Crawford who in expressing his happiness at their decision to Melville noted that 'neither they, nor such other lords as were in the Session', who had been omitted from the nomination, 'are in any caice desyred by the nation'.[45] 'Men of sound and sober principles, untained credit, tho' of meaner qualifications for the bench', it is declared, 'are more in the wishes of the people'.[46]

In a debate on the issue on 19th July 1689 it was claimed that in the case of an entire vacancy in the Session the nomination of new lords required parliamentary confirmation, the precedent of 1661 being cited in favour of this view.[47] Members also clashed over William's proclamation that the signet seal, the essential preliminary to the administration of justice, should be used henceforward.[48] With tempers frayed, the House was adjourned with the proviso that the signet

[38] Ibid., nos. 39–40, 79–80.
[39] Balfour-Melville (ed.), *Proceedings of the Estates*, I, pp. 85–9, 160; *Acts Parl. Scot.*, IX, Appendix, p. 133.
[40] *Leven and Melville Papers*, nos. 112, 116.
[41] Ibid., no. 121.
[42] Ibid., no. 120.
[43] Balfour-Melville (ed.), *Proceedings of the Estates*, I, p. 148.
[44] *Leven and Melville Papers*, no. 67.
[45] Ibid., no. 70.
[46] Ibid., no. 70.
[47] Balfour-Melville (ed.), *Proceedings of the Estates*, I, pp. 173–4.
[48] Ibid., I, pp. 173–4.

should remain shut until the members could consider the matter further.[49] They did so three days later when it was further argued that the constitution of the College of Justice required the president of the Session to be elected by the lords.[50] The contention was also made that the signet could not be opened until there were lords of Session and as yet there were none until the House approved of the king's nominations.[51] Precedents ranging from the original foundation of the College in 1534 through the total vacancies of 1641 and 1661 were quoted in support of this view, as was an act of James VI which declared that the president was to be elected by the lords, a procedure followed until 1661.[52]

The removal of Stair as lord president was the principal objective of this attack. This was supported by all but eighteen MPs, with many of the king's supporters joining in the campaign for the passage of the Act which was achieved on 23 July while the signet remained closed.[53] On this issue the estates were, however, to be thwarted by William's determination not to yield for, during the parliamentary recess of winter 1689–90, he made a re-nomination of the Session with Stair as lord president.[54] He and two of the lords – Baird of Newbyth and Swinton of Mersington – were to confirm the appointments of their fellow judges.[55] Ethically and constitutionally William was undoubtedly wrong in his action, probably taken on the advice of Dalrymple, but politically it paid dividends; the opposition was discomfited and its attempt to persuade the advocates not to plead before the new judges quite unsuccessful.[56] Although the judges were accompanied by a troop of dragoons at their first sitting, to protect them against the wrath of the Edinburgh mob, the verdict of one of the lords – Sir William Anstruther – that he found 'the generality of the people ... vere well pleased with the sitting down of the Session' has a note of authenticity.[57]

If effectively prevented from implementing its programme on these two issues, 'the club' reserved its most tenacious opposition for the campaign to abolish the lords of the articles which the Articles of Grievances had declared was 'a great grievance to the nation'. They further asserted 'that their ought to be no committees of parliament but such as are freely chosen by the statutes to prepare motions and overtures that are first made in the house'.[58] As this com-

[49] Ibid., I, p. 174.
[50] Ibid., I, p. 176.
[51] Ibid., I, p. 176.
[52] Ibid., I, p. 176.
[53] Ibid., I, p. 181; *Leven and Melville Papers*, nos. 133, 137.
[54] Balfour-Melville (ed.), *Proceedings of the Estates*, II, pp. 35–7.
[55] Ibid., II, pp. 35–7.
[56] H. C. Foxcroft, *The Life and Letters of Sir George Savile, Bart., first Marquis of Halifax* (2 vols., London, 1898), II, p. 236; *Leven and Melville Papers*, no. 251.
[57] Sir John Dalrymple, *Memoirs of Great Britain and Ireland* (3 vols., Edinburgh, 1771–88), I, pp. ii, 80; *Leven and Melville Papers*, no. 251.
[58] *Acts Parl. Scot.*, IX, p. 45.

mittee had been the means whereby Scottish monarchs had controlled parliamentary business for almost two centuries, it was inevitable that William should try and retain it. To this end William, in advance of Parliament's meeting on 5 June, proposed on 31 May that the committee should remain in being with a membership of twenty-four chosen by the estates, but still retaining the officers of state as *ex officio* members.[59] As in the past the committee was to prepare matter for debate and draft legislation. It was conceded, however, that the House might discuss issues rejected by the committee.[60]

These concessions proved insufficient on several counts. The proposed size of the committee caused some protests while others contended that each estate should be allowed to choose its own members.[61] Most controversy, however, centred around the inclusion of officials who had not been elected by the estates.[62] In the event, when Parliament re-assembled on 17 June the demand for the abolition of the committee was unequivocal, and remained so on the day following, despite an adjournment of the day's business.[63] Vigorous debates, in which the opposition appear to have had the best of the argument, took place over a period of days without any agreement being reached although a Council decision on 20 June that business might be introduced into the House compromised the case for the committee's retention, a point which did not escape Dalrymple's notice. He protested to Melville that this was tantamount to dispensing with the royal assent to the abolition of the committee.[64] Conflict between Crown and Parliament was predicted, but every effort on Dalrymple's part to reach a compromise proved unavailing and the Act for the committee's abolition passed with not more than ten votes against it on 25 June.[65] Royal assent was, however, withheld as Hamilton claimed that he did not have instructions to that effect.[66]

William's reaction left no room for doubts; he was determined to resist and on 3 July he informed Halifax that he 'would not agree to take away the articles, but would reform them ... [and] ... would yield no more neither there, and if the Parliament in Scotland did not like it, he would dissolve it and get another'.[67] On the following day his proposals were announced. It was now suggested that the committee should consist of thirty-three members elected

[59] *A Collection of Scarce and Valuable Tracts* (Lord Somers), cited here in the later version, ed. W. Scott (13 vols., London, 1809–15), XI, pp. 479–82; Balfour-Melville (ed.), *Proceedings of the Estates*, I, p. 133.
[60] Balfour-Melville (ed.), *Proceedings of the Estates*, I, p. 133.
[61] Ibid., I, p. 137.
[62] Ibid., I, p. 137.
[63] Ibid., I, p. 135; *Leven and Melville Papers*, no. 57.
[64] *Leven and Melville Papers*, no. 60.
[65] Ibid., no. 70.
[66] Balfour-Melville (ed.), *Proceedings of the Estates*, I, p. 140.
[67] Foxcroft, *Life and Letters of Halifax*, II, p. 223.

equally by the three estates at monthly or more frequent intervals.[68] To this number, however, the offices of state were still to be added, but although it could be argued that such a minority would not be able to influence the committee's deliberations, the opposition refused to compromise their principles on this issue.[69] Dalrymple's powers of persuasion were unavailing against the eloquence of Montgomery who rejected William's proposals out of hand laying blame for their suggestion upon Stair and claiming that the king 'wold certinly have granted all, if he had not been ill advysed'.[70] Appraised of the likely outcome of any vote, Hamilton adjourned the House without a division.[71]

An impasse had been reached with the estates taking their revenge by decreeing that no committee would be elected without acceptance of their demand for the abolition of the Articles.[72] Parliamentary procedures became slow and cumbersome; royal authority had been successfully challenged both in terms of Parliament and the judiciary. The abolition of prelacy on 22 July, while welcomed, did not assuage political demands, from which the only escape was the adjournment of the House on 2 August without any grant of supply.[73] The tactics employed by the king's ministers during the 1689 session had proved singularly inept. This was not to be repeated when Parliament reassembled on 15 April 1690.

On this occasion, every effort was made to placate Parliament, partially to obtain supply deemed necessary to maintain a standing army to meet any further Jacobite attempts to regain the throne by force, but also as a means of withdrawing support from 'the club'; a task made easier by Mongomery's indiscreet association with known Jacobites which had matured during the recess.[74] In that interval 'the club' had suffered another setback when an attempt to further their ends by the presentation of an address repeating their demands to the king had been initially rebuffed on 14 October and when finally presented on the following day had only succeeded in provoking William's ire.[75] As efforts to destroy the unity of 'the club' began to bite, Montgomery became increasingly isolated and resolved to maintain his parliamentary majority by allying with the Jacobites who planned to take the oath and attend Parliament to restore King James in a constitutional manner.[76] Opinions have differed as to the practicality of the Montgomery plot and certainly its discovery not only ruined its

[68] *A Collection of Scarce and Valuable Tracts* (Lord Somers), XI, pp. 479–82.
[69] Ibid., XI, pp. 479–82.
[70] *Leven and Melville Papers*, no. 111.
[71] Ibid., no. 111.
[72] *Acts Parl. Scot.*, IX, Appendix 132; Balfour-Melville (ed.), *Proceedings of the Estates*, I, p. 181.
[73] *Acts Parl. Scot.*, IX, p. 104.
[74] Balfour-Melville (ed.), *Proceedings of the Estates*, I, p. 193; *Acts Parl. Scot.*, IX, Appendix 38.
[75] *A Collection of Scarce and Valuable Tracts* (Lord Somers), XI, pp. 477ff; *Leven and Melville Papers*, nos. 185, 104.
[76] W. Fraser, *Annandale Family Book* (2 vols., Edinburgh, 1894), I, p. clxvi; Fraser, *Melvilles Earls of Melville and Leslies Earls of Leven*, I, p. 211.

author's political career but led in turn to his exile and premature death in France.[77] In the short term, however, more harm was done to the opposition's cause by a steady defection from the ranks of 'the club', occasioned by royal patronage in the form of financial inducements and official appointments.[78] Most significant of all, however, was the appointment of Lord Melville, a moderate Presbyterian, as royal commissioner to Parliament and his well-publicized instructions to make concessions when he thought fit.[79] Thus when Parliament reassembled and 'the club' demanded that the royal assent should be given to the Act abolishing royal supremacy over the Church, this was readily conceded on 25 April.[80] A repetition of the call for the abolition of the committee of the Articles was received in a similar manner and after a favourable vote, it too was touched with the sceptre on 8 May.[81] Such concessions had the desired effect: a bill designed to secure 'personal liberty and freedom of speech' for MPs was quietly forgotten and, more importantly, Parliament proceeded to establish committees, including one to consider the granting of supply, this being achieved on 7 June.[82] If the issue of church government remained to be resolved, the constitutional crisis which had threatened the royal prerogative was basically at an end.

With whom did this victory lie? Constitutionally the Revolution settlement has frequently been seen as a turning-point, with royal control over Parliament diminished through the abolition of the Committee of the Articles.[83] Likewise, while Parliament might at its discretion still appoint special committees, the officers of state (while still possessing the power to propose motions and debate issues) were debarred, unless they were noblemen, from voting. In this respect it can be argued that the Scottish Parliament secured some measure of freedom from monarchical control in 1690,[84] for the achievements of 'the club' led to the development of new techniques which allowed for more settled legislative procedures and debates upon important issues.[85] The threat to withhold supply became a powerful weapon in the event of a conflict of wills between Crown and Parliament.[86] This new-found independence would, however, lead to problems in the future and would in time precipitate the constitutional crisis ultimately resolved by the Treaty of Union of 1707.[87] Therein lies the apparent paradox

77 Halliday, 'The Club and the Revolution', pp.156, 158–9.
78 Ibid., pp. 156–8.
79 *Leven and Melville Papers*, nos. 341, 344, 346, 359, 359–60.
80 Balfour-Melville (ed.), *Proceedings of the Estates*, II, pp. 141–2, 145.
81 Ibid., II, pp. 145, 158–9.
82 Ibid., II, pp. 158, 166, 171, 175, 187–8, 189–91.
83 P. W. J. Riley, *The Union of England and Scotland* (Manchester, 1978); T. C. Smout, 'Union of the Parliaments', in G. Menzies (ed.), *The Scottish Nation* (London, 1972), pp. 150–1.
84 R. S. Rait, *The Parliaments of Scotland* (Glasgow, 1924), pp. 101–5, 280–3, 386–9.
85 Ibid., pp. 412–3, 429–33.
86 Andrew Fletcher, *Political Works* (London, 1749), p. 194.
87 Riley, *The Union of England and Scotland*, pp. 8–26.

of the Revolution settlement: that which had been hailed as a notable achievement led to the suppression of the very institution it had sought to free from external control. The truth is perhaps less dramatic. Constitutionally William may have surrendered some control over Parliament, but in political terms indirect influence could still be exercised through political management. The Crown's right of appointment of officers of state and above all of privy councillors who corporately exercised considerable legislative, judicial, and executive powers also ensured the continuity of royal authority.[88] In this respect the Crown's control over day-to-day Scottish affairs should have remained virtually unassailable. If in practice the irresponsibility of the Scottish magnates made royal authority less than complete, the means of asserting control was always present. If in a crisis Parliament still had a vital role to play, patronage, venality, and apparent concessions could be used to effect royal wishes, as the passage of the Act of Union, a standing testimony to the hollowness of the constitutional gains of 1689–90, readily exemplifies.[89]

On eccclesiastical issues, however, crown policies were less easily implemented. From the outset Presbyterian pressure was brought to bear upon William as a means of reinforcing claims made to him in the Netherlands that 'if Scotland was left to their free choice, of three parts two would be found Presbyterian'. It was, however, by no means certain that the King would justify the confidence shown by the large number of exiled Scottish politicians and churchmen who accompanied him on his journey to England.[90] William's own upbringing as a Calvinist meant less to him than has often been supposed. Supporters of a moderate episcopal system were more numerous than William had been led to believe and may, indeed, have been in the majority.[91] Moreover, he quickly realized the value of the bishops to the Crown, both as a means of controlling the Church and administering the state.[92] In the circumstances the maintenance of episcopacy was a possibility not to be denied. Much, however, depended upon the attitude of the Church itself.

The established Church confronted by the effect of James VII's policy of toleration and the threat of Catholicism had not been unmindful of its position.[93] In December 1688 the bishops had appointed two of their number, Edinburgh and Orkney, to proceed to London to safeguard their interests.[94] In the event only William Rose, bishop of Edinburgh made the journey south where he found

[88] *Reg. Privy Council*, 3rd ser. XV, pp. vii–ix, xvi–xvii, 19, 101, 196, 263, 277, 285–8.
[89] W. Ferguson, 'The Making of the Treaty of Union of 1707', *Scottish Historical Review*, 44 (1964), pp. 89–110.
[90] Wodrow, *History*, IV, p. 436.
[91] I. B. Cowan, *The Scottish Covenanters* (London, 1976), pp. 137–8.
[92] *State Papers and Letters addressed to William Carstares*, p. 43.
[93] R. Keith, *An Historical Catalogue of the Scottish Bishops down to the year 1688* (Edinburgh, 1755) cited hereafter in the later edition, ed. M. Russell (Edinburgh, 1824), p. 65.
[94] Ibid., pp. 65–6.

on his arrival that James had fled and William was soundly entrenched.[95] Rose could get little advice from the English bishops while a request to the king that he should receive a deputation of Scottish bishops, nobility, and gentry was rejected 'lest that might give jealousy and umbrage to the Presbyterians'.[96] On the other hand William would not encourage the Presbyterians to come to him in numbers, and he would not, he stated, 'allow above two of either party at a time to speak to him in church matters'.[97] The king did, however, inform Rose through Compton, bishop of London, that

> he now knows the state of Scotland much better than he did when he was in Holland, for, while there, he was made believe that Scotland generally all over was Presbyterian, but now he sees the great body of the nobility and gentry are for Episcopacy, and tis the trading and inferior sort that are for Presbytery; wherefore he bids me tell you, that if you will undertake to serve him to the purpose that he is served here in England, he will take you by the hand, support the Church and Order, and throw off the Presbyterians.[98]

To this Rose replied that he had no instructions to act for the Scottish Church in the circumstances.[99] Bishop Compton is said to have approved of his honesty – but added that he (Rose) had not waited on the king nor had any of the Scottish bishops sent an address to him.[100] Compton added significantly: 'the king must be excused for standing by the Presbyterians'.[101] The next day in a brief interview with William at Whitehall, Rose went far to seal the fate of the episcopal Church when, in answer to the Prince's comment that he hoped affairs in Scotland would follow the example of England, Rose replied: 'Sir, I will serve you so far as law, reason, or conscience shall allow me.'[102]

In later life Rose was to ruminate on whether William would have kept his promise to overthrow the Presbyterians and felt that this would have been the case as,

> by gaining as he might presume to gain, the Episcopal nobility and gentry which he saw was a great party, and consequently that King James would be deprived of his principal support; Then he saw what a hardship it would be upon the Church of England, and of what bad consequence, to see Episcopacy ruined in Scotland, who, no doubt, would have vigorously interposed for us, if we, by our carriage, could have been brought to justify their measures'.[103]

The option was not, however, in Rose's keeping, for in giving his reply to William,

[95] Ibid., p. 66.
[96] Ibid., pp. 66–7, 69.
[97] Ibid., p. 69.
[98] Ibid., pp. 69–70.
[99] Ibid., p. 70.
[100] Ibid., p. 70.
[101] Ibid., p. 70.
[102] Ibid., pp. 70–1.
[103] Ibid., pp. 71–2.

Rose was only foreshadowing the attitude adopted by the Scottish bishops in general.[104] Many ministers followed their lead and although a proclamation of 13 April 1689 ordering public prayers for the new king and queen brought few deprivations of episcopal clergy, yet another of 6 August which invited members of congregations to denounce defaulters to the Council, brought the number of deprivations by 7 November to 182.[105]

In the meantime the Presbyterians had continued to mount pressure for their own recognition. If at the meeting of the estates on 14 March there was a strong episcopal representation with two archbishops and seven bishops, including Rose, they soon withdrew, maintaining their allegiance to James, so leaving the field open for the Presbyterians who thereafter pressed home their advantage.[106] On 11 April the Claim of Right had declared

> That Prelacy and the superiority of any office in the Church above Presbyters is, and hath been a great and unsupportable grievance and trouble to the Nation, and contrary to the inclinations of the generality of the people, ever since the Reformation (they having reformed from Popery by Presbyteries) and therefore ought to be abolished.[107]

Two days later the passage of the Articles of Grievances reinforced the ecclesiastical ideal of the Revolution settlement in its reaffirmation of the rejection of episcopacy by claiming that the Act of Supremacy of 1669 was 'inconsistent with the establishment of the church government now desyred and ought to be abrogated'.[108]

In Parliament this desire was overwhelming and explains much of the support for other opposition policies. To this end William was anxious to settle the ecclesiastical issue. Nevertheless, he was anxious not to alienate the Church of England, a fact which explains his expressed reservation (later withdrawn) to the last clause of the Scottish coronation oath offered to him by the earl of Argyll on 11 May 1689.[109] On being asked to swear that 'he shall root out all heretics and enemies to the true worship of God that shall be convicted by the true Kirk of God of the foresaid crisis', he paused and replied: 'I will not lay myself under any obligation to be a persecutor.'[110] Since the oath was obviously directed against adherents of the episcopal Church, William was expected to agree to their persecution; a course to which he was unwilling to commit himself. Indeed as late as June he was being advised that while the Presbyterians were 'more zealous and hotter', the episcopal party were 'more

[104] Balfour-Melville (ed.), *Proceedings of the Estates*, I, pp. 8, 14, 16, 26.
[105] *Reg. Privy Council*, 3rd ser., XIV, pp. xvii–xxi, 77–8.
[106] *Acts Parl. Scot.*, IX, p. 3. Balfour-Melville (ed.), *Proceedings of the Estates*, I, p. 14.
[107] *Acts Parl. Scot.*, IX, p. 37.
[108] Ibid., IX, p. 45.
[109] Balfour-Melville (ed.), *Proceedings of the Estates*, I, pp. 85–9.
[110] J. Cunningham, *The Church History of Scotland* (2nd edn, 2 vols., Edinburgh, 1882), II, p. 163.

numerous and powerful'.[111] In Parliament the presence of burgh commissioners allowed for a Presbyterian majority, but the major part of the nobility and barons were 'not for Presbitry'.[112] The solution advocated by the king's advisers was essentially for a compromise which would effectively place both parties on an equal footing. William was urged to

> allow the ministers in evry presbitry who owne the Presbiterien government, according to the modell of 1592 or 1641 to meet Presbiterially evry fortnight, and Synodically once in the yeare as owners of the Westminster Confession; and to allow those ministers who are not for the modell, and owne the Articles of the Confession of the English Church, to meet also Presbiterially and Synodically, as said is; and that it be allowed to the one to elect a Moderator at every meeting, and the other to be allowed to elect a constant Moderator or Overseer.[113]

Such a solution was unlikely to find favour with the Presbyterians, and a further stipulation that 'no Generall Assembly of ether models be called or meet, except by the King's speciall call, in such numbers, and such places, as shall be by his Majesty appointed' would have been totally unacceptable.[114]

Time was, however, running out for compromise as on 2 July 1689 a draft bill was introduced by the earl of Annandale for the abolition of prelacy and 'of all superiority of office in the Church above presbyters, reserving to their Majesties to settle the presbyterian government in the way most agreeable to the inclinations of the people and the word of God'.[115] The royal commissioner requested a copy of the draft, presumably for perusal by the king, while at the same time an attempt was made by the episcopal synod of Aberdeen, through the earl of Kintore, to present an address, agreeing to pray for King William, expressing a desire for union with all their Protestant brethren who differed from them only on matters of church government and asking for a free General Assembly; a view not favoured by the Presbyterians who wished parliamentary establishment before the calling of an Assembly.[116]

Meantime, the phraseology of the original draft bill was under revision. The word 'presbyterian' was excised from the description of church government desired, while the settlement was only to conform to the inclinations of the people, nothing being said about the word of God.[117] This Act became law on 22 July.[118] If the abolition of prelacy constituted a major step forward the Act did not satisfy the aspirations of the Presbyterians, for a final settlement had not only been delayed but power to effect it was still very much a matter

[111] *Leven and Melville Papers*, no. 89.
[112] Ibid., no. 89.
[113] Ibid., no. 89.
[114] Ibid., no. 89.
[115] Ibid., no. 97; Balfour-Melville (ed.), *Proceedings of the Estates*, I, p. 149.
[116] Balfour-Melville (ed.), *Proceedings of the Estates*, I, p. 149.
[117] *Leven and Melville Papers*, no. 97; Balfour-Melville (ed.), *Proceedings of the Estates*, I, pp. 153–4.
[118] *Acts Parl. Scot.*, IX, p. 104.

of royal and ministerial concern. Thwarted in this respect, the opposition proceeded immediately to implement a fresh demand for the abolition of royal supremacy over the Church.[119] Despite the bill's passage the king's commissioner, Hamilton, refused for no apparent reason to grant royal assent.[120] Even William himself criticized his behaviour, commenting to Halifax on Hamilton's 'many very contrary stops' and remarking that the commissioner 'might have hindered some votes if he would'.[121] Nevertheless, it seemed that William was delaying the establishment of Presbyterianism. He was still in contact with the episcopal clergy who were being dispossessed of their benefices.[122] Resolutions on behalf of the burghs and barons passed during the adjournment of Parliament in August 1689 had little effect despite the promise that if Presbyterian church government was established they would 'serv him with life and fortun, and giv him a suply'.[123] The earl of Crawford in turn urged Lord Melville that 'it is in vaine to expect peace in this nation untill the Presbiterian government be settled'.[124] Whatever William's hopes, the Jacobite sympathies of the episcopal clergy precluded any reliance upon the allegiance of the episcopal clergy. At this time too came the revelation of the Montgomery plot by William Dunlop, the brother-in-law of William Carstares who conveyed the news to the king.[125] Thereafter the king was more well disposed to the Presbyterians as expressed in a letter of Carstares to Dunlop who assured him: 'You had done good service to your country, and a good king who is very willing and desirous we should be happy. He is sensible that the Presbyterians of that kingdom are his best friends, and will, I doubt not treat them as such'.[126]

When Parliament reassembled Melville had replaced Hamilton as commissioner, part of the intention behind this appointment being to placate the Presbyterians who had been in correspondence with him throughout the crisis and wrote to him as early as 4 September 1689 that 'wee, the Presbiterian partie expects ye will take us by the hand'.[127] Melville for his part bound himself to the Presbyterians who placed their trust in the new commissioner to whom instructions were forwarded by William after consultation with Carstares.[128] The establishment of Presbyterianism was conceded, but it was to be a moderate settlement and there was to be toleration of episcopal supporters loyal to the Crown. In this respect it was William's desire that 'Such as are of the Episcopall

[119] Ibid., IX, Appendix 139; Balfour-Melville (ed.), *Proceedings of the Estates*, I, p. 154.
[120] *Leven and Melville Papers*, no. 105.
[121] Foxcroft, *Life and Letters of Halifax*, II, pp. 233–4.
[122] *Leven and Melville Papers*, no. 231.
[123] Ibid., no. 174.
[124] Ibid., no. 181.
[125] R. H. Story, *Life of William Carstares* (Edinburgh, 1874), p. 18.
[126] Ibid., p. 18.
[127] *Leven and Melville Papers*, no. 207.
[128] Ibid., no. 366.

persuasion in Scotland have the same indulgence as Dissenters have in England provided they give security to live peaceably under the Government and take the Oath of Allegiance.'[129] As a show of goodwill the bills previously refused royal assent were touched with the sceptre and in this way the Act of Supremacy of 1669 was abolished, a meeting of the General Assembly appointed, and ministers ejected from their livings in 1662 were reinstated.[130] On 7 June 1690 an Act was passed restoring Presbyterian government to the Church on the model of 1592.[131] The omission of the Covenants is striking; the Confession of Faith was recognized, but not the catechism and the directory of worship.[132] Nevertheless, if the settlement, including the Erastian procedures for calling an Assembly, were questionable, the Presbyterians were confident that when they met in assembly they could then promote the intrinsic rights of presbytery.

To this extent Melville faithfully carried out the king's instructions. He was, however, deemed to have overstepped the mark in agreeing to Presbyterians' demands for the transfer of ecclesiastical patronage from private individuals to heritors and kirk sessions. William, who had instructed Melville to pass such an act 'if the Parliament shall desire the same', nevertheless felt that his commissioner had shown undue zeal in allowing this motion to go forward; a view which was shared with his ecclesiastical adviser, William Carstares, who felt that vesting the right of patronage in congregations would plunge the Church into chaos.[133] Melville, however, responded to Presbyterian pressure, and the Act passed on 19 July 1690 stipulated that on payment of compensation of 600 marks to the patron, the right to present ministers to vacant charges was to pass to the heritors and elders of the parish.[134] The magnates were displeased by this attack on their privilege and set about scheming with the aid of the displaced Hamilton for Melville's dismissal from office.[135]

The opportunity occurred at the General Assembly of 16 October 1690, the first since 1653, which consisted of about 180 ministers and elders, none of whom were drawn from the area north of the Tay.[136] The king's commissioner was Lord Carmichael who had firm instructions to maintain the royal prerogative and rights, but lest he should be unmindful of his responsibilities, Carstares was also present with letters of instruction from the king, and was in constant

[129] Ibid., no. 366.
[130] Ibid., no. 341; *Acts Parl. Scot.*, IX, p. 111.
[131] *Acts Parl. Scot.*, IX, pp. 133–4.
[132] T. Maxwell, 'William III and the Scottish Presbyterians', *Records of the Scottish Church History Society*, 15 (1965), pp. 184–5.
[133] *Leven and Melville Papers*, no. 341; *State Papers and Letters addressed to William Carstares*, pp. 47–9.
[134] *State Papers and Letters addressed to William Carstares*, p. 49; *Acts Parl. Scot.*, IX, pp. 196–7.
[135] *State Papers and Letters addressed to William Carstares*, p. 51.
[136] *Acts of the General Assembly of the Church of Scotland MDCXXXVIII-MDCCCXLIII* (Church Law Society, 1843), pp. 221–35; Cunningham, *Church History of Scotland*, II, p. 177.

attendance upon the Assembly although not a member of it.[137] From the outset it was made clear that the king wished compromise. In his letter to the Assembly he wrote:

> A calm and peaceable procedure will be no less pleasing to us than it becometh you. We never could be of the mind that violence was suited to the advancing of true religion; nor do we intend that our authority shall ever be a tool to the irregular passions of any party. Moderation is what religion enjoins, neighbouring churches expect from you and we recommend to you.[138]

Nevertheless, the Assembly, presided over by Hugh Kennedy a former protester, as moderator, proceeded to set up machinery to purge episcopal incumbents.[139] All ministers, probationers, and elders were required to subscribe to the Westminster Confession, private communion and baptism were forbidden, and two commissions (one to operate north of the Tay and the other south of it) were appointed to proceed against recalcitrant clergy, although the full force of their powers was not to become evident for some months to come.[140] The commissioner appears to have been satisfied with the conduct of business and although he seems to have intervened, made motions and proffered suggestions which were a 'stumbling to many', no offence appears to have been taken.[141] A discordant note was, however, struck at the end of the Assembly with a clash of wills over the date and means of summoning its successor. Some proposed June, some August. The commissioner, however, rose and declared in the king's name the Assembly dissolved. He then appointed the next Assembly to meet on 1 November 1691.[142]

In the event there was no meeting in 1691; a royal proclamation adjourned the Assembly until 15 January 1692.[143] This move not only underlined the king's authority in this respect, but also reflected William's growing displeasure with the operations of the northern commission who were deposing recalcitrant clergy on the slightest pretext while universities were likewise being purged.[144] Appeals for moderation to the 1692 Assembly fell on deaf ears and brought about a head-on collision which led to the commissioner dissolving the Assembly without naming a date for its reconvention, an omission rectified by the moderator who asserted on behalf of his brethren that

> he could not forebear to declare that the Office-bearers in the house of God have

[137] *Acts of the General Assembly*, pp. 221–2; Maxwell, 'William III and the Scottish Presbyterians', p. 186.

[138] *Acts of the General Assembly*, p. 222.

[139] Ibid., pp. 223–35.

[140] Ibid., 225–34.

[141] R. Wodrow, *Analecta: or materials for a history of remarkable providences; mostly relating to Scottish ministers and Christians*, ed. M. Leishman (4 vols., Maitland Club, 1842–3), I, p. 201.

[142] *Acts of the General Assembly*, p. 235; Wodrow, *Analecta*, I, pp. 203–4.

[143] Ibid., p. 235n.

[144] Cunningham, *Church History of Scotland*, II, pp. 183–4.

> a spiritual, intrinsick power from Jesus Christ, the only Head of his Church, to meet in Assemblys about the affairs thereof; the necessity of the same being first represented to the Magistrate. Therefore he craved that such a dissolution might not be to the prejudice of yearly General assemblys, granted by the laws of the kingdome.[145]

The members then agreed to meet on the third Wednesday of August 1693.[146]

This direct challenge to the authority of the Crown did not pass without response. The very existence of the Assembly was threatened: William retaliated with a parliamentary enactment in 1693 which promulgated an Oath of Assurance acknowledging William as king *de jure* as well as *de facto* which had to be sworn by all churchmen of whatever persuasion.[147] Both supporters of presbytery and episcopacy objected, but appeal to the Privy Council only produced a decree that the oath must be taken by all prospective members of the next Assembly.[148] Objections to the Erastian nature of this demand further threatened relations between the Crown and the Church and although some ministers attempted to convene as arranged they found the doors of their normal meeting place closed against them.[149] Only tact on William's part saved the day. On receipt of a vague promise that episcopal ministers loyal to the Crown would be accepted by the Presbyterians, he facilitated the appointment of a meeting for 6 December which was subsequently altered to 29 March 1694.[150] Even then the meeting was not assured: the taking of the oath as a condition of membership of the Assembly was a condition which few prospective members were prepared to meet.[151] The commissioner-designate, Lord Carmichael, urged William to relax his demand, at first to no avail, but his reluctance was eventually overcome and the meeting went ahead as planned.[152]

If this Assembly endorsed the 1693 Act, it also insisted upon acceptance of the Westminster Confession and of Presbyterianism as the only form of church government.[153] Every impediment was placed in the way of conformist episcopal ministers; a number of northern ministers were deposed and the cathedral of Aberdeen seized.[154] William's displeasure was expressed in a reluctance to allow a meeting in 1695, a series of royal proclamations changing the date of the opening of the Assembly from April to July, then to November and finally to

145 Wodrow, *Analecta*, I, pp. 201–2.
146 Ibid., I, p. 204.
147 *Acts Parl. Scot.*, IX, pp. 262–4.
148 Ibid., IX, p. 303; *State Papers and Letters addressed to William Carstares*, p. 57.
149 W. McMillan, 'The Lord High Commissioner to the General Assembly', *Records of the Scottish Church History Society*, 6 (1938), p. 268.
150 *Acts of the General Assembly*, p. 235n.
151 *State Papers and Letters addressed to William Carstares*, pp. 57–8.
152 Ibid., pp. 58–61.
153 *Acts of the General Assembly*, pp. 239–40.
154 Ibid., p. 321.

December.[155] Members who had honoured the July appointment were turned away and this Erastian note was confirmed when the Assembly finally met and the royal commissioner informed the gathering that they were met 'in this Assembly conform to the King's appointment'.[156] If the issue was again fudged, the question of royal authority continued to perplex Presbyterians whose consciences on the issue were further touched by the Cameronian reminders of their desertion of 'the intrinsic' right of presbytery.[157] Echoes of this dissatisfaction are found in the unremitting objection by Presbyterians to toleration, and their declaration in the Assembly of 1698. This repudiated the view that the Church was founded on the inclination of the people and acts of Parliament, and instead asserted: 'We do believe and own that Jesus Christ is the only Head and King of this church.'[158]

If this was more restrained than a declaration by the 1703 Assembly which informed Queen Anne that 'presbyterian government is settled, as agreeable to the Word of God ... and, therefore, to be the only government of Christ's Church within this Kingdom' and a subsequent declaration which following the introduction into Parliament of a toleration bill in 1703 which opposed 'any legal toleration to those of prelatical principles', the post-Revolution Church had nevertheless effectively obtained a settled constitution which was to persist with minor modifications to the present day.[159] Despite threats to the continuance of Assembly meetings the king's promise of 1695 that through his commissioner they would be summoned annually at a suitable time and place has been honoured ever since.[160] Stability was also provided by the passage of a 'Barrier Act' in 1697 which laid down the method by which legislation was to be passed through the General Assembly. All desired legislation was to be first proposed to the Assembly as an 'overture' and, if approved, was to be sent to presbyteries for their consideration. If supported by a majority of presbyteries, the measure would then be brought before the Assembly for a final decision.[161]

This achievement was, however, obtained at a price; the Erastian nature of the settlement left a legacy of discontent, intensified after the parliamentary union of 1707 by the passage of a Toleration Act and Patronage Act of 1712.[162] The latter, which reversed the decision of 1690 and restored individual rights of patronage, became a grievance around which all others, real and imaginary, could gather. In many instances patronage was the excuse rather than the underly-

[155] Ibid., p. 245n.
[156] Ibid., p. 247.
[157] Cunningham, *Church History of Scotland*, II, p. 201.
[158] Ibid., II, pp. 201–2.
[159] *Acts of the General Assembly*, p. 321; T. Stephen, *History of the Church of Scotland* (4 vols., London, 1843–48), III, pp. 649–50.
[160] I. A. Dunlop, *William Carstares and the Kirk by Law Established* (Edinburgh, 1967).
[161] *Acts of the General Assembly*, pp. 260–1.
[162] Ferguson, *Scotland, 1689 to the Present*, pp. 110–111.

ing reason for the secessions which split the Church of Scotland asunder in the period before 1843.[163] To this extent the Revolution settlement brought problems which were not fully resolved until the abolition of patronage in 1874 and the final concession of spiritual independence by the state in acts of 1921 and 1925.[164] Nevertheless, the Revolution settlement pointed firmly in that direction and was in the upshot to have more lasting consequences than the more ephemeral political concessions.

This judgment is, however, made with the benefit of hindsight. To many members of the Convention and Parliament during the traumatic years, 1689–90, the political and ecclesiastical consequences of their actions must have seemed of equal importance. Indeed, set as they were against the possibility of a Jacobite restoration, either by armed force or parliamentary reinstatement as envisaged by the Montgomery plot, the political reform may have appeared more immediate. If in the upshot these hopes were not to be fully realized, for a few years at least the Scottish Parliament became a more meaningful institution. With its demise in 1707, the focal point for many of the nation's hopes and aspirations passed to the Church which, without the achievements of the Revolution settlement, would have lacked the forum through which the Scots have frequently expressed their nationhood. If in the twentieth century the General Assembly no longer represents a consensus of the nation's will, its call for a Scottish Assembly reflects current political opinion north of the Border.[165] Sir James Montgomery and his compatriots would surely have concurred in a demand so reminiscent of their own political ambitions in the Revolutionary era.

[163] Ibid., pp. 121–7, 226–9, 306–12.
[164] Ibid., pp. 380–1.
[165] J. Brand, *The National Movement in Scotland* (London, 1978), pp. 127–35.

Chapter 5

The Williamite Revolution in Ireland, 1688–91

D. W. HAYTON

The traditional Whig interpretation of English constitutional history depicted the Glorious Revolution as a triumphant defence of liberty against the sinister encroachments of arbitrary monarchy. Such heroic simplicities soon vanish, however, when we examine the events of 1688–9 through an alternative lens, and indeed modern scholarship, focusing on the Revolution from several different perspectives, has almost succeeded in turning the image upside down. The most drastic revision, an anti-history of the Revolution, casts King James in the unlikely role of proto-liberal and William as the would-be tyrant.[1] This is not a particularly persuasive case, since it depends upon isolating James' commitment to religious toleration from other aspects of his rule, and seeking out the least attractive elements in William's kingship. But although the pro-Jacobites spoil their argument by exaggeration, they perform a valuable service in drawing attention to facets of the Revolution that Whig historians preferred to ignore, and which other recent authors less committed than they themselves to the rehabilitation of King James have also pointed out, the calculations of *Realpolitik* that lay behind William's invasion, for example, and, more significant still, the extent to which the Revolution ushered in a period of rapid growth in the resources and institutions of government. Rather than marking a crucial defeat for the monarchy and a victory for the freedom of the individual, the ultimate consequences of 1688, whatever one's view of the change in relations between Crown and Parliament, amounted to an increase and not a decrease in the power

My general approach to questions of Anglo-Irish governance owes much to the example (for an earlier period) of Dr Steven Ellis, and more directly to discussions with Dr Ellis over several years. However, no one but myself should be held responsible for the opinions expressed or the sins (of omission and commission) perpetrated in the present essay.

1 This I take to be the interpretation adumbrated in Eveline Cruickshanks, 'Religion and Royal Succession–The Rage of Party', in Clyve Jones (ed.), *Britain in the First Age of Party 1680–1750* (London, 1987), pp. 22, 26–7, and intended to be set forth in the recent collection of essays on the Revolution edited by the same author from the proceedings of a colloquium sponsored by the Royal Stuart Society, *By Force or By Default? The Revolution of 1688* (Edinburgh, 1989): see esp. p. v. However, it is neither followed, nor indeed borne out, by all the contributors to that volume.

of the state.[2] This interpretation gathers weight if we consider the Revolution in its wider, British context. Both in Ireland and in Scotland the Williamite victory meant in the long run a gain for the centre at the expense of the periphery, and an extension of English influence over the Gaelic peoples of Ireland and the Scottish Highlands.[3] It can be regarded as a critical moment in the expansion of English control over the other parts of the British Isles; a step towards empire, rather than towards constitutional democracy.

There was, of course, a Whig interpretation of the Glorious Revolution in Ireland, as a triumph for Protestantism and liberty over popery and arbitrary power. So ran the Williamite polemic of the seventeenth and eighteenth centuries. But as time passed this view proved more difficult for English Whigs and liberals to sustain, as their party took up the cause of Catholic emancipation and eventually Home Rule. Certain facts stuck in the craw, namely the denial in Irish Whig ideology of political rights to the majority Catholic population and the erection by the Protestant Irish Parliament of a savage code of discriminatory legislation. In the case of W. E. H. Lecky, the great liberal historian whose *Ireland in the Eighteenth Century* remains a classic, the intellectual torment in discussing the penal laws is almost palpable.[4] There was also the embarrassing fact that the adjective 'bloodless', so proudly attached to the Revolution in England, was rendered ridiculous as soon as the Irish war was taken into consideration. Gradually Williamite rhetoric, and the very image of King William the 'deliverer', came to be left to committed unionists. Thus English historians have tended to regard the Revolution settlement in Ireland either as a regrettable lapse from constitutional progressivism or as proof of the expansionist nature of the English state.[5] In this they have swum with the mainstream of modern Irish historiography, where the traditional nationalist account of the Jacobite period as a last bid for independence against a tightening colonial grip has been modified but not overthrown. Revisionist historians, while emphasizing the limited political objectives of the Irish Catholics in 1688–91, and the dissensions on both sides, have still presented the Revolution as in essence a struggle for supremacy between 'English' and 'Irish' interests, Williamites and Jacobites con-

[2] There is agreement on this point from two contrasting books: J. C. D. Clark, *Revolution and Rebellion: State and Society in England in the Seventeenth and Eighteenth Centuries* (Cambridge, 1986); and John Brewer, *The Sinews of Power: War, Money and the English State, 1688–1783* (London, 1989).

[3] Michael Hechter, *Internal Colonialism: The Celtic Fringe in British National Development, 1536–1966* (London, 1975), ch. 4, provides a general, and by now near classic, statement of this view.

[4] W. E. H. Lecky, *A History of Ireland in the Eighteenth Century* (5 vols., London, 1892), I, pp. 117–71.

[5] For some instances, see G. M. Trevelyan, *England under Queen Anne* (3 vols., London, 1930–4), III, pp. 160–71; David Ogg, *England in the Reigns of James II and William III* (Oxford, 1955), pp. 10, 249, 255, 259; John Carswell, *The Descent on England* (London, 1969), p. 235; and John Miller, *The Glorious Revolution* (London, 1983), p. 95.

testing for possession of the apparatus of state power, rather than striving for the liberty of the subject against arbitrary rule.[6]

Such an interpretation seems to accord with what we know to have been the major issues at stake. Naturally, each side claimed to be fighting for constitutional principles. Magna Carta and the cap of liberty featured prominently on Williamite medals; and William himself told the Dublin Protestants in 1690 that he had come 'to deliver you from ... tyranny ... and to restore your liberties and properties'.[7] For James and his followers what was to be vindicated was the divine hereditary right of the anointed monarch against the impious violence of a usurper and the treachery of rebels.[8] But both sets of protagonists also saw themselves as engaged in a war of religion, the climax of the Reformation and of the long struggle for supremacy in Ireland between Protestant and Catholic. Religious zeal was blended with political, social, and economic rivalry. However James may have prized the ideal of religious toleration, his Irish adherents hoped to obtain for themselves and their Church a dominant position in Irish society. Landed proprietors deprived by the Cromwellian confiscations looked for the recovery of estates and political influence; merchants for the readmission to lost privileges; poets for the revival of the native language; while laymen from all walks of life, as well as the clergy, aspired to the re-establishment of Catholicism and the restoration of the religious orders. On the other side Protestant planters and parsons were bent on maintaining their ascendancy against what they viewed as the latest in a series of insurrections against the English interest. A predominance in landownership, a Protestant church establishment, and a monopoly of political power were the bulwarks to be defended. Those sermons, speeches, and pamphlets in which Protestants were urged to stand fast spoke either in biblical terms of the war between true religion and the Antichrist, or in national-cum-racial terms of the defence of English power in Ireland against native insurgency.

The opposing ambitions of Jacobites and Williamites, and the language

[6] Aside from the work of J. G. Simms, and especially his *Jacobite Ireland 1685–91* (London, 1969), by far the best account of the period and on which I have drawn freely, few modern Irish historians have chosen to confront the still contentious events of the Revolution, unless obliged by the requirements of textbook writing. Some recent examples are: David Dickson, *New Foundations: Ireland 1660–1800* (Dublin, 1987), pp. 22–40; R. F. Foster, *Modern Ireland 1600–1972* (London, 1988), pp. 138–53; and Brendan Fitzpatrick, *Seventeenth-Century Ireland: The War of Religions* (Dublin, 1988), pp. 246–55.

[7] E. Hawkins, *Medallic Illustrations of the History of Great Britain and Ireland to the Death of George II*, ed. A. W. Franks and H. A. Grueber (2 vols., London, 1885), I, pp. 634–5, 638, 641, 669, 673; *The Speech of the Right Reverend ... Anthony, Bishop of Meath, when the Clergy Waited on His Majesty at His Camp near Dublin, July 7, 1690* (London, 1690). I have surveyed both Williamite and Jacobite propaganda in 'The Propaganda War', in W. A. Maguire (ed.), *Kings in Conflict: The Revolutionary War in Ireland and its Aftermath 1689–1750* (Belfast, 1990).

[8] P. K. Monod, 'For the King to Enjoy His Own Again: Jacobite Political Culture in England, 1688–1788', Yale University, PhD thesis (1985), pp. 89–116.

through which they were expressed, tell us clearly what contemporaries thought the Revolution and the ensuing war were about. And indeed, if we take the long view, the history of early modern Ireland is most easily comprehended as a pattern of English conquest and colonization. The process of political incorporation, which began with the assumption by Henry VIII of the title of king (rather than lord) of Ireland, and ended with the Act of Union in 1800, was accompanied by an attempt at social and economic integration and the cultural assimilation of the Gaelic Irish to English language, law, and customs. The underlying motives were fear and greed. English monarchs were afraid that a weak position in Ireland would render them vulnerable to attack in the rear by a foreign enemy. At the same time they coveted the treasure in taxes and men-at-arms that a compliant Ireland might offer, or saw a painless way to reward those adventurers among their subjects whose avarice was tempted by the prospect of Irish lands. The Reformation acted as a catalyst. As Protestantism and English patriotism came to be identified, Catholics in Ireland were regarded with increasing suspicion, even those of Anglo-Norman ('Old English') as against 'Old Irish' descent. From the late sixteenth century onwards a series of attempted plantations introduced a body of 'New English' Protestant settlers who in order to safeguard their own position and squeeze concessions from the English government acted as a more or less permanent pressure-group advocating aggressive policies against papists.

It would be wrong, however, to portray the process of conquest and anglicization as continuous and inevitable. Rather, it went on by fits and starts.[9] Periods of intense activity were followed by spells of administrative languor. The Catholic community was alternately coerced and conciliated. Such variations in temperature were only to be expected, given the principal motive forces dictating English strategy. Thus the long war with Spain sharpened Elizabeth's resolve to complete the subjugation of Ireland and encouraged her successor to embark on the systematic plantation of the most troublesome province, Ulster. In a different political context Charles I's desperate need for money resulted at one point in the auctioning of royal favour to Catholics as well as Protestants. After the Civil War English policy reached new heights of militancy as a consequence of an enhanced sense of domestic and international vulnerability. The violence of the Cromwellian reconquest and the thoroughness of the ensuing schemes of land redistribution and Anglo-Irish political union may be ascribed to the crisis of uncertainty that beset the fledgling English commonwealth. Similar fluctuations in approach can be found too among the 'New English' in Ireland, governed not only by

[9] For the background to English policy in the sixteenth and early seventeenth centuries, see the various accounts in T. W. Moody, F. X. Martin, and F. J. Byrne (eds.), *A New History of Ireland. Volume III: Early Modern Ireland 1534–1691* (hereafter *New Hist.*) (Oxford, 1976), chs. II–IV, VII–XIV; Steven G. Ellis, *Tudor Ireland: Crown, Community and the Conflict of Cultures, 1470–1603* (London, 1985); and Nicholas Canny, *From Reformation to Restoration: Ireland 1534–1660* (Dublin, 1987).

changes in the political climate but by differing local and family circumstances. Recent studies have detected an improvement in relations between some natives and newcomers in the early Stuart period, observing a genuine, if tentative, mixing of cultures as Protestant planters interested themselves in Gaelic customs and traditions. This proved to be a false dawn, dispelled by the Ulster rising of 1641.[10] But even after the outbreak of the rebellion, pronounced divergences in outlook can be discerned between sub-groups in the settler community, some of whom were even sharply antagonistic towards each other: 'old' and 'new' Protestants, Cavaliers and Puritans, and especially Anglicans and Dissenters.[11]

In terms of governance, the restoration of Charles II marked a return to pragmatism in Ireland. Royal policy swung like a weathervane, responding to developments in England.[12] Favouritism and factionalism at court made and unmade viceroys, and initiatives begun by one ministry might be abandoned or even reversed by the next. Beneath the tergiversations, however, lay a fundamental principle: in Charles' case, greed rather than fear. The king's objective, consistently held if not consistently pursued, was the mobilization of Irish resources for the aggrandizement of the monarchy. Relatively few impediments stood in the way. 'Here the king may be obeyed if he will', wrote the duke of Ormonde, the leading Anglo-Irish magnate, and lord lieutenant for much of the reign.[13] Ireland was to provide money and troops, in that order, and without the inconvenience of an Irish Parliament to rehearse grievances and tamper with subsidies. After 1666 the Parliament in Dublin ceased to be called. Charles tried farming the Irish revenues, but eventually fell back on the usual method of direct management of the hereditary customs duties. As in England, a trading boom in the 1670s multiplied the yield, and enabled the Irish treasury to remit surpluses to London.[14] Some contemporary wisdom attributed this commercial success

[10] Nicholas Canny, *The Upstart Earl: A Study of the Social and Mental World of Richard Boyle, First Earl of Cork, 1566–1643* (Cambridge, 1982); Raymond Gillespie, *Colonial Ulster: The Settlement of East Ulster 1600–1641* (Cork, 1985), pp. 1, 9–12, 144–5, 150–2, 204–5; Michael McCarthy Morrogh, 'The English Presence in Early Seventeenth Century Munster', in Ciaran Brady and Raymond Gillespie (eds.), *Natives and Newcomers: Essays on the Making of Irish Colonial Society* (Dublin, 1986), pp. 188–90.

[11] *New Hist.*, chs. XIV, XVII; T. C. Barnard, 'Planters and Policies in Cromwellian Ireland', *Past and Present*, no. 61 (1973), pp. 31–69.

[12] *New Hist.*, ch. XVII; J. C. Beckett, 'The Irish Viceroyalty in the Restoration Period', *Transactions of the Royal Historical Society*, 5th ser., 20 (1970), pp. 53–72; James I. McGuire, 'Why Was Ormond Dismissed in 1669?' *Irish Historical Studies*, 17 (1972–3), pp. 295–312; Liam Irwin, 'The Suppression of the Irish Presidency System', ibid., 22 (1980–1), pp. 21–32; R. Hutton, 'The Making of the Secret Treaty of Dover, 1668–1670', *Historical Journal*, 29 (1986), pp. 308–10.

[13] Thomas Carte, *The Life of James, Duke of Ormonde ...* (2nd edn, 6 vols., Oxford, 1851), V, pp. 162–3.

[14] On Irish finance in the Restoration period, see T. J. Kiernan, *History of the Financial Administration of Ireland to 1817* (London, 1930), ch. IV; and Sean Egan, 'Finance and the Government of Ireland, 1660–85', Trinity College, Dublin, PhD thesis (1983). On the Irish army, see J. C. Beckett, 'The Irish Armed Forces, 1660–1685', in John Bossy and Peter Jupp (eds.), *Essays Presented to Michael Roberts ...* (Belfast, 1976), pp. 41–53; and K. P. Ferguson, 'The Army in Ireland from the Restoration to the Act of Union', Trinity College, Dublin, PhD thesis (1981).

in part to the enterprise of Catholic and dissenting merchants, which confirmed the king's personal preference for a more relaxed regime in Ireland, against the wishes of determined Anglicans on both sides of the Irish Sea.[15] Under Charles Irish Catholic interests made moderate gains; not so much at the Restoration itself, when Protestant land claims were largely upheld, but subsequently. In particular the commercial and professional classes, the 'townsmen' and 'gownsmen' (lawyers), prospered and entered the land market. Briefly the furore over the Popish Plot obliged government to return to the ways of persecution, but the law was not imposed in its full rigour.[16] Protestant Dissent also reinforced itself, especially the 'Scotch colony' in Ulster, which by immigration in the 1650s and 60s recovered the ground lost by the failure of the Jacobean plantation.[17] Dissenters too suffered oppression during the loyalist reaction of 1681–5, though this was not inspired by government so much as by the local representatives of the Anglican ascendancy. Indeed, the Crown stood to gain from the Dissenters' reliance on royal protection, a fact recognized in Charles' grant to the Presbyterian ministers of a pension of £1,200 a year, the *regium donum*.[18]

James II's approach to questions of Irish policy was determined by much the same considerations as his brother's had been, with one important and obvious exception, that the new king was an avowed Catholic. Like his brother, James appreciated the contribution the Irish treasury and army could make towards strengthening the monarchy. It would, of course, have been surprising if his own experiences as the king's commissioner in Scotland had not opened his eyes to the advantages to be obtained for the Crown by effective management of the subordinate kingdoms. We may therefore interpret his first move in Ireland, the replacement as viceroy of the ageing and now less than dynamic Ormonde by an English Tory, the earl of Clarendon, as an effort to tighten up the administration in Dublin, and perhaps also to integrate it more effectively with government departments at home, where Clarendon's brother Lord Rochester (originally intended by King Charles for the viceroyalty himself) was proving

[15] E.g. *HMC Ormonde*, new ser., VII, 121, 464. For a local example of the association of reviving prosperity with the return of Catholic merchants, see James Hardiman, *The History of the Town and County of... Galway* (Dublin, 1820), pp. 149–51.

[16] Benignus Millett, 'Survival and Reorganization, 1650–95', in P. J. Corish (ed.), *A History of Irish Catholicism* (26 fascicles, Dublin, 1967–), III, ch. 7; P. J. Corish, *The Catholic Community in the Seventeenth and Eighteenth Centuries* (Dublin, 1981), pp. 52–72; John Hanley (ed.), *The Letters of Saint Oliver Plunkett 1625–1681 ...* (Dublin, 1979), pp. 529–33.

[17] L. M. Cullen, 'Population Trends in Seventeenth-Century Ireland', *Economic and Social Review*, 6 (1975), pp. 149–65; W. Macafee and V. Morgan, 'Population in Ulster, 1660–1760', in *Plantation to Partition: Essays in Ulster History in Honour of J. L. McCracken* (Belfast, 1981), pp. 46–63; Philip S. Robinson, *The Plantation of Ulster: British Settlement in an Irish Landscape, 1600–1670* (Dublin, 1984), esp. ch. 4.

[18] J. S. Reid, *History of the Presbyterian Church in Ireland*, ed. W. D. Killen (3 vols., Belfast, 1867), II, pp. 306–42; Daniel Szechi and David Hayton, 'John Bull's Other Kingdoms: The English Government of Scotland and Ireland', in Clyve Jones (ed.), *Britain in the First Age of Party 1680–1750: Essays Presented to Geoffrey Holmes* (London, 1987), pp. 262–3.

a highly competent treasury minister. But Clarendon was not only a staunch 'King's man'; he was an Englishman and a staunch Anglican, and his appointment thus carried more than one message. What the Irish Catholics were meant to read into it was made clear by James, who, according to Clarendon, declared his intention to

> support the English interest ... which was one reason of his sending me ... that the world might see he would do so; that though he would have the Irish see, that they had a king of their own religion, and that they should enjoy all the freedom thereof; yet he would have them see too, that he looked upon them as a conquered people; and that he would support the settlements inviolably, but I must endeavour to find out some way to help him to relieve some of the Irish, who had deserved well of him.[19]

Here is stated the basic dilemma on which the king's Irish policy was impaled. On the one hand, James was an English monarch who wished above all to exploit Ireland to reinforce his position at home; on the other, his own religious affiliation and the exceptional value he placed on personal fealty disposed him to do all he could to relieve his Irish Catholic subjects of their disabilities and to reward his best friends. The most thoughtful modern analysis of James's handling of Irish affairs, by Dr Miller, presents the king as faced with a choice between an 'English' and an 'Irish' policy; either the maintenance of Protestant supremacy in Ireland and the constitutional and economic subordination of Ireland to England, or the advancement of the Catholic interest, which would require as a corollary some weakening of the Anglo-Irish political nexus and a recognition of the separate needs of Irish agriculture and trade.[20] This is perhaps unduly reductionist. What confronted James was not so much a choice between policies as a conflict between mutually irreconcilable objectives. Some of his aims might be put at risk by radical change, for example the commercial prosperity upon which a full Irish treasury depended. He was also wary of inflaming English public opinion, which regarded the native Irish Catholics as savages. Perhaps above all he cherished his own authority too much to indulge the Irish administration or Parliament in any greater independence. Like his father and brother James was a centralizer. He had not come to terms with all the potential strategies for governing a multiple kingdom to the best advantage of the monarch, but persisted in identifying his own interests with those of England. At the same time he knew that the Irish Catholics would give him well-nigh unconditional loyalty – 'His Majesty had reason to place greater confi-

[19] *The Correspondence of Henry Hyde, Earl of Clarendon, and of His Brother Laurence Hyde, Earl of Rochester with the Diary of Lord Clarendon from 1687 to 1690* (2 vols., London, 1828), II, p. 25.

[20] John Miller, 'The Earl of Tyrconnel and James II's Irish Policy, 1685–1688', *Historical Journal*, 20 (1977), pp. 808–10. See also idem, *James II: A Study in Kingship* (Hove, 1978), pp. 216–18.

dence in their fidelity and adherence to him, as having the greatest interest in his support';[21] recognized their numerical strength and that they offered military recruits in abundance; and realized too that Catholic emancipation in England could scarcely exist alongside repression in Ireland, especially when the Irish Protestants were, in his eyes, so much more susceptible to 'republicanism' than their English counterparts.

Between 1686 and 1688 James was by stages persuaded to promote the cause of the Irish Catholics to a degree beyond anything he attempted in England, granting not only freedom of worship and the right to hold office but a predominance in national and local government, so that by November 1688 Catholics controlled the administration in Dublin, the Irish judiciary, army, militia, commissions of the peace, and borough corporations. Clearly the king had come to believe that the benefits of entrusting power to ultra-loyalists outweighed the various dangers. As time went by he became in general less mindful of English opinion, and less fearful of the impact of his policies on trade. But he was not allowed to forget these considerations altogether. His political strategies in England, whether they involved High Church Anglicans or nonconformists, always necessitated showing at least some concern for the fate of Protestants in Ireland, while his courtiers were never slow to remind him of the threat to his own revenues implicit in any extreme measures. James repeatedly insisted on fair treatment for his Irish Protestant subjects, ordering that no one be deprived of office merely because of religion, and that the Ulster Presbyterians not be disarmed (which reflected his lingering belief in the possibility of creating an anti-establishment alliance of Catholics and Dissenters), and prevaricating over what to do about the Restoration land settlement. Significantly, he was at his sharpest in demanding from the Irish the proper enforcement of the Navigation Acts.[22] The Catholic counter-revolution in Ireland was less his own work than that of his Irish Lord Deputy, Richard Talbot, earl of Tyrconnel. Dr Miller has shown how Tyrconnel achieved an ascendancy over James, first remodelling the Irish army as a kind of special adviser, then intriguing against Clarendon to obtain the deputyship, and finally convincing the king in a personal interview to endorse his restructuring of the Irish administration. Throughout it would seem that Tyrconnel, who for all his propensity to bluster could be 'a cunning, dissembling courtier' when occasion demanded, was able to play upon James' religious bigotry and rather simplistic views of human nature to undermine the warnings of the king's English advisers.[23]

Given that James' Irish policies came increasingly to originate in Ireland rather than at court, it follows that they can only be properly understood if some

[21] J. S. Clarke, *The Life of James the Second* ... (2 vols., London, 1816), II, pp. 59–60.
[22] Miller, 'Tyrconnel and James II's Irish Policy', pp. 808–9.
[23] Ibid., pp. 805–16.

endeavour is made to trace the political configurations of the Irish Catholic community. This, however, is no easy task. Source materials are scarce, especially for the viewpoint of the 'Old Irish', and those that do survive, for example the Gaelic poetry upon which much critical attention has been lavished, present problems of interpretation. Another difficulty is that a great deal of the contemporary discussion of political differences between Catholics was retrospective, and influenced by developments during and after the Revolutionary war. The conduct of the war, and more particularly the question of when to sue for peace, gave rise to conflict between militants and moderates, between those determined to fight to the end and those anxious to secure what they could from a peace treaty. Once the war was over the bitterness of defeat and exile wrought upon members of the 'war party' until they believed their cause had been betrayed, and that all along there had been a fundamental opposition between themselves and the moderates, the 'peace party', some of whom had indeed succeeded in retaining their lands, if not their political influence, under the ensuing settlement. Diehards interpreted moderation as the vested interest of 'new purchasers', those *arriviste* merchants and professional men who had bought lands since the Restoration. Often they represented the divisions between Catholics in racial terms, as another manifestation of the latent hostility of Old English for Old Irish, such as had bedevilled the Catholic confederacy in the 1640s. Colonel Charles O'Kelly ascribed the moderates' hunger for peace at any cost to the 'inveterate hatred' nurtured by the Old English 'to the old Irish race, lest they might be restored by the recovery of Ireland to their ancient grandeur'. Another soldier of Old Irish descent, Hugh 'Balldearg' O'Donnell, offered an even more traditional interpretation, not only distinguishing between an Old English and an Old Irish political interest, but identifying the latter with his own native province of Ulster, which he saw leading the way again as it had done in 1641.[24] Such views were not necessarily representative of the Old Irish at large: both these men hailed from the north-west of the country, where Old English families had always been scarce, and both had spent their formative years in foreign service and were somewhat out of touch with more recent developments in Irish society.

In fact the divergence in outlook between Old English and Old Irish, while it undoubtedly continued to exist, was far less pronounced than O'Kelly or O'Donnell would have had their readers believe, certainly before the Revolution and in the early stages of the war, while the Jacobites were on top. There was

[24] Charles O'Kelly, *Macariae Excidium, or the Destruction of Cyprus*, ... ed. J. C. O'Callaghan (Irish Archaeological Society, Dublin, 1850), p. 104; John T. Gilbert (ed.), *A Jacobite Narrative of the War in Ireland, 1688–1691* ... (Dublin, 1892), pp. 267–72. Biographical notices of both O'Kelly and O'Donnell may be found in J. D.'Alton, *Illustrations ... of King James's Irish Army List 1689* (Dublin, 1855), pp. 118, 549–50. For a discussion of the best known statement of post-war Old English attitudes, see Patrick Kelly, '"A Light to the Blind": The Voice of the Dispossessed Elite in the Generation after the Defeat at Limerick', *Irish Historical Studies*, 24 (1984–5), pp. 431–62.

tension, and an occasional flash of animosity, as when two of Tyrconnel's henchmen, Old English noblemen, were heard disparaging the 'Os' and 'Macs' they hoped to exclude from the remodelled Irish army.[25] But since the leading lights in the war party were Old English officers like Patrick Sarsfield, it must be clear that any simple equation of the two main political tendencies, as they emerged during the war, with racial groupings, will not work. Indeed, the racial distinctions themselves might not always have had much meaning. Gaelic poets, especially those from Munster like Daibhi O'Bruadair, with Old English patrons, may sometimes have labelled the Old English aristocracy as 'foreign protectors' of the Irish but more often blurred racial and national differences in praising the champions of the Catholic cause.[26] And in practice the Old Irish and Old English landed classes shared much of the same culture and many of the same attitudes. The Jacobite general Justin MacCarthy, Old Irish by race, had similar cosmopolitan experience as a soldier of fortune, and similar courtly connections in England, as the Old English Tyrconnel.[27] Equal if not greater importance might have attached to other kinds of divisions between Catholics: regional and factional rivalries, for instance; antagonism between 'old proprietors' who had lost their lands under Cromwell and the 'new purchasers'; between the landed and landless, squires and merchants, or laity and clergy. Many of these divisions would have cut across each other. Not the least significant was the contrast between those who had lived away from Ireland and those who had stayed at home. Residence abroad might well have encouraged a more uncompromising political stance, through exposure to the influence of Counter-Reformation Catholicism on the continent, or to discrimination and persecution in England (although in some cases a prolonged spell at court might equally well have led an ambitious man like Tyrconnel to identify himself primarily with the monarchy he served rather than with his native country). Potentially, therefore, the political 'structure' of Catholic Ireland was very complex, and as the Catholic interest came under increasing strain during the war the various cracks began to appear.

This being said, it must be emphasized that, as far as our sources indicate, the situation in 1688–9 was still relatively simple. There were a few Irish Catholics

[25] HMC *Stuart*, VI, 6.

[26] J. C. MacErlean (ed.), *The Poems of David O Bruadair* (3 parts, Irish Texts Society, XI, XIII, XVIII, London, 1910, 1913,1917), pt 3, pp. 135, 137, 139, 153. See also P. S. Dineen and T. O'Donoghue (eds), *The Poems of Egan O'Rahilly* (2nd edn, Irish Texts Society, III, London, 1911), pp. 11, 51, 57, 151. On this general point, see T. J. Dunne, 'The Gaelic Response to Conquest and Colonization: The Evidence of the Poetry', *Studia Hibernica*, 20 (1980), pp. 22–3; and Nicholas Canny, 'The Formation of the Irish Mind: Religion, Politics and Gaelic Irish Literature, 1580–1750', in C. H. E. Philpin (ed.), *Nationalism and Popular Protest in Ireland* (Cambridge, 1987), pp. 65–7.

[27] J. A. Murphy, *Justin MacCarthy, Lord Mountcashel* ... (Cork, 1959), pp. 4–11; Philip W. Sergeant, *Little Jennings and Fighting Dick Talbot* (2 vols., London, 1913), I, pp. 17–315; Sir Charles Petrie, *The Great Tyrconnel: A Chapter in Anglo-Irish Relations* (Cork, 1972), chs. III–VI.

who told the king that they were unhappy at Tyrconnel's advancement, and warned James of the perils of extremism. On the other side we hear of some, probably priests, who wanted James and his deputy to move faster, especially on the breaking of land settlement and the freeing of Irish trade from English-imposed restrictions.[28] But on the whole there was unanimity and enthusiasm for Tyrconnel's reforms. Catholics were united by religious loyalty, and by gratitude at the chance to turn the tables on their oppressors. The evidence of the poetry suggests that it was the disarming of the Protestants and the recruitment of Catholic troops that gave the greatest satisfaction. The hue and cry after Catholic traitors at the time of the Popish Plot, and the execution of some scapegoats, had induced in Irish Catholics a genuine fear for their lives if left at the mercy of local Protestants. They now rejoiced at the opportunity to protect themselves and perhaps wreak some vengeance of their own.[29]

The Revolution and King James' flight from England changed this picture in several important ways. For one thing James now 'wholly depended' on his Irish Catholic supporters, as he himself was to put it.[30] In fact he also relied to a large extent on French help to regain his throne in England, but the Irish Catholics represented his largest popular following. By 1689 Tyrconnel had established a firm grip on Dublin and on most of the country, except for the districts controlled by the voluntary associations of Protestants in Ulster and north Connaught. When, under French pressure, James agreed to sail for Ireland to take personal charge of affairs there, he was to some extent putting himself into the hands of his Irish adherents. At this stage the French had sent only a small force, almost entirely officers.[31] From his port of disembarkation James enjoyed a majestic progress to Dublin, but the hard realities of his position were soon apparent. His first thought, in which he was encouraged by English and Scots advisers, was to cross quickly to Scotland, to link up with Viscount Dundee. The strategic disadvantages of becoming bogged down in Ireland were obvious. His main concern was to regain the English Crown, and even if he defeated William on Irish soil he would still have had to mount another invasion. But the French ambassador d'Avaux, whose voice carried the weight of a paymaster's, argued successfully that James should first consolidate his position in Ireland and mop up resistance in the north, where the important port of Londonderry held out against Jacobite siege.[32] From the French point of view, a lengthy

[28] Clarke, *Life of James the Second*, II, p. 61; *Correspondence of Henry Hyde*, II, p. 67; William King, *The State of the Protestants of Ireland under the Late King James's government* ... (London, 1691), pp. 360–73.

[29] For example, MacErlean (ed.), *Poems of O Bruadair*, pt. 3, pp. 117–21, 127–41.

[30] Clarke, *Life of James the Second*, II, pp. 360–1. For general accounts of James' travails in Ireland, see Simms, *Jacobite Ireland*, chs. IV–VIII; and Miller, *James II*, ch. 15.

[31] Simms, *Jacobite Ireland*, pp. 58–62.

[32] James Hogan (ed.), *Négociations de M. Le Comte d'Avaux en Irlande 1689–90* (Dublin, 1934), pp. 59–63.

stay in Ireland, whatever the ultimate outcome for James, was preferable to a swift defeat in the Highlands. The longer he could occupy William's attention, away from the main theatres of war, the better for them. Next it was the Irish who raised difficulties. With James' arrival among them, their political demands had escalated. Attention was focused on the Restoration land settlement, and despite some differences of interest between 'old proprietors' and 'new purchasers', the current of opinion in the Catholic community ran strongly for repeal. Besides its practical significance, in having altered the balance of economic and political power between Catholic and Protestant, the land settlement had taken on a figurative importance, as a symbol of the degradation of Catholics at the hands of the Cromwellians. For James, conscious of the potential propaganda value such a step might have for William, this turn of the screw of Irish Catholic political extremism seemed another obstacle in the way of recovery of his English Crown.

The increasing stridency of Catholic opinion found expression in the Parliament which James' financial necessities obliged him to call in Dublin in May 1689. Unlike the Irish Parliaments of the 1660s, which the Protestants had dominated, this was an assembly with an overwhelming Catholic majority. The election of Catholics to the Commons had been facilitated by the flight of so many Protestant gentlemen to England in 1688; it was further assured by the preparations Tyrconnel had been making ever since 1687 to pack Parliament, by remodelling borough charters, bringing the corporations under closer royal control and purging their membership.[33] It was also alleged by his opponents that the deputy had interfered directly with the elections in 1689, by enclosing recommendations of his own with the election writs. The result was a House of Commons in which as few as a dozen of the 230 MPs were Protestants. (Counties Donegal, Fermanagh, and Londonderry had made no returns, and neither had a number of Ulster boroughs.) The Lords too enjoyed a substantial Catholic, and Old English, majority. James caused resentment among his supporters, however, in summoning the Church of Ireland bishops as spiritual lords. His principal motive was probably the encouragement of sympathetic Protestant opinion in Britain, the Jacobite, Nonjuring tendency in England and the Episcopalians in Scotland. To this end he had sought to procure loyal addresses from the Anglican clergy in Dublin and from Trinity College. He would also have been aware of the usefulness of the Protestant episcopate as a counter-balance to 'Irish' interests in the upper House, should Ireland's constitutional and economic subordination be brought into question. In the event only four bishops

[33] Simms, *Jacobite Ireland*, pp. 35–6; idem, 'The Jacobite Parliament of 1689', in D. W. Hayton and Gerard O'Brien (eds.), *War and Politics in Ireland, 1649–1730* (London, 1986), pp. 66–7. The remodelled corporations are detailed in Walter Harris, *The History of the Life and Reign of William-Henry, Prince of ... Orange, King of England ...* (Dublin, 1749), Appendix, pp. iv–xvi.

attended, headed by Dopping of Meath, but even this handful of votes was of some help to James' purposes.[34]

The history of the Jacobite Parliament is only partly known. The main sources, Williamite pamphlets, are neither full nor unbiased. We have details of the composition of the Parliament, and of the measures passed, but otherwise comparatively little. The degree to which there was any management by James' ministers, for example, remains obscure. Certainly the presence of a large number of army and civilian officers, perhaps augmented by those owing their election to the lord deputy's nomination, would have provided the nucleus for a formidable court party. It may be, however, that, as Professor Jones observes in his essay, James himself did not care to buy parliament-men, and considered it more honourable to rely on disinterested loyalty.[35] Matters may have been complicated by factionalism: Tyrconnel, for one, enjoyed a massive personal following of kinsmen and dependants, and the same may have been true of other magnates and prominent figures like Justin MacCarthy, ennobled during the Parliament as Lord Mountcashell. Such men would not necessarily share the views of the king or his English and Scottish councillors. Some might take a stronger line on religious issues (over which Tyrconnel was a notorious bigot) or on the land question, as well as having their own concerns to promote. Whatever the reasons, it appears that James could count less on the Commons than on the Lords, and that he used the upper House as a long-stop to frustrate unacceptable proposals emanating from below. The king's travails can be observed through d'Avaux's correspondence.[36] The stiffest battle was over the repeal of the land settlement. In this James had a personal stake, having been given a vast estate by his brother out of lands once held by the regicides. He received support from some 'new purchasers' and perhaps from Tyrconnel and his connection, since the deputy had been a 'new purchaser' himself. In the Lords the few Protestant temporal peers and the bishops spoke against repeal. But after a delaying action James was at last forced to accede to a modified version of the repeal bill put forward by the Commons. Under this Act the 'new purchasers' and the king himself received compensation, but the Protestants, including those who had stayed loyal to James, were uniformly losers. A subsequent Act of Attainder completed the means for destroying the Protestant interest by outlawing those who had fled to England or joined the northern associations. James' response was a fit of anger so strong as to make his nose bleed. He was affronted almost as much by the Declaratory Act, which weakened the Irish Parliament's

[34] Simms, 'Jacobite Parliament', pp. 67–9; O'Kelly, *Macariae Excidium*, pp. 34–6; [King], *State of the Protestants*, pp. 150–2; [Charles Leslie], *An Answer to a Book Intituled, The State of the Protestants in Ireland under the Late King James's Government* ... (London, 1692), pp. 111–12; BL, Stowe MS 746, fo. 111.

[35] See above, p. 50.

[36] Hogan (ed.), *Négociations*, pp. 185, 190–4, 199, 215–18, 225–6, 237, 242, 255, 340–2.

dependence on the English and denied that English legislation could apply to Ireland. Again he was obliged to acquiesce. However, he refused consent to the repeal of Poynings' Law, which would have diminished his own control over Irish parliamentary procedure, and defeated the schemes of the French to place themselves in the same kind of favoured position *vis-à-vis* the Irish economy that England had hitherto enjoyed. D'Avaux wrote of the king: 'he has a heart too English to take any step that could vex the English'. Even in the settlement of religion, James showed some concern for English opinion. The Act for Liberty of Conscience did not, as the Commons had hoped it would, repeal the Elizabethan Act of Uniformity. James provided freedom of worship for Catholics, and alleviated their grievance over tithes, but to the disappointment of the clergy and many laymen he did not substitute a Catholic religious establishment for a Protestant one.[37]

Despite James' pious optimism, and sometimes strenuous political efforts, he had not succeeded in removing the fear and distress felt by his Protestant subjects in Ireland at the course of events under Catholic rule; nor, it goes without saying, had he put at ease the profoundly disturbed feelings of the generality of Protestants in England. Williamite propaganda, some of it officially inspired, reported atrocities committed against Protestants by Irish and French troops: arbitrary imprisonment and execution, occasionally at James' personal behest.[38] Unofficial rumours reaching England were even wilder.[39] Whatever answers or excuses English Jacobites might have made were effectually scuppered by the report of the passage of the acts for repeal of the land settlement and for attainting rebels. For the exiled Irish Protestants too this news marked a point of no return. Convinced that their own estates were either seized by the Jacobites or laid waste, and their co-religionists threatened with massacre, they now busied themselves in seeking to persuade King William to take personal charge of the Irish war. The situation for those Protestants remaining in Ireland was rather more complicated. In the north and north-west were the associations, staunchly resisting King James. Elsewhere Protestant landowners isolated in areas controlled by the Jacobites and looking for protection from the depredations of lawless

[37] Simms, 'Jacobite Parliament', pp. 69–81; idem, *Jacobite Ireland*, pp. 77–94; Clarke, *Life of James the Second*, II, p. 353; O'Kelly, *Macariae Excidium*, pp. 34–6.

[38] See, for example, *An Account of a Late, Horrid and Bloody Massacre in Ireland, of Several Thousands of Protestants* ... (London, 1688); *A Relation of the Bloody Massacre in Ireland, Acted by the Instigation of the Jesuits, Priests and Friars* ... (London, 1689); *A Short View of the Methods Made Use of in Ireland for the Subversion and Destruction of the Protestant Religion and Interest* ... (London, 1689); *A True Discovery of Lord Tyrconnel's Design to Surprise and Massacre all the Protestants in Ireland* ... (London, 1689); *The Sad Estate and Condition of Ireland* ... (London, 1689); and *A True Narrative of the Murders, Cruelties and Oppressions Perpetrated on the Protestants in Ireland by the Late King James's Agents* ... (London, 1690).

[39] See, for example, Dr Williams' Library, Bloomsbury, London, Morrice MS R (Roger Morrice's ent'ring book), pp. 19–20, 147; Narcissus Luttrell, *A Brief Historical Relation of State Affairs from September 1678 to April 1714* (6 vols., Oxford, 1857), I, p. 609; H.M.C., *Kenyon MSS*., p. 224.

elements on the Catholic side were trying to be inconspicuous, or neutral, or both.[40] A small minority of Protestants actively supported the Jacobite cause: Nonjuring bishops and clergy, complaisant office holders, Anglican squires in the high-flying cavalier tradition, and others who were recent converts from popery, perhaps, and who retained not only many Catholic connections but their Old English or Old Irish political attitudes.[41] James had hoped to win over the Protestant Dissenters, and at the beginning of his reign had cultivated the earl of Granard as an intermediary between his government and the Ulster Presbyterians. Dissenters had benefited from his policy of toleration, and seem to have been included in numbers in the remodelled borough corporations. With the possible exception of the Quakers, this strategy failed to win a substantial body of support, for on the whole Dissenters were even more virulently anti-papist than Anglicans, but it did ensure that individual nonconformists stayed loyal to James for a time.[42] What happened in the Irish Parliament of 1689 killed that loyalty. A further polarization occurred in Irish politics, confirming the associating Protestants in their determination to resist, and causing many 'collaborators' (if one may use such a pejorative term) to rethink their position and to cross over to the Williamite side.[43]

The events of 1688–9 exercised a critical influence over what can be seen as a reformulation of Irish Protestant political ideology in the Revolution period. In the first place there was an obvious hardening of approach towards the Catholics. The ease with which Tyrconnel had created a Catholic army and bureaucracy; the speed with which the Catholic clergy, secular and regular, had re-established themselves; the size of the Catholic professional and commercial classes that swarmed to take advantage of the lifting of restrictions: all testified to what David Dickson has called the 'remarkable regenerative potency' of Catholic Ireland, and this despite a century or more of confiscation and plantation.[44] On its own such a shock would probably have been enough to account for the severity of the penal code which was to be the post-Revolution Protestant Ascendancy's answer to the Catholic question, given that there had already been calls for the tightening of legislation against popish priests and to restrict the

[40] Trinity College, Dublin, MS 3821/298 (Crosbie MSS); Public Record Office of Northern Ireland, T2812/4/7, 9, 15 (O'Hara MSS), Henry Dillon to Kean O'Hara, 24 Sept. 1690, Connor O'Donnell to same, 10 Oct. 1690, Lord Galmoy to same, [10] Jan. 1690–1; J. F. Ainsworth (ed.), *The Inchiquin Manuscripts* (Irish Manuscripts Commission, Dublin, 1961), pp. vii, 16–33, 39–40, 628–9.

[41] [Leslie], *An Answer*, pp. 111–12; J. I. McGuire, "The Church of Ireland and the 'Glorious Revolution' of 1688", in Art Cosgrove and Donal Macartney (eds.), *Studies in Irish History Presented to R. Dudley Edwards* (Dublin, 1979), pp. 147–9; PRO Northern Ireland, D.638/26 (De Ros MSS), lords justices to [?Lord Sidney], n.d.

[42] Reid, *Presbyterian Church*, II, pp. 342–54; J. C. Beckett, *Protestant Dissent in Ireland 1687–1780* (London, 1948), pp. 20–6; [King], *State of the Protestants*, p. 204. For Granard, see DNB and J. Forbes, *Memoirs of the Earls of Granard*, ed. Earl of Granard (London, 1868), esp. pp. 72–9.

[43] Granard, for one, was to go over.

[44] Dickson, *New Foundations*, p. 42.

admission of Catholic merchants into ports.[45] But the eighteenth-century penal laws were also a conscious response to the Jacobite Parliament's attempt to extirpate the Protestant landed interest. Furthermore, despite the best efforts of James' administration in 1689–90 to preserve order and defend law-abiding Protestants, there was still some repayment of old scores at local level. Throughout the prolonged civil war, the maintenance of public order proved an insuperable problem, and the 'rapparees', rural bandits who had thrived even in the more settled conditions before 1688, enjoyed a heyday of plunder. They attacked Catholics as well as Protestants, but as they were themselves for the most part native Irish, their activities were interpreted as a systematic anti-Protestant terror.[46] This was certainly what Protestants in exile in England were persuaded to believe. Indeed, it would be true to say that in general the further away from events in Ireland a Protestant happened to be, the more credence he would give to the claims of Williamite propagandists that the horrors of 1641 were being re-enacted. Significantly, the *ad hoc* committee formed by Protestants in London to co-ordinate their activities contained many who were later to be among the most vigorous advocates of a hard-line Protestant policy.[47]

At the same time as their fear of papists was being confirmed and enhanced, Irish Protestants experienced something of a change in their attitudes towards England and the Anglo-Irish political connection. They became more self-aware and in some respects self-reliant. It would be foolish to exaggerate, but the beginnings may be detected of a sense of separateness from England and an awareness that their best interests might not always coincide with those of the English monarchy and Parliament. The betrayal of Protestantism by King James had sown the seed. But the behaviour of William and the English Parliament had also done much to foster the suspicions that the Irish Protestants felt in their dealings with the English, who after all had demonstrated in the 1660s a willingness to sacrifice the Irish economy to domestic English pressure-groups. It was not easy to elicit a response from William to pleas for succour to the Protestant cause in Ireland. He was advised by self-appointed 'experts' on Irish affairs, who appeared often to be self-interested as well.[48] Moreover, to listen to the parliamentary debates on the condition of Ireland in 1689–90 was to be regaled with stories of dilatoriness and corruption in the conduct of the war, and then to be confronted with English arrogance and selfishness of the 'let

[45] See, for example, HMC *Ormonde*, new ser., VII, 92–3.

[46] Simms, *Jacobite Ireland*, pp. 198–200; Robert H. Murray (ed.), *The Journal of John Stevens, Containing a Brief Account of the War in Ireland 1689–91* (Oxford, 1912), pp. 61–2; MacErlean (ed.), *Poems of O Bruadair*, pt. 3, pp. 169–71; [King], *State of the Protestants*, p. 91.

[47] Richard Caulfield (ed.), *Journal of the Very Rev. Rowland Davies, LL. D. Dean of Ross* ... (Camden Society, LXVIII, London, 1857), pp. 59–62.

[48] *Correspondence of Henry Hyde*, II, pp. 238–41, 265; Cambridgeshire RO, Huntingdon, ddM52/1 (Manchester MSS), Oliver St John to Francis St John, 11 Mar. 1688 [–9].

us keep England, whatever becomes of Ireland' variety.[49] Of course, William did eventually take command of the forces in Ireland, and with his victory there became the Protestant hero. Before then, in August 1689, he had sent Marshal Schomberg with over twenty regiments, including Dutch and Huguenot infantrymen, to relieve the associations in Ulster. Schomberg too achieved a reputation, albeit for no more than 'masterly inactivity' in refusing battle. But although in the long run the Irish Protestants undoubtedly owed their deliverance to William and to the crack foreign troops provided by the English tax-payer, they did not fully recognize the fact of their dependence, believing, with some justification, that the heroics of the volunteers in the north had played a crucial part in facilitating William's triumph, by retaining a foothold for him in the island. At Londonderry in 1689 King James had been defied to his face, and the garrison had endured dreadful privations before Williamite ships broke the boom across the lough and raised the siege; and at the battle of Newtownbutler Jacobite forces under Justin MacCarthy had suffered a stunning reverse, with the general himself held prisoner for a spell afterwards. To this sense of moral victory, in having through their own efforts kept some part of Ireland free from Jacobite control, must be added the prevailing dogma that the fortunes of the reformed religion were in the hands of divine providence.[50] William was God's instrument, not England's and even without English taxes and soldiers the Protestants might still count on more effectual, providential assistance.

By the winter of 1689–90, therefore, the two communities in Ireland, Protestant and Catholic, had become more deeply alienated from each other, more militant in their demands, and more sharply aware of their own separate interests. Of course, there were degrees of militancy, and future events were to demonstrate the potential for divisions among Catholics. Nor, it must be said, did either Protestant or Catholic political activists yet envisage an independent Ireland, removed from the sovereignty of the English Crown. Protestants would not be in a position to contemplate political autonomy for another century. For Catholics, allegiance to James as the rightful, anointed monarch remained the basis of their actions, even for those whose hopes of reform he had obstructed, who resented his foreign advisers or who had formed, as many indeed had, an unfavourable impression of his political and martial talents. It is just possible that, before the birth of the Prince of Wales, Tyrconnel had conceived the idea that Ireland might become a protectorate of the French monarchy in the event

[49] Anchitell Grey, *Debates of the House of Commons from the Year 1667 to the Year 1694* (10 vols., London, 1769), IX, pp. 276–80, 347–9, 355–6, 388–94, 404–6, 422–3, 447–57, 461–73, 480–90, 534–6; X, pp. 36–40, 93–4, 99–101, 128–9, 131–2.

[50] I owe this point to Dr Thomas Bartlett. For some instances, see John Vesey, *A Sermon Preach'd to the Protestants of Ireland in and about the City of London ... Octob. 23. 1689* (London, 1689), p. 8; *The Speech of the ... Bishop of Meath ... July 7, 1690*; Nicholas Brady, *A Sermon Preached ... the Thanksgiving Day for the Preservation of the King and the Reduction of Ireland, 26 Nov. 1691* (London, 1692), pp. 2, 4, 15–17, 23–4.

of James dying without a Catholic heir.[51] The evidence is slight, and in any case the contingency soon became improbable.

As for the two kings themselves, each had demonstrated in his own way a lack of interest in Ireland *per se*. James, in his dealings with the Irish even before the Revolution, had always been concerned to trim his policies so as to give as little offence as possible to his English subjects. His attitude towards the Irish Parliament in 1689 gave a clear indication that he wished to maintain the constitutional and economic subordination of the kingdom to England. Moreover, for sound strategic reasons he could scarcely wait to be out of Ireland, which he and his court regarded as no more than a sideshow, and to be invading the British mainland. His military failures in 1689 rendered the situation critical. During the following winter and spring Tyrconnel wrote time and again to James' queen, providing her with arguments to lay before the French for sending ships and money to enable a 'descent'. To fight the war on Irish soil invited disaster. William would come over with a superior force, and there would be an end of the Jacobites. The best plan would be for Tyrconnel to occupy William in Ireland while James slipped over to England. 'I leave your majesty to judge', he remarked,

> whether the king's struggling to keep this poor kingdom with so much trouble to himself and his people be worth his pains, if thereby he did not hope to be master of England in some reasonable time, which if not done this year, I fear his friends there will despair of it, and consequently secure themselves.[52]

Not surprisingly, the French preferred James where he was. What Tyrconnel was asking was too great an expenditure in resources, and they trusted neither James' judgment nor his so-called English supporters. Instead they sent 7,000 French troops, but only in exchange for the same number of Irish soldiers, under Justin MacCarthy (whom Tyrconnel, regarding him as a rival, was glad to be rid of). It is hard to think that Louis XIV believed he was getting appreciably the worse of the bargain.

William was even less interested in Ireland. His prime objective was to wage war on the continent, but he could not afford to leave James poised with a large force to attack him in the rear. After an abortive attempt to negotiate with Tyrconnel early in 1689,[53] he had hoped that Schomberg's expeditionary force would have achieved a breakthrough. Now he had to suffer the 'terrible mortification' of going to Ireland himself, and being for a whole campaign 'as

[51] Miller, 'Tyrconnel and James II's Irish Policy', p. 821.
[52] 'Letter-Book of Richard Talbot', ed. Lilian Tate, *Analecta Hibernica*, 4 (1932), p. 127.
[53] Gilbert Burnet, *History of His Own Time* (6 vols., Oxford, 1833), III, pp. 368–73. Cf. H. C. Foxcroft, *The Life and Letters of Sir George Savile, Bart., first Marquis of Halifax* (2 vols., London, 1898), II, pp. 77–9.

Derde Deel. Fol. 109.
ictorieus geregt van Koning William tegens den gewesen Koning Iacobus in Irland den 8 Iuly 1690.
ning William 2. de Hartog van Schomburg 3. Passeren op drie plaatsen door't Water tot de Middel en swemmende 4. dringen op't Vyands leger in 5. die sy op de Vlugt krygen en Slaan.

12 *The Battle of the Boyne* (1 July 1690).
The engraving shows the three separate Williamite attacks across the river. The main crossing, by the Dutch Guards, followed by the Danes, took place in the centre. Schomberg (marked '2') is in the foreground. King William (marked '1') is depicted centre left.

it were out of knowledge of the world'.[54] To ensure that he would be able to do the job quickly he took great care over his preparations, and landed near Belfast in June 1690 with about 15,000 more troops and an artillery train, outnumbering and outgunning his enemies, as Tyrconnel had predicted.

Thus it was that two kings, neither of whom was especially concerned about the ultimate destiny of Ireland, came to fight their decisive battle at the Boyne water on 12 July, New Style. William's victory was owing not a little to his own courage and superior generalship. The result of the battle opened the way to Dublin and effectively gave him control of the south-east of the country. The Jacobite army retreated westwards, beyond the River Shannon, making Limerick its headquarters. William followed, but his progress was hampered

[54] N. Japikse (ed.), *Correspondentie van Willem III en Hans Willem Bentinck, eersten Graf van Portland* (5 vols., The Hague, 1927–37), III, p. 158.

13 *The Capitulation of Waterford to Williamite Troops and William III's Raising of the First Siege of Limerick (September 1690).*

by the operations of a Jacobite flying column, skilfully led by Patrick Sarsfield, who was emerging as Catholic Ireland's best military hope. William arrived at Limerick too late in the season to reduce the city, and departed for England

14 *William III's Triumphal Entry into London after his Irish Campaign (20 September 1690).*
Note the triumphal arches. William and Mary, the king holding a sceptre, are in the open carriage marked '8'. Lord Halifax is in the carriage marked '11'.

having, as he thought, broken the back of Jacobite resistance.[55] James, meanwhile, had quickly reassessed his position and decided to cut and run, even before his army's retreat to Limerick. The reason he gave for flight was that he saw the opportunity to pass behind William and reach England, with French help of course, which as usual was not forthcoming.[56] Rather than dispatch good money after bad, the French withdrew their troops from Limerick, leaving the Irish Catholics to their own devices. Tyrconnel went with them.

Without King James' presence in Ireland the Jacobite cause lost cohesion and purpose, and divisions opened up on the Catholic side.[57] It was at this point, in the autumn and winter of 1690–1, that conflict broke out between a 'peace party', willing to accept such terms as the Williamites might offer, in lieu of

[55] Simms, *Jacobite Ireland*, pp. 155–73.
[56] Clarke, *Life of James the Second*, II, pp. 407–8. Cf. Miller, *James II*, pp. 232–3.
[57] For what follows, see Simms, *Jacobite Ireland*, pp. 185–97; and O'Kelly, *Macariae Excidium*, pp. 71–113.

the alternative of unconditional surrender, and a 'war party', which drew comfort from William's failure at Limerick, and Sarsfield's successful raids, and believed that the war could still be won, or at least that it could be prolonged until the French came to their rescue. After all, it was conceivable that William would be beaten in Europe and be forced to make concessions over Ireland as part of a general peace. Some even began to think along the lines of trying to set up a separate Irish state under French protection or suzerainty.[58] The peace party seems to have been made up of Old English peers and gentry, together with lawyers and other 'new purchasers', that is to say those who would not necessarily have suffered in a return to the status quo prior to 1685. The war party comprised younger army officers, contemptuous of the pusillanimity of the politicians, particularly of the absentee Tyrconnel, whose residual hold over the Jacobite administration they were eager to break. The Catholic bishops, not surprisingly, seem to have joined in urging continuance of the war, for they had few prospects under a Williamite regime. It was the war party who made the running. Conscious that the real power to determine strategy lay with Louis XIV, they appealed directly to the French. A deputation was sent to request the removal of Tyrconnel and the duke of Berwick, James' illegitimate son, who had been left in command of the Jacobite armies and was regarded as a puppet of the deputy. Sarsfield was the favoured replacement. At the same time, Balldearg O'Donnell, engaged in what had become almost a private war for the liberation of Gaelic Ulster, wrote to denounce the Old English and pledge himself to fight on.[59] By way of material help the French sent only a general, St Ruth, to take over from Berwick. But the arrival of the deputation had alarmed and to some extent intimidated Tyrconnel, who decided to return to Ireland himself and conciliate Sarsfield and the war party. An indication of his change of heart came when the peace party obtained from the Williamites an offer of a settlement in December 1690. Tyrconnel was still in France then, but it was presumably with his approval that Berwick complied with Sarsfield's demand and arrested the peace party leaders, including Lord Riverston, the secretary of state, and a judge, Denis Daly, who had all along been the principal spokesman of the 'new purchasers'.

The events of the 1691 campaign were to prove this success of the war party's to have been a Pyrrhic victory, for the year ended with the final capitulation of the Jacobite army. The fateful battle took place at Aughrim, in County Galway, on 12 July, Old Style, after Williamite troops had breached the line of the Shannon by forcing a crossing of the river at Athlone. In fact, Aughrim was a close-run thing, and the advantage had at first seemed to lie with the Jacobites, until

[58] Murphy, *Justin MacCarthy*, p. 37

[59] Gilbert (ed.), *A Jacobite Narrative*, pp. 267–72; J. G. Simms, 'County Donegal in the Jacobite War, 1689–91', in Hayton and O'Brien (eds.), *War and Politics*, pp. 145–6; and idem, 'Sligo in the Jacobite War, 1689–91', in ibid., pp. 177–8.

St Ruth fell, decapitated by a cannonball, whereupon the forces he had led lost direction and allowed their opponents to sweep the field. There were 7,000 Jacobite losses, and the war was over. The Williamite commander, Ginkel, proceeded to Galway, where the townsmen, already inclined towards peace, were soon brought to terms, thereby earning the contempt of the war party. The main Jacobite army was now at Limerick, like Londonderry a natural citadel. French opinion, in which Tyrconnel was happy to concur, favoured holding out for as long as possible, in order to occupy William's troops. Tyrconnel's death, and Ginkel's bold stroke in effectively cutting the city off from its hinterland and thus its supplies, paved the way for the peace treaty the Williamite administration wanted. Sarsfield, now in command, was at last brought to admit defeat.

A negotiated settlement had been the aim of King William, his ministers, and his general ever since the rebuff at Limerick the previous year. William's main concern was quickly to release as much as possible of his military investment in Ireland for use on the continent. For his English ministers, the problem was money. The Irish war was expensive, and the longer it dragged on the more damage would be done to an Irish economy already ravaged by the armies of both sides. Instead of remitting funds to the English Treasury, post-war Ireland appeared likely to become a drain on the English government – bankrupt, and with little prospect of raising its customs revenue to the levels of the early 1680s. William's administration in Ireland, military and civil, was equally anxious for peace, even after Aughrim. Ginkel would have preferred not to have had to fight in 1691 at all, and certainly wished for a rapid end to the war once the battle was won. By the time he reached Limerick his supplies were running low, and the campaigning season was nearly over.[60] Back in Dublin the civil government was struggling to cope with escalating rural violence, perpetrated not only by the rapparees, whose ranks had been swollen by disbanded and deserting soldiers (Williamite as well as Jacobite) but by the ill-disciplined and sectarian militia that had been mobilized to suppress them.[61] Moreover, the senior lord justice, Lord Sidney, believed that the Irish Catholics could be won over by a policy of conciliation.[62] With the backing of officials in Dublin Castle Ginkel had vainly tried in the preceding winter to secure a negotiated settlement, when he had unwittingly precipitated the downfall of the Jacobite peace party. At

[60] Simms, *Jacobite Ireland*, pp. 189–91, 248; idem, 'Williamite Peace Tactics, 1690–1', in Hayton and O'Brien (eds.), *War and Politics*, pp. 185–8, 190–6.

[61] BL MS Add. 28877, fo. 16; 30149, fos. 20, 61, 71, 73, 76, 80–1; *CSP Dom. 1691–2*, p. 56. The depredations of units of the Williamite army were also a cause of much distress. See, for example, the complaints of the inhabitants of Youghal, County Cork, that they had been robbed by the Danish troops stationed in the town: Richard Caulfield (ed.), *The Council Book of the Corporation of Youghal* ... (Guildford, 1878), p. 387; BL MS Add. 38847, fo. 274.

[62] PRO Northern Ireland, D.638–14–49, Lord Sidney to Lord Coningsby, 4 June 1692. See also Simms, 'Williamite Peace Tactics', p. 196.

that time, besides the hostility of Sarsfield and the war party to such proposals, Ginkel was hamstrung by the limited nature of the terms he could offer. William himself was not disposed to liberality in granting pardons or guarantees about lands; he wished to have something with which to reward his courtiers, and the estates of Irish rebels were the most obvious and cheapest gift. There were political considerations as well: the English Parliament coveted Irish land, to compensate 'the public' for the heavy expenditure on the war, while opposition MPs at Westminster scented, in the possibility of generous peace terms to the Catholics, a highly promising issue. For the king, these considerations did not extend to a denial of Catholics' civil rights. William seems to have been prepared to allow full religious toleration in Ireland, partly out of principle, and partly for the traditional reason (reinforced by his own experience as ruler of the principality of Orange) that such a policy would give him a broader base of support in Ireland and encourage economic development there.[63] To some degree, the eventual peace conditions reflected royal preferences. Freedom of worship, but only as it had obtained in Charles II's reign, was guaranteed to all Catholics; indemnity and property rights were permitted to a limited number, the inhabitants of Galway and Limerick, and those in the countryside still under the protection of the Jacobite army, provided that they remained in Ireland and swore allegiance to William. The alternative, transport to France to fight for King Louis, was in fact preferred by 12,000 out of the 15,000 men in arms under Sarsfield, doubtless fearing reprisals if they stayed. They duly left Ireland with their general, in what has come to be known as the flight of the 'wild geese'.[64]

The terms of the Treaty of Limerick and the relative speed with which the conflict in Ireland had been ended were satisfactory to William, although he may have regretted the loss of so many proven soldiers to the armies of his enemy. However, the treaty was much less acceptable to Irish Protestants, especially the more radical elements in Ulster and among the exiles returning from England. Their disgust at what they considered unnecessary leniency towards the Catholics was compounded by suspicion of William's Irish ministers, who were widely attacked for corruption, mismanagement, and for favouring Catholics and those Protestants who had 'collaborated' with the Jacobite regime. 'The Irish flatter so well', observed one disgruntled Protestant, 'that they will still be courtiers. I hear the Castle is almost as crowded now with them as in Tyrconnel's time.'[65] This was the height of alarmist exaggeration, but in

[63] I am greatly obliged to Mr G. C. Gibbs for enlightenment on this point.

[64] Simms, *Jacobite Ireland*, pp. 254–60; idem, 'The Treaty of Limerick', in Hayton and O'Brien (eds.), *War and Politics*, pp. 203–24; *New Hist.*, pp. 506–7.

[65] Lord Macaulay, *The History of England from the Accession of James the Second*, ed. C. H. Firth (6 vols., London, 1913–15), V, pp. 2309–12; PRO Northern Ireland, D.638–6–8, Lord Ranelagh to Coningsby, 27 Oct. 1690; D.638–12–65, Ginkel to same, 22 Dec. 1691; D.638–14–34, 38, 43, Sidney to same, 8, 19 Mar., 4 Apr. 1692; BL MS Add. 28876, fos. 251–2; Trinity College, Dublin, MS 20008a/190 (Lyons MSS), Bishop King to James Bonnell, 4 Dec. 1691.

the political atmosphere of 1691–2 it was readily believed. Every blunder committed by government, every bribe taken, was interpreted as part of a sinister campaign to undermine the Protestant interest. The result was that when William's financial requirements, and desire to establish his regime on a basis of unquestionable constitutional legality, led him to call an Irish Parliament of his own in 1692, with Sidney as his lord lieutenant, the House of Commons in particular proved quite unmanageable. Such difficulties were not unexpected. The then lords justices had warned William as early as September 1690 to take care to hold a parliament while towns were still overawed by military garrisons and could be bullied into electing army officers. In their view, the Irish Protestants could not be relied on.[66] By the time the king got round to issuing writs, planter interests had resumed sway in the constituencies, so much so that in the 1692 general election some officials found it hard to obtain a seat. The Parliament itself lasted only four weeks, delaying the subsidy bills and pursuing enquiries into maladministration, with even the threat of impeachment. It was dissolved without granting money, and William ruled without an Irish Parliament, and in financial straits, for three years.[67] Meanwhile the Irish opposition took its grievances to England, unsuccessfully bringing impeachment proceedings at Westminster against two former lords justices, Lord Coningsby and Lord Chancellor Sir Charles Porter.

The resolution of this crisis came with the lord deputyship of an English Whig, Lord Capel, in 1695–6. Capel's party naturally sympathized with the fears and prejudices of militant Protestants in Ireland, and he himself established close relations with the leaders of the opposition in the 1692 Parliament, some of whom were taken into office by him and transformed into managers for the court party. In return for the vote of 'additional duties' needed to restore the Irish Treasury to solvency and pay for the large standing army kept in Ireland as a strategic reserve, these new 'undertakers' expected not only a share in the distribution of places and pensions, but a voice in government policy, something that in the circumstances of the 1690s they could hardly be denied. Using their privileged access to government to buttress what was already a position of considerable strength in the Irish House of Commons, they began to chip away at the Catholic civil rights the Treaty of Limerick had supposedly guaranteed, procuring the passage in 1695 of bills to prohibit the sending of children abroad to be educated, and for the disarming of Catholics. Their influence over the Castle administration did not expire with Capel in 1696, and in the following year came the most serious anti-popery act thus far, for the banishment of

[66] Nottingham University Library, Portland (Bentinck) MSS, PwA 299a, Sidney and Coningsby to Lord Portland, 27 Sept. 1690.

[67] James I. McGuire, 'The Irish Parliament of 1692', in Thomas Bartlett and D. W. Hayton (eds.), *Penal Era and Golden Age: Essays in Irish History, 1690–1800* (Belfast, 1979), pp. 1–31.

Catholic bishops and regulars.[68] Such infringements of the Limerick articles were made possible by the fact that the Irish Parliament had never been called upon to give formal approval to the treaty. English ministers now decided to press for ratification, primarily in order to settle the legality of the forfeitures of estates they themselves had received, although the king, under pressure from his ally the Emperor Leopold to make good his promises of toleration for the Irish Catholics, may have hoped to prevent the passage of any further penal laws. What happened was quite the reverse. Irish MPs grasped the chance to amend the articles of Limerick to suit their purposes: the clause promising freedom of worship was omitted entirely, and pardon and property rights were confined to Catholics in arms at the time of the surrender of Galway and Limerick. Those under the protection of the Jacobite armies were excluded, which opened the way to further outlawries and forfeitures.[69] In the long run the more militant of Irish Protestants, abetted by Whig interests in the English administration, had achieved the kind of settlement they wanted, rather than the more conciliatory terms William himself would have preferred. The Catholics had every right to feel cheated.

The outcome of the Williamite Revolution in Ireland was the destruction of the Irish Catholics as a political force for over a century. Another round of confiscations had reduced the extent of Catholic landownership in Ireland to a mere 14 per cent, and completed the work of the Cromwellian land reforms. Admittedly in many areas the scarcity of Protestant tenants obliged new landowners to let to Catholics, some of whom were former chief tenants or even proprietors and who were thus able to recover their old standing and local influence by acting as middlemen and sub-letting to Catholic under-tenants.[70] Some major landowners retained their broad acres, even under the proliferating penal laws of the eighteenth century, but while families like the Brownes in Kerry or the O'Conors in Roscommon kept house, demesne, and faith intact, they did so by abandoning political activity for many decades.[71] Others dropped by the wayside, either converting to Protestantism to save their estates, like the Burkes in Galway, or subsiding into a morass of debt like the Mayo Brownes.[72] A similar fate befell Catholics in the professions, especially the law-

[68] Wouter Troost, *William III and the Treaty of Limerick (1691–1697): A Study of his Irish Policy* (Leiden, 1983), chs. III–VI; J. G. Simms, 'The Bishops' Banishment Act of 1697 (9 Will. III, c.1)', in Hayton and O'Brien (eds.), *War and Politics*, pp. 235–49.

[69] Simms, 'Treaty of Limerick', pp. 212–17; Troost, *William III and the Treaty of Limerick*, pp. 182–3.

[70] David Dickson, 'Middlemen', in Bartlett and Hayton (eds.), *Penal Era and Golden Age*, pp. 171–2; L. M. Cullen, *The Emergence of Modern Ireland, 1600–1900* (London, 1981), p. 33.

[71] Gareth W. Dunleavy and Janet E. Dunleavy (eds.), *The O'Conor Papers* (Madison, Wisconsin, 1977), pp. x–xii; Edward MacLysaght (ed.), *The Kenmare Manuscripts* (Irish Manuscripts Commission, Dublin, 1942), pp. xi–xiii.

[72] J. G. Simms, 'Connacht in the Eighteenth Century', in Hayton and O'Brien (eds.), *War and Politics*, p. 290; Raymond Gillespie, 'Lords and Commons in Seventeenth Century Mayo', in *'A Various Country': Essays in Mayo History 1500–1900* (Westport, 1987), pp. 63–5.

yers who had helped staff Tyrconnel's bureaucracy, although those in trade and commerce seem to have survived the vagaries of punitive legislation rather better.[73] But above all it was the loss of the Catholic nobility and gentry, either killed or exiled, which reduced the Old English and Old Irish political interests to impotence: men like MacCarthy, Sarsfield, and even Balldearg O'Donnell (who at last gave up his crusade, took a Williamite pension, and returned to Spain) were hard to replace. As one Protestant remarked, as early as 1704, the Catholics no longer presented a threat, since 'their youth and gentry' had been 'destroyed'.[74] Irish Jacobitism has been aptly described as one of the 'dogs that did not bark in the night' in the eighteenth century, and the lack of Jacobite activity at the time of the '15 or the '45, or at any point in between, cannot simply be explained as the product of successful repression. It is testimony to the emasculation of the Catholic cause. On the whole, eighteenth-century Irish Catholics preferred peace and quiet to the risk of execution, and while some continued to idealize the exiled Stuarts, others reflected sourly on King James II as the careless instigator of all their misfortunes.

As a general conclusion, it would be reasonable to argue that the Williamite Revolution resulted in the preservation and reinforcement of English control over Ireland. The constitutional relationship remained the same. Poynings' Law was still in place, and the act of the Jacobite Parliament to prevent Westminster legislating for Ireland was declared null and void. Indeed, in 1699 the English Parliament flexed its powers by passing a bill to restrict the exporting of Irish woollens, thereby emphasizing Ireland's economic subservience. Within Ireland itself the English landowning interest had been strengthened, and was being given a monopoly of political power and government office. William was able to make use of Ireland for his own purposes, despite the poverty of the kingdom in the wake of a civil war. The large force he stationed in Ireland allowed him to maintain a standing army in spite of the vehement objections of English MPs.

Several important qualifications would have to be entered, however. The most obvious is that neither of the contending parties viewed the 'war of the two kings' as a struggle between England and Ireland, or between core and periphery. For William, his rival's presence in Ireland was a purely strategic problem. The continental war took priority, and he resented having to waste time attending to the second front the French had opened behind him. Equally, James never made Ireland his main concern. Before the Revolution he had regarded the country as a useful resource to be exploited. During his stay on Irish soil he seems to have been impatient to leave for his real work elsewhere. He resisted

[73] Maureen Wall, 'The Rise of a Catholic Middle Class in Eighteenth Century Ireland', *Irish Historical Studies*, II (1958–9), pp. 91–115; and, in general, Louis Cullen, 'Catholics under the Penal Laws', *Eighteenth-Century Ireland*, I (1986), pp. 23–36.

[74] Leicestershire RO, Finch MSS, box 4965, Ire. 9, 'The Case of the Sacramentall Test . . .'.

reforms to make Ireland less dependent on England and sought to keep up and if possible increase the powers of the English monarchy. Even the Irish Catholics, with whom demands for greater independence originated, were politically divided and more interested in land redistribution and the defeat of Protestantism than in political devolution.

Secondly, although the Catholic interest was effectively disabled as a consequence of the Williamite victory, it was neither extirpated nor wholly Anglicized thereafter. Pleas from some Irish Protestants for a systematic policy of colonization, using the newly forfeited estates to settle military veterans in the style of Cromwellian schemes, fell on deaf ears.[75] The only instances of such plantations were private enterprises involving Protestant refugees from Europe, the Huguenots in Queen's County and the 'poor Palatines' in Cork and Limerick, who could not be accommodated in England because of political prejudice. They were not always welcome in Ireland either, especially to High Church Anglicans, who saw them as recruits to Protestant Dissent.[76] There was a large influx of Protestants in the 1690s, but these were Scottish Presbyterians, who flooded into Ulster to escape starvation at home. Far from strengthening the English interest, they were viewed as an even greater threat to the establishment than the defeated Catholics. Animosity between Anglicans and Presbyterians, which had been a feature of the early 1680s, had not disappeared in the dark days of James' reign, and flared up again as soon as William appeared to have won the war.[77] Such a formidable accretion of numbers to the Presbyterian side, by heightening the fears of churchmen, proved profoundly divisive. By the accession of Queen Anne, Protestants in Ireland had split on party lines, as in England, with a substantial body of High Church Tories prepared even to oppose further oppression of the Catholics as the lesser of two evils.[78] Perhaps for this reason Protestant evangelism made little headway in the post-Revolution decades. Reformist clerics in the Church of Ireland, who might have done much to alleviate the poverty and shortage of manpower that thwarted Anglican pastoral work, were diverted by party squabbles and theological disputes with Presbyterian

[75] See, for example, HMC, *Portland*, III, 479–81; University College, Cork, Southwell MSS, presentment of County Cork grand jury, 1694 (copy at PRO Northern Ireland, T.3046–4–1); *The True Way to Render Ireland Happy and Secure* ... (Dublin, 1697).

[76] *CSP Dom. 1691–2*, pp. 67, 543; *1693*, p. 194; *1694–5*, p. 401; *1695*, pp. 211–12, 225–6; *1696*, pp. 4–6; Grace Lawless Lee, *The Huguenot Settlements in Ireland* (London, 1936); Raymond Hylton, 'The Huguenot Settlement at Portarlington, 1692–1771', in C. E. J. Caldicott, H. Gough, and J.-P. Pittion (eds.), *The Huguenots and Ireland: Anatomy of an Emigration*, (Dun Laoghaire, 1987), pp. 297–320; D. L. Savory, 'The Huguenot-Palatine Settlements in the Counties of Limerick, Kerry and Tipperary', *Proceedings of the Huguenot Society of London*, 17 (1947–52), no. 2, pp. 127–9; Cullen, *Emergence of Modern Ireland*, pp. 78–9; *A Representation of the Present State of Religion* ... (Dublin, 1712), pp. 14–15.

[77] Reid, *Presbyterian Church*, II, pp. 419–21. For an example of harassment of Presbyterians at local level, see BL MS Add. 30149, fo. 111.

[78] D. W. Hayton, 'Ireland and the English Ministers, 1707–16', Oxford University, D Phil. thesis (1975), pp. 104–48.

ministers.[79] And the devout among the laity, who in England formed the nucleus of the Protestant voluntary societies, were in Ireland too complacent about the expected decline of popery, assuming that it would naturally follow from the institution of the penal laws.

Indeed, the very completeness of the Catholics' political defeat encouraged Irish Protestants to assert themselves in defence of their political and economic interests. It would not do to make too much of this occasional truculence and slowly maturing independent-mindedness. The relaxed confidence which characterized some Protestant attitudes towards the supposed danger from popery could still be exploded by reports of agrarian disturbances or Jacobite activity, especially if the latter were backed by news of French naval manoeuvres. Probably of greater importance was the fact that after 1691 the English monarchy and the Protestant Ascendancy in Ireland were bound together by indissoluble ties. The exclusively Protestant character of the monarchy, confirmed by the Act of Settlement in 1701, rendered inconceivable a return to James II's policy of relying on Catholics rather than Protestants in Ireland; nor, without at least a potentially strong Catholic interest, would it have been feasible for any king to have tried to play one community off against the other. The role formerly played by the Catholics in this respect could not have been filled by the Ulster Presbyterians, for as Scots of a particularly radical kidney their loyalty to the English Crown was equally dubious. Of necessity, William and his successors depended upon the Anglicans. Naturally, in the last resort the English government could count on being able to force through its decisions. But in normal circumstances monarchs and ministers tended to avoid confrontation, and Irish politicians were often able to get their own way, as the final shape of the ratified Treaty of Limerick bears witness, unless of course they were opposed by the English Parliament, which rarely allowed itself to be restrained on Irish questions by considerations of diplomacy. In due course this awareness of the altered balance of Anglo-Irish relations, alongside a belief in the providential destiny of Irish Protestantism, encouraged the eighteenth-century Ascendancy to develop notions of colonial autonomy. Paradoxically, the defeat of one form of separatism was a step in the evolution of another.

[79] Ibid., pp. 17–20; J. C. Beckett, 'The Government and the Church of Ireland under William III and Anne', in idem, *Confrontations: Studies in Irish History* (London, 1972), pp. 87–110.

Chapter 6

The Revolution of 1688–9 in the American colonies

RICHARD R. JOHNSON

The Protestant wind that sped William of Orange's Dutch and English forces across the English Channel in November 1688 did not subside once it had landed the invading army at Torbay. It blew on across the Atlantic, bringing political upheaval to Englishmen in America as far afield as Boston and Barbados. In its wake, as in England, came a need to explain and defend what had occurred. 'No man', argued two writers in Massachusetts, one of three colonies where upheaval took the form of armed insurrection, 'does really approve of the *Revolution* in *England*, but must justifie that in *New-England* also; for the latter was effected in compliance with the former'. We took up arms, declared the rebels in Maryland, 'to Preserve, Vindicate, and Assert the Sovereign Dominion, and Right, of King William and Queen Mary to this Province'. 'Our only design and intentions', protested the New York city militia, 'was to secure ourselves and country to be wholly devoted to your Majestyes will and pleasure in the disposing of our Government.'[1]

Such pleas rang true, yet they deliberately papered over a more complex reality: the colonists had their own reasons for celebrating William's invasion and their own agenda to fulfil. Behind the swiftly resolved dilemma of adherence to James or William lay the more imponderable issue of the extent and nature of England's sovereignty over its American dominions. Did the character of William's success, promising a restoration of liberties to Englishmen everywhere, invite a new and closer dependence upon the Crown? Or did it license a resumption of the large measure of autonomy from England that James Stuart's government had sought to curb? How far might a more self-conscious loyalty to an English identity require submission to metropolitan power? In the event, each colony's particular needs and circumstances dictated different answers to these questions. Simulta-

[1] E[dward] R[awson] and S[amuel] S[ewall], *The Revolution in New England Justified* (Boston, 1691), in William H. Whitmore (ed.), *The Andros Tracts* (3 vols., Boston, 1868–74), I, p. 71; *The Declaration of the Reasons and Motives For the Present Appearing in Arms of Their Majesties Protestant Subjects in the Province of Maryland* (London, 1689), in Charles M. Andrews (ed.), *Narratives of the Insurrections 1675–1690* (New York, 1915), p. 312; Address of the New York militia, June 1689, in Michael G. Hall, Lawrence H. Leder, and Michael G. Kammen (eds.), *The Glorious Revolution in America: Documents on the Colonial Crisis of 1689* (Chapel Hill, N.C., 1964), p. 110.

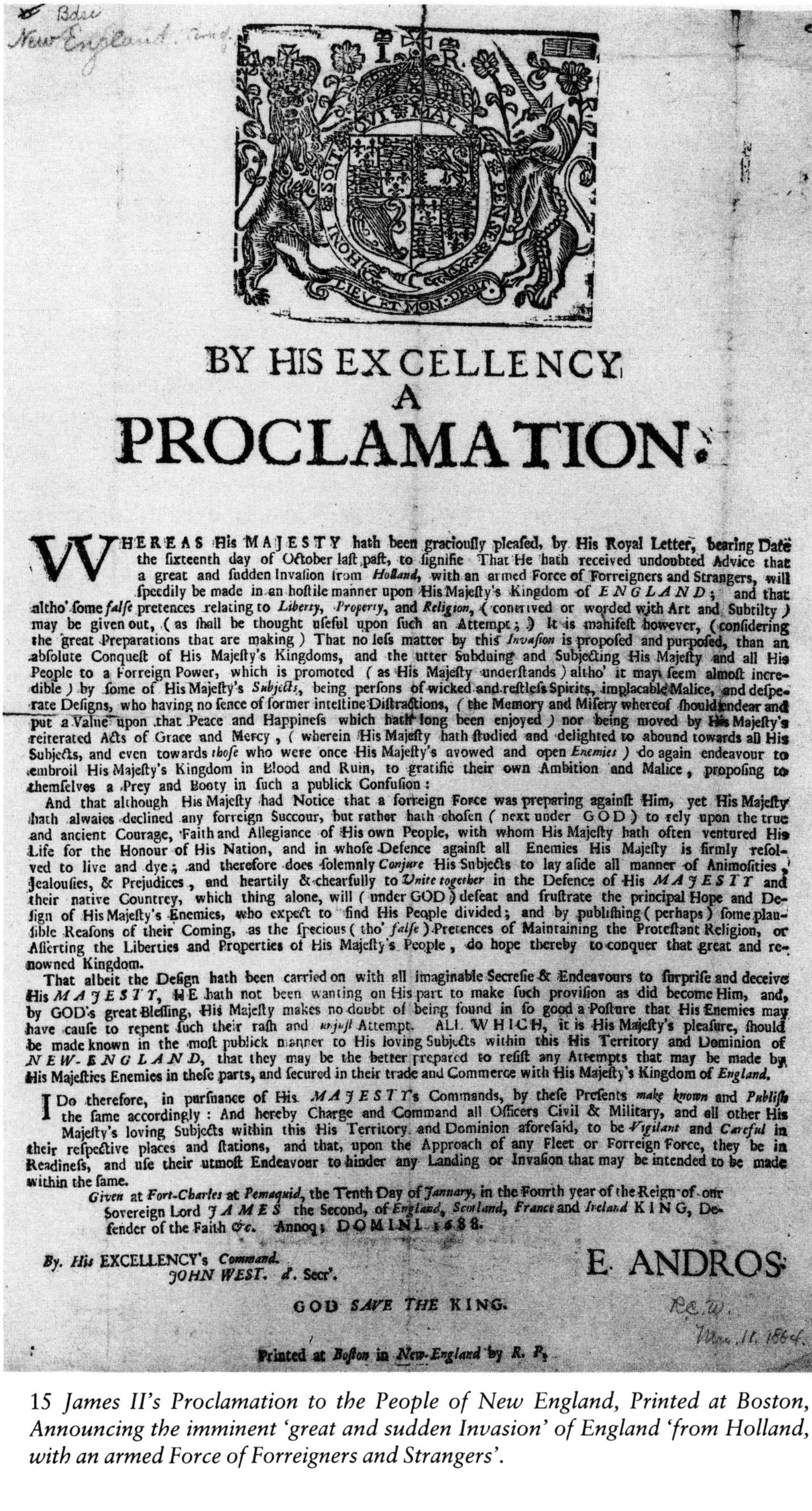

BY HIS EXCELLENCY.

A

PROCLAMATION.

WHEREAS His MAJESTY hath been graciouſly pleaſed, by His Royal Letter, bearing Date the ſixteenth day of October laſt paſt, to ſignifie That He hath received undoubted Advice that a great and ſudden Invaſion from *Holland*, with an armed Force of Forreigners and Strangers, will ſpeedily be made in an hoſtile manner upon His Majeſty's Kingdom of *ENGLAND*; and that altho' ſome *falſe* pretences relating to *Liberty*, *Property*, and *Religion*, (contrived or worded with Art and Subtilty) may be given out, (as ſhall be thought uſeful upon ſuch an Attempt;) It is manifeſt however, (conſidering the great Preparations that are making) That no leſs matter by this *Invaſion* is propoſed and purpoſed, than an abſolute Conqueſt of His Majeſty's Kingdoms, and the utter Subduing and Subjecting His Majeſty and all His People to a Forreign Power, which is promoted (as His Majeſty underſtands) altho' it may ſeem almoſt incredible) by ſome of His Majeſty's *Subjects*, being perſons of wicked and reſtleſs Spirits, implacable Malice, and deſperate Deſigns, who having no ſence of former inteſtine Diſtractions, (the Memory and Miſery whereof ſhould endear and put a Value upon that Peace and Happineſs which hath long been enjoyed) nor being moved by His Majeſty's reiterated Acts of Grace and Mercy, (wherein His Majeſty hath ſtudied and delighted to abound towards all His Subjects, and even towards *thoſe* who were once His Majeſty's avowed and open *Enemies*) do again endeavour to embroil His Majeſty's Kingdom in Blood and Ruin, to gratifie their own Ambition and Malice, propoſing to themſelves a Prey and Booty in ſuch a publick Confuſion:

And that although His Majeſty had Notice that a forreign Force was preparing againſt Him, yet His Majeſty hath alwaies declined any forreign Succour, but rather hath choſen (next under GOD) to rely upon the true and ancient Courage, Faith and Allegiance of His own People, with whom His Majeſty hath often ventured His Life for the Honour of His Nation, and in whoſe Defence againſt all Enemies His Majeſty is firmly reſolved to live and dye; and therefore does ſolemnly *Conjure* His Subjects to lay aſide all manner of Animoſities, Jealouſies, & Prejudices, and heartily & chearfully to *Unite together* in the Defence of His *MAJESTY* and their native Countrey, which thing alone, will (under GOD) defeat and fruſtrate the principal Hope and Deſign of His Majeſty's Enemies, who expect to find His People divided; and by publiſhing (perhaps) ſome plauſible Reaſons of their Coming, as the ſpecious (tho' *falſe*) Pretences of Maintaining the Proteſtant Religion, or Aſſerting the Liberties and Properties of His Majeſty's People, do hope thereby to conquer that great and renowned Kingdom.

That albeit the Deſign hath been carried on with all imaginable Secreſie & Endeavours to ſurpriſe and deceive His *MAJESTY*, HE hath not been wanting on His part to make ſuch proviſion as did become Him, and, by GOD's great Bleſſing, His Majeſty makes no doubt of being found in ſo good a Poſture that His Enemies may have cauſe to repent ſuch their raſh and *unjuſt* Attempt. ALL WHICH, it is His Majeſty's pleaſure, ſhould be made known in the moſt publick manner to His loving Subjects within this His Territory and Dominion of *NEW-ENGLAND*, that they may be the better prepared to reſiſt any Attempts that may be made by His Majeſties Enemies in theſe parts, and ſecured in their trade and Commerce with His Majeſty's Kingdom of *England*.

I Do therefore, in purſuance of His *MAJESTY*'s Commands, by theſe Preſents *make known* and *Publiſh* the ſame accordingly: And hereby Charge and Command all Officers Civil & Military, and all other His Majeſty's loving Subjects within this His Territory and Dominion aforeſaid, to be *Vigilant* and *Careful* in their reſpective places and ſtations, and that, upon the Approach of any Fleet or Forreign Force, they be in Readineſs, and uſe their utmoſt Endeavour to hinder any Landing or Invaſion that may be intended to be made within the ſame.

Given at *Fort-Charles* at *Pemaquid*, the Tenth Day of *January*, in the Fourth year of the Reign of our Sovereign Lord *JAMES* the Second, of *England*, *Scotland*, *France* and *Ireland* KING, Defender of the Faith &c. Annoq; DOMINI 1688.

By. *His* EXCELLENCY's *Command.*
JOHN WEST. d. Secr'.

E. ANDROS.

GOD *SAVE THE* KING.

Printed at *Boſton* in *New-England* by *R. P.*

15 *James II's Proclamation to the People of New England, Printed at Boston, Announcing the imminent 'great and sudden Invasion' of England 'from Holland, with an armed Force of Forreigners and Strangers'.*

neously, however, the elements of a common response emerged, one that would enshrine the Revolution of 1688–9 in ways that at once strengthened and yet circumscribed the colonies' relationship with the mother country.

To understand this interplay of particular and common responses requires a glance back at the pattern of colonial development in the years preceding James' overthrow. By the 1680s, English America's white population had grown to almost a quarter of a million people, the survivors and descendants of the approximately four hundred thousand migrants who had left the British Isles for America during the course of the seventeenth century. The most densely settled areas remained the three first colonized: the islands of the eastern Caribbean, coastal New England, and the shores of Chesapeake Bay. Since mid-century, however, a succession of further colonizations and conquests – Jamaica, the Carolinas, Pennsylvania, New Jersey, and New York – had extended the thin white line of English settlement almost the full, 3,000-mile length of the North Atlantic seaboard. The variations of soil and climate within this vast expanse fostered an increasing societal diversity, especially as the cultivation of sugar in the Caribbean and tobacco around the Chesapeake by large numbers of white indentured servants and black slaves created plantation economies quite different from the subsistence family-centred agriculture predominant north of the Chesapeake. Yet each enjoyed exceptional social and economic growth. By 1689, one royal official estimated that the American colonies provided 'a full third part of the whole Trade and Navigation of England'. Chesapeake tobacco alone, production of which had risen twentyfold since 1640, was reckoned to yield £200,000 a year in customs duties to the Crown.[2]

Politically, the colonies displayed an equal diversity, the legacy of their founding for motives ranging from a thirst for land and instant wealth to the quest of a succession of religious groups – Puritans, Separatists, Catholics, and Quakers – for freedom to establish their own particular orthodoxies. By comparison with the tight rein exerted over French and Spanish America by Paris and Madrid, London's hand had been light to the point of absence: in 1660, Virginia was the only English colony directly governed by the Crown. By then, however, Englishmen both in and out of government were looking to turn the fruits of colonial growth to the mother country's advantage. Beginning in the 1650s and

[2] [Sir Robert Southwell?] to the Earl of Nottingham, 23 Mar. 1689, in Hall, Leder, and Kammen (eds.), *Glorious Revolution*, p. 67; PRO, Report of the Commissioners of Customs [4 Sept. 1689], Colonial Office Papers (hereafter CO) Class 324, vol. 5, p. 120. Southwell's estimate does not seem wide of the mark given that it combined the approximately one sixth (in value) of England's foreign trade that was derived from imports from the American colonies with the trade in goods exported to America and the substantial quantities of colonial products re-exported to Europe: John J. McCusker and Russell R. Menard, *The Economy of British America, 1607–1789* (Chapel Hill, N. C., 1985), pp. 40, 121.

continuing under the restored Stuart monarchy, Parliament enacted a succession of measures designed to ensure, among other commercial goals, England's monopoly of the bulk of the colonies' imports and exports. The desire to exploit ran ahead of the bureaucratic capacity to do so, but by the mid-1670s Whitehall's more methodical collection of information about conditions in America and its creation of a network of customs officials there had established the rudiments of a regular supervision of colonial trade. Commercial regulation in turn fostered political intervention, as attempts at enforcement met with half-hearted support from local governments. One measure of London's growing involvement was its appointment of royal governors to several of the Caribbean colonies, overriding the proprietorial regimes of the founding years in favour of direct crown rule; a second was the dispatch of 1,000 English troops to Virginia in 1676 to put down a rebellion that endangered the Crown's authority and its tobacco revenues.

During these years, for the most part, London's interest in America followed the path of most immediate profit. Officials and contemporary commentators alike pointed to the contrast between the staple-producing colonies and those (as in New England) whose subsistence agriculture and preference for trading on their own account made them less directly valuable to the mother country. A brief attempt in the late 1670s to curb the power of the Virginia and Jamaica assemblies to initiate legislation was dropped once the Crown's immediate objective of obtaining more reliable revenues was satisfied. No effort was made to take government in Maryland, the Carolinas, and New York out of the hands of their proprietors; to the contrary, a further great proprietary province, Pennsylvania, was created in 1681.[3] Plainly, Whitehall was seeking a more regular and informed relationship with America, but its actions remained piecemeal and haphazard, responding to the needs and demands of others rather than conforming to any single strategy.

During the last years of Charles II's reign, however, events and circumstances combined to shape a more comprehensive and far-reaching imperial policy. As English merchants chafing at colonial competition pointed out, a full control of trade required that loopholes be closed even in the furthest reaches of the system. Whitehall was also drawn deeper into American affairs by local dissidents and office seekers looking to the rising sun of royal aid and patronage. The ensuing confrontations with provincial regimes accustomed to a large degree

[3] For interpretations suggesting a greater coherence in royal policy, and of longer standing, see Philip S. Haffenden, 'The Crown and the Colonial Charters, 1675–1688', *William and Mary Quarterly*, 3d ser., 15 (1958), pp. 297–311, 452–66; and Stephen S. Webb, *The Governors-General: The English Army and the Definition of Empire, 1569–1681* (Chapel Hill, N.C., 1979).

of autonomy from external control bred a clash of wills soon cast as a test of royal authority over America.[4]

Massachusetts became the precipitant and proving ground for this new policy. Its Puritan heritage endowed it with a lively suspicion of Stuart intentions, and its stiff-necked magistrates – one royal emissary angrily noted that half of them refused to doff their hats at the reading of a letter from the king – were convinced that its charter of 1629 gave them full powers of self-government. 'The lawes of England', stated the Massachusetts General Court in 1678, 'are bounded within the fower seas, and does not reach America.'[5] In addition, the Bay Colony's aggressive defence of its boundaries and sectarian orthodoxy had raised up a host of opponents – Quakers, royalists, land speculators, and others – eager to pursue their grievances at Whitehall. Investigation escalated into confrontation and after seven years of negotiations marked by Boston's steely refusal to accept any form of compromise, crown officials forced a nullification of the colony's charter by legal process in the autumn of 1684.[6]

Massachusetts' stubborn resolve 'to spinn out the case to the uttermost' had important consequences for the broader constitutional settlement that followed, one still evolving at the moment of William's descent upon England. Before moving against the colony's charter, royal officials had spoken of sending a 'general governor' to supervise the various New England colonies. Boston's intransigence, however, allowed and encouraged a more fundamental reorganization just at the moment of the marked revival of the Crown's political fortunes within England that followed the end of the Exclusion Crisis and the exposure of the Rye House Plot. The disciplining of Massachusetts now parallelled the larger remodelling of English borough charters designed to secure a compliant Parliament. Nonconformists on both sides of the ocean lay open to the revenge of a resurgent royal prerogative. Thus emboldened, in the autumn of 1684, crown officials abruptly consolidated Massachusetts with its neighbouring provinces of Maine, New Hampshire, Plymouth, and part of Rhode Island into a single royal government, to be ruled by a crown-appointed governor vested with broad and arbitrary powers, among them that of dispensing with an elected assembly. Delayed by Charles II's death and James II's accession, this 'Dominion of New England' supplanted charter government in Massachusetts in the spring of 1686. Over the next two years, its boundaries were steadily extended to include Connecticut, the rest of Rhode Island, and then New Jersey and New

[4] For fuller acccounts of these years, see Wesley Frank Craven, *The American Colonies in Transition, 1660–1713* (New York, 1968); and David S. Lovejoy, *The Glorious Revolution in America* (New York, 1972).

[5] Edward Randolph to the king, 20 Sept. 1676, in Thomas Hutchinson, *Hutchinson Letters* (2 vols., Albany, 1865), II, p. 241; Nathaniel B. Shurtleff (ed.), *Records of the Governor and Company of the Massachusetts Bay in New England* (5 vols., Boston, 1853–4), V, p. 200.

[6] Richard R. Johnson, *Adjustment to Empire: The New England Colonies, 1676–1715* (New Brunswick, N.J., 1981), pp. 17–42.

York, forming a single royal government stretching from Maine to Delaware Bay.

To the end of James' reign, the Dominion remained the single concrete accomplishment of the new turn in royal policy. Still larger plans were in train, as proceedings were ordered against every remaining colonial charter. The king, one well-placed English bureaucrat told a colonial correspondent soon after James' accession, was resolved to 'reduce all Proprieties and Independent Government to an Imediate Dependence upon the Crown'.[7] Given time and opportunity, James may have planned to consolidate all the notoriously fractious American colonies into a few great viceroyalties on the model of French Canada or New Spain. Plainly, the cautious pragmatism and sense of constitutional propriety that had hitherto governed London's relationship with America had given way to a thirst for order, uniformity, and the unfettered exercise of the Crown's prerogative powers. Here lay the script for the scenario perceived by Whig politicians then – and Whiggish scholars since – of a tyranny framed to encompass the entire English-speaking world.

Yet two qualifications must be appended to this script if we are to understand what did – and did not – occur in 1689. First, while Stuart hostility to parliamentary institutions was real, it should not be exaggerated: only within the Dominion of New England did royal policy extend to abolishing local assemblies, a measure prompted in part by Boston's exceptional intransigence and in part by James' perception from his years as proprietor of New York of the need for a full union of the northern colonies to defend against French and Indian attack. Other colonies to the south were permitted to retain their elected assemblies. Better, as in England, to bring such bodies to heel than to expunge them altogether. Second, whatever the full extent of James' plans, they were frustrated by events at home compounded by the inefficiencies of an overtaxed bureaucracy. The proceedings threatened against the chartered colonies south of the Delaware River were never pursued during the remaining months of his reign. To the contrary, the king and his advisers turned to solicit the support of such proprietors as Catholic Lord Baltimore and Quaker William Penn against an Anglican establishment alienated by the Crown's domestic policies.[8]

In consequence, the colonists most directly confronted by the shift in royal policy after 1684 were precisely those least receptive to closer ties with Whitehall. South of Pennsylvania, the colonies traditionally more dependent upon England for their trade and government were barely touched by the new policies; north of the Delaware, by contrast, colonists long accustomed to guarding their own

[7] William Blathwayt to Lord Howard of Effingham, 6 Mar. 1685, Blathwayt Papers, XIV, Colonial Williamsburg, Va.

[8] Johnson, *Adjustment to Empire*, pp. 54–63; Jack M. Sosin, *English America and the Restoration Monarchy of Charles II* (Lincoln, Neb., 1980), pp. 297, 307–9.

affairs and heritages – New Englanders convinced that submission to a Stuart king amounted to suicide and sin, and Dutch New Yorkers still at odds with the English conquest of thirty years before – found their cherished liberties and powers of self-government abruptly under attack. Here were the ingredients for a pattern of sharply differing responses to the news of James' overthrow that would shape the course of events through 1689 and beyond.

Chronologically, as Ian Steele has shown, the first colonies to receive reliable advice of William's invasion and subsequent success were those in the Caribbean – furthest from London in terms of distance but closest by reason of 'the gigantic North Atlantic clockwise circuit' of winds, currents, and trade.[9] Here, as elsewhere, the piecemeal transmission of the unfolding drama of invasion, flight, abdication, and succession allowed most colonial leaders to adjust to events in gradual fashion and turn their collective coats in time. In Jamaica, for example, a colony split by factional rivalries, acting governor Sir Francis Watson declared martial law in February 1689 and ruled criticized but unchallenged until the accession of William and Mary could be proclaimed with certainty at the end of May.[10] Even such known supporters of James II as Governors Edwin Stede of Barbados and Sir Nathaniel Johnson of the Leeward Islands retained their authority during these uncertain months, though Johnson followed his proclamation of the new monarchs with a dignified request to resign his post on grounds of his adherence to the high Anglican doctrine of non-resistance.[11] Through 1689, as during America's revolt a century later, the Caribbean colonists shied away from challenging authority in the presence of a black majority and the threat of French or Spanish attack.

To the north, in Virginia and Pennsylvania, a full account of events in England arrived more slowly but with equally peaceable results. Despite early rumours of William's success, his accession was not formally acknowledged in Philadelphia until November of 1689, a year after the Prince's landing at Torbay. Some scattered disturbances broke out in Virginia's Stafford and Rappahannock counties close to the border with Maryland, fed by rumours of a combined Catholic and Indian conspiracy against Protestantism, but order was restored by a swift proclamation of the new reign and the deployment of the local militia.[12]

Within the Dominion of New England, by contrast, where tensions had been screwed highest by the events of the last five years, the response to the news from England was far more dramatic. There, James' appointed governor, the

9 Ian K. Steele, *The English Atlantic, 1675–1740: An Exploration of Communication and Community* (New York, 1986), p. 96.

10 Nuala Zahedieh, 'The Glorious Revolution in Jamaica', in *The Glorious Revolution in America–Three Hundred Years After. A Conference at the University of Maryland, College Park* (April 1988).

11 Gov. Johnson to the Lords of Trade, 24 May, 15 July 1689, *CSP Col. America and the West Indies 1689–92*. nos. 143, 255.

12 Lovejoy, *The Glorious Revolution in America*, pp. 263–4.

veteran soldier Sir Edmund Andros, had embarked upon the most abrupt and sweeping changes attempted anywhere in the English-speaking world since the days of the 1640s. Within a few months of his arrival in Boston in 1686, Andros had levied taxes without representative consent, banned town meetings, challenged existing land titles, and displaced Puritan Congregationalism from its privileged legal position in favour of a policy of religious toleration. Scorning local advice, he governed his extensive state through a clique of intimates drawn mostly from his previous government of New York. Opponents were summarily fined and imprisoned: 'Either you are Subjects', the governor informed one timid critic, 'or you are Rebels'.[13]

William's success suddenly opened the way for New Englanders to be both. Andros made the fatal mistake of trying to suppress rather than temporize with the reports reaching Boston, thereby heightening suspicions that he was plotting to hold the Dominion for King James. On the morning of 18 April 1689, a sudden uprising in the town effected a bloodless coup d'état, capturing the governor and his principal subordinates and forcing the surrender of the royal frigate moored in Boston harbour. Within days, the Dominion fell apart into its component pieces, as magistrates who had served under the old charter governments stepped forward to reassume the reins of power. Only in New York, governed by James as his proprietary province before its inclusion in the Dominion, did something resembling a power vacuum develop. It was filled by the most revolutionary regime, in terms of the rise to power of men with little recent experience of government, that appeared in the course of 1689, a group headed by Jacob Leisler – German-born, formerly a soldier in the service of the Dutch West India Company, and now a wealthy member of New York's Dutch community and a captain of the city militia. Leisler's success was more the consequence of the blunderings of the Dominion's lieutenant-governor, Francis Nicholson, another veteran English soldier, than of any deliberate design. Like Andros, Nicholson tried in vain to play down the news from England, and his hot-headed threat to fire the city rather than allow any challenge to his authority aroused alarm bordering on hysteria. On 31 May the militia took possession of the city's fort and a few days later Nicholson took ship for England, leaving an informally chosen committee of safety headed by Leisler in effective charge of the province.

In only one colony outside the Dominion did events compare with what had taken place in Boston and New York. For years, Maryland's Catholic proprietors, the Lords Baltimore, had experienced a troubled relationship with its majority of Protestant settlers. A miniature civil war in the 1650s had been followed

[13] [Sewall and Rawson], *The Revolution in New England Justified*, in Whitmore (ed.), *Andros Tracts*, I, p. 90; Johnson, *Adjustment to Empire*, pp. 73–83.

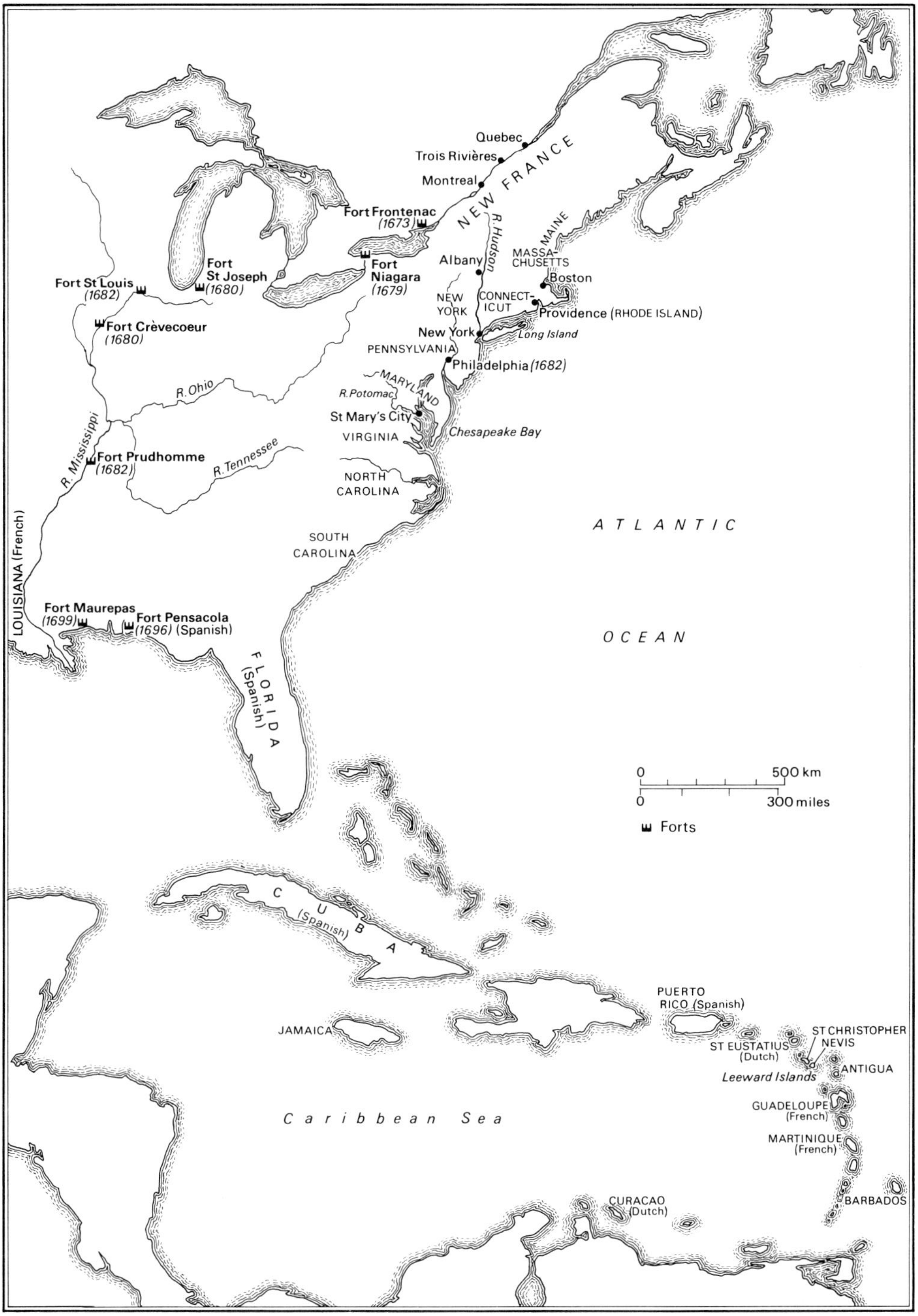

Map 3 The English and French settlements in North America at the time of the Glorious Revolution.

by a string of protests at the disproportionate patronage allotted to Catholics and the proprietors' attempts to maintain the all but absolute powers conferred by the colony's charter. Further discontent surfaced in the 1680s concerning economic conditions and the marketing of tobacco. Lord Baltimore's response, however, only echoed James' authoritarian policies in England, reasserting his proprietorial powers and augmenting Catholic domination of the Maryland council. His new governor, William Joseph, arrived in the autumn of 1688 and promptly affronted the majority of his new subjects with a stiff lecture on the Divine Right of kings and proprietors.[14]

The reports of William's invasion provided the spark needed to ignite this pile of kindling. In the absence of Lord Baltimore, his council greeted the news by calling in the public arms with the intent of confiding them to hands loyal to Baltimore and King James. Opponents responded by spreading rumours similar to those circulating in northern Virginia, of a Catholic plot aimed at inciting the local Indians to slaughter Protestants. Governor Joseph and his council worked hard to rebut these stories but held back from deploying the weapon most effective in Virginia, a prompt proclamation of the new reign. Finally, in mid-July of 1689, Protestant leaders in the counties along the Potomac gathered a small army and marched on St Mary's City in the name of King William and Queen Mary and a redress of a wide range of grievances against Baltimore's rule. Proprietorial forces melted away as rapidly as James' in England eight months before, and by August a new Protestant regime was in place, its bloodless coup accomplished.

In all three colonies – Massachusetts, New York, and Maryland – where 1689 brought armed insurrection, it was triggered by the failure of those in power to proclaim the new reign before popular feeling erupted. In all three, hydra-headed rumours of a conspiracy to frustrate what promised to be peaceful change bred faster than they could be suppressed. Yet there were other colonies, such as Pennsylvania and those in the Caribbean, where similar conditions arose. What turned uncertainty into revolt was the existence in Maryland and the Dominion of governments convinced that James' fall would probably precipitate their own together with opposition groups ready and eager to profit by any half-legitimate opportunity to seize power. In Maryland, for example, many of the rebels had participated in earlier protests, and three of the four principal leaders – John Coode, Nehemiah Blakiston, and Kenelm Cheseldyne – were the sons-in-law of a planter who had revolted against the proprietary regime

[14] Lois Green Carr and David William Jordan, *Maryland's Revolution of Government, 1689–1692* (Ithaca, N. Y., 1974), pp. 28–9, 35–45. For a selection of documents, with commentary, see Hall, Leder, and Kammen (eds.), *Glorious Revolution*, pp. 143–91.

thirty years before. In Massachusetts, the body of old charter magistrates stood poised to resume what many still believed was rightfully theirs. Puritan correspondents in London, headed by Boston minister Increase Mather, were already reporting success in lobbying Whitehall to curb Andros' reforms, and although the actual timing of the Boston revolt seems to have been spontaneous, it was plainly anticipated: the leaders who gathered in Boston's Town House on the morning of the governor's capture professed their surprise at events and then produced a sonorous and well-prepared indictment of his rule. On the side of government, meanwhile, Andros, Nicholson, and the Maryland councillors were committed by their own strong royalism or Catholicism to hoping against hope that the tales of James' fall would prove as false as those spread four years earlier in America of his overthrow by the Duke of Monmouth. Mounted in the saddle of unpopular, authoritarian regimes, they could not afford to dismount part way.

Yet there remains the question of what force or forces could be so strong as to overcome the powerful instinctive sanctions among Englishmen on both sides of the Atlantic against overthrowing – as opposed to criticizing – duly constituted authority. As in the England of the Convention Parliament, the explanations given after the event – once treason had prospered and none dare call it such – cannot be considered a wholly reliable guide to the motives that precipitated action. For the colonists, the matter was further complicated by the delicacy of explaining to England just how they had demonstrated their loyalty to the mother country by overthrowing the authority that England had set up. What emerged had a central consistency but with some elements more immediately significant and others acquiring greater significance over time in the light of changing circumstances and the reassessment by contemporaries and subsequent historians of the real legacy of revolution.

Of these forces, the most powerful and immediate – and subsequently downplayed – was that of religion. In the months before the events of 1689, something resembling a Great Fear spread through English America, of a Catholic plot designed to dash the fruits of the Protestant saviour's victory from the lips of suffering colonists. Its roots lay back in the cultural heritage brought across the ocean, in Foxe's *Book of Martyrs*, the 1640s slaughter of Protestants in Ireland, the Popish Plot, and James' policies, all links in the chain that made 'popery and slavery' synonymous with arbitrary rule. It was powerfully reinforced by events in America – the interplay of Catholicism and proprietary power in Maryland, the scattering of papists raised to office in the Dominion, and, most pervasively, by the French influence, 'a premediated Jesuiticall device complotted long before', seen behind Indian resistance to English territorial expansion. Andros, it was charged, had agreed to betray New England to the governor of French Quebec. Battalions of Frenchmen or their Indian and Catholic Irish allies lurked along the frontier. These were potent imperatives, sounding the need for action lest worse befall.[15]

Yet religious fears were also expressed in ways that revealed more provincial motives. In all three insurgent colonies, the line of division was not just between Catholic and Protestant but also between 'true' Protestants and those deemed still tainted with Romish practices. In Massachusetts, for example, Governor Andros had founded New England's first Anglican church and packed juries with its adherents to enforce his policies. So closely did the Church of England become identified with the regime, that Boston's Anglicans were swept into prison along with Andros and his officials on the day of the revolt, and then again a few weeks later on suspicion of setting fires in the town.[16] As the victims heatedly pointed out in letters to England, such treatment gave the lie to Puritan attempts to justify their revolt as a copy of the mother country's, for how could the triumph of the Church of England in one country be its persecution in another?

In New York, too, differences among Protestants were a significant motive for revolt. Of all the 1689 uprisings, what became known as Leisler's Rebellion has excited the most scholarly disagreement, principally because of the array of rivalries and cleavages uncovered by analysis of the colony's exceptional heterogeneity and social fluidity – English conquerors versus Dutch subjects, Dutch collaborators versus resistors, rich versus poor, Albany versus New York, and merchants versus farmers.[17] Such divisions appear and reappear at different moments during the crisis. Plainly, the paralysis and sudden collapse of the Dominion government allowed a takeover by a coalition of men of middle rank and status, not the 'rabble' portrayed by their opponents, but including very few who had recently held positions of authority. As Leisler sought to consolidate his power, moreover, the rebellion assumed a more openly ethnic cast as the Dutch majority in the city of New York plundered the estates of leading English merchants and clashed with the English settlers on Long Island who had initially helped spark the revolt. Yet throughout ran the cry of Protestantism in danger, and at the top level of leadership, recent research has shown, Leisler and his closest associates were distinguished by their ardent Reformed Calvinist beliefs,

[15] James P. Baxter (ed.), *Documentary History of the State of Maine*, VI (Portland, Me., 1900), p. 111; Whitmore (ed.), *Andros Tracts*, I, pp. 79–80, 163, II, pp. 5, 11; Declaration of Bartholemew le Roux, 26 Sept. 1689, *CSP Col. America and the West Indies 1689–92*, no. 458; Lovejoy, *The Glorious Revolution in America*, pp. 281–6.

[16] Johnson, *Adjustment to Empire*, pp. 99, 105.

[17] Compare, for example, Jerome Reich, *Leisler's Rebellion in New York: A Study of Democracy in New York, 1664–1720* (Chicago, 1953); Thomas J. Archdeacon, *New York City, 1664–1710; Conquest and Change* (Ithaca, N.Y., 1976); Robert C. Ritchie, *The Duke's Province: A Study of New York Politics and Society, 1664–1691* (Chapel Hill, N.C., 1977); and John M. Murrin, 'English Rights as Ethnic Agression: The English Conquest, the Charter of Liberties of 1683, and Leisler's Rebellion in New York', in William Pencak and Conrad Edick Wright (eds.), *Authority and Resistance in Early New York* (New York, 1988), pp. 56–94.

their resolve to sustain the cause of 'true Protestant Religion' resurgent in the miraculous triumph of the Prince of Orange.[18]

The second and interrelated theme running through the colonial uprisings of 1689 should come as no surprise to a student of contemporary events in England or early modern 'revolutions' in general: from the first, the insurgents insisted that they acted to restore legitimate rule. The Dominion was an alien incubus imposed upon them by a crew of 'strangers' led by a 'Guernsy-man' (Andros) in defiance of English liberties and the rule of law; Baltimore and his Catholic crew had conspired to subvert Maryland's ties with the English Crown.[19] Yet this in turn raised the question of whose past, and what species of legitimacy, was to be restored. In the aftermath of revolt, each of the new regimes expressed its willingness to wait for a settlement ordained by England. Yet each then charted a course that revealed its own peculiar circumstances and heritage. In Massachusetts, the two months following the April uprising witnessed a spirited debate over the form of government to be adopted. The Council of Safety created to receive Andros' surrender summoned a special convention of town representatives and then, foreshadowing the consultation involved in the drafting of the Massachusetts state constitution eighty years later, called upon the town themselves for advice. Few were willing to await a decision from England and the great majority favoured a return to charter rule, yet no more than in England's simultaneous debate on James Stuart's 'abdication' was there a consensus on how this could be justified. A radical minority insisted that Massachusetts had entered something approaching a state of nature: 'the *Sword* now rules' and 'in violent Changes the people can as well authorize *Civil* as military Government.' Others saw no need for such potentially disruptive fluidity: with the Dominion's illegality excised, charter rule could lawfully resume as if it had never been suppressed. Had not the Prince of Orange proclaimed a general restoration of English liberties, charters, and magistrates unjustly put out? The convention's final pronouncement frankly straddled the issue: it ordained a resumption of charter rule 'that this Method of Government may be found amongst us when Order shall come from the higher Powers in England' while stressing that 'the Method of Settlement of the said Government in the present Juncture lieth wholly in the People'.[20] Elsewhere in New England, Massachusetts' neighbours likewise returned to their pre-Dominion form of rule.

[18] David William Vorhees, '"In Behalf of the True Protestants' Religion": The Glorious Revolution in New York', New York University, PhD thesis (1988). Vorhees finds the divisions within the Dutch community in New York parallelling the split between the Cocceian 'States Party' and Voetian Orangist faction in the Netherlands, with Leisler advancing the views of the latter.

[19] Thus Hall, Leder and Kammen (eds.), *Glorious Revolution in America*, pp. 42–53, 109–11, 171–86.

[20] Whitmore (ed.), *Andros Tracts*, II, p. 200; Philo. Angl., *The Case of Massachusetts Considered*, CO 5/855, no. 4; *At a Convention of the Representatives ... [May 24, 1689], ibid.*, no. 17iv; and, generally, Johnson, *Adjustment to Empire*, pp. 100–7, and Robert Earle Moody and Richard Clive Simmons (eds.), *The Glorious Revolution in Massachusetts: Selected Documents, 1689–1692* (Boston, 1988), *passim*.

The PLAIN CASE STATED
Of Old -- but *eſpecially* of *New-England*, in an *Addreſs* to His *HIGHNESS*
THE PRINCE OF ORANGE

HAil noble Prince, in whom our Joy and Love
Unite, and (as to their own Center) move.
In whom thoſe Royal Qualities combine
Which may erect a Second *Conſtantine.*
Among the Songs which *Britain's* joyful dayes
To You preſent, accept *New-England's* Praiſe:
VVe alſo boaſt our ſelves of *Engliſh* Race :
And from our Anceſtors, who ſtock't this place,
The name of ſtricter *Proteſtants* derive,
And in Your faith and favour hope to live.

We heard, (and it to us did Sorrow bring)
The much-lamented death of the late King ; .
And, with but too much Truth, did calculate
From thence of all our woes, the wretched Date
Then *James*, with Papal Benediction
And Popiſh principles aſſum'd the Throne :
A Prince whom Nobler Vertues ne're did yeild
Fitter, the Sceptre of the World to wield :
But to what *Ills* can *Popery* perſwade !
And to what *Ruin* do its Maxims lead !
And what a *Hackney* is a *Bigot* made !
Under his umbrage did the Birds of Night
Sing their *damn'd notes*, and ſang them with delight;
And Locuſts of the Pit, grac't with his Smile,
In ſwarms invaded our (once happy) Iſle.

Heroick *El'ſabeth* for us, in vain,
Bafled the fraud of *Rome* and pride of *Spain.*
Whilſt Jeſuited *James* did readvance
The twiſted policies of *Rome* and *France.*

A *Nuncio* from the old Rogue of *Rome*
Muſt with Applauſe to *England's Palace* come,
A *Nuncio*, which a Century or more
Of reform'd *England* never ſaw before;
And we, in grateful ſort, muſt ſend again
On humble *Embaſſy* good *Caſtlemain*,
And, by a *Proxy* kiſs his Worſhip's *Toe*,
Whence *unknown* ſtreames of *unknown* Bleſſings flow.

From *Innocent* our plotted Ruin came,
Guilty in *Fact*, tho *Innocent* in *Name.*
From *France's* Don, whoſe *Papal-Romiſh* trade
Of Blood and Ruin has ſuch havock made,
That his *one* Perſecution has done more
Than the *ten* under pagan-*Rome* before.
From Jeſuits a brood, hatch't by the Devil,
To be the Propagators of all evil,
Incarnate Fiends, to Lucifer ally'd,
And heirs to all his cruelty and pride :
From *theſe*, our *James*, devoted to the Cauſe
His Meaſures took, their Counſels were his Laws :

Our *Sanguinary Laws*, tho' few yet good,
And juſtly merited by men of Blood,
And thoſe with milder penalties inforc't.
Were with a *Prorogation* indors't.
Thoſe Laws, which Parliaments had made to live,
Were laid in duſt by Grand Prerogative ;
And *Teſts* were uſeleſs grown, *Diſpenſing Power*
Diſarm'd their Force, that they could ſtrike no more.
Popery bare-fac't ſtalk't our injur'd ſtreets,
Juſtled the Reformation where it meets,
And Cells of *Maſs* under our noſes grew,
And daring Prieſts did eagerly purſue
Their Patron's Orders with unbounded joy,
Or to deceive us *Her'ticks*, or deſtroy.
Diſſenting Proteſtants they ſtrove to pleaſe
And wheadle, by a ſhort *deluſive* eaſe.
Th' eſtabliſh't Church trampled, againſt all Law,
And, *Jehu*--like, *drove* where they could not draw.
Whilſt Renegado-*Papiſts* were preferr'd,
And had their King's peculiar Regard.
The Snare was laid, the pointed hour drew nigh,
Wherein our *Name* and *Cauſe* was doom'd to die.
Great were his *hopes* (who, when the Stroak was gi- [ven
Claim'd for *Reward* a *double* ſhare of Heaven)
To ſacrifice in one brave funeral Pile,
The numerous HERETICKS of either Iſle.

Nor could the Vaſtneſs of this damn'd deſign
The Limits of his Popiſh Rage confine,
But or'e the Ocean to *this* world it flew ;
Reform'd *America* muſt ſuffer too.
That *we* were muſt'red in this bloody Roll
Our *Suffrings* tell (who then could us cajole ?)
We, by *Papiſtick* wiles, may well believe
Were mark't a lingring Ruin to receive.
They grug'd that we ſhould harmleſly poſſeſs
With Eaſe and Freedom this our Wilderneſs.
Which our religious Anceſtors (who ſought
God in a Deſart Countrey) dearly bought.
Our Charter, which freely we had injoy'd
In three ſucceſſive Reigns, is firſt made void ;
Condemn'd for forged Crimes we never knew.
Nor at this diſtance could er'e anſwer to.
Condemn'd unheard ; their fraud would not admit
A clear Defence and Legal ; nor was't fit
In a Court where *Aſtraa* nere' did ſit.
And thence were we annex't t' a Popiſh Crown,
By which we were deſign'd to be undone.

Then came a man to be our Preſident,
As well againſt the *Law* as our Content :
But he, Alas, did only ſmooth the way
For a Superior Lord, who made no ſtay.

Soon came the *Jerſy* Knight, crafty and Stout,
And for his Maſter's Intereſt cut out.
Soon did he and his Creatures let us know
Whence all our miſeries were like to grow.
Knaves, Beggars, *Papiſts* form'd the triple League
Which carry'd on the ruinous Intreague.
We were not treated by th' inſulting Knaves
As free-born *Engliſh*, but as poor *French* Slaves.
Taxes were rais'd, without Mercy, or Meaſure,
To keep us low, and fill our *Tyrant's* Treaſure.
To MAGNA CHARTA we coul'd claim no Right,
Neither our own, nor *Engliſh* Laws would fit,
But ſuch as by Diſtortion, and Abuſe,
Would ſtill advance the Plot to ruin us.
New Laws by a ſmall ſhabby Juncto fram'd,
And then ſo ſurreptitiouſly proclaim'd,
As if they choſe (Oh when were Laws ſo made !)
They rather ſhould be *broken* than obey'd :
So, if we *kept* or *broke* them, 'twas by chance ;
They made advantage of our *Ignorance* :
Strain'd their own Laws beyond their true Intent,
To our great Coſt, Sorrow and wonderment.

All that we counted dear was made a Prize
To th' raging Luſt and hungry Avarice
Of a few tatter'd Raſcals from *New-York*,
More inſolent than ever was *Grand Turk*.
Their debauch't tricks the harmleſs Countrey ſaw,
But vainly ſought a juſt redreſs by Law.
The Law, which ev'n our ſmalleſt Trips could find
Diſtinguiſh't Friends, and in *their* Cauſe was *blind.*
Their Luſt on Honour ſtrange Excurſions made :
Their Avarice did our Eſtates invade.
Our Lands, for which we to the Natives gave
Their *own Demands* theſe new-come Beggars crave,
Our Lands, which we had peaceably poſſeſſ't
For Sixty years, they with ſtrange flaws moleſt.
It would diſturb our Father's peaceful Graves,
Saw they their poor Poſterity made ſlaves,
Or knew our Lives or Liberties betray'd,
Or knew our Lands to forreign Foes convey'd.
Yet thus with grief might poor *New-England* cry,
We *our own Lands* with *our own Coyn* muſt *buy* ;
And *Patents* take, or elſe ſome ſordid Knave
Soon intercepts, and needs but *ask and have.*

The Secretaries *Houſe of Office* told
(And Courts of Juſtice) where our Rights were ſold,
New Tricks they found, and Fetches with rare ſkill,
To bring more Griſt to their inſatiate Mill.
Money we paid, for what we could not know,
Except to Feed their ever-craving maw,
But never full, for fill we might, as well,
As ſoon the gaping mouthes of *Death* & *Hell.*
Law at a price, and Juſtice we muſt buy,
Each ſmall Court-Officer gapes for his Fee,
Elſe Law would be deny'd, and Right delay'd,
Whatever Madam *MAGNA CHARTA* ſaid,
Our *Penal Acts* their *ſcores & hundreds ſlew*,
Through curſed aid of an informing Crew.
Theſe in our hated Courts did boldly tread,
Villains, who daily damn'd themſelves for bread:
Rogues, who for mony (I in plainneſs think)
Would ſwear the *Sun a bottle full of Ink.*
Theſe, Juries muſt implicitly believe,
And by *their* Teſtimonies Verdicts give,
The Senſe of *Thinking-men* they muſt forego,
And, as the Court directs them, blindly do,
Elſe they're turn'd back, and for their honeſt Strife
Muſt forfeit the Conveniences of Life.
Juries were pack't out of their own vile lump
To *ſerve a Turn*, and *turn* them up a *Trump*,
Men of ſmall Senſe, and ſmaller Honeſty,
Their knotty roguiſh Cauſes to untye.
From Freedom of *Diſcourſe* our Tongues were mor'd,
For we were made Offenders for a word.
When, Mighty Prince, we of Your *Landing* heard,
Tho Hopes & Wiſhes were on Tip toes rear'd
Yet *we* our Hopes could *whiſp'ring* only tell ;
And bold was he who dar'd to wiſh You well :
Him ſhall I ſtyle true *Ben*, who hither came,
To ſave his Life & an untainted fame ;
Harris was he, whom Parliaments had known
T' have been by Popiſh rage & frauds undone,
Yet *here* he could not ſcape the Lion's Paw,
Only for wiſhing well to *WILLIAM o' Naſſau.*

Our *laſt* great Grievance, which we could not bear
(With *Grief* we *tell*, and Oh, with *Pity hear* !)
Was a perplex't myſterious *Indian-War*,
For which with mighty Forces we prepare.
We, who a *Hundred*, in the dayes of yore
Could beat a *Thouſand Indians* and fight *more*,
An Army now a thouſand ſtrong muſt ſend,
With a poor Handful Hundred to contend ;
In horrid Woods where no Proviſion grew,
Sneaking moneths after moneths to ly *perdue.*
Our Officers were Popiſh men of blood,
Whoſe Principles could nere conſult our Good.
Our Scatt'ring Foes but ſeldom came in ſight,
Or if they had, we had no power to fight ;
No War was ere *proclaim'd* ; what could we do?
We dare not kill, the *Law* would then purſue.
Mean time a tedious *Winter* paſt our head,
Our Suffrings ſuch, we envy'd ev'n our *dead.*
And they not few by ſore Diſeaſes went.
Hunger and *Cold*, and how could this content ?

And thus things ſtood, and thus the Plot went on,
From earth to root our Her'tick Nation
Here, and in our beloved Native Iſle ;
Till Heaven on us caſt a propitious ſmile ;
Piti'd our wrongs and on their Counſels frown'd,
And rais'd a man their Empire to confound.
'Twas YOU, Great Sir, whom Heav'n did elevate
To make more famous this our *Eighty Eight*
Than that wherein brave *El'ſabeth* did quell
The jointed pow'rs of *Spain* & *Rome* & *Hell.*
YOU, us with gallant Forces did Invade,
(By long Succeſſes formidable made)
Our wiſhes join'd and met our hearts half way,
Whilſt Terror ſeiz'd our popiſh foes that day.
One bloodleſs month our happy Nation freed
From popiſh Plots, by which we fear'd to bleed;
Pounded a crew of mercenary Knaves.
Jeſuits & *Prieſts*, tools uſ'd to make us Slaves.
Frighted our ſtubborn King, who would not part
From his dear *Bantling*, nor his *Bigot*-heart.
Conven'd our Countrey's Repreſentative,
By whoſe ſage Counſels we now hope to live.

This hearing, by Your great Example ſway'd,
A *juſt* Attempt *oppreſt* New-*England* made,
Not to revenge our wrongs but ſet us free
From *arbitrary Power* and *Slavery* :
This did Heav'n bleſs, and on our Action ſmile,
Befool'd our foes, and brought them to the Toyl.

Sir, Your Protection we hope and crave ;
Condemn not the Succeſs Your Courage gave.
For this our Songs ſhall Your brave Triumphs meet,
Laying our Lives and forunes at Your Feet :
For *this* Your Name will conſecrated be
In *Engliſh* Hearts to late Poſterity.
May ſtill Succeſs Your great Atchievements crown !
Go on to *Conquer*, as You have begun.

BOSTON, Printed *for* and Sold *by*
Benjamin Harris at the *London Coffee-houſe.*

16 *'The Plain Case Stated' Printed for, and Sold by, Benjamin Harris at Boston.* Harris was a prominent English Whig bookseller pilloried in 1680 for publishing in support of Monmouth. He returned to England from Boston in the 1690s after publishing colonial America's first (and promptly suppressed) newspaper, *Publick Occurrences.*

The same delicate triangulation between raw power, local tradition, and royal sovereignty took place in New York and Maryland although – lacking Boston's self-discipline and printing presses – with less philosophizing and greater indecision. Nether colony possessed so usable a past as Massachusetts for its insurgents' purposes: to adopt the Boston formula of a simple return to pre-Dominion days would mean restoration of the very sort of proprietary rule that had helped prompt the act of revolt. Both, therefore, looked for justification to their colonists' broader heritage as loyal Protestants and Englishmen, a rationale that further reinforced their awaiting more passively than Boston for solutions out of England. In each colony, the rebels formed themselves into a Protestant 'Association' resembling those created in England during William's invasion and held a convention of their supporters to bolster their claims to rule. Such conventions conferred a veneer of consent and even popular sovereignty of the kind debated in Boston. Yet to judge from the surviving (and, admittedly, English-oriented) evidence, both Marylanders and New Yorkers put more stock in legitimacy derived from England: in Maryland, the rebels' attempts to form a government met with considerable, if largely passive, resistance until a royal letter of authority arrived in May of 1690, while in New York a fierce dispute erupted over whether the Leislerians or those previously in power were entitled to take possession (and, hence, advantage) of a cautious directive from Whitehall entrusting government in the colony to whomever 'for the time being' held power.[21]

Increasingly, therefore, as the need to justify revolt became a larger search for settlement, its main focus moved out of the colonies and into the corridors of Whitehall. Maryland forwarded a petition begging that 'our religion, rights and Lyberties may be secured, under a Protestant Government by your Majestyes gracious direction especially to be appointed'.[22] Later, fearing a restoration of Baltimore's rule, the colony sent a pair of agents to London to plead its case for a direct royal government. From New York, where the Leislerians' energetic attempts to extend their authority throughout the colony had aroused fierce resentment, came a stream of emissaries and refugees bearing contradictory tales designed to enlist the Crown's support. Within Whitehall, factions of merchants and planters contested to influence the choice of governors to be appointed to such colonies as Virginia and Jamaica.

[21] Carr and Jordan, *Maryland's Revolution of Government*, pp. 63–64, 102–111; Ritchie, *Duke's Province*, p. 209.

[22] W. H. Browne *et al.* (eds.), *Archives of Maryland* (72 vols., Baltimore, 1883–1972), XIII, p. 232; also VIII, pp. 110–11, 137–47.

Most revealing of the turn towards English authority, in light of its prompt resumption of charter rule and its history of refusing to negotiate with the Crown, was the arrival in London in the spring of 1690 of agents from Massachusetts. Though restricted by their instructions to obtaining the Crown's 'full confirmation' of charter rule, their coming was nonetheless a watershed in the colony's relationship with England.[23] Ideologically, it revealed that even Boston's Puritans now felt a renewed sense of kinship with the mother country. Brought back to the forefront of the Protestant crusade by the events of 1688, England seemed once more worthy of New England's allegiance. More practically, the agents' arrival also testified to the enduring impact of the policies of James Stuart. In Massachusetts, as elsewhere within the late, unlamented Dominion, the Crown's assault on charter and proprietary rule had revealed how unexpectedly fragile were the traditional bases of colonial authority. Some who had long chafed at the restrictions of Puritan rule now claimed that charter government was legally dead, and could only be resuscitated in England. The magistrates themselves felt uncertain of their authority. Moreover, James' final legacy to his American colonies was war with France. Already, French and Indian raids upon the borders of New England and New York had revealed the urgent need for aid from England in settling the colonies' internal divisions and mounting a united counter-attack against French Canada. Now, as for the next three-quarters of a century, the threat of a foreign enemy served to contain imperial dissensions within the loyalties of a larger English nationalism.

Along Whitehall's corridors, meanwhile, colonial affairs lay well down the agenda. With England's own political settlement still in doubt, sea-battles in the Channel, and Scotland and Ireland aflame, America stood last in line for attention and resources. What there was of either was first directed to protecting the valuable Caribbean colonies. In addition, the continuity of personnel from James' reign worked against any prompt settlement: such knowledgeable bureaucrats as William Blathwayt and Sir Robert Southwell were quick to argue that to allow America's 'Republicans' to resume their former ways would destroy the ties of dependence so laboriously constructed over the past decade and damage England's trade.[24] The ambivalence of the colonists' position was graphically illustrated in a hearing held in April, 1690, to consider charges of misgovernment brought against former governor Andros and several of his subordinates by the agents of Massachusetts. On the one hand, Tory member of Parliament Sir Robert Sawyer, acting for Andros, tried to circumvent the charges by rehears-

[23] Whitmore (ed.), *Andros Tracts*, III, pp. 58, 60.

[24] [Southwell?] to the Earl of Nottingham, 23 Mar. 1689, in Hall, Leder, and Kammen (eds.), *Glorious Revolution*, p. 67.

ing the story of the colony's defiance before the creation of the Dominion and blaming Andros' overthrow on 'the Rabble spirited by the faction'. On the other, the agents' English supporters, led by Whig solicitor-general, Sir John Somers, firmly credited the revolt to 'the Country ... the people of the place' who had risen 'like Englishmen and good subjects' and 'as we did here' to overthrow oppression. One privy councillor present compared the seizure of Andros to the capture of the garrison at Hull during William's invasion – a capture, as all present knew, directed by the very marquis of Carmarthen (then earl of Danby) now presiding over the hearing. Soon afterwards, Carmarthen abruptly adjourned the proceedings and presented a report that shelved the charges against the accused.[25] The longer that colonial settlement was delayed, the more it became an embarrassing reminder of events that England's political leaders now wished to put behind them.

Over the months following William and Mary's accession, however, Whitehall slowly began to put its colonial house in order. Its first impulse was to preserve continuity by means of the least possible expenditure of political capital and energy: all governors were authorized to remain in office, and those sent out to fill vacancies were of much the same calibre as those appointed earlier in the 1680s, English military officers likely to serve effectively in time of war. Among them were the two who most epitomized James' discredited policies, Francis Nicholson and Sir Edmund Andros, with the first appointed to command in Virginia in the autumn of 1689 and the second dispatched as his successor three years later. Plainly, just as men like Blathwayt and Southwell had survived the storms of 1688, so Whitehall was not to be distracted from making use of personnel known for their efficient loyalty to the Crown by the mere fact of their unpopularity in America.

These were stop-gap measures but ones that by default assumed the shape of policy. A turning-point came in mid-1689 with word of the uprisings in Boston and New York. The news blasted the hopes of English officials that the Dominion could be preserved as a bulwark against the French and a bridle for Massachusetts. It placed the onus of disturbing the status quo in the northern colonies back upon the shoulders of the Crown, and forced Whitehall to deal with the rebel governments on an individual basis. By the autumn, therefore, a royal governor, Colonel Henry Sloughter, had been ordered to New York along with two companies of British regulars sent to strengthen its northern frontier. Sloughter's appointment promised a quick end to the troubles touched off by Leisler's revolt, but the result was farce that turned to tragedy. In a classic example of how problems of transatlantic communication compounded bureauc-

[25] Elisha Cooke to Gov. Simon Bradstreet, 16 Oct. 1690, Massachusetts Historical Society, Boston, *Proceedings*, 45 (1911–12), pp. 647–9; Johnson, *Adjustment to Empire*, pp. 171–4.

ratic delay, Sloughter did not leave England until November, 1690. His ship became separated from the rest of his convoy and then ran aground in Bermuda. As a result, he did not reach New York until March of 1691, eighteen months after his appointment. By then, his troops and their commander had already stumbled into a bloody confrontation with Leislerian forces still convinced that papists and their minions were plotting to seize power. Sloughter arrested Leisler and his leading subordinates and, overborne by their local opponents' thirst for vengeance, pressed charges of treason and murder against them. On 16 May, Leisler and his son-in-law, Jacob Milborne, were hanged. Far from closing the drama, their deaths touched off a blood feud between Leislerian and anti-Leislerian factions that poisoned and polarised New York's politics for two decades to come.[26]

Maryland turned up next on Whitehall's agenda, as Lord Baltimore strove to regain authority over his province. But on this issue official policy coincided with rebel hopes, and the combination of anti-Catholic sentiment, a rebellion already accomplished, the insurgents' petition for royal government, and English officialdom's longstanding hostility to proprietary rule quickly extinguished Baltimore's hopes. Even before the colony's agents arrived, it had been decided that the Crown, and not the proprietor, would appoint a new governor – Lionel Copley, another of Carmarthen's soldier-protégés. This ran squarely in the face of Baltimore's powers by charter, but the Crown's law officers, fresh from the task of discovering the true legality of William's usurpation, found it justified 'in a case of necessity' and because of the proprietor's 'great neglects and miscarriages'.[27] When Baltimore protested, he lost most of his charter rights and revenues as well. What emerged by mid-1691 was a settlement similar in form to New York's with royal government replacing proprietary rule, but with the rebels' demands and most of their leadership confirmed in power and no one sharing Leisler's fate. It was a decidedly Protestant triumph. Catholics were henceforth excluded from voting and holding office. Not until 1715, and after the Baltimore family had converted to Anglicanism – judging Maryland to be worth more than a mass – would proprietary rule return to the colony.

There remained the matter of Massachusetts. A settlement here proved hard to reach, due in part to the high stakes involved and in part to the prominence and persistence of the players. In contrast to the case of Maryland, no broadly acceptable solution lay close to hand. The Massachusetts leadership sought nothing less than to keep intact the hedge around their holy vineyard; Whitehall officials were equally determined to bring the colony within the pale of direct royal government. True, Massachusetts contributed little of direct value to

[26] Patricia U. Bonomi, *A Factious People: Politics and Society in Colonial New York* (New York, 1971), pp. 75–8.
[27] Carr and Jordan, *Maryland's Revolution of Government*, pp. 154–61.

the Crown. Yet, as one official some years earlier had observed, 'the New England disease is very catching' and to allow one colony to retain its 'Common-wealth-like' ways might fatally infect the whole.[28] Nor was this a matter limited to a handful of colonists and officials. Many Englishmen still looked to New England as one of the last earthly fragments of the 'good old cause' of godly rule. Others more secularly minded identified the survival of Boston's liberties with their own. For almost three years, until the sealing of a new Massachusetts charter in October 1691, the colony's settlement became an issue in the larger national debate by which the English political nation decided what manner of revolution it had just accomplished.

Much of the credit for this strategy, as Whitehall officials ruefully acknowledged, belonged to one man, Boston minister Increase Mather. In England on Massachusetts' behalf since early 1688, Mather was not formally commissioned to act for the colony until the arrival of his fellow agents in the spring of 1690. By then, however, he had already established an extensive network of political allies through his friendships in London's dissenting community. Sympathizers secured him audiences with King James and several royal ministers, and then with King William and Queen Mary. Later, he solicited among the members of Privy Council who served on its committee for trade and plantations, and pleaded his case to leaders of the Convention Parliament, among them Philip, Lord Wharton, Sir Edward Harley, Sir John Somers, Paul Foley and his brothers, Hugh Boscawen, John and Richard Hampden, and Sir Henry Ashurst. Throughout, he expended hundreds of borrowed pounds on fees, lawyers, coach hire, printing of the several pamphlets he wrote and published, and 'dayly gratifications' to those guarding access to the mighty.

The details of Mather's quest have been told elsewhere.[29] Even a brief summary, however, reveals the increasing complexity of the ties of law and influence now linking the colonies with the Crown. At first, Mather sought to have the condemnation of the Massachusetts charter annulled by royal fiat. Later, he tried a course less dependent on the prerogative and more agreeable to his Whig advisers, the inclusion of New England in the Corporations Bill restoring forfeited municipal charters. This, too, failed in the face of rising Tory sentiment and a counter-attack mounted by officials in Whitehall. Among their ammunition were reports from New England of the charter government's difficulties in defending its borders against French and Indian attack, and several petitions from dissidents there – Anglicans, frontiersmen, and merchants – seeking royal assis-

[28] Observations on the proposals of Mr Secretary Ludwell of Virginia, [1674?], *CSP Col. America and the West Indies, 1675–6*, no. 403.

[29] Richard C. Simmons, 'The Massachusetts Charter of 1691', in H. C. Allen and Roger Thompson (eds.), *Contrast and Connection: Bicentennial Essays in Anglo-American History* (Athens, Ohio, 1976), pp. 66–87; Johnson, *Adjustment to Empire*, pp. 136–241; Michael G. Hall, *The Last American Puritan: The Life of Increase Mather, 1639–1723* (Middletown, Conn., 1988), pp. 212–54.

tance or a crown-appointed government.[30] An expedition launched at great cost against French Canada by land and sea in the summer of 1690 proved a humiliating failure. Buffeted by these storms on the homefront, Mather and his fellow agents finally had no choice but to turn back to Whitehall and treat with officialdom for a new charter for the colony. Intricate negotiations ensued as a first draft favourable to Massachusetts was savaged by Blathwayt and a Tory majority on the committee of trade, and the agents struggled desperately against the inclusion of a crown-appointed governor. At the last, King William's personal intervention upon his return from Flanders settled the matter in Whitehall's favour. Massachusetts was to have a royal governor with broad powers of patronage and the right to veto legislation, but one nominated by Mather and his allies. Puritan dominance would be curbed by provisions for religious toleration and a franchise extended to freeholders rather than church members, but the excesses of Dominion rule would be avoided by a guarantee of existing property titles and provision for a legislative assembly.

Increase Mather's return to Boston in the spring of 1692, bearing what he grandiloquently presented to his fellow colonists as a 'Magna Charta' for Massachusetts, brought to an end the first and most formative phase of the Revolution's settlement in America. Viewed in the longer context of imperial relations, it marked a further step in the extension of the forms and practices of royal government. In the wake of the governors sent to New York, Maryland, and Massachusetts, other colonies – the Carolinas, Georgia, Nova Scotia, and, briefly, Pennsylvania – were also brought under direct royal authority in the years ahead. New means were devised to tighten England's regulation of colonial trade, notably a statute of 1696 that strengthened the colonial customs service and established a network of vice-admiralty courts in America. By 1730, the great majority of the American colonies – all those in the Caribbean and seven of eleven on the mainland – were ruled by governors appointed by the Crown. If the revolt of the 1770s would shatter what has been called the first British empire, then the events of 1688–9 were a turning-point in constituting what had to be created before it could be overthrown.

Yet this assertion of royal authority had begun well before 1688; the more immediate significance of the post-Revolutionary settlement – and a prime reason for its prompt acceptance in America – lay in it formulation of what amounted to a synthesis between the virtual autonomy of the colonists' founding years and the radical centrism of royal policy in the 1680s. Where the Dominion had imposed a direct executive rule without representative consent, all the col-

[30] Johnson, *Adjustment to Empire*, pp. 183–90. For the odyssey of one individual's turn towards royal government during these years, see Richard R. Johnson, *John Nelson, Merchant Adventurer: A Life Between Empires* (New York, 1991).

onies settled in the wake of 1689 (with the single exception of the military outpost of Nova Scotia) were endowed with a legislative assembly. There were no further threats to abolish assemblies or uproot existing land titles. And although Whitehall continued to dabble with the notion of appointing a single general governor to command some or all of the northern colonies, it never repeated its experiment of consolidating them into a single administrative unit. A compromise – or, more accurately, a mutually acceptable coagulation of the imperial political structure – had emerged. This was due in part to the new sophistication of colonial pressures and persuasions as Increase Mather's remarkable embassy set a pattern for the work of other agents skilled in advancing their colonies' interests at court. But it was more immediately the consequence of Whitehall's return to a policy of seeking an effective balance between preserving 'a due dependence' upon the Crown and provoking colonial upheaval in ways that might threaten trade and distract the mother country's attention and resources from its more important concerns in Europe and at home. A return, because it restored much of the continuity of royal policy as it had existed at the beginning of the 1680s. James Stuart's unusual – and unusually disturbing – interest in English America now proved more aberration than prologue.[31]

From this synthesis, when allied with the unity forged by William's triumph and the struggle with France, came a perceptible strengthening of the colonists' ties to the mother country. The events of 1688–9 may have divided Britain while uniting England but they drew England's provinces in America into greater dependence upon the centre.[32] More than ever before, political leaders looked across the Atlantic for legitimacy, military aid, and political patronage. The appointment (and unseating) of governors, for example, became a complex process of lobbying and persuasion in which the colonists themselves learned to play an influential part.[33] Increasingly, too, they phrased their political goals in terms derived from their relationship with England. As scholars have noted, the upheavals of 1689 resounded with colonial calls for the vindication of their rights and privileges as Englishmen.[34] Even the Massachusetts colonists, hitherto intent upon shaping their bible commonwealth around the duties of a saint,

[31] A different view, seeing a continuity of royal policy from James' reign, is advanced by Stephen S. Webb, 'Army and Empire: English Garrison Government in Britain and America, 1569 to 1763', *William and Mary Quarterly*, 3rd ser., 34 (1977), pp. 1–31.

[32] Jennifer Carter, 'The Glorious Revolution in England from 1688 to the 1760s', and Thomas Bartlett, 'The Glorious Revolution and Ireland', papers given at 'Liberty, Rights, and the American Revolution, A Liberty Fund Symposium', Williamsburg, Va., 9–12 Mar. 1989. Compare, for example, William Molyneaux's *The Case of Ireland's Being Bound by Acts of Parliament in England Stated* (Dublin, 1698), with what might be termed its Virginian American counterpart, [Benjamin Harrison III?], *An Essay on the Government of the English Plantations on the Continent of America (1701)*, ed. Louis B. Wright (San Marino, Ca., 1945).

[33] As, for example, Stanley N. Katz, *Newcastle's New York: Anglo-American Politics, 1732–1753* (Cambridge, Mass., 1968), pp. 39–58; and Alison Gilbert Olson, *Anglo-American Politics, 1660–1775: The Relationship between Parties in England and Colonial America* (New York, 1973), pp. 75–141.

[34] Thus Lovejoy, *The Glorious Revolution in America*, index, *sub*, 'Rights, of Englishmen'.

found that the experience of the Dominion and its attack upon their liberties could induce a new acceptance of a middle way of secular, English-style freedoms guaranteed by charter. 'I am a true Englishman', declared the brother of the Puritan diarist Samuel Sewall to London in 1696, 'and a Loyal Williamite'.[35] Several colonies drafted declarations of their rights as Englishmen, some echoing England's Petition of Right in its rehearsal of the phrasings of Magna Carta.[36] The parallel with English political practice was deliberate and heeded even in colonies not directly ruled by the Crown, as evidenced by the shift from unicameral to bicameral legislatures, the claims made for parliamentary privileges, and the heightening of the powers and status of their executives.

This legacy took time to form. Not until well into the following century was it evident that the political arrangements pieced together in the 1690s would prove enduring and hence worthy to be revered. Gradually, however, as in England, memories of the enmities and accommodations of 1688–9 gave way to rosier visions of a 'Glorious Revolution' – bloodless, wholehearted, immaculately conceived and delivered – that had miraculously transformed the course of English history. From that moment, wrote a New York essayist of 1734 already oblivious of the Leislerian troubles, dated 'the original of our present Happy Constitution'; to it, forty years later, Massachusetts patriot Joseph Warren attributed a settlement 'by which all the liberties and immunities of BRITISH SUBJECTS were confirmed to his Province, as fully and absolutely as they possibly could be by any human instrument which can be devised'.[37] Indeed, perhaps the most enduring and still potent legacy of 1688–9 within America lay in making the terms 'revolution' and 'constitution' what they had not been before – common watchwords of political discourse and standards (however variously defined) by which to assess the politically proper.[38] Each sustained and validated the other; and together they came to encapsulate in colonial minds that array of liberties – such as the right to representation, to jury trial, to the security of property, and to pity foreigners – that all colonists could claim to possess by virtue of their birth or naturalisation as Englishmen. These were, of course, not new but refurbished rights; and the deep-rooted belief in antiquity and inheritance as proof of constitutionality ensured that 1688–9 would never become a Year One in the French sense, an intellectual deluge eradicating previous points of constitutional reference. On both sides of the Atlantic, nonetheless, the Glori-

[35] Stephen Sewall to Edward Hull, 2 Nov. 1696, CO 5/859, no. 40.

[36] Johnson, *Adjustment to Empire*, pp. 393, 419.

[37] *New-York Gazette*, 21–8 Oct. 1734; Joseph Warren, *An Oration Delivered 5 March 1772* (Boston, 1772), p. 8.

[38] As James Otis, *The Rights of The British Colonies Asserted and Proved* (Boston, 1764), pp. 37, 70; Thomas Jefferson, *A Summary View of the Rights of British America* (Philadelphia, 1774), p. 18; and, generally, Gordon S. Wood, *The Creation of the American Republic, 1776–1787* (Chapel Hill, N.C., 1969).

ous Revolution became the greatest single such point for the century that followed, far more so than the confused and disreputable events of 1640 to 1660.[39]

This said, the genesis and precise nature of these colonial constitutions remained as controversial as those of their fabled English counterpart. Pushed to the point of definition, crown officials refused to endorse colonial claims to the full panoply of English rights and some continued to deny that the colonies possessed constitutions independent of the grace and favour of the Crown. Colonial spokesmen, for their part, cited their charters and the manner of their first settlement as conferring contractual or purchased rights that London was bound to respect.[40] These differences, perhaps, have caught the eye of modern historians more than they determined the actual course and stability of colonial politics. But they document the extent to which, as in nineteenth-century America, ambiguities remained in the wake of what was held to be a conclusive constitutional settlement that would furnish grounds for conflict and secession.

Compounding these ambiguities, as Bernard Bailyn has pointed out, was the fact that, however much the colonies' political structures now resembled England's in form, they still functioned differently in practice.[41] Bailyn draws, I would argue, too sharp a portrait of England's eighteenth-century political stability contrasted with America's 'milling factionalism'. Yet his analysis of the claims and powers of the different branches of colonial government remains an exceptionally cogent introduction to the workings of 'inter-revolutionary' constitutionalism. For it re-emphasises the divergence between, on the one hand, England's progressive interweaving of Crown and Parliament under the rubric of king-in-parliamentary sovereignty and the reality of ministerial control and, on the other, the mounting antagonism that characterized executive–legislature relations in America.

This antagonism owed much to the way in which physical separation – an ocean's breadth – compounded the differences in the sources of authority empowering each branch of government, yoking an England-appointed executive to a locally elected legislature. Yet it was more immediately defined and inspired by the twin and ultimately conflicting themes we have already seen emerging from the Glorious Revolution's American settlement – its accelerated reception of the traditions of English constitutionalism coupled with an extension in theory and practice of control by the English Crown. The result, as patriot lawyer John Dickinson observed, was government 'not only *mixt*, but *dependent*', similar

[39] Thus the Whig views cited by H. T. Dickinson, *Liberty and Property: Political Ideology in Eighteenth-Century Britain* (New York, 1977), pp. 141–2.

[40] The best recent summaries of these views are found in Jack P. Greene, *Peripheries and Center: Constitutional Development in the Extended Polities of the British Empire and the United States, 1607–1788* (Athens, Ga., 1986), chs. 2–3; and John Phillip Reid, *Constitutional History of the American Revolution: The Authority of Rights* (Madison, 1986), chs. 14–18. All the declarations of English rights passed by colonial legislatures in the 1690s were disallowed by the Crown.

[41] Bernard Bailyn, *The Origins of American Politics* (New York, 1968), pp. 63, 66.

in form to England's renowned balance of estates and branches but subject to an externally derived imperial authority.[42] Had the Crown been willing to admit Parliament into administering the colonies in the years immediately after 1689, had that body shown any capacity to recognise the issues and the opportunity, this dependence might have assumed more binding and enduring form. For a brief moment in the early eighteenth century, in the wake of several bills introduced into Parliament to regulate colonial affairs, it appeared that London might establish – and the colonists accept – a form of imperial authority mixed in the further sense of being given statutory, king-in-parliamentary force.[43]

But it was not to be, as the very interweaving and ambivalence of the post-revolutionary relationship between Crown and Parliament inhibited the one from further radical policies in America and failed to empower the other. It would be the 1760s before Parliament tried to implement in America what it had come to claim within England, only to run full tilt into the now entrenched position of assemblies claiming constitutional parity as fellow legislatures. By then, too, colonial advocates like Benjamin Franklin stood braced to challenge the unquestioning belief of most Englishmen that the Glorious Revolution had enshrined the full supremacy of king-in-parliamentary authority. To the contrary, colonial writers argued, the Revolution had merely ratified customary arrangements whereby Parliament held back from attempting any internal government or taxation of America.[44]

Such contrasting views of the Revolution's meaning suggest the danger of attaching too great a weight to each invocation of its principles – like motherhood and apple pie, the Glorious Revolution became so universally venerated as to form the common coin of every sort of political appeal. Just as English leaders claimed its blessing for causes as contrary as Whig parliamentary reform and Tory resistance to Catholic emancipation, so colonial factions paid homage to William's 'Glorious Enterprise' in pursuit of a variety of different goals.[45] Yet even ritual veneration leaves imprints of its particular forms, and for all the debasement of the coinage of 1688, we should also note its persistent and configurative effects. The colonists' embrace of the Glorious Revolution cemented their ties to England and English authority. But it also furnished wholly respectable grounds for defining that relationship in terms that protected local autonomy and limited executive excess. The colonists' social and political Anglicization did not dictate submission to – rather, it equipped them to resist and with the greater strength derived from a more uniform political culture – any extension

[42] John Dickinson, *Letters from a Farmer in Pennsylvania, to the Inhabitants of the British Colonies* (Philadelphia, 1768), p. 58.

[43] Greene, *Peripheries and Center*, pp. 58–61.

[44] Ibid., pp. 115, 67; and Bernard Bailyn, *The Ideological Origins of the American Revolution* (Cambridge, Mass., 1967), pp. 175–229.

[45] John Clive, *Macaulay: The Shaping of the Historian* (Cambridge, Mass., 1987), pp. 90–2.

of English authority infringing on their rights as Englishmen. What derived from being English could be turned to limit England's power. The Massachusetts charter of 1691, for example, once a symbol of submission to the Crown, became in the eyes of patriots like Warren and John Adams a compact shielding the colony against further imperial regulation. The overthrow of Andros or Baltimore's proprietary rule was no longer an event that had rendered further upheavals unnecessary but a precedent for repeating the process should need arise.[46]

In this scenario the well-known 'rise of the assemblies' has an important place, especially in the minds and dispatches of querulous colonial governors.[47] But a longer look suggests that such legislative encroachment might better be set within the larger theme of the greater demands upon (and consequent growth of) government itself. In a society experiencing spectacular economic development, access to political power – for garnering status, war contracts, land grants, commissions, offices, and control of human and other kinds of property – mattered a great deal, more even than in England, and the competition was correspondingly fierce. One more legacy of 1689 was a proliferation of the strategies for such advancement – through the Board of Trade, well-placed ministers, the bishop of London, crown-authorised land companies, and mercantile interest groups – over and above those within the colonies themselves. The matter needs further study, but it would seem that, where government in Augustan England grew primarily at the local level, it expanded most in eighteenth-century English America at a level local from London's but central from the colonists' perspective, as in Kingston, Charlestown, Williamsburg, Boston, and New York. Competition for power, given that reverence for the mixed constitutions left by the Revolution prevented the issue from being wholly resolved in favour of either the Crown or internal independence, spawned checks both rhetorical and procedural upon its exercise – 'limiting the business of government became a part of the business of government'.[48] The way was prepared for the adoption during America's rebellion of the concepts recovered from seventeenth-century England – of the people as constituent power and of a fundamental law that placed bounds upon what any branch of government could do – that would set American constitutionalism on a different course from that of the mother country.

Plainly, we cannot credit all these developments to the events of 1688–9. An earlier English constitutional heritage, the forms and usages established during the founding years of settlement, England's political realignments, and colonial America's exceptional socio-economic opportunities and growth all played a

[46] Theodore B. Lewis, 'A Revolutionary Tradition, 1689–1774: "There was a Revolution here as well as in England"', *New England Quarterly*, 46 (1973), pp. 436–8.

[47] As Jack P. Greene, *The Quest for Power: The Lower Houses of Assembly in the Southern Royal Colonies, 1689–1776* (Chapel Hill, N.C., 1963).

[48] Johnson, *Adjustment to Empire*, p. 390.

part in shaping the years that followed. A fuller picture awaits more comparative study of early eighteenth-century colonial political development and of its relationship, in turn, to the new complexities being discovered in English politics for the years after 1715.[49] We need a more complete accounting of the local costs and consequences of the century of conflict with France touched off by the Revolution's diplomatic realignments.

Yet certain conclusions have emerged. The Glorious Revolution was surely English America's most broadly experienced and immediately celebrated event prior to the Great Awakening of the 1740s, and its first direct participation in what might be termed a happening of truly international dimensions. It committed the colonies to a century of full partnership in the conflict of nations. Sanctified as 'an Era of Renown unperishing, and to every true *Briton* ineffably precious', it became an enduring touchstone of political propriety and Protestant supremacy.[50] It drew together and wove into a single imperial fabric the hitherto disparate threads of early America's constitutional development. In hindsight, we may also see ways in which the Revolution helped that fabric to unravel. By recasting the colonists' conceptions of their various liberties (i.e. particular privileges) into a more uniform political language, it pointed the way towards their formulation of a more modern and politically potent concept of liberty, one that would lead them beyond their rights as Englishmen into the more turbulent waters of the rights of man. It refurbished the rationale for English colonial government, but in ways that ultimately exposed that rationale's ambiguities. By the 1760s, the evolution of the parliamentary authority that to most Englishmen within England represented a revolutionary settlement fulfilled would appear to many colonists as evidence of a settlement corrupted and betrayed. Yet this is to pass too quickly from '88 to '76. For much of the eighteenth century, the Glorious Revolution's legacy lay more in institutional definition and political practice than in ideological formation, more in habit than in thought. It thereby underwrote three-quarters of a century of constitutional stability in America along with many of the terms by which that stability would eventually be – quite literally – reconstituted.

[49] As, for example, J. C. D. Clark, *Revolution and Rebellion: State and Society in England in the Seventeenth and Eighteenth Centuries* (Cambridge, 1986).

[50] William Livingston and others, *The Independent Reflector*, ed. Milton M. Klein (Cambridge, Mass., 1963), pp. 322 (16 Aug. 1753).

Chapter 7

The Revolution of 1688–9 and the English republican tradition

BLAIR WORDEN

I

Perhaps my title calls for explanation.[1] The work of J. G. A. Pocock has familiarized us with the existence and with the importance of a 'republican tradition'. But no one would claim that republican ideas exerted any positive influence on the course of the Revolution of 1688 in England. Such effect as they had was negative, for the fear of republicanism contributed to the wariness of constitutional innovation that characterized the Revolutionary settlement. And if republicanism made no positive contribution to 1688, what did 1688 do for republicanism? Is not the simple answer that the Revolution, by laying the foundations of constitutional monarchy, made republicanism redundant?

The simple answer has a point. Yet the tradition with which Pocock has acquainted us shows vigorous signs of life long beyond 1688.[2] The Revolution brought not the end of republicanism, but a shift within it. It made it in some respects a tamer or softer body of ideas than before, in some ways a more difficult one to define and identify. But it did not make it a less influential one. A movement which before the Revolution had been essentially critical of the English constitution became essentially a friend to it, even if always a critical friend. It came to hope, not for a novel system of government, but for the purifica-

[1] This essay is the revised text of a lecture given at a conference of the History Faculty of Cambridge University in May 1989 to commemorate the tercentenary of the Revolution. I have occasionally drawn on material in other essays of mine, where the reader would sometimes find fuller discussion and documentation of points made here: the introduction to my edition of Edmund Ludlow, *A Voyce from the Watch Tower* (Royal Historical Society, Camden fourth series 21, London, 1978); 'Classical Republicanism and the Puritan Revolution', in H. Lloyd-Jones, V. Pearl and B. Worden (eds.), *History and Imagination* (London, 1981), pp. 182–200; 'The Commonwealth Kidney of Algernon Sidney', *Journal of British Studies*, 24 (1985), pp. 1–40; 'English Republicanism', in J. H. Burns and Mark Goldie (eds.), *The Cambridge History of Political Thought 1450–1700* (Cambridge, 1991), pp. 443–75; 'Milton's Republicanism and the Tyranny of Heaven', in G. Bok, Q. Skinner and M. Viroli (eds.), *Machiavelli and Republicanism* (Cambridge, 1990), pp. 225–45.

[2] For the development of Pocock's thesis, see particularly his *The Ancient Constitution and the Feudal Law* (Cambridge, 1957); *The Machiavellian Moment* (Princeton, 1977); *Virtue, Commerce, and History* (Cambridge, 1985); and his edition of *The Political Works of James Harrington* (Cambridge, 1977). Although other writers have found good grounds for questioning some of Pocock's emphases, his insights remain luminous and profound.

tion of the ancient one. It explained the nation's political defects in terms less of its laws than of its manners. Those changes did not occur abruptly at the Revolution. They were under way before 1688 and remained incomplete for long after it. Nonetheless, the Revolution of 1688 gave a decisive impetus to those changes. To explore its consequences, we shall need to place the Revolution within the long development of republican ideas from the sixteenth century until the nineteenth.

'It has always been the political craft of courtiers and court-governments', observed Tom Paine in *The Rights of Man*, 'to abuse something which they called republicanism; but what that republicanism was, or is, they never attempt to explain'.[3] If English republicanism has a modern historical image, it is probably that of bombs and socialism, an image formed in the Victorian age when a movement which convulsed the continent cast but a pale and crankish shadow in England. Victorian republicanism is a different animal from the tradition I shall be exploring. It is indeed a symptom (perhaps even a cause) of the death of that tradition. But if republicanism meant something different before the nineteenth century, the word was not used to mean anything more polite. 'Republicanism', at least until well into the eighteenth century, is a term of abuse.[4] Few men in early modern England called themselves republicans. In the same way, few men called themselves Puritans: a parallel worth reflection. The term Puritanism, which in most modern scholarship has yielded its abusive function to a neutrally descriptive one, has in the process encountered serious problems of application. Yet we have not been able to manage without it; and if we study the political thought and action of early modern England we may find it difficult to do without the term republicanism. In both cases there is a movement which needs a word. The republican movement being less well known than the Puritan one, we need first to establish its contours.

The movement to which I shall apply the word republicanism, and of which I shall be examining its English form, is the movement of intellectual protest which opposed the rise of the Renaissance and Baroque monarchies of early modern Europe, and which, in articulating that opposition, drew extensively on the political writings and political practices of classical antiquity. It is a movement whose modern origins lay in Italy, and whose principal modern guide was Machiavelli, but which in the seventeenth century made its most profound and most enduring contributions to political and intellectual history not on the continent but in England. The 'new monarchies' which arose or evolved across

[3] Tom Paine, *The Rights of Man*, ed. H. Collins (Harmondsworth, 1969), p. 200.

[4] The term 'republic' did not normally suffer that disadvantage before the middle of the seventeenth century, when its primary usage was a neutral one, as the English of *respublica*: J. H. Hexter, *On Historians* (London, 1979), p. 292. For the century or so following the English republic of the 1650s, however, the noun was usually (though not always) as pejorative as the adjective.

Europe from the later fifteenth century – in France, in Burgundy, in Germany and the imperial lands, in Spain, in Italy, in England – were held by republicans to have extinguished liberty and to have corrupted virtue. That process was effected, and in the seventeenth century extended and accelerated, by the swelling of patronage, by venality, by the enervation of independent nobilities and of representative institutions, by the servility, luxury, and effeminacy of courts, and in some instances by standing armies.

I have broadly defined republicanism and soon I shall name some republicans. But we must be careful. The republican writers of early modern England did not form a self-contained category, clearly distinguishable from other categories. They wrote in order to influence events, and adapted their language and their arguments to the preconceptions of the audiences they hoped to sway. Their republican assertions mingled with other political arguments – arguments about political or social contracts, arguments about popular sovereignty or natural rights, arguments justifying resistance or tyrannicide, arguments appealing to Scripture or to medieval history and precedent – which were advanced no less strongly by men in whose minds the republican critique of modern monarchy, if it was present at all, was much less prominent.

The Renaissance, which brought the new monarchies to Europe, was also the source of its republicanism. Underlying the classic texts of republican thought is the wide base of educated lay knowledge of the ancient world that was created by the educational practices of the Renaissance. Of course, the political lessons of antiquity were not always republican ones. Early modern Europe may have contained as many admirers of Augustus Caesar as of Marcus Brutus. Tacitus and Machiavelli stimulated arguments in favour of statecraft as well as criticisms of it. But it was the critics who won the intellectual arguments, even if not always the political ones.

Pocock maintains that in political thought the Renaissance came late to England: that, before the civil wars of the mid-seventeenth century, English interpretations of constitutional conflict were circumscribed by insular conceptions of custom and law and of the 'ancient constitution'; and that republicanism, with its classical preoccupations and its alien models, made its impact only in the 1650s, when the ancient constitution had broken down. If we look only at treatises of political theory, then Pocock's argument needs no qualification. The only well-known treatise written before the civil wars to have described the English polity in classical terms, the *De Republica Anglorum* of Sir Thomas Smith (1565), comfortably contains that analysis within a conventional account of, and a conventional tribute to, Tudor rule. Yet at least as early as the reign of Henry VIII aggrandizement of royal power was prompting, if not republicanism, then ideas on which republicanism would come to draw. Sir Thomas More, in whose writings during the second decade of the sixteenth century the evils of tyranny are a recurrent theme, invented in *Utopia* a political system where the office of king is elective rather than hereditary and where the ruler may be deposed for 'suspicion of tyranny'.[5] The same preoccupations, and similar recommendations, are present in Thomas Starkey's *Dialogue between Pole and Lupset*, written in the 1530s, the decade when the verse of Sir Thomas Wyatt cries out against the servility, the degradation, and the tyranny of the courts of the continent and against the 'bloody days' of the Henrician Reformation.[6]

Sir Walter Ralegh paid Henry VIII a terrible tribute of a kind which writers of early modern England more normally bestowed upon Nero or Domitian: 'if all the pictures and patterns of a merciless prince were lost in the world, they might all again be painted to the life out of the story of this king.'[7] In the anti-monarchical literature of the seventeenth century Henry would be 'that monster of mankind', 'one of the most violent princes we ever had'.[8] To Bolingbroke in the eighteenth century, Henry's would be the most 'severe' of 'tyrannies'.[9] Yet it was not under Henry VIII but under his daughter Elizabeth that we find the first representation of distinctively republican concerns. It lies within the great pastoral work written by Sir Philip Sidney around 1580, *Arcadia*. Sidney's *Arcadia* will repay our attention, for – with the capacity of art to anticipate life – it prefigures with uncanny exactness the dilemmas that would face republicans during the Revolution of 1688 – and indeed (though never more tantalizingly) at other crises of Stuart rule.

Within the 'hidden form' beneath the surface of his romance, Sidney discloses his dissatisfaction with the English system of rule. His inability to win the queen's favour, and the failure of his political circle (principally his uncle the earl of Leicester and his father-in-law Sir Francis Walsingham) to convert her to the cause of international Protestantism, encouraged his belief that under monarchy 'public matters had ever been privately governed', and led him to reflect 'how great dissipations monarchal governments are subject unto'.[10] Sidney was steeped in the resistance theories of the Marian exiles and of the Monarchomachs; he was a student of Tacitus and Machiavelli and Guicciardini; his mentor

[5] Book II, 'Of the Magistrates' (Ralph Robinson's translation, 1556). For More's preoccupation with tyranny see Alistair Fox, *Politics and Literature in the Reigns of Henry VII and Henry VIII* (Oxford, 1989), pp. 113ff.

[6] T. Starkey, *A Dialogue between Pole and Lupset*, ed. T. Mayer (Royal Historical Society, Camden fourth series 37, 1989), p. xiii (and works there cited); Wyatt, *The Complete Poems*, ed. R. Rebholz (Harmondsworth, 1978), pp. 155, 186–9, 442.

[7] Quoted in C. H. Herford and P. and E. Simpson (eds.), *Ben Jonson* (11 vols., Oxford, 1925–52), IX, p. 590.

[8] Ludlow, *Voyce from the Watch Tower*, ed. Worden, p. 7; Algernon Sidney, *Works* (London, 1772), 'Discourses', p. 345.

[9] Lord Bolingbroke, *The Works* (4 vols., Philadelphia, 1841: Gregg International Publishers reprint, 1969), II, p. 94.

[10] M. Evans, (ed.), *Arcadia* (Harmondsworth, 1977), p. 766.

was that stern critic of sixteenth-century monarchies Hubert Languet, the orchestrator of international Protestantism. With the lessons of those teachers in mind, Sidney addresses in *Arcadia* the question what would happen if, as seemed all too likely, Elizabeth were to die with the succession to the throne unresolved. There were, it must have seemed, two main possibilities: the one, the submergence of England into religious wars akin to those of France and the Netherlands; the other, the succession of Mary Queen of Scots and the resumption of the Catholic proscriptions of Mary Tudor. In 1553 the families of both of Philip Sidney's parents – the Sidneys and the Dudleys – had faced a comparable problem, and had met it by committing themselves, disastrously, to Lady Jane Grey. Would Philip and his friends respond to the end of the present reign any more effectively?

The question is faced at the point of the story, near the end of Book Four, where Basilius, the King of Arcadia, appears to have died, an event clearly intended to foreshadow the death of Queen Elizabeth. Instantly the Arcadian state is on the brink of dissolution. The divided counsels of its leaders 'brought forth a dangerous tumult. ... For some there were that cried to have the state altered and governed no more by a prince: marry, in the alteration, many would have the Lacedaemonian government of few chosen senators; others, the Athenian, where the people's voice held the chief authority.' How intently such ideas were discussed by Sidney's circle we can only speculate. What is clear is Sidney's realization that on Elizabeth's death they would be at best superfluous. For the Arcadian advocates of Spartan or Athenian models 'were rather the discoursing sort of men than the active'. Their republicanism, in a phrase borrowed by Sidney from Tacitus, was 'a matter more in imagination than practice'. For 'they that went nearest the present case (as in a country that knew no government without a prince) were they that strove whom they should make' – that is, whom they should enthrone.[11] Those politicians who have an eye to the possible, instead of 'discoursing' about classical republics, recognize the hold of the monarchy, and of the nation's laws and customs, on Arcadian minds, and concentrate on advancing their candidates for the Crown. The death of Elizabeth would be no occasion for returning to the constitutional drawing-board. The only hope for such 'forward' Protestants as the Sidney circle, whatever their anxieties about monarchical rule, would be to agree on a Protestant heir and to support his (or her) claim more effectively than that of Jane Grey in 1553. Once he was enthroned, there might even be pressing arguments not for restricting his constitutional authority, or for implementing even the most desirable of republican principles, but on the contrary for enlarging the powers that would enable him to defy the Catholic menace. That perception, which confronted the Sidney circle in the 1580s,would re-emerge in a no less uncomfortable

[11] Ibid., p. 767. Cf. Bolingbroke, *Works*, II, p. 120. I hope to write elsewhere about the political content of *Arcadia*.

form in the 1680s, when republicans were delivered from the Catholic James II by the Protestant William III.

II

In the event the death of Elizabeth passed off peacefully. The only challenge to the monarchical system in 1603, the eccentric attempt by Sir Robert Basset and Nicholas Hill to establish a hermeticist utopia on the unpromising soil of Lundy Island, seems not to have been indebted to republicanism.[12] From 1603 to 1640, a period when the succession to the throne was clear and safe and the constitution unchallenged, republicanism was confined to speculation. The rage of 'Tacitism' in the late sixteenth and early seventeenth centuries found ample reflection in private commonplace books or in the plays of Jonson and Massinger, but republican insights were normally balanced – as they had been balanced in *Arcadia* – against their opposites; and while parallels between ancient and modern practice were often at the forefront of writers' minds, they remained the preoccupation of 'discoursing sort of men'. From the 1620s, of course, England experienced acute constitutional tensions. Yet their effect was to make the Crown's critics less intellectually enterprising and more insular. The growing fear of 'popery', though it fostered mistrust of the Crown, simultaneously strengthened the case for a monarchy powerful enough to defend Protestantism at home and abroad. When civil war came in 1642, republicanism bore very little relevance to events: an impotence that might not have characterized it if (say) the succession had broken down at some point between 1580 and 1620.

If republicanism did not cause the civil wars, it contributed little more to the execution of King Charles I in 1649 or to the establishment of a 'commonwealth and free state' four months later. In sections of the Cromwellian army and among some of its supporters there did flourish a rhetoric which saw in all regal power a 'lordly interest' distinct from, and incompatible with, the rights of the people, while a small group among the regicides had probably been influenced by their knowledge of classical or foreign republics. The principal impetus of the revolution of 1649, however, was hostility not to kingship but to a particular king. The revolutionaries cut off King Charles' head and wondered what to do next. In that quandary they saw no practicable alternative to the abolition of monarchy, but they brought little intellectual self-confidence to that task. It is not the victories of the Roundheads, but their failures, that explain the fertility of republican thought in the 1650s, the decade of Puritan rule. The impermanence of the successive improvised regimes of the Interregnum brought home the need to look more deeply into the principles on which a durable constitution might be built.

[12] H. R. Trevor-Roper, *Catholics, Anglicans and Puritans* (London, 1987), ch. 1.

The writers who met that challenge were not king-haters. James Harrington, the greatest of them, was a servant and friend of Charles I who composed his great work *Oceana* in an effort to come to terms with the new facts of power.[13] He argued that the origins of the civil wars lay in the transfers of property under Henry VII and Henry VIII that had produced the rise of the gentry at the expense of the Crown and of the peerage, and in the subsequent failure of the constitution to give the House of Commons a political power commensurate with its economic power: an explanation that absolved King Charles I of moral responsibility for the conflict. Of course, Harrington's proposals – the agrarian law that would correct the balance between political and economic power; the adoption of Venetian schemes of rotation and of balloting to eliminate corruption; the separation, in political decision making, of the power of debate from the power of resolution – would have terminated the ancient constitution of which the royalists portrayed themselves as the defenders. Yet Harrington was anxious to restore the franchise to the royalists, without whose participation the government must be the rule of 'a party', not 'a commonwealth'. Henry Nevile, Harrington's literary partner and his close friend, played no part in the regicide, and although he sat in the Rump Parliament which governed England from 1649 to 1653 he regarded it as a mere 'oligarchy', an arbitrary regime with no basis in principles of political wisdom. Algernon Sidney (Sir Philip's great-nephew), another member of the Rump, condemned the regicide as a mere military coup. The journalist Marchamont Nedham, whose editorials introduced classical principles of government to a wide readership, was a royalist in 1649.

It was only under Charles II that the analytical perceptions of republican theory were harnessed to incendiary purposes. The long exile of Algernon Sidney gave him ample time for the study of classical republics – and for the plotting of revenge. His chance came (or seemed to come) in the Exclusion Crisis of 1679–81, which prompted him to compose his *Discourses concerning Government*: a work eloquent in its praise of classical liberty and virtue, still more eloquent in its denunciation of Stuart tyranny and in its calls for its violent overthrow, but imprecise about the forms of government by which that tyranny should be replaced. Sidney's *Discourses* was not the only substantial republican response to the Exclusion Crisis, which also produced Henry Nevile's *Plato Redivivus*, an attempt to apply Harrington's diagnoses and cures to the reign of Charles II. Nevile's purpose, unlike Sidney's, was not incendiary. He urged Charles, as Harrington had urged Cromwell, to acknowledge the inherent instability of his regime. Let him be a modern Theopompus: let him yield his untenable prerogatives, assist the re-designing of his country's constitution, and thus

[13] B. Worden, 'Andrew Marvell, Oliver Cromwell, and the Horatian Ode', in K. Sharpe and S. Zwicker (eds.), *Politics of Discourse* (Berkeley and Los Angeles, 1987), p. 200.

exchange the ephemeral blessings of power for the lasting glory of a lawgiver. Charles was no more tempted by such a prospect than Cromwell before him. The hopes of Nevile as of Sidney were dashed. Just as, in the 1650s, republicans had depended for their success on their co-operation with members of the Rump and of Cromwell's army – men who, like them, called themselves 'commonwealthmen' – so at the crisis of Charles II's reign they were dependent on the Whig party; and by the time of Charles' death in 1685 the Whig party had been virtually extinguished. The power of the Stuart monarchy was at its height, its prerogatives apparently impregnable. The 'deliverance' of 1688 was unimaginable.

To the political exiles of Charles II's reign, many of whom spent time in Holland and sought the support of the republican party of Johan de Witt for their cause, the House of Orange was as inimical to liberty as the House of Stuart. Its seizure of power in 1672 was, to their minds, a 'usurpation'.[14] In 1688 the usurper became a deliverer – and so presented republicans with a dilemma with which, for a hundred years, they would struggle awkwardly and which they were never to resolve. The republican combination of gratitude for 1688 and criticism of it was at its plainest in the reign of William III, one of the most fertile periods, but also perhaps the most tortured one, in the republican tradition. The works of Robert Molesworth, Walter Moyle, John Trenchard, John Toland, and (in Scotland) Andrew Fletcher, found ample scope for criticism. Although the immediate threats of popery and absolutist rule had been removed, the appearance of freedom obscured, as they believed, the heightening of dangers from other quarters. The expansion of the executive, the influence of placemen, and the contention of parties combined to erode the independence, and therefore the representative function, of Parliament. William's resolve to maintain a standing army after the Peace of Ryswick in 1697 added, to the menace of corruption, the threat of force. Allies of the commonwealthmen in the 1650s and of the Whigs in the 1670s, republicans made common cause in the 1690s with the 'Country party' which, under the leadership of Robert Harley, gave bitter vent to its fears and suspicions of the executive in the 'standing army controversy' of 1697–9. To influence that debate, republicans produced effective pamphlets to show the incompatibility of standing armies with liberty and virtue. They also produced editions of the works of their seventeenth-century forebears – works by James Harrington, Henry Nevile, Algernon Sidney, John Milton, and Edmund Ludlow – which would form the republican canon of the eighteenth century and give an ideological foundation to the eighteenth-century ideal of the independent country gentleman. But there were inevitable limits to the radicalism of a Country party, or an independent party. The backbench country gentle-

[14] Ludlow, *Voyce from the Watch Tower*, ed. Worden, p. 12.

men whom republicans cultivated might be persuaded that the English constitution was being abused or that legislation was needed to restore or to secure its proper operation. They would not countenance criticism of the constitution itself. From 1688 republicans – even those of most iconoclastic temperament – remembered to genuflect to 'our admirable constitution', 'the old English constitution', a constitution 'the best, the most equal, and freest in the world'.[15]

The creation of a republican canon, and its adaption to Country party perspectives, were completed by the critics of the Whig oligarchy after 1714: by Trenchard and by Thomas Gordon, the authors of *Cato's Letters*, and by Bolingbroke. Republican thought would receive a fresh stimulus from the constitutional anxieties of the early years of George III's reign, not only in England but more significantly across the Atlantic, where Bernard Bailyn and others have established its place in *The Ideological Origins of the American Revolution*.[16] Within England, republicanism would thereafter acquire a new character, and a new meaning, under the pressures of popular radicalism and of the movement for parliamentary reform. Yet even then, the preoccupations of earlier republicans proved more persistent than we might expect.

It is, indeed, one of the most striking features of English republicanism that it so often repeats itself. Our chief concern will be with the adjustments of republicanism to historical change, and particularly to the changes wrought by the Revolution and to shifts within the legacy of that Revolution. But before we examine the changes we must inspect the continuities.

III

Republican man is a citizen, not (like Hobbes' man) a subject. His citizenship is dependent on the free exercise of his virtue and of his reason, and upon his participation, as an elector of representatives and as an arms-bearer, in the communal affairs of his country. It is threatened when rulers act not as the instruments of his wishes or of his interests but in distinction from them or in opposition to them. Or it is threatened when the rule of law yields to the rule of will and lust, or when the sovereignty of reason in government is usurped by passion. Monarchy is not the only form of government which can be turned to arbitrary purposes, but it is subject to weaknesses which, in the minds of early modern republicans, constitute the fundamental political problem of the age. Hereditary monarchy is especially vulnerable to abuse. Many of the rulers

[15] [John Trenchard and Walter Moyle], *An Argument showing that a Standing Army is inconsistent with a Free Government* (London, 1697), p. 13; John Toland, *The Art of Governing by Parties* (London, 1701), p. 33; John Toland, *Paradoxes of State* (London, 1702), pp. 4–5.

[16] Bailyn's seminal work was published at Cambridge, Mass., 1967. I have not dwelled, in this essay, on the influence of English republicanism in the eighteenth century on the continents of North America and Europe: a large subject.

it produces are infant, or inept, or insane. Even an hereditary king who is none of those things will be surrounded by flatterers, who exaggerate his powers and prerogatives and encourage him to regard his kingdom not as a trust but as a possession. Elective monarchy may be generally less objectionable, but can be a nursery of ambition and of civil war.

Yet it would be an over-simplification, and in important respects an error, to equate republicanism with opposition to kingship. First, republicans mostly subscribed to the principle of political consent, and acknowledged a nation's right to consent to monarchy. They accepted unanimously that in 1660 the English people had chosen to restore the Stuarts. To republican minds the choice was foolish, parallel in its folly to that with which the Israelites had set up kingship, and it was legitimate to urge the English to change their minds; but until they did so their decision must be respected. Secondly, republicans, who agreed with Aristotle about so much else, concurred with his principle of distributive justice, which awards political power in proportion to merit and is therefore ready to entrust a supremely wise and virtuous man with kingship. That principle was too remote from the everyday principles and practices of politics, and indeed from other components of republicans' thinking, to surface frequently in their proposals. Yet it helps to explain a feature of their writings which may initially seem surprising, but which had its logic: the occasional readiness of men who attributed so many of the world's evils to wicked kings to find faith in the beneficial capacity of good ones. Here republicans are the heirs of Machiavelli, a republican who found a redemptive role for the prince. We see the image of the Machiavellian prince – of the prince who exemplifies *virtù* – crossing the minds of Algernon Sidney and of his successors of the 1690s when they contrast the constitutional and military enfeeblement of England with the animation that had been brought to French arms and French administration by Louis XIV.[17] We see the image again when Bolingbroke spots the chance of toppling the Whig oligarchy not through a backbench revolt but through a 'patriot king'. And we shall see it exerting a spell in 1688–9.

Such arguments for kingship were on the periphery of, if not in contradiction to, the main thrust of republican thought. Others were nearer its centre. Republicans knew from Aristotle and Polybius that all pure forms of government – monarchy, aristocracy, democracy – tend to degenerate, and that the best form lies in a judicious balance or mixture of the three. Most of them therefore accepted the desirability of a monarchical component in the constitution, and felt that the title to be given to the 'single person' was a matter of words. But words could be important. For mixed governments, in republican understanding, were

[17] Algernon Sidney, 'Court Maxims Refuted and Refelled', MS, Warwickshire RO, pp. 149–57; *Plain English: or, an Enquiry into the Causes that have frustrated our Expectations from the late Happy Revolution* (London, 1691), p. 8.

properly named according to the element – monarchical, aristocratic, democratic – which predominated. No republican wanted the monarchical element to predominate, and after 1688 it was essential to the republican case that within the English constitution, as properly and anciently understood, it did not predominate. The aim of republicans was to secure the predominance sometimes of the aristocratic element, sometimes of the democratic element, sometimes of a mixture of the two. After 1688 the more tenacious of them protested against the application of the term 'mixed monarchy' to the new order by its Whig supporters.[18] They preferred to call it a 'mixed government' or 'mixed form'.[19] None of them, however, risked the assertion to which their logic pointed: that the English constitution should properly be called a mixed aristocracy or a mixed democracy.

Their caution on that front, as on so many others, is expressive of the permanent ambivalence within the republican tradition: the ambivalence of a movement at once critical of contemporary political assumptions and yet dependent for its influence on its ability to play on them – and indeed to share them. In their most penetrating or most confident moments – most of them moments which occurred in the seventeenth century rather than the eighteenth – republicans argued that the whole language of English political thought was too insular, too obsessed with precedent, too wanting in abstract formulation to be fitted to the development of a healthy state. But republicans were Englishmen who fought battles for English liberties, and fought them alongside men – often their friends or their fellow sufferers – who were suspicious of alien ideas and practices. It can be hard to know how much we should ascribe to tactics, and how much to conviction, when we find republicans diluting their republicanism: when (for example) we find Algernon Sidney repeatedly conceding the validity of 'mixed' or 'limited' or 'regulated' monarchy; or stressing that his target is not kingship, only tyranny; or declaring that the English monarchy had been 'legitimate', even healthy, at least until 1485, perhaps even to 1603. There is a comparable difficulty in interpreting some passages of Henry Nevile's *Plato Redivivus*. What we can say is that Sidney and Nevile made statements that were surely intended to bridge a philosophical gap between them and their intended audiences.

Pocock calls republicanism a language rather than a programme, and so it was. The forms of constitutions mattered less to republicans than their spirit, and once Harrington's generation has passed there is ever less emphasis (though there is always some) on the dependence of a healthy spirit upon healthy forms. If there is one principle that informs their conception of a healthy constitutional

[18] See Robert Molesworth's preface to his edition of *Franco-Gallia* (London, 1721), p. viii; and Toland, *Art of Governing*, pp. 32–3.

[19] E.g. J. Toland (ed.), *Works of James Harrington*, (London, 1700), p. viii; *A Collection of Scarce and Valuable Tracts* (Lord Somers), cited here in the later version, ed. W. Scott (13 vols., London, 1809–15), X, p. 199. For a more cautious view see [Trenchard and Moyle], *Argument*, p. 2.

spirit more than any other, it is the principle of reason, of which liberty and virtue are the expressions, and which republicans contrast with passion, the root of slavery, and vice. Politics are the public projection of the battle, fought within every man, between reason and passion for mastery of the soul. Algernon Sidney was shocked by the appeal of his opponent, the Tory patriarchalist Sir Robert Filmer, to the 'natural instinct' which Filmer held to justify absolute monarchy, for, wrote Sidney, 'this instinct (if there be any such thing) is only an irrational appetite, attributed to beasts, who know not why they do any thing'.[20] Rationalists in politics, the republicans are rationalists too in religion. To a man they reject the Calvinist doctrine of predestination, and move instead toward teachings which allow room for man's dignity and for his reason in his attainment of salvation. Seventeenth-century republicans are Arminians and Socinians (anti-trinitarians). After 1688, like Toland and Bolingbroke, they are deists and freethinkers. In the late eighteenth and early nineteenth centuries they are often Unitarians (and scientists and mathematicians).

Reason likewise asserted its supremacy in the republicans' reading of history. They saw history – classical history, European history, English history – as a vast storehouse of political and moral instruction: as philosophy teaching by examples. They found in it a series of parallels between past and present – most particularly the parallel between the period of the early Roman Empire and their own: between the extinction of senatorial independence in Rome and the decline of noble and parliamentary independence in early modern Europe. When it suited them they would, like most politicians, find in English history precedents or sanctions for their claims. Yet the general effect of their historical studies – often extensive studies – was to liberate them from the tyranny exerted by English history over so much political debate. Moving with ease from one country or period to another, they looked for universal principles which transcended national rights and customs. They came to admire the landmarks of English liberty, like Magna Carta, less because of their antiquity or their legal authority than because they gave expression to principles of reason written in the hearts of men. Algernon Sidney asserted, in terms close to John Locke's, the authority of 'not so much that which is most ancient, as that which is best'.[21] Certainly it might be desirable, in a political crisis, to renew a constitution, in accordance with Machiavelli's teaching, by returning to ancient principles which had become corrupted. Yet it was equally open to any community to 'add' new constitutional provisions which would take account of social evolution or of the discoveries of reason. It was no less open to it to abandon its constitution and adopt a fresh one: a point which republicans frequently felt able to make

[20] Sidney, *Works*, 'Discourses', pp. 104–5.
[21] Ibid., p. 404.

before the Revolution, and which they made boldly during it, but with which they were much less free in the century that followed.

IV

Whatever the changes that republicans hoped to bring, how could they effect them? The problem which confronted Sir Philip Sidney's discoursing Arcadians on the demise of King Basilius remained the problem of English republicanism too. Late in the eighteenth century James Mackintosh, arguing for 'popular government', invoked Machiavelli's principle of constitutional renewal by a return to first principles. Yet, he observed, such renovation could only be achieved in 'a period of convulsion', for 'no hope of great political improvement ... is to be entertained from tranquillity'.[22] Only a 'convulsion' would supply what Machiavelli had called the *occasione* – the occasion or opportunity – upon which men's actions would determine the future liberty or slavery or their country. Perhaps Mackintosh was right. Yet the graver the convulsion, the more anxiously most men would cling – as the Arcadians had clung – to the political institutions and assumptions they already knew. For that reason the history of English republicanism is a history of missed *occasioni*. The paragraphs ahead will cite a number of instances when the words 'opportunity' and 'occasion' were used to describe the turning-points – or the missed turning-points – of seventeenth-century English history. There is no need to suppose – what is highly unlikely – that most of the writers who will be quoted had Machiavelli in mind (though some of them probably did). What they did share with Machiavelli was the sense that history offers rare moments when the happiness and liberty of the nation, for generations or even centuries to come, are won or lost.

The seventeenth century saw three such opportunities: those of 1649, of 1679–81, and of 1688–9. The most boldly created was the first. In 1649 the New Model Army had prepared a fresh constitution, or at least a new set of constitutional principles, in the *Agreement of the People*. The Levellers, who had urged the *Agreement* on the army's leaders, would lament that its abandonment had cost the nation the '*opportunity* which these 600 years has been desired, but could never be attained, of making this a truly happy and wholly free nation'.[23] Milton, too, saw 1649 as an epochal opportunity. He saw in it the chance to introduce, not the army's programme, but the principles and practices of classical antiquity. Watching that chance slip through his countrymen's fingers, he found a parallel in the withdrawal of the Romans from Britain, an event at which, he recalled, the English had 'such a smooth *occasion* given them to free themselves as after ages have not afforded'. The 'ill husbanding of those

22 James Mackintosh, *Vindiciae Gallicae* (London, 1791), pp. 107–8.
23 J. McMichael and B. Taft (eds.), *Works of William Walwyn* (Athens, Ga., 1989), p. 336.

fair *opportunities*' had deprived the nation of more than a thousand years of political well-being. Now, in 1649, Milton asks whether the English are any better equipped to create 'a just and well-amended commonwealth to come'. His answer is melancholy. Stuck in insular postures, intimidated by enemies at home and abroad, England's new rulers are merely propping up what is left of the ancient constitution.[24] Eleven years later Milton recalled that in 1649 'the form of a new commonwealth should indeed have forthwith been framed, and the practice thereof immediately begun, that the people might have been satisfied and delighted with the decent order, ease and benefit thereof ... this care of timely settling a new government instead of the old, too much neglected, hath been our mischief'.[25]

By then another *occasione* had gone begging: that offered by the decline and fall of the Cromwellian protectorate in the spring of 1659. For then the bankruptcy of puritan political thought was made plain. The soldiers and MPs who collaborated to bring down the protectorate could agree on no alternative save the restoration of the same Rump Parliament that had been left in power in 1649 and had clung to it until 1653. Its deficiencies as a political system – its failure to separate executive from legislature, its arbitrary assumption of judicial powers, its inability to devise a satisfactory scheme for fresh elections – had provoked its indignant dissolution by the army that was now reduced to restoring it. In such circumstances the arguments of Harrington and Nevile acquired a practical force. The ancient constitution had been destroyed – and, given the power of the Cromwellian army, there was no prospect of its reconstruction, at least without a prior return to civil war. Surely the time was ripe to adopt the fresh constitutional machinery devised by Harrington, machinery which offered the promise not merely of stability but of permanent stability. In March 1659, when the authority of Richard Cromwell was shaken by Parliament, and again early in May when he was overthrown, such ideas were widely canvassed. Once they had been rejected, republicanism became, in the period which remained before the Restoration, a matter of mere talk, the subject of distinguished debate at the Rota Club but having little impact upon the political process which destroyed political Puritanism and brought back the ancient constitution. Yet even in the spring of 1660, that time of fresh 'convulsion' which

[24] D. M. Wolfe (ed.), *The Complete Prose Works of John Milton* (8 vols., New Haven, Conn., 1953–82), V (i), pp. 441–3. I have discussed the dating of Milton's remarks in my essay 'Milton's Republicanism and the Tyranny of Heaven'. Milton's associates John Hall and Marchamont Nedham, who like him wrote on behalf of the new republic, portrayed 1603 as a missed republican 'opportunity': Hall, *The Grounds and Reasons of Monarchy* (1650), reprinted in James Harrington, Works (London, 1700), pp. 27–8; Nedham, *The Excellency of a Free State* (1656, repr. London, 1767), pp. xv, 146. Thomas Starkey had warned his countrymen not to 'let slip' the republican 'occasion' offered by the Reformation parliament: Starkey, *A Dialogue between Pole and Lupset* [n. 6 above], pp. 17, 142.

[25] Wolfe (ed.), *Complete Prose Works of John Milton*, VII, p. 430.

preceded the king's return, Milton saw another *occasione*: 'Now is the *opportunity*, now the very season wherein we may obtain a free commonwealth and establish it for ever in the land'.[26]

The reign of Charles II gave republicans time and cause to reflect on the missing of opportunities. From 1660, a year which produced a coup for monarchy not only in England but in Denmark, the sky appeared to republicans to darken across Europe. Regarding the Exclusion Crisis as a last chance to forestall the expiry of liberty, they urged their countrymen, in phrases which became a regular feature of republican exhortations, to act 'in time', before it was 'too late'. Astonishingly, in less than a decade, the English would be granted one opportunity more: indeed, in republican eyes, the greatest opportunity of all. It was also, in their eyes, to be one more opportunity missed.

That republican interpretation of 1688 may arouse modern scepticism. The Revolution, a monarchical coup by an invading Prince, surely gave much less scope to republicans than the regicide four decades earlier. In any case, whatever the Revolution failed to achieve, it did put an end to extra-parliamentary absolutism. The invading Prince and the English politicians who combined to curb it did take their 'opportunity', with courage and decisiveness. Yet the second great revolution of the seventeenth century impressed itself more firmly on republicans as a failed opportunity than the first. *Now Is the Time*, proclaimed the title of a pamphlet of 1689 which argued that 'there is now one thing we have *opportunity* to obtain which we can never again recover if it be lost, ... the delivery of the people from slavery, which can never be done effectually and radically but upon this advantage'; the English 'have such an *opportunity* which ... they are never like to see but once'.[27] Another pamphlet of the Revolution claimed that to build a government which would 'last for ages' would be 'easy, and prudent' if attempted now, unattainable if the enterprise were postponed.[28] An MP told the Convention that 'Since God hath put this *opportunity* into our hands, all the world will laugh at us if we make a half settlement.'[29] The Convention, thought John Locke, had 'an *opportunity* offered to find remedies, and set up a constitution that may be lasting': an '*opportunity*', he repeated, which must not be missed, for there was now 'an *occasion* not of amending the government, but of melting it down and making all new', of creating 'a right scheme of government'.[30] There is no more tantalizing a gap in the history of English political thought than Locke's failure to indicate what scheme he had in mind.

[26] Ibid.

[27] *A Collection of Scarce and Valuable Tracts* (Lord Somers), X, pp. 200, 202.

[28] *A Collection of State Tracts Publish'd on Occasion of the Late Revolution in 1688, and during the Reign of King William* (3 vols., London, 1705), III, I, pp. 151, 162.

[29] Quoted in Mark Goldie's article – which is indispensable to the student of republican thought in 1688 and beyond – 'The Roots of True Whiggism', *History of Political Thought*, 1 (1980), p. 33.

[30] Quoted by Julian Franklin, *John Locke and the Theory of Sovereignty* (Cambridge, 1978), p. 121.

The opportunity was squandered, and for a hundred years republicans would lament its loss. The nation paid the price, as John Toland put it, for 'the insufficiency of our hasty bill of rights',[31] a judgment with which successive writers would concur. In 1744 the historian James Ralph complained that at the Revolution 'such an *opportunity* was lost of resettling our old constitution as England is not like to have again'.[32] In 1760 Tobias Smollett regretted that the revolutionaries had neglected 'the fairest *opportunity* that ever occurred' to retrench the Crown's prerogatives.[33] And in 1773 a contributor to the *London Evening Post* saw the Revolution as 'the best *opportunity* we ever had of establishing our liberties upon a permanent foundation'.[34]

In what, then, had the opportunity consisted, and why had it not been met? The republicans of 1688–9 suffered defeats both of procedure and of substance. The Convention which enthroned William and Mary, like its predecessor of 1660, was named a convention rather than a parliament because there had been no king to summon it. Republicans wanted the Convention – or a more representative version of it – to be not a lesser thing than a parliament but a greater one. In their view the removal of King James had dissolved the constitution. Power had thereby reverted to the people, whose exercise of it required the summoning of a national constitutional convention. The decisions of that convention would be binding on future governments and on future representatives.[35] The people now had the right 'to set up what government they please': they 'may erect a new one, either according to the old model ... or any other that they like and approve of better'.[36]

If such a convention had assembled, what proposals would republicans have submitted to it? Here the evidence is sadly thin. 'Many speak, in coffee houses and better places, of fine things for you to do', one MP sardonically told the Convention.[37] Perhaps the coffee houses included the Grecian, where Henry Nevile would hold court in the early 1690s, but what the 'fine things' were we have largely to guess. Harringtonian analyses of the relationship of power to property, and Harringtonian arguments for the rotation of office, found their

[31] Toland, *Paradoxes of State*, p. 2.

[32] J. Ralph, *The History of England* (2 vols., London, 1744), II, p. 5.

[33] T. Smollett, *The History of England from the Revolution to the death of George II* (5 vols., London, 1788 edn), I, p. 3.

[34] Quoted by H. T. Dickinson, 'The Eighteenth-Century Debate on the "Glorious Revolution"', *History*, 61 (1976), p. 41.

[35] Goldie, 'True Whiggism', pp. 214–15; Franklin, *John Locke*, p. 121. Goldie and Franklin believe that this argument was inherited from George Lawson, the political thinker of the Puritan Revolution, but it may alternatively (or also) have derived from Harrington and Nevile: see Caroline Robbins (ed.), *Two Republican Tracts* (Cambridge, 1959), pp. 10–11. Tom Paine would argue for a national constitutional convention in 1792. See too *Mercurius Politicus* 2–9 Oct. 1651, p. 1111.

[36] *A Collection of Scarce and Valuable Tracts* (Lord Somers), X, p. 195; *Collection of State Tracts* I, p. 162. This position is very close to Algernon Sidney's earlier in the decade: Sidney, *Works*, 'Discourses', p. 485.

[37] Anchitell Grey, *Debates of the House of Commons from the Year 1667 to the Year 1694* (10 vols., London, 1769), IX, p. 32.

way into the radical pamphlets of 1689.[38] Yet they look tentative and hastily assembled: a weakness understandable amidst such fast-moving and unpredictable events, but fatal to any hopes republicans might have had of shaping them. The truth is that the Revolution had caught republicans unprepared. As they would admit, it 'came on too soon'.[39] And it occurred at a time when the intellectual resources of republicanism were at a low ebb. The Tory reaction of the early 1680s, which had brought Algernon Sidney to the block and driven other critics of the Stuart regime into exile, had done its work. The bold theorists among the Whigs of the Exclusion Crisis found themselves, from 1683 to 1688, deprived of a public audience. Sustained only by a sense of martyrdom, despairing of deliverance from the 'Stuart revenge' by any means short of assassination, they saw no point in, and were in no position and no mood to attempt, the rational political persuasion of their countrymen. Although republican ideas were far from dead in 1688, the Revolution did occur during an interval in their development. The older generation, schooled by the experiences of Cromwell and Charles II, was dying or demoralized. The younger generation which would be so vigorous in the 1690s had yet to emerge.

Two ageing writers, both survivors of Cromwellian politics, did bridge the gap of generations: Henry Nevile and John Wildman, collaborators in Charles II's reign and again in William III's.[40] But nothing published in1688–9 is known to be Nevile's. He may have published anonymously, as many of the radical pamphleteers of the Revolution found it prudent to do. Yet even if he did, neither he nor anyone else in 1688–9 wrote a work comparable in stature to the classic literature of political opposition which in the Exclusion Crisis had been produced by Sidney, Locke, James Tyrrell, and Nevile himself. Wildman did play an identifiable (although anonymous) part in the Revolutionary debate; and although the persistent political opportunism of his career may cast doubt on the sincerity of the Harringtonian proposals which he advanced, his readiness to advance them indicates his belief in their potential appeal. Yet it is Wildman, more than anyone, who reveals the essential dilemma which faced republicanism in 1688–9: the dilemma which Sir Philip Sidney had confronted a century earlier. Like the more realistic critics of monarchy in *Arcadia*, Wildman sees the case, amidst the grave uncertainties of 1688–9, for a strong and friendly monarch. His difficulty in knowing which way to jump becomes plain in the transparent inconsistency of a pamphlet in which he argues for a radical curbing of the prerogative and yet ends by lauding the benefits which 'absolute and arbitrary monarchy' might bring if entrusted to William, 'the prince'.[41] Another pamphle-

[38] Goldie, 'True Whiggism', p. 213; *A Collection of Scarce and Valuable Tracts* (Lord Somers), X, p. 197; *Collection of State Tracts*, I, pp. 156–7 (cf. *ibid.*, I, p. 381, II, pp. 604–5, 631, 645).
[39] Goldie, 'True Whiggism', p. 235.
[40] For their consociation see Robbins (ed.), *Two Republican Tracts*, pp. 16, 18.
[41] *Collection of State Tracts*, I, p. 162.

teer, recommending a Harringtonian scheme for rotation of office, injected into it the hope that William, 'the prince', would be 'the glorious author of the Britanick liberty'.[42]

The presence of John Wildman in the republican ranks of 1688–9 points us to a feature of their thought that may initially surprise us: its affinities with the Leveller ideas of the late 1640s and the 1650s which Wildman had done so much to influence. The republicans of 1689 affirmed, in clear echoes of the Levellers, that 'all power is originally or fundamentally in the people'. They envisaged the constitution that they wanted to emerge from the national constitutional convention as an 'agreement of the people', who would retain 'reservations of liberty' akin to the rights which, in the Leveller *Agreement of the People* of 1647, were 'reserved by the represented to themselves'.[43] The pamphleteers of 1689 likewise called for measures of electoral reform that would emulate the Leveller programme, not least in shifting power away from the leaders of the county communities towards the small property-owners of the 'hundred' and the 'wapentake'.[44]

What should we make of the common cause of republican and Leveller ideas in 1688–9? The Revolution is often described as an aristocratic coup, and so, in its power politics, it may have been. Yet it depended for its success on the acquiescence of a political nation which was at least as broad and as knowledgeable as that of the civil wars, and which, now as then, republicans and Levellers alike addressed. It is true that in the 1650s the two groups had gone separate ways. Levellers had shown little if any interest in classical commonwealths. Harrington disliked Leveller notions of unlimited popular sovereignty, which seemed to him to carry as high a risk of tyranny as did unlimited monarchy. Yet he was sympathetic to the Levellers' proposed social reforms, and like them he spoke the language of the 'good old cause'. Like them he spoke the language of 'an equal commonwealth' and of 'popular government'. So would the republicans of the 1690s; so would *Cato's Letters* in the 1720s, which argued, as Harrington had done, for an agrarian law that would prevent extremities of wealth; and so in the 1730s would Bolingbroke.[45]

There is, it is true, a strain in the republican tradition which admires the aristocracy and admires wealth. There is the feudal component of what Pocock calls the 'neo-Harringtonianism' of Charles II's reign, which inverts Harrington's democratic preoccupations.[46] There is the readiness of the critics of standing

[42] *A Collection of Scarce and Valuable Tracts* (Lord Somers), X, p. 197.

[43] Ibid., X, pp. 195, 197, 198, 199; S. R. Gardiner (ed.), *Constitutional Documents of the Puritan Revolution* (London, 1889), p. 334.

[44] Franklin, *John Locke*, p. 119; B. Worden, *The Rump Parliament 1648–1653* (Cambridge, 1974), p. 146. Goldie, 'True Whiggism', p. 215, observes that Wildman 'was probably the author of a pamphlet of 1659 called *The Leveller*, which . . . combined Leveller and Harringtonian theories'.

[45] *Cato's Letters* (2 vols., London, 1733), II, p. 16; Bolingbroke, *Works*, II, p. 122.

[46] J. G. A. Pocock, *Politics, Language and Time* (London, 1971), ch. 4.

armies in the late 1690s to idealize the feudal array, or their insistence that only the choice of 'rich' MPs[47] by a restricted and economically independent electorate could prevent the corruption of Parliament. Yet most republicans – even Bolingbroke – wanted the predominant form of the constitution to be democratic. The series of major republican editions produced in the later years of William III's reign were distinguished, as their editor remarked, by 'their democratical schemes of government'.[48] Even Algernon Sidney, who differed from other republicans in wishing for an aristocratic rather than a democratic commonwealth, understood by a true nobility not the peerage of his own time but what he believed to have been the much larger class of Anglo-Saxon warrior leaders.[49] The modern nobility, by contrast, was often criticized by Sidney and by other republicans as parasitic and oppressive.

The republican concept of democracy was not our own, but nor was the Leveller one. 'Leveller', too, was a pejorative term. Few of those we call Levellers wanted a universal male franchise. Many of them were concerned less with the extent of the electorate than with the inequalities of its distribution: with the difference in the franchise between one borough and the next, or with the geographical unevenness that gave representation to under-populated communities and denied it to over-populated ones. Nervous of enfranchising servants or other economically dependent groups, the Levellers were the friends, as the republicans were, of a property-owning democracy.[50] John Wildman was among the writers who after 1688 proposed to restrict rather than to widen the electorate.[51] Republicans distinguished sharply between democracy and the anarchy with which it was often associated. John Toland, editing Harrington's *Oceana* in 1700, declared that the work supplied 'a full answer to those who imagine there can be no distinctions or degrees, neither nobility nor gentry, in a democracy', while Thomas Gordon would mean by 'the people ... not the idle and indigent rabble' but 'all who have property, without the privileges of nobility'.[52] Those statements are not so distant from the Levellers' desire that 'every man may with as much security as may be enjoy his propriety', or from their repudiation of the charge 'that we would level all men's estates, that we would have no distinction of orders and dignities amongst men, that we are indeed for ... popular confusion'.[53]

When republicans referred to the democratic element in the English constitu-

47 *Collection of State Tracts*, II, p. 650; Toland, *Art of Governing*, pp. 165–6.
48 Ludlow, *Voyce from the Watch Tower*, ed. Worden, p. 31.
49 Worden, 'Commonwealth Kidney', p. 23.
50 Though its shortcomings have been much remarked, there remain important insights in C. B. Macpherson's discussion of the Levellers in his *The Political Theory of Possessive Individualism* (Oxford, 1962).
51 Goldie, 'True Whiggism', p. 214.
52 Toland (ed.), *Works of Harrington*, p. xxiii; T. Gordon (transl.), *The Works of Tacitus* (2 vols., London, 1728–31), II, p. 109.
53 McMichael and Taft (eds.), *Writings of William Walwyn*, pp. 337–8.

tion they meant the House of Commons. The beneficiaries of their electoral proposals would have been – as the beneficiaries of the reforms proposed by the Levellers in the 1640s and implemented by Cromwell in the 1650s had been – the smaller gentry and the independent freeholders who resented the electoral patronage of the court and of the great nobility. It was to those groups that the republicans looked, from the 1690s onwards, in their attempts to build a Country party philosophy. Many of the Levellers had come from families of minor gentry or substantial freeholders,[54] and there is a sense in which the Levellers – who wished to restrict the powers of any executive, whether monarchical or parliamentary or both, over the people – are the first Country party in English history. In the succeeding Country parties, of the later seventeenth and of the eighteenth centuries, the ideological backbone would be supplied not by Levellers, whose names and writings came almost to disappear from view, but by republicans. In the late eighteenth century, the movement for parliamentary reform would assume a new character that would gradually expose the limits of earlier republican or Leveller concepts of democracy. Even so, the republicans may have been largely responsible for the inheritance by the late eighteenth century of a language of equality that the popular radicals were to put to such different uses.

Yet that language, though present in the pamphlets of the Revolution, made no impact on its events. There were many Whigs in the Convention – 'old Whigs' or 'true Whigs', men to whom republicans naturally looked for support – who were eager to impose restrictions on the Crown. They wanted to curb its veto, its power of making war and peace, its control of the summoning and dissolving of parliaments. Such changes would indeed have altered the balance of the constitution in the direction republicans favoured. But in the main the interest of backbench Whigs was less in political or constitutional theory than in achieving security of liberty and property. They wished to make it impossible for William and his successors to repeat the misdemeanours of their seventeenth-century predecessors, and to that end they wished to impose the 'limitations' which, they believed, should have been enforced in 1660. Their programme rapidly succumbed before William's unwillingness to listen to it, and the republican programme succumbed with it.

A century later James Mackintosh would put his finger on the problem which the radicals of 1689 had faced. The policy of 'limitations', he argued, had been the right one – but had been pressed on the wrong king. 'Fortunate would it have been for England, if the person of James II had been retained while his authority was limited. ... The odium of personal misconduct would have kept alive a salutary jealousy of power', and the people would not have been 'compelled to entrust their new sovereign with exorbitant strength to defend

[54] G. E. Aylmer, 'Gentlemen Levellers?', *Past and Present*, 49 (1970), pp. 120–5.

their freedom and *his* contested throne.'[55] Mackintosh's observation, of course, had more logic than realism. It could scarcely have been formulated before the effective extinction of the Jacobites. If any members of the Convention had thoughts on preserving James II under limitations, they were Tories. William was indispensable to the Whigs, and so, once he had shown his determination to preserve it, was the ancient constitution. The 'old Whig' John Hampden assured the Convention that 'I am not for a commonwealth, in the posture now of affairs we are in'.[56] Next year the Whig MP Sir Thomas Littleton told the Commons that 'your government is not strong enough to try experiments upon; you have too many already'.[57] It became easy to mock 'whomsoever they are ... who prefer a commonwealth before a monarchy', and to deride writers who wished to exchange England's 'form of government', which 'the wisdom of past ages' had 'moulded', 'for some Utopian state, or other vain chimeras'.[58] The swift deportation of the regicide Edmund Ludlow, who in 1689 returned to England from his long exile to greet the hour of deliverance, removed all possibility of republican illusion.

Republicans reacted to defeat with a sense of disenchantment and of betrayal. In their eyes the failure of the settlement to secure fundamental constitutional change ensured that the conflict between William and James would be a conflict merely about the occupancy, as distinct from the powers, of the Crown, and would prove as protracted and destructive as the wars of York and Lancaster. The Revolution, thought Robert Molesworth, had been 'a piece of good luck, and that's the best that can be said for it'; and the ensuing settlement had done nothing to cure the basic weakness of modern English politics, 'the necessity of a civil war once or twice an age'. England owed her deliverance, observed Trenchard and Moyle, not to virtue or wisdom but to a fortuitous 'combination of causes (which may never happen again)'. The remedy had been as hazardous as it had been lucky, for, as Andrew Fletcher remarked, England had been rescued by 'a foreign force ... and how dangerous a remedy that is, the histories of all ages can witness'.[59]

V

Yet even as the republicans complained about the limits and about the insecurity of the alterations wrought by the Revolution, their strategy showed how profound those alterations had been. In the 1690s the language of consti-

[55] Mackintosh, *Vindiciae Gallicae*, p. 193.
[56] Goldie, 'True Whiggism', p. 216.
[57] John Kenyon, *Revolution Principles* (London, 1977), p. 38.
[58] *Plain English*, pp. 25–6. Cf. *Collection of State Tracts*, II, p. 381.
[59] Robert Molesworth, *An Account of Denmark as it was in the year 1692* (London, 1694), preface, sigs. a6v–a7r; [Trenchard and Moyle], *Argument*, p. 16; *The Political Works of Andrew Fletcher* (London, 1737), p. 27. Cf. Bolingbroke, *Works*, II, p. 86.

tutional conflict was redefined, and the language of republicanism changed with it. The prolonged seventeenth-century quarrel between Crown and Parliament was yielding to a new struggle, between the Crown-in-Parliament and the nation. The menace of prerogative was yielding to the menace of corruption. New opportunities were open to the republicans if they could exploit the fresh sources of mistrust of the executive. They could appeal not only to 'old' or 'true' Whigs, who felt as betrayed as they did by the settlement and by the apparent apostasy of the 'junto', but to backbench MPs of no party allegiance or even of Tory allegiance. Robert Harley's Country party crossed the existing party lines. Yet if republicans were to supply its ideology, they must observe new decencies. They must appear friends, not enemies, of the Revolution. They must refer to William, at least from time to time, as a glorious deliverer. They must complain, not that 1688 had exchanged old evils for new, but merely that more fundamental curbs on the prerogative were needed if the Revolution were to be given the stability and security it deserved.

The republican progress towards respectability, although uneven, was soon evident. One example will illustrate the change. In 1675 Henry Nevile, publishing his translation of the works of Machiavelli, had attached to them a 'letter', written ostensibly by Machiavelli but really by Nevile, in which the Florentine's lessons were subtly adapted to the political problems of Charles II's reign. The letter was perhaps the first, and perhaps the most inventive, of a series of publications to emerge from the history factory so enterprisingly operated by the republicans of the later seventeenth century. In 1691 the letter was reprinted – but with discreet alterations. Nevile's – ostensibly Machiavelli's – preference for a 'commonwealth' over other forms of government is silently eliminated. His renunciation of the doctrine of resistance is underlined. And where the earlier version refers to 'the plague of princes', the later one narrows the target to 'the plague of tyrants'.[60] After 1688, when resistance theory became predominantly Jacobite theory, republicans normally distanced themselves from what Tories called 'that popish republican doctrine of resistance to princes'.[61]

By the end of William's reign, republicans were in retreat. The death of the duke of Gloucester in 1700 threw the Protestant succession into uncertainty, and helped to persuade the Whigs to heal their differences. John Toland, who in the 1690s had done as much as anyone to keep republican hopes alive, pointed out in 1701 that 'not one single person among the real or reputed republicans' had embarrassed the Whig leadership by opposing the Act of Settlement, and announced in 1702 that 'all the republican pretences are quite out of doors'.[62]

[60] The authorship of the letter is identified, and its publishing history described, by Felix Raab, *The English Face of Machiavelli* (London, 1964), appendix B.

[61] Kenyon, *Revolution Principles*, p. 152.

[62] John Toland, *Anglia Libera* (London, 1701), pp. 48–9; Toland, *Paradoxes of State*, p. 4.

Republicans, it now emerged, had been critics never of monarchy, only of 'the Turkish and French forms of monarchy'. Admittedly the events of the seventeenth century had sometimes tempted them to despair of 'the very name' of a king, but now 'the republicans enjoy liberty under a king, though they once thought [a king and a republic] dissociable things and scarce to be reconciled'.[63] A pamphleteer of 1698, who accepted Harrington's reading of the relationship of power to property in the Stuart age, observed nonetheless that, since 'the common good of the people' had been achieved by the Revolution, 'he is fit only for a madhouse who will endeavour to pull down the established form only to introduce a new one'.[64] Of course, criticism of the Revolutionary settlement persisted. Yet in expressing it republicans became careful to say only that the constitutional improvements of the settlement had yet to be 'perfected', an outcome that could be trusted to time and experience.[65] Under Queen Anne republicans became more cautious still, and during the Tory reaction of her last years they either kept their heads well down or, if they tried to raise them, found difficulty in getting their work published. The Hanoverian succession of 1714 overthrew the Tories, but did nothing to strengthen republicanism among the Whigs.

Republicans were not necessarily losing their energy or their commitment. Rather, they were changing their emphases. The alliance of republicanism with resistance theory, evident in Sidney and in the pamphlets of 1688–9, was dissolving. Ideas of contract and consent, with which Sidney and the pamphleteers of 1688–9 had challenged the prerogative, were now invoked by republicans to justify the rule of William. Republican criticism of the new order concentrated instead on the corruptive properties of courts. Thus the Revolutionary settlement had enjoyed the consent of the people, and so had given 'the best of kings ... the best of titles', but 'fatal experience has now more than enough convinced us, that courts have been the same in all ages'.[66] Under Cromwell and Charles II a good 'commonwealthman' had been distinguished primarily by his willingness to resist tyranny. His distinguishing feature after 1688 was his incorruptibility: his distaste for, and detachment from, political intrigue, his vigilant mistrust of faction and of placemen, his immunity to the temptations of favour and advancement. During the Exclusion Crisis Henry Nevile's *Plato Redivivus* had made a criticism of some MPs which would look anachronistic when the work was republished in 1698. He rebuked members who were opposed to the Stuart tyranny, but who were allowing their wish to preserve their independence of judgment, and their freedom from party, to preclude them from effective political

[63] Toland, *Anglia Libera*, pp. 48, 83.
[64] *Collection of State Tracts*, II, p. 635.
[65] Toland, *Anglia Libera*, p. 18; Toland, *Clito* (London, 1700), preface.
[66] *Collection of State Tracts*, II, p. 640–1.

commitment.[67] After 1688 republicans hailed such abstinence as a virtue. The Machiavellian virtue of civic participation, prominent in Harrington and Sidney, was yielding to the virtue of Stoic detachment. In recommending it to Harley's Country party and to its eighteenth-century successors, the republicans delicately adjusted the mantles of their heroes. Algernon Sidney's incendiary propensities and his hostility to prerogative were played down, his scorn for corruption and venality played up. 'The picture of corrupt government', declared Toland, 'was never so well drawn to the life as by the great Colonel Sidney', who 'sums up the character of evil ministers, charging them with the most detestable traffic in procuring or disposing of preferments'.[68] Walter Moyle refuted the charge that Sidney's *Discourses* 'makes the grounds and obligations of subjection and obedience to government too precarious and loose'. 'This objection', he maintained, 'seems to be taken from some incorrect expressions which have fallen from his pen, and do not arise from the regular hypotheses he advances':[69] a profoundly misleading statement which, whether or not it helped to shape the predominant image of Sidney in the eighteenth century, certainly accorded with it. Thomas Gordon repeated Moyle's tactic. Accused of a 'republican' purpose in quoting Sidney in *Cato's Letters*, Gordon replied that

> the passages I take out of his book are not republican passages, unless virtue and truth be republican. ... Mr. Sidney's book, for the main of it, is ... agreeable to our own constitution, which is the best republic in the world, with a prince at the head of it. ... I hope ... never to see any other form of government in England than that which is now ... if this be the style and spirit of a republican, I glory in it.[70]

The adjective most commonly applied to Sidney after the Revolution was 'disinterested' – at least until the embarrassing revelation, in 1773, that Algernon had taken bribes from the French ambassador Barillon.

In claiming the principle of Stoic incorruptibility for their cause, the republicans of the late seventeenth century made an enduring contribution to English political ideology. In making it, they put their history factory on to overtime. In 1697 it manufactured another 'letter', this one ostensibly written by Algernon Sidney at the Restoration. Emphasizing Algernon's aversion to 'bribery', the document was universally taken as authentic, was widely read, and would be frequently reprinted.[71] The following year, which saw the first publication of Sidney's *Discourses*, also produced, from the same editor and the same publisher, the *Memoirs of Edmund Ludlow*, in which the autobiographical manuscript bequeathed by that violent millenarian was ruthlessly re-written so as to present

[67] Robbins (ed.), *Two Republican Tracts*, pp. 196–7.
[68] Toland, *Art of Governing*, pp. 112–13.
[69] *The Whole Works of Walter Moyle* (London, 1727), p. 58.
[70] *Cato's Letters*, I, pp. 195–6, 204, II, p. 28.
[71] Worden, 'Commonwealth Kidney', p. 29.

Ludlow as a polite, reflective, 'disinterested' country gentleman, blessed with 'the virtues of Scipio and Cato',[72] watchfully suspicious of, and inflexibly resistant to, the corruption of Oliver Cromwell's court. In the eighteenth century – to use a contemporary term – the 'politing' of republican heroes was taken further. It was not only English heroes who were redeemed from their insurrectionary pasts. Thomas Gordon, in praising Marcus Brutus, concentrated less on his assassination of Julius Caeasar than on Julius' venality and on Brutus' subsequent refusal to be bought off by Octavian.[73] Gordon, the tamer of Brutus, tamed Tacitus too. In the seventeenth century the Elizabethan translation by Henry Savile had kept alive the terse irony and the epigrammatic ambivalence of Tacitus' portraits of imperial tyranny. Now Gordon's smooth, leisurely translation turned Tacitus into – in Gordon's words – 'an upright patriot' with 'the good sense and breeding of a gentleman'. Gordon, scoffed a critic, had turned Tacitus into 'an independent Whig'.[74] While virtuous Romans were Anglicized, virtuous Englishmen were Romanized. By the middle decades of the eighteenth century the insurrectionary republicans of the seventeenth – Sidney, Ludlow, Milton – are being measured for their togas and paraded in classical engravings in the dignified publications of Richard Baron and Thomas Hollis.

Taming its heroes, republicanism tamed itself. Yet in the case of some republicans, at least, that result may have differed from their aim. After all, if respectable Country party heroes were to be created, why choose rebels or regicides like Ludlow and Sidney and Brutus? The only perceptible explanation of some apparent inconsistencies in republican writings lies in a gap between conformist profession and subversive intention. In the works of John Toland, the writer who did most to redesign pre-Revolutionary republicanism for post-Revolutionary audiences, there lies the purpose not of disguising the radicalism of his heroes but of making it respectable. He wished to demonstrate that under the evils of Stuart tyranny even the most disinterested and Stoical men of virtue had understood the need for extreme measures. He implied that if such evils recurred – as, without constitutional reform and without an end to corruption, was all too possible – similarly virtuous men ought to reach similar conclusions. Toland's pamphlets oscillate bewilderingly between tactical concessions to conventional thought and spirited defiance of it. Even when praising King William he is capable of calling him 'this king' rather than as elementary decencies required 'his Majesty'. Passages which imply that the troubles of 1688 could be explained merely by James II's departure from a healthy constitutional norm jostle – as they would

[72] Ludlow, *Voyce from the Watch Tower*, ed. Worden, introduction, p. 47.

[73] Worden, 'Commonwealth Kidney', p. 31.

[74] Ibid. The ground for Gordon's approach to Tacitus had been prepared in the later seventeenth century, particularly by the influential commentaries of Amelot de la Houssaie. See e.g. *The Compleat Courtier: or, the Morals of... Cornelius Tacitus concerning Flattery* (London, 1700).

jostle in the works of Bolingbroke – with statements which suggest that the English constitution had been gravely defective at least since 1603, perhaps since 1485.

Although Toland and Bolingbroke both emphasized the corruption of politics after 1688 rather than the principle of contract, both found in the corruption of Parliament an argument for resistance no less pressing than that which Sidney had drawn from contract theory in opposing Charles II. Toland observes that if Parliament, through its corruption, betrays the trust which the electorate has 'delegated' to it, then the people may 'defend themselves against their legislators'.[75] Bolingbroke's oscillations are no less remarkable. The Country party reader of his works would have found much to reassure him. There are Bolingbroke's professions of 'gratitude' for the 'deliverance' of 1688; there is his apparent pleasure in recording that in 1689 'republican and other whimsies' had been spurned and the settlement built on a broad cross-party base; there is his assurance, in which he follows Toland, that since 1689 the constitution had merely required 'perfecting'. Yet in almost the same breaths he can tell us (like Toland before him) how inadequate had been the Bill of Rights, a measure passed in that 'honeymoon' when 'the essentials of British liberty' had been 'almost wholly neglected'; how remote a prospect the attainment of 'perfection' remains; and how events since 1689 have weakened rather than enhanced the cause of freedom.[76] And like Toland, Bolingbroke slips in, almost subliminally, the doctrine of resistance. If Parliament yields its delegated powers to the executive, the balance of the constitution will be destroyed and the government thus dissolved: a pronouncement in which Bolingbroke's words resemble, with a proximity that seems too close for accident, the radical literature of 1689. Upon such a dissolution 'the nation hath a right to resist; and a people who desire to enjoy their liberty, will find the means'. In finding them the people would 'return to their original ... right ... of restoring the same constitution, or of making a new one'.[77]

Toland and Bolingbroke, then, did not so much abandon radicalism as wrap it in respectable packages. But packages can be more alluring than their contents. By the middle of the eighteenth century the very skill of republican packaging had rendered republicanism politically innocuous. The virtues of Algernon Sidney were now invoked by men of all persuasions.[78] In the public mind he had become an architect, not of the Rye House Plot, but of 1688: a misconception of a kind that became increasingly feasible as the Revolution slipped beyond the reach of living memory. For a variety of reasons republicanism found it

[75] Toland, *Anglia Libera*, pp. 4–5.

[76] Bolingbroke, *Works*, I, p. 341, II, pp. 9, 70–1, 75, 86, 96, 99, 110, 156, 227–8.

[77] Ibid., II, pp. 150–1. For Bolingbroke's interest in the literature produced by the Revolution, see also ibid., II, p. 99.

[78] Caroline Robbins, *The Eighteenth-Century Commonwealthmen* (Cambridge, Mass., 1959), pp. 46, 287–8.

ever more difficult to find a distinctive voice. Because the Whig oligarchy claimed 1688 as the sanction of its rule, and because republicans had conceded that the Revolution, whatever its defects, had been essentially beneficial, the differences between the Walpolean and the republican position seemed less than fundamental. Bolingbroke's acknowledgement that 'the Revolution is looked upon by all sides as a new era'[79] – as the basis of fresh political rules and fresh political obligations – admits the extent of the ground shared by all but the Jacobites. In other respects the differences between Walpole's Whigs and the republicans seem smaller still. The Polybian and Harringtonian concepts of the balanced constitution, which in the seventeenth century the republicans had come close to making their own, were appropriated by the Walpoleans and became the vindication of their oligarchy. It may, ironically, be in that appropriation that republican theory made its largest contribution to the mainstream of English political thought.[80] The words 'republic' and 'republican' began to lose something of their pejorative character. It became possible – perhaps through the influence of Montesquieu – to conceive of the English constitution not as a monarchical as opposed to a republican government but as a combination of monarchical and republican elements. The idolatry of kingship, which republicans had criticized so boldly in the age of Milton and Sidney, ceased to be a distinctively republican target. As David Hume wrote when he reflected on the changes of intellectual climate that had occurred since 1688, 'most people, in this island, have divested themselves of all superstitious reverence to names and authority. ... The mere name of king commands little respect; and to talk of a king as God's viceregent on earth, or to give him any of these magnificent titles which formerly dazzled mankind, would but excite laughter in everyone.'[81] Bolingbroke concurred:

> The whole bulk of the people hath been brought by the Revolution, and by the present settlement of the crown, to entertain principles which very few of us defended in my younger days. The safety and welfare of the nation are now the first and principal objects of regard. The regard to person and to families of monarchs hath been reduced to the second place.[82]

Can the influence of republican writing claim credit for the weakening of political idolatry? Does the explanation lie rather in broader intellectual developments of the age of reason? Or should we be content to find it in the successive

[79] Bolingbroke, *Works*, II, p. 27.
[80] Cf. John Brewer, *Party Ideology and Popular Politics at the Accession of George III* (Cambridge, 1976), p. 241.
[81] David Hume, *Essays, Moral, Political, and Literary*, ed. T. H. Green and T. H. Grose (2 vols., London, 1875), I, p. 125. (Hume is describing the view of other people, but appears to confirm it.)
[82] Bolingbroke, *Works*, I, pp. 308–9.

demonstrations – in 1649, in 1660, in 1688, in 1714 – of the nation's capacity to hire and fire its kings? Whatever the answer, the change deprived republicanism of its cutting edge. Theories of resistance and contract were likewise losing their distinctiveness, so that even Hume, that *bête noire* of Whiggism, could concede that Algernon Sidney's principles were 'such as the best and most dutiful subjects in all ages have been known to embrace': principles which he summarized as 'the original contract, the source of power from a consent of the people, the lawfulness of resisting tyrants, the preference of liberty to the government of a single person'.[83] There was, admittedly, a wide distance between arguing that resistance had been warrantable in 1688 and proposing, as Toland and Bolingbroke did, that it might still be warrantable after it, a position as unorthodox as the first had become conventional. Even so, the flirtation of Toland and Bolingbroke with resistance theory was less conspicuous than it would have been before the Revolution. Bolingbroke's own testimony again concurs with Hume's: the arguments which had been invoked to warrant Stuart absolutism, he thought, had been 'so exploded' by the Revolution 'that they are entertained by no set of men, whose numbers or importance give them any pretence to be reckoned among our national parties'.[84]

As the tenets of republicanism became less distinctive, so there became more evident the weaknesses inevitable in any argument addressed to a Country party: the limits of its appeal to men in search of power. In the 1750s, in the person of the elder Pitt, republicans found, as it seemed, a man after their own hearts: Pitt the patriot, Pitt the incorruptible, Pitt who called himself 'the Oldest Whig in England' and who read and recommended Ludlow and Algernon Sidney, Pitt whom Thomas Hollis claimed as 'a friend to liberty' – but whose career was to illustrate the incompatibility of political advancement with Roman aloofness.[85] Horace Walpole, learning of Pitt's acceptance of a pension, acknowledged himself to have been 'a dupe to virtue and patriotism. I adored Mr. Pitt, as if I was just come from school and reading Livy's tales of Brutus...Alack! Alack!'[86] The corruption of politics, it seemed, had become ingrained; and the more widely it was detected, the easier the Country party found it to lay the blame for their failure upon it. The republican legacy became a consolation for the 'outs'. Yet its influence was not confined to the defeated. In imaginative literature, criticism of the English court had long been – as it was in More and Wyatt and Sidney – a courtly genre: a safety-valve which, like that allowed to republican writers by the Emperor Augustus, enabled courtiers to release

[83] Worden, 'Commonwealth Kidney', p. 31.
[84] Bolingbroke, *Works*, II, pp. 23–4, 114.
[85] Robbins, *Eighteenth-Century Commonwealthmen*, p. 274; *Memoirs of Thomas Hollis* (2 vols., London, 1780), I, p. 186; Brewer, *Party Ideology*, p. 79.
[86] Brewer, *Party Ideology*, p. 104.

their resentment at their servitude and to reconcile it with their self-respect. There is a comparable phenomenon in the eighteenth century. Those who then absorbed republicanism included not merely 'old Whigs' or independent backbenchers but establishment Whigs, who turned to republican ideas in their thinking moods.

If eighteenth-century republicanism seems bland in comparison with that of the seventeenth century, a part of the explanation lies in that very stability of the Revolutionary settlement which republicans insistently questioned. Constitutional conflict was less frightening in the eighteenth century (at least after 1714) than in the seventeenth. Men can feel the threat of corruption keenly, but perhaps never quite as immediately as the threat of force. Under William III the standing army controversy brought the issues of corruption and force together, but in the eighteenth century, even though backbench mistrust of the standing army remained endemic, the dangers it threatened never seemed quite as grave or imminent as those of the 1650s, the 1670s, or the 1690s. Likewise, the corruption of Parliament, though a powerful theme of post-Revolutionary politics and one which republicans powerfully exploited, could never arouse anxieties quite as profound and widespread as those which the treatment of Parliament by Charles I or James II had provoked. Bolingbroke subtly rewrote the history of early modern tyranny in England so as to imply that its distinguishing features – under Henry VIII, and then under the Stuarts – had been the prevalence of faction and the corruption (rather than the attempted suppression) of Parliament.[87] Yet whatever the fears on which Bolingbroke played, his readers knew that, since 1689, an institution whose very being had previously depended upon the whims of kings had become an essential and regular feature of the constitution.

As the eighteenth century progressed, the teaching of republicanism became ever less precise, its appeal ever more amorphous. The movement became ever more a language, ever less a programme. It spoke less and less of particular constitutional defects, more and more of 'public spirit' and of 'the spirit of liberty'. Political health seemed more a matter of a nation's manners and morals than of its constitution. The study of history had less to do with institutions, more to do with the location of virtue and vice. Increasingly the energies of republicanism were concentrated on education: on the inculcation into young gentlemen of political virtue through the selective study of Roman and English history and through the emulation of the heroes – the 'patterns' – which history afforded. Republican publication consisted more and more of republication: of the reprinting, in handsome folio volumes fit for country-house libraries, of seventeenth-century treatises which had first appeared in less elegant forms.

[87] Bolingbroke, *Works*, I, pp. 353–4, 363, II, p. 9.

If repetition is one limitation of eighteenth-century republicanism, another is insularity. A movement which in the seventeenth century had been a plea for foreign ideas and models became from 1688 a celebration of Englishness: a development aided by the standing army controversy, when republicans lined up with the advocates of an isolationist foreign policy, and when the greatest compliment republicans could bestow was to discern 'the character of a true Englishman'. Republicanism did not wholly lose its continental dimension. Pieter de la Court's *The True Interest of Holland* was published in England in 1702, in a translation which recommended the government of 'a republic' with a freedom that native writing rarely risked. About the same time Sidney's *Discourses* was translated into French, Ludlow's *Memoirs* into French and, apparently, into Dutch.[88] John Toland and his friends were occasionally willing to praise the freedoms enjoyed by the citizens of the United Provinces,[89] and perhaps would have done so more often had William's Dutch advisers, and perhaps even the king himself, been better liked. But the general trend was towards introversion. Whereas, before 1688, the advances of Stuart tyranny had seemed part of a European trend, England's deliverance in 1688 – however fortuitous or insecure republicans believed it to be – made her an exception to the European rule of absolutism. Trenchard and Moyle declared that Englishmen remained 'freemen and not slaves in this unhappy age, when ... we see most nations of Europe overrun with oppression and slavery'.[90] As England became more powerful and self-confident abroad, so comparisons with the politics of ancient Rome became at once less humble and more superficial. In the middle of the eighteenth century they almost went out of fashion, at least for a time. Dr Johnson was contemptuous of Thomas Blackwell's republican study of Augustus Caesar in 1756: 'He is come too late into the world with his fury for freedom, with his Brutus and Cassius. We have all on this side of the Tweed long settled our opinions.' Six years later an 'old Whig', pleading for reform of the militia, remarked that his case 'carries its own conviction, without resorting to Greece and Rome'.[91] The classical republics were to be imitated in spirit but not in form: a principle encapsulated by Charles James Fox when he commended the early leaders of the Long Parliament because 'they never conceived the wild notion of assimilating the government of England to that of Athens, of Sparta, or of Rome. They were content with applying to the English constitution, and to the English laws, the spirit of liberty which had animated and rendered illustrious the ancient republics.'[92]

[88] Ludlow, *Voyce from the Watch Tower*, ed. Worden, p. 1.
[89] E.g. Toland, *Anglia Libera*, pp. 61–2, 150–60; cf. Bodleian Library, Carte MS 81, fo. 766v.
[90] [Trenchard and Moyle], *Argument*, pp. 2–3. Cf. *Collection of State Tracts*, II, p. 645; Bolingbroke, *Works*, II, p. 108.
[91] Both quotations are from J. A. W. Gunn, *Beyond Liberty and Property* (McGill, 1983), p. 29.
[92] Fox, *History of the Reign of James II* (London, 1846 edn), p. 294.

Should we say, as we observe the growing tameness and imprecision and insularity of republicanism, that the republican tradition had become moribund? I think not. There was nothing new – as a reading of Machiavelli will remind us – about the republican concern with corruption and with public spirit. Admittedly eighteenth-century republicanism supplied no rivals to Machiavelli's sharpness of mind, or indeed to the sharpness of Harrington or Nevile or Sidney. Yet it may be that it is in its least precise, its least contentious, even its least distinguished form that the republican tradition exerts its broadest influence: that it imparts classical ideas of liberty and independence and public responsibility to a ruling class which would never have imbibed the pure milk of republican theory, but which absorbs them, in their diluted forms, into the ideal of the gentleman. They are ideas which, with the passage of time, came to lose their intellectual dimension. In Britain's boarding-schools, in the evolution of whose principles they have surely been influential, they may even have taken some anti-intellectual forms. Yet behind them lies a tradition of the reading of classical history which the republicans did as much as anyone to shape.

I have drawn a comparison between republicanism and Puritanism. In assessing the influence of republicanism let me compare it with another 'ism', Renaissance humanism: another term not used by its adherents, and another movement dependent on, and interacting with, a broader lay interest in the classical world. In its early stages, when humanism is the movement of a minority and when its targets of ignorance and superstition are conspicuous, its practitioners can be identified and its teachings defined, as can the earlier practitioners and teachings of republicanism. Soon, admittedly, humanism forms an alliance with Protestantism, which is muddling, because not all humanists are Protestants and not all Protestants humanists (a difficulty analogous, if we like, to that created by the alliance of republicanism with contract theory). But the real problems of definition arise when the two movements, humanism and republicanism, have so far broadened their appeals (humanism by the later sixteenth century, republicanism by the eighteenth), have so far mingled or merged or argued with other – sometimes fresher – intellectual developments, have won so many victories over the idolatries they have denounced, that their contributions are no longer distinguishable. We do not ordinarily call Gibbon a republican, and it would no doubt be a mistake to do so. Yet as he struggles to find his subject – will it be the history of Swiss liberty, or the conflict between virtue and corruption in republican Florence, or the collapse of senatorial values in Rome? – there is a persistent republican preoccupation. The works of the English republicans were in Gibbon's library (among them those of Walter Moyle, who influenced his reading of Roman history); and the place of Machiavellian concepts of civic virtue and corruption in his explanation of Rome's decline is unmistakable. We do not ordinarily call Hume a republican, but the tradition of civic virtue is manifest in him too, as is the influence of Harrington's analysis, which he so admired, of the relationship of power to property.[93]

VI

The freedom of republican influence in the middle decades of the eighteenth century was curtailed near its end. The French Revolution revived Englishmen's fears of regicide and of resistance. Whigs of the late eighteenth and early nineteenth centuries retreated from abstract political theory, and maintained that resistance, even on the rare occasions when there might be legitimate grounds for it, was warrantable only if it was likely to succeed. The combination of propriety and expediency which had justified the resistance of 1688 had, they maintained, been exceptional, perhaps unique. Algernon Sidney, whom posthumous conflation had turned into a hero of 1688, was now rebuked for the 'speculative' and intransigent temperament which had led him first to demand a utopian 'republic' and then to conspire prematurely against the Stuarts.[94] Not all Whigs, admittedly, welcomed the new caution or the new pragmatism. In 1808 Francis Jaffray lamented that, as a result of the French Revolution,

> a sort of tacit convention was entered into, to say nothing, for a while, of the follies and vices of princes, the tyranny of courts, and the rights of the people. The Revolution of 1688, it was agreed, could not be mentioned with praise, without giving some indirect encouragement to the Revolution of 1789; and it was thought as well to say nothing in favour of Hampden, or Russell, or Sydney, for fear it might give spirits to Robespierre, or Danton, or Marat.[95]

If the French Revolution made orthodox Whigs nervous of mentioning 1688, radicals attacked it with a fresh freedom. Tom Paine thought that in 1688 an oligarchy had 'imported' the 'detestable' William and Mary, just as it later 'sent for' George I, in order to preserve the oppression of the people.[96] The Bill of Rights, he claimed, had been 'more properly a bill of wrongs, and of insult'.[97] Paine rejoiced to observe that the reputation of 1688 was 'already on the wane, eclipsed by the enlarging orb of reason, and the luminous revolutions of America and France. In less than a century mankind would scarcely believe that a country calling itself free, would send to Holland for a man, and clothe him with power, on purpose to put themselves in fear of him'.[98] Until the American Revolution, Paine maintained, there had been no true revolutions, merely 'changes of persons'

[93] H. Russell Smith, *Harrington and his Oceana* (Cambridge, 1914), pp. 146–8; Duncan Forbes, *Hume's Philosophical Politics* (Cambridge, 1975).
[94] Henry Hallam, *The History of England* (2 vols., London, 1914 edn), II, pp. 413, 418.
[95] *Edinburgh Review*, 12 (1808), p. 278.
[96] Paine, *Rights of Man*, pp. 148, 257; M. Foot and I. Kramnic (eds.), *The Thomas Paine Reader* (London, 1987), p. 458. Cf. J. T. Rutt (ed.), *The Diary of Thomas Burton* (4 vols., London, 1828), II, p. 452n.
[97] Paine, *Rights of Man*, p. 215.
[98] Ibid., p. 113.

which 'worked within the atmosphere of a court, and never on the great floor of a nation'.[99] Besides, 1688, together with 1714, had tied England to 'the destructive system of continental and foreign intrigues, and the rage for foreign wars and foreign domination', to which hereditary kings and hereditary nobles had sacrificed the blood of their impoverished subjects.[100] Set against such criticism, the reservations which republicans had expressed about the Revolution during the previous century were less noticeable than their record of general support for it. Paine, for whom the use of the term republicanism held no fear, altered its meaning and claimed it for the principles of parliamentary representation and popular sovereignty. Equipped with that definition, he cut through the earlier republican language of the mixed constitution. As John Adams, whose philosophy owed so much to the republican tradition, nervously remarked, Paine's system was 'so democratical, without restraint or even attempt at any equilibrium or counterpoise, that it must produce confusion and every evil work'.[101] The radicals of the late eighteenth and early nineteenth centuries – Paine, Mackintosh, William Godwin, John Rutt – were at one: the vaunted system of constitutional balance was 'farcical', a mask for corruption, 'a government not of check, but of conspiracy'.[102]

Admittedly the repudiation of 1688 by the radicals was not clear-cut. After all they did celebrate the centenary of the Revolution, although that was before the events of 1789 had offered a neighbouring model so much more attractive. Yet even before 1789, movements were at work which lowered the radicals' estimation of 1688. The first was their rejection of historical sanctions and their appeal instead to principles of natural rights. Earlier republicans, as we have seen, subordinated history to reason, but normally saw the two as allies. Many of the new republicans (though by no means all of them) saw historical appeals as at best irrelevant. 'It is not because we *have* been free', remarked Mackintosh with a swipe at the devotees of Anglo-Saxon liberty, 'but because we have a right to be free, that we ought to demand freedom ... Let us hear no more of this absurd pedigree of freedom.'[103] Classical and medieval landmarks of liberty proved chimerical. 'The people of England in their collective capacity', declared John Rutt, 'were as little concerned by Magna Charta, as the numerous slave-populations of Greece and Rome were protected by the free institutions' of 'the mis-called free states of antiquity.'[104]

Mackintosh and Rutt were themselves historians of stature. However much

[99] Ibid., pp. 183, 189.
[100] Ibid., pp. 253–4.
[101] Bailyn, *Ideological Origins*, pp. 288–9.
[102] Foot and Kramnick (eds.), *Thomas Paine Reader*, p. 69; Mackintosh, *Vindiciae Gallicae*, p. 340; William Godwin, *History of the Commonwealth of England* (4 vols., London, 1824–8), II, pp. 496–7; Rutt (ed.), *Diary of Thomas Burton*, III, p. 148n; cf. Gunn, *Beyond Liberty and Property*, p. 172.
[103] Mackintosh, *Vindiciae Gallicae*, p. 306.
[104] Rutt (ed.), *Diary of Thomas Burton*, I, p. 406n, III, p. 147n.

history had lost of its argumentative authority, it remained a source of instruction and inspiration. Yet the radicals were coming to find instruction and inspiration where their republican predecessors had hesitated to seek them: in the Revolution, not of 1688–9, but of 1640–60. Some earlier republicans had been prepared to defend the actions of the Long Parliament as far as 1641, or even 1642 or 1646, and some had glorified the victories of the Commonwealth abroad. But regicide, military usurpation, and the rule of the saints were different matters. From the middle of the eighteenth century attempts were made to link the two Revolutions, to suggest that a continuous cause joined Pym in the 1640s to Algernon Sidney in the 1680s.[105] In the late eighteenth century the champions of the Puritan cause became bolder, although it is not until the 1820s that we find Godwin and Rutt, who helped to lay the modern foundations of civil war studies, describing Charles I as a 'convicted criminal' and adulating the rule of the Rump Parliament.[106] Now that republicanism had abandoned its belief in checks and balances, the undivided sovereignty of the Rump was no longer a defect. To Godwin the Rump was the high point of English history, the Restoration the low. The Revolution of 1688 'to a certain degree reduced the disease' which the later Stuarts had inflicted on the body politic, but 'it is possible the nation has never recovered that tone of independence, strong thinking and generosity which the Restoration operated so powerfully to destroy ... The Revolution under King William was far from being characterised by anything preeminently friendly to freedom in a political view, or to heroism of character.'[107] Indeed,

> From the moment that the grand contest excited under the Stuarts was quieted by the Revolution, our history assumes its most insipid and insufferable form. It is the history of negotiations and tricks, it is the history of revenues and debts, it is the history of corruption and political profligacy, but it is not the history of genuine independent man.[108]

What prompted the interest of the radicals in the Puritan Revolution? They may have had a sense that 'the middling and lower orders' had been on Parliament's side. Godwin and Rutt showed some interest in the Levellers, who, they agreed, had been true republicans ('probably the only consistent republicans of their time', thought Rutt) – although Godwin saw Lilburne less as a social reformer than as a martyr to liberty, a seventeenth-century John Wilkes.[109] Perhaps the new interest owed something to the revival of religious earnestness

[105] Worden, 'Commonwealth Kidney', pp. 34–5; cf. Rutt (ed.), *Diary of Thomas Burton*, III, p. 110n.

[106] Godwin, *History of the Commonwealth*, II, p. 688; Rutt (ed.), *Diary of Thomas Burton*, III, p. 422n.

[107] Godwin, *Lives of Edward and James Philips* (London, 1815), pp. 267–8.

[108] Godwin, 'Of History and Romance', in Godwin, *Caleb Williams*, ed. M. Hindle (London, 1988), appendix iv, p. 367.

[109] Godwin, *History of the Commonwealth*, II, p. 447; Rutt (ed.), *Diary of Thomas Burton*, I, p. 49n. For a similar treatment of Lilburne see John Thelwall, *The Tribune* (3 vols., London, 1795–6), III, p. 229. (Godwin thought that Lilburne had taken his opposition too far.)

in the earlier nineteenth century, when Godwin and John Forster were glad to discover that the civil wars – whose Puritanism republicans of previous generations had usually overlooked and had sometimes concealed – had been wars of religion.[110] But the primary appeal, at least for Godwin and for Rutt, was to their republicanism: a republicanism which on inspection proves closer to that of the eighteenth century than they may have realized.

It is true that the charms of Stoic detachment had worn thin. As we enter the age of Napoleon and of Carlylean hero-worship, we find that incorruptibility becomes an insufficient ground for admiration. The term 'patriot', previously applied to defenders of their country's constitution, is now bestowed on agents of national self-assertion.[111] Heroes must be men of action, aiming not at mere 'negative liberty' – a goal, Godwin concedes, to which a republic may not be well suited – but at the higher moral and civic fulfilment which only a republic can accommodate.[112] Republicanism has returned from the Stoical to the Machiavellian ideal. For Godwin, John Hampden was 'the great English patriot' because he 'dismissed the thought of a solitary and retired meditation, and became a citizen after the purest model'.[113] Yet, amidst so many changes of emphasis, how many of the earlier republican assumptions have survived! The qualities which Godwin admires among the 'great spirits' of the Rump – men of 'a Greek or a Roman spirit', men characterized by 'independence', 'disinterestedness', 'public virtue', 'public spirit', 'frankness and unalterable sincerity' – are to him distinctively 'republican virtues'.[114] They are precisely the virtues for which, since 1688, republicans had praised their predecessors. Indeed, when Godwin and Rutt studied the Rump they saw it through the eyes of Sidney, of Ludlow, of Milton, of Roger Coke, authors whose works they read in the versions which the republicans of the 1690s had prepared for a Country party readership. The break of parliamentary and popular radicalism with the republican tradition is less marked than it looks. Perhaps that should not surprise us, for is not Paine, as much as Harrington or the Levellers, the friend of the independent freeholder and the advocate of a property-owning democracy? The old republican language of independence – the language which celebrates classical virtue and which contrasts it with the evils of courtly influence, of corruption, of standing armies – has a place of substance, not of mere rhetoric, in the writings of the first generation of popular radicalism:[115] in the publications of the Society for Constitutional Information, or in the tracts of Major Cartwright or James Burgh – or of John Thelwall, who edited the works of Algernon Sidney and christened

[110] Godwin, *History of the Commonwealth*, III, pp. 443–4; J. Forster, *Historical and Biographical Essays* (2 vols., London, 1858), I, pp. 308–9. Rutt (ed.), *Diary of Thomas Burton*, IV, p. 432n.
[111] Peter Karsten, *Patriot-Heroes in England and America* (Madison, Wis., 1978), esp. ch. 6.
[112] Godwin, *History of the Commonwealth*, II, p. 499, III, pp. 188–90.
[113] Ibid., I, pp. 12, 15.
[114] Ibid., II, p. 202.
[115] Worden, 'Commonwealth Kidney', pp. 32–3; Pocock, *Politics, Language and Time*, pp. 145–6.

his son Algernon Sidney. Where earlier republicans had contrived to read Sidney's *Discourses* as the work of a Stoic, their successors found in them an argument for electoral reform.

Yet in the appropriation of Sidney by popular reformers there is a new note: a note close to condescension. There is sometimes the same note in their discussions of 1688. Beside those reformers who, with Paine, condemned the Revolution out of hand were writers who were willing to allow it faint praise. In doing so they took account of the emerging concept of evolutionary progress, which could explain the deficiencies of the Revolutionary settlement as an understandable reflection of the limitations of its age. Thus Mackintosh, perceiving that 'the public mind' of the seventeenth century had not been 'sufficiently enlightened' to grasp 'the science which teaches the rights of man', found it forgivable that the Revolution had not satisfactorily 'reformed institutions', that its 'immediate effects on the government of England' had been inadequate. It had nonetheless exerted a significant 'indirect influence on the progress of human opinion', and had 'established principles' which made possible the larger enlightenment, and the more enlightened revolutions, of the present. It had 'sanctified ... the general principles of freedom'; it had made England 'an asylum of freedom of thought' from which the more sophisticated notions of freedom of the eighteenth century would develop; and thus it had 'accelerated' the 'progress of light'.[116] Here was the theme that Macaulay would soon make his own.

Macaulay had little time for republicanism. Algernon Sidney seemed to him hopelessly utopian and inflexible. Nineteenth-century radicals had become equally impatient, and had learned to manage without the republican canon. But where Macaulay followed Mackintosh down the road to 1688, other historians, principally Carlyle and John Forster, took the route marked by Godwin to the years of Puritan rule. Forster found it 'a grave reproach to English political biography that the attention rightly due to statesmen who opposed Charles I, in themselves the most remarkable men of any age, should have been suffered to be borne away by the poorer imitators of their memorable deeds, the authors of the imperfect settlement of 1688'.[117] In our century that battle for the soul of the seventeenth century has been fought again. Half a century ago G. M. Trevelyan, marking the passage of 250 years since the event, published *The English Revolution, 1688–1689*. The following year, in 1940, he was answered by the young Christopher Hill in *The English Revolution 1640*. Since that time it is Hill's cause that has prevailed. Is that because the conflict that produced the Levellers has seemed more in tune with a democratic age than the aristocratic

[116] Mackintosh, *Vindiciae Gallicae*, pp. 294, 309, 328–30. Cf. William Enfield, *A Sermon on the Centennial Commemoration of the Revolution* (London, 1778), pp. 17–18; Richard Price, *A Discourse on the Love of Our Country ... 4 Nov. 1789* (4th edn, London, 1790), p. 14; Rutt (ed.), *Diary of Thomas Burton*, III, p. 75n.

[117] J. Forster, *The Statesmen of the Commonwealth of England* (5 vols., London, 1840), I, p. lxxviii.

coup of 1688? Is it because so many historians of stature – Tawney, Trevor-Roper, Stone, Hexter, Hill himself – were drawn to the earlier conflict? Or is it because, since S. R. Gardiner and C. H. Firth, the earlier Revolution has possessed, as the later one has not, the firm chronological foundation without which large generalization is hard to sustain? Whatever the explanation, it now seems increasingly hard to argue that the first Revolution had the larger long-term consequences. The discovery during the past twenty-five years of deep-rooted provincialism and of apocalyptic hysteria among the Roundheads has made Puritanism seem less a revolutionary force than – both politically and intellectually – a reactionary one. At the same time fresh light has streamed on to the later Revolution, not least on to the battle of ideas which attended it. In the world around us it has become not always obvious that the relations between classes – the dominant theme of civil war studies from the 1930s to the 1960s – is more significant than the relationship of the state to the citizen, which remains the central theme of the later conflict. If, in fifty years' time, a book about the seventeenth century is published with the title *The English Revolution*, which event will it describe?

PART II

Background and world impact

Chapter 8

Freedom in seventeenth-century Dutch thought and practice

E. H. KOSSMANN

Jacques Basnage was a distinguished Huguenot minister who fled to Rotterdam in 1685 where he met two friends from his student days in Sedan, Pierre Bayle and Pierre Jurieu. He died in 1723 at The Hague, seventy years old. He had spent most of his time writing multi-volume books, pamphlets, and articles about theology and ecclesiastical history. But in his later years, apart from his work in the Walloon Church, he also served the Grand Pensionary of Holland, Heinsius, as an intermediary in negotiations with the French and it was due to this connection that he received in 1715 an official commission by the States of Holland to write the history of the Dutch Republic from roughly the Peace of Münster in 1648 to the time of his writing. Basnage did not have the time to complete the book – his narrative did not reach beyond 1676 – but as the book was on the whole not particularly satisfactory this can hardly be called regrettable. The best part of the two volumes which appeared are the introductory chapters in which the author analysed Dutch political institutions.[1]

Of course, Basnage, who lived almost forty years in the Netherlands, who knew the language and who was permitted to publish whatever he liked, highly appreciated the country of his exile. Yet he remained an expatriate and never in his life did he give up his preference for royal absolutism in the style of Louis XIV, though he believed, of course, that it should be tempered by the religious toleration which the great king had erroneously and tragically abolished when repealing the Edict of Nantes. This did not prevent Basnage from characterizing the history of the Republic in laudatory terms long current in the Dutch tradition. The inhabitants of the United Provinces, he told his readers, had since time immemorial cherished their freedom and defended it in incessant warfare. Freedom and war were the pivotal elements of their history. Their sense of liberty was such that each province of the federation, concluded in 1579 in the so-called Union of Utrecht, had retained its original sovereignty. In religious matters the Dutch had firmly decided not to use force against people

[1] Jacques Basnage, *Annales des Provinces-Unies depuis les Négociations pour la Paix de Munster, avec la Description de leur Gouvernement* (2 vols., The Hague, 1726). See G. Cerny, *Theology, Politics and Letters at the Crossroads of European Civilization. Jacques Basnage and the Baylean Huguenot Refugees in the Dutch Republic* (Dordrecht, 1987), pp. 269ff.

who refused to adopt the true creed. Hence the comprehensive toleration and the resulting proliferation of sects which shocked foreigners, but which, according to Basnage, should in fact be appreciated as humane, wise, in harmony with God's principles, and, moreover, economically profitable.[2]

Basnage had previously studied the problem of toleration in his *Traité de la Conscience* published in two volumes in 1696. His recent biographer, Gerald Cerny, analyses the book and determines its position in the furious debate then going on among the Huguenot refugees in Holland about the concept of toleration interpreted as liberty of conscience.[3] Basnage took a middle way between Bayle, who thought that someone whose conscience obliged him to think and do things that were wrong did not necessarily commit a sin – his *conscience errante* being caused by bad information or a limited intelligence and not by sheer wickedness – and those Calvinists who regarded all deviation from orthodoxy as a positive evil. It is far beyond the scope of this essay to consider the philosophical merits of the numerous books then produced about this exceedingly tricky issue. The discussion was profound and important. Moreover, it had practical implications, for it obviously concerned toleration. The reason why I refer to it is purely negative: it is the fact that Dutch writers did not take part in it. It was in their country that the debate took place; it was the remarkably tolerant attitude to sects prevailing in Holland that was under discussion, yet no Dutch author felt the need to intervene in the dispute. A few years before the situation had been similar. It had been at the request of a Remonstrant minister, Philip van Limborch, that Locke wrote in 1685 in Amsterdam his *Epistola de Tolerantia* and it was Limborch who published it in 1689 in Gouda. The Dutch remained silent. Is it not as if they handed both the theory of their toleration, which served as a paradigm to Europe, and the study of their past and their recent achievements over to foreigners to whom they extended hospitality and sympathy? What they themselves provided was the idea that the Dutch formed a people which had always wanted to be free and independent as well as the practice of a toleration that allowed most inhabitants of the Republic a religious and intellectual freedom not granted anywhere else in the world of that time. By 1700 they left it to exiles residing in their free country to work out such themes in a more detailed and profound manner.

From the late sixteenth century onwards the Dutch had developed a set of ideas and worked out a set of ways to implement them that were eminently practical and, though unsystematic, nonetheless not incoherent. This is the astonishing aspect of the Dutch seventeenth century. Its history is full of incidents, odd contradictions, uncompleted tendencies. Yet in retrospect we can organize this past quite easily in such a way that it looks as if it possessed a logic of

[2] Cerny, *Theology, Politics and Letters*, pp. 281, 284.
[3] Ibid., pp. 297ff.

its own. Although we know that freedom in the sense of independence, of provincial sovereignty or particularism, of a non-monarchial, republican form of government and religious and intellectual freedom are different conceptions not necessarily belonging together, it is as if in the Dutch seventeenth century they are quite naturally united in an organic whole. But not only later observers had this impression. Basnage and others, as we have seen, suggested the same thing. Freedom, Basnage thought, was the leading principle of the Dutch Republic, in all spheres of human endeavour, religious, and economic as well as political. It was therefore essentially the same freedom which manifested itself in all those fields. The Dutch concept of freedom was comprehensive, coherent, and consecrated by the nation's immemorial tradition. It is both easy and correct to qualify this as illusion and myth. It is evident that the various freedoms may not be looked upon as aspects of one single superior principle. One should, however, not accuse the authors of the late seventeenth century who proposed such views of producing hollow rhetoric for there is some reason to take them seriously. Let us then examine the history of Dutch freedom.

During the period in which the Dutch Republic emerged – let us date it from the 1560s to the early 1590s – the course of history was dominated to such an extent by unforeseeable incidents that it is unwise to try to detect in it what we like to call 'developments' or 'tendencies'. Historians have stopped debating about the main causes and the true nature of the Revolt. A series of disturbances stretching over various decades cannot, they think, be explained by means of such imperialistic conceptions. Fortunately, the question whether the various freedoms for which the Dutch Republic later came to stand were already during the Revolt beginning to be considered a more or less coherent whole can be answered even if we do not claim to know, and do not hope ever to be able to know, what the Revolt as such intended to perform. The point is that already in the early 1560s, when Calvinism began to spread in the Netherlands and Philip II showed signs of being uncertain about the method he should use to enforce religious uniformity, the opposition to his policies started to develop ideas about the right of the representative assemblies to participate in legislation concerning religious affairs. Both from the religious and from the constitutional point of view this was an important moment in the history of Dutch freedom and we should therefore consider it somewhat more closely.

In August 1559 Philip II, who had resided in the Netherlands since the abdication of Charles V in 1555, left for Spain. The newly appointed regent Margaret of Parma sought the regular advice of the formidable Antoine Perrenot, later Cardinal Granvelle who, originating from Franche Comté and thus considered a foreigner, made himself hated. The high nobility in the Netherlands reacted with deep disgust to his elevation to the highest dignity in the Church of the Netherlands. Philip II gave way to the vehement protests about this man's policies and in March 1564 Granvelle left the country. From that moment to the arrival of the duke of Alva in 1567 the provinces lived through a period of unprecedented chaos. Granvelle's departure was the signal for many militant emigrants to return from their refuges in Germany and England. Many lawyers and judges and the public in general considered the old edicts against heresy to have lost validity and were not prepared to apply them any longer. Persecution was generally stopped. At the same time Calvinism made its entry into the Netherlands and it rapidly drew large audiences especially in the industrial towns and countryside of southern Flanders. This added immeasurably to the complexity of the problems. The government, now largely dominated by the high nobility, was extremely weak and as it did not get clear orders from Madrid it was unable to give direction to the king's subjects. Would the king be prepared to withdraw the severe legislation against heresy and grant some form of toleration so that Protestants in the Netherlands would be given the means of survival which were then, or were soon to become, available in a major part of central and western Europe? People hoped for it, perhaps some of them genuinely expected it. But then, at the end of 1565, the king suddenly reaffirmed his decision to maintain the Inquisition, refusing all proposals to the contrary made to him by representative personalities and councils in the Low Countries. The reaction was intense. A section of the nobility drew up a document, eventually signed by some hundreds of them, in which they promised each other full assistance with the purpose of preventing the Inquisition from being introduced again. This was in January 1566.[4] In April 1566 this group presented to the governess at Brussels a petition which is worth considering.[5]

The nobles felt obliged, they declared, to warn the king against the rebellion which they feared would result from his refusal to mitigate the religious edicts. The regent was asked to send an ambassador to Madrid with this message:

> And so that the king may have no reason to think that we, who only seek to obey him in all humility, would try to restrain him or to impose our will on him ... we implore His Majesty very humbly that it may please him to seek advice and consent of the assembled States General for new ordinances and other more suitable and appropriate ways to put matters right without causing such apparent dangers.

The nobles, one sees, expressed themselves carefully. They did not suggest that the States General had the right to take part in the legislation itself, they did not even suggest that they had the right to give the sovereign advice in this matter, they just stated that it was necessary for the sovereign to collaborate with the States if he wished to prevent the Low Countries being disturbed by,

[4] E. H. Kossmann and A. F. Mellink, *Texts concerning the Revolt of the Netherlands* (Cambridge, 1974), pp. 59–62.
[5] Ibid., pp. 62–5.

as they expressed it, 'a universal rebellion bringing ruin to all the provinces and plunging them into utter misery'. For the first time it was quite openly stated by a large group of distinguished personalities, Catholics as well as Protestants, that royal policy was catastrophic and should be revised with the help of a local representative assembly better equipped to judge what was beneficial to the provinces in the given circumstances. And it was taken for granted that the States General would, either for religious reasons or for political expediency, plead on behalf of toleration. In pamphlet material from this time authors tended to go somewhat further than the nobles and vaguely hinted that there were ancient privileges and freedoms which seemed to suggest that the sovereign's religious policy had always been subject to approval by the States General. What is clear in all this is that the religious problem was associated with the constitutional problem and that the representative assembly, a political body, was expected to take sides with the religious opposition without necessarily opting for the Protestant cause as such.

However, the sovereign pertinently refused to convene the States General which had not met since 1559. They did in fact not meet till 1569, when the duke of Alva, immensely powerful at the time, assembled them because he needed their financial support. He did not permit them to discuss the religious question. Alva's successor, Don Luis de Requesens, was no longer able to prevent them from doing so. It was during his short governorship (1573–6) that the States General at long last had the opportunity to give their opinion about this matter. They then claimed to possess even more rights than the nobles, not ten years previously, had ventured to claim on their behalf, stating explicitly that they were entitled to consider and to take decisions on all matters, religion included. This was a bold assertion and the more remarkable because the by then openly rebellious provinces of Holland and Zeeland were of course not represented. Holland had in 1572 virtually disengaged itself from the Brussels government. The States of that province, meeting without royal consent, had confiscated ecclesiastical property and declared all confessions to be free. Although in fact the Catholics were during the following years not permitted to hold their services it was initially the principle of total freedom that the States, considered to be the representative of the people, proclaimed.

It is unnecessary to study the complicated history of the Revolt and the forming of the Seven United Provinces of the north as a separate republic. What matters to us is the simple fact that thanks to the conditions prevailing in the Netherlands in the 1560s and 1570s the constitutional and the religious problems came to be united in a way not to be found in other parts of Europe. Toleration and a form of provincial autonomy in the face of the central government appeared as two aspects of the same principle. Of course, there was still a third aspect, although this was not openly mentioned in these decades: liberty in the sense of independence. This theme only came to the fore in the 1590s. Then the matter was, though provisionally, settled: in 1596 France concluded an official treaty with the States General of the northern provinces, thereby recognizing its status as a more or less independent power. Hence, Dutch liberty consisted of three elements: independence, provincial autonomy, and religious toleration. There is no logical link between these aspects; they were united by accident, by unpredictable historical events. A fourth element was – but not before the 1650s – added to this triangle of liberties: the conviction that the independent, federal, and tolerant state should have a clearly defined republican form of government if it wished to be truly free.

Let us look at these elements in the form in which they were adopted during the seventeenth century. Two of them, toleration and republicanism, turn out to be in practice and in thought highly ambiguous and puzzling phenomena; the other two, independence and provincial autonomy, are much easier to understand. It is in retrospect by no means difficult to see why the state slowly emerging in the late sixteenth century should have become a federal state. The Burgundian rulers who had in the Low Countries collected as many principalities as they could and had attempted to govern them as much as possible from the centre established in Brussels had in the provinces not abolished the old institutions, regulations, instruments, and habits of mind but merely superimposed a federal structure upon them. In the various provinces those who objected to the central government and succeeded in withdrawing their region out of its reach were able to use the traditional local governmental systems. In other words, it was what has often too critically been called 'particularism' that made the whole Revolt possible and it is in no sense astonishing that provincial sovereignty should have been maintained after the decision taken in the late 1580s to try to solve the formidable problems of that period by accepting the fact that the United Provinces had become a virtually independent state. But why, one may well ask, did the province of Holland, which in the seventeenth century was in all respects, in wealth, in power, in the greatness and lustre of its culture, far superior to its partners in the federation, not make use of its hegemony to transform the Republic into a more united state under its own leadership? Most of the allies, after all, were Holland's dependencies rather than its equals and yet Holland left them a far greater say in the affairs of the Union than their contribution to it justified. It is impossible to answer this question adequately because in the seventeenth century it was never put in this form. The population and its leaders were apparently satisfied with the prevailing constitutional rules, however unsatisfactory they may seem to later generations. There was, moreover, one factor which may have made an alteration undermining the principle of provincial sovereignty unattractive to Holland. If Holland had institutionalized its ascendancy by establishing greater unity in the loosely constructed state, this might have resulted in an increase in power not only of that province but also in that of its Stadholder, the Prince of Orange. That Holland did not want to risk. However, this is pure speculation. The only fact which matters is that Holland happily abided by the system of provincial sovereignty and obviously did not consider it inimical to its interests, although it permitted its partners to exercise a political influence out of all proportion to their real importance.

The republican component of the Dutch concept of freedom was more ambiguous, for various reasons. The first one is simply that people in the Netherlands had no experience with republican government and tended to look upon it as something alien or even unnatural. In the course of the Revolt when it became clear that the provinces would eventually decide to abandon Philip II some pamphleteers considered the merits of republicanism but without transforming their reflections into a concrete proposal or programme. During a short time in the 1570s the city of Ghent, dominated by the Calvinists, experimented with the Genevan model but the adventure ended in disaster.[6] In 1583 a writer praised the Swiss system more generally[7] but he was immediately rebuked by another one.[8] The second illustrious example of republican government, Venice, was only rarely mentioned during the Revolt. The critic of the Swiss system did not think the Venetian model applicable to the Netherlands either: a country so accessible geographically should not copy the government of an island-state.[9]

Some years later the political situation developed in such a way that it became difficult to deny the republican character of the governmental system then prevailing in the northern Netherlands. The search for a new sovereign – in England, in France? – had led the Dutch nowhere, with the result that the states were forced to acknowledge that sovereignty had apparently reverted to themselves. This was not a moment of triumph for the republican idea but rather one of resigned acceptance of a no longer disputable fact. Both in theory and in practice, however, the most was made of the new circumstances. In a famous declaration, written by François Vranck, the Pensionary of Gouda, and voted by the States of Holland on 16 October 1587, they made it clear that in Holland sovereignty had for eight centuries resided with the States which had entrusted government to counts and countesses only provisionally and on strict conditions. This had on the whole, they stated, been a very successful arrangement thanks to which 'the state of Holland and Zeeland was never conquered by the sword or brought into subjugation as a result of foreign or civil wars' and they doubted 'whether

[6] Ibid. (1578), p. 162.
[7] Ibid. (1583), pp. 243ff.
[8] Ibid., pp. 249–50. See also Nicolette Mout, 'Ideales Muster oder erfundene Eigenart. Republikanische Theorien während des niederländischen Aufstands', in H. G. Koenigsberger (ed.), *Republiken und Republikanismus im Europa der frühen Neuzeit* (Munich, 1988), pp. 169–94.
[9] Kossmann and Mellink, *Texts*, p. 249.

this can be said of any other country except Venice'.[10] In practice the republican system worked satisfactorily. In ten years' time (1588–98) the Republic was consolidated. It was becoming a real state that concluded treaties with foreign powers and organized its internal affairs with more efficiency than had been possible during the previous decades.

Dutch diplomacy was generally not eager to underline the republican character of the state it represented. Treaties were made by the States General of the 'Vereenighde Nederlantsche Provintien', or the 'Vereenighde Nederlanden' or the 'Geunieerde Provincien', or the 'Vrije Vereenighde Nederlanden', etc. In the text of the treaties the country was often called 'this State', 'the State of these countries', or even simply 'the State'. Only in treaties with other republics was the word 'republic' used with any regularity. In a treaty with the 'Serenissime Republique van Venetien' of 1619 the expressions 'both republics' or 'this republic and the other one' occur frequently, but the contracting parties were indicated as on the one hand the Republic of Venice and on the other the States General of the United Netherlands Provinces. In the treaty of 1654 ending the first Anglo-Dutch War it is the States General of the United Provinces which make peace with the lord protector of the republic of England, Scotland, and Ireland. Although the text of the treaty contains the expressions also used in the Venetian one ('both republics', 'this republic and the other one', etc.), the United Provinces were never called 'The Republic of the Netherlands' or 'The Dutch Republic'. In Anglo-Dutch treaties after 1660 the word 'republic' is no longer used. In the treaty of 'Confoederatie ende Vriendschap' (September 1662) between Charles II and the States General and the Breda Treaty (1667) terminating the second Anglo-Dutch War, the word 'republic' occurs only once to indicate the Netherlands, as a relic, apparently, for both article IV of 1662 and article XIII of 1667 in which it appears are almost identical with article VII of the treaty of 1654.[11]

In the early seventeenth century neither the Dutch statesmen nor the Dutch intellectuals sought to provide a theoretical foundation for the republican government which most of them admitted now did exist. Few analysed its character or praised it for any particular merit. One of them was Hugo Grotius in a celebrated book *De antiquitate Reipublicae Batavicae* (1610) also published in Dutch (*Tractaet van de Oudheyt vande Batavische nu Hollandsche Republique*). Grotius used the word republic as an equivalent of state rather than of a specifically non-monarchical state, just as Jean Bodin had done. The English writers of his time translated Bodin's 'république' as 'commonweale' and this indeed

[10] Ibid., p. 275.

[11] The Dutch texts of these (and many other) treaties are reprinted in *Groot Placaet-Boeck* (9 vols., The Hague, 1658–1796). The treaty with Venice in IV, pp. 283ff, with Cromwell, II, col. 522ff, with Charles II (1662), II, col. 2867ff; Peace of Breda (1667), III, pp. 325ff.

must have been the sense in which Grotius too understood it.[12] Yet it is obvious that Grotius' treatise was written to praise the republican form of government which Holland had possessed since its birth 1,700 years ago. Grotius elaborated ideas put forward in 1587 by François Vranck and the States of Holland in the declaration which has already been mentioned. While taking account of the long rule of the counts of Holland, the theory sought to depict these as mere executives entrusted with government by the sovereign States. It is true, they had occasionally far exceeded their legitimate competence but fundamentally Holland had always been a mixed state with a tendency towards aristocracy rather than monarchy.[13] This interpretation of Holland's history and constitution remained for decades to come so generally acceptable in the eyes of the provincial patriciate that it did apparently not require further development. But this was not, and could not be, a dynamic vision. It was profoundly and unyieldingly conservative. According to Grotius the system of government prevailing in Holland – he did not write about the other provinces – had always been what it was in his own time and, as it stood even the test of the struggle with Spain, it was expected to endure forever. Obviously Grotius' short book could not serve as a theoretically valid plea for republicanism. Other writings in this spirit could not either. Moreover, such writings were rare and – as is well known – Grotius himself soon modified his view and in his *De Jure Belli ac Pacis* (1625) held monarchy in higher regard than he had in 1610; indeed, in the 1640s he admitted that the views which he had expounded in the *De Antiquitate* were exaggerated. In other words, though *De Antiquitate* was a useful book that propped patrician self-esteem it was not a work of universal significance and did not form the starting-point for republican theorizing.

In the universities of the early seventeenth century professors and students did not show much interest in republics. They acknowledged their presence in reality as well as in Aristotelian politics and hastily studied some of their characteristics but tended to consider them as rather exceptional constructions which might work adequately in certain circumstances but were not as fit for general use as monarchy, the oldest and in most cases the best form of government. But, the students were told, monarchy should be distinguished from despotism. In Europe all monarchies were limited, some admittedly more so than

[12] Bodin's *Les Six Livres de la République* (1576) appeared in English (1606) as *The Six Books of a Commonweale*. See for an erudite and enlightening analysis of the history of the word 'republic' the long study by Wolfgang Mager in *Geschichtliche Grundbegriffe*, V (Stuttgart, 1984), pp. 549–651. The Dutch sources confirm his opinion (pp. 580ff) that in seventeenth-century Latin 'res publica' retained its old meaning whereas in the contemporary vernacular it stood most often for non-monarchical government. In Latin 'libertas' was sometimes used to indicate the non-monarchical republic and so was Dutch 'vrijheid'.

[13] For the position of Grotius in the historiography of his time see E. O. G. Haitsma Mulier, 'Grotius, Hooft and the Writing of History in the Republic', in A. C. Duke and C. A. Tamse (eds.), *Clio's Mirror. Historiography in Britain and the Netherlands*, Britain and the Netherlands, VIII (Zutphen, 1985), pp. 55ff.

others, but nowhere did one find here the despotic regimes which prevailed in Turkey, Asia, and Africa. This conventional wisdom led the teachers to conclusions which allowed them considerably to reduce the originality of their own state. All European monarchies were limited monarchies; that is, they had mixed forms of government. So had the Dutch Republic where the Stadholder's function was interpreted as constituting the monarchical element alongside the aristocracy represented by the various provincial States and the democracy of which some vestiges were still discernible in the urban administrations. It needs no commentary that this view was inadequate and unrealistic. It is, however, interesting to see that the Dutch universities of the early seventeenth century did not attempt to claim any exceptional quality, or status, for the state in which they functioned and to which they owed their existence. It is true, some of the teachers claimed that their state was exceptionally free; but that was not because it was a genuine republic, it was because it was more thoroughly mixed than other European states and the more mixed a state the freer it is.[14]

Only in the second half of the seventeenth century did some Dutch writers develop an elaborate republican theory. The best, and best known, among them were Johan (1622–60) and Pieter (1618–85) De La Court and Spinoza who used their work.[15] The De La Court brothers were businessmen in Leiden who felt deep contempt for the political views circulating in the universities. They admired Machiavelli, Descartes, and Hobbes, intellectual radicals and realists in their opinion, and spurned the eclecticism, vagueness, dullness of traditional Aristotelianism, and the authoritarian conservatism of Calvinist orthodoxy. It is impossible to summarize their often unsympathetic but delightful impromptu argumentation in a few words without blunting its edge and making it more coherent than it was. According to them the so-called mixed state could not exist. The original form of government was democracy. All monarchies in Europe, America, Asia, or Africa were despotic. There had never been a limited monarchy. All monarchies exploited the population to make it possible for the kings and their court to spend enormous amounts of money on debauchery, war, and useless conquests. Human nature was such that no man or woman elevated to royal status was able to discipline his or her passions, with the result that

[14] Cf. E. H. Kossmann, *Politieke theorie in het zeventiende-eeuwse Nederland* (Amsterdam, 1960), pp. 17ff.

[15] I tried to summarize the main arguments put forward by the brothers and to indicate their sources in my *Politieke theorie*, pp. 36–58. Recent studies have added new insights. See E. O. G. Haitsma Mulier, *The Myth of Venice and Dutch Republican Thought in the Seventeenth Century* (Assen, 1980), pp. 120ff. Idem, 'The Language of Seventeenth-Century Republicanism in the United Provinces: Dutch or European?', in A. Pagden (ed.), *The Languages of Political Theory in Early Modern Europe* (Cambridge, 1986), pp. 179ff. H. Schilling, 'Der libertär-radikale Republikanismus der holländischen Regenten', *Geschichte und Gesellschaft*, 10 (1984), pp. 498ff. H. W. Blom and I. W. Wildenberg (eds.), *Pieter de la Court in zijn tijd (1618–1685)* (Amsterdam, 1986), print a number of interesting papers. I. W. Wildenberg, *Johan en Pieter de la Court (1618–1660 en 1618–1685). Bibliografie en receptiegeschiedenis* (Amsterdam, 1986), gives a bibliography of the works of the brothers and analyses the commentaries on them since their publication.

all of them necessarily became frivolous, cruel, and irrational. Republican government, if wisely ordered, contained the checks needed to control the wild vagaries disturbing our souls. Only the republican form of government brought liberty, peace, and wealth and it should be the primary concern of statesmen to withstand attempts by military men or ambitious civilians to grasp power. The Princes of Orange should not be allowed any longer to exercise the functions of Stadholder and captain-general which they had held before, in the 1650s, the Grand Pensionary of Holland, Johan de Witt, abolished their traditional posts. Did the De La Court brothers look upon the Dutch Republic as an anomaly? Certainly not, for although they recognized that in the Europe of their days the republican idea was on the wane they were convinced, on historical as well as rational grounds, that the republic was the original form of government which had until recently prevailed in Europe. Not the Republic but monarchy was anomalous. For absolute monarchy as it had developed in the previous decades no rational or historical excuse was conceivable. In their eyes it was a thoroughly corrupted and exceedingly dangerous system of government.

The influence of the books published by the De La Courts, mainly during the 1660s, should certainly not be overrated.[16] It is true, Spinoza drew inspiration and profit from them but his work did not immediately make a great impression either (apart from the acerbic polemic it occasionally gave rise to). Moreover, Johan de Witt's experimenting with what was called 'true liberty' ('ware vrijheid'), that is, genuine republicanism not allowing any interference in political matters by the Orangist court, ended in 1672 with his assassination and the start of William III's Stadholdership. Yet, although the success of the De La Courts was limited, some of the theses they had propounded with such unusual vigour and extremism were in a mitigated form taken up by large sections of the elite. That monarchy, whatever its shape, was inherently bellicose came to be a commonplace in Dutch opinion and the view that the Republic was better equipped to further peace, trade, prosperity, and all the arts gracing Dutch civilization was generally accepted. It is remarkable that when, at the time of his triumph in 1675, William at his own instigation, was offered the sovereignty over Gelderland from which Louis XIV's troops had just withdrawn, by the States of that province conferring upon him the ancient title of 'Duke', even his most loyal adherents in Holland and Zeeland took alarm at the implications. The outcry was so general that William III felt obliged to decline the honour. In Zeeland his own supporters declared that arbitrary government (which was the inevitable outcome of all forms of one-headed government – the stock argument of Dutch republicans) was likely to destroy confidence in the commercial and financial institutions of the Republic such as the great trading companies and the public

[16] Cf. Wildenberg, *Johan en Pieter de la Court*, pp. 46ff.

banks and thus ruin Dutch prosperity. Subsequently, the idea that the Republic should not be transformed into a semi-monarchical state – irrespective of one's stance on the Stadholderate as such because to do so would irreparably damage both liberty and the economy – was not again seriously challenged, even by the Princes of Orange themselves.[17] Clearly, by the second half of the seventeenth century, republicanism had become an integral part of the package of components held to constitute 'Dutch freedom'.

Scarcely less enigmatic than Dutch republicanism was the principle and practice of toleration in the seventeenth-century Republic. During the first stage of the Revolt the concept had been relatively easy to formulate, for it was just what it was described as being – permission by the government for non-Catholics to hold religious services, in private or in public, in their own manner. The principle of toleration was justified by a variety of arguments some of which were evidently improvised by serious men and women desperately trying to defend themselves against charges of heresy and rebellion as well as to put their own conscience at rest. Toleration was supposed to be one of the manifold traditional rights and liberties enjoyed by the inhabitants and guaranteed in contracts with the sovereign, but it was also represented as a privilege, or as a fundamental universal right given to all men. During the 1570s Protestant rebels succeeded in obtaining power in various areas and were thus in a position to implement the principle of toleration they had in the previous decades declared to be superior to religious uniformity. In Holland in 1572 – it has already been mentioned – religion was left entirely free although the Catholic Church was dispossessed of its property – the income being used for paying the salaries of Calvinist ministers and schoolmasters or helping the poor – and, from 1573, Catholic services were forbidden. This, however, it was said, was not because conscience was unfree, it was because the Catholics were politically untrustworthy, potential traitors not accepting the new situation and not supporting the new rulers in their extremely precarious fight against the Spanish foe.

When in 1576 the seventeen provinces, all of them thoroughly embittered by Spanish mismanagement, resolved on a common effort to drive the Spanish troops away (this was the so-called Pacification of Ghent), they drew up a document in which they declared all edicts against heresy to be provisionally suspended but they left it to a later meeting of the States General to take final decisions concerning the religious issue. For the time being a sort of religious status quo should be maintained, with Holland and Zeeland being allowed to preserve their Protestantism but forbidden to spread it over the rest of the Netherlands. This did not work at all. After the main purpose of the Pacification had been

[17] In the perceptive paper which H. H. Rowen read at a conference at Washington University, St Louis, in October 1989 and of which he kindly sent me a draft ('The Idea of Freedom in the Dutch Republic') he reaches exactly the same conclusion.

achieved – the Spanish army left the country – the provinces involved fell into disagreement and new alliances were concluded, notably the Union of Utrecht of 1579 which in the Dutch Republic came to be looked back on as a fundamental constitutional event and text.[18] Article XIII dealt with religion. It stipulated that Holland and Zeeland would act at their own discretion whereas the other provinces were given the choice between various options, one of them being that each of them might introduce such regulations as it considered proper: it is hardly necessary to say that it was this possibility they chose. But all individuals would enjoy freedom of religion, and no one might be persecuted or questioned about his religion. In other words, the only principle held to be universally valid was that all inhabitants of the northern Netherlands were free in their consciences and none of them might be forced to conform to whatever religion was declared by the authorities to be the right and the dominant one.

In 1579, Dirck Volckertszoon Coornhert, the great Dutch writer on toleration – but he was at the same time a poet, an engraver, an etcher, a printer, a notary public, and so much more – was 57 years old. He still had eleven years to live. During the 1560s he had participated in opposition to the Habsburg government; in 1568 he had been forced into exile in Germany where he waited till 1572 before being able to return to Holland. He became secretary of the States of Holland but not for long. His vehement criticism of the cruelties perpetrated by the so-called Sea Beggars was responded to with such threats that he was once again compelled to seek refuge in Germany. But in 1577 he returned to Haarlem where he resumed his work as a public notary. He could, however, not remain silent. From 1577 to his death in 1590 he was engaged in constant debate with the representatives of the Calvinist Church. He was, of course, not a Calvinist. Calvin himself had as early as 1562 called him 'ce brouillon, ce pourceau, ceste beste sauvage' and twenty years later the Calvinist theologian Lambert Daneau, a Frenchman who in the early 1580s taught for a very short time at Leiden, declared in Latin that Coornhert was a rabid dog, an uncircumcised Goliath, the fan of Satan, the prince of the libertines. Yet the libertine sects did not like him either and he in his turn was extremely critical of many of the theological ideas they propounded. His own Christianity was undogmatic and optimistic. He was convinced that thanks to Jesus Christ all human beings are capable of obeying God's orders and of 'perfecting' themselves. Dogma, sacraments, ritual, sermons, etc., are of only secondary importance compared to the essence of the Christian faith, which is love. Deeply influenced by Senecan and Ciceronian Stoicism and by Erasmian evangelism, he refused to subject himself to the discipline of any church and claimed each man's right to follow his own path to perfection.

[18] Kossmann and Mellink, *Texts*, pp. 165–73.

The poignancy of the situation is obvious. The plea for toleration made during the 1560s and 1570s by people in fear of persecution at the hands of the Catholic Church and the Catholic sovereign was not heard; to obtain a measure of liberty those opposing the Spanish Habsburg government had in the 1570s set up local governments of their own and granted the Calvinist Church much power. Coornhert had backed the rebellion and served William of Orange because in his view this was not a struggle between hostile churches but between coercion and freedom. However, given the circumstances in Holland after 1572, his fiery defence of freedom was no longer directed against the Catholics but against the Calvinists. Now it is not unusual among nineteenth- and twentieth-century historians to praise Coornhert as by far the greatest author on tolerance in the Netherlands. They may well be right. At the same time they suggest that his writings inspired and influenced the ruling classes in Holland during the seventeenth century and thus may be studied as the theoretical legitimation of the extremely tolerant policies favoured by the regents.[19] If this is true we would have to conclude that the Dutch Republic while professing to be a Protestant state based its religious policy on a theory which was shaped by, and drew its impetus from, an anti-Calvinist rather than an anti-Catholic bias.

Does the study of the facts bear this out? But what are the facts? According to the liberal interpretation of Dutch history the battle about toleration was indeed one between the Calvinist Church on the one hand and the libertarian urban patriciate mainly in Holland on the other. The Calvinists accepted that conscience was free; they did not want persecution to be introduced again; they did not wish to transform their Church into an established Church; they thought the state must finance their Church but leave it free within its own spiritual responsibilities. At the same time, however, it was the duty of the state to prohibit the non-Calvinist part of the population – and that was the majority – to compete with the eternal truth laid down in Calvinist dogma. All ungodly activities should be stopped. Calvinist censors should be appointed by the state to prevent unorthodox writings being sent to the book shops. No dissidents should be allowed to hold religious services outside their own house. In public, Dutch society should conform to the Calvinist ethic with, among other things, strict Sunday observance. All officials, urban, provincial, federal, should be members of the Calvinist Church; and so should be all schoolmasters.

The answer which the ruling patricians gave to these and other claims was, so runs the liberal interpretation, cautious. They could hardly deny that the new state was in a sense a Protestant state even though there was no established

[19] See, for example, in the great work by Cd. Busken Huet, *Het land van Rembrandt. Studies over de Noordnederlandsche beschaving in de zeventiende eeuw* (1st edn., 1882–4), the passage on p. 400 of the most recent edition (Amsterdam, 1987). See also H. A. Enno van Gelder, *Vrijheid en onvrijheid in de Republiek. Geschiedenis der vrijheid van drukpers en godsdienst van 1572 tot 1789*, I: *Van 1572 tot 1619* (Haarlem, 1947), p. 221.

state Church. They knew, moreover, that Calvinism constituted a formidable force which it would be extremely risky to alienate. So they gave in and when urgently asked by the Church to act against dissident views, books, speeches, services, against the theatre, against Descartes, against Spinoza, against all the innumerable phenomena shocking the puritan conscience, they issued strongly worded edicts – and there were very many of them, enacted by diverse authorities, the States General, the States of the various provinces, the urban governments. Most of these texts were carefully formulated. They normally did not consider the religious significance of the forbidden abuses but merely stated that they might stir unrest or even sedition and should therefore be stopped. Yet in reality they were hardly ever stopped. When the Church protested against the negligence of the political authorities in enforcing obedience to their own orders, these answered that this was highly regrettable but that they did not possess adequate means to enforce them more strictly. They then patiently waited until the Church started another campaign and if this became sufficiently powerful they issued some new, equally ineffectual edicts. In fact, many of the patricians in the towns and in the States felt some contempt for the Calvinist ministers and their *furor theologicus*.

This corroborated the view of the patricians that the Church should not be given too much independence. In fact, there were strong links between state and Church. In return for the money provided by the state out of confiscated property of the former Roman Catholic Church the political rulers possessed concrete power in the Church itself, just as they had in the universities all of which were Protestant, founded by the provinces, and subjected to the authority of the provincial States. The ultimate goal of political interference in what was going on both in the Church and in the universities was to pacify conflicts, to lower the temperature of the often extremely heated discussions between theologians, philosophers, jurists so that the social order would not be disturbed by intellectual debates which no one might expect to be concluded satisfactorily. This was the spirit that prevailed: conciliate the Church when it protested against the wicked outer world by verbose prohibitions; terminate abstract debates by forbidding the participants to speak and write about the issues under discussion. It was, so the liberal historians suggest, a wise, cautious, somewhat sceptical but thoroughly civilized behaviour which achieved in practice what it refrained from putting as principle: a measure of freedom more generous than anywhere in the world of that time. And indeed, there were no censors in the Republic; the universities enrolled students without requiring them to mention their religious affiliations (in most universities the professors, however, were asked to subscribe to the articles of the Dordt Synod), marriages contracted in Remonstrant, Lutheran, Baptist Churches were considered legal; of those consecrated in the Catholic Church the magistrate needed to be notified; as for the officials, every one knew that in the countryside but also even in the towns Catholics, Remonstrants, Lutherans held positions of importance although it is true that in the higher ranks of the bureaucracy the presence of non-Calvinists would in the course of the seventeenth century possibly have come to seem too eccentric to be continued for long. But strict legal objections to the participation of non-Calvinists in the government did not exist. In the towns the old methods of appointing members of the councils and the burgomasters by co-option were maintained and attempts by some higher authority to put limits to the towns' freedom of action in this matter by obliging them to elect only Calvinists would have been interpreted as an intolerable form of interference in local affairs, an onslaught on local autonomy and thus a betrayal of the values the towns had fought for during the Revolt.

There is much to be said for this interpretation of Dutch history. Moreover, there is a mass of material that may be used to confirm it. It is easy enough to collect numerous passages in books and pamphlets which indicate that their authors were doubtful about the significance of theological debate, as ultimate truth was beyond human understanding and could not be definitively established by any creed or any dogma. And, of course, the assertion that a commercial society cannot survive if it refuses to welcome all sorts of people, views, religious practices served as a most effective argument in discussions about whether or not to prohibit the sermons of a sect or the publication of a book. But notwithstanding their respect for the historians[20] who analysed Dutch history and more specifically the history of Dutch freedom in ways similar to the admittedly simplified summary I have sketched, other historians cannot suppress a feeling of uneasiness about this representation of seventeenth-century reality.[21] According to them, the liberal view is anachronistic. I share this feeling. Is it really conceivable that seventeenth-century rulers, regents, patricians were, though unwillingly, prepared to issue edicts against heterodox sects and books just because the Calvinist Church pressed them to do so but without the intention of seeing to it that they were obeyed? Do we know enough about the culture of the politicians to ascertain that they were influenced by Erasmus and by Coornhert? Must we assume that the orthodox Calvinists among the regents – and, of course, there were many of them although nobody has as yet tried to calculate their

[20] The major representative of this liberal historiography in our century was H. A. Enno van Gelder (1889–1973). His last monograph *Getemperde vrijheid. Een verhandeling over de verhouding van Kerk en Staat in de Republiek der Verenigde Nederlanden en de vrijheid van meningsuiting in zake godsdienst, drukpers en onderwijs gedurende de 17e eeuw* (Groningen, 1972) is, although the title does not indicate this, the second volume of the book mentioned in n. 19. See for an excellent brief review of his life and work I. Schöffer, 'Herman Arend Enno van Gelder', in *Jaarboek van de Maatschappij der Nederlandse Letterkunde te Leiden, 1975–1976* (Leiden, 1977), pp. 110–21.

[21] See in particular the short but most pertinent remarks by W. W. Mijnhardt in the book he edited in 1983, *Kantelend geschiedbeeld. Nederlandse historiografie sinds 1945* (Utrecht), pp. 165ff. A. Th. van Deursen's *Het kopergeld van de Gouden Eeuw* (4 vols., Assen, 1978–80) contains many important passages relating to the issue.

number – were virtually impotent as soon as the moment arrived to carry the ordinances against heterodoxy into effect? Is it likely for responsible people bearing fairly heavy responsibilities – many of them educated in the law schools of the universities – and eager to emphasize the fullness of their power to make laws which they hoped and expected not to be implemented? Should we even try to look for a single underlying principle in the chaos of measures taken, executed, withdrawn, or left dormant by all sorts of federal, provincial, and local authorities in a bewildering variety of circumstances? The answer to all these questions is probably: no. Without denying that patricians and writers regularly advanced enlightened ideas about the value of toleration, it was generally speaking not the logic of a principle but the force of a situation which brought about the freedom prevailing in the Netherlands. Even if dominant Calvinism might have succeeded in driving Protestant dissenters to the margin of social acceptability, this was totally impossible in the case of the Catholics. There were simply too many of them – in the middle of the century, more than 40 per cent of the not yet 2 million inhabitants of the Republic and about one third of the population of Holland alone. Although the majority of the politicians undoubtedly thought Catholic sacraments, ritual, and the role of the priest shocking or merely silly they were perfectly aware of the fact that it was not enough for a Catholic to be free in his conscience because he needed a church and a clergy to obtain salvation. Could one deny him these without risking disturbances and bloodshed? Probably not, which means that if the various authorities in the Republic had insisted on drawing practical conclusions from their ordinances, they should have had to equip themselves with considerably more armed forces than they had and wanted to have. But a Protestant government not prepared or able to prohibit Catholic religious services and drive the Catholic clergy away did not, of course – or, if it did, only occasionally – feel itself bound to put Protestant Dissenters under heavy pressure to stop their activities.

So far so good. But does this bring us nearer to the spirit of the Dutch seventeenth-century government? Only in a limited way, for we remain confronted with the enigma of massive legislation, not, or only rarely, carried into effect by people whose primary concern was civil obedience. Let us not worry too much about it. This essay does not claim to decipher the mystery of the Dutch seventeenth century. It just wishes to indicate the character of its freedom. And in relation to that phenomenon we may attempt to draw a conclusion. It can be short. We do not need romantic notions about the nature of the Dutch people to see why the various freedoms it cherished came to be regarded as a coherent whole. They resulted from practice rather than principle and perhaps we may even say that in the Dutch seventeenth century the rulers used freedom, that is, independence, provincial autonomy, republicanism, and toleration, as an instrument to maintain a precarious equilibrium in an economically, politically, and culturally dynamic society that was in constant danger of being disrupted by the multifarious interests, ideals, convictions, ambitions, and traditions which characterized it. The Dutch experience showed that liberty is an excellent tool to keep a society going.

Chapter 9

William III, Brandenburg, and the construction of the anti-French coalition, 1672–88

WOUTER TROOST

INTRODUCTION

Many historians have claimed that William's expedition to England in the autumn of 1688 was an extremely hazardous venture: bad weather could have easily destroyed the fleet, while at the same time the frontiers of the Dutch Republic were left undefended against a possible French attack. They argue that Louis XIV could have easily moved his troops from the Rhineland towards the Republic, a policy which was actually advocated strongly by the French ambassador at The Hague, the comte d'Avaux, who regarded William's absence from the Republic as a golden chance for his king to invade the home base of his main rival.[1]

Professor Ragnild Hatton, however, has shown that when William left for England, the frontiers of the Dutch Republic were not without troops. The rulers of Brandenburg, Brunswick, Hesse, and Württemberg had finalized treaties with William III in September 1688, undertaking to compensate for the number of Dutch troops that William took to England.[2] Frederick III, the Elector of Brandenburg, supplied 6,000 men to an auxiliary army of 14,000 men placed under the command of Count Waldeck, which, in William's absence, helped defend the line 's-Hertogenbosch-Deventer.[3] Brandenburg's support for the whole operation was indeed crucial. The agreement of September 1688 was based on a treaty reached on 23 August 1685 between the Dutch Republic and Frederick William, the Great Elector of Brandenburg, and renewed by Frederick William's son, Frederick III, on 30 June 1688 after the Elector's death on 9 May 1688.

I would like to thank Dr Robert Cribb of the Australian National University, Canberra, who stayed with me at NIAS, Wassenaar during the term 1988–9, for his helpful comments on an earlier draft of this paper.

[1] For the remark of d'Avaux see N. Japikse, *Prins Willem III, de Stadhouder-koning* (2 vols., Amsterdam, 1930–3), II, p. 248.

[2] R. Hatton, '1688 in Europees Perspectief', *Oranje Nassau Museum Jaarboek 1988* (Zutphen, 1988), p. 10. I wonder whether Ernst August, duke of Hanover really promised military support. See G. Schnath, *Geschichte Hannovers im Zeitalter der neunten Kur und der englischen Sukzession, 1674–1714* (4 vols., Hildesheim, 1938), I, p. 430.

[3] See p. 107 above; J. Carswell, *The Descent on England* (London, 1969), p. 173. Schnath, *Geschichte Hannovers im Zeitalter der neunten Kur*, I, p. 429.

The balance of power doctrine seemed to make Brandenburg's entry into the anti-French alliance in 1688 almost inevitable, but this essay will show that during the period 1672–88 close relations between the Republic and Brandenburg could not be taken for granted.

In 1672 relations seemed good. As we shall see, when Louis XIV attacked the Republic, Frederick William came to the aid of the Dutch, and during the war the Elector also fought France's northern ally Sweden, conquering West Pomerania (Vorpommern) and the port of Stettin. It was Frederick's victory over the Swedes at Fehrbellin in August 1675 that added the adjective 'Great' to the title of Elector. The allied front, however, was broken by the Dutch, who negotiated a separate peace with France at Nijmegen in August 1678. As a result the French were able to put pressure upon Brandenburg to return Western Pomerania to the Swedes. This put relations between Frederick William and the Republic's leader William III under great strain.

Although the Republic had concluded peace with France, it will become clear that William III still regarded Louis XIV as a threat to peace in Europe. He therefore tried to forge tight links with the Elector once again. At first William did not succeed. In order to revenge himself on his former allies and to safeguard his own security, the Elector had established friendly relations with Louis XIV. By closely aligning himself with the French king, Frederick William hoped to retake Stettin, this time as an ally of France.

However, the relationship between France and Brandenburg never became cordial. Louis XIV distrusted the Great Elector, while Frederick William's disapproval of Louis' *Réunions* policy and his religious policy towards the Huguenots ensured that the two rulers kept their distance. The Elector nevertheless remained in the French camp as he regarded the anti-French alliance of the Republic, Sweden, the German Empire, and Spain and Saxony, which William III had been building since October 1681, as not strong enough to stand up to Louis XIV successfully. Whether the entry of the English king, Charles II, into the League of Association, for which William III strove hard but to no effect, would have overcome the Elector's objections against entering the Alliance remains a point of speculation. Frederick William remained a reluctant ally of Louis XIV, because he feared that if he joined the League of Association war in Germany would become inevitable, and would lead to a total defeat of the anti-French powers. His original motive for becoming an ally of France, namely the desire to reconquer Stettin, was gradually subordinated to this consideration. For fear and not for love of France the Elector agreed with the French proposal to conclude a separate peace between France and the German Empire and accepted Louis XIV's 'judicial' conquests in the empire.

It is therefore no surprise to see that when the Twenty Years' Truce of Regensburg realized the peace in Germany which Frederick William had wished for and gave him renewed freedom of action, he moved closer to his Dutch nephew and joined the other anti-French powers once again. His regard for this alliance was reflected in the pass-words he gave to his palace guards on the two last days of his life, 'Amsterdam' and 'London'.[4]

A PRELUDE TO THE ESTRANGEMENT BETWEEN THE REPUBLIC AND BRANDENBURG: THE GREAT ELECTOR AND THE PEACE OF NIJMEGEN, 1672–8

At the end of 1671 the Dutch States General decided to send Godard Adriaan van Reede van Amerongen to Berlin in order to seek the Elector of Brandenburg's support against Louis XIV, who seemed to be on the point of attacking the Netherlands. Van Amerongen belonged to the nobility of the province of Utrecht. He had been on several earlier diplomatic missions on behalf of the States General and, although he was not regarded as a top diplomat, his diligence, perseverance, and sangfroid made him an obvious choice for the job. His strong support for the young William III, who was appointed captain-general of the Dutch forces in January 1672 for one season only, told strongly in his favour for the post, as Frederick William had strong family ties with the Orange family: his mother had been a grand-daughter of William the Silent and during his youth he had stayed in the Republic and had married an Orange princess, Louisa Henrietta, daughter of the Dutch Stadholder Frederick Henry. As an uncle of William III, Frederick William had repeatedly urged the Dutch 'regenten' to restore his nephew into the dignities that had belonged to William's forefathers and, indeed, precisely for this reason, the Grand Pensionary of Holland, Johan de Witt, distrusted the Elector. Thus it was not de Witt but the States General who initiated Van Amerongen's mission. Van Amerongen for his part did not keep de Witt informed about his negotiations, but corresponded only with the clerk of the States General and after July 1672 with William III.[5] William's role in foreign policy formulation was ambiguous. In July 1672, a popular rising against the 'regenten', who were blamed for having neglected the country's defences to the point where the French took control of most of the territory of the Republic, brought him greater power in all areas of government and the States General gave him an important share in the making of Dutch foreign policy. As a Stadholder he was nevertheless still a servant of the provincial estates and, although the majority of the Dutch provinces usually backed William, the constitutional rule that decisions in the States General should be taken unanimously made William III very dependent on the Republic's most

[4] C. E. Maurice, *Life of Frederick William, the Great Elector of Brandenburg* (London, 1926), p. 177, and B. Cloger, *Friedrich Wilhelm, Kurfürst von Brandenburg* (Berlin, 1984), p. 351.

[5] A. Waddington, *Le Grand Electeur Frédéric Guillaume de Brandenbourg. Sa Politique extérieure 1640–1688* (2 vols., Paris, 1905), II: *(1660–1688)*, p. 251.

powerful province, Holland, in general and its leading city, Amsterdam, in particular. Much as Holland's leading politician, the Grand Pensionary Caspar Fagel, who succeeded de Witt in 1672, and William III shared the same view on foreign policy, we shall see that Amsterdam and some other cities were able to frustrate William's foreign policy at certain times.

In Brandenburg, on the other hand, the Elector was in complete control of foreign policy making. When he commenced his reign in 1640, Frederick William's power had been very weak, but since then this convinced Calvinist had been striving to strengthen his own position and to forge his scattered territories of Prussia, Brandenburg, Halberstadt, Minden, Cleves, and Mark into greater unity.

In order to achieve this aim he deemed the formation of a standing army absolutely necessary. The Nordic War (1655–60), in which Frederick William initially supported Sweden and then defected to its enemy, Poland, gave him the opportunity to recruit an army. With this army he forced the various provincial estates to vote for the necessary expenses of war. When the war was over, the Elector did not disband his troops, but used them to bring pressure upon the estates to agree to the introduction of a new permanent tax, the Excise (a Dutch idea). This made Frederick William financially independent of the estates and increased his authority enormously.

In administering the country, this hot tempered ruler was assisted by a Privy Council of about fifteen members, which since 1651 had constituted the central governing body of all the Elector's territories.[6] At first, all aspects of government policy were dealt with in the Privy Council, but this practice did not lead to a speedy dispatch of business. Therefore the Elector began to take counsel with only a few members of the Privy Council. Especially towards the end of his reign, when Frederick William was plagued by regular attacks of gout which made writing and walking impossible, he used to consult only a few intimi. A few privy councillors advised him especially on foreign affairs, but no one ever reached the rank of minister of foreign affairs like in France. The Elector made sure that he never became too dependent on any one privy councillor and in fact sometimes actually encouraged rivalry between his councillors, because it gave him the opportunity to steer his own course.[7] In France foreign ambassadors seldom visited the king and if they did it was only at an official audience. In Berlin, or in Potsdam where he often stayed, Frederick William conferred with foreign ministers incessantly.

When Van Amerongen arrived in Berlin, he found the Elector very worried about the rising power of France and the almost certain attack on the Nether-

[6] C. Hinrichs, 'Der Grosse Kurfürst', in *Preussen als Historisches Problem. Gesammelte Abhandlungen herausgegeben von Gerhard Oestreich* (Berlin, 1964), pp. 227–53.

[7] G. Pagès, *Le Grand Electeur et Louis XIV, 1660–1688* (Paris, 1905), p. 32.

lands. In spite of French offers intended to buy his neutrality, Frederick William decided it was in the interest of Brandenburg, the empire, and his Dutch co-religionists to help the Republic, although a majority of the members of the Privy Council preferred a policy of wait-and-see.[8]

It nevertheless took almost six months of tough negotiations before Van Amerongen could succeed in concluding a defensive treaty with the Elector. In exchange for 220,000 thaler recruitment money and a Dutch guarantee to pay half the cost of Frederick William's army of 20,000 men, the Elector promised to have an army ready within two months of payment of the recruitment money. He then would march towards Westphalia and join the forces of the Republic. The allies agreed that neither power would negotiate, or conclude, a separate peace with the enemy.[9]

Having obtained Frederick William's support, William III turned to the emperor, signing a treaty with Leopold I in July 1672. Originally the emperor had wanted to remain neutral, but the French invasion of the Republic caused great concern in Vienna. The French occupation of the Elector's territory of Cleves was regarded as a violation of the German Empire and used as a justification for Leopold's entry into the allied camp.[10]

A combined Austrian–Brandenburg army could have gone a long way towards halting the French attack on the Netherlands. Frederick William sent his Master of the Horse, Bernard Baron von Pöllnitz, to William III to confer on what military action should be taken. Von Pöllnitz suggested a rendezvous of the Austrian and Brandenburg armies in the middle-Rhine area. The two armies would then cross the Rhine and meet William's army at Maastricht. This move would cut off the French army in the Netherlands from its home base and force it to withdraw.[11]

William III and the States General approved of the plan but it was never carried out, because of obstructive actions by the Austrian army. The Austrian commander, Raimondo di Montecuccoli, had received strict orders from Vienna not to cross the River Rhine. The Austrian Grand Chamberlain Prince Lobkowitz, head of the 'Eastern' faction at the Austrian court, regarded the Turks as a greater danger to the empire than France and had convinced the German emperor to avoid open warfare with the French. He went as far as to tell the French ambassador in Vienna, Grémont, that the expedition to the Rhine was merely for show.[12]

[8] Ibid., p. 289, and F. Schevill, *The Great Elector* (Chicago, 1947), p. 299.

[9] Th. von Moerner, *Kurbrandenburgs Staatsverträge von 1601 bis 1700. Nach den originalen des Königl. Geh. Staats-Archiv* (Berlin, 1867), pp. 360–3.

[10] L. Hüttl, *Friedrich Wilhelm von Brandenburg, der Grosse Kurfürst, 1620–1688. Eine politische Biographie* (Munich, 1981), p. 382.

[11] M. Philippson, *Der grosse Kurfürst Friedrich Wilhelm von Brandenburg* (3 vols., Berlin, 1897–1903), II, p. 268.

[12] J. Spielman, *Leopold I of Austria* (London, 1976), p. 59.

When the joint army arrived at Koblenz in September 1672, the Elector of Trier refused it permission to cross the river, and Montecuccoli used this as a pretext to march instead towards Frankfurt. William urgently requested Van Amerongen, who was accompanying the Elector, to encourage Frederick William to cross the river 'without using so many detours' but to no avail.[13] Fagel compared the march of the Austrian–Brandenburg army to 'the journey of the Jews from Egypt to Canaän, who when they had reached the frontier of the promised land returned to Egypt'.[14]

The States General now accused Frederick William of breaking his treaty with them, of failing to fulfil his obligations. The Elector indirectly agreed with them, remarking to Van Amerongen 'he would not be fooled around with any longer by the Austrians',[15] but he was unable to have his plans prevail in the war council. When, however, the Dutch stopped paying their war subsidy, Frederick William was most displeased and lack of money forced him to break yet another provision of the treaty, negotiating a separate truce with Louis XIV in April 1673. This act led to heated reactions from Fagel and the Prince. The Grand Pensionary admitted that the subsidies had not been paid punctually, but 'the non-fulfilment of his [Frederick William's] treaty obligations is the main reason why the provinces have not paid their subsidies, because they could not be persuaded to pay money for which they got so little in return'.[16] William shared his Pensionary's thoughts: 'if only the Elector had done half the work I did, state affairs would have been in a better posture'.[17]

Louis XIV, of course, was delighted that the Elector of Brandenburg had been compelled to abandon his struggle against France and offered him lenient peace conditions in order to win him to the French side. In the Treaty of Vossem of June 1673 the French king restored to Frederick William most of the fortresses he had captured in Cleves and Mark, adding a French subsidy of 800,000 livres in return for the Elector's promise to keep his army behind the River Weser and to remain neutral for the rest of the war.[18] This peace, however, did not mark the beginning of friendly relations between the two countries and attempts of Louis XIV to negotiate a treaty with Frederick William failed. The Elector did not envisage breaking away completely from the Republic and Austria, where the government had taken a more anti-French course after Lobkowitz had fallen into disgrace. These two countries extended their alliance concluding a treaty

[13] William III to Van Amerongen, 24 Oct. 1672, *Urkunden und Actenstücke zur Geschichte des Kurfürsten Friedrich Wilhelm von Brandenburg* (23 vols., Berlin, and Leipzig, 1864–1930), III, p. 305.

[14] The Pensionary to Van Amerongen, 24 Oct. 1672, *Urkunden und Actenstücke*, III, p. 309.

[15] Van Amerongen to the clerk of the States General, 27 Oct. 1673, *Urkunden und Actenstücke*, III, pp. 315–16.

[16] The Pensionary to Van Amerongen, 11 Mar. 1673, *Urkunden und Actenstücke*, III, p. 382.

[17] William III to Van Amerongen, N. Japikse (ed.), *Correspondentie van Willem III en Hans Willem Bentinck, eersten Graf van Portland* (5 vols., The Hague, 1927–37), I, part 2, p. 193.

[18] Pagès, *Le Grand Electeur*, pp. 327–9.

with Spain and the exiled duke of Lorraine, Charles IV, at The Hague on 30 August 1673, that bore fruit almost at once. In September William III captured Naarden and in November the town of Bonn had to surrender to an army of Austrian, Dutch, and Spanish troops, forcing Louis XIV to withdraw from the Netherlands.[19]

Frederick William was delighted. He was no friend of France and the French subsidy had fallen far short of financing his armed neutrality, so he began to wonder whether his former allies would be prepared to pay him substantial subsidies for his services again. Thus at the end of 1673, when William III asked his uncle to enter the alliance of the emperor, the Republic and Spain, claiming that 'the bond between the House of Orange and Brandenburg is as indissoluble as the bond between heaven and earth',[20] the Elector did not turn a deaf ear to his request.

The renewed negotiation, however, did not run smoothly. The capture of Naarden and Bonn had changed the diplomatic situation to the Republic's advantage. Moreover, Dutch parsimony and the Elector's passion for money did not go well together. The Dutch originally offered to pay half the cost of a Brandenburg expeditionary force to consist of 12,000 men only, while Spain was to pay the other half.[21] The Elector thought such an army far too small and proposed a force of 20,000 men, to be paid for by the allies. He also claimed 630,000 thaler, as the outstanding debt of the Republic to Brandenburg under the 1672 treaty.[22] The Dutch States General refused to contribute to a larger army and rejected the 630,000 thaler as outrageous, arguing they owed the Elector only 190,000 thaler.[23]

When, however, the French vacated the Brandenburg fortresses of Wesel and Rees at the beginning of May 1674 and promised the Elector large subsidies if he did not rejoin his former allies,[24] the Dutch became more conciliatory, finally agreeing along with Spain to support a Brandenburg army of 16,000 men, while each of them would contribute a further 100,000 thaler towards its equipment. In paying this sum the Dutch evidently presumed that the problem of their outstanding debt to the Elector had been solved. The new treaty between Brandenburg and the Republic, which tied the Elector also to the emperor and Spain was concluded at last on 1 July 1674.

Article 24 of the treaty, included at the request of the Elector, stipulated that each partner in the coalition had the right to conclude peace separately as far

[19] Japikse, *Prins Willem III*, I, p. 314.
[20] J. H. Hora Siccama, *Schets van de diplomatieke betrekkingen tusschen Nederland en Brandenburg, 1596–1678* (Utrecht, 1867), p. 268 n. 4.
[21] *Urkunden und Actenstücke*, III, pp. 423–4.
[22] Ibid., III, pp. 432 and 436.
[23] Ibid., III, p. 441.
[24] Hora Siccama, *Schets*, p. 270.

as it did not bring a loss upon the other allies and on the condition that they were informed in time.[25] Having violated an earlier treaty with the Dutch in 1673 by concluding a separate treaty with the French, Frederick William now made sure he could not be censured again if he negotiated a separate peace, and indeed the Dutch and Austrians suspected the Elector of wanting to quit the alliance whenever it suited him. What the Elector did not realize, however, was that this clause could also be used against him.

In the middle of July 1674 the Elector, at the head of an Austrian–Brandenburg army of 50,000 men decided to march towards the River Rhine, cross it, and move into the Palatinate, a territory that had been invaded by the French marshal de Turenne in April 1674. William III's proposal that the Elector should join the allied forces in the Spanish Netherlands, where the army under Louis de Bourbon, prince de Condé, was much larger than that of Turenne, was ignored.[26]

The army crossed the Rhine on 13 October. Turenne, with an army of only 25,000 men, withdrew into Alsace, and the Elector's hope of defeating the French in battle was frustrated. Once again the Austrians sabotaged military operations. This time, the delaying tactics of the Austrian commander Bournonville, Montecuccoli's mediocre subordinate,[27] saw to it that Turenne got away. Frederick William, who admittedly did not have the reputation of being a calm, well-balanced person anyway, was filled with rage: 'we could have destroyed him [Turenne] if only Bournonville, the villain, had not prevented it'.[28] In the middle of November the Elector withdrew towards Kolmar, while Turenne, who in the meantime had reinforced his troops to 35,000 men, succeeded in forcing the allied army back over the Rhine.

While wintering in Franconia, the Elector, whose mental state had worsened with the death of his eldest son Carl Emil, received the news that general Wrangel, at the head of a Swedish army of 15,000 men, had invaded the Uckermark, a part of Brandenburg north of Berlin.

Like Brandenburg, Sweden had a reputation of using up political allies rapidly. In 1668, after the War of Devolution, Sweden had joined with England and the Republic, but Louis XIV had quickly succeeded in disbanding this Triple Alliance. The secret Treaty of Dover of June 1670 brought Charles II into the French camp and in April 1672, in exchange for a liberal subsidy, the Swedes promised Louis XIV to fight any German State that rendered assistance to the Dutch Republic.[29]

[25] Waddington, *Le Grand Electeur*, II, p. 346, and Cloger, *Friedrich Wilhelm*, p. 239. See also the letter of the Dutch ambassador Van Achtienhoven to William III, 23 Apr. 1674, *Urkunden und Actenstücke*, III, p. 432.
[26] *Urkunden und Actenstücke*, XIII, pp. 638–9.
[27] Spielman, *Leopold I*, p. 79.
[28] Philippson, *Grosse Kurfürst*, II, p. 325.
[29] Schevill, *The Great Elector*, p. 295.

The Swedes had not had to bring their army into action against Brandenburg in 1672, since Frederick William had concluded peace with the French within a year. When, however, the Elector decided to take up the armed struggle again in July 1674, the French envoy in Stockholm, Isaac de Feuquières, reminded the Swedish government of the French–Swedish treaty of April 1672.

The Swedes did not really want to start a war, as their finances were too fragile to maintain a large army. Their main object was to keep their German conquests including Western Pomerania, Bremen, and Verden without getting involved in hostilities. The Swedish government nevertheless remained loyal to the alliance with France, fearing that if they broke with France, Denmark, Sweden's prime enemy, might become an ally of France.[30] The Swedes, thus, gave in to French pressure although, since they made no formal war declaration on Brandenburg,[31] one may surmise that they wanted to avoid a complete rupture between the two countries.

To the Elector, however, the Swedish attack meant not only a military threat, but also an opportunity. His reaction was 'The Swedes have invaded the Mark, now I might be able to get the whole of Pomerania'.[32] The Elector, already in the possession of Eastern Pomerania, looked forward to capturing Western Pomerania in general and the Swedish port of Stettin in particular. During his stay in the Netherlands, Frederick William had been very impressed by the commercial activities of the Dutch merchants, but Western Pomerania's position, blocking Brandenburg's access to the sea, was an obstacle to his following their example. If he succeeded in taking Stettin, the Elector thought, he might also be able to start a policy of commercial expansion.

First of all, however, the Elector needed his allies. Their support was by no means automatic, since they were unlikely to approve of the diversion of Brandenburg troops from the Rhine to Pomerania. On 30 December 1674 Frederick William therefore asked William III 'not to leave him in the lurch, but to attack Bremen and to entreat Denmark to declare war on Sweden'.[33]

William III reacted favourably[34] but the States General were reluctant to plunge into a new war, complaining that the war efforts of the emperor and Spain were clearly insufficient, that the war costs were unbearable, and that Dutch business was stagnant.[35] In order to put pressure on the Prince and the States General, Frederick William himself travelled to The Hague and there

[30] G. Rystad, 'Sweden and the Nijmegen Peace Congress' in J. A. H. Bots (ed.), *The Peace of Nijmegen, 1676–1678/79* (Amsterdam, 1980), p. 134.
[31] Hüttl, *Friedrich Wilhelm*, p. 400.
[32] Ibid., p. 402.
[33] Quoted by L. von Orlich, *Geschichte des Preussischen Staates im siebzehnten Jahrhundert; mit besonderer Beziehung auf das Leben Friedrich Wilhelms des Grossen Kurfürsten* (3 vols., Berlin 1933–9), II, p. 147.
[34] Hora Siccama, *Schets*, p. 274.
[35] *Urkunden und Actenstücke*, III, pp. 455–6.

on 15 May 1675 the Prince of Orange, the States General, and the envoys of the other allies – the emperor, Spain, Brandenburg, and the dukes of Brunswick–Lüneburg – decided to declare war on Sweden on 15 June 1675. Denmark would be asked to launch an attack on Sweden with 16,000 men. The allies would send a squadron of nine ships in order to assist the Danish navy; the Danes would be asked to equip sixteen ships themselves, to which the allies would contribute 600,000 guilders.[36] Frederick William was delighted with the promised support. He decided to concentrate himself fully on the war against Sweden, leaving only a small part of his army, two cavalry regiments, on the Rhine.

The Elector's campaign against Sweden was rather impressive. He defeated the Swedes at Fehrbellin at the end of June 1675, he conquered Stettin in December 1677, and about a year later was master of the whole of Pomerania. The Elector, however, should have realized when he started his Pomeranian venture that the future of Pomerania would not be decided by Brandenburg and Sweden alone. A victory over Sweden could be easily undone by the military supremacy of France, Sweden's western ally. The real outcome of the war was still to be decided in the Spanish Netherlands and on the Rhine.[37]

In the west, the armies of the allies were no match for the French generals in the campaigns of 1676 and 1677. The Dutch suffered most. Their army bore the brunt of the French attacks, and the Elector refused William's request to send more troops to the Low Countries because he needed them against the Swedes.[38] As financial exhaustion struck the Republic, the payment of the promised subsidies to the Elector quickly became irregular,[39] and in December 1676 the States General decided to suspend payments altogether from 1 January 1677.[40]

The Elector's annoyance with the Dutch had already grown when the States General resolved on 26 September 1676 to start separate negotiations with France unless the envoys of the allies met at Nijmegen by 1 November.[41] The Elector was very suspicious of this move as he realized that such negotiations might lead to a separate peace which could be detrimental to his interests. In April 1677, in a lengthy discussion at Wesel, Fagel succeeded in reassuring the Elector for the time being. The Grand Pensionary repeated the Republic's wish to conclude a general peace. The States General and their envoys, Fagel said, 'would do their utmost to enable him to occupy the whole of Pomerania. They would

[36] *Urkunden und Actenstücke,* XIII, pp. 806–9.

[37] See the article of R. Pillorget, 'La France at les Etats Allemands au Congrès de Nimègue (1678–1679), in Bots (ed.), *The Peace of Nijmegen*, pp. 225–36. See also E. Opgenoorth, *Friedrich Wilhelm, der Grosse Kurfürst von Brandenburg. Eine politische Biographie* (Göttingen, 1978), II, pp. 196–7.

[38] *Urkenden und Actenstücke*, XVIII, pp. 149 and 150.

[39] Ibid., III, p. 482.

[40] ARH SG 8607, res. 12 Dec. 1676.

[41] Waddington, *Le Grand Electeur*, II, p. 382.

not separate themselves from their allies, but remain in the alliance until a general peace was concluded'.[42] Frederick William was also told that it was inability rather than unwillingness that made Dutch payment of subsidies irregular. Fagel sketched a gloomy picture of the Dutch finances. At the end of the war against Spain the outstanding debt of the State had been 15 million guilders, but the figure had now risen to 40 million.

Despite Fagel's assurances, however, rumours that the States General wanted to negotiate a separate peace continued to circulate and the Elector began to worry that his Pomeranian venture might become a failure.

Frederick William could have counteracted Dutch war weariness by sending a large part of his army to the Rhine after the capture of Stettin in December 1677, but he did not do so. The Elector explained to the Prince: 'my troops have been worn out during the long and difficult siege. If I had been promptly paid, more could have been done'.[43] He ignored Van der Tocht, the Dutch Ambassador in Berlin, who reminded him of 'his promise to fight against France as soon as he had captured Stettin' and he warned the Brandenburg ruler of the danger that France, taking more and more towns in Flanders, could bring 'his Highness into a situation in which his conquest of Pomerania would be of little help to him'.[44]

And Van der Tocht's warning came true. The Elector's claim that 'he would be included only in a peace treaty which gave him the whole of Pomerania'[45] was made futile by the French capture of Ghent on 27 February 1678, which made it imperative for the Dutch to end the war.[46] Although the Republic and Brandenburg renewed their 1674 defensive alliance on 8 March 1678 and promised to maintain friendly relations after the war, this could not stop the Republic from concluding a separate peace with France, albeit against the wishes of William III, at Nijmegen on 10 August 1678.

On the day the Dutch signed peace with France, Frederick William lost Pomerania.[47] He could not understand why the Republic had negotiated a treaty not only without the allies, but also against them. He had apparently forgotten that it had been his own particular wish to insert a paragraph into the treaty of 1 July 1674 which allowed each individual ally to conclude a separate peace on the condition he inform his other allies.[48]

In spite of the Dutch opting out of the war, the Elector still hoped to continue the struggle against France with the help of the emperor alone, but Leopold's

[42] *Urkunden und Actenstücke*, XVIII, pp. 164–71.
[43] The Elector to the Prince, 18 Jan. 1678, *Urkunden und Actenstücke*, XVIII, p. 188.
[44] Van der Tocht to the clerk of the States General, 12 Jan. 1678, *Urkunden und Actenstücke*, III, pp. 512–13.
[45] Kurfürst to Somnitz, 26 Nov. 1677, *Urkunden und Actenstücke*, XVIII, p. 183.
[46] S. Baxter, *William III* (London, 1966), p. 152.
[47] Schevill, *The Great Elector*, p. 332.
[48] Cloger, *Friedrich Wilhelm*, p. 264.

17 *Allegory on the Peace of Nijmegen* (1678).

stronger fear was of Brandenburg not of France. The emperor was unperturbed by the prospect of the Elector losing his Pomeranian conquests. Crockow, the Brandenburg ambassador in Vienna, was told by the Austrian Chancellor, Johan Paul Hocher, 'The emperor has no wish to see the rise of a new king of the Vandals on the Baltic Sea'.[49] So in February 1679 the emperor concluded peace with France, renewing the Treaty of Westphalia and implicitly restoring West Pomerania to Sweden. Relations between the emperor and Frederick William reached a new low point.

Before the peace between France and the emperor had been concluded, the Elector himself tried to negotiate a separate peace with France on the basis that West Pomerania would remain part of Brandenburg. The French king, however, remained a loyal ally of Sweden and refused to conclude peace with

[49] Von Orlich, *Geschichte des Preussischen Staates*, II, p. 323.

the Elector unless he returned West Pomerania to Sweden. In order to show the Elector he was in earnest, Louis XIV sent an army into Cleves in March 1679. To his great dismay Frederick William realized that his former allies, having all concluded peace with Louis separately, had exposed him to the full might of France. Urgent requests by the Elector to the States General for military support met with a refusal on 28 March: 'The States General regret that their peace with France forces them to maintain a strict neutrality; it is impossible for them to render assistance to the Elector'.[50]

So the Elector had to accept the loss of West Pomerania. All his war efforts had been in vain. But he would have his revenge, as he wrote to the Danish king on 3 July 1679, four days after he had negotiated the Treaty of St Germain with the French. Christian V, who had also been compelled to conclude peace with France after his former allies had left him, was told: 'I want to separate France from Sweden and I would like us to get close to France not only for security reasons, but also for the sake of revenging ourselves on those who have abandoned us so shamefully.'[51]

CLOSE TIES BETWEEN BRANDENBURG AND FRANCE FRUSTRATE VAN AMERONGEN'S EFFORTS TO IMPROVE RELATIONS BETWEEN THE REPUBLIC AND THE ELECTOR, DECEMBER 1679–SEPTEMBER 1681

All historians agree that Brandenburg's rapprochement with France was devoid of any feelings of real sympathy for that country and Frederick's own words confirm this. On 11 August 1679, in a letter to Otto von Schwerin, president of the Privy council, Frederick William wrote: 'There is no reason why we should have a special affection for France or promote her aggrandizement, for we are well aware of her yoke'.[52]

On the motives that underlay Frederick William's rapprochement towards France, however, there is no such consensus. Pagès, Waddington, and Schevill maintain that the Elector negotiated the French alliance because he wanted to replace Sweden as France's northern ally and to conquer Stettin once more as an associate of France. The reconquest of Stettin and his bitterness towards his former allies were constant factors determining the Elector's foreign policy at the beginning of the 1680s.

Professor Opgenoorth, however, argues that Frederick William's acrimony towards his allies faded away fairly soon. Even the reconquest of Stettin, although remaining an important issue, lost its top priority. Opgenoorth believes that

[50] *Urkunden und Actenstücke*, III, p. 544, and XVIII, p. 232.
[51] Pagès, *Le Grand Electeur*, p. 411.
[52] Von Orlich, *Geschichte des Preussischen Staates*, III, p. 304.

it was concern for Brandenburg's security that forced the Elector into entering the French alliance.[53]

Security was certainly the most striking point in the letter to Von Schwerin mentioned above: 'but as the allies negotiated separate treaties with France, matters have gone so far that France has become the arbiter of Europe, so there will be no security without the friendship of and close association with France'.[54] As the duke of Celle, a former ally of Brandenburg, was trying to rob the Elector of Minden and Halberstadt, and the Elector of Saxony had his eyes on Cleves and Magdeburg,[55] such protection was essential for Frederick William.

The task of bringing about this alliance (*nähere Alliantz*) with France was given to Franz Meinders. Although the son of an obscure tax collector, he had studied the classics, and was familiar with the literary and learned culture of contemporary France.[56] Meinders had already concluded the Peace of Vossem of 1673 and during the period when the Elector was closely aligned with France, Meinders was the most influential of the privy councillors.

The French king, for his part, had little trust in his former opponent. He had not forgotten that the Elector's adherence to the Peace of Vossem had been particularly brief and the French king was consequently rather cautious. Louvois, the French minister of war, told Meinders: '[one] could not move from war towards an intimate liaison so soon, things should therefore not be precipitated'.[57]

The French became more sympathetic towards an alliance with Brandenburg when Denmark and Sweden concluded peace at Lund on 26 September 1679 and negotiated an alliance on 7 October. The Swedish king, Charles XI, had reduced the influence of his pro-French minister Magnus de la Gardie and appointed Johann Gyllenstierna who advocated an alliance with Denmark. A marriage between Charles XI and the Danish princess Ulrike Eleonore, a sister of the Danish king Christian V, confirmed the new bond between the two former rivals, although as it turned out this was not to last long.[58] From France, Meinders reported that the French 'in public profess not to be jealous about the alliance and the marriage, but it is easy to sense that they are worried by it'.[59]

To preserve their interests, the French decided to negotiate a treaty with Brandenburg, Sweden's main rival in the Baltic and on 25 October 1679 at St Germain they signed a second and this time secret treaty with Meinders. The French, knowing how urgently the Elector wanted the alliance, bought it for a mere

[53] Opgenoorth, *Friedrich Wilhelm*, II, p. 209.
[54] Von Orlich, *Geschichte des Preussischen Staates*, III, p. 304.
[55] Pagès, *Le Grand Electeur*, p. 428.
[56] H. Rosenberg, *Bureaucracy, Aristocracy and Autocracy. The Prussian Experience, 1600–1815* (Cambridge, Mass., 1958), p. 61.
[57] Meinders to the Elector, 18 Aug. 1679, *Urkunden und Actenstücke*, XIX, p. 342.
[58] Philippson, *Grosse Kurfürst*, III pp. 259–60.
[59] Meinders to the Elector, 27 Oct. 1679, *Urkunden und Actenstücke*, XIX, p. 377.

trifle: the Elector was given 100,000 livres per year during a period of ten years, while the French would protect his territory against hostile neighbours. In return French troops were to be allowed to cross Brandenburg territories whenever they wished. For the French king, however, the most important clause was the one that dealt with the election of a new emperor. Rumours that the health of Leopold I was declining gave rise to the speculation that a new emperor might have to be chosen soon,[60] and the Elector promised the French king to support the French candidate if it came to an election.[61] Frederick William was not really satisfied with the treaty, but it gave him the security he wanted and was, as Meinders put it, 'the beginning of something more'.[62] Under these circumstances it is readily understandable that Dutch efforts to improve relations with the Elector failed.

During the summer of 1679 the Elector had written various letters to the States General and the Prince complaining about their treatment of him. He argued that the Republic, in spite of repeated promises not to do so, and without giving him the slightest notice beforehand, had negotiated a separate peace with France. As a result he had been left to his fate: the French had invaded his territory of Cleves, and now Frederick William claimed 'damages for the losses sustained'.[63]

The Prince proposed consultations which he suggested might remove false impressions and improve relations between the two countries[64] and on 21 October 1679 Van Amerongen received instructions once more from the States General to make his way to Berlin. He was told to enlarge the 'old and trusted friendship with the Elector', as embodied in the 1678 treaty. Van Amerongen had established friendly relations with the Elector during his 1671–2 negotiations and the Elector in turn had called at Amerongen Castle during his visit to the Republic in 1675, so Van Amerongen was perhaps the Republic's best chance for reconciliation.

The instructions to Van Amerongen dealt with the two main issues between the Republic and the Elector: indemnification of sustained losses and the outstanding debt of the Republic to Brandenburg, but the fact that their contents did not come close to meeting the demands of the Elector did not augur well for his negotiations.

Van Amerongen had to inform the Elector that the States General refused to pay any indemnification for the Elector's losses in his Cleves territory. They

[60] Hüttl, *Friedrich Wilhelm*, p. 430.

[61] A. Waddington (ed.), *Recueil des instructions données aux ambassadeurs et ministres de France depuis les traités de Westphalie jusqu'à la Révolution Française*, XVI: *Prusse* (Paris, 1901), p. 212.

[62] 'dass einmal etwas daraus werden sollte'. Meinders to the Elector, 24 Oct. 1679, *Urkunden und Actenstücke*, XIX, p. 375.

[63] Elector to William III, 22 Aug. 1679, *Urkunden und Actenstücke*, XXI, p. 10.

[64] Prince to Elector, 22 Sept. 1679, *Urkunden und Actenstücke*, III, pp. 553–4.

argued that Cleves had not sustained any damages until 1678, after the treaty was signed. The French invasion had only taken place after the Republic and France had concluded peace at Nijmegen which the Elector had refused to join. Without saying it so explicitly, the States General regarded the destruction of Cleves as the Elector's own fault. To the Elector's reproach that they had not informed him of their decision to negotiate peace separately, Van Amerongen was instructed to reply by pointing out that the States General, in a conference with the representatives of the allies in June 1678, had announced that concluding peace was unavoidable for them and had suggested joint negotiations with France. Romswinckel, the Brandenburg envoy, however, had rejected the suggestion and therefore the Republic had gone ahead on its own. If the Elector complained that the States General had stopped the war and negotiated peace on conditions that were not acceptable to him, Van Amerongen was to tell him that it had been impossible for them to continue the war and that the 1674 treaty did not compel the States to guarantee the Elector's Pomeranian conquest, but only the *status quo ante bellum*.

As regards the outstanding debt of the Republic to Brandenburg, Van Amerongen had to inform the Elector that the States General would pay their outstanding debts up till the end of 1676. In December 1676, because of the bad financial situation, the States General had resolved to stop paying subsidies from 1 January 1677. Therefore the Elector's request to receive Dutch subsidies which would have been due until the time he had concluded peace with France in June 1679 should be refused.[65]

When Van Amerongen arrived in Berlin in December 1679, the Elector dismissed the Dutch arguments. Naturally enough, the French alliance freed the Elector of the need to take a lenient view of the matter, but the inflexibility of the States General especially on the issue of the outstanding debt of the Republic to Brandenburg – regarded by Van Amerongen as the 'most controversial and difficult' issue –[66] made the chance of agreement remote. In lengthy negotiations with the privy councillors Franz Meinders and Frederick Jena, a former law professor at the University of Frankfurt who had been the Elector's top aide in the 1660s but had since then been succeeded by Meinders,[67] Van Amerongen failed to convince either of these of the Dutch case.

The outstanding debt included what was soon to be called the 'indisputable and disputable subsidies'. The former were the subsidies from 1674–6 which the States General had promised to pay. The disputable subsidies, covering the financial aid from 1677 onwards, were claimed by the Elector but refused by

[65] *Urkunden und Actenstücke*, III, pp. 556–7.
[66] Van Amerongen to Fagel, 10 Apr. 1680, *Urkunden und Actenstücke*, III, p. 568.
[67] Rosenberg, *Bureaucracy*, p. 61.

the States General on the basis of their resolution of December 1676. Jena and Meinders argued that the latter decision had been unilateral; although the Elector had shown his concern for the Republic's financial difficulties during his conversation with Fagel in Wesel in April 1677, he had never formally agreed on the States General's decision not to pay the subsidies after 1676.[68] They pointed out that the 1678 treaty did not hold any clause that entitled the Republic to suspend payment of their subsidies after 1676.[69]

The refusal to pay the indisputable subsidies, a sum of 82,000 thaler, enraged the Elector and was proof in his eye of bad faith. Fagel's remark that the Republic would not pay them 'as long as they were not convinced of the Elector's friendship'[70] was indeed unreasonable.

Frederick William, nevertheless, came to meet the Dutch to some degree with new proposals on 3 July 1680. He argued that if the States General showed their willingness in principle to pay the disputed subsidies, he would be satisfied with payment of the amounts due up until the end of 1678 instead of June 1679, when he had concluded peace with France. As regards the indemnification of his losses in Cleves, the Elector suggested that some compromise should be reached.[71] When in July 1680 the province of Zeeland paid 54,000 thaler as their part of the undisputed subsidies, Van Amerongen, who knew nothing about the October 1679 alliance between France and Brandenburg, wrote to the Prince that he hoped 'the old friendship could be restored'.[72]

This Franco-Brandenburg alliance would have prevented any such thing from happening, but delayed reactions to the Elector's new proposals and the side-effects of a major conflict between Brandenburg and Spain saw to it that Dutch–Brandenburg relations did not get a chance to improve further.

The Spanish owed the Elector 1,800,000 thaler under the 1674 treaty, but showed no willingness at all to talk about their outstanding debt. In order to have his revenge on them, Frederick William ordered his Dutch marine director, Benjamin Raule, to organize an attack on Spanish merchant ships.[73] On 18 September 1680 the Brandenburg navy, mostly manned with Dutch sailors, captured the *Carlos II*, a Spanish ship loaded with linen, at Ostend. This row could have developed into a major war, since on 10 June England had negotiated a defensive treaty with Spain, which had also had an alliance with the Republic since 1673, while Louis XIV could have become involved too, having given the Elector permission for his ships to shelter in French harbours.

The conclusion of the defensive treaty with Spain was part of an English

[68] Van Amerongen to Fagel, 30 June 1680, *Urkunden und Actenstücke,* III, p. 582.
[69] Van Amerongen to Fagel, 22 May 1680, *Urkunden und Actenstücke*, III, p. 575.
[70] Fagel to Van Amerongen, 11 May 1680, *Urkunden und Actenstücke*, III, p. 570.
[71] Van Amerongen to Fagel, 3 July 1680, *Urkunden und Actenstücke*, III, pp. 583–4.
[72] Van Amerongen to the Prince, 24 July 1680, Japikse (ed.), *Correspondentie*, II, part 2, p. 352.
[73] Philippson, *Grosse Kurfürst*, III, p. 278.

diplomatic offensive against France. Since the beginning of 1680 Charles II of England had tried to negotiate alliances with Celle, Hanover, Brandenburg, and the empire. Professor Jones speaks about Charles' 'insincere and cosmetic anti-French foreign policy',[74] but the earl of Sunderland, Charles' secretary of state, seems to have been sincere at least in initiating this anti-French coalition in order to appease parliamentary opposition to the duke of York, the future James II, who had been excluded from the succession to the throne by the English House of Commons in May 1679.[75] By negotiating an anti-French coalition the English government tried to show Parliament it was conducting an anti-French foreign policy, implying there was no need to be afraid of James who was identified with Roman Catholic and absolutist France.

In order to support this English diplomatic initiative, William III decided to visit the two dukes of Brunswick–Lüneburg too. George William, duke of Celle, and his brother Ernst August of Hanover, had been William's allies during the war against France, but the two brothers had been forced to conclude peace with France after the Peace of Nijmegen. William now went to them in order to improve relations and to ask them to negotiate with England, which they, however, refused to do.

Before going to Celle, William III had expressed a wish to visit his uncle in Berlin. His purpose was to attempt to bring the Elector too into the alliance with England, a move for which the English ambassador in Berlin, Sir Robert Southwell, had been striving since his arrival in Brandenburg in the spring. William's request to be allowed to visit had been accepted but he did not succeed in convincing his uncle of the need to align with England. In fact, at the time of William's visit, Frederick William was negotiating a new alliance with France, because he needed French support in his actions against Spain[76] and he kept the French ambassador in Berlin, Rébenac, well informed of William's negotiations with him. Rébenac wrote to Louis XIV that William had told his uncle that he did not doubt the Elector would join the English alliance, 'puisque le danger serait trop manifest pour lui de s'attacher à la France'. William's effort to soften his uncle by suggesting that he would make Prince Louis, Frederick William's third son, his sole heir did not work. The Elector judged there would be no accommodation between the king and his Parliament, and that England was therefore not to be relied upon as an ally.[77]

William was therefore not very satisfied with his trip. He had received a warm welcome, the Elector had accepted English–Dutch mediation in the row with Spain over the capture of the *Carlos II* and, under the 1678 treaty, had promised

[74] J. R. Jones, *Britain and the World* (London, 1966), p. 125.
[75] J. P. Kenyon, *Robert Spencer, Earl of Sunderland, 1641–1702* (London, 1958), p. 41.
[76] Rébenac to Louis XIV, 13 July 1680, *Urkunden und Actenstücke*, XX, first part, pp. 466–7.
[77] Rébenac to Louis XIV, 26 Oct. 1680, *Urkunden und Actenstücke*, XX, first part, pp. 498–504.

to return the fortress of Schenkenschans to the Dutch at last; but the effort to bring Frederick William into the anti-French coalition had failed. A new alliance with France in January 1681 and a new row with the Dutch about his activities in Africa prevented the 'restoration of the old friendship' for the time being.

In the twentieth article of the new secret alliance of 11 January 1681, France trebled its yearly subsidy of 100,000 livres to 100,000 thaler and promised to protect Brandenburg if Spain started hostilities against Frederick William in retaliation for his capture of the *Carlos II*. It was France again, however, that benefited most from the new treaty. Although officially called a defensive alliance,[78] it was potentially an offensive one because the fifth article stated that the partner that was asked for help had to provide it, without the right to consider whether the petitioner had caused the 'Differenz' or was the victim of aggression.[79] This was very important to Louis XIV, who wanted to strengthen his north-eastern boundary and had set about doing so by his so-called *Réunions* policy. In Metz, Breisach, and Besançon Louis XIV set up Chambers of *Réunion*, law courts in which French judges examined the claims to various parcels of territory in Lorraine and Alsace and pronounced in favour of France. French troops thereupon moved in. Since these territories were part of the empire, Louis expected trouble from the emperor and although no love was lost between Leopold and Frederick William, a firm alliance with the Elector was a useful precaution.

Relations between France and Brandenburg, however, were hardly warm. The Elector had wanted a larger subsidy, and during 1681 he became annoyed with France several times. In June 1681 France captured Chiny, a property belonging to William III but which had been promised to Prince Louis under the 1681 treaty.[80] Frederick William was also very much enraged about the persecution of the French Huguenots.

The capture by the Dutch West Indian Company (WIC) of a Brandenburg ship, *Das Wappen von Brandenburg*, off the coast of Guinea in August 1681 was, however, equally bad for Dutch–Brandenburg relations.[81] The Elector, keen on developing colonial trade, planned a maritime expedition to Guinea. He informed the WIC of his plan in September 1680, but the Dutch company reacted by saying that under international law Brandenburg ships had no right to enter this Dutch chartered area. The company claimed, and its claim was taken up by the States General, that the Elector's ships employed mostly Dutch sailors who, as they were enlisted by a foreign power, were forbidden to enter

78 Moerner, *Kurbrandenburgs Staatsverträge*, p. 418.
79 Philippson, *Grosse Kurfürst*, III, p. 283.
80 Ibid., p. 288.
81 Van Amerongen to the clerk of the States General, 27 Aug. 1681, *Urkunden und Actenstücke*, III, p. 608.

Dutch chartered areas.[82] The Elector reacted furiously when his ship was captured. Van Amerongen, who had written in June 1681 that 'times are more opportune now than before to start the important work',[83] had very little reason to be optimistic about Brandenburg–Dutch relations when he returned home for consultations at the beginning of September 1681. If he had known about the French–Brandenburg treaty he would have been even more depressed.

THE ELECTOR'S REFUSAL TO ENTER THE LEAGUE OF ASSOCIATION, OCTOBER 1681–NOVEMBER 1682

During Van Amerongen's stay in the Republic an important new development in European politics took place. After the death of Johann Gyllenstierna in June 1680, his successor Bengt Oxenstierna gave up the idea of the Scandinavian Union with Denmark. He was convinced that the rising power of France should be contained by a coalition between Sweden, the Republic, England, and the emperor.[84] The Swedish king, Charles XI, was won over to Oxenstierna's cause in August 1681 when Louis XIV annexed the duchy of Zweibrücken, which Charles had inherited in April 1681 after the death of its duke, Frederick William.[85] As a result the Republic and Sweden concluded the so-called Association Treaty on 10 October 1681.

In this treaty the two countries promised to uphold the peace settlements of Westphalia and Nijmegen and to use, if necessary, military force against countries that violated them. Other countries, including France, would be asked to join the League of Association, but it was clear that the League was directed against France. According to Sweden and the Republic, France's *Réunions* policy had violated the Treaty of Nijmegen, most clearly on 30 September 1681, when Louis XIV occupied Strasburg. According to Professor Hatton this action was 'not the prelude to the establishment of control over the Empire or of universal monarchy', but at the time France's neighbours thought quite differently.[86]

The Association Treaty meant a success for William III's anti-French policy. A leading Amsterdam regent, Coenraad van Beuningen, was sent to England to urge Charles II to join the League, while Van Amerongen was instructed to convince the Elector of the necessity to do the same.

Neither Van Beuningen nor Van Amerongen succeeded in carrying out his

[82] Resolution of the States General, 16 Nov. 1680, *Urkunden und Actenstücke*, III, p. 597.

[83] Van Amerongen to the Prince, 17 June 1681, Japikse (ed.), *Correspondentie*, II, part 2, pp. 390–1.

[84] W. J. M. van Eysinga, 'Het Associatieverdrag van 10 October 1681', *Mededelingen der Koninklijke Nederlandsche Akademie van Wetenschappen*, nieuwe reeks, X (Amsterdam, 1947), pp. 157–71.

[85] G. Symcox, 'Louis XIV and the outbreak of the Nine Years War', in R. Hatton (ed.), *Louis XIV and Europe* (London, 1976), p. 181, and Carswell, *Descent*, p. 49.

[86] Van Eysinga, 'Het Associatieverdrag', p. 163, and R. Hatton, 'Louis XIV and his Fellow Monarchs', in Hatton (ed.), *Louis XIV and Europe*, p. 34.

instructions. The refusal of the States General to meet the Elector's wishes concerning the 'disputed subsidies' and the capture of *Das Wappen von Brandenburg*[87] must have raised doubts about the Republic's sincerity in wanting to improve relations with the Elector, but even if the States General had satisfied the Elector completely, it is doubtful whether Frederick William would have joined the League at that moment.

In a letter to Dijkvelt, one of William's closest confidants, Van Amerongen wrote that the Elector had told him that he would never conclude an alliance with Sweden, as he had been forced to restore to her the territories he had conquered during the last war. According to Van Amerongen 'this opinion has been so firmly fixed in his mind that I do not see him [the Elector] getting rid of it during his lifetime'.[88] The refusal of Charles II to enter the League also played an important role in Frederick William's refusal to join the anti-French forces. Charles II was strongly tied to France and although he told Van Beuningen at times that he would help Spain and the Republic if Louis XIV conquered an important town in the Spanish Netherlands, he did not call for a session of the English Parliament in order to obtain the money to fight France if necessary. Van Amerongen told Van Beuningen that in Berlin a session of the English Parliament would be seen as sufficient proof of Charles II's wish to contain French aggression. He ended by saying 'as long as this does not happen, I am afraid neither here nor anywhere else will anyone rely on that Crown'.[89] Moreover, the Elector thought that the emperor was not capable of showing strength towards France either, since a rebellion of the Hungarians against Vienna precluded any possibility that the Austrian government would be able to bring enough troops to the west.[90]

Although Van Amerongen knew Frederick William's objections against joining the League, from a Dutch point of view he still could not understand why Brandenburg obstructed 'the salutary work of conserving the peace'.[91] In a letter to Fagel on 14 January 1682 he mentioned rumours that the Elector was negotiating with France[92] and when Van Amerongen realized that these rumours were true, the Dutch ambassador understood that for the time being advice was wasted on the Elector.

Louis XIV was very annoyed about Sweden's entry into the anti-French coalition. Although France's support of Sweden at the peace negotiations in Osnabrück at the end of the Thirty Years War and Nijmegen led Louis XIV to say 'the true maxims of his [Charles XI's] Crown must always oblige him to

[87] *Urkunden und Actenstücke*, III, p. 620.
[88] Van Amerongen to Dijkvelt, 6 Dec. 1681, Huisarchief Amerongen, Rijksarchief Utrecht, I, no. 141.
[89] Van Amerongen to Van Beuningen, 4 Jan. 1682, Huisarchief Amerongen, I, no. 145.
[90] Van Amerongen to Fagel, 22 Nov. 1681, *Urkunden und Actenstücke*, III, p. 628.
[91] Van Amerongen to Van Beuningen, 14 Jan. 1682, Huisarchief Amerongen, I, no. 145.
[92] *Urkunden und Actenstücke*, III, p. 643.

prefer my alliance to all others',[93] the French monarch had to accept the fact that Sweden had left his alliance. He therefore turned to Brandenburg to get the Elector's support in maintaining his *Réunions*.

When Louis XIV occupied Strasburg, Frederick William strongly protested to Rébenac 'que tout l'Empire se trouvait obligé de s'opposer à un démembrement si considérable'.[94] Now, in order to win the Elector to his side, Louis promised to stop his *Réunions* and announced himself content with what he had conquered up to 1 August 1681, including Strasburg, although he had not occupied that city until September. He also held out the prospect of higher subsidies to Brandenburg as an incentive. Louis even offered to help the Elector in his quarrel with Spain and to protect his African company against the Dutch. It was tempting, and Frederick William decided to accept the French offer. The anti-French forces, he believed, were still not strong enough to withstand France successfully, so on 22 January 1682 he concluded a new treaty with France[95] and the Elector set about attempting to get the French *Réunions* accepted by the empire.

Van Amerongen soon found out that at the German Diet, in Frankfurt, Gottfried Jena, Frederick Jena's brother, was strongly advocating the French proposal to conclude peace with the empire on the basis that what France possessed on 1 August 1681, including Strasburg, she might keep. To the Prince and Van Beuningen the Dutch ambassador wrote that Brandenburg's policy was motivated by the argument 'that the empire at the present time is unable to take different measures'.[96]

To William's relief the German Diet did not accept the French proposal for the time being. A separate peace between France and the empire would have been disastrous for the Dutch because it would have allowed the French king to concentrate all his power in the Low Countries. To his second-in-command, Georg Friedrich von Waldeck, the Prince wrote: 'everything is lost, and our state in particular, if a treaty between France and the empire is not prevented'.[97] William was therefore delighted that the emperor joined the League of Association on 28 February 1682, followed on 2 May by Spain, which had had to contend with a French blockade of Luxemburg from November 1681 to March 1682. In the continuous struggle in Vienna between 'Westerners' and 'Easterners', Leopold this time opted for the former group. In spite of the threat of the Hungarian discontent under Imre Thököly, helped by the Turks, who were suspected

[93] A. Lossky, 'Maxims of State in Louis XIV's foreign policy in the 1680s', in R. Hatton and J. S. Bromley (eds.), *William III and Louis XIV. Essays 1680–1720 by and for Mark A. Thompson* (Liverpool, 1968), p. 12.

[94] Rébenac to Louis XIV, 15 Oct. 1681, *Urkunden und Actenstücke*, XX, first part, p. 589.

[95] Moerner, *Kurbrandenburgs Staatsverträge*, pp. 426–8.

[96] Huisarchief Amerongen, I, no. 145.

[97] P. L. Muller, *Wilhelm von Oranien und Georg Friedrich von Waldeck* (2 vols., The Hague, 1873–80), I, p. 135.

of wanting to attack Austria again after the expiry of the twenty years' truce of Vasvar of 1664, the Austrians decided to concentrate on the Rhine rather than on the Danube and set their faces firmly against making an agreement with France that would sanction the *Réunions*.[98]

The anti-French coalition gathered strength in October 1682 when Van Amerongen negotiated the Elector of Saxony's entry in the League of Association. Demoralized, he had left Berlin for Dresden in March 1682, after his effort to get the Elector of Brandenburg involved in the League had failed, but when he returned to Berlin in November he found Frederick William filled with rage against France as well, which seemed to make the prospect of Brandenburg's entry in the anti-French coalition look excellent at last.

FREDERICK WILLIAM'S DISILLUSIONMENT WITH FRANCE DOES NOT LEAD TO A GENUINE RAPPROCHEMENT BETWEEN BRANDENBURG AND THE REPUBLIC, NOVEMBER 1682–JULY 1683

Frederick William, who had never really trusted the French, had been extremely annoyed about the French occupation of William III's principality of Orange in August 1682 since this move in Van Amerongen's words 'could damage the rights of his descendants to the heritage of their Dutch relative'.[99]

Van Amerongen's impression that the Elector would now enter the League of Association after all was reflected in the words he wrote to Fagel: 'one has to strike the iron when it is hot'.[100] Paul Fuchs, who had originally been private secretary to the Elector, but whose political star had risen rapidly after the death of Frederick Jena in September 1682, urged Van Amerongen to return to The Hague for consultations with William III and Fagel. The apparent willingness of the Elector to enter the League[101] brought Van Amerongen back to The Hague and on 9 February 1683 Fagel gave him new instructions.

William III and Fagel wanted a general peace between Spain, the empire, and France. A separate peace between France and the empire would give France the opportunity to put more pressure on Spain, while a separate peace between France and Spain would have the same effect on Franco-German relations. Therefore, the Elector should be asked to enter a convention with the Republic and Spain, which confirmed the 1678 treaty between the Republic and Brandenburg.

[98] Spielman, *Leopold I*, p. 97.

[99] Van Amerongen to the Prince, 24 Nov. 1682, Japikse, *Correspondentie*, II, part 2, p. 505.

[100] Van Amerongen to Fagel, 12 Dec. 1682, *Urkunden und Actenstücke*, III, p. 650.

[101] See the remarks of the well-informed French ambassador in the Netherlands, the comte d'Avaux, on 8 Feb. 1683 in: E. Mallet (ed.), *Négociations de Comte d'Avaux en Hollande depuis 1679* (6 vols., Paris, 1752–3), I, p. 279.

Frederick William would have to promise to support Spain if it were attacked by France and he should also enter the League of Association and the Treaty of Dénombrement, which laid down the number of troops with which the allies were to assist each other.[102] In return, Van Amerongen was allowed to meet the Elector's claim on the 'disputed subsidies' halfway. The Dutch ambassador was instructed to offer Frederick William a lump sum of 400,000 guilders. The quarrel over the capture of *Das Wappen von Brandenburg* should be settled amicably.[103]

After his return to Berlin, however, Van Amerongen soon realized that in spite of the expectations he had raised at the end of 1682, the Elector neither wanted to help Spain nor to enter the League of Association. During Van Amerongen's absence Paul Fuchs had written a memorandum on Brandenburg's foreign policy, the result of which was incompatible with a policy of joining the anti-French coalition.

In the memorandum, written at the beginning of January 1683, Paul Fuchs offered three options on foreign policy: (1) a policy of closer association with France; (2) entry into the League of Association; and (3) a policy of temporization and keeping to the middle of the road until it had become clear whether the Turks would attack the empire or not. Fuchs did not recommend the first option although it would yield higher subsidies from France and might create the possibility of reconquering West Pomerania. If the Turkish war did not break out, the League of Association would threaten Brandenburg, and the Elector could not expect much support from France in his war against Sweden if Louis XIV himself were engaged in a war with the emperor. The French king might even occupy another part of Germany and that was clearly not in the interest of Brandenburg. Fuchs, however, had serious objections to joining the Association, because of the weakness and division among the allies, which had been clearly apparent during the last war. Fuchs believed that war with the Turks was inevitable, in which case the Elector and the other allies would have to wage war on two fronts without the hope of any military success. Moreover, France would stop the payment of subsidies immediately and would probably invade Cleves again. So, therefore, Fuchs advised the Elector to take the third option, which was clearly in line with the policy of non-intervention he had pursued before. The Elector, according to Fuchs, should gain time until it had become clear what the Turks were going to do. As war was to be avoided at all costs, his main objective should be the establishment of peace between France and the empire. Fuchs recommended a pendulum policy (*Schaukelpolitik*) between the two blocks, but the Elector should give the Association countries some hope

[102] F. A. Middlebush (ed.), *The Dispatches of Thomas Plott (1681–1682) and Thomas Chudleigh (1682–1685), English Envoys at The Hague* (The Hague, 1926), p. 217.

[103] Fagel to Van Amerongen, 9 Feb. 1683, *Urkunden und Actenstücke*, III, pp. 654–6.

of him entering their League by 'some sort of negotiation with Mr van Amerongen' ('eine espèce de négociation mit dem H. van Amerongen') in order to gain time.[104]

As a result Van Amerongen was kept on a string, and while the Elector was clever enough not to dash the Dutch ambassador's hopes completely, his objections against entering the League of Association saw to it that Brandenburg's inclusion in the anti-French coalition remained music of the future. Van Amerongen was told that the Elector could not support Spain as to do so would be incompatible with his French alliance.[105] The Treaty of Dénombrement was also used as an argument against joining the League, since it would allow Sweden, Brandenburg's arch-enemy, to transport troops to Germany.[106] Although Fagel repeatedly argued that the Elector should not separate Franco-German relations from those between Spain and France, since a separate peace between France and the empire would lead to the ultimate ruin of Brandenburg,[107] the Elector reacted by saying that he would not enter the League of Association until the French proposals at Frankfurt were accepted.[108] Although this remark seems to show Frederick William's preference for the anti-French forces, he regarded a rupture with France as too great a risk for his country. Fuchs told Van Amerongen that entry into the League of Association would be like 'de vouloir abandonner la conservation et la seureté de ses Etats qui en dépendent'.[109]

The Elector was confirmed in the rightness of his foreign policy when, in accordance with Fuch's prediction, the Turks launched their attack against the empire and besieged Vienna in July 1683. This made entry in the League even more unlikely since it would involve the League countries in a war with France and Turkey, which they could never win.

THE ELECTOR'S INSISTENCE ON A SEPARATE AGREEMENT BETWEEN FRANCE AND THE EMPIRE AS A CONSEQUENCE OF THE TURKISH WAR IS REJECTED BY THE DUTCH, JULY 1683–AUGUST 1684

With the empire involved in a war with the Turks, Louis XIV did not want to raise suspicion that the most Christian king was going to exploit the success of the Turkish infidels and he therefore moderated his claims on the empire. He renewed his offer of a full peace on the basis that what France possessed on 1 August 1681, including Strasburg, she might keep, and he offered as an alternative a thirty years' truce on the same basis. How much Frederick

[104] *Urkunden und Actenstücke*, XIX pp. 457–60, and Opgenoorth, *Friedrich Wilhelm*, II, p. 244.
[105] Van Amerongen to Fagel, 2 Mar. 1683, *Urkunden und Actenstücke*, III, p. 665.
[106] Van Amerongen to Waldeck, 4 May 1683, Huisarchief Amerongen, I, no. 144.
[107] Fagel to Van Amerongen, 13 Mar. 1683, *Urkunden und Actenstücke*, III, p. 673.
[108] Van Amerongen to the Dutch ambassadors in Denmark and Austria, Moeringh and Hamel Bruynincx, 15 May 1683, Huisarchief Amerongen, I, no. 146.
[109] Van Amerongen to Fagel, 28 Mar. 1683, *Urkunden und Actenstücke*, III, p. 684.

William wanted this separate deal between the empire and France emerges in his instructions of 2 August 1683 to the Prince of Anhalt, who at an earlier date had been sent to the emperor to offer Brandenburg's help for the relief of Vienna. If the emperor accepted the French proposals, Anhalt was to offer a relief force of 16,000–18,000 men.[110] Leopold, however, refused to accept Frederick William's conditions, and so Brandenburg troops were not present in the relief force with which Charles of Lorraine and John Sobieski defeated the Turks at Vienna in September 1683.

The Elector knew, of course, that William III and Fagel, like the emperor, were also against a separate agreement between France and the empire. The Dutch leaders wanted a general peace between the empire, Spain, and France, and they believed that France could be forced into this only by united action on the part of the other powers. They had, therefore, also rejected Louis XIV's suggestion that Spain should accept English arbitration to end the Franco-Spanish controversy separately. The Dutch leaders were aware of Charles II's sympathy for Louis XIV and realized that accepting English arbitration would be tantamount to giving in to France. They continued to maintain that only a united front against France would force Louis XIV into concessions.

Still, Frederick William ordered his special envoy to the Republic, Melchior von Ruck, to urge the Prince and Fagel to accept a separate peace between France and the empire. If they suggested a universal peace *Universalfriede* he was to say that Brandenburg also wanted such a settlement, but that 'there is no prospect of this now; Spain must accept France's proposal to refer Franco-Spanish controversies to English arbitration. Common sense calls for avoiding everything that can irritate France this moment'.[111]

Although the Elector and the Dutch leaders regarded the French king as an aggressor, they differed substantially in their methods of dealing with Louis. William and Fagel rejected Von Ruck's view that one should appease France, 'help the Emperor against the Turks and wait for better times'. The allies, they maintained, had to withstand France, for a separate peace between France and the empire 'will separate the allies. If France has made peace with the empire it will easily conquer the Spanish Netherlands'.[112]

During the following months the leaders of both countries tried to convince each other but to no avail. Relations between William III and Frederick William, already strained because of their differences on the question of what policy should be pursued towards France, reached their nadir at the beginning of 1684, when the Elector intervened in a major conflict between William III and Amster-

[110] *Urkunden und Actenstücke*, XXI, pp. 155–6.

[111] The Elector to Von Ruck, 29 July 1683, *Urkunden und Actenstücke*, XXI, pp. 61–2.

[112] Von Ruck to the Elector, 3 and 17 Aug. 1683, *Urkunden und Actenstücke*, XXI, pp. 63–4, and Fagel to Van Amerongen, 17 Aug. 1683, *Urkunden und Actenstücke*, III, pp. 743–4.

dam which erupted over the issue of whether to support Spain militarily against France. William III, always convinced he was in the right, was furious to see his uncle opposed to assisting Spain.

The disagreement arose after France had given Spain until 1 September 1683 to accept its demand for English arbitration. When this time had elapsed, Louis XIV sent troops into the Spanish Netherlands to put pressure on the Spanish government. Spain regarded this French move as an act of war and asked the Republic for help on the basis of the treaty concluded between the two countries a decade earlier on 30 August 1673. William III and Fagel proposed to raise an extra 16,000 men but, although most provinces gave their consent to their plan, it nevertheless broke down when Amsterdam refused to go along with it. The main opponent of William III's policy was Coenraad van Beuningen, one of the four burgomasters of Amsterdam. As we have noticed, he had been sent to England to persuade Charles II to enter the League of Association. His mission had failed and, although he remained an opponent of France, he thought that for the time being France was too strong to be contained, especially since England had refused to enter the anti-French coalition.[113] Van Beuningen believed 'the Prince wants to destroy himself and the state with his warlike plans'.[114] He thought that Spain should accept the offer of d'Avaux of 17 February 1684 in which the French ambassador offered a twenty years' truce to Spain and the empire on the basis of the retention during that time of what France had taken.[115]

This concession by France – the idea of separate peaces between France and Spain and the empire and France was abandoned – was a further source of disagreement between William and the Elector. It was not acceptable to William because it would have meant the loss of many territories. William was furious with the Elector. Frederick William, however, endorsed the French proposals and with that gave moral support to Amsterdam. The dispute almost led to a repetition of the 1650 armed conflict between William III's father, William II, and Amsterdam. When Paul Fuchs visited Amsterdam in March 1684 to express the Elector's delight with Amsterdam's refusal to contribute in raising the extra troops and subsequently to urge William III to accept the French proposals, an angry altercation between the two men took place. Paul Fuchs' remark that, although the Elector realized that a further increase in French power would be highly dangerous, 'the violent means which the Associates seem to prefer will be fatal to the whole of Christendom', fell on deaf ears. Angrily William

[113] M. A. M. Franken, *Coenraad van Beuningen's politieke en diplomatieke aktiviteiten in de jaren 1667–1684* (Groningen, 1966), ch. VII.

[114] See Paul Fuchs' report to the Elector about his conversation with Van Beuningen on 15 Mar. 1684, *Urkunden und Actenstücke*, XXI, pp. 67–8.

[115] M. E. Grew, *William Bentinck and William III (Prince of Orange). The Life of Bentinck, Earl of Portland from the Welbeck Correspondence* (London, 1924), pp. 75–6.

F A B E L

van de

Koeyen, de HERDER, en de WOLF.

De Wolf loerende op eenige vette Koeyen, vond al ſijn toeleg vergeefs, om dat haer Herder ſo wacker was; ſijn bloet-dorſt en vraet-ſucht, echter, trachtende eens te verſaeden, aen dat lecker aes, ſo gebruyckte hy 't Vosjen, door welke hy de vetſte en weeligſte van allen aldus liet aenſpreeken. Wat baet het u Nichte, dat gy tot de buyck in 't klaver gaet dat uwe uyers geſpannen ſtaen, dat gy ſo veel melck leevert, U Herder ſal u leevren aen een vleeshouwer wanneeer hy van u al de melk getrocken heeft, ſiet gy niet dat hy voor uwe melk, een nieuwe en ſwaerder ſtaf gekreegen heeft. Wat macht hebt gy voor de uytſteekentheyt, van de voordeelen die gy boven andere opgeeft. Och dat gy wijs waert, gy ſout na uw eygen ſin weyden en vry willen ſijn, dit is immers dat Herders knaepjen, dat ſo drae, gy maer uwe hoorns toonde, door dick en dun uyt de weyde vloot. Moet hy niet u ontſien? Gy hem niet, Neef de Wolf is van inborſt verandert, hy is u herte-vriend. Och was ick daer van verſeekert; antwoorde de Vette Koey; ick ſou my niet laten leyden, met de drift van mijn ſuſters, die hoewel droog, by mijn gelijk geſtelt werden, ik geef de meeſte melk, ik wil ſelf Herder ſijn en de Staf ſweyen over mijne ſuſters: Neef de Wolf weet wel dat ik de melk-emmers, dikmaels omgeſmeeten heb, om dat ikſe den Herder niet en gunde. De Wolf haer goede wille 't hemwaerts hoorende ſeyde, Mijne waerdſte en liefſte Nichte, onſe heymlijke vriendſchap is niet van heeden of giſteren, ick ſweer u by mijn woord, en eer, dat ick voor niemant ſo groote liefde heb als voor u, dat gy wilt en begeert, kan u niet miſſen noch ontſtaen, want geeft gy geen melk, hoe kan u Herder dan uwe mackers houden, en ſo gy met mijn ſamen doet, ſo kunt gy de Herder uyt uwe en andere weyden jagen, ſelfs, door mijn, Herder weeſen, ſoſe teegen u kanten, een voor een verſlinden, en dan blijft de heele weyde, voor u alleen, en ſo ſult gy, lieve Nicht, indienge nu wijs ſijt, door mijn hulp, tot u lang gewenſt oogwit raeken.

De Koey, gekittelt van die ſchoone inbeelding, loeyde en balckte, hier op vol hoveerdigheyt, beproefde haar hoornen, nu tegen deſe, dan tegen geene van hare Suſters 'tot dat ſy ſe alle gequeſt hadde; Noch meer dan opgeblaſen ſijnde, en krachtig onder de hand, van de Wolf onderſteunt, viel ſy haer eygen Herder teegen, ſy blies uyt haer neuſgaten, ſy ſchuymde in de mond, ſy ſchopte de aarde op met haer klaeuwen, ſette de kop met vlammende oogen tegen de grond en dreygde verveerdelijk met de hoornen, en liep recht tegen den Herder in, de Herder verdroeg na ſijn gewoone ſachtſinnicheyt die ſtuyp, en over de vonder gaende ſprack haer aen met reeden en deſticheyt. Hoe ſeyde hy, heb ick u niet verleden jaer gered van die dollen Dog, en den broeder van die Wolf, die hoe ſchoon hy u vleyt, doenmaels ondernomen had, uwe Schuyr in koolen te ſetten, de Kadijk van uwe Polder, door te ſteeken u Vlees ſijn ſelf tot een ontbijt te maken en de huyt, op de miſthoop te ſmijten? Immers is 't onreedlijk onvernuſtig en dul, met U geſlagen doot-vyand verbond aen te gaen, die voor al 't loon op ſijn beſt u laeſt ſou verſlinden, de Koeyen riepen alle tot een toe het ſelve, maer ten gold niet, ſy brulde onverſtaenlijk uyt, ick verſtae 't ſoo, ick verſtae 't ſoo, ik wil meeſter weeſen, wie kan mijn dwingen, vry ben ik, baes wil ik ſijn; 't looſe Vosjen, blijde van dit vuyr te ſien opgaen met die heevicheyt, beloofde haer de hoornen en klaeuwen te vergulden, en had het goud ook al gereed; Dit gaet te hoog riepen de andere Koeyen, den Herder, ſag de Wolf, greenikende van vreucht datſe de ſotte Koey ſo aen en opgeſet had; en watertandende vaſt na de vette brocken, wanneer hy ſijn Staf op hief, de andere Koeyen in poſtuur bracht, de Heyningen verſag en de dulheyt van de vette Koey met recht wilde toomen: dit verſtonden de andere nodig te ſijn, verſochten den Herder na ſijne bekende trouw en yver, die ſe met ſijn lijfs gevaer dickmaels beproeft hadden, dit ſette haer ſamen tegen de gemeene Vyand ſchrap, ſy riepen de Wolf toe, dat ſy ſijn wreetheyt en Reyntjes looſheyt kenden, haer Herder by ſouden ſtaen, en temmen haer Suſter,

en ſlooten haer dicht, in de Wolfs geſicht
om ſijn ſchelmſtucken te ſtuyten, ſtaert tegen ſtaert en de horens na buyten.

Tot AMSTERDAM, Gedruckt voor Coppen Heerſchops in de Spiegel voor de Raesheeren.

18 *The Fable of the Cows, Cowherd, and the Wolf* (1684).
By Romeyn de Hooghe. Seven cows representing the seven United Provinces stand in a circle to fend off a ravenous wolf (Louis XIV). However, the cow with a full udder in the foreground (Holland), distracted and misled by a fox (the French ambassador, d'Avaux) turns its horns instead against the herder (William III).

retorted 'one thing only pains me deeply, that the Elector, who has loved me from the cradle like a father, whom I honour as a son has ranged himself on the side of the city of Amsterdam, which prides itself on always opposing me'.[116]

It is in fact questionable whether military support from the Elector would have been able to turn the scales in favour of the allied forces. Spain was very weak and England pro-French, while the emperor after the relief of Vienna in September 1683 concentrated once more on the Turkish war and showed himself prepared to accept the *Réunions*, a price he had not been willing to pay in 1683.[117] In vain William asked for military support from his allies to relieve Luxemburg, the strong fortress Louis XIV blockaded in April 1684 to force his opponents into agreeing with his truce proposals. When Luxemburg surrendered in June 1684, William III washed his hands of the whole situation. Spain and the empire negotiated the Twenty Years' Truce of Regensburg on 15 August 1684 which gave France the *Réunions*, Strasburg, and Luxemburg. Apart from the fact that the Truce was not a separate agreement between the Republic and France like the Peace of Nijmegen and that it did not fully and definitely acknowledge the French conquests,[118] William III had suffered a crushing defeat, for which the Elector, in William's opinion, was to a large extent to blame.

THE TWENTY YEARS' TRUCE OF REGENSBURG ENABLES FREDERICK WILLIAM TO MOVE TOWARDS WILLIAM III AND THE ANTI-FRENCH COALITION, AUGUST 1684–MAY 1688

William III, of course, did not know that the policy of concluding a truce with France had never been part of an intrinsic pro-French policy on Frederick William's part. The truce actually gave the Elector room for manoeuvre and with the danger of war gone, induced him to make overtures to the Republic with which he shared a common dislike of France.[119] Under the lee of the truce he took the first steps to improve relations with the Republic.

The Electoral message was well understood. In October 1684 Van Amerongen realized that ideas on foreign policy in Berlin were changing.[120] When the States General wanted to recall him and other ambassadors to The Hague, the Elector asked Van Amerongen to stay on, to which William III and Fagel consented, arguing that he might be able 'to arrange something positive for the State'.[121] At the end of December, just before leaving Berlin, Van Amerongen wrote to

[116] *Urkunden und Actenstücke*, XXI, pp. 70–3. English translation in Grew, *William Bentinck*, p. 77.
[117] Spielman, *Leopold I*, p. 117.
[118] Franken, *Coenraad van Beuningen*, p. 233.
[119] Opgenoorth, *Friedrich Wilhelm*, II, p. 256.
[120] Van Amerongen to Dijkvelt, 31 Oct. 1684, Huisarchief Amerongen, I, no. 141.
[121] Dijkvelt to Van Amerongen, 14 Nov. 1684, Huisarchief Amerongen, I, no. 142.

Dijkvelt: 'I look forward to report to the Prince on matters I do not dare to commit to paper'.[122] When leaving Berlin the Elector told the Dutch ambassador: 'the trusted friendship can be confirmed more and more if the money dispute, this stumbling block with the Republic, were settled'.[123]

In the Republic, however, no ill-based doubts were raised about the sincerity of the Elector's policy. Some members of the foreign policy committee of the States General pointed out that two years ago the Elector had raised the same hopes of improving relations with the Republic, but that before Van Amerongen had reached Hamburg 'the compass had turned again'.[124] In spite of their recent disagreement with the Elector, the Prince and Fagel nevertheless decided to take up the challenge once again, and they reacted favourably to the Elector's suggestion to send Paul Fuchs once more 'to discuss his claims, the maintenance of the reformed religion and their mutual security'.[125] The Prince and Fagel, however, realized that Amsterdam had blocked their anti-French policy the year before, so they reckoned that a successful outcome of Fuchs' mission could be ensured only if Amsterdam and the Prince succeeded in formulating a common policy towards Brandenburg. Since Van Amerongen was on good terms with both the Prince and Van Beuningen, he was sent to Amsterdam to recommend Fuchs' mission and at the same time to try and restore confidence between the Prince and the city. The Amsterdam burgomasters Hudde, Witsen, Corver, and Van Beuningen showed their willingness to resolve the differences between the Elector and the State, but concerning a reconciliation with the Prince they observed 'last year's wound is so fresh that a full recovery is not in sight yet'.[126]

Although Paul Fuchs and the States General succeeded in negotiating a treaty on 23 August 1685, the outcome was partly clouded by the division between Amsterdam and the Prince. They did not clash on the financial settlement with the Elector. Holland and its leading city agreed to pay a lump sum of 440,000 thaler to the Elector, who in turn gave up his claim of the 'disputed subsidies', compensation for the loss of *Das Wappen von Brandenburg*, and the damages sustained in Cleves. Financially, it was clearly the Elector who profited. As we noticed before Van Amerongen had been instructed to offer 400,000 guilder to the Elector at the beginning of 1683. The States General had subsequently raised that amount to 400,000 thaler,[127] but now they also offered 40,000 thaler

[122] Van Amerongen to Dijkvelt, 26 Dec. 1684, Huisarchief Amerongen, I, no. 141.

[123] Frederick William's mandate to Van Amerongen in Huisarchief Amerongen, I, no. 183.

[124] Van Amerongen to Dr Ham, his secretary, who had been left in Berlin to take charge of running affairs, 3 Mar. 1685, Huisarchief Amerongen, I, no. 189.

[125] Elector to Diest, the Brandenburg envoy in the Republic, 9 Apr. 1685, *Urkunden und Actenstücke*, XXI, p. 84.

[126] Van Amerongen to Fagel and Pesters, 6 May 1685, Huisarchief Amerongen, I, no. 188.

[127] *Urkunden und Actenstücke*, III, pp. 747–8.

as compensation for the loss of *Das Wappen von Brandenburg*, although it had not been decided yet whether the capture had been illegal or not. From William III's point of view, however, this financial concession was fully justified by the renewal of the 1678 treaty between Brandenburg and the Republic, especially since a new clause was added to it. This fourth article stipulated that the two countries would maintain the peace in Europe against 'potential disturbers'.[128] This clause corresponded with the spirit of the Association Treaty and was therefore directed against France. Although Fuchs had told d'Avaux that his instructions did not contain anything that could weaken the friendship and alliance between France and the Elector, the French ambassador took offence at this article, because it contradicted the Franco-Brandenburg treaties of 1681 and 1682, the fifth article of the 1681 treaty making compulsory mutual help in any conflict without the right to consider whether the petitioner had caused the conflict or was the victim of aggression.

This fourth article sowed discord between William III and Amsterdam because d'Avaux, in order to frustrate the ratification of the new treaty, informed the Amsterdammers of its anti-French element. They reacted by saying 'ils ne vouloient rien faire que put donner le moindre ombrage a Votre Majesté'.[129] So the Amsterdammers, to William's dismay, once again clashed with him on his anti-French course and held up the ratification of the Dutch–Brandenburg treaty until October 1685. Then, however, by revoking the Edict of Nantes, Louis XIV showed his hostility to Calvinism and flouted d'Avaux's earlier warning that the Protestant religion 'est le seul foible [weak point] par où on les [the Amsterdammers] pourroit attaquer'.[130] The revocation of the Edict of Nantes caused a wave of protest across Europe and finally convinced the Amsterdammers of the need to take some precautions against the power of France.[131] So, ironically enough, Louis XIV himself helped bring about the reconciliation between William III and his opponents.

The Revocation of the Edict of Nantes cut the last ties binding the Elector to France.[132] He tried to avoid breaking with France openly and to heed Paul Fuchs' advice to move carefully, 'dissimulating everything and secretly taking steps to maintain the integrity and security of the State',[133] but although he denied to Rébenac that the Dutch–Brandenburg treaty had changed his relationship with France, the French ambassador knew better. French threats, however,

[128] Moerner, *Kurbrandenburgs Staatsverträge*, p. 470, and Schevill, *The Great Elector*, p. 360.
[129] Mallet (ed.), *Négociations*, V, pp. 134–5.
[130] Ibid., V, pp. 52–3.
[131] P. L. Muller, 'Een Brandenburgsche zending in Nederland in 1685', *Bijdragen voor Vaderlandsche Geschiedenis en Oudheidkunde*, nieuwe reeks, 6, (1870), p. 109.
[132] Spielman, *Leopold I*, p. 124.
[133] Fuchs to the Elector, *Urkunden und Actenstücke,* XXI, pp. 100–1.

did not work with the Elector and Rébenac's demand that the Elector should deliver a written statement in which he promised Louis XIV neither to conclude any new treaty nor to renew old ones without the prior consent of the king of France led to one of those notorious outbursts of anger from the Elector.[134]

So although Frederick William never formally revoked his treaty with France, he strengthened his links with the anti-French powers in the meantime. After issuing the Edict of Potsdam of 8 November 1685 in which he invited French Huguenots to come to Brandenburg, he offered the Emperor Leopold I 7,000 troops to fight against the Turks. Anti-French sentiments played a dominant role in concluding a defensive treaty with Sweden, Brandenburg's arch-enemy, on 20 February 1686, which was followed by a treaty with the emperor in the following month. In the summer of 1686 he visited William III in Cleves 'to discuss things with you in a better and more trusting manner'.[135] What the two men discussed is not known. Van Amerongen, who welcomed the Elector at Wesel, on behalf of the States General, on 30 July 1686, noticed the Elector's firm friendship for 'the state',[136] so one may assume that William and his uncle, unlike six years earlier, now shared the same perceptions about France. According to Rébenac, who had been at Cleves during the negotiations between William III and the Elector, there was no doubt that Frederick William was lost for France: 'Ainsi je ne puis, Sire, en aucune sorte avoir l'honneur d'assurer V.M. qu'il y ait encore un changement favorable dans l'esprit de M. l'électeur de Brandenbourg'.[137]

Still Frederick William did not press for any direct action during his lifetime. At the end of January 1688, when another European conflict was drawing nearer, the Elector wrote to William to tell him that he thought the time for action was not yet ripe. So William learned of his uncle's death in May 1688 with some relief,[138] especially since the new Elector, Frederick III, had already been advocating Brandenburg–Dutch co-operation at a time when his father was still in the French camp. The two countries promptly renewed their treaties of 1678 and 1685 on 30 June 1688 and William III very quickly started negotiating for Brandenburg's assistance, which had become more crucial than ever since William had now decided to cross over to England in an attempt to capture effective control over the conduct of government in order to withstand Louis XIV's expansionist policy more successfully.[139]

[134] See the draft of this statement in *Urkunden und Actenstücke*, XX, second part, p. 1044.
[135] The Elector to William III, 16 Apr. 1686, *Urkunden und Actenstücke*, XXI, pp. 114–15.
[136] Van Amerongen to the States General, 30 July 1686, Huisarchief Amerongen, I, no. 198.
[137] Rébenac to Louis XIV, 8 Aug. 1686, *Urkunden und Actenstücke,* XX, second part, p. 1140.
[138] L. Pinkham, *William III and the Respectable Revolution* (Cambridge, Mass., 1954), pp. 113–14, Baxter's remark in *William III*, p. 225, that William was pleased by the Elector's death is exaggerated.
[139] J. R. Jones, 'The Road to 1688', *Groniek. Gronings Historisch Tijdschrift*, 101 (1988), p. 62.

FREDERICK III SUPPORTS WILLIAM'S EXPEDITION TO ENGLAND, MAY 1688–NOVEMBER 1688

The Twenty Years' Truce of Regensburg was not granted a long life. It had been put to the test for the first time by the death of Charles II, the Elector Palatine, in May 1685. As the Elector died childless, the succession went to Philip William of Neuburg, duke of Jülich-Berg, a prince closely allied with the emperor and hostile to France. Louis XIV could not prevent the Neuburg claimant from taking over the Palatinate, but the French king put forward a claim to certain parts of the inheritance on behalf of his sister-in-law, Liselotte, 'Madame Palatine', who had married his brother, Philip of Orleans.[140] Louis did not press his claim by force, but the emperor and the Elector of Brandenburg nonetheless firmly rejected it. The former showed his dislike of France by signing the League of Augsburg with the kings of Sweden and Spain and the Electors of Bavaria, Saxony, and the Palatinate on 9 July 1686. As the emperor was still involved in his Turkish war, the League did not immediately serve any great purpose and for that reason William III and Frederick William did not join it, but they both approved of the anti-French objectives of the League as such.

The military position of the anti-French powers, however, took a turn for the better when the imperial army captured Buda in September 1686 and beat the Turks at Mohács in August 1687. It would now be possible to put an imperial army on the Rhine for the first time in years.[141] The French realized this too. Louvois, the French war minister wrote to Vauban, the engineer of siege works that 'the news which the King has just received of the defeat of the Turkish army has made him judge it necessary to bring his frontier towards Germany to the last stage of perfection.[142] The weakest point in the whole frontier was still Lower Alsace because of imperial control of Philippsburg on the Rhine. In November 1687 Vauban began to work on a fortress at Landau to block the route from Philippsburg into Alsace. Professor Symcox claims that Louis' answer to the mounting threat to his eastern border was primarily defensive,[143] but at the same time he tried to intimidate the emperor and the German princes into converting the Truce of Regensburg into a peace on his own terms.[144] Asserting fictitious claims in the Palatinate formed part of this policy, but Louis XIV, in January 1688, also succeeded in having William von Fürstenberg, his long-time German client and bishop of Strasburg, chosen by the pro-French chapter of the ecclesiastical Electorate of Cologne as coadjutor of the ailing pro-French archbishop Maximilian Henry. This meant that Von Fürstenberg would

[140] Symcox, 'Louis XIV and the Outbreak of the Nine Years War', p. 186.
[141] Baxter, *William III*, p. 222.
[142] Quoted by Symcox, 'Louis XIV and the Outbreak of the Nine Years War', p. 187.
[143] Ibid.
[144] Jones, 'The Road to 1688', p. 62.

succeed the archbishop when he died and keep the Electorate of Cologne within the French sphere of influence.[145] The emperor and Frederick William protested in vain against Von Fürstenberg's election, but this time the international political situation offered the emperor and the other anti-French powers the opportunity of trying to contain France without having to face almost certain defeat.

William III played a crucial role in organizing the opposition to Louis. In the early 1680s his anti-French policy had failed partly because of Charles II of England's refusal to enter the anti-French coalition. Now, once again, William needed English support, but this time it was his father-in-law, James II, who stood in his way. The new English king was openly intent on furthering the Roman Catholic cause in his country and ministers who refused to co-operate were dismissed. When Parliament emphasized that the penal laws against popery should be observed, it was prorogued and subsequently dissolved in June 1687. James then started a systematic campaign to pack the next House of Commons. Being so preoccupied with his English plans, James II had little opportunity to support his ideological ally, Louis XIV, even if he had wanted to. William III, however, feared that James might become an ally of Louis in order to crush domestic opposition in England. The Prince knew for sure that his father-in-law would not render him any assistance against France, since he had refused to endorse James' religious policy. As far as William was concerned English neutrality was unacceptable. He was determined that England would support his anti-French policy this time and therefore decided to invade England.

By taking a large force with him, however, William ran the risk of leaving the frontiers of the Republic inadequately defended against a possible French attack. He could not know beforehand that Louis intended to resolve the Cologne affair militarily and was to attack Philippsburg on 27 September 1688.[146] William therefore sent his most trusted favourite, Hans Willem Bentinck, to Berlin to ask the new Elector to fill the gap with his troops. The negotiations with Fuchs, however, caused some problems, because Eberhard von Danckelmann, the new leading minister of Frederick III, hoped that as a *quid pro quo* William could be induced to make some definite assignment of his rights in the Netherlands to Brandenburg.[147] Therefore William himself went to meet Frederick III and spoke to him in Hanover on 10 September 1688.[148] What they discussed we do not know, but William obtained the military help he needed without having promised to make a definite will in favour of Frederick III. So the future king of England could be confident that the United Provinces would be reasonably safe in his absence, among other forces shielded by a substantial contingent of Brandenburg and other Protestant German auxiliary troops.

[145] Schevill, *The Great Elector*, p. 400.
[146] J. R. Jones, *The Revolution of 1688 in England* (London, 1972), p. 281.
[147] Pinkham, *William III*, p. 123.
[148] Schnath, *Geschichte Hannovers im Zeitalter der neunten Kur*, I, pp. 429–30.

CONCLUSION

The start and finish of this essay focus on Brandenburg–Dutch friendship and co-operation, but it has also shown that this alliance was not to be taken for granted during the intervening years, because William III and Frederick William had a different view on how to conduct their foreign policy. William III's policy was straightforward: Louis XIV had to be contained at all costs. Any compromise in the field of foreign policy was rejected, as Amsterdam and Van Beuningen, to their anger and dismay, discovered in 1683–4. *Raison d'état*[149] prevented Frederick William from sharing William's obsession. He aimed at strengthening his own state and army and changed from one side to the other as the interests of his state seemed to demand.[150] When the Twenty Years' Truce safeguarded these interests sufficiently, the Elector moved closer to William, who must have been delighted that his uncle at last looked more favourably on his anti-French policy.

[149] E. N. Williams, *The Ancien Régime in Europe. Government and Society in the Major States, 1648–1789* (Harmondsworth, 1972), p. 326.

[150] F. L. Carsten, 'The Rise of Brandenburg', in F. L. Carsten (ed.), *The New Cambridge Modern History*, V, (Cambridge, 1969), p. 555.

Chapter 10

Of Providence and Protestant Winds: the Spanish Armada of 1588 and the Dutch armada of 1688

JONATHAN I. ISRAEL AND GEOFFREY PARKER

On 30 July 1588 Philip II's 'Invincible Armada', a huge force of 130 ships and some 25,000 men, arrived off the south-west coast of England.[1] It was an awesome sight which struck terror into many of those who observed it; and it has been vividly remembered ever since. But it failed: following a devastating attack by the Royal Navy, the Armada was forced to return to Spain via the North Sea and the Atlantic where severe storms destroyed perhaps one half of the ships and at least one third of the men. The English and their Dutch allies were jubilant, and saw the outcome as the direct intervention of Providence: 'God blew and they were scattered' was the message struck on a famous commemorative medal.[2] One hundred years later, on 15 November 1688,[3] another armada, this time assembled by the Dutch Republic, appeared off the same south-west coast of England under the personal command of Prince William III of Orange. This was an even more awesome sight: around 500 sailing ships carrying some 40,000 men and 5,000 horses. This time the 'Protestant wind' directed the invaders to a favourable haven – Torbay in Devon – while keeping the pursuing Royal Navy at bay for the crucial three days while the troops, horses, and artillery were landed.[4]

Some obvious points of comparison between the two armadas were noted even before the Dutch fleet set out. In October 1688, the Polish resident at The Hague reported that Europe was about to witness one of the most amazing enterprises in its history, and that:

> The Dutch are convinced that they will be as fortunate in their plan to attack

[1] We wish to thank Dr Peter Le Fevre for bringing some helpful references to our attention. So far as we are aware, the only modern attempt to compare the two invasions is J. L. Anderson, 'Climatic Change, Sea-Power and Historical Discontinuity: The Spanish Armada and the Glorious Revolution of 1688', *The Great Circle*, 5 (1983), pp. 13–23. This article concentrates largely on climate.

[2] 'Flavit deus et dissipati sunt'. In fact this was a Dutch medal: see details on this and other commemorations in M. J. Rodríguez-Salgado (ed.), *Armada 1588–1688* (London, 1988), pp. 276–7.

[3] All dates in this article are (unless otherwise stated) New Style, the system in use in Holland (and throughout most of the continent) after the 1580s. In Britain, however, dates were ten days earlier, and the year began on 25 March, until 1752.

[4] See details in J. L. Anderson, 'Combined Operations and the Protestant Wind: Maritime Aspects of the Glorious Revolution of 1688', *The Great Circle*, 9, 2 (1987), pp. 96–107.

> England as Philip II was unfortunate, when he sent his fearful fleet against Elizabeth in the month of August in the year 1588. There are few among them who are unaware of this period of history and who do not know by heart the inscriptions on the medals which were struck at that time.[5]

The similarities between the two expeditions were indeed numerous and striking. Both armadas ostensibly set out to reverse England's religious bias (militantly Protestant in 1588; allegedly tending towards Catholic in 1688) and to impose fundamental political changes in the interests of a major foreign power and at the invitation of certain factions in England. Both enjoyed some support from an assortment of European states but had to run the gauntlet of the ships and soldiers of a hostile neighbouring power (the Dutch in 1588; France in 1688) as well as those of England. Both armadas came logistically and mentally prepared to take on the Royal Navy, but both hoped to avoid a battle at sea as far as possible since they carried large invasion armies and had as their essential objective the disembarkation of those armies in England with as little loss and disruption as possible. Both attempted to succeed by stealth, attacking (like the Japanese at Pearl Harbor in 1941) in advance of a formal declaration of war. Above all, both armadas mobilized unprecedented reserves of shipping, supplies, equipment, munitions, and manpower so that, to some observers, the invasion fleets appeared almost inconceivably large. That of 1588 was, to a Florentine diplomat, 'The most numerous that has ever existed in these seas since the creation of the world'. And the English admiral Sir John Hawkins remained equally impressed even after his victory in the Channel: the Armada was, he assured his government, 'The greatest and strongest combination, to my understanding, that ever was gathered in Christendom'.[6] A century later Gregorio Leti, historiographer of the city of Amsterdam, had no doubt that the Dutch armada was 'a fleet the like of which has never been seen'; while the English ambassador at The Hague claimed that 'such a preparation was never heard of in these parts of the world'.[7]

At least some of these claims were true. Although the battle of Lepanto in 1571 had involved more vessels and more men on the Christian side, the 130 ships (of which about 25 were purpose-built warships), 2,431 guns and 25,000

[5] BL MS Add. 38495, fo. 28v, Moreau, Polish resident in the United Provinces, to the king of Poland, The Hague, 12 Oct. 1688; a contemporary French writer, Sainte-Marthe, also compared the Spanish Armada of 1588 with the Dutch armada of 1688, see Denis de Sainte-Marthe, *Entretiens touchant l'entreprise du prince d'Orange sur l'Angleterre* (Paris, 1689), pp. 89–93.

[6] Filippo Cavriana to B. Vinta, Paris, 22 Nov. 1587, in G. Canestrini and A. Desjardins, *Négociations diplomatiques de la France avec la Toscane* (6 vols., Paris, 1859–86), IV, p. 737; and Sir John Hawkins to Sir Francis Walsingham, 10 Aug. 1588, in J. K. Laughton, *State Papers concerning the Defeat of the Spanish Armada, Anno 1588* (2 vols., London, 1895), I, pp. 358–62.

[7] G. Leti, *Teatro Belgico o vero ritratti chronologici, politici e geografici delle Sette Provincie Unite* (2 vols., Amsterdam, 1690), I, pp. 353–6; BL MS Add. 41816, fo. 239, marquis d'Albeville to Middleton, The Hague, 15 Oct. 1688.

men – 18,000 of them soldiers (and 10,000 of them scheduled to land) – of the Spanish Armada certainly formed the largest naval concentration achieved to that date in Atlantic waters. And furthermore Philip II's fleet was instructed to join forces with an army of 17,000 infantry and 1,000 cavalry veterans gathered in the Spanish Netherlands and embarked aboard 215 barges and small warships.[8] The total size of the invasion force in 1588 was thus 345 ships and 43,000 men, of whom some 28,000 were scheduled to land. But the expedition of 1688 was still larger, for there were 53 warships – 32 medium and small 'capital ships', the rest small escort vessels[9] – some 10 fireships, and about 400 other vessels to transport the troops, supplies, and horses.[10] The army included 10,692 regular infantry and 3,660 regular cavalry: 14,352 men in all. In addition there were the gunners of the artillery train and several thousand volunteers. James II's ambassador in The Hague was close to the truth when he put the total strength of William's invasion army at 21,000, including some 5,000 volunteers.[11] But of course this figure did not include the crews

[8] On the Armada's size see C. Martin and G. Parker, *The Spanish Armada* (London, 1988), pp. 23, 258–9 and 285–6. However, the estimate of the men must be revised in the light of the more detailed calculations of M. Gracía Rivas, *Los tercios de la Gran Armada (1587–8)* (Madrid, 1989). On the size of Parma's fleet see G. Parker, *In the wake of the Spanish Armada: Essays and Sources* (New Haven and London, forthcoming, ch. 5. See also Rodríguez-Salgado (ed.), *Armada*, p. 36.

[9] The 'capital ships' consisted of thirteen with between sixty and sixty-eight guns, seven with between fifty and fifty-six and twelve with between forty and forty-eight. The Dutch deliberately held back their first- and second-rate ships, believing that they would prove unstable in the heavy seas to be expected so late in the season. See J. C. de Jonge, *Geschiedenis van het Nederlandsche zeewesen* (2nd edn, 5 vols., Haarlem, 1858–62), III, pp. 41 and 722.

[10] ARH SG 5625/2, memorandum of delegates of the Dutch admiralty colleges, The Hague, 16 Oct. 1688; *Hollandse Mercurius verhalende de voornaemste saken van staet en andere voorvallen die in en omtrent de Vereenigde Nederlanden en elders in Europa in het jaar 1688 zijn geschiet* (Haarlem, 1689), p. 277; Abraham van Poot, *Engelands Gods-dienst en vryheid hersteldt door syn Hoogheyt den Heere Prince van Oranje* (2 vols., Amsterdam, 1689), p. 108; A. Montanus, *Het Leven, bedryf en oorlogs-daaden van Wilhem de Derden, koning van Engeland, Schotland, Frankryk en Ierland* (4 vols., Amsterdam, 1703), III, pp. 108–10; de Jonge, *Geschiedenis*, III, pp. 41, 722; A. N. J. Fabius, *Het leven van Willem III (1650–1702)* (Alkmaar, 1912), pp. 29, 299; J. C. Mollema, *Geschiedenis van Nederland ter zee* (4 vols., Amsterdam, 1939–42), III, p. 107; and E. B. Powley, *The English Navy in the Revolution of 1688* (Cambridge, 1928), pp. 35–6, 71.

[11] BL MS Add. 41816, fo. 267, d'Albeville to Middleton, The Hague, 30 Oct. 1688. In the aftermath of the Glorious Revolution, it suited Williamite writers to play down the size of the Dutch army as they maintained that there had *not* been an 'invasion'. Most secondary authorities unconsciously follow this tendency asserting that William's invasion force was of only around 14,000 men, not realizing that the quoted figure of 14,352 refers only to the regular Dutch infantry and cavalry, omitting the Dutch gunners and the English, Scots, Huguenot, and Dutch volunteers, many of whom were professional soldiers. The most authoritative contemporary Dutch sources give the size of the invasion army as 21,000 men while Van den Bos gives 23,000: *Hollandse Mercurius 1688*, p. 275; Van Poot, *Engelands Gods-dienst en vryheid hersteldt*, I, pp. 107–8, states that 'de hele militie is sterk meer als 21 duisent man soo volontaires als mede de vluchtelingen'. See also Montanus, *Leven, bedryf en oorlogs-daaden*, III, pp. 108–10; *Engeland Beroerd onder de regering van Iacobus de II en hersteldt door Willem en Maria, Prins en Princesse van Orange* (Amsterdam, 1689), p. 170; Lambert van den Bos, *Leven en Bedryf van Willem de Derden, koning van Groot Brittanien* (2 vols., Amsterdam, 1694), I, p. 255 (gives 18,000 foot and 5,000 horse); and *The Expedition of his Highness the Prince of Orange for England* (1688), in *Harleian Miscellany* (London, 1744), p. 438, which also gives over 23,000. Thus the assumption that had there been a battle on Salisbury Plain the Dutch would have been outnumbered by two to one is incorrect; the Dutch would perhaps have been slightly outnumbered but were much superior to James' army in artillery, experience, and training, the States

of the warships – which numbered 9,154 men – and those aboard the transports – at least a further 10,000. The invasion forces gathered in 1688 thus totalled some 463 ships and 40,000 men.

It was clearly not possible to conceal preparations of this magnitude from the eyes of either domestic or foreign observers. When, in the last week of August 1688, the merchants of the Amsterdam Exchange suddenly grasped that the Republic was intending to attack Britain, frenzied dealing set off the second most catastrophic crash of the entire seventeenth century on the stock market. On 9 September the French ambassador at The Hague, the comte d'Avaux, appeared before the States General and delivered a blunt warning in the name of his master that the moment the Dutch moved against His Britannic Majesty, Louis XIV would immediately declare war on the Republic. But the preparations continued. In the days preceding d'Avaux's intervention there was still some doubt as to whether the vast armada was to be used against France or Britain, but the balance of opinion steadily shifted to the latter view. Thus on 7 September the English consul at Amsterdam reported to London that 'the discourses of, and reasons for, this equipage are very various – one day they say they will demand reason of France another that they will goe and cause a rebellion in England'; but a few days later the English consul at Hamburg reported that the 'alarm is yet hott here that the Dutch fleet is designed against England'.[12]

The news now spread rapidly: English agents everywhere detected ripples of the Grand Design. ''Tis no wonder that their going for England is no more a secret in these parts' wrote the English ambassador at The Hague: 'at Berlin the Elector's ministers speak of nothing else.' And ten days later: 'these forces, accompanied by many volunteers designe no less than a conquest of the three kingdoms [of England, Scotland, and Ireland]: never was an army better furnished with all necessaries.'[13] At Hamburg the residents of the Protestant princes told each other that the 'Prince of Orange is master of Amsterdam and London'; while in Vienna (according to James II's envoy) 'there is nothing more talk'd of here than the quarrel betwixt the Dutch and us', and in Lisbon 'wee have

General having sent over only their very best troops. Several modern historians have been misled into thinking that William III had only 'a fairly modest force for his expedition', of around 12,000 men, see J. R. Western, *Monarchy and Revolution: The English State in the 1680s* (London, 1972), pp. 259–60; Baxter calls it a 'little army', S. B. Baxter, *William III* (London, 1966), p. 238. The one department in which the Armada of 1588 definitely surpassed that of 1688 was in clergy: the 1588 Armada carried some 198 clerics while in 1688, apart from Burnet and a few regimental chaplains, the States General commissioned only six Calvinist preachers to accompany the fleet, see Rodríguez-Salgado (ed.), *Armada*, p. 36; ARH Raad van State 109, fo. 477.

12 BL MS Add. 41816, fo. 167, Petit to Middleton, Amsterdam, 7 Sept. 1688; BL MS Add. 41831, fo. 167. Peter Wyche to Middleton, Hamburg, 4 Sept. 1688.

13 BL MS Add. 41816, fo. 231, d'Albeville to Middleton, The Hague, 11 Oct. 1688. As late as Nov. 1688, however, Sir Robert Holmes still thought the Dutch fleet was designed to attack France: see J. Black, 'The Revolution and the Development of English Foreign Policy', in E. Cruickshanks (ed.), *By Force or by Default: The Revolution of 1688–89* (Edinburgh, 1989), pp. 135–58, at p. 150.

been here of late extremely alarm'd with the vast preparations that the Dutch have made of sea and land forces, it being the common discourse that their designs are against England'.[14]

The government in London was soon convinced and began to take preventive measures, strengthening the defences of the east coast towns and forts and sending the Royal Navy to Harwich with orders to prevent 'any approach of any fleet or number of ships from Holland upon any of our coasts, or their making any descent upon the same'; and 'to endeavour by all hostile means, to sink, burn, take and otherwise destroy and disable the said fleet'.[15] 'Whoever comes here', wrote Secretary of State Lord Middleton, 'shall not find us unprovided to receive them, and as the English nation hath been famous for their courage, so I doubt not at all, but on this occasion they will signalize their loyalty.'[16] In fact, of course, the opportunity never arose because James II and his advisers expected the invaders to land in either Essex or Yorkshire, whereas William actually made his descent in the south-west.

It is easy to be wise after the event. Most recent studies have found James' ministers and commanders guilty of either incompetence or disloyalty, and have praised William for his masterly control of his destiny. They have assumed that all talk of a possible landing by the invaders in the north was an elaborate feint. Thus a report of the English ambassador in the Hague (in late October) that the Dutch 'take all the colliers they can light on [to get experienced pilots and crews], which is a sign that they intend to sayle northwards' is interpreted as part of an elaborate smoke-screen: William ordered these pilots to be seized, it has been argued, simply because he wished the English to think he was aiming for Yorkshire.[17] Likewise the information brought to London by 'a Roman Catholick Pilott come this night from the [Dutch] fleet' that he had heard one of the English exiles with Prince William 'whisper to others ... that they must steer their course now towards the River Humber' is seen as part of a successful Dutch campaign of disinformation.[18] But there is no reliable evidence at all to show that William had decided the matter in advance. The only certain point is that the Prince was determined to avoid the south-east of England at all costs because that was where James had concentrated the bulk of his considerable

[14] BL MS Add. 41816, fo. 209, d'Albeville to Middleton, The Hague, 1 Oct. 1688; BL MS Add. 41828, fo. 91, Wyche to Middleton, Hamburg, 21 Sept. 1688; BL MS Add. 41841, fo. 88, Carlingford to Middleton, Vienna, 19 Sept. 1688; and ibid., fo. 234v, Scarborough to Middleton, Lisbon, 3 Nov. 1688.

[15] James' Instructions to Dartmouth dated 11 October are quoted by Powley, *The English Navy*, pp. 28–9.

[16] BL MS Add. 41816, fo. 75, Middleton to d'Albeville, London, 13/23 Sept. 1688. Middleton was a Scot, which may explain his gross miscalculation.

[17] BL MS Add., 41816, fo. 244, d'Albeville to Middleton, The Hague 16 Oct. 1688.

[18] From a letter sent by Samuel Pepys, secretary of the Navy, to Lord Dartmouth on 8 Nov., quoted in J. R. Tanner, 'Naval Preparations of James II in 1688', *English Historical Review*, 8 (1893), pp. 272–83, at p. 279 n. 57.

military and naval strength.[19] The essence of the Dutch strategy was therefore to land at a great distance from London. As Hans Willem Bentinck, the Prince's chief adviser, wrote some time in October: 'If the landing be northwards, it is conceived to be very dangerous to land any nearer to London than in some part of Yorkshire; and if the landing be westward, then no nearer to London than some part of Devonshire, the King's forces being all about London.'[20] At that point, therefore, perhaps only a few days before the first invasion attempt, the Prince had evidently not made his final choice between the two potential landing zones. And, indeed, when the force finally set out, after one false start sabotaged by storms, it sailed northwards before doubling back. It has usually been argued that this was a feint, largely on the strength of a cogent memorandum written by Admiral Herbert warning the prince of the extreme difficulty of disembarking a large army in winter on the Yorkshire coast.[21] But this point of view ignores a number of considerations: first, the Prince and his Dutch advisers normally seem to have paid little heed to Herbert's counsel; second, the minutes of a Council of War held aboard the *Leyden* on 11 November displayed a determination to land in the south-west *unless* the wind forced the fleet northwards – in other words, even at that late stage the Prince was content to let the wind ('Protestant' or otherwise) make the decision for him; third, at 1 p.m. the following day William wrote to tell Bentinck (who had been left behind when the fleet sailed) that they had after all taken 'the westerly route' – news which would scarcely have been necessary had that been the Dutch plan all along.[22] Finally, and most telling of all, another letter written by the Prince shortly after his descent upon Devon complained about the difficulty of communicating with Holland from the south-west of England and went on to regret that circumstances had forced him to sail west rather than north. 'If we had landed in the north of England', William remarked, 'we would have found various

[19] James' preparations are well discussed in J. Childs, *The Army, James II and the Glorious Revolution* (Manchester, 1980), pp. 171–81; and C. Jones, 'The Protestant Wind of 1688: Myth and Reality', *European Studies Review*, 3 (1973), pp. 201–22. For Dutch intelligence about them see, for example, the report sent to Holland in September by a Dutch agent in England, Jacob van Leeuwen, stating that James was concentrating his forces around London: N. Japikse (ed.), *Correspondentie van Willem III en Hans Willem Bentinck, eersten Graf van Portland* (5 vols., The Hague, 1927–37), I, part 2, p. 609.

[20] Bentinck to an unnamed agent in England, undated but from October 1688 in Japikse (ed.), *Correspondentie*, I, part 2, p. 619.

[21] See, for example, Anderson, 'Combined Operations'. However, the author has since modified his opinion: see J. L. Anderson, 'Prince William's Descent upon Devon, 1688: The Environmental Constraints', in S. Fisher (ed.), *Lisbon as a Port Town, the British Seaman, and Other Maritime Themes* (Exeter, 1988), pp. 37–55 – which argues that the key consideration was the need to land cavalry horses.

[22] The decision of 11 Nov. is recorded in Japikse (ed.), *Correspondentie*, I, part 2, pp. 623–4. The points for invasion were to be Southampton, failing which Poole, failing which Exmouth.

things easier; but the strong easterly wind that we encountered did not allow it.'[23]

So the unfortunate James II – however good his intelligence – could thus have received no accurate forewarning of the exact place of his enemies' descent since they themselves only made the critical decision at the last moment. The invaders held the initiative until the moment they reached the coast of England.

The same had been true in 1588. The build-up of naval and military forces in Iberian ports had been an open secret for over two years before the Armada finally set sail, with detailed reports on the precise disposition of Philip II's forces available to any spy – whether Catholic or Protestant – willing to pay for the information.[24] But, as in 1688, what the spies all failed to ascertain was the strategy to be followed and, above all, the designated point of disembarkation. Some thought that Plymouth was the target; others feared for the Isle of Wight. Others still remained convinced that the Armada was not destined for England at all but for a direct descent on Holland and Zealand![25]

But numerous as the similarities between the two invasions may have been, they were outweighed by the differences. Most obvious was the outcome: the invasion of 1588 proved an heroic and costly failure, that of 1688 a total and almost bloodless success (although both gave rise to an indecisive, costly, and long-running European war). And since the contrasting outcomes derived largely from the distinct strategies and logistics adopted by the invaders, it is worth examining them in some detail.

To begin with, there was major fighting in 1588, but – rather surprisingly – none in 1688. The contrast stemmed entirely from the different conduct of

[23] Herbert's memorandum, warning that the north-eastern coast was 'soe dangerex that I hardly think it practicable', is printed in Japikse (ed.), *Correspondentie*, I, part 2, p. 612. The low opinion of Herbert held by William and his entourage is discussed at pp. 354–5 below; the letter to Bentinck of 12 Nov. ('Vous voiés que je tiens la course en West, et passerons J'espère demain le pas de Calais') is in Japikse (ed.), *Correspondentie*, II, part 3, p. 53; William's own view of the two alternative landing sites is given in ARH Collectie Fagel 507, William III to Grand Pensionary Fagel, Exeter, 26 Nov. 1688.

[24] See J. de Lamar Jensen, 'The Spanish Armada: The Worst Kept Secret in Europe', *Sixteenth Century Journal*, 19 (1988), pp. 621–41. This admirable article only deals with 'leaks' to the enemy; the even more copious leaks to Spain's allies and potential allies are discussed in Parker, *In the Wake of the Spanish Armada*, ch. 6.

[25] As late as 15 Nov. 1587, in a letter filled with details about Parma's preparations, the earl of Leicester (governor-general of the Dutch Republic) still had no idea about their objective: H. Brugmans (ed.), *Correspondentie van Robert Dudley, Graaf van Leycester* (3 vols., Utrecht, 1931), III, pp. 284–6. And as the Armada prepared to weigh anchor, the French ambassador in Madrid remained convinced that it was bound for Zeeland (Bibliothèque Nationale de Paris (hereafter BNP), Fonds français 16 110, fo. 257, M. de Longlée to Henry III, 6 May 1588)!

the Royal Navy, for both invasion fleets were under strict orders to avoid battle if at all possible: as the two orders of battle make clear, the essential element in both armadas was the convoy carrying the army of invasion and its supplies. At all costs, both had to be preserved intact until they could get ashore.[26] But in 1588 the English warships, although taken by surprise when the Armada hove into view, managed to work their way out of harbour and harry the invaders from the moment they entered English territorial waters. A century later, by contrast, the Royal Navy failed to get to sea until the invaders were two days ahead of them and failed to catch up until the expeditionary force was safely landed and on the way to London. For this striking difference there are two explanations. First, and often forgotten, shipbuilding in Europe advanced markedly during the seventeenth century. The changes occurred less in ships-of-the-line, for the firepower and seaworthiness of (say) Medina Sidonia's Portuguese galleons or of (say) the *Ark Royal* were not so different to that of the third-rates involved in the 1688 campaign; but the quality of the transports was revolutionized. In 1588, both the English and Spanish commanders excoriated the poor performance of the merchantmen in their fleets, which reduced their overall speed (even with a following wind) to that of a rowing boat; a century later, William of Orange's fleet – larger and thus harder to keep together – covered the distance between the Channel and Torbay (also with a following wind) in one third of the time.[27] Thus the failure of the English to mount a hot pursuit in 1688 against a fleet travelling at top speed was far more serious than it would have been a century earlier. And some have therefore posed a second question: whether that failure perhaps stemmed from treachery rather than from ill-fortune or incompetence. James II, in retrospect, certainly felt he had been betrayed; and, equally certainly, there were some captains in his fleet who were unsympathetic to his cause. There was none of that enthusiastic, aggressive xenophobia that characterized Elizabeth's commanders against Spain. But, when all the evidence is considered, it would seem that James' admiral, Lord Dartmouth, and at least some of his captains fully intended to intercept and fight the enemy if they could. The two principal obstacles in their path were, first, the lateness of the season which made Dartmouth reluctant to take his fleet across to blockade the Dutch coast (as James counselled); and, second, the decision to station the navy at the Gunfleet, which was an excellent position from which to pursue

[26] AGS Estado 165, fos. 104–14, Instructions to Medina Sidonia, 1 Apr. 1588; Japikse (ed.), *Correspondentie*, I, part 2, pp. 613–17, Instructions for Arthur Herbert, 6 Oct. 1688.

[27] In 1588 the Armada passed Torbay on 1 August and reached Calais six days later; a century later the Dutch passed through the Straits of Calais on 13 November and began disembarkation at Torbay on the 15th.

an enemy sailing towards the coast of Yorkshire, but in certain circumstances dangerously ineffective against one sailing south for the Channel.[28] The central problem, in 1688 as in 1588, was that (as noted above) the invaders always held the initiative.

Now given England's traditional strength by sea, experience has shown that there are effectively only four strategies that might lead to a successful invasion. The first is a simultaneous combined operation by a navy strong enough to defeat the opposing English navy, and a convoy numerous enough to carry an army capable of effecting the Conquest. This was the technique successfully used by William I in 1066 and William III in 1688 and unsuccessfully attempted by France in 1759 and 1779. The second possible strategy is to assemble an army in secret, somewhere near the Channel, and then send out a fleet from some other port as a decoy (to lure away the Royal Navy) so that a squadron of light and nimble transports could ferry the army across the Channel virtually unescorted. This was the ploy favoured by Napoleon in 1804–5. The third possible strategy is a variant of this: to launch a diversionary assault on Ireland, which would lure away England's principal forces, leaving the mainland relatively open to invasion. The French tried this, with partial success, in 1760 and 1798. And, finally, it might be possible to make a surprise assault at a time when England was unprepared – as the French (yet again) were to attempt in 1743–4.[29] It is a tribute to the excellence of Philip II's advisers that all these possibilities were considered in the 1580s; it is a measure of the limitations of his methods of strategic planning that in 1587–8 he tried to undertake three of them at once.

In January 1586, in response to English attacks on Spanish possessions in Galicia, the Canaries, and the Caribbean, Philip II invited both the duke of Parma (commander of his forces in the Spanish Netherlands) and the marquis of Santa Cruz (admiral of his Atlantic fleet) to formulate a plan of attack on England.[30] Santa Cruz replied first, sending a draft proposal to court in mid-February, followed by a full plan on 22 March 1586. Unfortunately only the lists of necessary resources appear to have survived, but the immense detail of this document – ranging from the number of capital ships down to the last

[28] There are many discussions of this question, but in our view the best analysis of the available evidence – which concludes that the 'Naval conspiracy', although it existed, was not decisive in the outcome of the campaign – is that of D. Davies, 'James II, William of Orange, and the Admirals', in Cruickshanks (ed.), *By Force or by Default*, pp. 82–108.

[29] Based upon F. McLynn, *Invasion. From the Armada to Hitler, 1588–1945* (London, 1987), *passim*.

[30] See the documents printed in E. Herrera Oria, *La Armada Invencible* (Archivo documental español, II, Valladolid, 1929), pp. vii-ix.

pair of shoes required – make Santa Cruz's intentions perfectly plain.[31] It clearly corresponded to the third alternative strategy for the invasion of England: a diversionary attack on Ireland followed by a surprise attack on the mainland. Briefly stated, a fleet of some 150 great ships and 400 support vessels would be assembled in Iberian ports in order to transport 55,000 invasion troops – together with their equipment, munitions, and supporting artillery – direct to a landing point somewhere in the British Isles. It was to be an operation modelled on such earlier successes as the relief of Malta in 1565 and the conquest of the Azores in 1582 and 1583.

Early in April 1586, a meeting of top advisers was held at the Escorial at which Santa Cruz presented his plans in detail. Exactly which landing area he designated is not known, for no minutes of the meeting have survived; but it was most probably the port of Waterford in southern Ireland since this was the region mentioned in so many subsequent papers.[32] The attack was to be launched in the summer of 1587 and preparations were authorized in three areas: in Lisbon, where ships and men were to be assembled to form a strike force under the personal command of Santa Cruz; in Andalusia, whither the duke of Medina Sidonia (who had also been at court for the planning meeting) was dispatched to raise troops and assemble supply vessels which would later be sent to Lisbon; and in Vizcaya, where eight large merchantmen and four pinnaces were embargoed to serve as a new squadron under the command of Spain's most experienced Atlantic seaman, Juan Martínez de Recalde.[33]

However, just as preparations to implement the Santa Cruz plan were initiated, the duke of Parma completed his own strategic assessment. It was explained in a twenty-eight page letter dated 20 April 1586, and further details were entrusted to the special messenger who brought the letter to court. Parma began

[31] There is a problem of dating here. The original memorial (drawn up in the joint names of Santa Cruz and the Provisioner-General Bernabé de Pedroso) was thought to be lost, but in 1983 it appeared at an auction and was purchased for the Archives of Simancas, where it may now be consulted at AGS Guerra Antigua 221, fo. 1bis. Most – but not all – of this long document was printed in C. Fernández Duro (ed.), *La Armada Invencible* (2 vols., Madrid, 1884), I, pp. 250ff. It was undated, but Santa Cruz's covering letters were sent to Court on 22 March 1586. However, an earlier version – which has still not surfaced – was sent from Lisbon more than a month earlier (see Biblioteca de Heredía Spínola, *caja* 81, fo. 88, Santa Cruz to Don Juan de Zúñiga, 13 Feb. 1586, announcing its dispatch) and a précis of it was discussed by the Council of War on 23 Feb. (see AGS Guerra Antigua 190, fo. 314). This must have been the document seen by the Venetian ambassador in Madrid, and described in his letter back to the Doge and Senate on 22 Mar. 1586 (a major security breach!) since an ambassador in Madrid could not have seen a letter mailed in Lisbon that same day: *CSP Venetian 1580–89*, p. 147. Copies of the 22 Mar. document were also secured by several ambassadors: for Venice see ibid., pp. 193–5; for London see PRO SP 94/2, fos. 124–5; for Paris see BNP, Fonds français 16 110, fos. 130–6; and so on.

[32] Santa Cruz is known to have consulted detailed maps and descriptions of Ireland while preparing his plan: Duro (ed.), *Armada Invencible*, I, p. 23.

[33] See AGS Estado 2218, fo. 43, Don Juan de Idiáquez to Archduke Albert, 2 Apr. 1586, on the preparations at Lisbon; and G. Maura Gamazo, duke of Maura, *El designo de Felipe II y el episodio de la Armada Invencible* (Madrid, 1957), pp. 145ff, on Medina Sidonia's part; AGS Contaduría Mayor de Cuentas 2a época 1208 on the embargo of ships to form the squadron of Vizcaya 10 Apr.–7 May 1586.

by regretting the lack of secrecy concerning the king's intentions. According to him, even ordinary soldiers and civilians in Flanders were openly discussing how England could be invaded. Nevertheless, the duke believed, the enterprise might still be feasible provided certain basic precautions were taken. First, the king of Spain must be in sole charge 'without placing any reliance on either the English themselves, or the assistance of other allies'. Second, some assurance must be obtained that France would not interfere. Third, sufficient troops and resources must be left to defend the reconquered parts of the Netherlands against the Dutch even after the assault force had left.

If all this could be achieved, the duke considered that a force of 30,000 foot and 500 horse might safely be detached from the army of Flanders and ferried across the Channel to launch a surprise attack on England aboard a flotilla of sea-going barges. Provided his precise intentions remained a secret, 'given the number of troops we have to hand here, and the ease with which we can concentrate and embark them in the barges, and considering that we can ascertain, at any moment, the forces which Elizabeth has and can be expected to have, and that the crossing only takes 10 to 12 hours without a following wind (and 8 hours with one)', Parma felt sure the invasion could be undertaken with a fair chance of success. 'The most suitable, close and accessible point of disembarkation [he concluded], is the coast between Dover and Margate', which would permit a surprise march on London.[34] This was, in essence, the fourth alternative invasion strategy: a surprise assault.[35]

Philip II was thus confronted by two plausible plans. One was endorsed by his foremost naval commander; the other by his most experienced general. But which was the better?

To some extent, the appeal of Parma's strategy was reduced by the long delay which intervened before it arrived at court. The king had asked for it on 29 December 1585 and yet, despite a reminder on 7 February 1586, it was not sent until 20 April and was not received by the royal cypher clerks until 20 June. Four more days elapsed before the bearer, Giovanni Battista Piatti, was debriefed by the king's ministers: questions were asked about exactly what shipping was currently available in the ports of Flanders to ferry a major army

[34] AGS Estado 590, fo. 125, Parma to Philip II, 20 Apr. 1586; its arrival is noted in ibid., fo. 126 'Lo que dixó Juan Bautista Piata de palabra a 24 de junio 1586' (a document which itself contains additional information about the plan).

[35] Parma only devoted two paragraphs of his letter to the possibility of naval support from Spain, and even then he considered it only in the context of 'the worst possible scenario': that somehow details of his plan had become known in England. In that case, he suggested, since the king was being forced by Drake's exploits to mobilize a fleet to protect the Atlantic, perhaps this new navy could be used 'either to sail suddenly up here in order to assist and reinforce the troops who have already landed [in Kent] and keep open the seaway between the coasts of Flanders and England; or else – if your fleet is large, well-provided, well-armed and well-manned – it could create a diversion which will draw the English fleet away [from the straits of Dover]'; AGS Estado 590, fo. 125, Parma to Philip II, 20 Apr. 1586.

across the open sea, and about the possible advantage of seeking an alternative landing place in the Thames estuary, closer to London. Then the whole dossier was turned over to the king's leading adviser, Don Juan de Zúñiga.[36]

Zúñiga could draw upon a lifetime's experience of political and military affairs. He had fought in the Netherlands in the 1550s, and then rose through the ranks of ambassador to the papal court and viceroy of Naples to become in 1582 a councillor of war and state in Madrid. Now he presided over the Junta de Noche (the 'night committee'), formed to co-ordinate central government policy and advise the king on major affairs of state. He was totally undeterred by the conflict with the Santa Cruz plan already adopted. Instead he sought to amalgamate the two strategies. He proposed that the marquis's fleet should sail from Lisbon, carrying as many troops as could be mustered, together with most of the material needed for the land campaign, directly for Ireland. There it would put ashore its assault troops and secure a beach-head. This (Zúñiga anticipated) would threaten and disrupt Elizabeth's naval forces, thereby neutralizing their potential for resistance when, after some two months, the Armada suddenly left Ireland and made for the Channel. The main invasion force of 30,000 veterans would then be led by Parma in a surprise attack, sailing from the ports of Flanders to the beaches of Kent in a flotilla of flat-bottomed craft, while the Armada cruised off the North Foreland and secured the local command of the Narrow Seas requisite for a safe crossing. It would then off-load the siege artillery and supplies necessary for a swift march on London. Finally, once the two beach-heads had been established and the seas made secure, the fleet of supply ships already being concentrated by the duke of Medina Sidonia in the ports of Andalusia would bring up further reinforcements and replenishments. With significant parts of England and Ireland thus under Spanish occupation, Parma was to create an interim administration in London pending the arrival of the new ruler approved by both pope and king.[37] If, however, Parma proved unable to defeat and capture Elizabeth, he would be instructed to use his presence on English soil to secure three key concessions. First, there was to be complete toleration and freedom of worship for Catholics throughout the kingdom. Second, all English troops were to be withdrawn from the Netherlands, and the places they garrisoned were to be surrendered directly to Spain. Finally, England was to be made to pay a war indemnity and the invasion force was to remain in Kent until it was paid. With such high stakes, Zúñiga concluded,

[36] See AGS Estado 589, fo. 15, Philip II to Parma, 29 Dec. 1585, 590, fos. 117 and 125, Parma to Philip II, 28 Feb. and 20 Apr. 1586, and ibid., fo. 126, 'Lo que dixó Juan Bautista Piata'.

[37] Zúñiga suggested Mary Queen of Scots – preferably married to some more dependable Catholic prince, such as the duke of Parma. But after her execution in Feb. 1587 there was an extended and somewhat acrimonious correspondence between pope and king over the 'investiture': the king wished England to be ruled by his daughter Isabella and her future husband (probably an Austrian Habsburg), but the pope was reluctant to sanction this massive extension of Spanish political power in advance of the conquest.

and with such a complex operation, it would be futile to attempt anything in 1586; so he recommended that the *Enterprise* of England should be launched in August or September 1587.[38]

One wonders whether Philip II realized the enormity of the proposed change of plan. There was, in retrospect, much to recommend Santa Cruz's strategy. The events of 1588 were to prove that, once they got their Armada to sea, the Spaniards experienced little difficulty in moving 66,000 tons of shipping from one end of the Channel to the other, despite repeated assaults upon it; while the Kinsale landing of 1601 showed how easily a beach-head in southern Ireland could be secured and fortified. Likewise, Parma's concept of a Blitzkrieg landing in Kent, without any warning, also had much to recommend it: time and again, his troops had proved their invincibility under his leadership, and it is hard to see how the largely untrained English forces, taken by surprise, could have successfully resisted the army of Flanders as it marched on London.[39] The Armada's undoing was caused, ultimately, by the decision to unite the fleet from Spain with the army from the Netherlands as the obligatory prelude to launching the invasion.[40]

On 26 July 1586, Giovanni Battista Piatti was therefore sent back to the Netherlands with details of a masterplan for the conquest of England that embodied, in all essentials, the complex and subtle vision of Don Juan de Zúñiga. A parallel dossier was sent to Lisbon. But neither Parma nor Santa Cruz was invited to comment on the orders sent to them; they were merely instructed to carry them out.[41] The king, for his part, instructed all public authorities in Spain, Portugal, Naples, and Sicily to prepare troops, munitions, and other necessary equipment, while Spanish and Italian reinforcements were readied for

[38] AGS Estado 590, fo. 127, 'Parescer' of Don Juan de Zúñiga, holograph and undated (but early July 1586); partially published in Ch. Piot (ed.), *Correspondance du Cardenal de Granvelle* (12 vols., Brussels, 1877–96), XII, pp. 487–90.

[39] This argument is developed in more detail in G. Parker, *Spain and the Netherlands 1550–1650. Ten Studies* (London, 1979), ch. 7.

[40] But had Parma assembled enough vessels to transport all his troops in safety? He only had 45 ships and 170 barges for his 18,000 troops but, by contrast, when the Dutch army (also of 18,000 men) made a surprise seaborne attack on Flanders in 1600, no less than 1,266 vessels were assembled. See Martin and Parker, *The Spanish Armada*, pp. 151–2; and B. Cox, *Van den Tocht in Vlaanderen: de logistiek van Nieuwpoort, 1600* (Zutphen, 1986), pp. 32 and 146–57.

[41] The Instructions of 26 July have not survived, but can be surmised from AGS Estado 2218, fo. 52, Philip II to Parma, 18 July 1586, fo. 56, Don Juan de Idiáquez to Parma, 27 July 1586, and fo. 67, Philip II to Parma, 1 Sept. 1586. It is just possible that Piatti took only oral instructions with him on 26 July, for at much the same time Philip II criticized his ambassador in France for committing too much to paper. 'In future', the king warned, 'it would be better and more secure to entrust these secret matters to persons of confidence who will handle them by word of mouth, without writing them down.' (AGS Estado K 1448, fo. 64, Philip II to Don Bernardino de Mendoza, 5 Sept. 1586.) In his subsequent letters, the king and Parma never referred to details of the invasion strategy, only to 'la traza acordada' (the plan agreed).

dispatch to the army of Flanders, and shipping from all over Europe was lured towards Lisbon and Cadiz.[42]

And then the whole strategic scene was transformed when in April 1587 Queen Elizabeth, goaded by news of Philip's designs against her, decided to launch Sir Francis Drake with a powerful flotilla on what today would be called 'a pre-emptive strike' (and was then known as 'the singeing of the king of Spain's beard'). It was not the sack of Cadiz and the destruction of stores and ships that proved critical, but rather Drake's subsequent – and well-publicized – departure to intercept the returning treasure galleons from the East and West Indies. For that threat forced Santa Cruz to take his powerful fleet to sea, in July, not to Ireland as intended but to await the returning fleets off the Azores. Although he accomplished this feat brilliantly (losing only one East Indiaman to Drake) he was unable to return to Iberian waters until October, and by then his ships were storm damaged and his men sick. There was now no way the Armada could sail against England in 1587. The whole Grand Strategy required rethinking.[43]

Philip II worked hard. First the auxiliary fleet in Andalusia was ordered to sail to Lisbon and join forces with the warships of Santa Cruz (as soon as they returned from the Azores). Then on 14 September a detailed directive was issued for the Armada. There was now no talk of invading Ireland – indeed two whole clauses of the Instructions were devoted to explaining that, because of the delays caused by Drake's raid and the need to escort the treasure fleets, there was no longer time to secure a base in Ireland before invading England. The purpose of the enterprise, the king emphasized, remained unchanged: to restore England to the Catholic Church, to end English attacks on Spain's interests, and to secure an indemnity. Only the strategy had been modified.

Santa Cruz, together with the fleet of auxiliaries from Andalusia and a newly arrived squadron from Guipúzcoa, was now ordered to 'sail in the name of God straight to the English Channel and go along it until you have anchored off Margate head, having first warned the duke of Parma of your approach'. Then, the king continued, 'The said duke, according to the orders he has received, on seeing the Narrow Seas thus made safe by the Armada being either anchored off the said headland or else cruising in the mouth of the Thames, ... will immediately send across the army that he has prepared in small boats, of which (for transit alone) he has plenty.' The king went on to insist that, until Parma and his men had made their crossing, the Armada 'was to do nothing except make safe the passage, and defeat any enemy ships that may come out to prevent

[42] AGS Estado 1261, fo. 87, Philip II to the governor of Lombardy, 7 Aug. 1586, and 1088, fos. 210–12, to the viceroys of Naples and Sicily, 12 Nov. 1586. The towns of Spain were ordered to prepare to levy troops on 7 Oct. 1586 (AGS Guerra Antigua 189, fos. 119–68).

[43] On the raid, see Martin and Parker, *The Spanish Armada,* pp. 130–2, and the sources listed at p. 283 n. 9.

this'. He also loftily asserted that 'from Margate, you can prevent any junction between the enemy warships in the Thames and the eastern ports, with those in the south and west, so that the enemy will not be able to concentrate a fleet which would dare to come out and seek battle with ours'.

It all sounded highly convincing, but important questions were left unanswered. To begin with, would the Grand Fleet go across to the ports of Flanders to meet the army, or were the invasion barges expected to put out to meet the fleet in open water? And, in the former event, how would the deep-draught ships of the Armada negotiate the shallows and sandbanks which hugged the Flemish coast; in the latter, how could a fleet cruising some miles offshore protect Parma's vulnerable barges from the heavily gunned Dutch blockade squadron once they left the safety of Dunkirk and Nieuwpoort harbours? It was, to say the least, an unfortunate lacuna.[44]

Philip II also seems to have devoted little thought to moulding a favourable faction in England. Although there was no shortage of émigrés at his court (albeit not so many and of such eminence as at the court of William III a century later) clamouring for action, Philip made no effort to present his enterprise as a response to the pleas of the English for 'liberation' from religious and political oppression. Instead, propaganda to win local support was entrusted to the Catholic clergy in exile, headed by Cardinal William Allen who in July 1588 published an *Admonition to the People of England*, declaring Elizabeth deposed, promising the swift arrival of Parma and his army, and urging English Catholics to rise in arms in support.[45] After the conquest, the pope and Philip II intended Allen to take charge of the new Catholic state until the arrival of a mutually approved sovereign.[46] But the king's Instructions to the duke of Parma in April 1588 made clear that no uprising by the English Catholics in support of the invaders was to be expected.[47]

In the event, of course, it did not matter, for the invaders never managed to land: thirty-two heavily armed warships sent by the Dutch to blockade the Flemish coast kept Parma's barges confined to port, while the fireships, galleons, and guns of the Royal Navy possessed sufficient superiority over those of the Armada to ensure that although Medina Sidonia might lead his fleet relatively

[44] The Instructions may be found in AGS Estado 594, fo. 5, Philip II to Parma, 4 Sept. (*sic*) 1587; and Oria, *La Armada Invencible*, pp. 33–7, Instructions for Santa Cruz, 14 Sept. 1587. It was an oversight to which Parma, at least, frequently alluded, but without ever receiving an answer! Cf. AGS Estado 592, fos. 147–9, Parma to Philip II, 21 Dec. 1587, and 594, fos. 6–7, 189 and 197, idem, 31 Jan., 22 June, and 21 July 1588.

[45] It is worth noting that, despite all the effort expended on propaganda in England and all the promises of support issued by English political, ecclesiastical, military, and naval leaders, there was very little open support for William III in 1688 until it was clear that he had won.

[46] The role assigned to Allen in the interim government of England emerges clearly from Philip II's supplementary instructions to Parma on 5 Apr. 1588: AGS Estado 165, fos. 176–7. In general, see the excellent article of A. J. Loomie, 'The Armadas and the Catholics of England', *Catholic Historical Review*, 59 (1973), pp. 385–403.

[47] See AGS Estado 165, fos. 174–6, Instructions to Parma, 1 Apr. 1588.

intact to the Narrow Seas, he could not remain there long enough to effect his rendezvous with Parma. But if the immediate cause of the defeat of the Spanish Armada in 1588 was thus tactical, its roots were undoubtedly strategic.

Leaving aside the mistaken decision to place all trust in the union of the fleet from Spain with the army from Flanders before permitting the invasion to proceed, the king's forces were also seriously weakened by the fact that the supreme commander remained at the Escorial, hundreds of miles from the theatre of operations. This entirely removed the hot breath of royal urgency from the necks of those preparing the fleet. Where Philip II had to rely on messengers and letters to convey his orders to officials in Lisbon, William III and his close advisers were on hand to see for themselves.[48] And, conversely, where William of Orange in 1688, in conjunction with his political advisers and all the relevant military and naval commanders, could take last-minute decisions on the method and direction of attack in the light of changes in the sea and the weather, as well as of up-to-date intelligence from England, Medina Sidonia and Parma were both tied by strict instructions that were at best ambiguous and at worst incompatible.

Moreover, the viability of Philip II's Grand Design was also undermined by the snail's pace at which the necessary ships, men, and munitions were assembled. There was, in fact, never the slightest chance of finding all the resources listed in Santa Cruz's original masterplan of March 1586: 150 great ships, 400 support vessels, 55,000 men, and all necessary munitions were simply not to be had from a peninsular population of under 9 million people. Although troops were raised all over Spain and Portugal, and veterans were brought back from the Spanish garrisons in Naples and Sicily, there were still not nearly enough – hence, in part, the decision to involve the duke of Parma's forces in the Netherlands, where crack Spanish, Italian, Burgundian, Walloon, and German regiments (as well as several units raised from British exiles) could be used for the invasion.[49]

Even to concentrate the 130 vessels which finally sailed from Lisbon required constant effort and some illegality, with numerous ships (in effect) being commandeered on entering Iberian ports. Indeed, by the time the fleet sailed it was not a 'Spanish' Armada at all, since its ships and crews came from over a score of European ports stretching from Ragusa to Rostock; and when even that did not prove sufficient, in desperation the escort warships of the Indies fleet were

[48] This was particularly important in view of the tense international situation. In both cases, the invasion could only succeed if all other interested powers (and especially France) were temporarily distracted. Yet the desired conjuncture could not be expected to continue indefinitely: the blow had to be delivered swiftly. For the international conjuncture in 1588, see Parker, *In the Wake*, ch. 3; for 1688, see the excellent survey of J. Carswell, *The Descent on England* (London, 1969).

[49] For the troops aboard the Armada, see Gracía Rivas, *Los tercios*; on Parma's army, see H. O'Donnell y Duque de Estrada, *La fuerza de desembarco de la Gran Armada contra Inglaterra en 1588* (Madrid, 1989).

commandeered and christened the 'squadron of Castile' in order to bring the Grand Fleet up to strength.[50]

In the end it was only the organizational talents of the duke of Medina Sidonia, who had spent most of his professional life overseeing the concentration and dispatch of the convoys sailing from Seville to America, which got the Armada to sea at all.[51] But the duke had to scrape the bottom of the barrel: some of the food accumulated was putrid; several of the ships embargoed sailed barely faster than the speed of a rowing boat; many of the men raised were unserviceable; and a few of the big guns cast early in 1588 'in furious haste' (as the documents themselves state) were seriously defective, having either brittle or mis-bored barrels.[52]

What a contrast this logistical confusion made with the Dutch armada a century later! Although William III himself worried that the hiring of transports and seamen and the finding of supplies and equipment were not proceeding fast enough, almost everyone else considered the speed breath-taking. According to Gilbert Burnet 'Never was so great a design executed in so short a time ... All things as soon as they were ordered were got to be so quickly ready that we were amazed at the dispatch' – for, after all, the build-up began only in June and the fleet was ready to sail in October.[53] It seems ironic indeed that a state usually decried for its decentralized federal political structure should have been able to mobilize and deploy its financial, military, and naval resources with such efficiency; moreover, the feat was achieved by a relatively small team. Bentinck was involved in every aspect of the operation, assisted by Caspar Fagel, Pensionary of the States of Holland, and other key members of the provincial standing committee. Their chief executive officers were Job de Wildt, secretary of the Amsterdam Admiralty College, and Cornelis Evertsen, the senior Dutch naval commander. Because of the emphasis on speed, secrecy, and efficiency, the three outlying admiralty colleges (those of Zeeland, Friesland and North Holland) were only marginally involved in preparing the armada; more than half the ships and total naval manpower was provided by Amsterdam, and the only other major contribution was made by the naval authorities of

[50] On the disruptive effects of this exercise, which involved several large merchantmen from the returning Indies fleet of 1587 as well as their escorts, see H. and P. Chaunu, *Séville et l'Atlantique, 1504–1650* (9 vols. in 12 parts, Paris, 1955–60), III, pp. 404–10. It is worth noting that the English fleet of about 197 ships and almost 16,000 men were raised in just over three months.

[51] See the excellent new biography of P. Pierson, *Commander of the Armada. The Seventh Duke of Medina Sidonia* (New Haven, 1989), *passim*.

[52] Details from Martin and Parker, *The Spanish Armada*, pp. 158–9, 163, 204–5.

[53] Contrast Japikse (ed.), *Correspondentie*, I, part 1, p. 57; William III to Bentinck, 14 Sept. 1688, with Gilbert Burnet, *History of His Own Time* (6 vols., Oxford, 1833), III, p. 310. The Dutch public was also amazed by the dispatch with which the expedition was made ready according to G. Leti, *La Monarchie Universelle de Louys XIV* (2 vols., Amsterdam, 1689), II, p. 522.

19 *The Arrival of the Amsterdam Contingent of the Invasion Armada at Hellevoetsluis (28 October/6 November 1688).* Engraving by the Huguenot refugee artist Daniel Marot.

Rotterdam.[54] The Sephardi Jewish businessman Jacob Pereira, one of the two leading Jews under contract with the States General to act as 'provisioner-general' of the army at that time, also played a key role in providing the food and fodder sent out to the fleet from Amsterdam.

The major stages in the build-up were all accomplished smoothly and swiftly. In late July the States General voted to expand the Dutch navy by 9,000 men, virtually doubling its strength: these men were recruited in less than a month – thanks in part to the offer of very high wages by the admiralty colleges – and (according to James II's consul in Amsterdam) the Amsterdam squadron was so well supplied that 'they want no men for them and even runne out

[54] ARH SG 5625/ii, delegates of the admiralty colleges to the States General, The Hague, 4 Nov. 1688; ibid., Zeeland Admiralty College to same, Middelburg, 3 Nov. 1688; and de Jonge, *Geschiedenis*, III, pp. 44, 723–4.

some to take on better'.[55] Late in August, however, the same observer noted some shortages: 'the States have taken into their service most of the men that came home with the Smyrna fleet and some off the East India ships'; and, when that did not suffice, resort was made to impressment: 'Dutch vessels that goe in and out ... are visited, and such men as they lyke are taken out of them.'[56]

At the same time, manufacture of much special equipment began in Amsterdam, The Hague, and Utrecht (a city boasting numerous copper mills and metal workshops). It was reported that the government had ordered 'at Utrecht the making of severall thousand of pairs of pistols and carabins' whilst Amsterdam 'has undertaken to furnish 3,000 saddles in three weekes time' and 'they are also night and day employed at The Hague in making bombs, cuirasses and stinkpotts'.[57] In late August the hiring of transport vessels began (the event that seems to have triggered the stock market crash which began on 25 August) and within a month 400 vessels were hired at Amsterdam (at 670 guilders a month) to transport hay, provisions, etc.[58]

The range and quantity of specialized equipment loaded on the Dutch fleet in the weeks just before departure was prodigious. To begin with, many vessels were filled with horses (the Spanish Armada had carried virtually none).[59] Although there were only 3,660 cavalry troopers in the army of invasion, the Prince, his entourage, and many officers and gentleman volunteers brought spares. Furthermore, at least 200 four-horse wagons were required to carry

[55] BL MS Add. 41816, fo. 104, d'Albeville to Middleton, The Hague, 15 July 1688; ibid., fo. 157v, Petit to Middleton, Amsterdam, 24 Aug. 1689. For further details on the recruiting of the 9,000 seamen, see ARH SG 5625/i, Zeeland Admiralty College to the States General, Middelburg, 14 July 1688; *Res. Holl.* 19 Aug. 1688; and *Resolutiën van de Hoogh Mog. Heeren Staten Generael der Vereenighde Nederlantsche Provincien genomen in den jare 1688* (The Hague, n.d.), p. 481, res. 11 Aug. 1688.

[56] BL MS Add. 48186, fo. 159v, Petit to Middleton, Amsterdam, 27 Aug. 1688. Some 3,000 seamen had already been raised by 26 July when d'Albeville reported to London that 'there are at present but six thousand seamen to be raised, and this has been compassed with a great deal of patience and artifice and the Prince hopes by means of the late rear admiral Herbert [who had just arrived in The Hague from England] to gett over many of His Majesty's seamen: hitherto though they gott but very few or none at all'. (BL MS Add. 41816, fo. 124v, d'Albeville to Middleton, The Hague, 26 July 1688.) Impressment was extremely rare in the Dutch Republic at this time.

[57] BL MS Add. 41816, fos. 157v-8 and 165, Petit to Middleton, Amsterdam, 24 Aug. and 3 Sept. 1688.

[58] BL MS Add. 41828, fo. 91, Wyche to Middleton, Hamburg, 21 Sept. 1688. Needless to say, such an enormous mass of shipping was not hired so quickly by normal processes of commercial bargaining but through the systematic intervention of the admiralty colleges and the States of Holland: see Job de Wildt to Bentinck, undated but from Oct. 1688, in Japikse (ed.), *Correspondentie*, I, part 2, p. 618.

[59] There were perhaps 200 mules and horses on the Armada, mainly to help manoeuvre the big siege-guns ashore: AGS Guerra Antigua 221, fo. 64, 'Relación' of 16 Feb. 1588. The duke of Parma planned to embark some 1,000 cavalry troopers on his fleet of small ships, but they intended to secure their mounts from English stables after the landing: see H. O'Donnell, 'El secreto requisito para la Empresa de Inglaterra de 1588', *Revista de Historia Naval*, 2, no. 7 (1984), pp. 63–74.

provisions and ammunition for the army,[60] and further draught animals were needed to pull the 50 artillery pieces. According to Gilbert Burnet (an eye-witness), the fleet carried a total of 7,000 horses – though this is probably too high an estimate.[61] And then there were 'muskets, pikes of all sorts, bandoliers, swords, pistols, saddles, boots, bridles and other necessaries to mount horsemen; pickaxes, wheelbarrows and other instruments to raise ground' as well as 'a great many ... boats covered with leather to pass over rivers and lakes'.[62] The fleet also carried a mobile smithy, 10,000 pairs of spare boots, a printing press, and a large quantity of printing paper as well as tens of thousands of propaganda leaflets previously printed (in English) at The Hague, Amsterdam, and Rotterdam, intended to convince the English and the Scots that the armada had not come to invade and conquer the kingdoms, but merely to accompany the Prince of Orange in his proclaimed purpose of rescuing English and Scottish liberty and the Protestant faith.[63]

The invasion armada was immensely impressive but in one sense it was no more 'Dutch' than that of 1588 had been 'Spanish'. On the one hand, 3,710 of the invasion troops were drawn from the regular Scots and English regiments in the Dutch army, and many soldiers in the 'Dutch' regiments embarked were in fact German.[64] On the other, there were the 5,000 or so volunteers – mostly discontented English and Scots but also including 600 Huguenot officers and many other French adventurers as well as numerous men from different lands. Finally, there were also English pilots and sailors on the fleet, including the titular commander Admiral Herbert.

In some cases the cosmetic value of the English and Scots volunteers was greater than their military value. Even Herbert was regarded as potentially too fiery to be altogether reliable, being put in overall naval command, over the

[60] According to the supply contracts drawn up by the States General with the Amsterdam Sephardi 'Provisioners General' Antonio Alvares Machado and Jacob Pereira the following year, a Dutch field army of 20,000 men required for its provisions 200 wagons each drawn by 4 horses (see BL MS Add. 38695, fos. 73, 75v, copy of a supply contract dated The Hague, 22 Jan. 1689).

[61] Burnet, *History of His Own Time*, III, p. 299. There has been some dispute over the number of horses. The Polish resident reported that 90 transport vessels in the fleet carried 60 horses each – a total of 5,400: see BL MS Add. 38495, fo. 30v, Moreau to the king of Poland, The Hague, 12 Oct. 1688. According to a Dutch planning document, 120 vessels would be required to carry 36 horses each (sc. 4,320 horses in all); and the fleet was to carry 640,000 pounds of hay as rations for 4,000 horses at 16 pounds per day each: see the 'Memorie' of 19 Sept. 1688 in Japikse (ed.), *Correspondentie*, I, part 2, p. 606. In the end it would seem that some 4,000 horses were embarked for the cavalry, together with 2,000–3,000 draught animals, of which about 300 died during the first abortive invasion attempt, *Resolutiën van de Hoogh Mog. Heeren Staten Generael ... 1688*, p. 647, res. 8 Nov. 1688.

[62] BL MS Add. 41816, fos. 185 and 251, d'Albeville to Middleton, The Hague, 21 Sept. and 21 Oct. 1688.

[63] The Spanish Armada also had its own press but left it behind in Lisbon. The advance propaganda for the English was printed in the Low Countries and was to be carried over by the duke of Parma's forces: see Martin and Parker, *The Spanish Armada*, p. 153, and pp. 121–2, 349 above.

[64] BL MS Add. 41816, fo. 186, d'Albeville to Middleton, The Hague, 21 Sept. 1688; and F. J. G. ten Raa and F. de Bas, *Het Staatsche Leger, 1568–1795* (11 vols., The Hague, 1911–18), VII, p. 6.

head of Admiral Evertsen (who actually assembled the fleet and prepared it for action) mainly as a propaganda ploy designed to help encourage parts of the Royal Navy to defect or at least refuse to fight.[65] Moreover, the troops of the British regiments of the States General's army, though highly trained, were not necessarily as zealous as the British volunteers for combat against their royalist compatriots. Agents sent by the marquis d'Albeville, James II's ambassador at The Hague, to the Nijmegen–Arnhem area where many of the troops were assembled before being ferried down the rivers to the fleet, reported that they had 'seen many of the English and Scotch soldiers weep for being forc'd to goe to fight against their own king and country, that many declared they would not fight'; and while the previous assurance which the commander of the British regiments, Major-General Hugh Mackay, had given to d'Albeville that 'always he would retire and never draw sword against the king' may be taken with a pinch of salt (given his unshakeable loyalty to William) there is no reason to doubt that some of these protestations were genuine.[66] Furthermore, some of the British volunteers were radical Whigs subject to strong political passions which clashed with the moderate message (designed to appeal to the Tories) of the Prince of Orange's *Declaration*. Yet, while the British volunteers were a diverse, even motley, crew, and many fewer of them were professional military men than was the case with the Huguenots, they displayed no lack of bravado. 'The English and Scotch men who are lately come over and do embark', reported d'Albeville on 28 September, 'boast they will soone graize their horses in St James Park.'[67]

Moreover the few minor shortcomings in morale and discipline scarcely mattered in such a mighty expedition in which the majority of the invasion army consisted of crack regiments, the finest in the States General's army, including all the guards regiments, when the troops were equipped with the most modern muskets, 'artillery and that very good . . . in abundance', and prodigious quantities of supplies of every kind, when the armada carried '100,000 pounds in ready money', and when the men had all been paid in advance. 'One has to admit', wrote the Polish resident, 'that this undertaking could not have been vaster or better organized.' In fact, before they sailed, the troops were issued

[65] De Jonge, *Geschiedenis*, II, part 3, p. 51. The promotion of Herbert was very unpopular with the States General, as well as with Evertsen and the Dutch navy: see J. Wagenaar, *Vaderlandsche Historie vervattende de geschiedenissen der nu Vereenigde Nederlanden* (21 vols, Amsterdam, 1749–59), XV, p. 466. But William insisted, even though he too had his doubts – see his letter to Bentinck of 26 Sept. 1688: 'Ce n'est pas le temps de faire voir bravoure, n'y de se battre si l'on le peut éviter; je luy [sc. to Herbert] l'ay déjà dit, mais il sera nécessaire que vous le repétiez et vous le luy fassiez bien comprendre' (Japikse (ed.), *Correspondentie*, I, part 1, p. 58). It was hardly an expression of confidence! Indeed, no one really seems to have trusted Herbert: see Davies, 'James II, William of Orange, and the Admirals', pp. 87–90.

[66] BL MS Add. 41816, fo. 239, d'Albeville to Middleton, The Hague, 15 Oct. 1688. Apparently, a few Scotsmen did refuse.

[67] Burnet, *History of His Own Time*, III, pp. 308-9; BL MS Add. 41816, fo. 202, d'Albeville to Middleton, The Hague, 28 Sept. 1688.

with their wages to the year end; and 'for every merchant ship hired to transport soldiers, horse or foot, or ammunition' it was reported 'the Prince pays 1,500 guilders a month, a half in hand'.[68] It was a far cry from the financial world of Philip II, who was forced to spend a part of every Saturday morning in 1588 checking and correcting the statements of cash-in-hand forwarded by his treasury in order to see how many of his bills he could afford to pay. The weekly balance was rarely more than 150,000 guilders.[69]

But there is more to Grand Strategy than guns, money, troops, and sails. There is also luck or, as contemporary writers put it, Providence. One of the Spanish Armada's senior commanders had said – perhaps sardonically – that the Grand Fleet was sailing 'in the confident hope of a miracle'; and Philip II was certainly confident that, whatever shortcomings might exist in his plans, God would intervene directly to ensure the desired outcome. And so when the marquis of Santa Cruz complained that it was madness to launch the Armada against England in mid-winter, the king replied serenely: 'We are fully aware of the risk that is incurred by sending a major fleet in winter through the Channel without a safe harbour, but . . . since it is all for His cause, God will send good weather.'[70] And in June 1588, after a storm had damaged some of the Armada's ships, driven others into Corunna, and scattered the rest, the king remained tranquil. When Medina Sidonia suggested that these reverses might be a sign from God to desist, the king replied: 'If this were an unjust war, one could indeed take this storm as a sign from Our Lord to cease offending Him; but being as just as it is, one cannot believe that He will disband it, but will rather grant it more favour than we could hope.' 'I have dedicated this enterprise to God', the king concluded. 'Get on, then, and do your part!'[71] A better example of cognitive dissonance would be hard to find.

And yet it almost worked! In the event, a chastened and encouraged Medina Sidonia eventually led the entire Armada – with scarcely any losses – from Corunna to Calais in three weeks. At 4 p.m. on Saturday, 6 August 1588, the Grand Fleet anchored only 25 miles from Parma, its order unbroken by the English and its strength virtually intact. There they were liberally supplied with

[68] BL MS Add. 41816, fo. 209, d'Albeville to Middleton, The Hague, 1 Oct. 1688; ibid., 38495, fo. 45, Moreau to the king of Poland, The Hague, 2 Nov. 1688; and Burnet, *History of His Own Time*, III, p. 305.

[69] See the 'Relaciones de sábado' for 1588–9 in AGS Consejos y Juntas de Hacienda 249, carpetas 16–17.

[70] The sardonic captain was probably Martín de Bertendona: see Martin and Parker, *The Spanish Armada*, pp. 153 and 285 n. 27; AGS Estado 165, fos. 2–3, Philip II to the Archduke Albert, 14 Sept. 1587. Perhaps the triumphant November voyage of the Dutch armada a century later proves that God *could* send good weather when He chose.

[71] Quotations from Maura, *El designo*, pp. 258–61, Medina Sidonia to Philip II, 21 and 24 June 1588; and Oria, *La Armada Invencible*, pp. 210–14, Philip to Medina Sidonia, 1 July 1588.

victuals and provisions by the benevolent Catholic governor of the port. From their anchorage they could see the designated landing place just south of Ramsgate, where the Romans, Saxons, and Danes had all stormed ashore successfully in the past. Had they but known it, the English had absolutely no idea where the Spaniards would strike, and had stationed their main army at Tilbury, on the Thames. During the opening weeks of August, the world (with reason) held its breath: a landing at the Downs would have been opposed by only a few untrained militia units, their numbers daily dwindling through desertion. The dramatic success of the fireships on the night of 7 August, which far exceeded expectations, should not be allowed to obscure the fact that Philip II's grand strategy came within an ace of success.

A century later it was much the same. At first there was euphoria: in September, at The Hague, according to d'Albeville, 'Here are wagers lay'd that the Prince of Orange will be master of England before two months will be at an end.' Even the regents with all their *gravitas* seemed unaccountably confident: 'no doubt is made here of a speedy success', noted d'Albeville on 1 October, 'and of a speedy declaration of war [by England] against France, that if they were not sure of it they would not venture to send into England the flower and best part of their forces'.[72] As the flotillas of flat-bottomed boats specially hired to 'transport the soldiers from Nimighen unto the men-of-war and merchant ships' swept down the Maas and Waal to Rotterdam and Hellevoetsluis, they passed a vast throng of cheering burghers and farmers, the women with tears streaming down their cheeks.[73] A sense of elation filled the country. Yet when all was ready, with the troops, horses, and supplies embarked, but with a persistent, strong, westerly wind confining the invasion fleet to port, and giving the English time to get their battle fleet ready, the mood began to sour. Correspondingly, at King James' court, spirits began to rise. 'Though we long for your letters', Lord Middleton wrote to d'Albeville, 'yet we cannot be sorry that they are so long in coming, I mean, that the wind is westerly.'[74] The ambassador replied, on 11 October: 'the [Dutch] Catholics pray ardently for His Majesty's preservation and for the success of his army against his enemies; the wind continuing contrary all this while they call it a "popish wind". God continue it one month longer.'[75] And for that 'month longer' God seemed to listen: 'the continuance of this weather which is very tempestuous', d'Albeville wrote a week later, 'goes to the heart of the Prince and of all of them. The people begin to say, God does not prosper the design. The soldiers are quite dejected and

[72] BL MS Add. 41816, fo. 209v. D'Albeville to Middleton, The Hague, 1 Oct. 1688.
[73] [J. Whittle], *An Exact Diary of the Late Expedition of His Illustrious Highness The Prince of Orange* (London, 1689), pp. 11–12.
[74] BL MS Add. 41823, fo. 77v, Middleton to d'Albeville, London, 5/15 Oct. 1688.
[75] Ibid. 41816, fo. 231, d'Albeville to Middleton, The Hague, 10 Oct. 1688.

begin to curse the masters of the design: if they continue embark'd but eight days more, a third part of them will perish.'[76]

A week later the Polish resident at The Hague reported to Warsaw that so many people, Protestants included, were now saying 'the wind is papist' that the magistrates of the Holland towns were obliged to forbid anyone to say in public that 'the wind is papist' on pain of a heavy fine which was, in fact, exacted from a number of offenders.[77] In Holland during these tense weeks the

> common thing every morning, which was most used, was first to go and see how the wind sate, and if there were any probability of a change. When any person came unto a house, in the heart of their city, concerning any manner of businesse, the very first question by all was, Sir, I pray how is the wind to day? Are we likely to get an easterly wind ere long? Pray God send it, and such like. The ministers themselves pray'd that God would be pleas'd for to grant an East Wind.[78]

Meanwhile there was frenetic activity around the Thames estuary. On 8 October, as the Dutch embarked their forces, Lord Middleton wrote to d'Albeville from London: 'I hope our fleet shall be ready in time enough to oppose their landing: all the seamen and soldiers expresse their resolution of dying in doing their duty.'[79] By the end of October all was ready: 'our fleet will be at sea tomorrow', wrote Middleton on 26 October, 'in a much better condition than theirs'.[80] Nor was his confidence misplaced. Under most conditions, the Gunfleet was a secure anchorage at which to wait and intercept an invasion fleet crossing from the Netherlands and sailing either northwards or to the south. Nor did the English fleet lack fire-power, numbering some forty-one ships and, according to the *Hollandsche Mercurius*, mounting 11,565 men and 2,058 guns.

Furthermore, the bitterest blow to Dutch morale was yet to come. On the first attempt to emerge, the great fleet was driven back in disarray by a severe tempest on 30–31 October. Although actual damage was less than the Dutch propaganda machine pretended (to lull James into a false sense of security), ships, men, and especially horses were badly battered. Moreover, the regents now had an additional reason for acute anxiety. Louis XIV had warned them what he would do should they defy him by moving against England. As the Polish resident noted on the day of the storm: 'on attend à tout moment de voir la guerre declarée entre la France et cet état'.[81] Having been cooped up

[76] Ibid., fo. 247, d'Albeville to Middleton, The Hague, 19 Oct. 1688.

[77] Ibid., 38495, fos. 40v–1, Moreau to king of Poland, The Hague, 26 Oct. 1688.

[78] [Whittle], *An Exact Diary*, pp. 13–14; according to Whittle 'the total number of the fleet, as they sailed from the Brill, was about four hundred and odd ships' not counting some small craft and boats.

[79] BL MS Add. 41823, fo. 76v, Middleton to d'Albeville, London, 28 Sept./8 Oct. 1688.

[80] Ibid., fo. 78v, Middleton to d'Albeville, London, 16/26 Oct. 1688.

[81] Ibid. 38495, fo. 54v, Moreau to king of Poland, The Hague, 9 Nov. 1688.

Vertrek van zyn Koninglyke Hoogheyd met s'Lands Vloot naar Engeland. Den 8 November 1688.

20 *William III's First Departure with his fleet for England (30 October/8 November 1688).*

for weeks in appalling conditions, the Dutch troops were now desperate. According to the Prince's secretary, William himself now became 'melancholicq'.[82] The English for their part, considered the Dutch mad. As Lord Dartmouth wrote to the king: 'Sir, we are now at sea before the Dutch with all their boasting, and I can not see much sense in their attempt with the hazard of such a fleet and army at the latter end of October.'[83]

Then, all of a sudden, the picture was transformed. The prayers of the Dutch preachers were answered. The wind veered right round to a strong easterly, the famous 'Protestant Wind' of 1688 which pinned the English fleet helplessly to their anchorage in the Gunfleet and enabled the invaders to reach their disembarkation point swiftly and unmolested. Remarkably, the armada first proceeded northwards right past the Thames estuary and the English fleet, to the most northerly point at which it was still possible for William and his advisers to

[82] *Journaal van Constantijn Huygens, den zoon, van 21 Oktober 1688 tot 2 September 1696* (2 vols., Utrecht, 1876–7), I, pp. 5–8; N. Japikse, *Prins Willem III, de Stadhouder-koning* (2 vols., Amsterdam, 1930–3), II, p. 256.

[83] Quoted in Carswell, *Descent*, p. 178.

21 *William III's Second Departure with his fleet for England (3/13 November 1688).* By Romeyn de Hooghe.

change their minds.[84] In view of the strong wind and the inadvisability of landing in the north-east under such conditions, the Prince gave the order for the great fleet to turn round. It doubled back, passing Harwich and the estuary within sight of Dartmouth's fleet which was still unable to get out to intercept them. The arrival of the great fleet off Dover caused a sensation in London and a shock at court, where James and his advisers had been convinced that the Prince would opt for the north-east.[85] It also caused a sensation at Paris whither couriers sped from Dunkirk, Calais, and Boulogne. The passage of the vast armada through

[84] Alan Pearsall, 'The Invasion Voyage: Some Nautical Thoughts', in Charles Wilson and David Proctor (eds.), *1688. The Seaborne Alliance and Diplomatic Revolution* (Proceedings of the International Symposium held at the National Maritime Museum, Greenwich 5–6 October 1988), pp. 170–1.

[85] BL MS Add. 25377, fos. 104, 100, Terriesi to Bassetti, London, 5/15 and 9/19 Nov. 1688; according to Terriesi there was a total of 637 vessels in the Dutch armada; see also the *Correspondence of Henry Hyde, Earl of Clarendon and of His Brother Laurence Hyde, Earl of Rochester, with the Diary of Lord Clarendon from 1687 to 1690* (2 vols., London, 1828), II, p. 504.

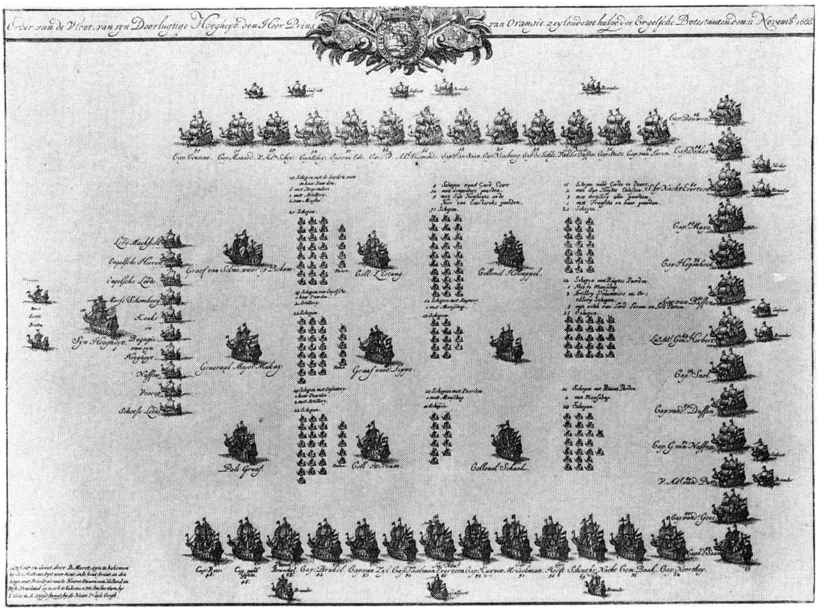

22 *The Order of the Fleet of His Highness the Prince of Orange (3/13 November 1688).*

the Narrow Seas presented a stunning spectacle.[86] First, there was a pause to enable stragglers to catch up. Then the Prince gave the signal 'stretching the whole fleet in a line, from Dover to Calais, twenty five deep'.[87] The Dutch went through 'colours flying', the fleet 'in its greatest splendour', a vast mass of sail stretching as far as the eye could see, the warships on either flank simultaneously thundering their guns in salute as they passed in full view of Dover Castle on one side and the French garrison at Calais on the other. The Dutch regiments stood in full parade formation on deck, as an English volunteer accompanying the expedition recorded, with the 'trumpets and drums playing various tunes to rejoice our hearts ... for above three hours'.[88] The boldest enterprise ever undertaken by the Republic of the United Netherlands was stage-managed with exquisite artistry. In all it took six hours for the incomparable mass of shipping to clear the straits. As the great fleet sped, driven by the strong winds, down the Channel, all available regiments in the London area were ordered

86 Abel Boyer, *The History of King William the Third* (3 vols., London, 1702), I, p. 237; [Whittle], *An Exact Diary*, pp. 30–1; *The Expedition of His Highness the Prince of Orange for England*, p. 437; Giovanni Gerolamo Arconati Lamberti, *Mémoires de la dernière révolution d'Angleterre* (2 vols., The Hague, 1702), I, pp. 561–3, 565; F. A. Kazner, *Leben Friedrichs von Schomberg* (2 vols., Mannheim, 1789), I, p. 287, and II, p. 269.

87 *The Expedition of His Highness the Prince of Orange for England*, in *A Fourth Collection of Scarce and Valuable Tracts* (Lord Somers) (4 vols, London, 1752), II, p. 258.

88 Ibid.

23 *The Prince of Orange Landing at Torbay (Exmouth Bay) on 5/15 November 1688.*

to proceed with the utmost haste, some clattering through London in the middle of the night, towards Portsmouth, the Isle of Wight, and the south coast. But the amazing luck which had pinned the Royal Navy to the Gunfleet held. The strong easterly wind carried the invaders down to the western reaches of the Channel too fast for James to be able to organize any opposition by sea or land. Then, having dangerously overshot the mark – Torbay being the last suitable and, apart from Teignmouth and Exmouth, the only undefended landing point capable of accommodating such an immense quantity of shipping for any length of time – the wind backed to southerly, sweeping the armada back towards safety, and then dropped to a calm, permitting easy and orderly disembarkation. Ignoring Herbert's advice one last time – Herbert, whose warships stood out to sea to fend off the expected English attack, sent word advising that William disembark at Exmouth[89] – William began landing his troops, horses, and supplies in Torbay on the evening of 5/15 November, the enormous operation continuing until late on 7/17 November. The English and Scots regiments of the States General's army came ashore first. Both Dutch regiments and English and foreign volunteers were under the strictest orders to behave civilly towards

[89] E. M. Thompson (ed.), 'Correspondence of Admiral Herbert during the Revolution', *English Historical Review*, 1 (1886), pp. 526–7.

the inhabitants they encountered and to pay for everything they procured 'without swearing and damning and debauching of women, as is usual in some armies'.

It is ironic that, until quite recently, it was the unsuccessful attack of 1588 that Britons chose to recall rather than the no less complex and in some respects even more imposing operation which so fundamentally altered the course of British history which took place exactly a century later. But then peoples, like individuals, often prefer to recall not what is crucial in their past but what best illustrates (and flatters) their own perception of themselves.

Chapter 11

The Glorious Revolution of 1688–9 and the House of Savoy

ROBERT ORESKO

In 1688, Vittorio Amedeo II, duke of Savoy, dispatched the conte Carlo Massimiliano Roero to the court of St James as his representative to congratulate King James II and Queen Maria Beatrice of England on the birth of their son James Edward, styled Prince of Wales. 'Les liens de sang qui nous unissent au

In addition to the archival abbreviations generally used in this volume, the following additional abbreviations are used in the footnotes to this chapter:

AST: Archivio di Stato di Torino	AAE: Archives du Ministère des Affaires Etrangères, Paris
LC: Lettere della Corte	CPR: Correspondance politique, Rome
LMF: Lettere Ministri Francia	CPS: Correspondance politique, Sardaigne
LMGB: Lettere Ministri Gran Bretagna	AEG: Archives d'Etat, Geneva
LMS: Lettere Ministri Spagna	RC: Registre du Conseil

Parts of this article were first presented as a paper in 1988 at the annual conference of the International Commission for the Study of Parliamentary and Representative Institutions held at the University of Durham. I am very happy to thank Dr John Rogister (University of Durham) for having invited me to deliver a paper, Professor Salvo Mastellone (Università degli Studi di Firenze) for having chaired the session, and the other participants, Professor H. G. Koenigsberger and Dr Dorothy Koenigsberger, Graham Gibbs, Prof. Dr Klaus Malettke (Phillipps-Universität, Marburg), Dr Lothar Höbelt (Universität Wien, Wien), Prof. Dr Armin Wolf (Max Planck Institut, Frankfurt-am-Main). Professor Ragnhild Hatton made many comments on the typescript, and it is difficult to find words to express my gratitude for her support. In addition several colleagues made important contributions: Le rév. Père Jean-Robert Armogarthe (Ecole Pratique des Hautes Etudes, Paris), Dott. Cesare Enrico Bertana (Soprintendenza per i monumenti storici, Torino), Dr Marie-Thérèse Bouquet-Boyer (CNRS, Paris), Dr Rohan Butler, Le rév. Père Jean-Marie Charles-Roux, Professor Giorgio Chittolini (Università degli Studi di Milano), Irene Cioffi, Dr Eveline Cruickshanks (History of Parliament, London), Dott.ssa Rosalba Davico (Università degli Studi di Torino), William Davies, the Rev. G. M. Dilworth (Scottish Catholic Archives, Edinburgh), Dr Lionel Glassey (University of Glasgow), Professor Jonathan Israel (University College, University of London), Dott. Sandro Lombardini (Università degli Studi di Torino), Professor Cesare Mozzarelli (Università degli Studi di Trento), Professor Geoffrey Parker (University of Illinois, Champagne-Urbana) and Dr Jane Parker, il Conte Prunas Tola, Dr Christine Shaw, and Dr Janet Southorn. My debt to my two closest colleagues in Piedmontese studies in the Anglo-American world, Christopher Storrs and Professor Geoffrey Symcox (UCLA, Los Angeles), is so large that it merits a sentence to itself. It is always the greatest pleasure to acknowledge the assistance of the staffs of the archives and libraries without whose help research would have been impossible; in the first place the entire staff of the Archivio di Stato di Torino, with special thanks to Dott.ssa Isabella Massabò Ricci, Dott. Marco Carassi, Dott.ssa Elisa Mongiano, Dott.ssa Federica Paglieri, Dott.ssa Anna Marsaglia, Dott.ssa Maria Gattullo, and Dott.ssa Elisabetta Giuriolo; and also to the equipe of the Archives d'Etat de Genève and to my dear friend Dr Barbara Roth-Lochner. The help given by the staffs of the Archives du Ministère des Affaires Etrangères, Paris; the British Library, London; the London Library, London; and the Public Record Office, London, has been invaluable. The encouragement given to my work on the House of Savoy by HM Queen Marie-José of Italy and HRH the Princess Maria Gabriella of Italy merits particular attention. To Nicholas Oresko, CMH, to Roger Clark, to Alexander Clark, and to Dr David Parrott (University of York) go the deepest thanks for their loving support and criticism. This article is dedicated to the memory of Harry Hatton.

Roy d'Angleterre ... nous a fait ressentir une joye infinie de l'heureuse naissance de M. le Prince de Galles', and the duke reminded Roero that James II 'est l'oncle maternal de Madama la Duchesse Royale',[1] Anna Maria d'Orléans, Vittorio Amedeo's consort. Such missions of courtesy to commemorate great dynastic moments, births, marriages, and deaths, were a commonplace of diplomatic intercourse in early modern Europe, but they should not be viewed as an empty ritual void of importance. The dispatch of an envoy to compliment or to condole with a crowned head enabled princes of the second and third ranks to draw public attention to the closeness of their blood links with those royal dynasties of the first rank, the Houses of Bourbon, of Habsburg, and of Stuart. Vittorio Amedeo may have had an additional reason for sending Roero as there is a suggestion that, not uncharacteristically, James looked with less than full favour upon his younger Savoyard kinsman. Certainly, Roero reported to his master that his initial audience with the king had been so warm that 'je sortis bien désabusé de ce que l'on m'avoit supposé à Paris. Il m'a dit avec plaisir ... qu'il consideroit M. le Duc de Savoye comme son meilleur amy et parent.'[2] As this interview took place early in October 1688, when James was anything but satisfied with the comportment of his immediate family, such expressions of affection for the House of Savoy may well have been more than rhetorical flourish.

Roero was caught up in all of the tumult surrounding William III's invasion and what can only be described as the panic at James II's court. Roero finally left London on 20 December 1688, taking with him, disguised as members of his suite, the papal nuncio and the Modenese envoy. Shortly afterwards, however, Vittorio Amedeo's minister in Paris, the marchese Dogliani, informed the court of Turin of Roero's arrest and detention at Canterbury and asked for instructions. Securing Roero's release posed considerable difficulties. The duke suggested that Dogliani write to the Maréchal Schomberg and request his intervention and enclosed a draft letter. This was necessary, Vittorio Amedeo explained, 'puisque nous n'avons aucun commerce de lettres avec M. le Prince d'Oranges ni avec M. le Prince de Dannemark,' the husband of Princess Anne Stuart.[3] A passport from William III eventually arrived.[4]

If in early 1689 there was no correspondence between the Prince of Orange

[1] AST, Materie politiche: Inghilterra, m. 1, no. 25: Istruzione al Conte Rovere (*sic*) mandato in Inghilterra per contratularsi sulla nascità del Principe di Galles.

[2] AST, LMGB, m. 7, Roero to Vittorio Amedeo II, 7 Oct. 1688. Many of Roero's dispatches were published in Ermanno Ferrero, 'La rivoluzione inglese del 1688: l'inviato di Savoia a Londra', *Memorie della Accademia delle Scienze di Torino*, ser. II, 32 (1880), pp. 113–53.

[3] AST, LC, m. 80, fo. 3410: Vittorio Amedeo II to Dogliani, [?1 Jan.] 1689.

[4] BL MS Add. 25377, fo. 221, Francesco Terriesi to the abbate Apollonio Bassetti, 31 Dec. 1688: 'Sono quindici giorni che arrestavono a Canterbury l'inviato di Pollonia e quello di Savoja ... ma ora sperarsi che partiramo, havendo questo giorno havuto quello [passaporto] del Principe d'Oranges.' I am grateful to Professor Jonathan Israel for directing my attention to the volumes of transcripts of the letters of Francesco Terriesi, the Tuscan minister in London, in the British Library, London.

and the duke of Savoy, who were second cousins[5], that situation changed dramatically during the following eighteen months. In July 1690, Vittorio Amedeo wrote directly to William, informing him that 'Les mouvements de coeur et les autres pressantes considérations qui me font souhaiter l'honneur de la protection de Votre Majesté m'engagent à ordonner au Président de La Tour de passer à Londres pour l'en supplier',[6] and on 20 October La Tour signed at The Hague, in Vittorio Amedeo's name, the treaty of alliance with England and the United Provinces which formally brought Savoy into 'la cause commune', war against Louis XIV.[7] With this treaty, the duchy of Savoy and its duke 'emerged for the first time into the limelight of European politics' and became a focus of British interest.[8]

Vittorio Amedeo followed the dramatic events of 1688 closely and demanded precise details from Roero, who had managed to send a copy in Italian of William's declaration,[9] and from Dogliani, who was kept well informed by the duke's father-in-law, the duc d'Orléans, Monsieur, Louis XIV's only brother. The young duke of Savoy fully realized at an early date that 'du succès de ce dessein [William's projected invasion] dépendent des suites de la dernière importance aux affaires présentes de l'Europe',[10] and his initial reaction to the unfolding events in England was characteristic of that of most Catholic princes, even those with good reason to welcome a change of regime in London.[11] He deplored the attack upon an anointed brother sovereign, and he feared for the fate of his Catholic co-religionists in Britain.[12] He paid to the marquis d'Arcy, Louis XIV's ambassador in Turin, 'mille compliments et dix mille douceurs pour V. M. de la gloire qu'Elle a de donner azile avec tant de generosité au Roy, à la Reine d'Angleterre et au Prince de Galles leur fils, dans les conjonctures présentes'[13] and he sent letters for Dogliani to present to James II and Maria Beatrice.

[5] William III's maternal grandmother, Henrietta Maria of France, queen of England, and Vittorio Amedeo II's paternal grandmother, Marie-Christine of France, duchess of Savoy, were sisters, the daughters of Henri IV, king of France, and Marie de'Medici of Tuscany.

[6] PRO SP 92, fo. 175, Vittorio Amedeo II to William III, 15 July 1690.

[7] PRO, SP 108–442.

[8] Stuart Woolf, 'English Public Opinion and the Duchy of Savoy', *English Miscellany*, 12 (1961), p. 211.

[9] AST, LMF, m. 122, Dogliani to the marchese San Tommaso, 8 Dec. 1688.

[10] AST, LC, m. 79, fo. 2086, Vittorio Amedeo II to Dogliani,16 Oct. 1688.

[11] Lothar Höbelt has analysed Emperor Leopold I's misgivings of conscience over James II's deposition in an as yet unpublished paper, 'Imperial Diplomacy and the Glorious Revolution', presented at the Durham conference in 1988. I am most grateful to Dr Höbelt for sending me a copy of his text. Other aspects of Habsburg policy in 1689 are addressed in Lothar Höbelt, 'Die Sackgasse aus dem Zweifrontenkrieg: Die Friedensverhandlungen mit den Osmanen 1689', *Mitteilungen des Instituts für österreichische Geschichtsforschung*, 97 (1989), pp. 329–80.

[12] AAE, CPS, vol. 88–9 (unpaginated, d'Arcy to Louis XIV, 30 Oct. 1688: '[Vittorio Amedeo] m'a tesmoigné ... du chagrin de ce que je luy appris en mesme temps qu'il estoit beaucoup à craindre que le Prince d'Oranges n'abolit entièrement la Religion Catholique en Angleterre s'il réussissoit à entrer dans ce pays-là.'

[13] AAE, CPS, vol. 88–9: d'Arcy to Louis XIV, 22 Jan. 1689.

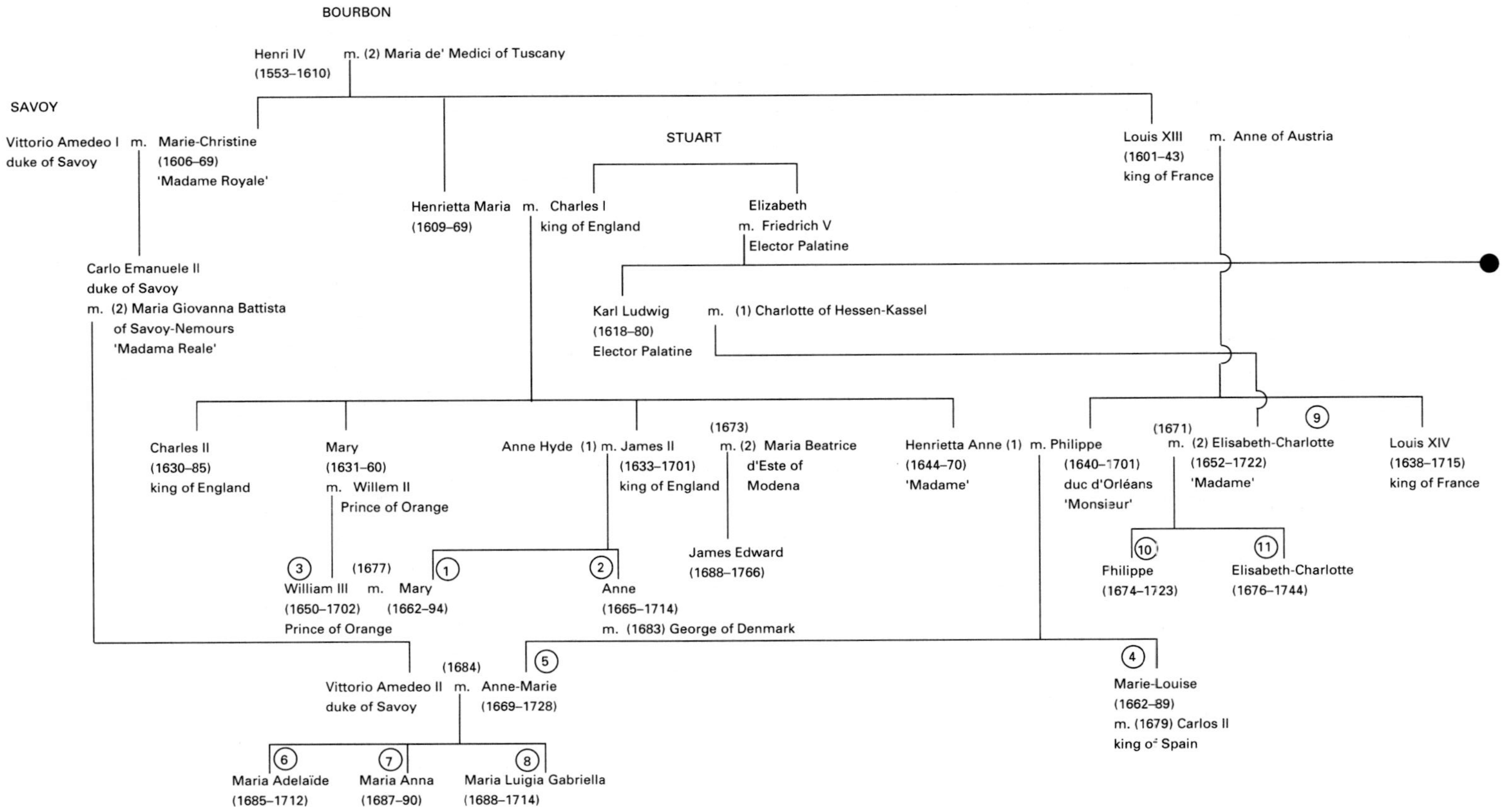
BOURBON
Henri IV (1553–1610) m. (2) Maria de' Medici of Tuscany
SAVOY
Vittorio Amedeo I duke of Savoy m. Marie-Christine (1606–69) 'Madame Royale'
Henrietta Maria (1609–69) m. Charles I king of England
STUART
Elizabeth m. Friedrich V Elector Palatine
Louis XIII (1601–43) king of France m. Anne of Austria
Carlo Emanuele II duke of Savoy m. (2) Maria Giovanna Battista of Savoy-Nemours 'Madama Reale'
Karl Ludwig (1618–80) Elector Palatine m. (1) Charlotte of Hessen-Kassel
Charles II (1630–85) king of England
Mary (1631–60) m. Willem II Prince of Orange
Anne Hyde (1) m. James II (1633–1701) king of England
(1673) m. (2) Maria Beatrice d'Este of Modena
Henrietta Anne (1) (1644–70) 'Madame' m. Philippe (1640–1701) duc d'Orléans 'Monsieur'
(1671) m. (2) Elisabeth-Charlotte (1652–1722) 'Madame'
9
Louis XIV (1638–1715) king of France
James Edward (1688–1766)
10 Philippe (1674–1723)
11 Elisabeth-Charlotte (1676–1744)
3 William III (1650–1702) Prince of Orange (1677) m. 1 Mary (1662–94)
2 Anne (1665–1714) m. (1683) George of Denmark
(1684)
Vittorio Amedeo II duke of Savoy m. 5 Anne-Marie (1669–1728)
4 Marie-Louise (1662–89) m. (1679) Carlos II king of Spain
6 Maria Adelaïde (1685–1712)
7 Maria Anna (1687–90)
8 Maria Luigia Gabriella (1688–1714)

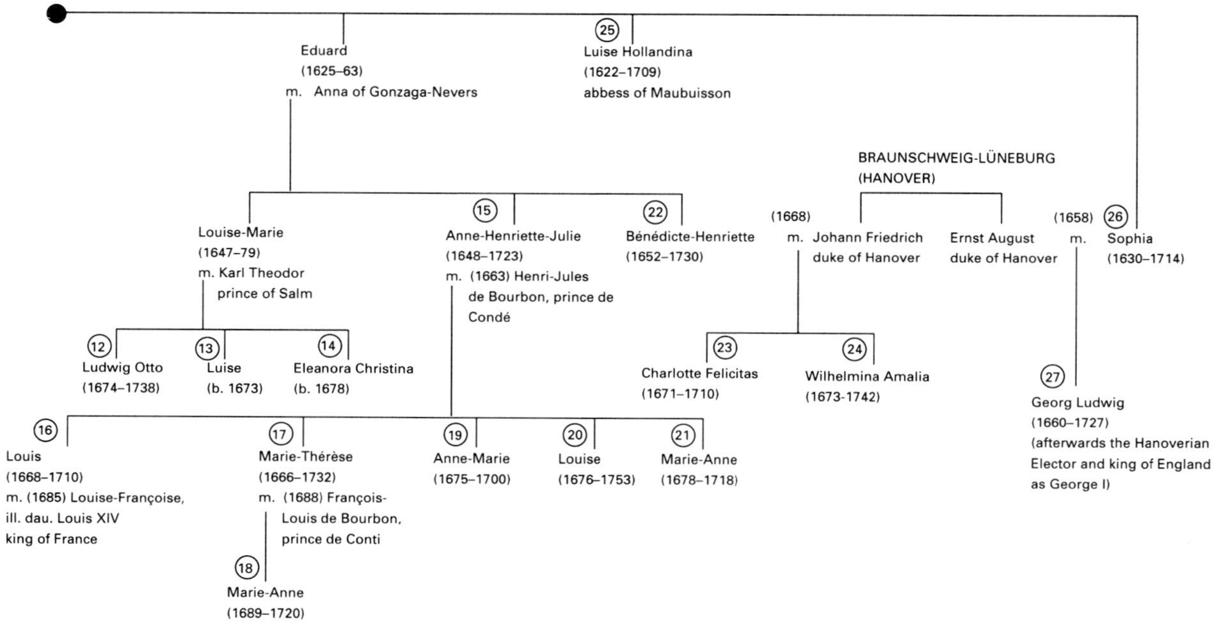

Genealogical table. The English succession at the time of the 'flight' of James II (December 1688).

Note: ringed numbers indicate the order of succession at the time of James II's flight.

Sources: Père Anselme, *Histoire généalogique et chronologique de la Maison royale de France* . . . (Paris, 1712); Ragnhild Hatton, *George I, Elector and King* (London, 1978); Wilhelm Karl, Prinz von Isenburg, and Frank, Baron Freytag von Loringhoven, *Stammtafeln zur Geschichte der europäischen Staaten* (Marburg, 1953–7); Pierre de La Condamine, *Salm en Vosges* (Paris, 1974); Conte Pompeo Litta, *Celebri famiglie italiane* (Milan, 1819–99); Adriaan Vliegenthart, *Bildersammlung der Fürsten zu Salm* (Zutphen, 1981); David Williamson, *Burke's Royal Families of the World*, I: *Europe and Latin America* (London, 1977).

This geneaological table presents the state of the English succession in December 1688–January 1689, just after James II's flight, and it proceeds on the assumption that both the king and the infant Prince of Wales were excluded from the succession. Reference to birth and death dates and to marriages which did not touch on the question of the English succession at this point have been eliminated, and the arrangement of the table has aimed at clarifying dynastic relationships rather than ensuring that an elder child always appears in a senior position to his younger siblings. Marie-Anne de Bourbon-Conti, not born until April 1689, has been included as no. 18, as her mother was advanced enough in her pregnancy to permit an addition to the list of possible claimants.

The Revolution of 1688 was, of course, anything but an overnight phenomenon, and it was only as 1689 progressed that the exact nature of the new settlement became clear, giving the European sovereignties time to adjust themselves to the radical changes in Great Britain. It was as late as July 1689 that Dogliani was able to inform Vittorio Amedeo that 'L'ambassade d'Espagne à Londres a enfin receu l'ordre de reconnoitre le Prince d'Orange Roy de Grande Bretagne',[14] and the duke followed closely the reactions of other princes, especially other Catholic princes, to the proclamation and the coronation of William III and Mary II as joint king and queen of Great Britain and to the official notifications of their accession sent to their brother sovereigns. Vittorio Amedeo had received such a letter, and he was especially eager to monitor the movements of his two Wittelsbach first cousins, the Bavarian elector, Max II Emmanuel, married to the Emperor Leopold I's daughter, and the Cologne Elector, Josef Klemens.[15] Early in June 1689 'Habbiamo osservato che cotesto Ser. Elettore di Colonia non ha pur anche risposse alla ... lettera del preteso nuovo re d'Inghilterra, desideriamo però di sapere se il Ser. mo Elettore di Baviera sospenda similarmente di rispondergli',[16] and in another letter of exactly the same date he stressed the need 'di sapere se gli altri elettori e principi dell Impero ... habbiano risposse alla ... lettera del preteso nuovo Re d'Inghilterra'.[17] By the end of July, 'non habbiamo stimato di dover rispondere ad una lettera colla quale ci ha participata la sua assuntione al trono d'Inghilterra',[18] and as late as September 1689 'stiamo sempre nell'impazienza di sapere se Illst. Elettore di Baviera come quello di Colonia, suo fratello, habbino risposto al Principe d'Oranges sopra la sua elevazione al trono d'Inghilterra'.[19] Recognition of William and Mary was inextricably linked to the densely complicated relationship of the duke of Savoy with the king of France.

The political revolution of 1688–9 in Great Britain coincided with and, indeed, may have helped to spur Vittorio Amedeo's efforts not so much to reverse his

[14] AST, LMF, m. 122, no. 239, Dogliani to Vittorio Amedeo II, 25 July 1689.

[15] Vittorio Amedeo's father, Carlo Emanuele II, duke of Savoy, and the electors' mother, Adelaïda Enrichetta, were brother and sister. Relations between the courts of Turin and Munich and, indeed, personally between Vittorio Amedeo and Max Emmanuel were particularly close in the last quarter of the seventeenth century, as was evidenced by the meeting of the cousins at the carnival in Venice of 1687 (V. Dainotti, 'Vittorio Amedeo II a Venezia nel 1687 e la lega di Augusta', *Bollettino storico-bibliografico subalpino*, 25 (1933), pp. 434–77). One sister of Max Emmanuel and Josef Klemens was the Dauphine Marie-Anne-Victoire-Christine, an important supporter of the House of Savoy at the court of her father-in-law, Louis XIV. In 1688, Roero, en route for the court of St James, passed through Paris, and Vittorio Amedeo's instructions for his visits to the court of Versailles specified that 'Madame la Dauphine conserve pour nous et pour cette royale Maison des sentiments de bonté que nous devons cultiver soigneusement ... Vous la supplierez instemment de vouloir rappeller le souvenir de ce que luy aura dit souvent feue Madame l'Electrice en notre faveur' (AST, Materie politche: Inghilterra, m. 1, no. 25).

[16] AST, LC. m. 80: Vittorio Amedeo II to the abbate Lauteri, 4 June 1689.

[17] AST, LC, m. 80: Vittorio Amedeo II to Cavour, 4 June 1689.

[18] AST, LC, m. 81: Vittorio Amedeo II to Gorone, 23 July 1689.

[19] AST, LC, m. 81: Vittorio Amedeo II to the abbate Lauteri, 17 Sept. 1689.

alliance system as to redefine the nature of his relationship with Louis XIV. Maria Giovanna Battista of Savoy-Nemours, the second Madama Reale, had, unwillingly, relinquished her regency in 1685, and, on assuming the direction of policy, Vittorio Amedeo, her only child, was faced with the problems created by his mother's dependence upon the French court for support against the factions in Turin opposed to her government. The young duke, who had inherited in full measure the energy and intellectual concentration of his formidable mother, gave early notice of his desire to diminish the level of consultation with Versailles before decisions were taken in Turin and to extract himself from the necessity of obtaining Louis' authorization before taking action. This need not automatically have implied entrance into an alliance hostile to France, and for much of 1688 and 1689 and, indeed, up to the entry of Catinat's army into Piedmont in the spring of 1690, Vittorio Amedeo seemed to be aiming at a position of neutrality in the armed conflict which had become, clearly, inevitable. Neutrality, however, obviously entailed establishing some form of relationship with both branches of the House of Habsburg, as well as maintaining an accord with the House of France, a situation which Louis XIV had taken pains to circumscribe during the regency of Madama Reale. Versailles viewed with irritation, followed by anger rather than alarm, the steps taken by the duke to establish contact with the courts of Madrid and Vienna and reacted violently to Vittorio Amedeo's negotiations with Leopold I for the purchase of a number of imperial fiefs enclaved within Savoyard territory and for the grant by the two Habsburg courts to Vittorio Amedeo of the *trattamento reale*, perhaps the central pylon of Savoy House policy from the accession of Vittorio Amedeo I in 1630. The recognition of the 'royal', as opposed to 'serene', status of the House of Savoy and of the right of its envoys to take their place as emissaries of crowned heads had the most important implications for territorial aggrandizement and dynastic advancement. In attempting to strike a balance between, on the one hand, Louis XIV of France, and, on the other, Emperor Leopold I and King Carlos II of Spain, Vittorio Amedeo was obliged to take into consideration the needs and sensibilities of the sovereign who was emerging as the most important ally of the Habsburg cause, William III, hereditary Prince of Orange, Stadholder of five and captain-general of all of the United Provinces and, from April 1689, crowned king of England.[20]

It is possible to observe, during the course of 1689, a number of adjustments to Savoyard policy aimed at eliminating any offence to William III, which, nevertheless, stopped short of formal recognition of his British titles, a step which would have entailed a definite break with France. In the first instance, Vittorio

[20] The alteration of the relationship of the duke of Savoy with the king of France is analysed in much greater detail in Robert Oresko, 'The Diplomatic Background to the Glorioso Rimpatrio: the Rupture between Vitorio Amedeo II and Louis XIV (1688–1690)', in *Dall' Europa alle Valli Valdesi* (Turin, 1990) (ed. Albert de Lange), the published acts of the 1989 conference held at Torre Pellice.

Amedeo began to distance himself from the exiled Stuarts. In January 1689, Dogliani was eager to pay an official visit to James II on his master's behalf to assure the king 'de la part singulier que V.A.R. prend en son malheur' and assumed that he would be received by the king as the envoy of a royal, crowned sovereign, that is to say, that the ambassador would have remained covered during the audience. 'Je fus surpris ... que le Roy me verroit tout seul dans son cabinet, sans me faire couvrir, ne pouvant me recevoir en ceremonie pour avoir promis au Roy de France de n'en faire ny d'en souffrir aucune pendant qu'il seroit dans ses états.'[21] The problem of etiquette proved insurmountable, but by May there was some possibility that Dogliani could be received incognito by Queen Maria Beatrice, and he wrote to Vittorio Amedeo to 'luy représenter qu'il me semble qu'il seroit à propos que je luy portasse quelque lettre de V.A.R. et comme celles que j'ay entre les mains pour leurs Mtés B. sont de trop vieilles dates, je les renvoy afin qu'on en mette une plus fraiche à celle de la Reine'.[22] Dogliani's audience with Maria Beatrice did not, however, take place until October and although he expressed verbally his master's sympathy for his exiled British cousins, he presented nothing in writing from Vittorio Amedeo 'Quoi que V.A.R. ne trouve plus à propos que je remette sa lettre à la Reine d'Angleterre.'[23] Throughout 1689, therefore, there was no epistolary contact between Vittorio Amedeo II and James II, and by the time that such contact became feasible, the duke of Savoy had become disinclined to make such a public statement of support for the House of Stuart.

But if, during this period, Vittorio Amedeo grew cooler to the exiled king of England, James, for his part, became increasingly eager to establish some rapport with his Savoyard kinsman. In April 1689, James had despatched Bevil Skelton on a mission to Venice and Vienna, with instructions to stop en route at Turin to solicit Vittorio Amedeo's support. Skelton's visit coincided with one of the more enigmatic episodes of Vittorio Amedeo's reign, his extended stay in the remote and isolated county of Nice. The 'viaggio a Nizza' may well have reflected the psycho-sexual crisis in the duke's private life, as retreat from Turin facilitated the *glissements* from coqueterie to consummation and then to commitment in his relationship with the contessa di Verrua, the wife of a member of the Scaglia family but also the daughter of the duc de Luynes and a Rohan princess.[24] The extended absence of the duke from his capital seems also to have had political implications, as Vittorio Amedeo was careful to include in his party his cousin, the deaf-mute principe di Carignano, the focus of Habsburg sentiment in Turin, while courteously but firmly blocking the participation

[21] AST, LMF, m. 122, no. 170, Dogliani to Vittorio Amedeo II, 24 Jan. 1689.
[22] AST, LMF, m. 122, no. 215, Dogliani to Vittorio Amedeo II, 23 May 1689.
[23] AST, LMF, m. 122, no. 296: Dogliani to Vittorio Amedeo II, 5 Dec. 1689.
[24] G. de Léris, *La comtesse de Verrue et la cour de Victor Amédée II de Savoie* (Paris, 1881), pp. 64–77.

of the pro-French Madama Reale.[25] D'Arcy, the French ambassador, noted that Skelton

> ayant trouvé que cette cour et moy en [from Turin] estions partis, il a pris la résolution d'escrire au marquis de Saint-Thomas pour le prier de temoigner à Monsieur le Duc de Savoye son déplaissir extrême, de ce que les affaires du Roy d'Angleterre qui l'appelloient incessement à Vienne, l'empeschoit de venir icy [to Nice], pour avoir l'honneur de l'y voir et pour s'acquitter de vive voix de la commission dont il estoit chargé du Roy son maistre auprès de ce prince.[26]

Vittorio Amedeo wrote that 'Nous luy avons fait faire une reponse fort obligeante sur laquelle il poursuivra son voyage',[27] but when Skelton passed through Turin a second time, in July, returning empty-handed from his visits to Venice and Vienna, he was disappointed yet again to find the duke still absent, and this neglect was noted by d'Arcy.

> M. Skelton partit de Turin pour retourner en France, après avoir demeurer en cette ville là plus d'une quinzaine de jours. (Il est étonnant que pendant tout ce temps là M. le Duc de Savoye, qui l'y sçavoit et pendant celuy qu'il y demeura lors qu'il vint il y a trois mois, ne luy aye fait faire aucune honnesteté ny offre de service. Il en receu toutes sortes de Madame Royale [Maria Giovanna Battista], dont je crois bien il se louera) jusques là qu'encore que (cette princesse n'ait qu'un revenu fort mediocre et borné. Elle a fait defrayer M. Skelton, sa famille et toute sa suite dans l'auberg où il a logé et mangé à Turin), tant lorsqu'il est venu que lorsqu'il est revenu principalement à cause qu' (elle sçait que c'est un ministre bien intentionné pour la France et que Votre Majesté protége de toute sa puissance son maistre malheureux. Pour le procedé de cette cour cy) à l'égard de M. Skelton, on peut remarquer (combien peu on s'y regle par ses véritables intérêts et par les sentiments de la bienseance, Madame la Duchesse de Savoye [Anna Maria] estant aussi proche heritière qu'elle est de la couronne d'Angleterre.)[28]

Vittorio Amedeo's reluctance to displace himself in order to see James II's envoy was thrown into sharper relief by his willingness to consider a lightning visit in May to Turin from Nice for reasons which d'Arcy could not fathom,[29] but which were, most certainly, not attached to Skelton's visit. D'Arcy also focused precisely upon the link between Vittorio Amedeo's reluctance to see Skelton and the proximity of the Duchess Anna Maria to the British thrones. Any public reception of Skelton was likely to offend William III, but not solely because he was the envoy of James II. Shrewd observer of political affinities that she was, Maria Giovanna Battista was not alone in marking out Skelton

[25] I shall address myself to the composition, the cost, and the purposes of the voyage to Nice in a future article.
[26] AAE, CPS, vol. 90, fo. 94, d'Arcy to Louis XIV, 20 Apr. 1689. D'Arcy had accompanied Vittorio Amedeo to Nice in order to keep him, as much as was possible, under French surveillance, as he had, in similar fashion, followed him to Venice in 1687 (Dainotti, 'Vittorio Amedeo II', p. 450).
[27] AST, LC, m. 80, fo. 3582, Vittorio Amedeo II to Dogliani, 15 Apr. 1689.
[28] AAE, CPS, vol. 90, fo. 204, d'Arcy to Louis XIV, 23 July 1689. Parentheses indicate de-ciphered passages.
[29] AAE, CPS, vol. 90, fo. 112, d'Arcy to Louis XIV, 10 May 1689.

as 'bien intentioné pour la France': in 1679 Charles II of England 'wanted to send Bevil Skelton to ... [The Hague], but the Prince [William III] and Pensionary Caspar Fagel refused to accept Skelton, because he had exhibited pro-French tendencies at Vienna'.[30] Although Vittorio Amedeo avoided receiving Skelton officially and ceremoniously in his capital, he, nevertheless, seems to have seen, under circumstances which remain unclear, one emissary from James II during the stay at Nice.[31]

Vittorio Amedeo's public attempt to distance himself from the Stuart cause was complemented by discretion on issues which could prove embarrassing for William III. In 1688, the abbé Jean-Paul de La Roque, who had, until 1687, been the editor of the *Journal des Savants*,[32] proposed writing an account of

[30] Phyllis Lachs, *The Diplomatic Corps under Charles II and James II* (New Brunswick, 1965), p. 60.

[31] James II's diplomatic activity in the years immediately following his flight from England has not been adequately studied. In April 1689, Vittorio Amedeo wrote to Gubernatis, his representative in Rome, that 'è capitato quà il milord di Porter qual habbiamo veduto volontieri' (AST, LC, m. 80, fo. 1877, Vittorio Amedeo II to Gubernatis, 26 Apr. 1689). A few days later, the duke reported that 'M. Porter est venue fort à propos dans le temps qu'il a passé icy de retour de Rome et qu'il a desiré de nous voir, disant qu'il en avoit ordre du Roy son maitre et de nous assurer de son amitié, nous l'avons vu volontiers et luy avons temoigné que nous prendrons toujours un interest tout particulier en [tout ce qui concerne] ... Sa Majesté' (AST, LC, m. 80, fo. 3898, Vittorio Amedeo II to Dogliani, 30 Apr. 1689). Vittorio Amedeo and his entourage had arrived in Nice on 15 April (de Léris, *La comtesse de Verrue*, p. 68). Dangeau recorded that 'Le Roi d'Angleterre envoie à Rome le chevalier Georges Porter, pour tâcher à faire entendre au pape [Innocente XI Odescalchi], qui est aussi difficile que jamais' (Philippe de Courcillon, marquis de Dangeau, *Journal du marquis de Dangeau*, ed. Eudox Soulié *et al.* (19 vols., Paris, 1854–60), II, p. 322: entry for 3 Feb. 1689), although it is clear that Dangeau was mistaken in one respect, as it was Francis Porter who was sent by James II to Rome (Bruno Neveu, 'Jacques II, médiateur entre Louis XIV et Innocent XI', *Mélanges d'Archéologie et d'Histoire de l'Ecole Française a Rome*, 79 (1967), pp. 741–2; and Jane Garrett, *The Triumphs of Providence: The Assassination Plot 1696* (Cambridge, 1980), pp. 32–3). It is clear, in spite of such confusions, that the Porter mission to Rome was a complete failure. According to Sourches, Porter 'assuroit que Sa Sainteté ne lui en [du secours] avoit pas voulu donner, disant qu'elle avoit besoin de son argent pour se défendre contre le Roi de France' (Louis-François de Bouchet, marquis de Sourches, *Mémoires du marquis de Sourches sur le règne de Louis XIV*, ed. Gabriel-Jules de Cosnac and Edouard Pontal (13 vols., Paris, 1882–93), III, p. 95: entry for 23 May 1689), while, subsequently, Lord Melfort urged the duc de Chaulnes, the French ambassador, to stress, in an audience with the new pope Alessandro VIII Ottoboni the 'sentiments peu favorables où estoient les Catholiques pour le feu Pape [Innocente XI] lors qu'ils sçeurent en Bretagne par le retour du sieur Porter qu'il n'avoit rien fait de tout pour le Roy d'Angleterre, qu'ils avoient exclamés contre feu Sa Sainteté et s'en étoient scandalizés au dernier point' (BL MS Add. 37660, fo. 114, Lord Melfort to Cardinal Rinaldo d'Este, 18 Feb. 1690). The proposed timetable for these confused and fumbling diplomatic exchanges between Vittorio Amedeo II and James II is, thus: 15 April 1689: the duke's arrival in Nice; immediately after 15 April: Skelton's arrival in Turin, en route to Venice and Vienna; no later than 26 April: the arrival in Nice of Porter, returning to France, with the details of his futile mission to Rome; July: second visit of Skelton to Turin, having failed to procure the aid of either the Venetian Republic or Emperor Leopold I. Vittorio Amedeo avoided seeing Skelton, deeply distrusted by William III, but saw Porter, in the relative obscurity of Nice, only on his return from his disastrous mission. The two versions of 'Instructions données à notre fidèle Jacques Porter et notre vice-chambellan', dated only February 1689 (AAE, CPR, vol. 326, fos. 44–7 and 58–62), deal exclusively with the papal negociations and make no mention of the duke of Savoy. It is a pleasure to record a special debt of gratitude to Dr Eveline Cruickshanks for her aid in helping me to unravel aspects of James II's diplomacy.

[32] Jean Segard, *Dictionnaire des journalistes (1600–1789)* (Grenoble, 1976). La Roque seems to have been particularly interested in questions of conversions, missions, and new churches, as evidenced by his article in the 11 December 1680 number of the *Journal des Savants*, and this may have attracted him to the subject of the Valdesi. Graham Gibbs, with characteristic generosity of spirit, drew my attention to elements of La Roque's career, and I am deeply indebted to his aid.

Vittorio Amedeo's armed expulsion of his Valdesi (Waldensian) subjects from their valleys. This military action had been demanded of the duke of Savoy by Louis XIV following the Revocation of the Edict of Nantes in 1685, and Vittorio Amedeo was, at most, a reluctant participant in the French king's quest for confessional homogeneity, more from a sharpened resentment of French bullying than from any anachronistic notions of toleration. Having been compelled to launch an attack upon his Protestant subjects, the duke was, characteristically, concerned to extract the maximum credit from the humiliation of obeying Louis' commands. Vittorio Amedeo gave his consent to La Roque's project in September 1688,[33] and, in reply to a request from La Roque for assistance in assembling the documents for his study, he observed that 'Nous ne sommes pas seulement bien aisés que ce partie d'histoire qui nous regarde soit l'ouvrage d'une plume aussi distinguée que la sienne, mais nous luy savons ... bon gré des sentiments d'affection et de zèle qui luy en ont inspiré le dessein. Nous ferons préparer tous les mémoires qu'il demande.'[34] England was still the subject of rumour and conjecture. As William and Mary's establishment became more secure, Vittorio Amedeo's enthusiasm for La Roque's adulatory éloge of his attempt to eradicate from his domains the presence of the new king and queen's co-religionists diminished correspondingly. By early July 1689, Cullet, the secretary of the Savoyard mission to Versailles, reported to Carlo Giuseppe di Carron, marchese di San Tommaso that 'J'ay prié M. l'abbé de La Roque de suspendre encore quelque temps de faire imprimer son livre',[35] and subsequent correspondence attests to La Roque's resentment at what was, quite clearly, the withdrawal of the duke's encouragement for celebrating an event which threatened to become a diplomatic embarrassment.[36]

As Vittorio Amedeo proceeded to detach himself from the Stuarts, he profited from a number of family ties to establish and to maintain contact with those courts aligned against Louis XIV. His cousins, Prince Eugene of Savoy and Ludwig Wilhelm, Markgraf of Baden-Baden[37] were firmly installed in imperial service, and his Wittelsbach cousins were also allies of the emperor. Within the first week of 1689, a prince of the House of Pfalz-Neuburg, a younger brother of

[33] AST, LC, m. 79, fos. 2995–6, Vittorio Amedeo II to Cullet, 25 Sept. 1688: 'nous sommes fort agrés que la reduction des vallées de Luserne y soit comprise et qu'elle soit publiée par une plume aussy illustre'.

[34] AST, LC, m. 79, fo. 3105, Vittorio Amedeo II to Cullet, 16 Oct. 1688.

[35] AST, LMF, m. 121, no. 165, Cullet to San Tommaso, 4 July 1689.

[36] AST, LMF, m. 121, no. 187, contains a number of letters from La Roque complaining of the court of Turin's revised attitude to his project and its lack of co-operation.

[37] Ludwig Wilhelm of Baden-Baden was the son of Luigia Cristina of Savoy-Carignano, the sister of Emanuele Filiberto, principe di Carignano, first prince of the blood of Savoy, heir apparent to the throne of Savoy as long as Vittorio Amedeo was without a legitimate son and leader of the Habsburg faction at the court of Turin, a role which paralleled that of Vittorio Amedeo's mother, Maria Giovanna Battista, as the principal animator of the French grouping.

Leopold I's consort, the Empress Eleanora Magdalene, had established himself in Turin, ostensibly to study at the academy.[38]

The duke of Savoy's initial relations with William III were less direct. As is obvious from the documentation surrounding the arrest of Roero, there seems to have been some correspondence between Vittorio Amedeo and Schomberg. Schomberg's third son, Meinhard, had, in 1683, married Karoline von Degenfeld, one of the morganatic brood fathered by the Elector Palatine Karl I Ludwig, thus making her a half-sister of Elisabeth Charlotte of the Palatinate, the second wife of Monsieur and, therefore, the step-mother of Vittorio Amedeo's consort, Anna Maria d'Orléans. The second Madame was on particularly good terms with both her Degenfeld half-siblings and with her younger step-daughter, to whom she wrote every week.[39] Indeed, she was also in epistolary contact with the Schomberg family, then in Berlin, in 1688, complaining of the silence of the maréchal and his wife.[40] The entourage of Monsieur, which, thanks to the presence of the chevalier de Lorraine, his lover and acknowledged favourite, had the possibility of access to Vienna,[41] and that of Madame, with her endearing enthusiasm for her 'German' relations, gave the circle at Saint-Cloud and at the Palais-Royal a dimension of supranational flexibility quite distinct from the court maintained by Monsieur's brother, Louis XIV, at Versailles. Vittorio Ame-

[38] This is a problematic episode. D'Arcy reported to Louis XIV that 'Un des plus jeunes princes de Neubourg est arrivé icy, qui presque aussitôt après est entré à l'Academie. Cette Academie se peuple fort de jeunes seigneurs allemands.' (AAE, CPS, vol. 90, fo. 9, d'Arcy to Louis XIV, 8 Jan. 1689.) Vittorio Amedeo was, immediately, more curious and made enquiries 'delle circonstanze concernenti la persona del Principe di Neuburgo e il di lui passaggio per cotestà città, sotto nome di conte di Vachtenta, professando di vivere del tutto incognito e così gionse giovedi in questa accademia e l'habiamo veduto hieri siera' (AST, LC, m. 80, fo. 3417, Vittorio Amedeo II to the conte di Landriani, 1 Jan. 1689). By March 1689, Maria Giovanna Battista was so agitated by the continued presence of the young Neuburg prince in Turin that she confided to the French ambassador information gleaned from her closest ally in Lisbon, the duque de Cadaval, that this 'cadet de la Maison de Neubourg, qui sous pretext de faire icy à l'Academie ses exercises n'y attendoit que l'ordre pour passer en Portugal' (de-ciphered passage) (AAE, CPS, vol. 90, fo. 55, d'Arcy to Louis XIV, 12 Mar. 1689) to marry the Infanta Isabel Luisa Josefa, the niece of Maria Giovanna Battista, who had initially been destined by Madama Reale to marry Vittorio Amedeo with the design of removing the young duke definitively from the duchy of Savoy (Geoffrey Symcox, *Victor Amadeus II* (London, 1983), pp. 82–9; and Louis Farges, 'L'Infante Isabelle de Portugal et ses dix-sept prétendants', *Revue d'Histoire Diplomatique* (1907), pp. 357–77). This already dense situation was complicated further by the fact that King Pedro II of Portugal, who had married first Marie-Françoise-Elisabeth of Savoy-Nemours, the sister of Maria Giovanna Battista, wed, secondly, in 1687, Maria Sophia of Pfalz-Neuburg, another sister of the Empress Eleanora Magdalene and of the Neuburg prince established in Turin. Even the precise identity of this Neuburg prince is uncertain, but Madama Reale's observation that he was a cadet of the bishop of Breslau probably means that it was either Friedrich Wilhelm (1665–89), killed in combat in July, or Philipp Wilhelm Augustus (1668–93). The numerous Neuburg children formed an important part in the matrimonial strategies of the House of Austria in the late seventeenth century.

[39] Dirk Van der Cruysse, *Madame Palatine* (Paris, 1988), p. 199.

[40] Madame Palatine (Elisabeth-Charlotte of the Palatinate, duchesse d'Orléans), *Lettres françaises*, ed. Dirk Van der Cruysse (Paris, 1989), pp. 81–3: 'Malgré toute la politesse et l'honnêteté dont vous couvrez votre longue silence, brusque et mal polie que [le] Seigneur m'a faite je me sens bien tentée de vous grondée un peu' (Madame to the maréchal and the maréchale de Schomberg, 11 Apr. 1688).

[41] In November 1689, for instance, the ailing Charles V, exiled duke of Lorraine, head of the imperial armies and the emperor's brother-in law, wrote to the chevalier, his kinsman, asking him to intervene with Louis XIV to arrange the dispatch of a French physician (Sourches, *Memoires*, III, p. 176: entry for 16 Nov. 1689).

deo's loveless marriage to the unexciting and self-sacrificing Anna Maria d'Orléans, therefore, brought, almost as an unspecified component of the dowry, both the goodwill of his father-in-law, Monsieur, with his constant access to the king of France,[42] and entry into the network of the 'German' protestant princes which was accorded to him by the princess who can only be described as his 'step-mother-in-law'. Madame's role was particularly important, for, in addition to securing the link with Schomberg, she opened up the access to the House of Hanover, at once the critical support for William III's invasion[43] and the primary opponent to any claims of the House of Savoy for the throne of England. The possibilities of such dynastic interchange had been abundantly clear at the end of 1688, when two of the younger Hanover princes, sons of Ernst August, and a Saxon prince visited the court of Turin on the specific encouragement of Madame and with her request to Vittorio Amedeo 'que V.A.R. leur feroit aussy beaucoup d'honnestetés'.[44] Louis XIV's vigilant efforts to regulate Vittorio Amedeo's relations with other princes, especially with those moving into alliance against France, were constantly frustrated by the workings of the dynastic system to which the duke belonged, by the geographic position of Turin as a natural stopping place en route to Italy and by the presence of the academy which acted as a magnet for foreigners.

It is still unclear precisely how, within this complex web of possibilities, Vittorio Amedeo made his accommodation with William III. The official letter of recognition, addressing William as 'Monseigneur', is dated 2 June 1690 and cites 'La providence divine qui a élevé V. M. au Trone.' The reference to the 'pressantes considérations qui ont fait une contrainte à mon coeur pour renfermer jusqu'à présent les sentiments devoués qui m'intéressent dans le bonheur de V.M.'[45] may well indicate that this was the first epistolary contact between

[42] The political role of Monsieur, a figure too frequently dismissed as an insignificant cipher, is discussed in greater detail in Oresko, 'The Diplomatic Background to the Glorioso Rimpatrio'. Nancy Barker, *Brother to the sun King: Philippe, Duke of Orléans* (Baltimore, 1989), attempts, not always successfully, to offer a much more subtle approach to the question of Monsieur's power and influence than any preceding biography.

[43] Ragnhild Hatton, *The Anglo-Hanoverian Connection, 1714–1760* (The Creighton Trust Lecture) (London, 1982), p. 8.

[44] AST, LMF, m. 122, no. 126, Dogliani to Vittorio Amedeo II, 1 Nov. 1688. Dogliani reported on 27 Dec. 1688 that 'Monsieur et Madame m'ont témoigné en presence de toute la cour des sentiments d'une parfaite reconnaissance de tant de honnestetés que V.A.R. avoit eü la bonté de faire aux princes d'Hannovre, qui ont écrit icy le plus obligeament du monde ... se louant infiniment de toutes les generosités de V.A.R. Madame m'a chargé de l'en remercier particulièrement de sa part' (m. 122, no. 155).

[45] AST, LC, m. 82, Vittorio Amedeo II to William III, 2 June 1690. The letter is also transcribed in Mario Viora, 'Notizie e documenti sugli interventi diplomatici dell' Inghilterra in favore dei Valdesi durante il regno di Vittorio Amedeo II', *Studi urbinati*, 2 (1928), p. 86. The French also acquired a copy of the letter, undated with slightly different wording, which is mis-filed in AAE, CPS, vol. 88–9, literally tucked into the back of this volume, which deals exclusively with 1688. A third version exists in BL MS Add. 38146, fo. 198, and a fourth copy was sent by Terriesi to Cosimo III de' Medici (BL MS Add. 25380, fo. 172) on 4 July 1690. I have yet to find the original letter in the Public Record Office, London.

the two princes.[46] Vittorio Amedeo went on to note 'que Dieu l'a choisie [i.e. Votre Majesté] comme un des principaux instruments pour arrêter la violence des puissances voisines', an obvious reference to Louis XIV, and this theme was subsequently elaborated upon by La Tour in his November audience with William. Once France was rendered powerless by the proposed invasion 'loin de saccager et de brûler, il faudroit au contraire publier par un manifeste ... qu'on veut rendre au Royaume son ancienne splendeur, restablissant les Estats Generaux dans tous leurs droits et les anciennes pairies de France en faveur des princes du sang et autres pour servir à l'avenir de barrière contre la puissance arbitraire et despotique'.[47] Early in June, the duke had also written to the States General of the United Provinces referring to the 'pauvres Vaudois mes sujets' and to his willingness to follow 'vos recommendations en faveur desdits Vaudois'.[48] Any appreciation of Vittorio Amedeo's rapid conversion to principles of restraint upon royal power and to some form of religious toleration must be tempered by the consideration that the principal beneficiaries of such an extraordinary constitutional restructuring of the French monarchy as proposed by La Tour would have been the duke's own father-in-law and brother-in-law, Monsieur and the duc de Chartres.

William III replied promptly to Vittorio Amedeo's letter, which he began, significantly, with the words 'Mon frère'. He had received the duke's missive

> avec une satisfaction très particulière, d'autant que j'ay considéré comme je devois la manière dont vous vous expliquez à l'égard de la puissance qui depuis bien du temps est la cause des malheurs de l'Europe. Je souhaiterois fort pour son repos que les autres princes d'Italie, jugeant comme ils devroient de l'honneur que vous est dû pour des résolutions si généreuses, voulussent entrer dans des sentiments semblables aux vôtres.[49]

William's letter underscored an important stand in his continental policy, as he hoped to profit from the coincidence of papal hostility to Louis XIV with a rare moment of Wittelsbach–Habsburg accord[50] to open the alliance to

[46] Camille Rousset, *Histoire de Louvois et de son administration politique et militaire* (4 vols., Paris, 1879), IIV, pp. 358–9, produces a transcription of Louis XIV's initial manifesto against Vittorio Amedeo, dated 22 June 1690, beginning with the words 'Le roi fut averti, vers le mois d'octobre dernier, que le prince d'Orange recevoit souvent des lettres de M. le duc de Savoie, et qu'il traitoit quelque chose entre le duc de Savoie et lui.'

[47] AST, LMGB, m. 8, La Tour to Vittorio Amedeo II, 24 Nov. 1690.

[48] BL MS Add, 38146, fo. 200, Vittorio Amedeo II to the States General, 2 June 1690.

[49] BL MS Add. 38146, fo. 198, William III to Vittorio Amedeo II, 26 June 1690.

[50] The traditional antagonisms and rivalry between the House of Wittelsbach, particularly the Bavarian branch, and the House of Habsburg were reconciled only temporarily during the seventeenth century, during the Thirty Years War when the electoral dignity was transferred from Heidelberg to Munich, and, in the 1680s and 1690s, when Elector Max II Emmanuel's son from his marriage to the Archduchess Maria Antonia, Leopold I's daughter by the Infanta Margarita Teresa, seemed to offer the best hope for the resolution of the problem of the Spanish succession. As soon as the prospect of further dynastic advancement receded or was removed, the Bavarian Wittelsbachs resumed their usual orientation towards France as a counterpoise to imperial power. In drafting instructions for a secret mission in 1691 to detach Max Emmanuel and Vittorio Amedeo from the anti-French alliance, Louis XIV stressed the need to make 'une forte grande impression dans l'esprit d'un Electeur de Bavière qui

a wide range of Catholic sovereignties in southern Europe. The adherence of Vittorio Amedeo II to the league ranged against Louis XIV was an important advance for this policy, and Terriesi reported to Cosimo III de' Medici, grand duke of Tuscany, that 'ora che s'è dichiarata contro la Francia pure la Savoja, credano tutti quelli [qui] . . . che Vostra Altezza Serenissima, Portogallo, li Veneziani, li Genovesi etc. non potranno di meno di non fare l'istesso'.[51] Indeed, in August 1690, Terriesi was informed that 'non vede il Gran Duca di poter più lungamente sospendere a Sua Maestà [William III] il rispetto dovuto di riconoscerla per regnante il quel trono'.[52]

William had, in fact, for some time appreciated the advantages, military as well as diplomatic, of attracting the duke of Savoy into the league against Louis XIV. No later than September 1689 he had written to Heinsius 'dat sij hoop hebben den hartog van Savoye in de partij te brengen',[53] and, strikingly, this letter coincided with a warning from Jules-Louis Bolé, marquis de Chamlay to Louvois to 'Prenez garde à la conduite de M. le Duc de Savoie; je sais . . . que le prince d'Europe qu'il estime et honore le plus, et qu'il souhaiteroit d'imiter davantage, est M. le Prince d'Orange'.[54] The strategic importance of the duke's adherence to the alliance was summarized in a mémoire originating from Zurich and dating from June 1690.

> Dans le dessein qu'ont les alliés d'humilier la France, il ne pouvoit rien arriver, après l'affaire d'Angleterre, de plus utile et de plus avantageux que le déclaration que le duc de Savoye vient de faire en leur faveur. Car pour venir facilement à bout de la France, ce qui est nécessaire dans une ligue, qui, ordinairement, ne

doit plus craindre qu'aucun autre l'augmentation de la puissance de l'empereur' (Horric de Beaucaire, *Recueil des instructions données aux ambassadeurs et ministres de France: Savoie-Sardaigne et Mantoue* (2 vols., Paris, 1898–9), I, p. 147: 'Mémoire du Roi pour servir d'instruction au sieur comte de Rébenac s'en allant vers les princes et états d'Italie pour le service de Sa Majesté' (13 Sep, 1691).

[51] BL MS Add. 35380, fo. 166, Francesco Terriesi to Cosimo III, 4 July 1690. There is a strong suggestion in Terriesi's correspondence that the reactions of the Portuguese and Tuscan courts to William III had been severely complicated by the death of the Dauphine in April 1690, as both the House of Bragança and the House of Medici had eligible princesses whom they were eager to marry to Louis XIV's widowed heir.

[52] BL MS Add. 25380, fo. 217, instructions sent to Francesco Terriesi, 22 Aug. 1690. The events of 1688–9 in Great Britain had significant implications for a number of the Italian sovereignties and they placed Cosimo III de' Medici in a particularly awkward position. Along with Leopold I, the Grand Duke enjoyed, deservedly, a reputation for piety and devotion, and, as the with emperor, William III's invasion and his assumption of the Crown caused him, for a variety of reasons, severe spiritual anxiety. Louis XIV's instructions to Rébenac for dealing with Cosimo during his 1691 mission, accordingly, stressed confessional elements in the military conflict: 'l'obstination de ce Prince [Vittorio Amedeo] à vouloir ruiner son pays et même la religion, l'ayant précipité dans le malheureux engagement où il se trouve, toute l'Italie se voit aujourd'hui remplie . . . d'une infinité de religionnaires [i.e Protestants] françois et de toutes les autres nations qui ne songent qu'à s'y introduire pour y établir leur erreur' (de Beaucaire, *Recueil*, p. 152). Against the claims of his own conscience and his desire to marry his favourite child, Anna Maria Ludovica de'Medici, to the dauphin, Cosimo III had to balance the decisive importance of British trade for the port of Livorno.

[53] G. Groen van Prinsterer, *Archives ou correspondance inédite de la maison d'Orange-Nassau*, 3rd ser. (1689–1702), ed. F. J. L. Krämer (5 vols., Leiden, 1907–9), I, p. 36: William III to Anthonie Heinsius, 20–30 Sept. 1689.

[54] Rousset, *Histoire de Louvois*, IV, p. 286, citing a letter in the Archives de la Guerre (Service historique de l'armée de la terre), Vincennes, dated 26 Sept. 1689.

> dure pas longtemps, il faut attaquer dans le coeur du royaume, ce qui est le seul moyen pour la réduire au point qu'on souhaitte.

The French-speaking lands of Vittorio Amedeo, principally the duchy of Savoy, offered three routes of penetration into France: through Bresse, 'où l'on peut aller en Franche-Comté [et] profiter de la bonne disposition où sont les Comtois de secouer le joug de France'; through Pont-Beauvoisin, leading, via the Rhône, to Lyons or Vienne; and through Montmélian, opening the way to Grenoble.

> La porte à entrer en France que les alliés trouvent par la Savoie ... est d'autant plus favourable que ... [le duché de] Savoie joint la province de Dauphiné, où celles de Languedoc et des Cevennes et Vivarais sont contigues, qui sont remplies de mécontents de l'une religion ou de l'autre, mais surtout de la religion reformée ... Le seul diocèse de Nimes contentant 98 mille âmes de cette religion.

The mémoire finally advised that 'il faut un prince qui soit à la teste des troupes françaises [the Huguenot troops] et le comte Charles de Schomberg pour capitaine-general'.[55] Invasion from the duchy of Savoy thus brought the additional possibility, as Terriesi viewed the situation from London, to 'formentare nel cuore della Francia una mortale guerra civile'.[56]

William III's evolving position in 1689 had obviously added tremendous weight to the cause of the League of Augsburg, with two of the members of which, the emperor and the king of Spain, Vittorio Amedeo was also in negotiations. When he was compelled to make the final break with Louis XIV, in the summer of 1690, the duke of Savoy turned immediately to the Protestant allies of his new Catholic allies for support and aid. In terms of military strategies and financial subventions William III and Vittorio Amedeo II had much to offer each other, and the exchanges leading to their alliance shed much light on the political assumptions, rhetoric, and aspirations which framed the creation of the most formidable coalition yet arrayed against Louis XIV. But if William III's transformed European position helped to facilitate the detachment of Savoy from a smothering French alliance which threatened to become a military protectorate, it also brought the king of England and the duke of Savoy into a relationship which made a notable impact on areas of Vittorio Amedeo's policy and outlook which extended well beyond those implicit in his membership in the new European system.

Nervousness over the abbé de La Roque's proposed paean to Vittorio Amedeo's

[55] PRO SP 8 [King William's Chest]/7, no. 43: Mémoire pour l'entrée dans la France, 'à Zurick, le 31 de mai (v.st.)'. The role of members of the Schomberg family as mediators between varying confessional elements of the European polity is underscored by the suggestion of the appointment of Charles Schomberg. Charles Schomberg was the fourth son of the maréchal, Friedrich Heinrich Schomberg, first duke of Schomberg, whom he succeeded as second duke, in preference to his elder brother, Meinhard, married into the Degenfeld family, who had not yet been naturalized at the time of their father's death in 1690. Meinhard succeeded as third duke at Charles' death at Turin, following the battle of Marsaglia, in 1693.

[56] BL MS Add. 25380, fo. 217, Francesco Terriesi to the segretaria di Firenze, 24 June/4 July 1690.

attempt to exterminate his Protestant subjects pointed to the first changes required by the emergence of William III in the duke's political thinking, as he had allied himself not only to the king of England but also to a prince who presented himself publicly as a defender of Protestantism. Vittorio Amedeo's treaty of alliance with England and the United Provinces, signed at The Hague on 20 October 1690, also contained a secret clause protecting the rights and privileges of the Valdesi, who had forced their way back into their valleys in September 1689 and who remained, despite their trials, a loyal and effective element in the duke's military planning.[57] From this point on, British governments assumed a benevolent protection of the Valdesi during those, not infrequent, periods, when Turin and London were in alliance, and the British ambassador to the court of Savoy, even into the reign of Vittorio Amedeo's son, Carlo Emanuele III (1730–73), appropriated the right to be consulted on any measures which affected the Valdesi and to pass on to London any complaints the Protestants chose to confide to him about their treatment by the central government in Turin.[58] Moreover, this policy of intervention in the confessional arrangements within Savoy–Piedmont was replicated by the other signatory of the October 1690 treaty, the United Provinces.[59]

William III also emerged speedily as a rather closer neighbour than Vittorio Amedeo might have anticipated, for, once king of England, he took a heightened interest in the affairs of the Helvetic Confederation and the various sovereign entities linked to it by pacts of 'co-alliances' and 'combourgeoisie', most notably, the city of Geneva. Duke Charles III of Savoy had lost his lands in the Vaud and his distinctive position within Geneva in the 1530s as a result of his war with the canton of Berne. Recovery of at least part of this missing inheritance remained an *idée fixe* of the policy of his descendants, even long after the calamitous escalade of 1602. On one level, Vittorio Amedeo II strove to safeguard his residual rights in the Vaud through such actions as attempting to exert his disputed privilege to nominate the absentee Catholic bishop of Reformed Lausanne.[60] On another level, it seemed that a less juridical and a more straightfor-

[57] PRO SP 108, 442.

[58] Viora, 'Notizie e documenti'.

[59] Mario Viora, 'Documenti sulle assistenze prestate dall'Olanda ai Valdesi', *Bollettino storico-bibliografico subalpino*, 30 (1928), pp. 282–305, for the transcriptions of documents.

[60] D'Arcy informed the French king that 'L'Evesché de Lausanne, auquel le Père Peyra, Theatin, avoit esté nommé il y a longtemps par cette cour, ne luy a point esté conféré, mais au Prévost de Fribourg. Il est vray que le Pape a fait entendre à Monsieur le Duc de Savoie ... que s'il vouloit la [Sa Sainteté] prier de conférer cet Evesché à ce Prévost de Fribourg, pour lequel Sa Sainteté estoit entrée dans des engagements indispensables, on le luy donneroit de cette manière, ce qui a esté résolu au conseil d'icy d'accepter pour qu'il ne fust pas fait tort à la prétention de nomination ... sur cet evesché' (AAE, CPS, vol. 90, fo. 5, d'Arcy to Louis XIV, 1 Jan. 1689). D'Arcy observed, one month later (fo. 27, 5 Feb. 1689), however, that 'la nomination de M. le Duc de Savoye à l'evesché de Lauzanne n'a jamais esté bien establie et reconnue'. Such claims to appoint absentee bishops of Reformed dioceses in the Vaud and the Genevois were far from empty exercises of privilege, and Vittorio Amedeo I, Marie-Christine, as regent, and Vittorio Amedeo II intervened actively in the elections of bishops of Geneva, resident at Annecy, in, respectively, 1639, 1661, and 1697 to obtain the see for candidates

ward assertion of Savoyard interest in those lands north of Lake Léman was under serious consideration. In late November 1688, Berne alerted Geneva to its fears of 'quelque diversion du costé de cette ville et de leur pays de Vaud et qu'ils nous prient de veiller exactement sur tous les mouvements qu'on pourroit faire aux environs de nous et de faire bonne garde',[61] while at the end of October 1688, Dogliani, from Paris, was remarking 'qu'on n'est guères content icy des Bernois et qu'on n'a pas un meilleure volonté pour Genève ... les conjonctures permettront de faire quelque démarche contre ces deux hydres d'hérésie, V.A.R. puisse ... tirer raison des droits contre ces usurpateurs'.[62] Louis' manifesto against Vittorio Amedeo referred to a proposal 'à remettre Genève sous l'obéissance du duc de Savoie',[63] and in July 1690, the French king had taken care to inform Messieurs de Genève 'que si le Roy avoit voulu nous nuire il en auroit trouvé par ci-devant des occasions plus favourables que dans ces dernières conjonctures, lesquelles luy avoient été insinuées par le Duc de Savoye'.[64]

Much of this may reflect only the speculative tradition of Savoyard enthusiasts or the rumours of imminent assault which frequently splashed around Geneva and which have left ample trace in the documents. The very rhetoric of such schemes, however, and, indeed, an entire strand of thought in Turin which continued to view Geneva and the Vaud as recoverable or of compensating the duke for his lost rights were, necessarily, dislodged by the emergence of William as an international force with a keen interest in affairs in the Helvetic Confederation. In the first place, members of the Dohna family, to whom he was closely related through his grandmother, Amalia von Solms-Braunfels,[65] were living in Geneva in a position of considerable respect and standing.[66] Gilbert Burnet was an active supporter of Genevan interests, and as early as March 1689, the Council of Geneva wrote to William and Mary 'pour les féliciter' with letters 'addressées à Mons. le Docteur Burnet. . .auquel on doit aussy écrire pour le prier de remettre les dittes lettres à LL. MM. et le féliciter aussy de la nouvelle dignité que luy a esté conférée'[67] as bishop of Salisbury. By July Burnet himself had written to the syndic Jean-Jacques de La Rive and 'luy dit par exprès que Leurs Majestés parlent de Genève avec tant d'affection et s'intéressent si fortement en tout ce

approved by the court of Turin (F. Perron, 'Les Evêques d'Annecy', *Annesci*, 7 (1959), pp. 65, 75, 87).

[61] AEG, RC, vol. 188, fo. 433, 20 Nov. 1688.

[62] AST, LMF, m. 122, no. 124, Dogliani to Vittorio Amedeo II, 29 Oct. 1688.

[63] For the same transcription by Camille Rousset see, above, n. 46.

[64] AEG, RC, vol. 190, fo. 246, 29 July 1690.

[65] Amalia von Solms-Braunfels' sister, Ursula, had married Christoph von Dohna, who became governor of the principality of Orange, a post also held by their son, Friedrich von Dohna. See J. J. Poelhekke, *Frederik Hendrik, Prins van Oranje: een biografisch drieluik* (Zutphen, 1978), p. 569.

[66] The dowager Gräfin von Dohna, Friedrich's widow, requested places in the Temple de Saint-Gervais (AEG, RC, vol. 188, fo. 371, 14 Sept. 1688), and, on her death in 1690, condolences were sent by the Council of Geneva to her son, the Burggraf von Dohna (AEG, RC, vol. 190, fo. 193, 21 July 1690).

[67] AEG, RC, vol. 189, fo. 141, 18 Mar. 1689.

qui la regarde que les plus zélés pour notre état n'ont rien à faire que de proposer les moyens pour faire éclatter leur amitié et leur bienveillance'.[68] The signal means suggested by London to 'faire éclater' the concern of the new king and queen for the city of Calvin was the proposed establishment of a permanent British resident in Geneva, heretofore the exclusive diplomatic preserve of the court of Versailles.[69] Indeed, Lord Melfort, James II's representative at Rome, deployed William's efforts 'pour venir à bout de ses desseins en Suisse, à Genève' in his attempt to persuade the recently elevated Pope Alessandro VIII Ottoboni to aid his master.[70] At the same time that William was increasing diplomatic vigilance in a traditional area of Savoyard interest, he was also using his new position to assert his dynastic rights, a rather neglected aspect of his policy,[71] to a strategically important co-alliée of the Helvetic Confederation, the sovereign principality of Neuchâtel. Throughout the 1690s, he used his claims as the ultimate heir of the House of Châlons to protect the position of the duchesse de Nemours as sovereign princess from attempts to establish the prince de Conti in Neuchâtel, on which the principe di Carignano also had rights,[72] while reserving the possibility of putting forward these claims in the future whenever the childless Mme de Nemours should die.[73]

From one point of view, therefore, the events of 1688–9, by enlarging William's international role, introduced a complicating factor in the perceptions of the duke of Savoy, establishing a tacitly accepted Anglo-Dutch protectorate over his Valdesi subjects, one maintained by subsequent rulers of Great Britain, while

[68] AEG, RC, vol. 189, fo. 306, 22 July 1689.

[69] I shall address myself more fully elsewhere to William III's attempts to establish a diplomatic presence in Geneva, a move which caused acute embarrassment in the city, reluctant to offend either the king of Great Britain or the king of France, who reacted angrily to such an intrusion. Sourches, in his entry for 26 April 1689, reported the dispatch of the British envoys 'aux Cantons des Suisses et à la ville de Genève, quoique les Rois d'Angleterre ne leur en eussent jamais envoyé, et par là on voyoit clairement qu'il ne perdoit aucune occasion de travailler contre la France' (Sourches, *Mémoires*, III, pp. 79–80). This episode is considered in a more general context in L. A. Robertson, 'The Relations of William III with the Swiss Protestants, 1689–1697', *Transactions of the Royal Historical Society*, 4th ser., 12 (1929), pp. 137–62.

[70] BL MS Add. 37660 [Lord Melfort's letter book], fo. 68: Mémoire to Mgr Robini, the papal secretary of state, 18 Jan. 1690.

[71] A recent study devoted to one aspect of the dynastic policies of the House of Orange is W. F. Leemans, 'Enkele brieven van Mary Stuart, de Princesse Royale, in het geschil over het Prinsdom Oranje', *Oranje-Nassau Museum Jaarboek 1988*, which includes a letter from Vittorio Amedeo's grandmother, Marie-Christine of France, duchess of Savoy, written in 1659 in her Stuart niece's favour (p. 120).

[72] C. Robert, 'Etudes sur la succession de Neuchâtel, 1694–1714: la renonciation du prince de Carignan en faveur du Roi de Prusse (Traité secret du 16 octobre 1707)', *Musée neuchâtelois*, 46 (1909), pp. 37–43.

[73] The literature on the Neuchâtel succession dispute is voluminous: the standard account is Jonas Boyve, *Annales historiques du comté de Neuchâtel et Valangin*, (5 vols., Berne and Neuchâtel, 1854–9), IV. This should be supplemented by numerous articles in the journal *Musée neuchâtelois*, notably Armand du Pasquier, 'Les Ambassadeurs Amelot et Puysieulx et la succession de la Maison de Longueville' (pp. 57–130) in the issue of 1931. In the event, Marie d'Orléans-Longueville, duchesse de Nemours, concurrently involved in a second separate inheritance dispute with Vittorio Amedeo's mother, outlived her benefactor, William III, and on her death, in 1707, the investiture of Neuchâtel was awarded to Friedrich I, king in Prussia on the basis of the recognition of the Hohenzollern as William III's closest heirs.

obliging him to take the initial steps towards a diplomatic reconciliation in the subsequent century with Geneva and with those cantons in the Helvetic Confederation which had, since the 1530s, been viewed as hereditary enemies. From another point of view, however, these difficulties were more than compensated for by the new prospect of the English succession. Much of Vittorio Amedeo's thinking about this aspect of policy became sharply focused by the coincidence of William's invasion and James' flight with a second dynastic event of capital importance, the sudden death, under circumstances which have never been clarified,[74] in Madrid on 12 February 1689 of the childless queen of Spain, Marie-Louise d'Orléans, the elder sister of Vittorio Amedeo's wife, the Duchess Anna Maria of Savoy. The death of the alert and lively Marie-Louise, described by Dogliani as 'fort exagerée contre l'entreprise du prince d'Orange',[75] eliminated from the scene the leader of the French party at the court of Carlos II and, immediately, opened up the possibility of selecting a new queen with political affinities more attuned to the situation in 1689.[76] Marie-Louise's death without issue, coming only a matter of weeks after the Savoyard envoy reported that Monsieur 'avoit quelque espérance que la Reine d'Espagne fut grosse',[77] also concentrated in the hands of her sister, the duchess of Savoy, all of the rights belonging to their mother, the last child of Charles I of England, Henrietta Anne Stuart, duchesse d'Orléans. Putting to one side the question of James II and the infant Prince of Wales, Anna Maria, following Louise-Marie's death, found herself in a position in which only three people had stronger claims than hers to the British thrones, William and Mary, married barrenly for over eleven years, and Princess Anne Stuart, whose marriage to Prince George of Denmark had produced four children, all dead by 1689, although she was known to be pregnant again early in the year. At the death of the queen of Spain, Anna Maria was not yet twenty but already the mother of three living princesses, all of whom were barred from the Savoyard succession, but were capable of the British succession and were, thus, harbingers of hope for future male issue.

The proximity of the blood ties between the courts of Madrid and Turin necessitated in terms of dynastic etiquette, as had the birth of the Prince of Wales in the previous year, the dispatch of an 'extraordinary embassy', this time one of condolence. Such a mission, however, would bring an envoy of Vittorio Amedeo into direct contact with Carlos II and his ministers at a time

[74] This death may have been an instance when the always frequent rumours of poisoning surrounding an early or sudden death had some substance, with the guilty act popularly attributed to another member of the House of Savoy, Mazarin's niece, Olympe Mancini, comtesse de Soissons, the mother of Prince Eugene (M. Bassenne, *La Vie Tragique d'une reine d'Espagne: Marie-Louise de Bourbon-Orléans* (Paris, 1939), pp. 273–95; and Max Braubach, *Prinz Eugen von Savoyen*, I: *Aufstieg* (Vienna, 1963), p. 146).

[75] AST, LMF, m. 122, no. 164, Dogliani to Vittorio Amedeo II, 10 Jan. 1689.

[76] The choice fell upon yet another Pfalz-Neuburg princess, Maria Anna, sister of both the Empress Eleanora Magdalene and Queen Maria Sophia of Portugal.

[77] AST, LMF, m. 122, no. 168, Dogliani to Vittorio Amedeo II, 24 Jan. 1689.

when Spain was in open confrontation with France, still Savoy's principal ally, albeit an overbearing one. Vittorio Amedeo, realizing both the importance and the delicacy of this question, proceeded with great caution and approached Louis XIV through Monsieur,[78] whose customary role of intermediary between Turin and Versailles was, in this instance, greatly enhanced by the fact that he was the late queen of Spain's own father. Louis had considerable misgivings in consenting to a Savoyard embassy to an enemy court, but was unable to abridge the requirements of the ceremonies of royal mourning and the notions of familial bienséance. He did, however, take the precaution of ordering d'Arcy to 'bien faire entendre au Marquis de Saint-Thomas ... que je m'assure que l'envoyé du Duc de Savoye à Madrid ne sera chargé que des compliments de condoleance sur la mort de la Reyne d'Espagne et qu'après qu'il s'en sera acquit, il retournera à Turin'.[79] Vittorio Amedeo, however, ignored these restrictions, and his envoy, the conte di Martiniano, remained in Spain much longer than Versailles thought appropriate. Martiniano's mission in the spring and summer of 1689 coincided roughly with the periods of the duke of Savoy's protracted absences from Turin, and during the time he spent at the court of Carlos II he raised a number of points of critical interest to the House of Savoy. Among the most important were Vittorio Amedeo's own rights to the Spanish inheritance,[80] and, in September, Martiniano reported the extraordinary news that 'Il re di Spagna è nostro ... che S.A.R. sia stato nominato alla successione di questo Regno.'[81]

While pursuing the duke's claims in Madrid, Martiniano was also charged with protecting those of the duchess. Anna Maria's interests in her sister's estate touched upon a variety of points. There was the question of the late queen's personal property, and early rumours had suggested a significant bequest of jewellery to the duchess of Savoy. In the event, Dogliani reported that 'le legs que Sa Majesté [the Queen of Spain: Marie-Louise] a fait à M.L.D.R. [Madame la Duchesse Royale: Anna Maria] n'est pas fort considérable' consisting only of a 'garniture de toute sorte de pierres qu'elle luy a laissé'.[82] Expectations both of the Orléans circle at Saint-Cloud and of the court of Turin were disappointed by Marie-Louise's will which named her husband, Carlos II, as her universal heir. The chancellor of the House of Orléans 'm'a aussy assuré que ... Monsieur seroit bien fondé d'impugner la validité de ce testament par plusieurs raisons',[83] and Vittorio Amedeo was, clearly, eager that Dogliani should explore 'les droits de la feue Reine d'Espagne provenants de feue Madame sa mère

78 AST, LMF, m. 122, no. 188, Dogliani to San Tommaso, 14 Mar. 1689.
79 AAE, CPS, vol. 90, fos. 69–70, Louis XIV to d'Arcy, 8 Apr. 1689.
80 Vittorio Amedeo's very strong claims on the Spanish Crowns were based upon descent from his paternal great-grandmother, the Infanta Catalina Micaela, the younger daughter of King Philip II and the wife of Duke Carlo Emanuele I of Savoy.
81 AST, LMS, m. 34, Martiniano to Vittorio Amedeo II, 5 Sept. 1689.
82 AST, LMF, m. 122, no. 210, Dogliani to Vittorio Amedeo II, 9 May 1689.
83 Ibid.

[Henrietta Anne Stuart], dont elle n'a pas disposé par son testament'.[84] The duke was particularly concerned to 'eclaircir de ce dont la couronne d'Angleterre doit encore au mariage de feue Madame' and to obtain copies of the marriage contracts of Henrietta Anne and Philippe d'Orléans and of Marie-Louise d'Orléans and Carlos II.[85] Monsieur's unwillingness to pursue this line of enquiry obliged Vittorio Amedeo to follow suit,[86] but at the same time as these points of the queen of Spain's inheritance were discussed, another, vitally important, aspect of her inheritance came into sharp focus.

The French ambassador, d'Arcy, had, as noted above, underscored the proximity of Anna Maria to the English throne at the time of Skelton's unsuccessful attempt to see Vittorio Amedeo,[87] and, at an early date, the House of Hanover's eagerness to press its own claim[88] concentrated the attention of the court of Turin upon the rights of the young duchess. Dogliani reported from Paris the arrival in London in June 1689 of an envoy from Hanover who

> tâche de faire appeler à la couronne le Duc de Hanovre à l'exclusion de M.L.D.R. [Madame la Duchesse Royale: Anna Maria] pour estre catholique, au cas que le Prince d'Orange et celuy de Dannemarck viennent à mourir sans enfants. Mais quelque declaration que les deux chambres puissent faire, elles ne pourront en rien préjudicier en son droit, n'étant pas au pouvoir d'un peuple rebelle de changer l'ordre de la succession de ses légitimes souverains, outre que la personne du prince de Galles sera un autre obstacle.[89]

Vittorio Amedeo replied promptly that 'Nous seront ... bien aysés de sçavoir les suites de la négociation qu'on attribue à l'envoyé de la Maison de Lunebourg par laquelle vous nous mandez qu'il tâchoit à faire appeller à la couronne le Duc de Hanovre à l'exclusion de M.L.D.R.',[90] and early in August Dogliani sent back word of the 'plusieurs contestations entre les deux Chambres sur le project d'acte pour régler la succession de la couronne d'Angleterre pour sçavoir si la duchesse d'Hanovre [Sophia] y seroit appellée à l'exclusion de M.L.D.R. au cas que la princesse de Dannemarck n'eust point d'enfants'.[91] Thus, by the summer of 1689, only a matter of months after the coronation of William III and Mary II, the interested parties in an eventual English succession had begun to assemble their arguments, and the question of the Savoy claim began its long

[84] AST, LMF, m. 122, no. 203, Dogliani to Vittorio Amedeo II, 25 Apr. 1689.
[85] AST, LC, vol. 80, fo. 3852, Vittorio Amedeo II to Dogliani, 15 Apr. 1689.
[86] AST, LC, vol. 80 (folio numbers cease), Vittorio Amedeo II to Dogliani, 21 May 1689.
[87] See above n. 28.
[88] Georg Schnath, *Geschichte Hannovers im Zeitalter der neunten Kur und der englischen Sukzession, 1674–1714* (5 vols., Hildesheim, 1938–82), II, pp. 233–4; and Waltraut Fricke, *Leibniz und die englische Sukzession des Hauses Hannover* (Hildesheim, 1957), p. 11.
[89] AST, LMF, m. 122, no. 229, Dogliani to Vittorio Amedeo II, 27 June 1689.
[90] AST, LC, m. 80 (not numbered), Vittorio Amedeo II to Dogliani, 9 July 1689.
[91] AST, LMF, m. 122, no. 243, Dogliani to Vittorio Amedeo II, 8 Aug. 1689.

life, assuming a prominent role in discussions during the 1690s[92] and maintaining some impact in British thinking even after the Act of Settlement in 1701.[93]

The claim of the House of Savoy, which really coalesced only in 1688–9 with the elimination of James II and his son from the political equation and with the death of the queen of Spain, merits slightly further consideration. As we have seen, at precisely the same time that Dogliani was warning of the approach of the Hanoverian envoy, Martiniano, in Madrid, was discussing the duke's rights to the Spanish thrones, and the claims of the House of Savoy to Spain also played a large role in discussions during the decades on either side of 1700. Both claims, to England and to Spain, were, moreover, part of a larger dynastic strategy. Throughout the second half of the seventeenth century, the House of Savoy had sought recognition as kings of Cyprus, on the basis of the fifteenth-century Lusignan resignation, and this pretension had poisoned diplomatic relations between the Italian states.[94] Descent from the House of Paleologus brought to the House of Savoy strong claims to the Monferrato, a strategically important marquisate which also evoked the Byzantine imperium, and there were impressive titles to the Crown of Portugal as well. A fundamental element of the early modern dynastic mentality was the maintenance and assertion of all possible claims, however remote their realization at any given moment might seem, in order to avoid the appearance of having permitted the pretensions to have lapsed. The hope of eventual recognition of titles was, however, balanced by the concept of compensation, renunciation of rights in return for concrete, material advantage elsewhere. The tenacity with which the House of Savoy claimed the *trattamento reale*, their recognition as 'royal highnesses' and the reception of their ambassadors with those of crowned heads, was anything but a dispute over empty ceremonial form and etiquette. It played an important role in the dynastic advancement and territorial aggrandizement of the House, and the acquisition of a convincing claim to the English throne as a result of the events of 1688–9 added a strong card to Vittorio Amedeo's hand. The proximity of the House of Savoy to so many royal thrones, especially those of England and Spain, certainly had a considerable part to play in the accession of Vittorio Amedeo, in 1713, as king of Sicily.

[92] In the first half of the 1690s, during discussions for a possible marriage between the king of the Romans and Vittorio Amedeo's elder daughter, Maria Adelaïda, the Savoyard representative stressed 'la convenance du mariage avec une princesse catholique, parente au degré successible de la reine d'Angleterre', Mary II (comte d'Haussonville, *La Duchesse de Bourgogne et l'alliance savoyarde sous Louis XIV: La réconciliation avec la Savoie et le mariage de la duchesse de Bourgogne* (Paris, 1899), p. 60).

[93] Hatton, *The Anglo-Hanoverian Connection*, p. 19 n. 3, observes that Anna Maria's claim 'was still regarded as potentially damaging in 1720' and cites Jeremy Black, 'British Travellers in Europe in the Early Eighteenth Century', *Dalhousie Review*, 61 (1982), n. 26, as her source.

[94] Carlo Contessa, *Per la storia della decadenza della diplomazia italiana nel secolo XVII: anedotti di relazioni veneto-sabaude* (Turin, 1906) (also published as an article in the *Miscellanea della storia italiana* of 1906).

In 1969, John Carswell publicly reclaimed the Glorious Revolution for international history,[95] and this retrieval was convincingly confirmed in the subsequently published work of Ragnhild Hatton.[96] It is important to remember, however, that the events of 1688 had an influence on an area beyond northern, Protestant Europe and that their effect was felt significantly in the Catholic south, by the pope, by the emperor, by the kings of Spain and Portugal, and, among Italian princes, most of all by the duke of Savoy. Indeed, in the role they played in Savoy's detachment from France, in the eventual readjustment of the duke's relations with his Valdesi subjects and with his Helvetic neighbours and in the advance of the House of Savoy, which quickly emerged as an important factor in European power politics, the results of William III's invasion made upon Vittorio Amedeo II a greater impact than they did upon, with the obvious exception of Georg Ludwig of Hanover, most other European princes.

[95] John Carswell, *The Descent on England* (London, 1969).
[96] Ragnhild Hatton, *George I. Elector and King* (London, 1978).

Chapter 12

Sequel to Revolution: The economics of England's emergence as a Great Power, 1688–1712

D. W. JONES

For Europe, the most important consequence of the Glorious Revolution was that England relatively quickly, within the space of a few years, gained Great Power status for the first time. Once the newly crowned William III had brought her in to fight a great European war against Louis XIV's France, England, in a manner wholly unprecedented for her, sent ever more ships and men, and ever more money to pay for foreign troop hirings, to fight abroad in European theatres of war. Quite astonishingly, in the space of little more than two decades and by no means solely because of Marlborough's great military victories, England emerged as one of the greatest European military powers, rivalled only by the defeated French. Yet England's population at this time was little more than some 5 million as compared with a French population nearly four times as great.

The story of the European consequences of the Revolution would thus seem to be an epic in which David slew Goliath. It is all the more surprising, therefore, that outside the specialist field of military history, so much of this story has, until very recently, remained to be told.[1] To be sure, we have long possessed excellent studies of England's Financial Revolution that followed the Revolution of 1688; and these have just been joined by a scintillating synthesis of the development of England's state apparatus more generally to meet the mounting administrative requirements of war.[2] Adequate finance and sound administration were certainly *necessary* conditions of success. However, when war is on the agenda – that realm of human activity, to quote Clausewitz, 'so continuously [and] universally bound up with chance [which] makes everything more uncertain and interferes with the whole course of events'[3] – an over-concentration on the necessary conditions at the expense of the sufficient is peculiarly dangerous, and especially so of England's war effort of the post-Revolution decades. For

[1] D. W. Jones, *War and Economy in the Age of William III and Marlborough* (Oxford, 1988).

[2] E. L. Hargreaves, *The National Debt* (London, 1930); E. Hughes, *Studies in Administration and Finance, 1558–1825* (Manchester, 1934), ch. 5; P. G. M. Dickson, *The Financial Revolution in England, 1688–1756* (London, 1967); John Brewer, *The Sinews of Power: War, Money and the English State* (London, 1989).

[3] C. von Clausewitz, *On War*, ed. M. Howard and P. Paret (Princeton, N.J., 1976), pp. 85, 101.

in addition to inspired generalship, the sufficient conditions were not that resources should have been effectively raised and rationally financed in England (even if, as necessary conditions they certainly needed to have been), but that once raised, these resources, in the face of the actions of an implacable enemy, should then have been effectively managed and deployed to fight two great wars (the Nine Years War, 1689–97, and the War of the Spanish Succession, 1702–12), both of which were fought abroad and not at home.

Incorporating war into any scheme of historical causality and explanation is never easy. But it is almost as if historians have side-stepped this difficulty by annexing England's role in the wars of the Grand Alliance to her financial and administrative history. The precise details of the military role played by England in Europe have never been comprehensively presented; the nature and character of England's war effort over the years 1689–1712 thus remain unclear. It is also symptomatic, perhaps, that the so-called Recoinage Crisis of the years 1695–7 has never been fully explored for the light it might throw on the dangers of the war effort for England. Yet the crisis which followed the decision taken early in 1696 to recoin what, by then, had become the heavily clipped silver coin of pre-1663 mintage (the so-called 'hammered' coin as distinct from the milled coin of post-1663 mintage) was certainly the most critical of the century. Recoining was bound to take time so that in the midst of a critical war situation, the years 1696–7 suffered a grave shortage of circulating media once all the old hammered silver coin had been taken in for reminting and until it could re-emerge as a much smaller face-value amount of newly minted, full-bodied, milled coin. English payments to her Flanders army virtually failed totally between late June and early October 1696 while over the years 1696–7 economic activity at home was severely hit.[4]

In short, the total war situation and of the play of the contingent and the unforeseen have largely been neglected. At the very least this has risked a mild Whiggery. All too readily, England's success in the wars can be presented as resulting solely from financial and administrative innovations emerging ineluctably, seemingly, from the financial and administrative necessities that called them forth. At its worst, however, the failure to confront the wars in their totality can lead to the facile assumption that victory was almost inevitable thanks to England's greater wealth successfully mobilized for war by the financial and administrative innovations. Again, these latter were certainly important necessary conditions; but in terms of the sufficient conditions – to do with how resources raised at home were then successfully, or otherwise, projected abroad – nothing could be further from the truth.

The character of England's war effort emerges clearly from the details of her

[4] For a reconstruction of this episode, see Jones, *War and Economy*, pp. 20–6, 244–7.

military commitments in Europe.[5] In part this is simply a matter of their remarkable extent and scale. To start with, it is true, most of England's efforts over the years 1689–91 had to be devoted to the war in Ireland. Even over these years, however, England did send some thousands of her officers and troops to join the allied army fighting in the Low Countries. Also, £600,000 provided by the Dutch States General to help finance William's invasion of England in 1688 was repaid and two subsidies were commenced, the first, one of some £20,000, paid annually to Brandenburg for her troops to fight in the Low Countries (though these troops were not directly on English establishment); and the second, one of some £95,000 annually, to the duke of Savoy fighting in Italy. Further sums were also paid for imperial and Bavarian troops to go to the aid of the duke when hard-pressed by a French offensive under Catinat in 1691. In the meantime, a massive naval building programme was begun, this lasting throughout the Nine Years War.[6]

Once the Irish War was over, England started to do much more in Europe. Over the years 1692–3 an army of some 41,000 officers and men was paid for in Flanders. Of these 28,900 were subject, and the rest foreign officers and troops hired directly onto English establishment from Denmark, Hanover, and Wolfenbüttel, all of whom also received subsidies from England. Further subsidies of £25,000 and £35,000 each were paid to Saxony and Hesse Cassel for yet more troops to fight in the Low Countries, though like the Brandenburg troops, these again were not directly on English establishment. Both 1692 and 1693 saw the launching of two massive 'Descents' (i.e. conjoint military and naval operations) against St Malo and Brest respectively; while in 1693 two naval squadrons were sent to operate in the Mediterranean approaches off Cadiz. Over the autumn and winter of 1693–4 as many as possible of the navy's ships were sent to intercept ships carrying corn to France following the disastrous harvest failures there of 1692–3 and 1693–4. Though no further 'Descents' were attempted after 1693, England's commitments continued to increase, reaching their peak over the years 1694–5, at which level they were more or less maintained for the rest of the war. From 1694 onwards, the English army in Flanders, counting officers and men but not the Brandenburg, Saxon, and Hessian 'subsidy' troops, was some 68,000–69,000 strong (48,000 subject, 20,500 foreign). During 1694, also, the bulk of the English navy was sent under Admiral Russell to operate in the Mediterranean. Overwintering at Cadiz 1694–5, this fleet did not return home until the end of 1695. Taking the naval and military sides together, from 1694 onwards – or but some four years on from the Revolution – England was quite clearly doing more in Europe than any of her other allies (Spain, the Dutch Republic, and Austria).

[5] Reconstructed in ibid., pp. 7–11.
[6] J. Ehrman, *The Navy in the War of William III* (Cambridge, 1953), pp. xx, 630–2.

England's role in the War of the Spanish Succession was even more substantial, even if the forces paid for by England in the Low Countries, having commenced in 1702 at some 52,000 strong (of whom fully 31,000 were now foreign hirings and for whom subsidies were again paid), never surpassed the levels of the previous war. At their peak of 69,000 officers and men (42,500 foreign) over the years 1710–11, they only just about equalled the maximum levels sustained in the 1690s over a longer period. Nonetheless, the new war, with its contest for the Spanish possessions in Italy as well as Spain itself, necessitated far more extensive operations in southern Europe. Already in 1702 an English naval force was dispatched to attempt to disrupt Spain's lifelines with her American colonies. And once Portugal and Savoy came over to the allied side in 1703, England commenced paying substantial annual subsidies to them of £150,000 and £160,000 respectively for the rest of the war (and Savoy's subsidy was to be increased by a further £100,000 from 1706 onwards). Quite quickly, too, over the years 1704–5, English military forces were sent to operate both in Portugal and in Catalonia, where they joined those of the Archduke Charles, the Austrian claimant for the Spanish Succession and who also received a substantial annual subsidy from England. From 1704 onwards nearly half the ships of the English fleet were committed to operate in the Mediterranean whence they did not return until late 1707.

England's commitments in the south then steadily increased. First, more funds had to be sent to Savoy and the Austrians to help stave off a dangerous French offensive in Italy over 1705–6; while early in the latter year the Austrians were permitted to raise a massive £250,000 loan for the Italian theatre on the London capital market. In 1707 when an English force was disastrously defeated at Almanza in Spain, the English navy assisted the Austrian conquest of the Spanish possessions in Italy before then participating in a joint, though wholly abortive, attack on the French naval base at Toulon. Finally, the years 1708–11 witnessed a steady English military build-up in Catalonia, in vain pursuit of 'No Peace without Spain'. By 1710–11, England had an army of some 52,000 officers and men in Catalonia (roughly half subject, half imperialists and Portuguese) while a further 6,000 of Charles' troops were paid for out of the subsidy he received.

Taking the northern and southern war theatres together and also counting the forces indirectly paid for by English subsidies: over the years 1710–11, England was in fact paying for fully 171,000 officers and men (58,000 subject and 113,750 foreign) to fight abroad in Europe. In 1710, also, the Austrians had been permitted to raise a further loan, one of £87,000, in London to finance troops, this time in the Low Countries.

The great extent and scale of England's war effort is thus apparent. But thanks to contradictions lying at the heart of the chosen war strategy it was also extremely hazardous. At the same time that England maintained armies abroad and subsidized her continental allies she also much of the time deployed her navy on forward operations. On their own the forward naval operations coupled with the massive naval build-up associated with them would have been dangerous enough. By the later seventeenth century England was a major trading nation, enjoying trading surpluses with Europe amounting to some £500,000–£600,000 annually.[7] But these surpluses depended to a considerable extent on being able to ship in sugars, tobaccos, dyestuffs, and East India textiles from her Atlantic colonies and trading stations in India, and then on re-exporting a substantial proportion of these for sale in Europe. In fact the bullion that had to be bought in Europe to run the India trade usually just about balanced the East India goods sold as re-exports to Europe.[8] But the Atlantic trades were quite different. What these trades yielded as re-export sales of sugar, tobacco, and dyestuffs, plus sales of Newfoundland cod sold direct in the Iberian peninsula (the proceeds being remitted back to England), was greater by some £800,000 annually than the naval stores and the linens and metalwares that had to be bought in Europe to run these trades each year.[9] (The naval stores to build, equip, and re-equip the ships upon which these trades were so dependent; and the linens and metalwares for shipping back to the colonies.)

Naval manning requirements, however, were bound to starve the Atlantic trades of the men required to serve them. Also a dangerously unseasonal pattern of sailing could well be forced upon them were priority given to naval manning by preventing trading ships from going out before the end of the navy's manning season, early in May, and requiring their return before it commenced, early in February. For the Atlantic trades, along with others, this would bring ships into dangerous tropical waters during the hurricane season and enforce their return through stormy, winter, European waters. Finally, given the navy's forward operations, far too few ships of the line were apt to be spared to protect both departing and incoming ships from the privateering attack that the French were only too likely to launch against English commerce.

The forward naval deployment on its own was thus likely to be damaging for the economy. England could all too easily lose those European trade surpluses that annually vouchsafed a high level of economic activity at home by bringing in a flow of bullion (gold mainly) to be minted into coin at the London mint. But the loss of these surpluses would be doubly damaging since favourable trade balances provided the only way that England could maintain her forward military

[7] For a discussion of England's balance of payments surpluses, see Jones, *War and Economy*, pp. 211–16. The estimated surpluses given here are based on net monetary inflow.

[8] Ibid., pp. 55, 219, 226.

[9] Ibid., pp. 55, 219, 226.

commitments without subverting economic stability at home. England's difficulty was that in an age when, in western Europe at least, it was no longer possible to maintain armies and meet foreign commitments by levying *Kontribution*, neither was it possible for England to subsist her armies and meet her other military commitments by shipping the necessary supplies directly from her shores. Instead, England was obliged to remit funds abroad for her troops and allies to spend largely as they saw fit. Hence the danger of England's position: in transmitting funds across the foreign exchanges whereby taxes and net loans were spent abroad and not at home where they had been raised, England's balance of payments and employment stability were put at risk. Only had direct supply been undertaken would these dangers have been avoided.

That direct supply would not have threatened stability is clear enough. For then the taxes and net loans raised to provide for the military commitments would have been spent at home, internally redeploying resources freed by them out of English consumption: the stability of home employment and output would thus have been preserved.[10] At the same time shipping the supplies out instead of remitting across the foreign exchanges would have obviated any disturbance to the balance of payments. But direct supply was impractical. Shipping the quantities involved, an estimated 245,000 tons[11] of supplies annually to supply the Flanders army alone, would have been beyond the shipping and port facilities of the day and would have presented the French with an inviting target to attack. In any case, while it was better for the officers and men to be able to buy fresh bread and meat locally, the horses when on summer campaign had to be provided with green fodder close to where they were campaigning. Otherwise, operations would have been hopelessly bogged down had any attempt been made to bring the vast quantities required from magazines in the rear.[12] Supplies were also cheaper locally, and particularly so in the Low Countries where there were also local entrepreneurs – notably the firm of Machado and Pereira – long-versed in the business of supplying armies.[13] For the subsidies that England paid (very important in the 1700s), there was no choice anyway, contracted to be paid as these were in money.

Hence the need to remit and the attendant dangers of this. Spending the proceeds of taxes and loans abroad had to mean that the home-spending which under direct supply would have been present to take up the resources first freed out of home consumption would now be absent. Spending would thus be deficient and the stability of home employment and output put at risk. At the same time,

[10] For the purposes of a short paper, there is some oversimplification here: see ibid., pp. 97–109.
[11] Ibid., pp. 30–1, 33–4.
[12] G. Perjés, 'Army Provisioning, Logistics and Strategy in the Second Half of the 17th Century', *Acta Historica Academiae Scientorium Hungarica*, 16 (1970), pp. 6, 8, 12, 14–17; D. Chandler, *The Art of Warfare in the Age of Marlborough* (London, 1976), p. 17.
[13] V. Barbour, *Capitalism in Amsterdam* (Baltimore, 1950), pp. 30–1.

remitting across the foreign exchanges risked a balance of payments deficit and so a money outflow and money squeeze at home, which would further intensify the disturbance to home output and employment. Moreover, in view of the very narrow range within which exchange rates could fluctuate, the money outflow would be likely to occur with devastating speed.[14] To be sure, had there been trade surpluses big enough to handle the remittances then still there would have been no difficulty. For not only would the necessary foreign exchange thus have been available, there would have been no disturbance to home employment either. For saving is always the counterpart of trade surpluses, keeping imports lower than could have been afforded. Accordingly, a government able to use a surplus to remit implies that its taxes and loans would, in effect, have appropriated this saving, not current spending, and so leaving home employment and output undisturbed. Much the same effect, it is worth noting for its later relevance, might also be achieved by England's India trade which, as we have just seen, yielded re-export sales in Europe that usually just balanced the bullion that had to be bought back from Europe for shipment out to India. This bullion represents investment, and thus saving, which will generate imports and thus re-exports some time into the future. Accordingly, although the effect might not last very long, a halting of this investment would mean that a flow of re-exports, as the fruit of past investment, could continue earning foreign exchange for some time but in the absence now of the usual offsetting bullion purchases. Again, therefore, foreign exchange would have been made available; and again savings (not current spending) would have been appropriated.

Unfortunately, however, as the accompanying table shows, the remittances were so vast that they would have outstripped England's peace-time balances, let alone the smaller balances likely in wartime. Thus, taking the years 1694–7 and 1708–12: remittances were at least twice, and nearly four times, greater respectively than the £500,000–£600,000 surpluses of peace-time trade; they also amount to some 25 per cent of England's *total* annual European earnings in the 1680s, and to some 40 per cent of total earnings over the years 1699–1701.[15] For the 1690s, moreover, the position is complicated by the prohibition of Ireland's French trade which in the 1680s played an important part in England's balance of payments. Ireland had debts to pay to England of some £200,000 annually; and these she settled by making over to England the surpluses she enjoyed on her trade with Europe, and especially France.[16]

Even with remittances of this size, all might not be lost, of course. The spending abroad might either come back for goods bought from England (butter, cheese, and grain for bread making and brewing the beer, say); and/or it might divert

[14] Jones, *War and Economy*, pp. 123–5.
[15] Ibid., pp. 37–8, 53.
[16] Ibid., pp. 55–7.

Table 1. *England's remittances to troops and allies abroad 1688–9 to 1712* (inclusive of loans raised for foreign powers on the London capital market)

Year	Total spent abroad	Net borrowings abroad	Remitted from home	To the north	To the south
1688–9	169,335	—	169,335	169,335	—
1689–90	795,547	—	795,547	795,547	—
1690–1	557,866	—	557,866	426,200	131,666
1692	788,420	—	788,420	732,420	56,000
1693	876,114	—	876,114	781,032	95,082
1694	1,508,137	150,000	1,358,137	1,254,137	104,000
1695	1,255,621	17,000	1,238,621	1,099,821	138,800
1696	1,174,717	133,000	1,041,717	966,717	75,000
1697	806,922	100,000	706,922	706,922	—
1702	*c.* 900,000	—	*c.* 900,000	900,000	—
1703	1,296,609	—	1,296,609	1,071,809	224,800
1704	1,622,309	—	1,622,309	1,088,888	533,421
1705	1,614,475	—	1,614,475	1,115,690	498,785
1706	2,107,109	—	2,107,109	924,215	1,182,893
1707	1,782,318	—	1,782,318	826,630	955,688
1708	2,000,969	—	2,000,969	970,889	1,030,079
1709	2,068,457	—	2,068,457	785,687	1,282,770
1710	2,467,671	150,000	2,317,671	1,054,395	1,263,276
1711	2,546,358	30,000	2,516,358	1,595,360	920,998
1712	1,527,112	—	1,527,112	999,472	527,640

Note: figures for 1688–91 are for Michaelmas years.

the consumption abroad of some of England's erstwhile imports (linens and wines bought by officers and troops, say). Both these effects would obviously help correct any instability of employment and payments by enabling trade, in the shape of rising export and reduced import, to achieve virtually the same as direct supply would have done. Unfortunately, neither effect was at all likely to occur, at least to anything like the required extent even jointly. Bearing in mind that bread, meat, and fodder had really to be bought locally, the proportion of what even could realistically come back as sketched above was quite small anyway, amounting to no more than some 36 per cent in the 1690s and to but some 25 per cent in the 1700s.[17] (This latter, smaller, proportion simply reflects the much larger subsidy payments of the decade.) And far less than this was likely to be achieved. Supplies were cheaper locally while beyond stipulating that the bread contractors in Flanders had to export out of England an

[17] Ibid., pp. 112–14.

amount of grain equivalent to the grain they used in making the bread (only some £90,000 at most annually),[18] the government could exercise no control over how its officers, troops, and allies spent the money received from England. Thanks to the river system, the Dutch Republic was very well placed to supply the English army in Flanders; and there French goods (notably wines) prohibited in England, were also readily available to entice the officers' spending.[19] In the meantime, Revolution Finance was of too recent a foundation, and thus too unknown a quantity, for it to have provided a major attraction for foreigners to have lent England the resources she needed abroad.[20]

Nor is it easy to see, finally, how the government could have done much to encourage the one thing that would provide a solution to England's problems – namely, an export boom simultaneously making available the required foreign exchange while restoring home employment by taking-up labour and skills thrown out of employment at home by the spending abroad.[21] Though we shall have to mention export bounties paid on corn exports, a thoroughgoing subsidization of English exports would have been expensive, and thus unlikely on top of heavy war expenditures. (For early modern governments it would also have been unprecedented.) In any case, English grains and woollens, the two major items upon which any export boom would have to be based, faced stern competition. European grain markets had long since been supplied by Baltic wheat and rye coming via Danzig and Riga while major centres of competing woollen production were located at Leiden in Holland; in and around Tilburg, Eindhoven, and Helmond in the south of the Dutch Republic; in and around Verviers in the bishopric of Liège; in and around Dresden, Leipzig, and Zwickau in Saxony; in and around Bautzen, Görlitz, and Zittau in Lusatia (a province of Saxony); and in and around Lissa, Fraustadt, Glogau, and Breslau in Silesia. Unless something wholly untoward happened to these competitors, a boom in English exports was not to be expected.[22]

We have moved far, evidently, from the relative certainties of administration and public finance. The economic side of England's war effort was clearly as

[18] BL MS Add. 10123, fol. 106. For the bread contracts, see: Salop Record Office, Shrewsbury, 112–75, 186; BL MS Add. 38707, fols. 162–5; PRO T48–12, T64–132.

[19] J. de Smet, 'Commerce et Navigation de Bruges et Ostend', *Bulletin de la Commission Royale d'Histoire*, 94 (1930), pp. 180–97; F. van Kalken, *La Fin du régime espagnol aux Pays-Bas* (Brussels, 1907), pp. 107–8.

[20] For the limited role of foreign borrowings, see Jones, *War and Economy*, pp. 21, 22–3, 25–6, 225 and n. 18.

[21] For a detailed analysis of the limits of government action, see D. W. Jones, 'Economic Policy, Trade, and Managing the English War-Economy, 1689–1712', forthcoming in *Britain and the Netherlands*, X.

[22] Jones, *War and Economy*, pp. 61–4, 198.

much an 'uncharted sea full of reefs'[23] as Clausewitz thought battles to be. On the one hand, without very careful management, the forward naval deployment could all too easily destroy the very trade performance upon which any successful forward military deployment would depend. On the other hand, good management alone would not be sufficient since the remittances were far greater than the favourable balances of peace-time trade. England thus risked a serious dislocation of home employment when very little of the spending abroad was likely to come back and with a money squeeze only too likely to follow the resulting deficit on the balance of payments. Only good luck, in the form of an export boom which was neither likely nor easily encouraged by government policy would seemingly see England through.

The aptness of this analysis, with its emphasis on good luck, is certainly borne out by the facts of the matter. Quite fortuitous and far-flung developments throughout the then known world all worked to make the 1700s a near miraculous success story despite the fact that England's commitments were now roughly double those of the earlier war. The 1690s, on the other hand, culminating with the Recoinage, were a near disaster from which only clipping the coin, as an improbable dénouement, provided a very lucky escape. The near-disaster of the 1690s was, perhaps, predictable. Ireland's earnings with France (which boosted sterling as we have seen) were immediately lost not only because of the mutual trade prohibitions between England and France, but also because the military campaigns in Ireland caused severe economic disruption.[24] To give priority to naval manning requirements, draconian controls were imposed limiting the men and tonnage that the longer distance trades could employ to below half what they had employed in the 1680s.[25] And ships were indeed not permitted to depart before the end of May and obliged to return before the following February.[26] Trade was seriously disrupted by the massive hirings of ships for the Irish campaigns 1689–91 and for the two 'Descents' of 1692 and 1693 while throughout, to ward off the relentless privateering attack that the French duly mounted, far too few ships of the line were indeed spared for commerce protection.[27] As a result, English trade and shipping suffered enormous pressures and loss. The massive naval manning requirements allowed foreign shipping to take over a large share of England's European trades while simultaneously reducing the volume of her maritime commerce with the wider world.[28] Other than in the east coast coal trade, attempts to relieve the pressure by relaxing

[23] Clausewitz, *On War*, p. 120.

[24] Jones, *War and Economy*, pp. 140–1; L. M. Cullen, *Anglo-Irish Trade 1660–1800* (Manchester, 1968), pp. 40–1; idem, *An Economic History of Ireland since 1660* (London, 1972), pp. 27–34.

[25] PRO CO 389–12, fos. 28v–30v, 108, 151, 222, 249, 279; 389–13, fos. 1–2, 143.

[26] W. A. Shaw (ed.), *Calendar of Treasury Books* (London, 1904–61), IX and X: index, s. v. 'Embargo'.

[27] Jones, *War and Economy*, p. 156.

[28] Ibid., pp. 156–8.

Navigation Act regulations to permit the employment of more foreign seamen on English ships failed.[29] Thanks to the dangerously unseasonal pattern of sailings imposed on trade and the inadequacy of trade protection, English maritime commerce suffered further heavy losses from storms and at the hands of the French privateers.[30]

No comprehensive listing of the losses exists, but it is clear that along with the India trade, the Atlantic trades (unsurprisingly) suffered greatly. Some idea of the scale of these losses for the London mercantile community can be gained from the fact that over the years 1695–6 alone, the Royal Africa Company suffered losses of cargo (i.e. excluding the value of the ships) of £57,219; the Jamaica, New England, and Leeward Island merchants, cargo losses of £320,500; and the Barbados merchants, a massive loss of £387,100.[31] Of this latter, £187,000 had been suffered through storm, the rest in the Channel Soundings at the hands of a French naval squadron commanded by Nesmond. The departure of the Barbados ships from England had been delayed for five months, so that they were obliged to be leaving Barbados at the height of the hurricane season. Nineteen of the Barbados ships were lost through hurricane as compared with sixteen taken by Nesmond.[32] Nor were the Barbados merchants slow to point out the grim significance of the losses they had suffered, and of the shattering effect for England's re-export trade with Europe. They represented to Parliament that:

> The losses from the plantations are double for the nation being all goods that would have been exported to have supplied the army with the proceeds, and kept up the exchange ... for if we have not effects to pay our army, the foreigners will have our silver to be sure, for the exchange is governed by the balance of trade.[33]

Elsewhere, in the meantime, developments were hardly more encouraging. From the start, there was little chance of the India trade helping much during the 1690s. The Company which controlled the trade had overreached itself over the first half of the 1680s, undertaking massive investments to fight off an interloping attack mounted against it both by London merchants and its own servants in India.[34] Accordingly, its much reduced investments of the later 1680s were far too low to have contributed much in the 1690s, even had the war losses not intervened. The trading position in the 1690s was improved by the ending

[29] J. A. Johnston, 'Parliament and the Navy, 1688–1714', Univ. of Sheffield PhD thesis (1968), pp. 335–43; *House of Lords Manuscripts* (hereafter *HLMSS*) (15 vols., HMSO London, 1887–1962), *1693–5*, pp. 537–9; *CJ*, X, pp. 514, 535; XI, pp. 283, 291; 2 William and Mary s. 2, c. 7.

[30] Jones, *War and Economy*, pp. 158–61.

[31] *HLMSS 1695–7*, pp. 64, 79–82, 87–8.

[32] Ibid., pp. 64, 65, 66, 76–7, 88.

[33] Ibid., p. 77.

[34] Jones, *War and Economy*, pp. 286–95.

of French trade which had been a deficit trade for England;[35] on the other hand, since nothing untoward happened to European competitors, English exports grew very little over the decade.[36] Moreover, earnings were somewhat reduced on England's woollen textile exports to the Low Countries and Germany when a progressively higher proportion of these now went out undyed (dyestuffs being cheaper abroad thanks to the rebate of duties on their re-export from England).[37] Earnings on these exports were also further reduced when, following the ending of the Merchant Adventurers' monopoly in 1688 (though the pressures of war might also have played a part), a progressively higher proportion now went out for the accounts of foreign principals abroad with a consequent loss of the profits accruing to English principals previously handling the business.[38] Above all, far from the spending of the Flanders' army helping either by coming back for English supplies and thus boosting exports, or by helpfully diverting imports, most of it ended up in the pockets of the Dutch and French. Richard Hill, deputy paymaster of the army in Flanders, provides a graphic description of the position. Towards the end of 1695 he described how:

> There has been little help from Trade since the war, and none at present, for Hollande supplys allmoste everything which is wanting for ye use and consumption of the Army ... they send butter and cheese and Bread, Rhenish wines and fish and foreage, spices and rice and Everything for the subsistence of their own and our Troops, and of all Brabant and Flanders ... and this year has been so plentifull in corn and other provisions that allmost nothing of that kind can come from England; and ye Trade to France being opened with those provinces their goes more of our money in France at present for wines, brandies and baubles than there goeth to England or Ireland for any kind of provisions.[39]

Relative to the remittances, therefore, there had been a near-total failure of trade. Accordingly, the 1690s were years of depreciating exchange and, culminating with a huge export in 1694 of nearly £700,000's worth of silver, of massive silver bullion outflow[40] which greatly accelerated the clipping of the hammered silver coin. The outflow of 1694 (most of it molten silver) so reduced the metal content of the hammered coin that confidence in it was lost early in 1695, thus precipitating the currency crisis. Clipping the coin had certainly been well established, particularly in the north of England, by the mid-1680s.[41] Once no new hammered silver coin was being minted after 1663, the public was having to accept it as an increasingly worn coin anyway. And it was this which made

[35] Ibid., p. 53.
[36] Ibid., pp. 134, 224–5.
[37] *CJ*, X, p. 770; XI, pp. 96, 212; XII, pp. 275–6.
[38] I William and Mary c. 32; Jones, *War and Economy*, pp. 80–1, 253–60.
[39] BL MS Add. 10153, 'Considerations about the Payments of His Majesties Armyes in Flanders from Mr Hill, 1695', fos. 124r-v, 126.
[40] Jones, *War and Economy*, pp. 128, 131, 228, 232–3.
[41] Ibid., pp. 228–33, for an account of the clipping trade based mainly on Northern Circuit Assize depositions (PRO ASSI 45).

it possible, probably, to profit by clipping off small slivers of metal from the coin for sale to be melted down as *bona fide* bullion: the newly clipped coin could then be passed on at face value. Hence the basis of the trade which quickly became highly organized between, first, all kinds of dealers who culled their cash receipts for heavier coin to put out to be clipped; secondly, clippers who actually did the clipping; and third, goldsmiths who received the clippings for melting into bullion, paying clipped money for it. The clippers were then able to return this plus the coin they had clipped to the dealers at the rates agreed with them. (The clippers, though, obviously retained some of the coin as their profit.)

Clipping the coin was already causing some official concern in the mid-1680s. But when the sampling of excise receipts was instituted in 1684 to monitor the position, a deficiency of no more than some 13 per cent metal content was found,[42] which is relatively trivial since taxes provided an obvious opportunity for off-loading the worst coin. From the late 1680s onwards, however, and throughout the 1690s down to the end of the 1695, the pace of clipping accelerated markedly. To start with this was probably related to a currency debasement – the so-called *schellingen* 'plague' – in the Dutch Republic which put up silver prices there.[43] But from about 1690 onwards, it was clearly the failure of trade and the need to find bullion to pay England's debts that fuelled the business. As goldsmiths sought ever more bullion for export, the metal deficiency of the silver coin as measured by the excise receipts reached some 40 per cent by midsummer 1694, and some 50 per cent by midsummer 1695.[44] It was hardly surprising, therefore, that confidence should have been lost in the silver coin early in 1695.

That clipping, a criminal activity and one that was soon to necessitate the dangerous Recoinage of 1696–7, can be presented as the saviour of the situation in the 1690s must, at first sight, seem surprising. But this must certainly have been the case for it was only through clipping the coin that England, at least down to the end of 1695, was enabled to escape the penalties of having failed to get trade to pay for her military commitments abroad. With a favourable trade balance virtually non-existent and with little of the spending abroad coming back to help in the ways earlier sketched, England should have been suffering a serious deficiency of spending at home and thus a grave dislocation of home output and employment. And with bullion flowing out, this dislocation should have been intensified, had money been sound, by a severe money squeeze. However, as an industry newly established and booming in the land, clipping generated

[42] BL Lansdowne MS 801, fo. 39.

[43] E. Enno van Gelder, *Munthervorming tijdens de Republiek* (Amsterdam, 1949), pp. 133–4; J. G. van Dillen, *Van Rijkdom en Regenten* (The Hague, 1970), pp. 442–3.

[44] BL Lansdowne MS 801, fo. 39.

new income, and thus spending, to take the place of the spending lost abroad; at the same time the continued passing on of an increasingly clipped coin at face value meant that no effective contraction of the money supply was occurring. Finally, melting the clippings supplied the bullion that would otherwise have been unavailable and so enabled England to pay debts that otherwise she could not have paid. True, clipping did lead to the onset of a currency crisis in 1695; but the immediate effect of this was to make 1695 a year of inflationary hyperactivity. And it was this which enabled the war effort to be kept going for one more, vital, year when William III retook Namur and so gained a crucial opening card for his negotiations with Louis XIV.

Survival down to the Peace of Rijswijk which ended the war in 1697 had evidently been very close-run. But what had worked once could not work again; the milled coin into which the old hammered coin was reminted by the Recoinage could not be clipped. During the War of the Spanish Succession, therefore, there could not again have been clipping to provide an escape had England once more failed to get trade to pay for war abroad. Yet failure must certainly have been the likelier outcome. The external spending was now roughly double that in the earlier war: all the greater, correspondingly, the potential dislocation of home output and the potential severity of the money squeeze. Fortunately, however, and thanks largely to extraordinarily favourable and lucky circumstances abroad, England did succeed to get trade to pay for war in the 1700s and thus escape what should otherwise have been a rerun of the 1690s, but worse. During the War of the Spanish Succession England's exports boomed; the India trade contributed a great deal; the exchange rate remained remarkably steady; bullion export was negligible.[45]

Placing the emphasis on lucky circumstances abroad is not to deny that the management of the war effort at home may have improved somewhat in the 1700s. In the War of the Spanish Succession the draconian controls on shipping of the 1690s were not re-introduced while Navigation Act requirements were relaxed to permit the employment of a higher proportion of foreign seamen.[46] No 'Descents' like those of 1692 and 1693 were attempted; moreover it was now easier to provide cover for trade when so many military and naval movements – notably to the Iberian peninsula and into the Mediterranean – ran parallel to major branches of English commerce.[47] It is also possible, though by no means certain, that trade protection improved, thus reducing losses at the hands of the French privateers. Certainly, at no time during the 1700s apart

[45] Jones, *War and Economy*, pp. 131, 134, 217, 222–4.

[46] Johnston, 'Parliament and the Navy', pp. 385–6, 412; 2 & 3 Anne c. 11, 6 Anne c. 64; *HLMSS 1706–8*, pp. 227–8; *LJ*, XVIII, p. 362.

[47] Between April 1703 and October 1707 it had been possible to arrange twenty-nine convoys for the Portugal trade alone (*LJ*, XVIII, p. 407).

from possibly 1704–5[48] were the sort of 'across the board' losses of the 1690s suffered. Since at times, however, the old problems did recur and notably in 1706–7,[49] it may well be the somewhat lower intensity of French privateering that was the crucial factor. Judging from the closing two-and-a-half years of the Nine Years War, the French annually fitted out more privateers in the 1690s than they did at any time during the 1700s.[50]

Still, better management would only ensure that England's war-time surpluses in the 1700s would more closely approach the size of her peace-time surpluses than had been the case during the 1690s. During the War of the Spanish Succession much more than this was actually achieved, England's trade surpluses frequently doubling, and occasionally nearly tripling anything achieved before.[51] For the causes of this striking improvement it is to the very fortunate circumstances abroad that we must look. Of these, Brazil gold and the boost this gave to English exports provides perhaps the most obvious example. In 1698 communications between São Paulo and the newly established mines in the interior were improved so that thereafter ever increasing quantities of gold, amounting to over a million pounds' worth in some years of the 1700s, reached Lisbon.[52] From the ensuing boom in Brazil, English woollen exports benefited enormously and since English imports from Portugal grew very little during the 1700s, so did England's trade balance with Portugal. During the War of the Spanish Succession, Portugal became one of two important channels of remittance (the other being via Italy) to Catalonia.[53] (These remittances, though, did mean that very little Brazil gold reached England during the 1700s and thus could not have helped England's military payments elsewhere had this been required.)

Of even greater importance was the manner in which the unprecedented warfare of the 1700s worked to favour English exports. There were two aspects to this. First, England was numbered amongst the greatest producers of 'military' textiles – that is of such woollens as kerseys, bays, and broadcloths suitable for making uniforms (plus serge for linings); and was reputed to be the best.[54]

48 Jones, *War and Economy*, pp. 163, 168; *LJ*, XVII, pp. 466, 470, 584, 622–4, 627, 643, 649; XVIII, p. 466.

49 *LJ*, XVIII, pp. 341–419, 466–72; *HLMSS 1706–8*, pp. 99–226; *CJ*, XV, pp. 404–5.

50 A conclusion reached by subtracting the figures given by J. S. Bromley, 'The French Privateering War 1702–1713', in H. E. Bell and R. L. Ollard (eds.), *Historical Essays 1600–1750 Presented to David Ogg* (London, 1963), pp. 302–26, from those supplied from 1695 onwards by J. Delumeau, 'La Guerre de course Française sous L'Ancien Regime', 'Course et Piraterie': papers of the San Francisco Conference (1975) issued by the Commission Internationale d'Histoire Maritime, Paris, pp. 274–5.

51 Jones, *War and Economy*, pp. 215, 221.

52 V. Magalhães Godinho, 'Portugal and her Empire, 1680–1720', *The New Cambridge Modern History*, VI, ed. J. S. Bromley (Cambridge, 1970), p. 534; H. V. Livermore, *A New History of Portugal* (Cambridge, 1966), p. 206; C. R. Boxer, 'Brazilian Gold and British Traders in the First Half of the Eighteenth Century', *Hispanic American Historical Review*, 49 (1969), p. 429; M. Morineau, 'Or Bresilien et Gazettes Hollandaises', *Revue d'histoire moderne et contemporaine*, 25 (1978), p. 15.

53 Jones, *War and Economy*, pp. 87–8.

54 Ibid., pp. 201–3.

When, therefore, there was an unprecedented mobilization of armies in the 1700s, taking the number of men under arms higher than ever before, English woollens were bound to benefit from the demand for uniform cloth. English woollens dominated the supply of the Russian army which, under Peter the Great, was now being uniformed, systematically, for the first time.[55] Attempts made by Holland and Zeeland to preserve the clothing of the troops they paid for in the Dutch army to their own indigenous producers seem to have failed, while the foreign troops paid for by England and serving in the Low Countries appear to have been clothed in English woollens as a matter of course.[56]

The second aspect of how war worked to favour English exports was that it crippled England's competitors and thus created room for a growth of England's exports greater even than the expanded market for military textiles. Woollen textile production in the Low Countries was disrupted when in 1702 Marlborough had had to campaign straight through that region of woollen production centred around Eindhoven, Tilburg, and Helmond with serious effects for production.[57] Then in 1703 Marlborough had to lay siege to Verviers, Liège, and Limburg with similar results for textile production there.[58] Further afield there were the disruptive effects of the Great Northern war which, going on quite independently of the War of the Spanish Succession, was being fought between Charles XII of Sweden, on the one side, and Peter the Great of Russia and Augustus of Saxony, on the other. Woollen production in the great Saxon and Lusatian centres of production was disrupted by the excises levied by Augustus, and by his recruitment of weavers into the army.[59] More serious disruption then followed when Charles XII occupied Saxony (including Lusatia) from late 1706 until early 1708.[60] In the meantime, Silesian production was disrupted both by these operations, and earlier when Charles had struck westwards late in 1704.[61] Little wonder, then, that English woollen sales to both the Low Countries and Germany boomed during the War of the Spanish Succession.

The campaigns of Charles XII, together with those of Peter the Great to oppose him, also explain at least part of how England's grain exports also boomed

[55] A. I. Jucht, 'Russkaya promylenost' i snabzenie armii obmundirovian i armuniciez', *Poltava, k 250-letiiu Poltavskogo srazhenia. Sbornik Statei* (Moscow, 1959), pp. 211–27. (I am indebted to my friend and colleague, John Parker, for translations of the relevant parts of this.)

[56] *Groot Placaet-Boeck* (9 vols., The Hague, 1658–1796), V, pp. 132–3, 134–6, 145–7, 162–4, 183–5, 195–6, 196–8; Shaw (ed.), *Calendar of Treasury Books*, XVIII, pp. 133, 209; PRO T1/136/40.

[57] W. S. Churchill, *Marlborough. His Life and Times* (4 vols., London, 1933–8), II, pp. 136–8; Henry L. Snyder (ed.), *The Marlborough-Godolphin Correspondence* (3 vols., Oxford, 1975), I, p. 98.

[58] Ibid., I, pp. 236–44.

[59] Josef Leszczynski, 'Die Oberlausitz in den ersten Jahren des Nordischen Krieges (1700–1709)', in J. Kalisch and J. Gierowski (eds.), *Um die Pölnische Krone: Sachsen und Poland während des Nordischen Krieges* (Berlin, 1962), pp. 73–9, 82, 92.

[60] Ibid., pp. 82–7; A. Gunther, 'Das Schwedische Heer in Sachsen 1706–7', *Neues Archiv für Sachsische Geschichte und Altertumskunde*, 25 (1904), pp. 234, 247.

[61] R. Hatton, *Charles XII of Sweden* (London, 1968), pp. 201, 209; N. Davies, *God's Playground: A History of Poland* (2 vols., Oxford, 1981), I, p. 84.

during the 1700s. The great Baltic grain trades had never included barley and malt, so the growth in English exports of these must certainly be explained by the English export bounties first introduced during the 1670s, and then reintroduced in 1689.[62] These bounties only applied at or below certain fixed prices; and prices during most of the 1690s had been above these. Down to 1708, however, prices during the 1700s ruled very low, bringing the bounties into play to boost English grain export. From 1697 onwards, malt export had also been encouraged by the repayment to exporters of all excise duties irrespective of prices at home.[63] Bounties were also payable, of course, on wheat and rye exports, and were indeed paid during the 1700s down to 1708. But wheat and rye had formed the staples of the Baltic trade coming from Danzig and Riga. Accordingly, even allowing for the bounties, English export of wheat and rye must clearly have been assisted first by the devastating campaigns waged by Charles XII in the Vistula basin between 1702 and 1706, disrupting the Danzig grain trade; and second by Peter the Great's occupation in the early 1700s of Estonia, Livonia, and Courland in Riga's hinterland followed by his devastating of their resources when forced to leave by Charles XII's march eastwards into Russia in 1708–9.[64] A similar situation prevailed in Portugal where fighting in the Alentejo and Campo Maior also favoured English grain sales by disrupting grain production there and cutting off supplies from Spanish Extremadura.[65]

Finally, the India trade provides the last piece of the jigsaw in this tale of good fortune and luck. As already briefly mentioned, the Company controlling the trade had been under attack since the early 1680s. This attack had been made possible by the readiness of the Company's own servants in India to co-operate with interloping ships coming from London. The readiness of the servants to do this seems to have been related to a slump in the European diamond market after Louis XIV had been forced to retrench his purchases in the late 1670s.[66] Diamonds were the only permitted means of repatriating accumulated gains from India; so when diamonds could no longer be profitably sold back in Europe, the Company's servants were only too ready to remit their gains via goods carried by interlopers. Immediately before the War of the Spanish Succession, the struggle reached a decisive stage when a new, rival, Company was established in 1698, but leaving the old Company in existence. As a result, both Companies attempted to gain the initiative by undertaking massive invest-

[62] A. H. John, 'English Agricultural Improvement and Grain Exports 1660–1775', in D. C. Coleman and A. H. John (eds.), *Trade, Government and Economy in Preindustrial England* (London, 1976), pp. 47–8.

[63] 8 & 9 William III c. 22.

[64] Davies, *God's Playground*, I, pp. 262, 288, 314–15, 501; M. S. Anderson, *Peter the Great* (London, 1978), pp. 54, 57.

[65] Godinho, 'Portugal and Her Empire', p. 527; PRO T1/136/40.

[66] The fortunes of the diamond trade can be followed in North Yorkshire Record Office, Letter Book of John Cholmley and in PRO C 114–180, Letter Book of Daniel Chardin.

ments to India over the years 1698–1701. By the opening of the Succession War a veritable silver mountain of investment existed out in India. But obviously this was not sustainable and there would have to be retrenchment; during the War of the Spanish Succession the war with Spain made silver more difficult to get hold of anyway.[67] Thanks to the ensuing fall in bullion investments, therefore, and to the fact that there was a great deal of silver still out in India to generate a flow of imports (and thus re-exports) for some considerable time, what had been over 1699–1701 a significantly negative balance of bullion purchases over East India re-export sales turned into a moderately positive one during the 1700s (1709 solely excepted). Most years, indeed, this turnround contributed the equivalent of between a third and a half of the *improvement* in England's balance during the War of the Spanish Succession.[68]

It was in these ways and for these reasons, then, that England rose to Great Power status following the Revolution of 1688. The decline of Great Powers tends to attract historians more than their rise. However, the rise of England in the space of little more than two decades demands attention because for England the projection of military power was more, and not less, dangerous than for any other military power of the early modern period. Swedish military power fuelled itself uncomplicatedly on *Kontribution*; the Austrians and the Russians simply raised taxes in kind and supplied their armies directly with the supplies so raised; Dutch agriculture received back much of the spending in Flanders. Similarly, the French armies which for the most part operated directly adjacent to the French frontiers, and, in any case, during the War of the Spanish Succession France enjoyed better access than did her rivals to Spanish silver. But it is perhaps a comparison with Spain, whose position was the exact reverse of England's when she was *the* great military power roughly a century earlier, which is the most instructive. Spain certainly had much greater difficulty raising resources for war than England; but it was England, not Spain, who risked serious economic dislocation when transferring these resources for the purposes of war abroad. Spain had the silver of her empire to do so; England did not. It is little wonder, therefore, that luck had to play such an important part in England's success.

[67] *Records of Fort St George: Despatches from England 1701–1706* (Madras, 1925), pp. 55–6, 60, 65, 76; *1707–1710* (Madras, 1927), p. 59.
[68] Jones, *War and Economy*, pp. 221–2.

Chapter 13

The English and Dutch East India Companies and the Glorious Revolution of 1688–9

K. N. CHAUDHURI AND JONATHAN I. ISRAEL

The year 1688 was a watershed in British history. The period and context of the 'Revolution' also served symbolically and in real terms as a time-mark for significant changes in the nature of European presence in the Indian Ocean. The year was a decade short of the bicentenary of the Portuguese arrival in Calicut and it was close enough to be the centenary anniversary of the first Dutch and English voyages to the Further East. The directors of the English East India Company were fully aware by 1688 of the historical precedence and the legitimacy which their century-long trade with Asia had given to the Company. When a critical Parliament with the active support of William III resolved to set up a new East India Company and dismantle the old Company with its Jacobite overtones, the court embarked on a fierce political counter-campaign, observing 'our joints are too stiff to yield to our juniors'.[1]

It is not generally appreciated by the historians of early modern Europe that 1688 marked not only a 'revolution' in Britain but also one in the Indian Ocean. During 1687–8 the English East India Company, under the leadership of Sir Josia Child, decided to wage a war on the Mughal emperor and demonstrate to the VOC that its naval power was more than a match for the Dutch organization. Tactically, the war went badly for the Company but in the long run its strategic aims were fully realized. By 1689 the directorate had begun to sense that the political gamble undertaken in India had failed. The news of the defeat at the hands of the Mughal naval and military officers, combined with the arrival of William and Mary in England, proved to be a serious political setback for the East India Company, which had closely allied itself with James II. Soon the Company's rivals and enemies dubbed by the directors as 'interlopers' succeeded in persuading a parliamentary committee to investigate its affairs. This was only the beginning of a long public campaign at home to discredit and permanently remove the old managerial group from the control of the East India trade. Paradoxically, during the period the East India Company was preoccupied with its domestic problems, the VOC failed to maintain its relative status

[1] IOR EIC Despatch Book, 26 Aug. 1698, vol. 93, para. 12, p. 102.

in the Indian Ocean. By 1720, it was clear to all observers in England and Holland that the United East India Company was a rising commercial and naval power in Asia, while the VOC appeared to have lost its political and economic dynamism and become a relatively conservative stagnant operation. The Dutch Company retained its immense trading capital and financial influence. But the naval and imperial ambitions passed into the hands of the English and French East India Companies.

The change in English policy in Asia from peaceful to armed trading during these years is fully documented and brings out the gulf between ideology and historical events. In the 1670s the Company was still critical of the Dutch method of constructing fortified bases as a viable commercial policy.[2] In the 1680s and 1690s there was a dramatic turn round and the long-term policy considerations of a more politically active role in the Indian Ocean were gradually worked out by the East India Company and its directors led by Child. The example of the VOC played a major part in the change of course. Within fifty or sixty years, the East India Company would reap spectacular political dividends from an aborted naval war in India and largely displace the Dutch, though the French wars were yet to come. In the early 1680s the East India Company and perhaps even the VOC were 'mere merchants' in the Mughal Empire. By 1720 when the Mughal Empire was already well on its way to decline and disintegration, the two trading corporations with enormous capital resources at their command found themselves in a position of considerable political and economic influence.

Anglo-Dutch relations in Europe and Asia naturally featured as an important topic of discussion on contemporary public affairs. It is worth repeating the fact that the task of curtailing the maritime power of the Portuguese Estado da India took the VOC more than sixty years to accomplish. In the second half of the seventeenth century, with Malacca, Colombo, and Cochin in their hands the VOC had only Goa to contend with. The capital of the Estado da India was never seriously threatened by the Dutch who had more serious wars on their hands in Sulawasi and other parts of the East Indies. In any case, the VOC realized in the 1670s that the main threat to its trade and empire in the Indies came not from the already defeated Portuguese but from the merchants of commercially underdeveloped London. The rapidity with which the East India Company overhauled the VOC was a success story perhaps only equalled in our own times by the post-war record of Japanese industries. The concerted attempt to expand Asian trade by the two Companies produced predictable results: Europe was flooded with Indian, South East Asian, and Chinese goods. The revolution in western consumer tastes, it can be argued, laid the foundation of both the coming Industrial Revolution and the economic imperialism of the

[2] IOR EIC Despatch Book, 12 Dec. 1677, vol. 88, p. 492; 3 Dec. 1679, vol. 89, p. 115.

nineteenth century. If people did not wear Indian cotton textiles and drink Chinese tea and Arabian coffee, there would have been no need to set up mechanized cotton mills and look for coffee and tea plantations beyond the Yemen and China. American cotton plantations and the associated system of slavery might not have materialized. The boom in the import of Indian textiles, initiated and organized by the English East India Company, and the decisive shift from pepper and spices, took place in the decade 1680–90 and the trend proved to be a permanent one. At the time, however, neither the East India Company nor the VOC was fully aware of the long-term shift in the composition of the East India trade, though there was ample evidence that other rival commodities were beginning to displace pepper and spices from consumers' choice.[3]

The Company's decision to become armed traders in the Indian Ocean on the Dutch model was a major theme of policy making in both the outgoing and incoming letters. There were also three other important social images discussed at length. Political relations with the Asian states were evaluated in the light of a distinctive view of oriental, despotic governments which was played off against a mild and liberal English regime in Bombay and Madras. The unsatisfactory behaviour of the Company's own officials in living up to this idealized image and their failure to support wholeheartedly the Company's search for profits provided another theme. Finally, there was the question of how to treat non-English groups in Asia with whom the Company had to conduct its daily business. These groups included fellow Europeans, Catholics, Jews, Armenians, Hindus, Muslims, Malays, and the Chinese. Each set of ideas and attitudes had a preformed and permanent component which made them simultaneously mythological and real. The reality of day-to-day events, of course, determined the actual course of history. But no matter how contradictory the evidence, English attitudes in Asia remained largely invariant.

The East India Company's perception of the VOC up to the Revolution of 1688 was itself grounded in a contradiction. On the one hand, the Company saw its Dutch rival as a powerful commercial organization determined to destroy all European competitors trading in the Indian Ocean. On the other hand, during the leadership of Sir Josia Child, the VOC's political wisdom was much admired and a concerted attempt was made to copy the Dutch policy of trading from fortified military enclaves. The adoption of the new policy owed a great deal to the expansion in the volume and value of the East India Company's Asian trade which began in the early 1670s and continued to the middle of the next decade. There were two immediate reasons for the commercial and financial success of the Company. In the first place, the directorate had at long last succeeded in capitalizing the trade adequately with a semi-permanent joint-stock

[3] See K. N. Chaudhuri, *The Trading World of Asia and the English East India Company 1660–1760* (Cambridge, 1978), p. 322.

24 *The English Trade Factory at Surat.*

and with associated short-term finance raised in the form of fixed-interest bonds. Secondly, the commercial operations in the Indian Ocean were reorganized to make them more efficient. The increasing financial stake made it necessary to formulate a more positive political and naval policy in the Indian Ocean. As the Dutch war against the Portuguese moved into its final phase with the attack against Cochin, the East India Company at first feared that its trade in black pepper would suffer the same fate as the trade in cloves, nutmeg, and mace. For the Company had been effectively debarred from trading in the Spice Islands and its only source of cloves in the East Indies, Macassar, was under determined Dutch blockade.[4] However, it was not easy for the VOC to dislodge the Company from its major trading areas in the Mughal Empire. Not only was the Company strongly based in the great Mughal port of Surat and in the textile weaving districts of Gujarat but the possession of Fort St George, a fortified settlement on the Coromandel coast, underlined considerable political and commercial authority in an important area of inter-Asian trade. The confident mood of the East India directorate and the sense of diplomatic security which the company enjoyed in Restoration London were fully reflected in the following

[4] For the Company's perception of the Dutch intentions on the Malabar pepper trade see, IOR EIC Despatch Book, 22 Aug. 1659, vol. 85, p. 241, Factory Records Java, 28 Mar. 1660, vol. 3, part 3, p. 308, Original Correspondence, 28 Jan. 1664, vol. 28, no. 3019.

instructions given to the English chief of the Company's Bantam Factory in 1670.

> We take notice of what you write, concerning the Dutch proceedings at Macassar and their endeavouring to out us of all trade in the South Seas. If we can fully satisfy ourselves, how to direct you, what to act, in order to claim and re-enter our trade at Macassar (notwithstanding the late Articles between the Dutch and them) you might expect it before the close hereof. But as to your acting in other parts, where they may attempt to disturb us, either at Bantam, Jambi, or elsewhere, we have given you full directions in our former. The sum whereof was, that you should not at all be hindered in our trade, by their threats or protests, although they should make war with any place unless they do hinder us by force, to the breach of the peace, but to insist upon the last Articles of Peace, made at Breda and particularly, upon the first, second, third, and fourth Articles of the Marine Treaty (which Articles we now again send) ... for we may come to reckon with them, and have satisfaction from them, before they are aware, notwithstanding their high and lofty carriage in India.[5]

Furthermore, both the English and the Dutch had long realized that Bengal was a 'treasure-house' of fine textiles and other high-valued goods, alongside a prosperous trade in bulk items. This was a province in which the strength of Mughal administrative and military power was such that no single European trading company, including one as strong as the VOC, could even contemplate initiating monopolizing policies. In fact, the VOC actively assisted the Mughal authorities in Bengal with the loan of warships when they launched a campaign against local pirates in 1664–6.[6] But the VOC made no sustained attempt to restrain the highly successful trade which the English Company had succeeded in establishing in Bengal.

By 1680 the VOC and the East India Company had worked out a balance of trading power in the Indian Ocean which gave the Dutch a marked preponderance in the Indonesian archipelago, Ceylon, and the southern tip of India, while the English trading organization in the rest of the Indian subcontinent and in the Persian Gulf was established in real strength. The East India Company's trade in cotton textiles, Bengal silk, saltpetre, coffee, and other commodities competed well with the Dutch imports and the financial success of the Company was reflected in the number, armament, and the capital stock of its annual fleet sent to the Indies. But the relative spheres of the two great Companies' operations and influence were still sufficiently open for the English Company to be surprised by the onset of a concerted (and last) general drive by the VOC, in the 1680s, to consolidate its supremacy in Asian commerce. Dutch pressure during this decade was mainly directed against the principal threat to their ascendancy –

[5] IOR EIC Despatch Book, 9 July 1670, vol. 87, p. 355. See also J. I. Israel, *Dutch Primacy in World Trade, 1585–1740*, (Oxford, 1989), p. 334.

[6] Om Prakash, *The Dutch East India Company and the Economy of Bengal* (Princeton, N.J., 1985), p. 49.

the rapidly growing trade of the English; it was also directed against the French who were making some progress, if less than the English, in the sultanate of Bantam, at the western end of Java, and in Siam, as well as India, and the Danes, who were likewise active at Bantam and who, in 1688, had established what was now a thriving trade factory at Tranquebar, on the Coromandel Coast of south-east India.

Sir Josia Child commented on the increased belligerence of the Dutch in Asia in a letter to James II's secretary of state, the earl of Middleton, in September 1683, in the following terms:

> Besides their naturall avarice one thing hath necessitated them in these dangerous and daring attempts to the provocation of three such great kings of Europe [i.e. Charles II, Louis XIV, and Christian V of Denmark] at this time, I suppose, is the great increase of the English East India trade these few last years which did sensibly consume their stock. And my present thoughts are that they will endeavour to drive their designe of the sole trade of India through at any charge of hazard.[7]

In the 1680s it still seemed that the Dutch possessed a wide margin of military and naval superiority over their European rivals both in the Indonesian archipelago and the Indian subcontinent and that they were willing to use it wherever needed, to shore up their commercial supremacy, however prejudicial such a policy was bound to be to relations between the Republic and her powerful neighbours at home. The Dutch authorities at Batavia had long been irritated by the way the sultanate of Bantam had developed into a general depot for the spice and pepper trade, open to the English, French, and Danes alike. In February 1682, seizing the opportunity presented by the outbreak of civil war in the sultanate, the VOC intervened in Bantam with a strong force of troops, restored order, 'entered and ransack'd all the chambers in the English factory, carrying away whatever they found there', closed the English, French, and Danish factories, and forced the sultan henceforth to sell his pepper and spices exclusively to the Dutch, an arrangement subsequently formalized in the treaties of April 1684 and March 1691.[8] The English pepper traffic in the East Indies had been growing rapidly in recent years (see Tables 2–3). While they had not, with the occupation of Bantam, 'absolutely gained that trade to themselves', the Dutch had made a large step towards their goal. In 1685 the Dutch began to construct a substantial fortress at Bantam which they named Fort Speelwijk (after the governor-general at Batavia, Cornelis Speelman), completing the work the fol-

[7] BL MS Add. 41822, fo. 28, Child to Middleton, Wanstead, 6 Sept. 1683.

[8] Ibid., fos. 9–11, 'Relation of the Bantam business, March 1682'; J. E. Heeres and F. W. Stapel (eds.), *Corpus Diplomaticum Neerlando-Indicum* (4 vols., The Hague, 1907–53), III, pp. 555–6; Charles Boxer, 'The World of William and Mary in Asian Seas, 1688–1702', in Charles Wilson and David Proctor (eds.), *1688: The Seaborne Alliance and Diplomatic Revolution* (Proceedings of the International Symposium held at the National Maritime Museum, Greenwich, 5–6 Oct. 1988), pp. 102–3.

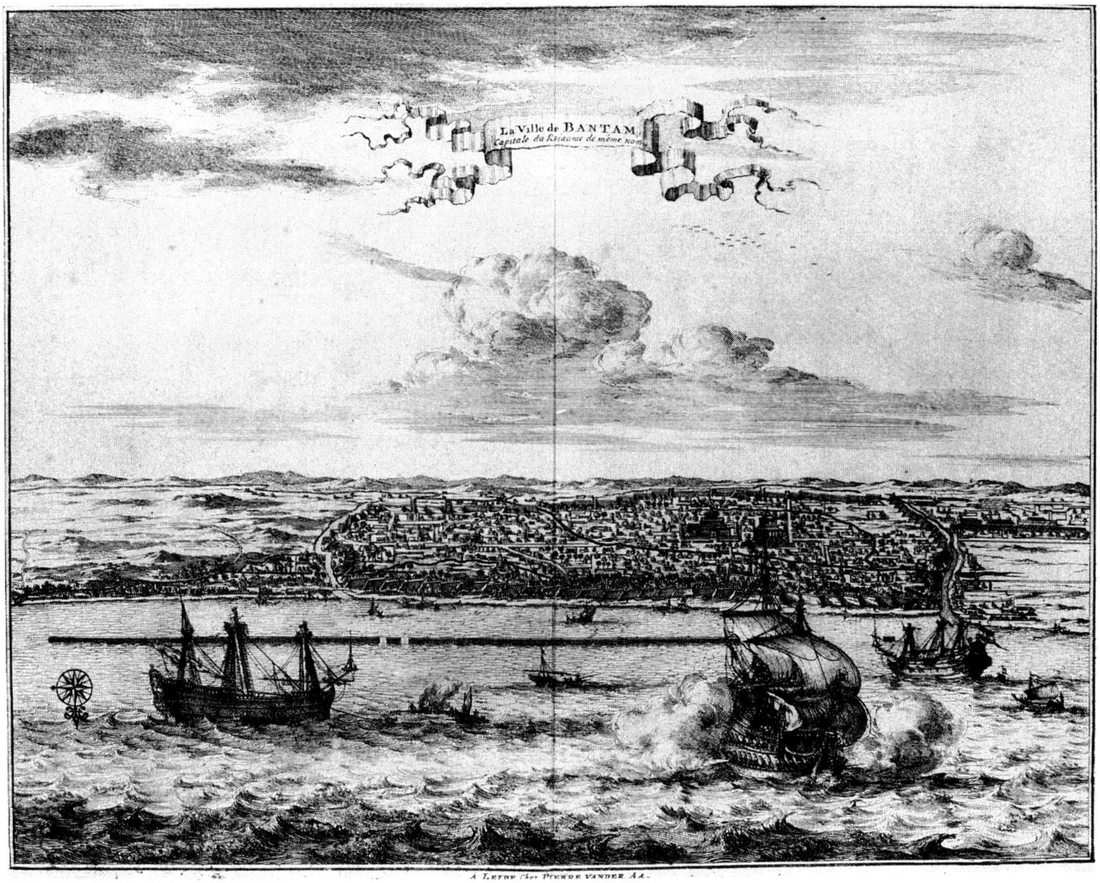

25 *The Town and Sultanate of Bantam.*
Situated at the western extremity of Java, occupied by the Dutch in 1682, Bantam was the foremost bone of both Anglo-Dutch and Franco-Dutch contention in Asia during the 1680s.

lowing year. The Dutch garrison at Bantam in 1690 stood at 563 men.[9] The sultan was reduced to what the English company's directors termed 'a mere slave', unable to 'stirr a step out of the castle without a guard of Dutch soldiers'.[10] At the same time that he reduced Bantam to subservience, Speelman put pressure on Palembang and Jambi, and the west coast sultanates of Sumatra, not to trade with the English, and other rivals of the VOC.[11] The English did retain

[9] Heeres and Stapel (eds.), *Corpus Diplomaticum Neerlando-Indicum*, III, p. 555.
[10] BL MS Add. 41822, fo. 48. The East India Company, the Court of Committees to Charles II, London, 9 July 1684.
[11] Heeres and Stapel (eds.), *Corpus Diplomaticum Neerlando-Indicum*, III, p. 479, IV, pp. 35, 39, 46, 52; Israel, *Dutch Primacy*, p. 334.

Table 2. *English East India Company: imports of black pepper (lb) from South-East Asia 1664–1720*

Year	Quantity imported	Value imported (£)	Year	Quantity imported	Value imported (£)
1664	899,519	11,559	1691	303,619	2,152
1665	1,479,262	16,595	1696	342,370	2,012
1667	24,646	369	1698	357,508	2,055
1669	2,683,349	33,287	1704	28,994	495
1670	3,684,570	40,506	1705	478,838	4,196
1671	2,080,932	23,116	1706	996,249	8,775
1672	7,120,882	75,678	1707	920,808	8,688
1675	4,011,170	43,083	1708	1,511,328	14,259
1676	3,003,059	32,157	1710	235,312	5,073
1677	7,030,937	74,926	1711	292,320	2,758
1678	3,734,056	38,923	1713	537,725	2,978
1679	2,760,146	27,190	1714	430,770	3,007
1680	2,702,546	28,835	1715	653,968	5,034
1681	4,239,118	46,538	1717	688,084	3,589
1682	915,272	10,049	1718	570,815	7,292
1687	401,047	2,877	1719	262,827	1,362
1689	166,550	945	1720	743,000	10,026
1690	1,631,679	8,703			

Source: IOR EIC, General Ledger and Commerce Journal.

several toeholds on the west coast of Sumatra and later founded a settlement at Bencoolen to organize the pepper trade. But there is no doubt that in the short and medium term their trade with the Indonesian archipelago was drastically reduced.[12] In the mid-1680s the Dutch consolidated their grip on Sumatra's west coast.

Child's efforts to organize a major armed counter-offensive against the Dutch in Asia were frustrated by Charles II who, in his declining years, had no wish to become embroiled in a fourth Anglo-Dutch war. But the Company's directors did not cease in their efforts to persuade the Crown to take a more forceful line. Child assured Middleton:

> My Lord, God knows, I doe not write this to provoke His Majestie against them ... but I know that the Dutch will lay their commonwealth at stake to accomplish the mighty conquest of the entire trade of India [i.e. of all the East Indies] unto

[12] ARH SG 5741/2, report of Jacobus Couper to SG, exhibitum 7 Dec. 1688, section on Sumatra. Chaudhuri, *Trading World of Asia*, p. 319.

Table 3. *English East India Company: imports of black pepper (lb) from the Malabar coast 1664–1720*

Year	Quantity imported	Value imported (£)	Year	Quantity imported	Value imported (£)
1664	268,476	6,711	1693	329,036	4,667
1665	745,733	12,457	1696	975,348	15,173
1667	169,529	3,547	1697	937,727	16,374
1669	358,654	7,329	1698	1,693,976	28,854
1670	611,132	9,874	1699	1,403,041	22,855
1671	793,497	13,417	1700	1,861,950	26,955
1672	465,352	5,991	1701	1,319,995	18,047
1673	844,687	14,078	1702	130,950	2,559
1674	1,347,384	20,935	1703	1,324,031	23,425
1675	426,054	5,407	1704	642,624	11,614
1676	1,554,047	20,262	1705	179,400	2,299
1677	1,096,828	15,148	1706	554,013	8,512
1678	643,023	9,898	1707	539,141	6,307
1679	22,881	285	1708	466,527	8,645
1680	328,835	5,717	1709	392,449	7,115
1681	870,227	13,273	1710	573,513	10,061
1682	1,386,736	17,226	1711	675,472	11,853
1683	1,279,818	17,819	1712	413,002	6,210
1684	1,318,231	18,956	1713	1,197,032	22,505
1685	1,836,825	25,366	1714	902,572	16,862
1686	454,151	7,458	1715	775,788	14,914
1687	1,022,355	14,981	1716	1,183,400	20,020
1688	1,820,804	23,599	1717	874,935	14,674
1689	219,370	4,333	1718	598,735	11,594
1690	1,905,161	27,509	1719	2,882,008	49,337
1691	960,354	14,094	1720	1,963,139	30,733
1692	461,318	7,862			

Source: IOR EIC, General Ledger and Commerce Journal.

> which they have made a great step if they can secure the sole trade of the South Seas which they are now in possession of.[13]

The Dutch position was strongest in Indonesia; but Child was scarcely less alarmed by the signs of increasing Dutch militancy also on the Indian subcontinent. Commercial rivalry between Dutch and English in Bengal was now fast and furious and it was feared in London that the Dutch designed to build

> a fort at the mouth of the Ganges and thereby stop the Mogull's salt-ships which

[13] BL MS Add. 41822, fo. 25v, Child to Middleton, London, 1 Sept. 1683.

supply the vast countreys bordering upon that great river until they should compel him to banish all other Europeans out of his country as the young king of Bantam has done by which they will be masters not only of the saltpetre trade but in effect of all the trade of India.[14]

In 1684 the VOC resumed the attempts undertaken intermittently since Ryklof van Goens' conquest of Cochin and Cannanore in 1662–3 to shut the English and French out of the trade with the Malabar coast of south-west India.[15] The Dutch were reacting to the establishment in 1683 of a new English factory at Tellicherry to add to the precarious Malabar foothold which the English had retained since 1664 as the guests of the anti-Dutch Zamorin at Calicut.[16] The VOC now placed the two English factories under psychological siege, stepping up their naval patrols along the Malabar coast. They also used their warships to stop 'all pepper-boats from coming to the English factories, prohibiting the natives from it by their publick edicts and afterwards shooting at and destroying all that they met with in the said trade'.[17] In terms of impact on the actual quantities of Malabar pepper which the English were obtaining through their stations at Calicut and Tellicherry the effect of all this was slight (see Table 2), as the Dutch themselves were perfectly aware. In a report of the VOC to the States General in The Hague, of May 1688, it was readily admitted that the VOC directors regarded their string of garrisons on the Malabar coast – with their four main bases at Cochin, Cannanore, Cranganore, and Quilon – 'a burden on the body of the Company' since expenditure on the bases and patrols consistently exceeded the profits accruing from the Dutch Malabar trade 'so that this commitment is kept up only out of political considerations'.[18] Nevertheless, one should not underestimate the psychological effect of the Dutch effort in Malabar in the mid-1680s either on the local rajas or on the English. The English at Tellicherry considered their position highly vulnerable 'not knowing', as they expressed it in a letter to Fort St George (Madras), in June 1687, 'how long we may be able to keep our station ... on the coast of Malabar if the Dutch resolve to pursue their long laid design of engrossing all the pepper trade of India by armes which our duty to our king and country obligeth us to prevent to the utmost of our power'.[19]

[14] Ibid., fo. 28, Child to Middleton, London, 1 Sept. 1683; see also ibid., fo. 25, where Child writes: 'and they threaten next yeare to expell all Europeans from the trade of Bengal which is more worth than all the rest of India, and I doe verily believe they intend it; because they will then be masters of all the Indian saltpetre and when they are soe they may within two years after expel all Europeans from the rest of India as easily as they did last year from the South Seas'.

[15] Heeres and Stapel (eds.), *Corpus Diplomaticum Neerlando-Indicum*, II, pp. 237–9, 246–51; M. A. P. Meilink-Roelofsz, *De vestiging der Nederlanders ter kuste Malabar* (The Hague, 1943), pp. 354–6.

[16] N. Rajendran, *The Establishment of British Power in Malabar (1664 to 1799)* (Allahabad, 1979), pp. 26,37,41.

[17] BL MS Add. 41822, fo. 80; see also ARH SG 5741/2, report of Jacobus Couper to SG, The Hague, 7 Dec. 1688, section on Malabar.

[18] ARH SG 5741/2, report of Daniel Braems to SG, The Hague, 26 May 1688, fo. 11v.

[19] Rajendran, *Establishment of British Power in Malabar*, p. 42.

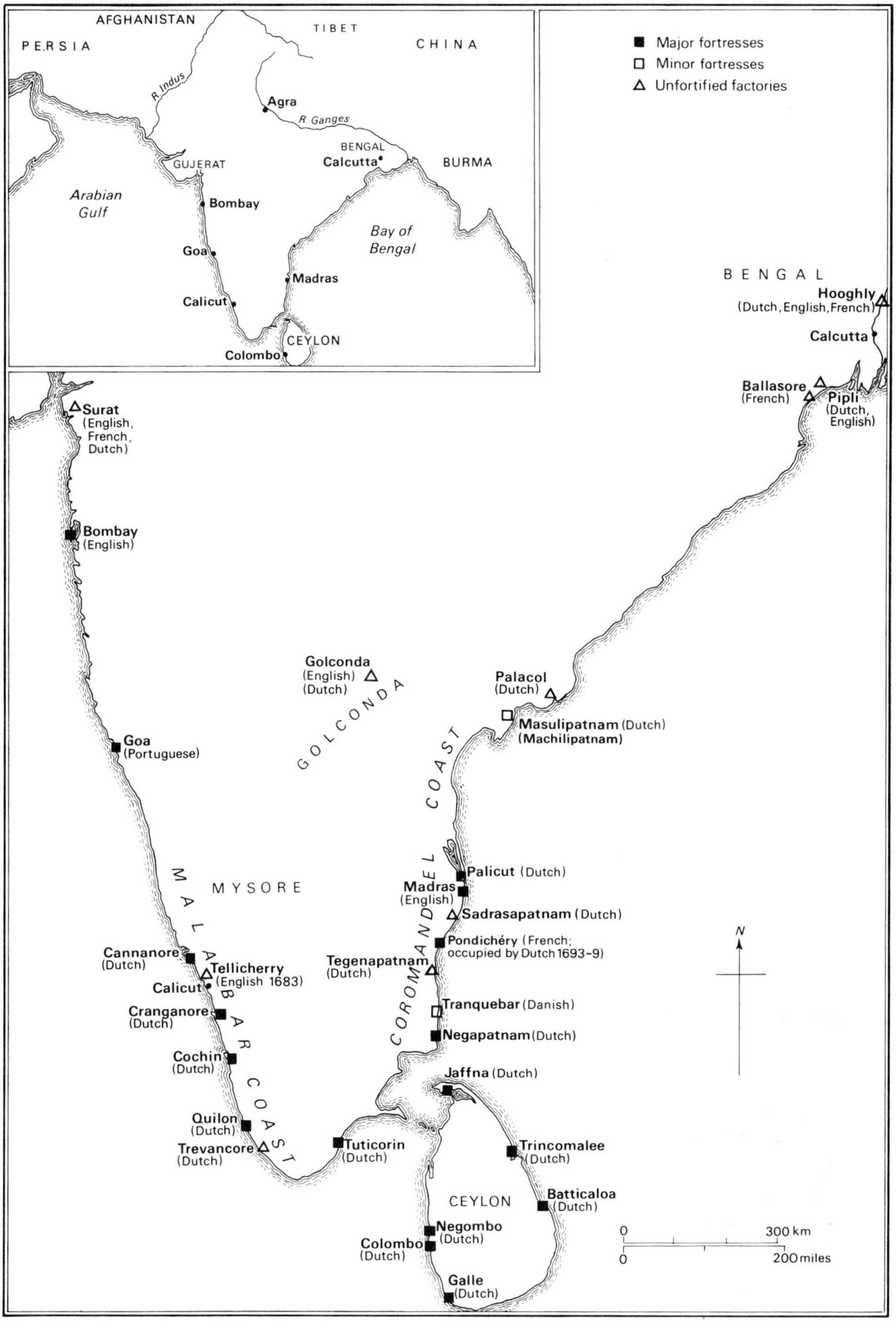

Map 4 European fortresses and trade factories in India and Ceylon at the time of the Glorious Revolution.

At times, the VOC directors, disheartened by the ineffectiveness of their efforts to monopolize the coastal trade of Malabar, had toyed with the idea of abandoning their bases there, or at least exchanging them for something more profitable. Aware of the growing importance of the China tea trade and the relative weakness of the VOC in that sector, the directors of the Amsterdam chamber of the Company suggested in 1682, in a series of discussions with the Sephardi Jewish 'Agent' of the Crown of Portugal at Amsterdam, Jeronimo Nunes da Costa, that perhaps the king of Portugal might like to have Cochin and his other former forts on the Malabar coast returned to him in exchange for Macao.[20] But in the end the Dutch always came back to those 'political considerations', their fear of relaxing their grip on the Malabar coast only to see their place taken by the English or French.

Anglo-Dutch tension in India was rising in the 1680s also on the Coromandel coast. The Dutch were jealous of the commercial success of Fort St George at Madras and dismayed by the relative decline of their base at Fort Geldria (Pulicut), though this was caused less by English competition than the political and economic turmoil along the northern Coromandel coast caused by the southwards expansion of Mughal power.[21] The English suffered the effects of this too; but the general deterioration of the Coromandel trade, and relative decline in importance of this trade compared with that of Bengal, did nothing to alleviate the perpetual friction between the English and Dutch. Both parties regarded every step taken by the other in the worst possible light. In July 1686 the Dutch governor of Fort Geldria, at that point still the VOC's headquarters on the Coromandel coast, established a garrison at the Dutch factory at Masulipatam as part of a dispute with the Nawab of Golconda.[22] The English were greatly alarmed as they had long plied a lively commerce with Masulipatam. In a letter to James II, Child claimed, with obvious exaggeration, that the Dutch 'have seized Metchlepatam [Masulipatam] after the same manner they did Bantam, and have forbid Your Majesty's subjects after eight weeks to trade there notwithstanding Your Majesty's East India Company have had a residence and factory there about eighty or ninety years'.[23] James II lodged a diplomatic complaint

[20] J. I. Israel, 'The Diplomatic Career of Jeronimo Nunes da Costa: An Episode in Dutch–Portuguese Relations of the Seventeenth Century', *Bijdragen en Mededelingen betreffende de Geschiedenis der Nederlanden* 98 (1983), p. 188.

[21] ARH SG 5741/2, report of Pieter van Dam to SG, The Hague, 24 Dec. 1692, fo. 5v; Sinnapah Arasaratnam, *Merchants, Companies and Commerce on the Coromandel Coast, 1650–1740* (Delhi, 1986), pp. 150–3, 173.

[22] BL MS Add. 41822, fos. 93–5, Fort St George Council to Dutch governor of Pulicut, Madras (undated 1686); Dutch governor at Pulicut to Fort St George Council, Fort Geldria, 3/13 Aug. 1686; ibid., fo. 120, Pieter van Dam to SG, The Hague, 4 Oct. 1687.

[23] Ibid., fo. 107, Child to James II, London, 29 June 1687. However, the English continued to trade actively at Masulipatam albeit now without having a factory there; the Dutch position was weakened in the aftermath of the Mughal conquest of the Kingdom of Golconda, see *Records of Fort St George: Letters to Fort St George 1686–1687* (Madras, 1919), pp. 87–9; T. Raychaudhuri, *Jan Company in Coromandel 1605–1690* (The Hague, 1962), p. 73.

in The Hague. The VOC directors advised the States General, in reply, that Dutch troops had been sent in to Masulipatam only as a result of the quarrel with the Nawab, not to eject the English or prevent them trading there, and that if the English, as a consequence of the ensuing turmoil, had felt unsafe and chosen to leave, that was neither the fault nor concern of the Dutch Company.[24]

Meanwhile Child complained bitterly also of the continuing growth of Dutch power on the west coast of Sumatra. From their main base at Palangh, the VOC were now systematically imposing local treaties right along the coast, forcing the inhabitants to sell their pepper exclusively to the Dutch. The English fort at Batancapas which, the Dutch considered, had been built provocatively close to one of their own was, in the VOC's eyes, rendered redundant when an exclusive trade treaty was imposed also on this locality in March 1686. As tension rose, both Dutch and English mobilized local factions against the other, the tussle ending with the English factory being attacked, pillaged, and closed.[25] Child in his usual dramatic style, conveyed to James II his horror that the Dutch in Sumatra had torn 'Your Majesty's flag ... in pieces, contemptuously ... by which it manifestly appears that the Netherlands East India Company are still pursuing their design of engrossing the whole East India trade by violence, injustice and oppression'.[26]

Naturally, the VOC also endeavoured to take advantage of the deteriorating relations between the English Company and the Mughal authorities in western India. At Surat where the VOC maintained a sizeable establishment, with some eight employees, and where Anglo-Dutch tension was acute, the Dutch were delighted when the Mughal governor arrested the head and nine other officials at the English factory and paraded them in chains through the streets. In February 1689, the month in which William and Mary were proclaimed king and queen of England, the VOC director at Surat wrote to the Mughal emperor to assure him that the Dutch had entered into no arrangement or collaboration with the English Company in India with respect to trade or anything else.[27]

The Dutch moves in the 1680s precipitated a pamphlet war at home and a series of fruitless two-power conferences in London, the only effect of which was to impress the Anglo-Dutch confrontation in Asia strongly on the consciousness of the public in both England and the United Provinces. Relations between the two countries during James II's reign were poor and friction over the East India trade was a major factor in this. In October 1688, with William III's invasion of England imminent, pro-government pamphleteers in London urged

[24] ARH SG 5741/2, Heren XVII to SG, The Hague, 4 Oct. 1687.
[25] Ibid., fos. 6v–7.
[26] BL MS Add. 41822, fo. 107, Child to James II, London, 29 June 1687.
[27] Heeres and Stapel (eds.), *Corpus Diplomaticum Neerlando-Indicum*, III, pp. 488–9.

the Protestant populace not to listen to the propaganda emanating from The Hague about England's liberties and the dangers facing the Protestant religion and to remember 'by what perfidiousness, over-reaching and barbarity, the Dutch have wormed us out of the trade of the East Indies'.[28]

With the Glorious Revolution the picture changed abruptly, almost overnight, not only on the surface but also in many fundamental ways, some of which took decades to become fully evident. All at once, the openly hostile propaganda ceased, the further use of force was ruled out, and, even though the directors of both the great Companies instructed their employees to hinder and obstruct the activity of the other with every means compatible with an outward show of friendliness, official communication between the two Companies was now transformed.[29] Inter-Company correspondence was now replete with reference to the 'friendliness' proper 'between two nations so closely bound to one another and allied in so good a cause' as the English directors put it, in November 1689, in a letter to the directors of Amsterdam Chamber of the VOC about an English vessel which, owing to unseaworthiness, had been forced to put in and land its cargo of pepper at Batavia.[30]

The underlying cause of the weakening in the VOC's position in Asian trade as a whole, from the 1680s onwards, was the shift in patterns of consumption and demand in Europe which dramatically increased the importance of Asian commodities such as cottons, calicoes, muslin, raw silk, and also tea and coffee, which came overwhelmingly from regions where there were no Dutch garrisons and where the VOC's naval might was of little or no relevance. The irony of the Dutch drive to supremacy of the 1680s was that it was, and perhaps could only have been, primarily directed towards securing the traditional Dutch aim of monopolizing the spice and pepper traffic, and this precisely at the moment when the balance tilted decisively against those commodities in the overall composition of Europe's Asian trade. It was thus not so much an effort doomed to failure, though in Malabar one might argue that it was, as one of decreasing relevance to the commercial realities of the time. In 1688 the supremacy of the VOC among the European companies trading with Asia appeared to be intact and to have been further enhanced. It was only gradually, in the years after 1688, that the way things had appeared to be in 1688 was shown to be deceptive. In mid-August 1688 the price of shares in the Amsterdam Chamber of the VOC on the Amsterdam Exchange reached 582 per cent of their face

[28] *The Dutch Design Anatomized, or, A Discovery of the Wickedness and Unjustice [sic] of the Intended Invasion* (London, 1688), p. 7.

[29] The Dutch governor of Ceylon evidently instructed his subordinates not to supply English vessels with provisions, sail-cloth, masts or other ships' stores or anything else other than 'water or firewood', see the *Memoir of Thomas van Rhee, Governor and Director of Ceylon for his Successor Gerrit de Heere (1697)* (Colombo, 1915), p. 54.

[30] ARH VOC 155, res. 5 Dec. 1689.

value, the peak for the entire century.[31] This was the culmination in a long climb in the VOC share price in progress since the beginning of the decade. The peak was not maintained for long, for once the merchants realized, at the end of August, what the preparations going on in the Dutch seaports were for, share prices slumped disastrously. But the recovery that began with the success of the Glorious Revolution failed to win back all the ground that had been lost. At the time of the battle of the Boyne, in 1690, the shares were trading in Amsterdam at only 490.[32] Indeed, the optimism about the prospects of the VOC evinced in 1687–8 was never fully to return.

The strategic implications of the Glorious Revolution in Asia were so vast that it was bound to take time to digest them. It was simply not clear whether these would, on balance, be favourable or unfavourable to the English or the Dutch. For both Companies there were advantages to be gained from the ending of the era of armed confrontation and of attacks on each other's factories and ships, if not of blatant incitement of native princes by the one Company against the other. Both sides could now take refuge when in need, from storm or the French, in the bases of the other. But in the past the VOC had relied on the military superiority, and had used it, to check the growth of English commerce in both the Indonesian archipelago and India proper and the impossibility of doing so in the changed circumstances was likely to be a serious drawback for them. The resurgence of English trade with the Malabar coast was evident as early as 1689.[33]

The one remaining political instrument with which the Dutch Company could hope to impede the progress of its English rival was by the surreptitious use of its influence with William III, now king of England as well as Dutch Stadholder, and his 'secret cabal of Dutchmen', as his close advisers in London were known. Ironically, the directors of the VOC became so afraid of the new English East India company that they seem to have decided that it was in their interest to help shore up the old Company – the Company which had been closely aligned with James II and preached a philosophy of armed confrontation with the Dutch – as an obstruction to the new.[34] There were even signs that the VOC, through the States General's ambassadors in London, induced William to give some support to the pretensions of the old Company.[35]

Thus, one major effect of the Glorious Revolution in India was a fundamental shift in the strategic balance between the Dutch and English in favour of the

31 BL MS Add. 41821, fo. 236v, 'News from The Hague' (13 Aug. 1688); J.I. Israel, 'The Amsterdam Stock Exchange and the English Revolution of 1688', *Tijdschrift voor Geschiedenis*, 103 (1990), p. 428.

32 PRO SP 84/221, fo. 157v, Aglionby to Warre, The Hague, 7 July 1690.

33 ARH SG 5741/2, report of Jacobus Couper to SG, 7 Dec. 1688, section on Malabar; W. Ph. Coolhaas (ed.), *Generale Missiven van Gouverneurs-Generaal en Raden aan Heren XV11 der Verenigde Oostindische Compagnie* (9 vols., The Hague, 1960–), V, p. 336.

34 N. J. den Tex, *Jacob Hop, gezant der Vereenigde Nederlanden* (Amsterdam, 1861), p. 161.

35 Ibid.

latter. On the Malabar coast the Dutch had to cease their harassment of the English factories and abandon all thought of monopolizing the pepper traffic of the region. The English were now free to strengthen their position largely unhindered. Although the Dutch tried to foil them indirectly, by inciting the local rajah against them, the English established themselves securely in a fortified base at Anjengo during the 1690s and, in 1703, began also to fortify their factory at Tellicherry.[36] At the same time, from 1689, there was a marked tendency for Dutch influence in the central and northern parts of the Coromandel coast to begin to give way to that of the English. Even the one aspect of the new strategic situation which seemed to favour the VOC eventually turned out to work to the Dutch Company's disadvantage. For if the Glorious Revolution ended the confrontation between the Dutch and English in Asia at sea and on land – even if not in the minds of the two Companies' employees – the Revolution appeared to isolate the French and present the VOC with a golden opportunity to eliminate them from the scene.

The Nine Years War (1688–97) in India was indeed essentially a contest between the Dutch and French and was never likely to be anything else. There were several reasons for this. In the first place, the French and English, ever since the French had first become a significant factor in Asia in the 1660s, had been on relatively friendly terms, both nations regarding the Dutch rather than each other as the main obstacle to their progress.[37] In the recent past, the French and English had jointly suffered the effects of Dutch aggression in Bantam. In the second place, the Dutch in Asia were much more accustomed than the English to use their naval power as a strategic instrument and to seek to deal with foreign competition by means of force. Finally, the French themselves considered that they had much more to gain by attacking the Dutch than the English. In 1688 the Dutch were still unquestionably the strongest European power in Asia; but Louis XIV's ministers, and the French director at Pondichéry, François Martin, were convinced that the Dutch empire in Asia, however imposing it might seem, was now on the wane and vulnerable to a well-aimed blow delivered from metropolitan France.[38] The potential of the sort of heavily armed expedition which had been sent out from France to India in 1672 (however unsuccessful on that occasion) continued to exert a powerful fascination at Paris and not without reason. The French view was that if they amassed a sufficient force they could appropriate much of what the VOC now possessed in Asia swiftly and relatively easily. Martin urged his masters in Paris to aim high and send expeditions not only against the Cape of Good Hope and Malacca, as well as to India, but against Batavia itself, expecting the capture of the VOC's

[36] Rajendran, *Establishment of British Power in Malabar*, pp. 45, 48.
[37] Paul Kaeppelin, *La Compagnie des Indes Orientales et François Martin* (Paris, 1908), pp. 286–7.
[38] Ibid., pp. 237, 270, 285.

headquarters in Asia to paralyse virtually the entire Dutch imperium in the eastern Indies.[39]

Nor, for their part, were the Dutch at all complacent about the French threat in Asia. They were not deceived by the relative ease with which they had eradicated the French from Indonesia in 1682. On the contrary, there was a perceptible anxiety amongst the Dutch leadership in Asia that the French might be capable of making very major inroads indeed. Thus far the French had established an overall ascendancy only in Siam.[40] But if they could coax the king of Siam into favouring themselves, and hostility towards the Dutch, what was to prevent the French repeating this feat elsewhere? The French possessed well-established trade factories at Surat and Pondichéry as well as in Siam and, since 1684, and particularly 1687, had also established themselves in the highly lucrative Bengal trade. Nor was the VOC unaware that the French Company had also been engaging in exploratory probing of the Malabar trade. It is true that the French commerce with Surat, Coromandel, and Bengal was, in 1688, still very small compared with that of either the Dutch or English. But the Dutch were abundantly aware that such an incipient traffic could very quickly be transformed into something far more formidable in propitious political and military circumstances.

The Franco-Dutch war in India in 1689–98 is not a topic which attracts much attention. Yet it was a major episode in the history of India. The VOC went full out to eliminate, or at least drastically weaken, the French presence. From the moment war between France and the United Provinces seemed likely, in 1688, the Compagnie des Indes Orientales concentrated its whole attention, and spent recklessly, on fitting out armed expeditions to fight the Dutch in India. As part of their overall strategy to counter the French threat while, at the same time, hoping to evade the adverse effects of Mughal expansion on the north Coromandel coast on commerce, the VOC decided at the outset of the war to transfer their headquarters on the Coromandel coast, and the substantial garrison based north of Madras at Fort Geldria to Negapatnam, a short distance from Pondichéry, at the southern end of the coast.[41] Over a million guilders were spent on the fortifications of Negapatnam in the years 1686–93 in the hope of turning the town into the most formidable European stronghold in the whole of India.[42] The main transfer of troops, equipment, and records took place in 1690.

[39] Ibid., p. 285; see also François Martin's memorandum of February 1700 in Pierre Margry (ed.), *Relations et mémoires inédits pour servir à l'historire de la France dans les pays d'Outre Mer tirés des archives du ministère de la marine et des colonies* (Paris, 1867), p. 122.

[40] ARH SG 5741/2, Pieter van Dam to SG, The Hague, 2 Nov. 1694; Kaeppelin, *Compagnie des Indes Orientales*, pp. 261–4.

[41] Coolhaas (ed.), *Generale Missiven*, V, pp. 332, 379; Pieter van Dam, *Beschryvinge van de Oostindische Compagnie*, ed. F. W. Stapel (4 vols. in seven parts, The Hague, 1927–54), II, part 2, pp. 110–11.

[42] Van Dam, *Beschryvinge*, II, part 2, pp. 110–11.

In the years around 1690 the concentration of Dutch power in India at the southern end of the Coromandel coast appeared to be well judged. Not only was the VOC now well placed to lay siege to Pondichéry, and to eliminate the French presence from southern India, they could also hope to compensate for the decay of trade along the northern Coromandel coast by means of heavy investment, and attracting weavers and work-people, to build up textile output in the comparatively unexploited, low-cost regions of Madura and Tinnevely, at the southern end of the coast.[43]

The war began well for the VOC with two French East India ships captured at the Cape of Good Hope, in May 1689, and turmoil in Siam temporarily disrupting the French military and commercial presence there. The French expedition which arrived off the Coromandel coast in 1690 failed to do the Dutch any real damage and as soon as it was gone, active planning began for laying siege to Pondichéry. Although various delays now ensued, the French garrison at Pondichéry felt themselves very much under siege in 1691–2.[44] As the manpower available to the Dutch in southern India was insufficient to mount the sort of operation required to capture Pondichéry which was defended by 163 French troops, some 400 native auxiliaries, and 69 cannon, the attack had to be co-ordinated from Batavia, drawing on troops as well as artillery and siege equipment from Java and Ceylon as well as the southern tip of India. Finally, in August 1693 a force of 17 VOC ships under the command of Laurens Pit, with around 2,000 seamen and 1,579 troops – 987 of these being Europeans and the rest Indonesian and Sinhalese auxiliaries – departed Negapatnam and closed on Pondichéry.[45] Although the siege lasted only sixteen days, there was a considerable amount of firing. On 9 September the French garrison surrendered. The Dutch then themselves garrisoned Pondichéry, sending the French prisoners to Batavia and Ceylon, and secured the surrounding area.

The fall of Pondichéry depressed French morale throughout India and adjoining areas of Asia. On François Martin's orders, the subsidiary French Coromandel lodge at Caveripatam was abandoned; the VOC arranged for the local rajah to demolish it.[46] The news of Pondichéry's fall, relayed via Aleppo, in Syria, reached Paris in June 1694. But, though dismayed, the French were in no mood to give up. Eager to restore French prestige in Asia, Louis assisted the Compagnie to fit out a new expedition to secure the French factories in Bengal whither the focus of the war now shifted.

By 1689 the French were established at three places in Bengal with their main

[43] Arasaratnam, *Merchants, Companies and Commerce*, pp. 159–60, 166, 177.
[44] Coolhaas (ed.), *Generale Missiven*, V, pp. 418, 480.
[45] Ibid., V, pp. 634–5; Van Dam, *Beschryvinge*, I, part 2, pp. 621–2; and II, part 2, p. 114; see also ARH SG 5741/2, Pieter van Dam to SG, The Hague, 2 Nov. 1694, fo. 8.
[46] Kaeppelin, *Compagnie des Indes Orientales*, p. 314.

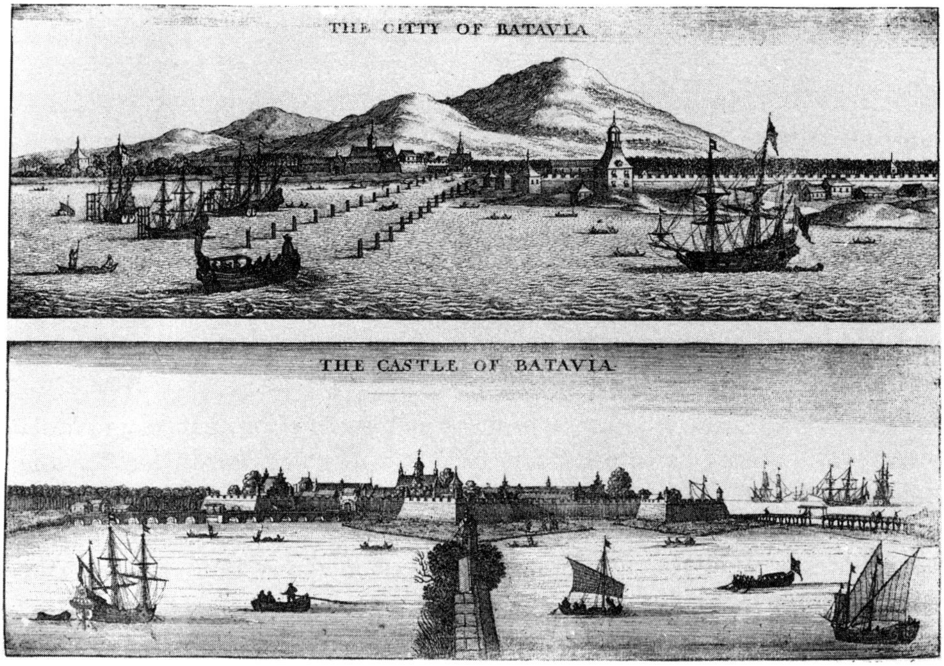

26 *The City and Fortress of Batavia (Jakarta), Headquarters of the VOC in Asia.*

factory at Hugli and two subsidiary *comptoirs* at Ballasore and Cassimbazar.[47] A Dutch squadron had already appeared and briefly blockaded Ballasore, on the Ganges estuary, in 1693. But the main blockade, co-ordinated by the Dutch factory at Hugli, began with the arrival of five VOC ships, from Pondichery, in 1694. [48] Besides the French lodges, three French vessels with valuable cargoes were trapped in the Ganges estuary. The blockade was sustained throughout the rest of the war, paralysing French activity in Bengal completely. The expedition sent from France set out from Surat to break the blockade. But after an inconclusive battle between the five French and eight VOC ships ten leagues north of Goa, in March 1696, the attempt to relieve the French factories in Bengal was abandoned.

Thus, in the mid-1690s, the VOC's strategy political, military, and commercial in India appeared to be triumphantly successful. VOC fleets were supreme on both the eastern and western coasts of India, with eight Dutch vessels regularly patrolling the coast of Malabar.[49] French trade with Bengal was all but destroyed

[47] Margry (ed.), *Relations et mémoires inédits*, p. 122; Henri Carré, *François Martin. Fondateur de l'Inde Français* (Abbaye S. Wandrille, 1946), p. 143.

[48] Jules Sottas, *Histoire de la Compagnie Royale des Indes Orientales, 1664–1719* (Paris, 1905), p. 388; Kaeppelin, *Compagnie des Indes Orientales*, pp. 324–33; Carré, *François Martin*, p. 144.

[49] Sottas, *Histoire*, p. 390.

Table 4. *Dutch military and civilian personnel in south-eastern India in 1694*

Location	Employees	Location	Employees
Negapatnam (fort)	389	Teganapatam	31
Pondichéry (fort)	147	Sadraspatnam	7
Tuticorin (fort)	91	Golconda	4
Calpetty (fort)	56	Daetcheram	4
Pulicut (fort)	45	Portonovo	4
Masulipatam (fort)	31	Palakol	4

Source: Coolhaas (ed.), *Generale Missiven*, V, p. 763.

and was never to recover.[50] Dutch primacy on both the Coromandel and Malabar coasts appeared to be intact. In 1695, the Dutch Company had a total of 645 employees on the Coromandel coast, 989 European and 740 native employees on the Malabar coast, a couple of hundred perhaps in northern India, 147 soldiers at Tuticorin and the extreme southern tip of India, and an army of 2,700 men in five main garrisons in Ceylon.[51]

Yet, somewhat paradoxically, the Dutch drive against the French in Southern India during the 1690s had the ultimate effect of weakening the VOC's position overall. The shift in the centre of gravity of Dutch activity on the Coromandel coast from Pulicut, which lies north of Madras, to Negapatnam, at the southern end of Carnatic, made strategic sense and enabled the Dutch to capture Pondichéry; but, at the same time, it effectively undermined the Dutch presence along the northern half of the coast.[52] This effect was further contributed to by the VOC's policy of minimizing the stocks of goods kept in the lesser factories, out of fear of French attacks, and keeping the main stocks in Negapatnam which was a safe and formidable stronghold but which turned out to be a rather poor base for commerce, most of the Coromandel textile trade being centred further north.[53] Fort Geldria, meanwhile, already obsolete and losing its commercial importance in 1688, decayed rapidly thereafter, its walls being described in 1697 as being in a deplorable state.[54] Furthermore, the VOC's original plan to keep Pondichéry was frustrated by events in Europe. At the Rijswijk peace conference,

[50] ARH SG 5741/2, report of Wouter Valkenier to SG, The Hague, 28 Aug. 1700, fo. 7v; Kaeppelin, *Compagnie des Indes Orientales*, pp. 316, 635.

[51] Coolhaas (ed.), *Generale Missiven*, V, pp. 141, 727, 731, 763, 807; *Memoir of Thomas van Rhee*, p. 52; the garrison on the Malabar Coast, consisting of only 350 troops in December 1687 had been considerably increased; in 1694, there were 82 Dutch employees at Surat and a probably slightly larger number in Bengal.

[52] S. Arasaratnam, 'The Dutch East India Company and its Coromandel Trade, 1700–1740', *Bijdragen tot de taal-land- en volkenkunde van Nederlandsch-Indië*, 123 (1967), pp. 326, 337, 346.

[53] Ibid., p. 337; ARH SG 5741/2, report of Pieter van Dam to SG, 23 Dec. 1693, section on Coromandel; François Martin, writing in 1700, dismissed the Dutch depot at Negapatnam as 'bien inutile en cet endroit. Le commerce est peu considérable de ce coste-là', Margry (ed.), *Relations et mémoires inédits*, p. 130.

[54] Coolhaas (ed.), *Generale Missiven*, V, p. 847.

the Dutch negotiators were under orders to sacrifice lesser commercial considerations to the overriding Dutch goal of obtaining a general reduction in the French tariffs on imports from the Republic and the Company had no choice but to fall in with the wishes of the States of Holland. The peace treaty consequently stipulated that 'le fort et habitation de Pondichery sera rendu ... à la Compagnie des Indes Orientales établie en France'.[55]

The delay in finalizing the Franco-Dutch tariff agreement enabled the Dutch to hang on to Pondichéry until 1699 but once the tariffs were agreed, the VOC had to hand the fortress back, the fortifications intact, as was done at a ceremony on 13 September 1699.[56] This was a double disaster for the Dutch Company for not only did the restitution of Pondichéry restore French influence in south-eastern India but, since 1693, the Dutch themselves had strengthened the fortifications so that Pondichéry was now one of the most formidable coastal strongholds in all India. The French were quick to see the enhanced value of their asset. In 1701 the French director-general and headquarters in India was transferred from Surat to Pondichéry which, a few years later, had a garrison of some 800 European troops, dwarfing Negapatnam, and, after 1713, became one of the most thriving European trade centres in the subcontinent.[57] Consequently, after 1699, the Coromandel coast from Pondichéry north became for the first time more of a French and English than a Dutch preserve.

Meanwhile the Dutch position on the Malabar coast was also now perceptibly in decline. According to François Martin the VOC did temporarily suppress the incipient French trade which, in 1688, had been concentrated especially in the Cannannore area, during the 1690s.[58] But it soon revived again around 1700, albeit rather sporadically, and, in any case, not only the English but also the Portuguese and Danes were all now increasing their activity in the region. The English traffic in Malabar pepper was particularly successful in the years 1696–1703 (see Table 3) and, although it then fell off markedly during the following years, there was a noticeable increase in English political and military effort.[59] The fortifications at Tellicherry were completed in 1708. The increasing obstructiveness of the Zamorin of Calicut to Dutch wishes was strongly encour-

[55] Heeres and Stapel (eds.), *Corpus Diplomaticum Neerlando-Indicum*, IV, p. 169, quoting article 8 of the Treaty of Rijswijk.

[56] Ibid., IV, pp. 168–74; several communications from Louis XIV to the States General demanding the return of Pondichery, under the terms of the peace treaty, feature in ARH SH 2497.

[57] Arasaratnam, 'Dutch East India Company', p. 336; G. B. Malleson, *History of the French in India from the Founding of Pondicherry in 1674* (London, 1893), pp. 34–6; Pondichery already surpassed Negapatnam as a military garrison as early as 1707 by which date there were 400 French there, see Kaeppelin, *Compagnie des Indes Orientales*, p. 634; according to Arasaratnam, Pondichery began to be a serious commercial threat to the Dutch and English from about 1710, Arasaratnam, *Merchants, Companies and Commerce*, p. 203.

[58] ARH SG 5741/2, report of Jacobus Couper to SG, The Hague, 7 Dec. 1688, section 'Malabar'; Margry (ed.), *Relations et mémoires inédits*, p. 120.

[59] Rajendran, *Establishment of British Power in Malabar*, pp. 48–52.

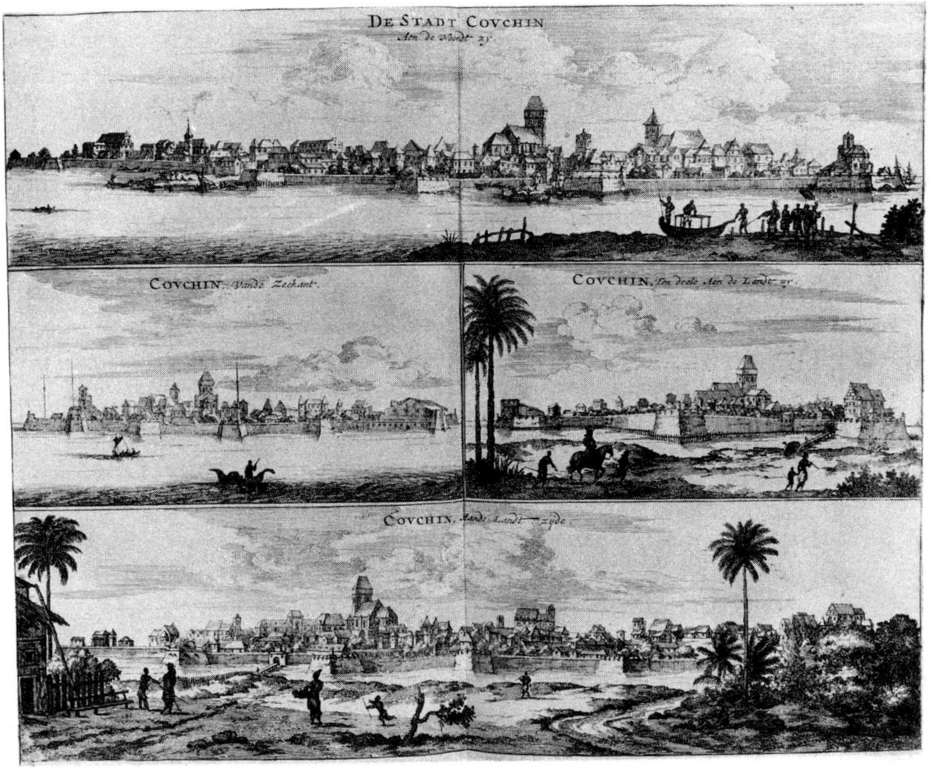

27 *The City and Fort of Cochin on the Malabar Coast.*
The Dutch commander Rykloff van Goens captured Cochin from the Portuguese in 1663. It remained in Dutch hands for 132 years until 1795.

aged by the English. Yet the VOC had not yet finally abandoned its ambition to be the undisputed master of the Malabar coast and a strategic decision was made that the Company could only boost profits, end the enervating drain of the Malabar garrisons on the Company's resources, and curtail English influence in the area, by using force to compel the Zamorin of Calicut to submit to Dutch domination. In the years 1708–10 the Dutch invaded the territory of Calicut and captured a number of strong points. In January 1710, the Zamorin was compelled to sign a treaty with the VOC undertaking to trade exclusively with the Dutch Company and expel the English as well as the French, Danes, and Portuguese from his dominion.[60] Briefly, it appeared that the Dutch were succeeding. English trade, until 1713, remained at a comparatively modest level compared with the 1696–1703 period. In October 1710, the States General in The Hague were informed that the state of the Dutch Malabar trade was

[60] Heeres and Stapel (eds.), *Corpus Diplomaticum Neerlando-Indicum*, IV, pp. 340–3.

now considerably healthier than a few years before.[61] The Dutch once again expanded their military establishment on Malabar and began to fortify Chetuwa.

But this final phase of general Dutch domination of the Malabar coast proved brief. In 1715, the Zamorin, stirred by the English, renounced his agreements with the Dutch and seized the unfinished fort at Chetuwa. The next year was one of intense drama in the region. Whilst the authorities at Batavia made preparations for an expedition to crush thoroughly the Zamorin's insubordination, the English strove as one of them put it to help 'prevent the Dutch designs to engross the pepper trade on that coast ... like on Sumatra'.[62] A Dutch army of 600 European and 1,000 native troops launched a counter-offensive, defeating the Zamorin's forces and recovering the fort at Chetuwa. Under the treaty of December 1717, the prince again undertook to exclude the English, French, Portuguese and Danes from his realm. Yet the victory proved a pyrrhic one. Within two years the Zamorin was again asserting his independence, selling large quantities of pepper to the English and resuming relations also with other Europeans.[63] In the 1720s there was a noticeable upsurge of French as well as English traffic. It was at this point that Batavia, and the directors in the Netherlands, for all practical purposes finally abandoned the policy initiated by Van Goens in 1663 of trying to monopolize the Malabar pepper and spice trade. In 1721 a strategic decision was taken that the Dutch forces would no longer intervene in the interminable conflicts between the rulers of Cochin and Calicut and that the Dutch military presence would be scaled down.[64] It was the end of an era.

While the Dutch Company was busy in the 1680s and 1690s formulating plans for the elimination of its European rivals in the Indian Ocean and putting those schemes into practice, English trade, political influence, and naval strength in the Mughal Empire steadily increased. Josia Child was convinced that the Company's formidable fleet put at sea in the aftermath of the fall of Bantam would enable it to seize a number of trading ports in the Mughal Empire and become, as he reminded the Bombay Council in 1689, a political nation in India. As for the VOC, the Secret War Committee hoped that 'we may continue to have peace with the Dutch, yet we must in prudence never look otherwise upon them in India than as an emulous and ambitious neighbour and make such provisions in peace as we may be able to defend ourselves in war ... and doubt not but this Company will be longer than our youngest grand-children can live'.[65] Any one who reads through the court of directors' letters during the early 1680s

[61] ARH SG 5742/1, Pieter van Hoorn, 'Rapport belangende den toestant van saken der Nederlandsche Compagnie in India' (17 Oct. 1710), fo. 30.
[62] Rajendran, *Establishment of British Power in Malabar*, p. 52.
[63] Ibid., pp. 54–7.
[64] Ibid., p. 54; William Logan, *Malabar* (2 vols., Madras, 1951), I, p. 350.
[65] IOR EIC Despatch Book, 11 Sept. 1689, vol. 92, p. 64.

will notice that a subtle change had crept into the tone of expressions used towards the Dutch Company. This particular letter was written nine months after the Company had reported to Bombay the events of late 1688. The old violence of terms used against the Dutch begins to lessen and the language becomes more cautious and restrained. In fact, as the East India Company struggled hard to retrieve the disastrous consequences of its Mughal war and fight off Whig opposition at home for its abolition, the perceived danger from the VOC seemed to recede. After 1709 when the two rival East India Companies officially merged, Dutch competition and political ambition in Asia are seldom mentioned in the English correspondence. The wheel seemed to have turned a complete circle and soon it was the turn of the VOC officials to complain about the aggressive policy of the English in India in promoting their private trade and invading areas which were hitherto reserved strictly for the Dutch. In the 1720s the East India Company would even elect a Dutchman, Sir Matthew Decker, as its governor. Decker was responsible for formulating policies which were to take the East India Company's trade beyond the scale of the VOC's commercial operations.

Although the naval strength of the VOC and its superior finances were an ever present anxiety to the English organization in the 1660s and 1670s, the real political danger faced by the Company came from a different direction. The Company had always faced criticism and opposition from fellow English traders who had been excluded from a share of the East India trade by the monopoly granted by successive royal charters and by the deliberate restriction of the size of the share capital in the 1670s. In order to combat such opposition, the East India directorate had forged close links with the king and his courtiers. The most tangible evidence of the connection between the East India Company and the royal support was a series of financial loans made to the government which amounted to £40,000 and £50,000 respectively in 1676 and 1677.[66] The loans were made primarily to pay for the expenses of the Royal Navy and therefore were national in spirit. But the corporate reward was the granting of fresh Letters Patent in 1677 which confirmed all the previous privileges, and the reason for the new charter was stated to be 'diverse transactions having happened, where the proceedings of the governor and company may be liable to some question, how far they are warranted, by the strict letter of the said charters and the charters themselves may be in danger of being impeached as forfeited for some misuser or non-user of rights'.[67]

The attack on the Company's management at home conducted through the shareholders' meetings and in printed pamphlets soon went beyond words and

[66] IOR EIC Court Book, 3 Oct. 1676, vol. 34, p. 58; Ibid., vol. 35, p. 59.
[67] IOR EIC *Charters granted to the East India Company*, A/2/3.

took on a more concrete form. From the late 1670s, rival merchants and commanders of ships began to organize actual trading voyages to the Indies which were interpreted by the East India directorate as a serious threat to the Company's economic and political survival. The corner-stone of the Company's long-term policy throughout its existence remained the defence of its monopoly but the Company was caught in a legal dilemma in the immediate post-Restoration years. The Company's charter was granted not by Parliament but by the king. According to English legal tradition, engrossing of goods and monopolies in general was illegal. If the Company turned to the law courts to defend its privileges against the interlopers, it was by no means clear that the judges would support claims which derived from royal prerogatives. The Company did go to court in 1683 in the celebrated case of Thomas Sandys. In the early days of interloping, however, the directors thought it more prudent to try and intercept the private traders in India, using its quasi-military forces in the various settlements.

In the 1670s all kinds of rumours were circulating in the trading world of Europe and the Indian Ocean that the iron stranglehold of the English and Dutch Companies on Asian trade was about to be broken. The Jewish merchants, it was reported, had offered Charles II £50,000 for the charter of a new company in which they would be entitled to own stock legally. The Surat Factory had received news from Europe in 1675 about an impending plan to set up a Portuguese East India Company, financed by the Jewish 'New Christians' of Lisbon and the Jewish merchants of Livorno, Genoa, Venice, and Amsterdam. The Company was disturbed at the news which on enquiry turned out to be 'groundless'.[68] The Jewish interest in the East India trade arose from their heavy involvement in supplying gold to the Company and the export of Mediterranean coral to the Middle East and India. The proceeds of these sales were invested in diamonds from the famous Golconda mines. From the 1680s the East India Company allowed the Jewish merchants to export silver on the Company's ships under licence. The most prominent leader of the English interlopers undoubtedly was Thomas Pitt. In February 1682, the directorate informed the Company's officials in Bengal that Pitt had left for India in the ship *Crown* and ordered them to have him arrested 'whatever it cost the Government or other natives'. When Pitt was in the Company's custody, care was to be taken to secure him in irons, 'he being a desperate fellow, and one that we fear will not stick in doing any mischief that lies in his power'.[69] The Bengal Council reported later in the year that, upon arrival in Bengal, Pitt had entered the trading port of Ballasore in a hostile manner with Portuguese, Rajput, and other guards armed

[68] IOR EIC Original Correspondence, 26 Jan. 1676, vol. 36, no. 4171; Despatch Book, 7 Mar. 1677, vol. 88, p. 404; W. R. Scott, *The Constitution and Finance of English, Scottish and Irish Joint-Stock Companies to 1720* (Cambridge, 1911), II, p. 142.

[69] IOR, EIC Despatch Book, 15 Feb. 1682, vol. 89, para. 6, p. 455–6.

with matchlocks and with trumpeters.[70] In the close-knit community of London merchants and ships' captains it was not easy for any particular group to take drastic action against trade rivals and it was soon clear that the Company's own officials were deeply involved in the clandestine voyages which breached the old Company's exclusive rights. When an official in India informed the Company that he would comply with the instructions to arrest the interlopers as far as the laws of England allowed him, Sir Josia Child replied with obvious anger that 'he expected his orders should be observed and obeyed as statutes, and that they were to be his rule and not the laws of England, which were a heap of nonsense compiled by a few ignorant country gentlemen, who hardly knew how to make laws for the guidance of their own private families much less for the regulating of companies and foreign commerce'.[71]

It is clear that there were many complex twists and strands in the politics of East India trade. The opposing factions were not strictly categorized by single, identifiable policy issues. The Revolution of 1688 certainly polarized the East India Company and the City of London along certain lines, leading eventually to the foundation of a new rival Company. The role of the Crown, and after 1690, that of Parliament, was critical in preserving or weakening the East India Company as a single organization delegated with semi-sovereign rights in the Indian Ocean and at home. Two major sets of policy issues dominated East India politics in the 1680s and 1690s. First, there was the question whether the company should carry on at all as a closed trading corporation with a permanent joint-stock as opposed to a more open organization with either terminable capital or sums contributed by individual members on the model of regulated companies. The second point concerned the Company's stated and long-held determination to act as neutral merchants concerned wholly with peaceful trading and avoiding the expenditures of fortified settlements and military forces. Thomas Papillon and Josia Child, both wealthy merchants and government contractors, headed two opposing factions in the East India House. In 1677 the Committee of Correspondence had declared in a letter to the Fort St George Council that 'our business is Trade not War' and two years later condemned the Dutch method of armed trading.[72] The letters were signed jointly by the members of the Committee which included Papillon and Child.

It is not quite clear whether Papillon was a leader of the anti-armed-trading faction in the directorate, although his advocacy of an open East India trade was to cost him the membership of the Company in 1682. Josia Child strongly supported and indeed initiated the change-over to the policy of armed trading

[70] IOR EIC abstract of a letter from the English Council of the Bay of Bengal in India, Original Correspondence, vol. 2, no. 4882.

[71] Quoted in C. N. Dalton, *The Life of Thomas Pitt* (Cambridge, 1915), p. 17.

[72] IOR EIC Despatch Book, 12 Dec. 1677, vol. 88, p. 492; Despatch Book, 3 Dec. 1679, vol. 89, p. 115.

and he was instrumental in formulating a commercial and political strategy which would put an end to the interlopers. The immediate context of the conflict between the East India factions led by Papillon and Child respectively was a petition submitted to the king (1680) by the Levant Company challenging the East India Company's monopoly and the restricted share capital. In its defence the Company mounted a vigorous propaganda campaign through pamphlets and in October 1681, the General Court decided to present the king with a present of 10,000 guineas in recognition of the prosperity of the joint-stock which 'next to the blessing of the Almighty, they must attribute to the singular favour, countenance, assistance, which upon all occasions His Majesty hath been graciously pleased to vouchsafe unto them'.[73] A similar annual gift continued to be made to the king until the Revolution of 1688. The tactics of the royalist faction were not without critics within the Company. Thomas Papillon moved a resolution in November 1681 when the petition to the king was being drafted that the subscription for a new joint-stock should be opened in three years' time with free membership and the joint-stock of 1657 should be repaid. Josia Child and his party opposed the amendment on the ground that it would 'do us a mischief'. The motion was lost and at the next year's annual election of directors, Papillon lost his membership of the board.[74] A contemporary tract noted that Sir Josia Child had at last forsaken 'all his old friends that first introduced him with great difficulty into the Committee' and that he had allied himself with the 'great ministers and chief men at Court'. His lavish presents to the courtiers enabled him to do what he pleased.[75]

The East India Company's powerful patrons included not only the king himself but also his brother the duke of York and future James II. The duke had decided to become a shareholder in the Company, although not being a member the shares were held in trust by Sir Benjamin Bathurst. In April 1684 the royal trustee reported to the court of Committees that the duke wished the shares amounting to £2,000 to be registered directly under his own name, and it was decided that James was to be made free of the Company.[76] Six months later the royal holdings were increased by another £1,000. Two years after James II's accession, the Company represented to the king that the annual present of 10,000 guineas should be commuted to a single payment of £7,000 worth of stock. The offer was accepted and the Company spent £13,583 in acquiring the necessary stock. Although the shares were held by the king as part of his privy purse, the dividends paid by the Company were not treated as private

[73] IOR EIC Court Book, 5 Oct. 1681, vol. 36, p. 164.
[74] A. F. W. Papillon, *Memoirs of Thomas Papillon, of London, Merchant* (London, 1887), pp. 80–3; W. W. Hunter, *A History of British India* (2 vols., London, 1899–1900), II, p. 285.
[75] *Some Remarks upon the Present State of the East India Company's Affairs* (London, 1690); Hunter, *A History of British India*, II, p. 286.
[76] IOR ETC Court Book, 30 Apr. 1684, vol. 38, p. 2.

property and brought into the Exchequer accounts.[77] These shares proved to be a valuable asset for James II when in exile at St Germains where he transferred them to the Keeper of his Privy Purse Colonel James Grahame in return for a loan of £6,000. The East India Company raised no objection to the transfer of James II's personal shares of £3,000 to Grahame but refused to register the £7,000 which had been presented to the now exiled king. Eventually, after court proceeding, these shares were paid into the Exchequer in the name of William III and Mary.

At the beginning of 1688 Josia Child and his victorious faction was in triumphant mood. Thomas Papillon and other opponents of Child in the Company had sold out their holdings. Court action was brought against Papillon in 1684 and damages worth £10,000 were awarded against him. Papillon mortgaged his estates in order to avoid complete bankruptcy and fled to Utrecht. The interlopers were also prosecuted at law and what was more damaging, the East India Company flooded the home and European markets with oriental goods and severely depressed prices. However, this was a double-edged weapon and the Court of Committees admitted as early as 1684 that the cost of the price war against competitors was a drastic fall in profits.[78] Josia Child and the directorate defended the policy as fully justified by the expectation of long-term gains and in 1687 decided that the elimination of commercial competition from English merchants should be followed up by a short and effective naval war against the Mughal Empire. The main aim of the war would be to make territorial conquests in the coastal areas of India and the new settlements would be fortified on the Dutch and Portuguese model.[79] The Secret War Committee hinted that the Company's full warehouses should take care of the possible interruption to normal trading caused by the outbreak of hostilities.

It was against this background of events at home and abroad that the East India Company found itself facing the change of regime in the autumn of 1688. In a letter dated 11 January 1689, the Committee of Correspondence reported to the Bombay Council that the Dutch army which the Prince of Orange had brought over from Holland was quartered in and around London, but the army behaved themselves civilly, paid for their quarters, and did no injury to the country. The political news concluded with the statement that

> the King and Queen are gone to France. The Late Lord Chancellor with many Jesuits and Priests and others most active in Promoting the Popish Religion and other Innovations are made prisoners in the Tower, Newgate and other prisons ... The coming of the Prince of Orange, and general fear forerunning it hath caused

[77] Scott, *The Constitution and Finance of ... Joint-Stock Companies*, III, pp. 534–7; W. Foster, 'Some Royal Stockholders', in his *John Company* (London, 1926), p. 134.

[78] IOR EIC Despatch Book, 30 Sept. 1684, vol. 90, para. 11, p. 363.

[79] For a description of these events see, Chaudhuri, *Trading World of Asia*, pp. 115–17.

a great deadness of trade all this winter. But we hope now the Nation is a little settled, trade will begin to mend.[80]

A month later the Committee once again returned to the possible political consequences of the Revolution on the Company and drafted a defiant message:

> You will hear of the great change that it hath pleased God by His wonderful Providence to make in the Government of this Nation, and before this ship departed, we may have occasion to write you more thereof when the Lords and Commons have bounded and finished the intended settlement of the Prince and Princess of Orange whom the Lords have voted to be King and Queen of the Realm. But now we only mention this in transitu for an occasion to tell you that the Interlopers and other Maligners of the Company, are very busy, and pretend great matters they will do shortly by complaints of the company's management. A lightness and vanity which they have always abounded in, especially upon every change of the Government or lesser changes of Ministers of State or favourites. But their boastings have always come to nought, and so they will now, all Governments being wiser than to be swayed by such irregular disorderly vain men, though they may sometimes seem to give them a little ear and countenance for reasons not be mentioned, as also for the enlargement of their own understanding in so abstruse an affair as that of the East Indies is to Noblemen and Gentry that have not been conversant in business of that nature.[81]

The letter urged the Company's officials to disregard any unofficial rumours.

Before the year ended, the East India directorate became uncomfortably aware that the magnitude of the opposition had been underestimated. Reports were circulating in the City in the summer of 1689 that the old Company and its board were to be dissolved altogether and subscriptions were opened for the capital stock of a new company. But the single most important event which served to discredit the old Company was the news of the disastrous defeat in India. The Company's officials had found themselves either closely besieged by the Mughal forces or been driven altogether off-shore. An independent eyewitness, Alexander Hamilton, a Scottish sea-captain, privateer, and trader in the Indian Ocean, recorded the sorry outcome of the Company's Mughal war:

> The ill success we had ashore with the Enemy, made our General sick, and in December, he dispatched two Factors to the Mogul's Court, with a Surat Merchant, called Meer Mezamie [Mir Nizamie]. He was our Friend, and had some interest at Court ... Mr George Weldon was first in Commission, and Abraham Navaar, a Jew was Second. In fifteen days they arrived at Court, being then at Jahanabad. They were received but coldly; but, about the Middle of April, by the special assistance of presents to the officers of the Court, they were admitted to Audience, but were brought to Aurangzeb's presence after a new Mode for Ambassadors, their hands being tied by a sash before them, and were obliged to prostrate. The King gave them a severe reprimand and then asked their demands. They first made

[80] IOR EIC Despatch Book, 11 Jan. 1689, vol. 92, p. 3.
[81] IOR EIC Despatch Book, 15 Feb. 1689, vol. 92, para. 26, p. 11.

> a confession of their faults, and desired pardon, then that their phirmaund [farman] which was forfeited, should be renewed, and that the Sedee [Sidi Yakub, the Mughal Admiral] and his army should be ordered off Bombay. Their submission he accepted of, and pardoned their faults, on condition that Mr Child [Sir John Child, the governor of Bombay] should leave India in nine months and never come back again, and the phirmaund to be renewed on condition that satisfaction should be given his subjects on account of debts contracted, robberies committed, and losses and damages made good.[82]

If these were harsh terms for an organization which had confidently boasted two years earlier that it was a sovereign power in India and not an association of mere merchants, worse was yet to come. The Indian Ocean was invaded in the 1690s, by a number of European privateers from the West Indies and the American colonies who were followed by ruthless outright pirates. The Company pleaded in vain that it was doing all in its power to suppress the pirates and, eventually, the Mughal government in Surat forced both the VOC and the East India Company to institute a system of protective convoys.[83] The disruption to the Company's trade, however, continued for nearly a decade and was compounded by the long war with France, which led to the loss of many East-Indiamen in home waters at the hands of French privateers.

At home the 1690s were marked by continued attacks on the old East India Company and by close parliamentary investigations of its financial affairs. It was a measure of the Company's inherent strength and entrenched position in the commercial life of the City that the opposition only succeeded in 1698 in serving parliamentary notice on the old Company for its formal dissolution (in three years' time) and in securing the foundation of a new East India Company. The historical details of the struggle between the opposing groups for the control of the East India trade are well recorded and there is no need to go over the same ground again.[84] However, it is worth noting that the constitution of the East India Company, especially the elective element in the Court of Committees, allowed it to change its managerial policies and modify the line which had been taken by Josia Child and his party. Although Child continued to be a member of the board until his death in 1699, he was not elected to the governorship after 1689. His personal wealth still allowed him to bribe the courtiers close to William III. That Dutch statesman had sufficient experience of the complex politics of international trade since his early days not to take drastic action against an organization which controlled a large number of heavily armed ships and had command over immense corporate funds.

[82] Alexander Hamilton, *A New Account of the East Indies* (first published in Edinburgh, 1727; modern text, ed. W. Foster, 2 vols., London, 1930), I, pp. 128–9.

[83] For an account of the Red Sea piracies and the system of convoy demanded by the Mughals see, A. Das Gupta, *Indian Merchants and the Decline of Surat c. 1700–1750* (Wiesbaden, 1979), ch. 2.

[84] See Scott, *The Constitution and Finance of .. Joint-Stock Companies*, III, pp. 150–66; Chaudhuri, *Trading World of Asia*, pp. 429–36.

The detailed financial investigations conducted by the parliamentary committees, of course, revealed practices on the part of the old East India directorate which were rightly regarded as objectionable if not fraudulent. Even so in 1693 the Company managed to reach an accommodation with the king and its parliamentary supporters succeeded in having the charter renewed. It is doubtful whether the foundation of the new East India Company would have been possible without the severe credit crisis in which the government found itself at the end of its decade-long foreign wars.[85] The title of the parliamentary bill which set up the new Company spelt out the connection between public finance and the East India trade: 'Act for raising a sum not exceeding two million, upon a fund for payment of Annuities after the rate of eight pounds per cent. per annum, and for settling a trade to the East Indies.'[86] The historical significance of the New East India Company can be viewed from three complementary perspectives. The size of the capital and the actual method followed in raising it showed that the share capital of the old Company was unduly restricted. English trade with the Indian Ocean could easily absorb £2m or £3m disbursed in the form of working capital and investment on ships, settlements, and reserve funds. The loan of its trading capital to the government also introduced a novel principle in financing purely commercial operations. Trading capital was raised through fixed-interest bonds secured against the Exchequer bills. The new East India Company had in effect become a banking institution. In this situation all the elements of a full-fledged capital and money market were present and it is clear that London was fast becoming an important European financial centre. On the other hand, the new Company ran into unexpected difficulties in making its actual trading operations profitable. The exports and imports of the old Company not only picked up after the end of the war but its servants were the 'sitting tenants' of Bombay, Madras, and the newly fortified settlement in Calcutta. It proved difficult to dislodge them from this position of power in the Mughal Empire.

The new East India Company was managed by directors and officials many of whom had been members of the old Company and had long experience of the trade. The commercial organization set up by the Company was modelled on the system followed by the old Company. During the first eighteen months of its existence the new Company was confident that it would easily take over the bulk of the India trade. But in March 1700 the directors informed Sir Nicholas Waite, the president of the Surat Council, that the old Company had a bill passed in both Houses of Parliament confirming its right to continue as a corporation; the bill soon received Royal Assent from William III. The directors urged the officials in India to follow efficient purchasing policies: 'While the Old Com-

[85] P. G. M. Dickson, *The Financial Revolution in England 1688–1756* (London, 1967), pp. 46–57.
[86] Scott, *The Constitution and Finance of... Joint-Stock Companies*, II, p. 165.

pany thus contend with us, our advantage will be to buy none but the best goods in their kind, endeavouring with all imaginable care and skill to get them as cheap as possible and to manage all our charges and expenses with the utmost frugality.'[87]

The existence of two separate legally constituted organizations trading with the Indies was a situation which the directors of both the Companies wished to avoid. The solution adopted was a classic one under semi-monopolistic conditions. In 1702 Sir Basil Firebrace negotiated a merger and seven years later the two Companies formally terminated their separate joint-stocks to become the United East India Company. In January 1702 the directors of the new Company wrote to John Pitt in India that the losses sustained by the Company had induced them to enter into negotiations with the Old Company for a possible 'treaty'.[88] The United East India Company began its commercial life under adverse war conditions. But its rapid progress and economic success after the Treaty of Utrecht (1713) underlined the basic strength of English trade in the Indian Ocean. The Company had acquired three semi-independent trading enclaves in Gujarat, Coromandel, and Bengal. Bombay, Madras, and Calcutta were substantial settlements protected by major fortifications. Madras was already a prosperous trading port and Calcutta was soon to become one. Only Bombay remained in the shadow of its great Mughal commercial neighbour Surat for nearly half a century. The growing naval strength of the United Company enabled the English traders in general to organize an active inter-port trade in the Indian Ocean. Some of the Company's officials made large fortunes through their private trade. The policy of armed trading was retained in theory but used only strategically. The court of directors reminded a militant Bombay Council in 1718 that reprisals against Asian shipping at high seas or against Mughal trading ports must be treated like 'extreme unction, never to be used unless in the last extremity'.[89] The injunction was not lightly treated.

[87] IOR EIC Despatch Book (English East India Company), 15 Mar. 1700, vol. 94, pp. 170–1.
[88] IOR EIC Despatch Book (English East India Company), 8 Jan. 1702, vol. 94, p. 380.
[89] IOR EIC Despatch Book, 8 Jan. 1718, vol. 99, para. 45, p. 375.

Chapter 14

William III and the Glorious Revolution in the eyes of Amsterdam Sephardi writers: the reactions of Miguel de Barrios, Joseph Penso de la Vega, and Manuel de Leão

HARM DEN BOER AND JONATHAN I. ISRAEL

In a solemn prayer recited by the Portuguese and Spanish Jews of Amsterdam in their magnificent synagogue on 27 October 1688, the God of Israel was implored to

> bless, guard, favour, aid, support, save, exalt, enhance, and raise to the most glittering peak of success the Noble and Mighty States of Holland and West-Friesland, the High and Mighty States General of the United Provinces, and His Highness the Prince of Orange, Stadholder and captain-general by sea and land of these provinces, with all their allies, and the noble and illustrious burgomasters and magistracy of this city of Amsterdam.

God was implored further to grant the Dutch armies victories and triumphs and, just in case anyone was in doubt as to what this was all about, the Almighty was asked to side with those 'who with their ships plough the waves' so that the stars favour them, good weather carry them forward, and 'triumphs make them immortal'.[1] The Jews were praying for an end to the persistently strong westerly winds which had locked William III's great invasion fleet in at Hellevoetsluis over the past three weeks and for the success of the expedition mounted by the Dutch government and the Stadholder which was to achieve the successful landing at Torbay two and a half weeks later.

It was not tact alone, or mere subservience, that moved the Sephardi Jews

We would like to thank the Netherlands Organization for Scientific Research (NWO) for its support of Harm den Boer's research on the Spanish and Portuguese literature of the Dutch Sephardi Jews.

1 'Oración que hizo la Nación Hebrea en su Sinagoga de Amsterdam, en 27 Octubre año 1688' quoted in Miguel de Barrios, *Atlas angélico de la Gran Bretaña* (Amsterdam, 1688/9), p. 67; the passage specifically referring to the expedition to England reads 'Pelee Dios como Soberano Señor de los Exércitos por los que surcan con sus navíos las olas, aprisione como benigno las çoçobras, para que las estrellas los cortejen, las bonanças los alienten, y los triumphos los immortalizen'; further on this prayer, see David Franco Mendes, *Memorias do estabelicimento e progresso dos judeus portuguezes e espanhões nesta famosa citade de Amsterdam*, in *Studia Rosenthaliana*, 9 (1975), p. 95; it is noteworthy that the community also paid to have the prayer translated into Dutch and published as a public sign of Dutch Sephardi Jewry's solidarity with the state and support for the invasion of England under the title *Gebedt, Gedaen op Woensdag sijnde den 27 Oktober 1688, door de Portugeese Joden in hare kerck, ofte synagoge, binnen Amsterdam* (Amsterdam, 1688) (Knuttel no. 12784a); the Jews were certainly not the only Dutch religious minority which recited special prayers for the success of the expedition to England; in Haarlem, besides the Dutch Reformed and the Huguenots, the Remonstrants, Lutherans, and Mennonites all recited special prayers, see GA Haarlem, Stad Haarlem 10 (Burgermeestersresoluties), no. 27, fos. 88–9, res. 13 Nov. 1688.

of Amsterdam to participate enthusiastically and conspicuously in the prayers and general fast decreed throughout the Republic for that day of 1688. For the Amsterdam Sephardi community had enjoyed the favour of the House of Orange since early in the seventeenth century and their synagogue had been honoured by visits by several of William III's forebears including, on one occasion, in 1642, his mother in the company of Prince Frederick Henry, William's grand-father, and Queen Henrietta Maria of England. Of course, Jews like members of the other religious minorities dwelling in the Republic had reason to be grateful for William III's disinclination to espouse the intolerant policies advocated by the orthodox wing of the Dutch Reformed Church and the Prince's well-advertised commitment to religious toleration. But there was also another, more direct reason why the Sephardi Jews of Amsterdam proved strongly supportive of the Prince's expedition to England: several leading members of the community were closely involved with the financial and other practical aspects of the Prince's ambitious statecraft. These included, in particular, the Baron Francisco Lopes Suasso who was involved in various aspects of the financing of the Dutch invasion armada and who, through his father-in-law in Hamburg, Manoel Teixeira, arranged the speedy transfer of the transit costs of the Swedish troops sent to assist the Dutch Republic in November 1688 from Pomerania and Sweden, Jeronimo Nunes da Costa who had various links with the Stadholder, Antonio Alvares Machado who had been handling the bread supply of the Dutch army since the 1670s and who, in 1688, was the main supplier of the Dutch army of the Rhine, Jacob Pereira who had organized the provisioning of the Amsterdam section of the invasion fleet and the latter's son, Isaac, who was already developing those links with the Stadholder which were to make him the main military contractor for the allied Protestant army fighting in Ireland in 1690–1.[2]

The prayer quoted above appears in the *Atlas angélico de la Gran Bretaña* (1688/9) by Miguel (Daniel Levi) de Barrios (1635–1701), one of several texts dedicated by Sephardi Jewish writers of Amsterdam to the Stadholder-king during

[2] In November 1688, Lopes Suasso was contracted by the States General's receiver-general, Cornelis de Jonge van Ellemeet, to advance an initial 188,000 guilders in local currency, via Hamburg, to be paid within ten days to the governor of Swedish Pomerania, to finance the transportation of the hired 6,000 Swedish troops to Dutch territory, see ARH SG 3318, fo. 488v, res. 30 Nov. 1688; on Alvares Machado's contract, negotiated with him by William III in October 1688, to supply bread, wagons, and ovens for the provisioning of the Dutch army on the Rhine during 1689, see ARH SG Raad van State 109, fo. 520v, res. 25 Oct. 1688, and, for a copy of the text of his contract, BL MS Add. 38695, fos. 72–3; on Jacob Pereira's victualling of the Amsterdam contingent of the invasion armada, see BL MS Add. 41816, fo. 229, and John Childs, *The British Army of William III, 1689–1702* (Manchester, 1987), p. 250; generally on the role of the Dutch Sephardi leadership in William III's statecraft, see D. J. Roorda, 'De joodse entourage van de koning-stadhouder', *Spiegel Historiael* (May 1979), pp. 258–61; J. I. Israel, *European Jewry in the Age of Mercantilism, 1550–1750* (Oxford, 1985), pp. 130–4; L. Schönduve, 'Antonio en Francisco Lopes Suasso: joodse baronnen in Holland', *Holland. Regionaal-Historisch Tijdschrift*, 20 (1988), pp. 175–85.

28 *The Baron Francisco Lopes Suasso.*

the years of the revolutions in Britain and Ireland (1688–91).[3] Before examining the picture which these texts project of the Stadholder, crowned king of England, and the events of the Glorious Revolution, let us first have a brief

[3] Besides the works by the three Dutch Sephardi writers discussed in this essay, a fourth, Duarte (Moseh) Lopes Rosa, also celebrated the Glorious Revolution with a literary flourish in his *Panegyrico sobre la restauración de Inglaterra* (Amsterdam, 1690); unfortunately neither author of this present essay has been able to locate a copy of this extremely rare publication.

look at the character and scope of the literature in Spanish and Portuguese produced by the Dutch Sephardi Jewish community.

The latter part of the seventeenth century and the beginning of the eighteenth are justly know as the Golden Age of Dutch Sephardi literature. Between 1650 and 1730 more than 250 literary works written in Spanish or Portuguese were published at Amsterdam, making up almost one third of the entire printed production in these languages in the northern Netherlands during the seventeenth and eighteenth centuries.[4] This output includes genres of every type: religious, moralistic, burlesque, and (above all) occasional poetry; religious and secular drama; and a wide variety of prose ranging from philosophical treatises and doctrinal works to rhetorical discourses and even a kind of novella. Among other indications of the importance of literary activity in Dutch Sephardi Jewish life, an importance to which the Italian Protestant city historiographer of Amsterdam, Gregorio Leti, strongly attests, is the evident popularity of Spanish *comedias*, performed for the Sephardi audience in warehouses and the existence (however briefly) of two literary academies based on the Spanish model.[5]

Although the Dutch Sephardi literature of this period has received a certain amount of attention, beginning with the studies of Meyer Kayserling and Jośe Amador de los Ríos,[6] it has, until now, been studied mainly as an aspect of Jewish life. Attention has consequently focused only on certain aspects of the subject, with a tendency to neglect that dimension which is purely secular. For Dutch Sephardi literature forms a dichotomy, with two quite distinct streams expressing, on the one hand, the newly strengthened sense of Jewish identity of the Dutch Sephardi community and, on the other, the wordly ambition and preoccupations of its secular leadership.[7]

This dichotomy becomes fully evident when we examine the Sephardi Spanish and Portuguese literary works of the period in terms of the readership to which they were presented. By studying their title pages, dedications, and prefaces, we see that one large category of works was directed almost exclusively towards a Jewish audience, familiar with the forms of synagogue life, while another substantial category was directed essentially to a general Spanish- and Portuguese-speaking and reading public.

In the first class of works authors present themselves under their Jewish, or

[4] For a recent general bibliographical survey of this literature, see Harm den Boer, 'Spanish and Portuguese Editions from the Northern Netherlands in Madrid and Lisbon Public Collections', *Studia Rosenthaliana*, 22 (1988), pp. 97–143, and 23 (1989), pp. 38–77, 138–77.

[5] Harm den Boer, 'El teatro entre los sefardíes de Amsterdam a fines del siglo XVII', *Diálogos hispánicos de Amsterdam*, 8 (1989), pp. 679–90.

[6] See Meyer Kayserling, *Sephardim. Romanische Poesien der Juden in Spanien* (Leipzig, 1859); José Amador de los Ríos, *Estudios históricos, políticos y literarios sobre los judíos de España* (Madrid, 1848), pp. 608–18; see also Cecil Roth, *A History of the Marranos* (New York, 1974), pp. 322–38.

[7] D. M. Swetschinski, 'The Portuguese Jews of Seventeenth-Century Amsterdam: Cultural Continuity and Adaptation', in F. Malino and Ph. Cohen Albert (eds.), *Essays in Modern Jewish History* (London and Toronto, 1982), pp. 56–80.

synagogue, names as do all the other persons mentioned on the title page or elsewhere in the book. The titles of these literary works usually have a specific Jewish content. These also, as a matter of course, specify Amsterdam as the place of publication and give a Jewish rather than Christian date in their *impressum*. In many cases approbation by the Mahamad, or board of governors of the Sephardi community, is also expressly stated on the title page or in the preliminaries. Finally, most of these editions mention the patronage of leading figures of the community. Patrons appear not only under their Jewish names but with reference to the offices which they held in the administration of the community and its charities.

In the other category of publication, Sephardi writers and other members of the community mentioned in the text or prefaces appear under their alternative secular names, as for example 'Miguel' for 'Daniel Levi' de Barrios, 'Francisco' for 'Abraham Isaac' Lopes Suasso, and 'Antonio Alvares' for 'Moses' Machado. From the titles of these works all specifically Jewish features are excluded. Sometimes the *impressum* specifies Brussels, Antwerp, or another Catholic city to conceal their origin in the 'apostatical' city of Amsterdam. These publications are dedicated or addressed to Christian statesman or royalty, or Sephardi patrons, in which case the latter appear exclusively in terms of their secular functions and dignities, usually a diplomatic function on behalf of a Christian king or other potentate. All these features indicate that these publications were directed to a Spanish- or Portuguese-reading public which was not exclusively Jewish and which included Spanish officials and soldiers in the southern Netherlands as well as readers in the Iberian Peninsula and, more marginally, hispanic America.

We could perhaps think of the latter class of literature as the expression of an Iberian identity, or as a mere extension of Spanish and Portuguese cultural life outside of the Iberian Peninsula, at any rate in the case of authors such as Miguel de Barrios or Manuel de Leão who were born in Spain or Portugal and raised in an Iberian cultural milieu. Barrios later served in the Spanish army of Flanders and became acquainted with numerous Spanish army officers in the southern Netherlands. Indeed, he continued to address poetry to friends and influential Spanish noblemen even after reverting to formal Judaism in Amsterdam. But other Sephardi authors such as Joseph Penso de la Vega were born in Amsterdam and raised in a specifically Jewish context and lacked personal relationships with Spaniards and Portuguese outside the Republic. The latter, however, still endeavoured to write a Spanish intended to be acceptable to a non-Jewish audience. In Penso de la Vega's case, we cannot speak of any direct personal or cultural links with the Iberian Peninsula other than his tireless dedication to the cultivation of a highly literary Spanish in the Sephardi diaspora. Being Spanish was simply part of his cultural identity and was socially more highly esteemed – even in the Protestant United Provinces – than being a Jew. In his case, as in that of so many others, this Iberian identity was unmistakably tinged with quasi-aristocratic pretensions. Among other things, this explains why Penso de la Vega prided himself on writing such a highly refined, fashionable Spanish, styling himself Don Joseph de la Vega.

One distinct group of Sephardi secular texts in Spanish and Portuguese addressed to Christian kings, princes, and statesmen which cannot be understood as being essentially either Iberian or Jewish in character are the occasional works dealing with contemporary European events, a literary phenomenon mainly of the last part of the seventeenth century. There is no obvious religious dimension to these writings. On the occasion of the defeat of the Ottoman Turks at Vienna, in 1683, by John III Sobieski, for example, both Barrios and Penso de la Vega immediately addressed themselves to the Polish monarch, congratulating him on this triumph.[8] This was not a victory of any particular benefit to the Jews of Vienna, or the Austrian lands, or of Jews more generally. How, then, should we explain the interest which writers such as Barrios and Penso de la Vega took in the event? The answer, we believe, is to be found in the relations which the Dutch Sephardi elite had developed by this time with various European courts, especially with courts allied with, or sympathetic to, the United Provinces in its continuing confrontation with the might of Louis XIV, such as the Holy Roman Emperor, the king of Spain, various German princes and – after the Glorious Revolution – the king of England. This literature, then, formed part of the refined aristocratic behaviour, and especially of the elaborate hospitality, with which leading members of the Sephardi community, such as Lopes Suasso, Alvares Machado, Nunes da Costa, and the Baron Manuel de Belmonte, agent-general of Spain at Amsterdam, honoured their noble and diplomatic guests and furthered their connections with European courts.[9] The prose and poetry written on the occasion of the Glorious Revolution belong clearly to this sub-group of the secular category of Sephardi literature.

MIGUEL DE BARRIOS: 'ATLAS ANGÉLICO DE LA GRAN BRETAÑA'

Miguel de Barrios is the best known writer among the Sephardi Jews of Amsterdam writing in Spanish or Portuguese. Born in Spain in the province of Córdoba, at Montilla, in 1635, he left his native country – probably through

[8] Miguel de Barrios, *Panegírico al Juan Tercero, Rey de Polonia* (Amsterdam, 1683), and Joseph Penso de la Vega, *Los triumphos del águyla y eclypses de la luna* (Amsterdam, 1684); Barrios also published an *Epístola y panegírico al ínclito y victorioso monarcha de Polonia Ivan Tercero* (Amsterdam, 1684); see also den Boer, 'Spanish and Portuguese Editions', *Studia Rosenthaliana*, 23, pp. 53, 59, 154.

[9] J. I. Israel, 'Gregorio Leti (1631–1701) and the Dutch Sephardi Elite at the Close of the Seventeenth Century', in A. Rapoport-Albert and S. J. Zipperstein (eds.), *Jewish History. Essays in Honour of Chimen Abramsky* (London, 1988), pp. 274–7.

fear of the Inquisition – and led a wandering life in Italy, the Caribbean, and the Spanish Netherlands where he served as a captain in the Spanish army, before settling in the Dutch Republic around 1663.[10] Here he joined the Talmud Torah community in Amsterdam, leading a somewhat threadbare existence until his death in 1701. His wayward poetical temperament inspired him to write poetry (in a highly cultivated baroque fashion) addressed to a variety of Christian noblemen (mostly Spaniards) as well as sovereigns. This brought the poet into a degree of conflict with the community and with co-religionists eager to bury their Christian past. But, at the same time, the adulatory verses he wrote to celebrate the most prominent members of the Talmud Torah community and its religious, charitable, and educational institutions earned him the unofficial position of poet laureate of Amsterdam Sephardi Jewry. It is in his poetry that both the Jewish and secular preoccupations of Amsterdam Sephardi literature were fully expressed. In his collection, the *Coro de musas*, the poet, styling himself 'the Captain Don Miguel de Barrios', published verse in the fashionable contemporary Spanish manner full of convoluted mythological allusions directed to a Christian public in which he not only concealed his own religious beliefs but, on occasion, praised the Catholic faith and, indeed, even the Inquisition! By contrast, in other verse works, as Daniel Levi de Barrios, he presented himself as the poetical champion of the Law of Moses and adversary of its Catholic detractors.[11]

The *Atlas angélico de la Gran Bretaña* is a curious mixture of both facets of the poet. To see how the two dimensions interweave in this compilation, we will consider how the work is presented to the reader. The title page presents the *Atlas angélico* as a 'declaration to [Great Britain's] great king James II, that Atlas was Enoch, son of Jared, before the Flood' and as a discussion of what Isaiah xix 'foretold ... until the present year 1688 and what is about to happen'.[12] The author is presented under his Christian name: 'Don Miguel de Barrios'. At first sight, the works appears to be dedicated to the Catholic king of England, James II. However, the title page is immediately followed by a passage from Isaiah (xix:7) in which Barrios elaborates on the spiritual significance of the birth of the Prince of Wales in June 1688, interpreting the event

[10] On Miguel de Barrios, see Kenneth Scholberg, *La poesía religiosa de Miguel de Barrios* (Madrid, 1963); I. S. Revah, 'Les Ecrivains Manuel de Pina et Miguel de Barrios et la censure de la communauté judeo-portugaise d'Amsterdam', *Tesoro de los Judíos Sefardíes (Otzar Yehude Sefarad)*, 8 (1965), pp. lxxiv–xci; W. Ch. Pieterse, *Daniel Levi de Barrios als geschiedschrijver van de Portugees-Israelietische gemeente de Amsterdam in zijn 'Triumpho del govierno popular'* (Amsterdam, 1968); also still well worth consulting is M. Kayserling, 'Une histoire de la littérature juive de Daniel Lévi de Barrios', *Revue des Etudes Juives*, 18 (1889), pp. 276–80.

[11] Thus amongst his writings is a satirical work on the pope and the Inquisition, the *Trompeta del juizio. Contra el Papa y la Inquisición* (Amsterdam, 1675).

[12] The title page reads 'Atlas angélico de la Gran Bretaña, declaración a su Gran Rey Jacobo Segundo, de que Atlante fue Henoch hijo de Jared, antes de Diluvio con la Monarchía Británica. Y de lo que predixo de ella Isaias cap 19. Hasta el presente año de 1688 y de lo que ha de ha contecerle [*sic*] hasta que sane de sus interiores heridas. Declarador Don Miguel de Barrios.'

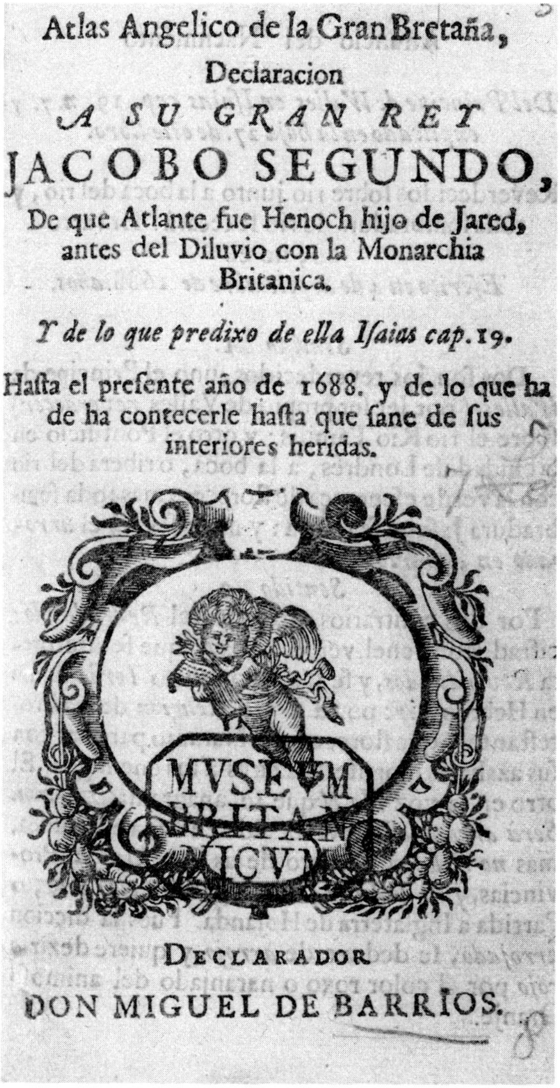

Atlas Angelico de la Gran Bretaña,
Declaracion
A SU GRAN REY
JACOBO SEGUNDO,
De que Atlante fue Henoch hijo de Jared,
antes del Diluvio con la Monarchia
Britanica.

Y de lo que predixo de ella Isaias cap. 19.

Hasta el presente año de 1688. y de lo que ha
de ha contecerle hasta que sane de sus
interiores heridas.

DECLARADOR
DON MIGUEL DE BARRIOS.

29 The title page of Miguel de Barrios' *Atlas angélico de la Gran Bretaña* (1688).

as a (hidden) defeat of popery in London and triumph of the Protestant religion whose cause is embodied by the Prince of Orange.[13]

After this 'prophecy' comes a dedication to the Creator. Here Barrios asserts that he writes the 'Angelic Atlas of Britain', consecrated to the Divine King, 'not to flatter any king, but for the Glory of 'He who is always One'.[14] The

[13] Barrios, *Atlas angélico*, p. 2.
[14] Ibid., p. 3.

poet was clearly caught up in the mood of political elation which swept the United Provinces at the time of the departure of the great invasion fleet to England. In a letter written to the Prince of Orange on 28 September 1688, just a few days before the embarkation of the Prince's army was due to begin, Barrios writes: 'the obligation and goodwill which we the Spanish Hebrews of this city owe to their [*Altipotencias*] and to Your Royal Highness prompt me to send you the still unfinished book *Angélico atlas de la Gran Bretaña*, because of the happy events announced there, explaining chapter xix of Isaiah'.[15] Thus, instead of dedicating his book about England to James II, the poet had decided, by September 1688, that it would be more judicious to submit it to the Almighty but at the same time, address it to the Prince of Orange.

The text of more than 150 pages contains in the first place an interpretation of the ancient origins of Great Britain. After specifying the virtues and shortcomings of democracy, monarchy, and aristocracy in turn, the author introduces the first biblical monarchy, that of Enoch, son of Yerek. The monarchy of Enoch, Barrios decides, from Scripture, was situated in the 'Atlantic Land', separated from the Netherlands on 4 November of the year 225 since the beginning of the world.[16] By the 'Atlantic Land' Britain is meant. The notion that Britain once belonged to the continent was, of course, not new. But the way Barrios develops the idea was, in a way, original. To illustrate his manner of reasoning, we may mention the story – recounted by William Camden in the *Atlas Maior o geografia blaviana* of Joan Blaeu – that when Henry II was in Scotland, a violent storm blew away the sand that had long covered the surface of the shore, revealing underneath a dark soil with black tree trunks (a petrified wood?). These were interpreted as the remnants of a former land washed away by a flood. Now, according to Barrios, in the Bible Britain was always called *Chus* meaning 'black' or 'brown'. The name Britain itself, he claims, confirms this since it is derived from the Germanic word *brein* – as the poet renders it – or 'brown'. William Camden moreover calls the Britons *Pretones* which Barrios derives from the Portuguese *preto*, meaning 'black'.[17] Continuing in this style, Barrios develops an elaborate account of the biblical origins of Britain.

The interpretation of the prophecies contained in Isaiah xix relies on a similar

[15] 'Epístola a su Alteza Real el Príncipe de Orange en Amsterdam a 28. de Septiembre de 1688. años', included in Barrios, *Atlas angélico*, pp. 3–4: 'La obligación, y benevolencia que devemos los Hebreos Españoles de esta Ciudad a sus Altipotencias, y a V.R.A. me animan a remitirle el libro aun no acabado del *Angélico Atlas de la Gran Bretaña*, por los felizes sucessos que le anuncian, explicando el capítulo 19. de Isaias: y espero que se cumplan sus anuncios, de que fueron vislumbres las dos celebres Victorias que alcançó la Armada de sus Altipotencias, a 7 y 14 de Junio de 1673'; in the battles of Schoonevelt, in June 1673, de Ruyter defeated the English and forced them to retreat back to English shores.

[16] Barrios, *Atlas angélico*, p. 9; Barrios here quoted from the Spanish version of Blaeu's great atlas, on which he and other Sephardi writers of Amsterdam had actively collaborated, see the volume entitled *Nuevo Atlas del reyno de Inglaterra* (Amsterdam, printed after 1672), p. 337.

[17] *Nuevo Atlas del reyno de Inglaterra*, p. 5.

technique. Barrios was deeply imbued with the idea that great contemporary political events such as the Glorious Revolution in England were of profound spiritual significance for all mankind and had been foretold and announced in Scripture, but that the revelation of such events in Scripture needs, before it can be understood, to be analysed and explained by a process of mystical, poetical, and etymological insight. Indeed, for years after 1688, the poet continued to see the Revolution, and events connected with it, as the fulfilment of the mystical prognostications of William III's triumph and 'Dutch salvation' which he had set out in 1688. In a letter to the financier and military contractor Jacob Pereira written at Amsterdam on 3 June 1692, for example, Barrios claimed to have foretold, as part of his more general foretelling of the Revolution, the great naval battle of La Hougue which had taken place off the French coast a few days before.[18] In the battle the French admiral Tourville with forty-four warships had again taken on the combined Anglo-Dutch fleets, comprising eighty-eight warships, hoping for a similar victory to that which he had achieved, owing to dissension and lack of co-ordination among the allies, at the battle off Beachy Head in 1690: but this time the French were defeated and the English and Dutch gained supremacy in the Channel. Strategically the battle was an important turning-point for both England and the United Provinces.

In the *Atlas angélico* Barrios develops an elaborate poetical prophecy concerning the birth of James, Prince of Wales, and the then imminent triumph of the Prince of Orange. The passage of Isaiah unravelled by Barrios is rendered: 'Flourished over the river, near the mouth of the river, and all the vegetation will dry up, *it* will be cast across, not *he*'.[19] Barrios develops his reading of this text in two stages. First, he explains that there are here two subjects which flourished: on the one hand, the Prince of Wales (rendered Walles) – since it is a characteristic of valleys (Sp. *valles*) to flourish – who 'flourished' in the vicinity of the River Thames; and, on the other hand, the world Catholic cause residing in London on the 'banks of the River Thames filled with the green hope of flourishing'. But, he continues, 'all Jesuitical seeds will dry up, while that which is produced [or blown over] in childbirth will not dry up.'[20] Barrios subsequently explains that the *flourished* will, and will not, dry up in two opposite ways, one ciphered in the verb *Arot*, which means 'flourish', and in the opposite

[18] GA Amsterdam PJG 334/680, pp. 740–1, Daniel Levi de Barrios to Jacob Pereira, Amsterdam, 3 June 1692; we are indebted to Edgar Samuel, Director of the Jewish Museum in London, for this reference.

[19] Barrios, *Atlas angélico*, pp. 2, 27: 'Anuncio del Nacimiento del Princípe de Walles en Isaias cap. 19 n. 7. y explicado en la hoja 27. de este libro'; the passage of Isaiah on which Barrios focuses he renders 'Reverdecidos sobre río junto a la boca del río, y toda sembradura de río se secará: será arrodo [*sic*], no el.'

[20] Ibid., p. 27: 'Escrito en 4 de Septiembre de 1688 años. Dos son los reverdecidos, uno el Príncipe de Walles (por ser propio de Valles reverdecer) sobre el río Río Támisis: y otro el Pontificio en la ciudad de Londres, a la boca, o ribera del río con la verde esperança de florecer: mas toda sembradura Jesuitica se secará: y no se secará el arrojado en el parto.

direction 'Torah', the Hebrew for 'Law'. The allusion, Barrios explains, is to the 'Law or Religion of the Protestants, flourishing in the Orange tree so as to forge with its flowers deadly destinies for its enemies'. The key contradiction is, then, contained in the words *no el* (not he) which, according to Barrios, refer to the *león* (lion). The meaning of the prophecy is that the 'flourished will be cast up in vain hope [i.e. the Prince of Wales], but not the arrowed Lion of the Seven United Provinces, and the thrown out [blown over] in childbirth [Sp. *parto*] – or departure [Sp. *partida*] to England from Holland'.[21] This is because, the poet explains, the '*arrojado* thrown [blown over] derives from *arrojo*, that is *a rojo* [red], because of the red, or orange, colour of the courageous Orange'.

Practically the whole of the text of the *Atlas angélico* consists of these intricate prognostications and etymological derivations. They are based on a technique which the poet employed increasingly from the 1680s onwards. Deeply impressed by cabala, and cabalistic methods of interpretation, Barrios combined cabalistic readings of Hebrew words and their Spanish equivalents in the early modern Sephardi Spanish translation of the Bible with an extreme form of *conceptismo*, a style within the Spanish baroque in which rhetorical devices such as paradox, paranomasia, and (often highly contrived) etymologies are used to establish affinities and correspondence between subjects. In Miguel de Barrios, however, these correspondences are often so far-fetched that it is not easy to take them seriously. However, the evidence we have strongly suggests that the poet believed in them. Although it cannot be denied that Barrios displayed a certain poetic ingenuity in combining and reconciling the most disparate allusions and texts, to the modern reader his derivations appear not only utterly unconvincing but confused and tiresome.

However, Barrios' poetic technique possessed one great advantage in enabling him to integrate the world of contemporary political events with the traditional Jewish zeal for uncovering the secrets of the biblical text. He celebrated William III's invasion armada of 1688 in verse as a great and ordained happening and judged the deposing of James II a just and necessary punishment of that king's active promotion of popery in England. The Prince of Orange is depicted (with considerable justification) as the champion of religious freedom generally and thus worthy to be helped by the God of Israel. 'To have a steadfast Faith, is pious love / and forcing the People that follow it, / is not to imitate God who gives free / will, and God will punish him who tries to force the consciences of others.'[22] It was precisely by seeking to force their Catholic faith on the Dutch that Spain lost the seven provinces, and the Ottomans, by mistreating

[21] Ibid., '*Será arrojado* lo reverdecido [the Prince of Wales] en vana esperança, mas *no el León flechero* de las siete Unidas Provincias, y *no se secará el arrojado en el Parto*, o Partida a Inglaterra de Holanda. Pues la dicción *arrojado*, se deduze de arrojo, y quiere dezir a rojo por el color roxo o naranjado del animoso Oranje.'

[22] Ibid., p. 41.

non-Muslims, lost Vienna. This all may seem rather unjust to James II who, after all pursued a policy of religious toleration in Britain, Ireland, and North America, but in 1688 the important point for Dutch Jews, as for the Dutch generally, was that James II was the protegé (and assumed ally) of Louis XIV, the perpetrator of the Revocation of the Edict of Nantes and the would-be enslaver of the United Provinces and all Europe. In this sense he saw James II as the enemy of religious freedom and Dutch Protestantism. At the same time, Barrios also sees the rest of the allied coalition ranged against the might of Louis XIV – the emperor, king of Spain and German princes – as in some sense committed, along with the Dutch Republic and William III, to the defence of freedom both religious and otherwise. Accordingly, the work is in part also addressed to these allied powers, particularly Spain. It contains, for example, a poem dedicated to Don Manuel Coloma, the Spanish envoy in the United Provinces, and his Austrian wife, Maximiliana Doratea, and a section of prose addressed to the Spanish ambassador in England, Don Pedro Ronquillo, who was a strong sympathizer with William III and the Glorious Revolution and, like other Spanish diplomats in northern Europe during the late seventeenth century, had links with Lopes Suasso, Belmonte, and other members of the Dutch Sephardi leadership. Assuming that either of these Spanish Catholic noblemen actually read Barrios' text, one can only wonder what they can have made of such a bizarre mixture of reaching out towards Spain, defence of Dutch Protestantism, and Jewish allusions.[23]

Many of the seeming contradictions in the *Atlas angélico de la Gran Bretaña* are resolved if we bear in mind that it was specifically a literary product of the crucial months of the Glorious Revolution. In the period that he wrote this work, both his poverty and the conviction that he was a great visionary encouraged Miguel de Barrios to address whoever he reckoned should be interested in his revelations, hoping that they would reward him accordingly. Thus, the work had clearly been originally intended to be presented to James II as a biblical history of Great Britain in which no aspersions would be cast on either the late Stuart dynasty or the Catholic faith. The work was unfinished in September 1688, when Barrios, along with the rest of the population of Amsterdam was profoundly excited by the prospects opened up by William III's pending invasion of England. He thereupon changed parts of the book and added his 'prophecies' which were in one sense rather typical of the confident and fervent speculation which characterized the Dutch public's intense excitement in the autumn of 1688, differing from other more run-of-the-mill prognostications about William

[23] However, it is apparent that Barrios intended that only his original version of the *Atlas angélico*, written before the Dutch invasion of England, and incorporated into his *Palma angélica de los Campos Elíseos* (Amsterdam, 1688) should circulate in Spain. (The only known copy of this work is to be found in the collection of the Hispanic Society of New York.)

III's prospects mainly in being dressed up in an elaborate pseudo-biblical garb. Writing to the Prince himself, more than six weeks before the successful landing at Torbay, Barrios could with all sincerity praise the Dutch enterprise, in his capacity as a Jewish writer, as a defence of religious freedom.

JOSEPH PENSO DE LA VEGA: 'RETRATO DE LA PRUDENCIA'

Joseph Penso de la Vaga (1650–92) presents analogies but also some notable differences when compared with Miguel de Barrios.[24] He too had an Andalusian background, his father having lived in Espejo in the region of Córdoba prior to emigrating to Amsterdam. Joseph may have been born in Spain but, if so, was still very young on being brought to the Dutch Republic. He spent the major part of his youth in Amsterdam where he had the benefit of the excellent Jewish education provided by the Talmud Torah community. At the age of seventeen he already made a literary name for himself with a drama in Hebrew which was one of the first to be published in that language.[25] Yet, though this work met with effusive praise, he preferred to write the rest of his interesting literary output in Spanish and, on one occasion, Portuguese. In contrast to Barrios, the literary oeuvre of Penso de la Vega was that of a personality raised and educated in a specifically Jewish milieu and thoroughly familiar with Hebrew, nevertheless like so many other Sephardi writers he chose to express himself chiefly in Spanish. He devoted himself exclusively to prose, cultivating a contrived, sometimes obscure style somewhat reminiscent of that of the great Spanish master of *conceptismo*-prose, Baltasar Gracián, though Penso de la Vega usually lacked the concision, terseness, and brilliance of the great Castilian. Besides some interesting novellas in his *Rumbos peligrosos* and *Ideas posibles*, Penso de la Vega wrote his now famous literary recreation of the Amsterdam stock exchange – the first detailed description of a stock exchange ever to be written – entitled the *Confusión de confusiones*.

As it happens the *Confusión de confusiones* was written during the year 1688 and the last of the four convoluted dialogues of which the work is composed deals with the great stock exchange crash of late August and September which resulted from the panic which ensued when the Amsterdam financial markets first realized that the Dutch state was about to attempt an invasion of England

[24] On Joseph Penso de la Vega, see M. F. J. Smith, 'Inleiding' to Joseph Penso de la Vega, *Confusión de Confusiones* (The Hague, 1939) (Dutch translation published together with the original Spanish text); Julio Caro Baroja, *Los judíos en la España moderna y contemporánea* (3 vols., Madrid, 1978), II, pp. 169–72; Yosef Kaplan, *From Christianity to Judaism. The Story of Isaac Orobio de Castro* (Oxford, 1989), pp. 288–90, 293–5, 297–302, 426–7; at the end of his life Penso de la Vega moved to Livorno where he was the secretary of the local Spanish literary academy among the Sephardim *Los Sitibundos*, see F. Aghib Levi d'Ancona, 'The Sephardi Community of Leghorn (Livorno)', in R. Barnett and W. Schwab (eds.), *The Sephardi Heritage*, II: *The Western Sephardim* (Grendon, Northants., 1989), p. 185; Penso de la Vega died in Livorno at the age of forty-two.

[25] Joseph Penso de la Vega, *'Asirey ha-Tiqvah* (Amsterdam, 1673).

in open defiance of Louis XIV as well as of James II.[26] At the close of this dialogue, Penso de la Vega, who himself belonged to a well-known Sephardi business family, urges his readership – mainly but not necessarily exclusively Sephardi Jews – to invest in East and West India Company shares only in a sober, responsible manner and, as far as possible, to support the *patria*, their Dutch homeland, and the great colonial Companies, by preferring to buy rather than sell!

Penso de la Vega's other work with a direct bearing on the Glorious Revolution is his *Retrato de la Prudencia y Simulacro del Valor* (*Portrait of Wisdom and Image of Valour*) which was published after William III's triumphs over James II in Ireland, in 1690.[27] Essentially, this work is a portrait of William III, and in places also of Mary, containing relatively little about the actual historical events of the Glorious Revolution and still less about its ideological implications. Apart from the work's obvious bias in favour of the Stadholder-king, there is nothing in it which reveals, or asserts, any affinity which a Sephardi Jew ought feel for the Williamite cause, no discussion of the Stadholder-king's religious policy for example. The title page bears the name of Don Josseph de la Vega, the name the author used when addressing a not exclusively Jewish readership. The title with its symmetric, two-part structure is typical of the Iberian baroque literature of the period. Being a literary portrait of William III, the work also carries a dedication to the Stadholder-king. In it the author declares his intention to illustrate with 240 passages of the 'Sacred Volume', the two essential qualities which characterized the sovereign: 'wisdom' and 'courage'.

Wisdom and courage, we read, are the two pillars on which monarchs base their achievements and heroes their triumphs. The people of Israel in their passage through the desert were supported by these pillars in the form of a pillar of cloud (wisdom) and a pillar of fire (courage). Likewise, King Solomon installed two pillars, representing wisdom and courage to support his Temple, pillars which Penso de la Vega sees as foreshadowing the coronation of William and Mary being adorned with roses and crowns: for roses feature on the arms of England while the two crowns prognosticate the crowns of William and Mary. The Bible, he claims, also foretold that the coronation would take place on a Tuesday: for Tuesday corresponds to the third day of the Creation on which God says *twice* that 'it was good!' thereby foretelling the dual crowning. Another example of this type of *conceptismo* in the work is the comparison of William

[26] Penso de la Vega, *Confusión de Confusiones*, pp. 286–7; Otto Pringsheim, *Don Joseph de la Vega. Die Verwirrung der Verwirrungen. Vier Dialoge über die Börse in Amsterdam* (Breslau, 1919), p. xiv; see also J. I. Israel, 'Een merkwaardig literair werk en de Amsterdam effectenmarkt in 1688: Joseph Penso de la Vega's *Confusión de Confusiones*', *De Zeventiende Eeuw*, 6 (1990), pp. 160–1.

[27] Joseph Penso de la Vega, *Retrato de la Prudencia y Simulacro del Valor* (Amsterdam, 1960), p. 13; de Boer, 'Spanish and Portuguese Editions', *Studia Rosenthaliana*, 23, p. 153; copies are to be found at the Royal Library in The Hague and the Bibliotheca Rosenthaliana and Ets Haim collections in Amsterdam.

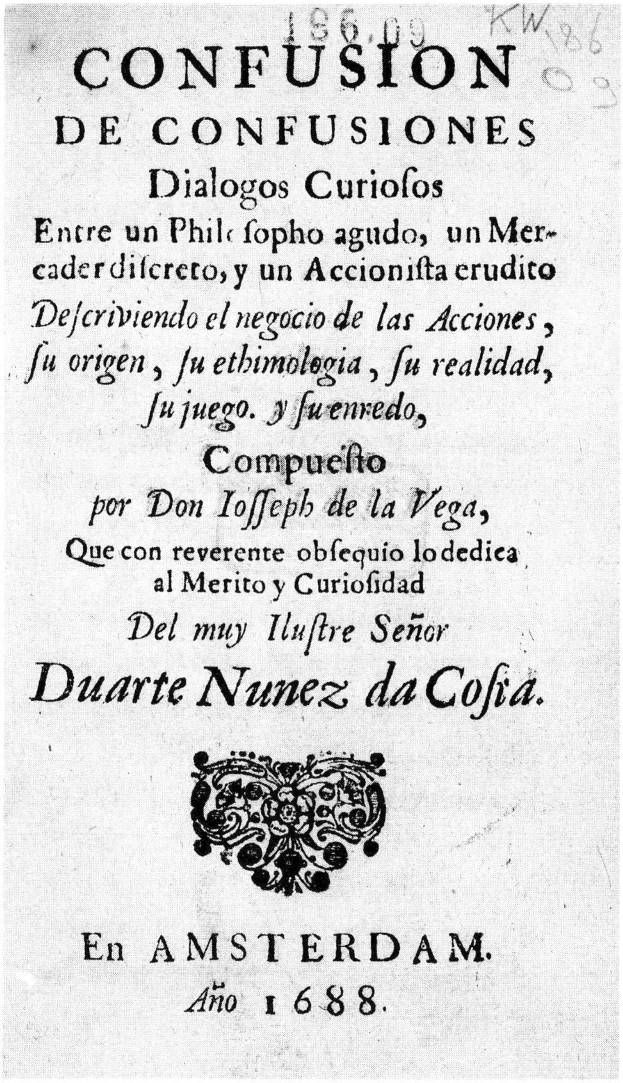

CONFUSION
DE CONFUSIONES
Dialogos Curioſos
Entre un Philoſopho agudo, un Mer-
cader diſcreto, y un Accioniſta erudito
Deſcriviendo el negocio de las Acciones,
ſu origen, ſu ethimologia, ſu realidad,
ſu juego. y ſu enredo,
Compueſto
por Don Ioſſeph de la Vega,
Que con reverente obſequio lo dedica
al Merito y Curioſidad
Del muy Iluſtre Señor
Duarte Nunez da Coſta.

En AMSTERDAM.
Año 1688.

30 The title page of Joseph Penso de la Vega's *Confusión de Confusiones* (1688), the first ever description of the workings of a stock exchange, dedicated to the eldest son of Jeronimo Nunes da Costa.

with David, a favourite theme amongst Dutch Calvinist and Huguenot preachers during the years of the Glorious Revolution. The biblical David whom the People of Israel chose to replace the formerly anointed but now rejected (and no longer deserving) King Saul (James) is characterized as wise, courageous and swift. 'David defeated Goliath', our author tells, 'whose name means 'slavery' and this fearless monarch defeated with courage and swiftness the slavery that was

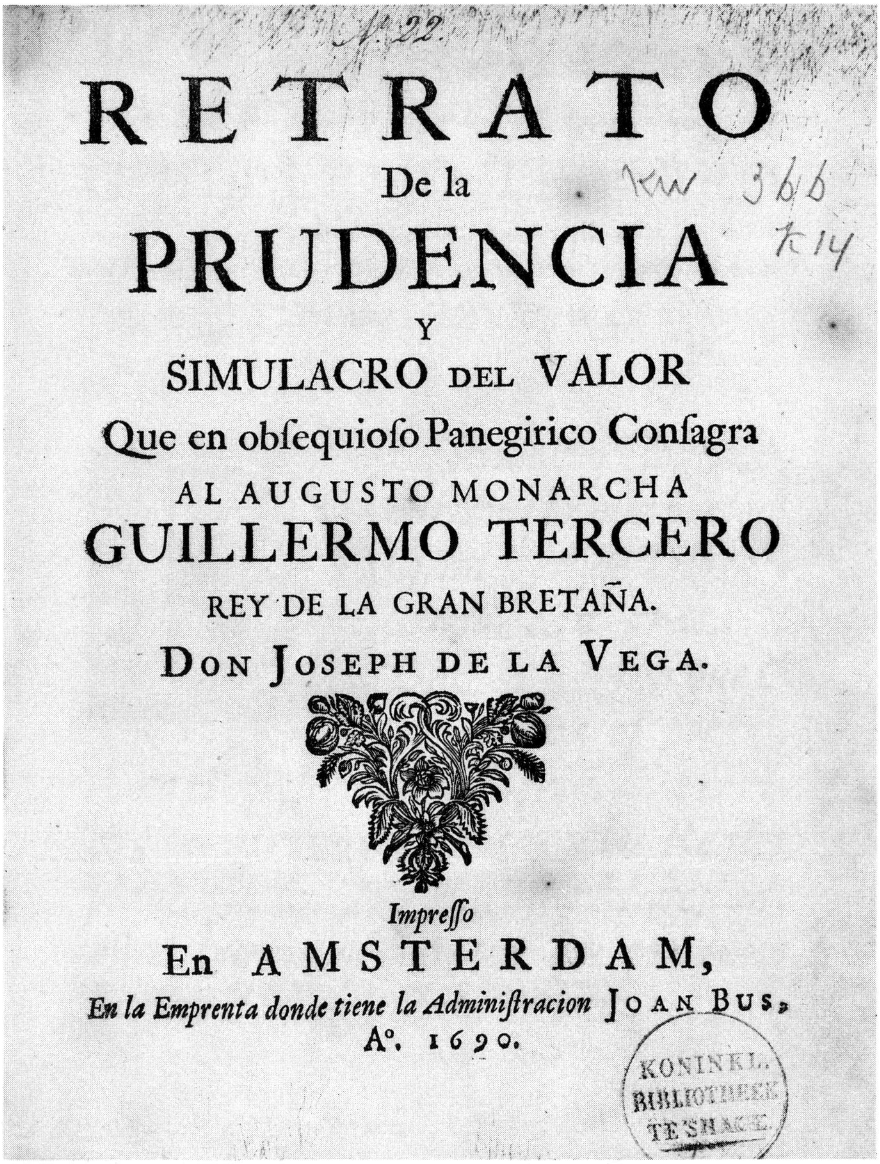

RETRATO
De la
PRUDENCIA
Y
SIMULACRO DEL VALOR
Que en obſequioſo Panegirico Conſagra
AL AUGUSTO MONARCHA
GUILLERMO TERCERO
REY DE LA GRAN BRETAÑA.
DON JOSEPH DE LA VEGA.

Impreſſo
En AMSTERDAM,
En la Emprenta donde tiene la Adminiſtracion JOAN BUS,
A°. 1690.

31 The title page of Joseph Penso de la Vega's *Retrato de la Prudencia y Simulacro del Valor* (1690).

being fostered against his religion and against his fatherland.'[28] David slew Goliath with five smooth (Sp. *lisas*) stones: these correspond to the five *fleurs de lis* in William's coat of arms. Furthermore, the author reminds us, Goliath was killed by hurled stones, the punishment for blasphemy.

[28] Penso de la Vega, *Retrato de la Prudencia*, p. 13.

Penso de la Vega, then, like Barrios, is convinced of the moral justification for the dethroning of James II in favour of William and May. The way both writers make extensive use of biblical passages and themes to depict and analyse contemporary political events might be held to be analogous. But there is a basic difference between the two writers' ways of working. Barrios assumes the role of prophet, and assumes that there are hidden secrets in passages of Scripture, relating to contemporary events, which can be revealed by means of poetic and etymological insight. Penso do la Vega by contrast is merely displaying his refined rhetorical skills to flatter the king and entertain the reader.

MANUEL DE LEÃO: 'EL DUELO DE LOS APLAUSOS, O TRIUMPHO DE LOS TRIUMPHOS'

Very little is known about Manuel de Leão. He did not participate in Amsterdam literary life in Amsterdam as described in 1684/5 by Barrios.[29] As the five texts he published do not reveal anything concrete about his religion, we do not know even whether he lived in Holland as a professing Jew. All we know for certain is that, from the late 1680s onwards, he had close links with Amsterdam and that he received the patronage of the Dutch Sephardi figures of the day – Jeronimo Nunes da Costa (Moses Curiel), agent of the Portuguese Crown in the United Provinces, and Francisco Lopes Suasso, baron of Auvergne-le-Gras.

Manuel de Leão's first work was the *Triumpho Lusitano, Applausos festivos* (1688) which, according to the *impressum* was published in Brussels but was probably in fact published at Amsterdam with 'Brussels' being given, to make the work more acceptable in Portugal.[30] The book was commissioned by Jeronimo Nunes da Costa who, in 1687, had played a large part in arranging the stately journey of Maria Sophia of Bavaria, daughter of the Elector Palatine, the new bride of King Pedro II of Portugal, from Heidelberg via the Dutch Republic to Lisbon as well as the banquets and festivities which marked her brief stay in Holland.[31] The book was embellished, presumably at Jeronimo's expense, with one of the most splendid title pages of all the works ever published in Spanish or Portuguese in the Low Counties. The book may indeed be said to be a sort of a celebration of the rapprochement in Dutch–Portuguese relations

[29] Miguel de Barrios, *Relación de los poetas y escritores judíos amstelodamos* (Amsterdam, 1684), and Miguel de Barrios *Academia de los floridos. Memoria plausible de sus juezes, y académicos* (Amsterdam, 1685); see also den Boer, 'Spanish and Portuguese Editions', *Studia Rosenthaliana*, 23, p. 45.

[30] M. Kayserling, *Bibliografia española-portugueza judaica* (Strasburg, 1890), p. 57; den Boer, 'Spanish and Portuguese Editions', *Studia Rosenthaliana*, 23, pp. 140–1.

[31] ARH SG 7015/1, Jeronimo Nunes da Costa to SG, The Hague, 21 Sept. 1686 and 11 Apr. 1687; Jeronimo's sons, Duarte (to whom Penso de la Vega dedicated his *Confusión de Confusiones*) and Alexandre Nunes da Costa travelled to Düsseldorf and accompanied Maria Sophia's party back from there to The Hague; see also Manuel de Leão, *Triumpho Lusitano, Applausos festivos* (Brussels [Amsterdam], 1688), dedication.

and William III's efforts to detach Portugal from the sphere of influence of Louis XIV.[32]

El Duelo do los Aplausos, Triumpho de los Triumphos is likewise clearly addressed to a secular and not necessarily, or even primarily, a Jewish audience. Its title page explains that it is a literary portrait of the 'unvanquished Augustus, William III British Monarch', and that it is a panegyric on his grand entrance to The Hague which took place on 5 February 1691, the first occasion that he returned to his Dutch homeland since his crossing to England in November 1688, an occasion marked by great festivities and the presence of diplomatic representatives of all the allied princes participating in the coalition against Louis XIV.[33] Manuel de Leão dedicates his 'metrical praise' to the princess of Soissons and Savoy, the mother of Prince Eugene of Savoy, and a lady with longstanding links with the Sephardi Jewish business elite of Amsterdam (and with the stock exchange).[34] The dedication is dated 20 February 1691.

In his dedication, the poet declares that the representatives of the illustrious princes of the coalition had gathered together in The Hague in the presence of the Stadholder-king for two purposes: one, of just vengeance against France, and, the other, of 'courtesy', and ceremony, in the salon of the Princess of Soissons. Manuel de Leão promises her that on a later occasion he will celebrate the heroic actions of her son, Prince Eugene, meanwhile offering this description of William III so that she will afterwards be able to compare the illustrious virtues of both heroes.

The metrical portrait of William III is written in *silvas*, the form in which Iberian pastoral poetry was written. The opening verses indeed allude to the *Soledades*, a much admired work by the great Spanish baroque poet, Luis de Góngora. In verse replete with classical comparisons, the poet celebrates William III's entry in the depths of winter to The Hague where the gods are gathered

[32] We see from the reports which Jeronimo Nunes da Costa sent to the Conde de Castelmelhor, in Lisbon, in the opening months of the Nine Years' War that he was certainly endeavouring to influence Portugal against France, claiming (for example) that the Anglo-Dutch alliance would be far superior to France at sea and that Anglo-Dutch sea-power would prevent France sending any significant assistance to James II in Ireland, see Biblioteca Nacional, Lisbon, MS Caixa 208, no. 45, Jeronimo Nunes da Costa to Conde de Castelmelhor, Amsterdam, 26 Feb. 1689; Jonathan I. Israel, 'The Diplomatic Career of Jeronimo Nunes da Costa: An Episode in Dutch–Portuguese Relations of the Seventeenth Century', *Bijdragen en Mededelingen betreffende de Geschiedenis der Nederlanden*, 98 (1983), p. 189; according to Gregorio Leti, Jeronimo was one of the most enthusiastic patrons of literature among the Amsterdam Sephardi patrician elite, Israel, 'Gregorio Leti (1631–1701) and the Dutch Sephardi Elite', pp. 274–6; Duarte Lopes Rosa wrote several eulogistic works in honour of Pedro II and the 'serene Princess Dona Maria Sophia of Neuburg' in the years 1687–91, doubtless also at the request of Jeronimo Nunes da Costa, see den Boer, 'Spanish and Portuguese Editions', 23, pp. 144–5.

[33] See the *Relation du Voyage de Sa Majesté Britannique en Hollande, et de la reception qui luy a été faite* (The Hague, 1692), with engravings by Romeyn de Hooghe; N. Japikse, *Prins Willem III, de Stadhouder-koning* (2 vols., Amsterdam, 1930–3), II, pp. 326–7.

[34] E. R. Samuel, 'Manuel Levy Duarte (1631–1714): An Amsterdam Merchant Jeweller and his Trade with London', *Transactions of the Jewish Historical Society of England*, 27 (1982), pp. 19–20.

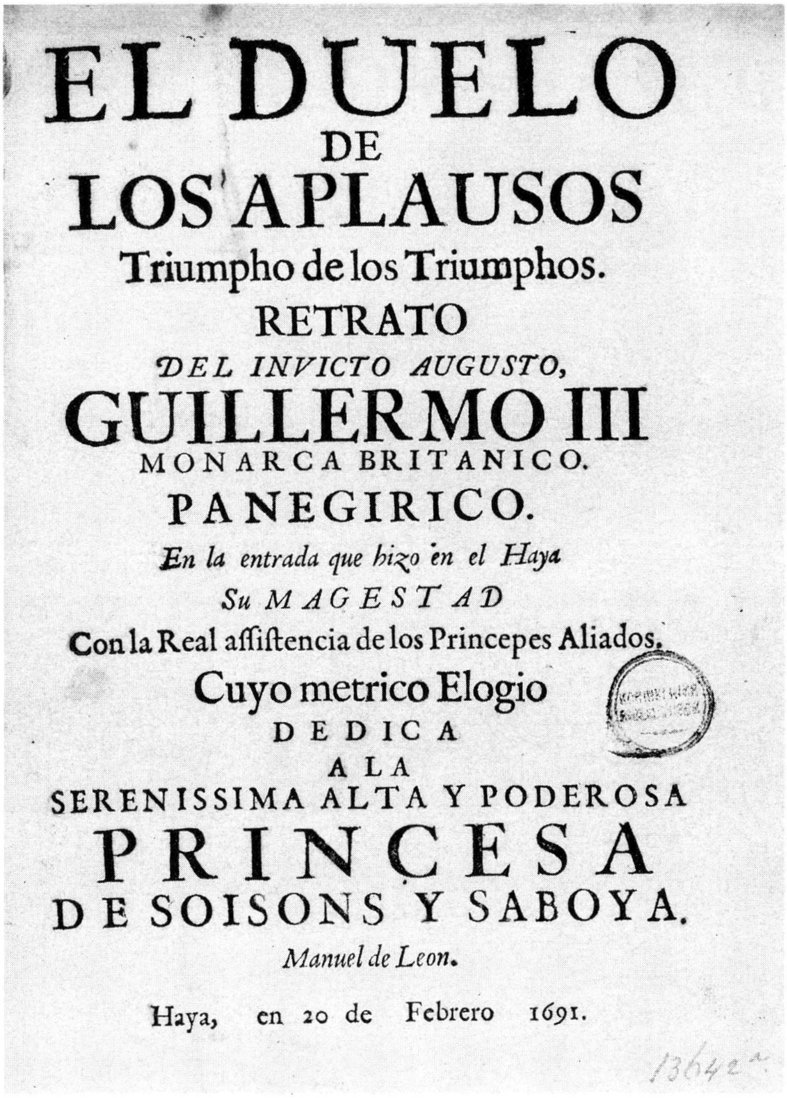
EL DUELO
DE
LOS APLAUSOS
Triumpho de los Triumphos.
RETRATO
DEL INVICTO AUGUSTO,
GUILLERMO III
MONARCA BRITANICO.
PANEGIRICO.
En la entrada que hizo en el Haya
Su MAGESTAD
Con la Real aſſiſtencia de los Princepes Aliados.
Cuyo metrico Elogio
DEDICA
A LA
SERENISSIMA ALTA Y PODEROSA
PRINÇESA
DE SOISONS Y SABOYA.
Manuel de Leon.
Haya, en 20 de Febrero 1691.

32 The title page of Manuel de Leão's *Duelo de los Aplausos* (1691).

together for a momentous reunion. The gods – Mars of England, Neptune of Holland, Jupiter of the empire, Phoebus of Spain, Hercules of Denmark and several less significant demi-gods (the German principalities) – have convened not only to receive the heroic William III following his triumphs in Britain and Ireland but to 'halt the furies of the Gallic Giant'.

The poet celebrates the unprecedented splendour of the festivities amid which the Stadholder-king was received which, according to Manuel de Leão, no pre-

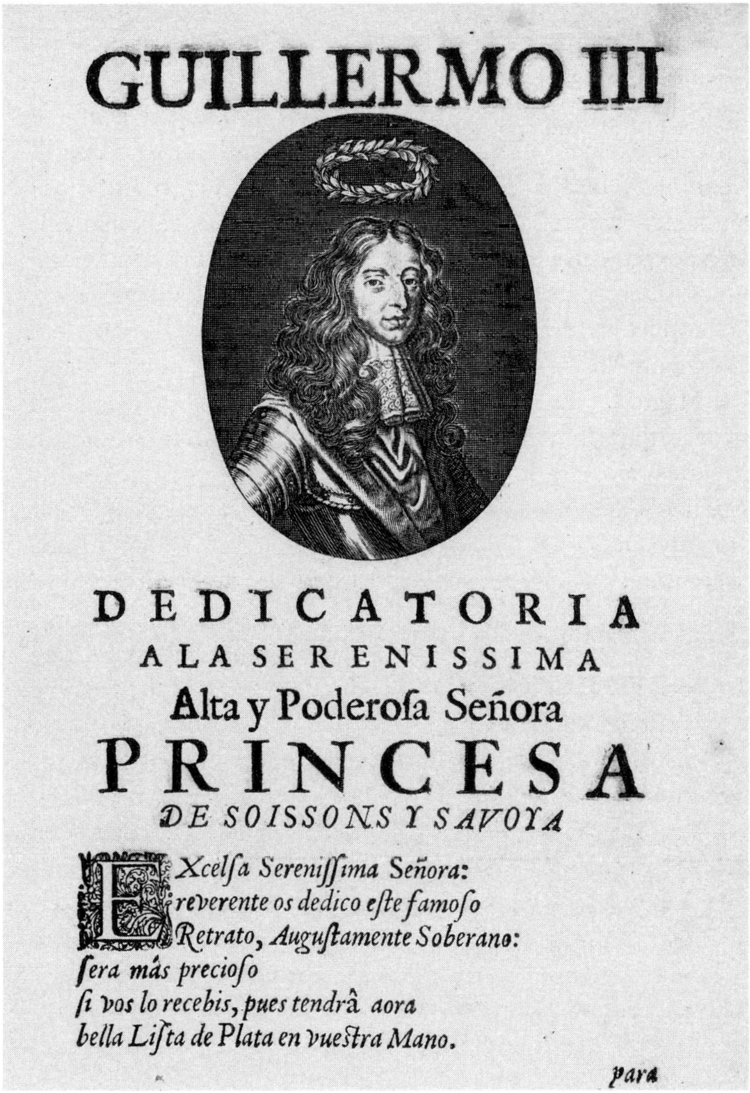
GUILLERMO III

DEDICATORIA
ALA SERENISSIMA
Alta y Poderoſa Señora
PRINCESA
DE SOISSONS Y SAVOYA

EXcelſa Sereniſſima Señora:
reverente os dedico eſte famoſo
Retrato, Auguſtamente Soberano:
ſera más precioſo
ſi vos lo recebis, pues tendrâ aora
bella Liſta de Plata en vueſtra Mano.

para

33 *Manuel de Leão's Dedication to the Princess of Soissons and Savoy, Headed by a Portrait of William III.*

vious triumphs could match. These were indeed very elaborate and were recorded for posterity at the time in a series of magnificent engravings by Dutch artists including Romeyn de Hooghe. In typical baroque fashion, the poet challenges other poets to a poetical contest. A 'duel of applauses' is celebrated and the 'canaille' of the Olympic Games, and the Saturnian and other feasts, required to submit; for theirs are but pagan spectacles inferior to the triumphs of William of Orange. The achievements of this great contemporary hero are compared with those of nine famous heroes of the past, the names of the latter being taken from the letters that form the name 'Guillermo'. Thus, if Ulysses, corresponding to the second letter of William's name, gained fame by refusing to fear the tempests of the sea, William III 'to the astonishment of the ages' acquired glory by braving Neptune when the latter was at his most angry. This, as we are informed in a note, refers not only to the rough winter crossing from England which William had just experienced, but all three of his crossings from England to Holland, his four crossings, thus far, from Holland to England, and his crossings from England to, and from, Ireland.

The 'triumph of triumphs' refers to the splendour of the Stadholder-king's grand entry into The Hague. No ancient hero was received with ceremony of comparable magnificence, though William's carriage was not drawn by elephants, like Caesar's, nor by lions, like Mark Anthony's, but rather by horses like that of Apollo: for like Apollo, William resembles a sun, shining in England, reflecting in Holland and casting rays in France. The three arches of triumph which formed the centre-piece of ceremonial decorations erected in the centre of The Hague, and adorned by leading artists (see Plate 34), surpassed in splendour Manuel de Leão tells us, the famous monuments of ancient Memphis, Babilonia, and Rhodes while the firework displays put on in The Hague surpassed the flashing of volcanoes and the very flames of Vesuvius.

El Duelo de los Aplausos, if possibly the most elegant of the eulogistic works we have discussed, is certainly also the most superficial as a comment on William III and the Glorious Revolution. It is merely a typical baroque panegyric of the late seventeenth century, a light entertainment in a classical mythological style, devoted to a monarch. It is mainly significant for us today as a cultural historical document illustrating the elaborate festivities which were put on at The Hague in celebration of William III's triumphs in February 1691.

CONCLUSION

The Glorious Revolution and the elevation of William and Mary to the three thrones of England, Scotland, and Ireland, was enthusiastically prayed for, and celebrated, by the Sephardi Jews of Amsterdam. A number of eulogistic and other occasional works written at this time by Miguel de Barrios, Joseph Penso de la Vega, Manuel de Leão, and Duarte (Moseh) Lopes Rosa reflect this support and enthusiasm.

In the case of the *Atlas angélico* of Miguel (Daniel Levi) de Barrios we may speak of Sephardi literature containing a discernible Jewish response to the triumphs of William III. Barrios includes in his book one of the several prayers which the Portuguese Jewish community of Amsterdam recited for the success

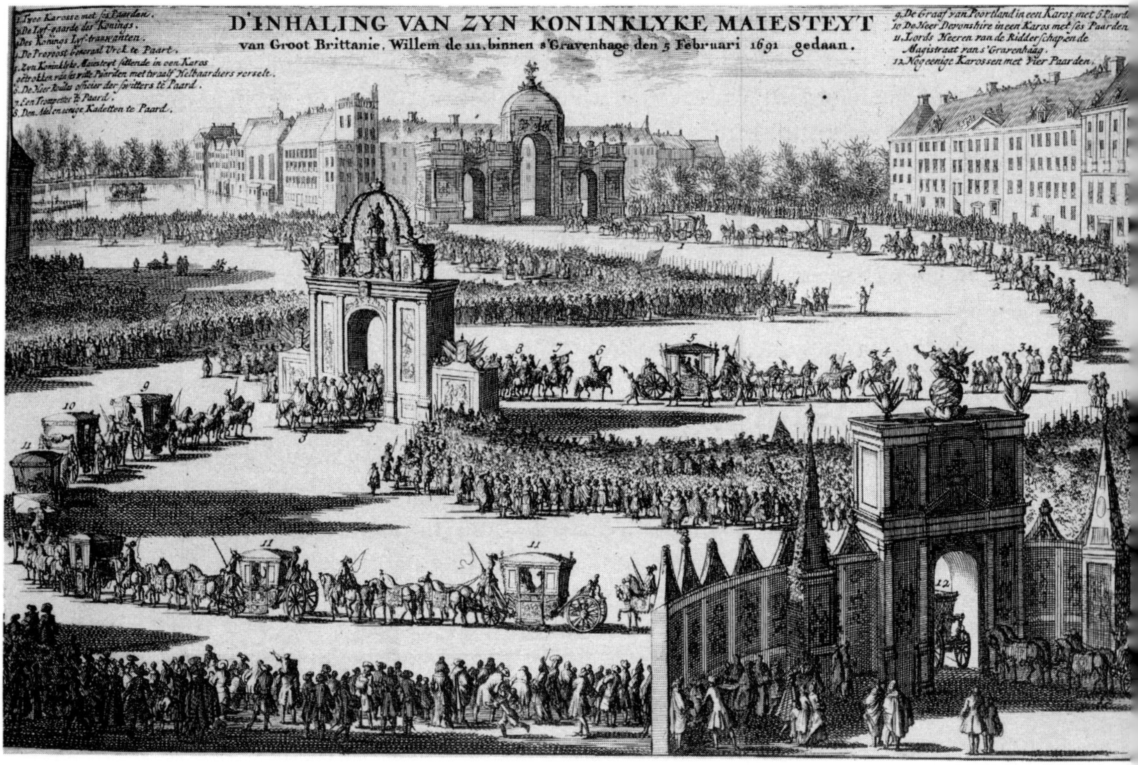

34 *William III's Triumphal Entry into The Hague on 5 February 1691.*
Note the several specially erected triumphal arches adorned with elaborate depictions of his victories. William is riding in the carriage marked '5', Bentinck, now Lord Portland, is in the carriage marked '9', Lord Devonshire is in the carriage marked '10'.

of the Stadholder, Dutch state, and their invasion armada in the autumn of 1688. Parts of his text reveal a definite sympathy for the Calvinist religion which William defended and aversion to the popery he defeated. More importantly, the penchant for cabalistic explanations rooted in etymology and biblical prophecies characteristic of this author impart an unmistakable Jewish flavour to his work. Despite the fact that it is clearly a reworking of a book originally intended to be dedicated to James II and designed to please that Catholic and absolutist Stuart monarch, there is no reason to doubt the sincerity of the pro-Revolution sentiments Barrios expressed in the revised version of the book, and privately.

By contrast, Joseph Penso de la Vega and Manuel de Leão avoided introducing any specifically Jewish overtones into their eulogies. They wrote elaborate, entertaining, courtly panegyrics of slight literary value doubtless but of considerable significance for the cultural historian. Of ideological content there is very little.

Even the defence of the international Protestant cause by the Stadholder-king is touched on only very lightly so as to avoid offending the sensibilities of the Catholic allies. The one key idea which is basic to all three of the works discussed in this essay is the three authors' common view of the Glorious Revolution and the dethroning of James II in favour of William and Mary as something important, and indeed necessary, for the Dutch Republic and Europe as well as Britain, events to be placed firmly within the framework of Europe's struggle against the insatiable tyranny of Louis XIV. The lack of Jewish content in the eulogies by Joseph Penso de le Vega and Manuel de Leão, indeed the fact that these works were written at all, has to be understood in the context of the political, financial, and diplomatic role of the Dutch Sephardi patrician elite. The leading figures of the community were eager to build on their links with the Stadholder-king, his entourage, and the ambassadors of his allies, and their patronage of the type of occasional literature the Sephardi writers of Amsterdam produced at the time of the Glorious Revolution was an integral part of what was at once a political, cultural, and social strategy: by increasing their ties with William III and his allies, the Dutch Sephardi leadership gained in influence and prestige in both Jewish and non-Jewish circles and further enhanced their quasi-aristocratic pretensions.

Chapter 15

A fateful alliance? William III and England in Dutch historiography, 1688–9 to 1988–9

P. J. A. N. RIETBERGEN

The history of Anglo-Dutch relations is long and characterized by almost continuous commercial rivalry.[1] On the political level periods of comparative peaceful co-existence were punctuated by such severe and disruptive crises as the four Anglo-Dutch Wars, bitter maritime and colonial struggles which the Dutch blame on, and name after, the English and the English call 'the Dutch Wars'.

There were only two moments when a close union between the two powers seemed a distinct possibility. Twice in the 1650s, the Lord Protector, Oliver Cromwell, approached the regents of the province of Holland, led by Pensionary Johan de Witt, and also the States General, with insistent proposals for a merger between the two Protestant republics. The Dutch were by no means enthusiastic and nothing came of the project.[2] Then, in the late 1680s, the Glorious Revolution placed the man who was the leading figure in Dutch domestic politics and in the formulation of Dutch foreign policy on the thrones of England, Scotland, and Ireland. If the marriage of William and Mary had been blessed with offspring, the course of European history, and not least the relationship between Britain and the Netherlands, would doubtless have been profoundly different from what it was. However, with Mary's death in 1694, the last, then already remote, possibility of achieving an enduring, close linkage between the two countries finally disappeared. For us today it is hard even to guess how such a personal union, linking two nations which had for so long seemed destined to be rivals, would have worked out.

The Glorious Revolution held out the promise of a close Anglo-Dutch partnership without removing the underlying tension between the two peoples. In 1694, an English pamphleteer, in a tract rather ominously entitled *Delenda Carthago or the True Interest of England*, wrote: 'it is interest that governs Kingdoms.

[1] A recent, if not always satisfactory, survey is K. H. D. Haley, *The British and the Dutch: Political and Cultural Relations through the Ages* (London, 1988).

[2] See Pieter Geyl, *Oranje en Stuart, 1642–1672* (Zeist and Arnhem, 1963), pp. 71, 73, 99–100; and G. Mitsukari, *Englisch-Niederländische Unionsbestrebungen im Zeitalter Cromwells* (Berlin, 1891).

Nations do not fall in love with one another as particular persons do.'[3] It is obvious that the English were perfectly well aware of this truth from the start while both the Dutch in William III's time, and not a few of their historians in following centuries, were in danger of ignoring this maxim. For the Dutch, the union, such as it was, failed almost from the start to live up to the great promise which initially it held out. Ever since 1689 Dutchmen have been endeavouring to interpret this failure and explain what went wrong.

It is the aim of this essay to chart Dutch views about the history of the Anglo-Dutch alliance forged in 1688–9 as expressed and, one might almost say codified in large-scale, standard Dutch historical works over the past three hundred years.[4] I have concentrated my analysis on the 'general' histories of the Netherlands published in the eighteenth, nineteenth, and twentieth centuries since this study is intended to be, in part, an evaluation of the political function of history. The historical works which I have selected for discussion were written for the general, educated public, the sections of society which might be expected to wield political influence. Consequently, they reflect the political and ideological functions of the writing of history rather more than do more specialized scholarly monographs.

The political and ideological functions of history and historiography are perhaps particularly obvious in the Dutch case where faith and ideological posture have always been potent factors behind the writing of history.[5] In this connection, I propose to use the term 'faith' in a double sense to mean both adherence to a particular religious creed and commitment to a particular stance in political life. In the Netherlands the two were quite often almost indistinguishably mixed.

Ever since the first years of its existence, the Dutch Republic had been characterized by a power structure which displayed a curious dichotomy and which, in its turn, had a bearing on practically all manifestations of political power. The at times quasi-monarchical but partly unconstitutional power of the Stadholders from the Houses of Orange and Nassau was nearly always at variance with the views held by factions within the regional elites of the seven supposedly sovereign provinces that constituted the confederation of the United Provinces. Admittedly, the successive Princes of Orange, Stadholders, that is officials appointed by the provincial States in five of the seven provinces, could rely, if they exploited the influence and resources of patronage available to them,

[3] Ch. Leslie, *Delenda Carthago, or the True Interest of England in Relation to France and Holland* (London, 1694), cited in what remains a very valuable study of English public opinion and the Dutch during William III's reign: G. van Alphen, *De stemming van de Engelschen tegen de Hollanders in Engeland tijdens de regeering van den koning-stadhouder Willem III, 1688–1702* (Assen, 1938).

[4] There is no up-to-date survey of the history of Dutch historiography. For the present purpose one might consult: E. H. Kossmann, *Politieke theorie in het zeventiende-eeuwse Nederland* (Amsterdam, 1960).

[5] See, for example, J. S. Bromley and E. H. Kossman (eds.), *Britain and the Netherlands*, V: *Some Political Mythologies* (The Hague, 1975).

on the support of powerful factions of their own. For whereas their 'structural' power lay in their great landed wealth and lordly status, their 'functional' power emanated from their role as captain-general of the army, and admiral-general of the navy supplemented by the right to elect or nominate a mass of local magistrates and other officials in some provinces and towns within provinces. Thus, there was always a strong Orangist faction, all the more effective owing to the consistent support which the House of Orange received from significant sections of the common people, frequently prompted by the ministers of the Dutch Reformed Church.[6] In this present context it is important to bear in mind that William III deliberately sought to make the most of this support, and expand it, by means of political propaganda, inspiring a stream of pamphlets and engravings presenting his political stance in vivid, strong, and emotive terms.[7] Yet despite the fact that the Orangist faction was a considerable force in Dutch politics, the actual power of the regent class, especially the urban patriciate of Holland and Zeeland, always seems to have been of comparable or even greater weight than that of the Stadholders. Even so, at times the regents had to accept that the Prince of Orange stood at the centre of the stage and was the presiding figure in Dutch politics, and at times accepted also that the Prince's power was increasing.

It was the danger posed by the growth of French power and the uncompromising policy pursued by Louis XIV against the insistent advice of his astute ambassador at The Hague, the comte d'Avaux, that paved the way for the further expansion of William's power inside the Republic in the late 1680s,[8] after a period of setbacks commencing with the Peace of Nijmegen (1678) which the regents had concluded against his wishes. In the late 1680s even the regents least sympathetic to the Stadholder's aims had to admit that in the face of the rising French threat, it was only William's Grand Design which stood between them and almost certain commercial ruin.[9] Thus, the Descent on England, of November 1688, was based on a relatively firm if obviously only temporary consensus among the Dutch power elites. Even those who were aware of the pitfalls inherent in linking the Republic's fortunes to England had to acquiesce for the time being, because of the international political situation and because

[6] A study that goes a long way towards explaining the ambivalent relationship between the House of Orange and Dutch Protestantism is: A. van Deursen, *Bavianen en Slijkgeuzen. Kerk en Kerkvolk ten tijde van Maurits en Oldenbarnevelt* (Assen, 1974), *passim.*

[7] For the role of pamphlets in William III's statecraft, see P. J. A. N. Rietbergen, ''s Werelds Schouwtoneel. Oorlog, Politiek en Economie in Noord-West Europa ten tijde van Willem III', in A. G. H. Bachrach *et al.* (eds.), *Willem III. De Stadhouder-koning en zijn tijd* (Amsterdam, 1988), pp. 51–87, esp. pp. 68–71.

[8] P. J. A. N. Rietbergen, 'William III of Orange (1650–1702) between European Politics and European Protestantism: The Case of the Huguenots', in H. Bots (ed.), *La Révocation de l'Edit de Nantes et les Provinces-Unies, 1685. Colloque international du Tricentenaire* (Amsterdam, 1987), pp. 35–50, esp. pp. 43–5.

[9] Ibid., pp. 45–6.

35 *Hans Willem Bentinck, Earl of Portland (1649–1709)*. Engraved portrait by J. Houbraken.
For more than thirty years Hans Willem Bentinck, a member of a Gelderland noble family, was William III's closest confidant and political accomplice. In 1678 he married Anne Villiers, one of the ladies who accompanied Princess Mary to the United Provinces. Together with William he was the chief planner of the expedition to England in 1688 and the Schomberg expedition to Ireland in 1689. In 1689, after William's elevation to the English throne, he was proclaimed Groom of the Stole, Treasurer of the Privy Purse, Intendant of the Royal Parks, and Chief Intendant of the Royal Houses, and created earl of Portland, Viscount Woodstock, and Baron Cirencester. He was a member of the Privy Council and the House of Lords, a general in the Dutch army, and through his possession of the Castle of Rhoon and other estates in Holland a member of the *ridderschap* of the States of Holland.

the Dutch Protestant common people had been won over by the effective exploitation by William's public relations machine of the religious argument for intervening in Britain. When the news that the Crown of England had been offered to William and Mary jointly reached the Republic, there was great public rejoicing. The States General ordered a general thanksgiving. The coronation of the Prince and Princess in Westminster Abbey, in April 1689, was widely celebrated in the Netherlands as well as in England, with salutes of guns, triumphal arches, bonfires, banquets, and literary recitals in all the major cities. To cite but one example of the Williamite fervour, a play put on in the Amsterdam civic theatre forecast in allegorical terms peace and prosperity as the outcome of the union between the two nations under William's glorious rule.[10] William himself communicated to the Amsterdam city council his satisfaction at the elaborate and costly celebrations which the city had laid on.[11]

It soon became evident, however, not least from the long, arduous and ill-tempered negotiations which preceded the signing of the military and naval alliance between the two powers in 1689 that Anglo-Dutch co-operation was likely to be fraught with many and serious problems. Some of the Holland regents, including the anti-Orangist faction at Amsterdam, resumed their efforts to gain popular support for their view that humiliating deference to the English was not exactly what they had had in mind when giving their consent to the plans for the invasion of England. But the argument remained rather muted owing to the firmness of popular Protestant support for the Stadholder-king and most of the Dutch pamphlets which appeared during the decade following the Glorious Revolution argued for rather than against William's policy. Nor was any large-scale historical work attempted with a view to documenting the standpoint of either the Stadholder-king or the anti-Orangist regents, restating any particular view of the nation's past and what was desired for the future.

With regard to the relatively large quantity of pamphlets written between 1688 and 1702 dealing with Anglo-Dutch relations, mostly the joint war effort, two pertinent observations may be made. First, this literature, often essentially reportage, apparently satisfied a deep-seated need for detailed, up-to-date information about the progress of the joint war against France. Secondly, it seems that William's propaganda machine successfully used the pamphlet medium to convey the message that co-operation between England and the Republic was a vital necessity for both. My (admittedly rather cursory) glance at the Dutch pamphlets certainly does not suggest that there was an anti-English climate in the Republic in any way comparable to the widespread, even virulent anti-Dutch feeling evident, as we see from G. van Alphen's study, *De stemming van de*

[10] Rietbergen, ''s Werelds Schouwtoneel', pp. 51–3.
[11] GA Amsterdam, archives of the burgomasters, oud num. 7, Witsen to Amsterdam *vroedschap*, London, 3/13 May 1689. I am indebted to Jonathan Israel for this reference.

36 *The Onset of England's Naval Supremacy: The Battle of La Hougue (29 May to 1 June 1692).* Engraving by J. Vianen.
The humiliation of the English fleet off Beachy Head, in 1690, was erased with the great victory, in which the English played the leading role, off the top of the Cherbourg Peninsula, from Barfleur to La Hougue, at the end of May 1692. In this decisive battle the Anglo-Dutch fleet – comprising forty-nine heavy English warships as against thirty-nine Dutch – severely defeated the considerably smaller (forty-four major warships) French fleet under Admiral Tourville. On the engraving, the figure of Fame (top right), sitting on a globe with captured French banners and insignia at her feet, extends a huge laurel wreath, encompassing the portraits of William and Mary, to the two allied naval commanders Admiral Russell and Admiral Philips van Almonde (1644–1711). In the centre are views of the battle and on the columns on either side individual scenes of the defeat of fifteen destroyed or captured French warships.

Engelschen tegen de Hollanders in Engeland tijdens de regeering van den koning-stadhouder Willem III (1938), in the English pamphlets of the period.

In the Dutch Republic in the 1690s there was a certain amount of grumbling about the growing naval supremacy of England and about the impact of the joint Anglo-Dutch trade embargo against France on the Dutch carrying trade, as we see in a pamphlet such as the *Consideratien over de huydendaagsche commercie*,[12] of 1690. But these adverse developments were not blamed directly on the Republic's political involvement with England; nor is blame affixed to William. On the contrary, even if we set aside obvious works of Orangist propaganda such as the long, tedious panegyrics of a poetaster such as Lucas Rotgans, who never missed an opportunity to sing William's praise, we encounter numerous publications which extol the virtues of the alliance and close links between England and the Republic, mostly esteeming the new relationship on grounds of mutual religious *and* commercial interests. An interesting example is the pamphlet *Hollants Heyl in haar Eenigheit met Engeland gelegen* (1689)[13] which reviews the evolution of Anglo-Dutch relations over the centuries, refers to Cromwell's efforts towards an Anglo-Dutch union, and concludes that it is only by standing together with England that the Dutch can save themselves, with William III, the new Gideon, leading the two nations. The Dutch should simply give way to the English on points of ceremony and so forth, England being, after all, a kingdom.

It is only after William's death in 1702, and the inevitable loosening of the links with England that followed, that a more critical tone is encountered. The pamphlet *Het Waare Interest van Europa* (1702),[14] published soon after William's death, stresses the indispensability of the alliance with England to the Republic but is disparaging about the late dynastic bond, referring to the Prince as the 'royal Stadholder in the Republic' and, interestingly, the 'Stadholder royal in England'. Characteristic of the upsurge of new republican sentiments in the United Provinces following the Prince's death is the pamphlet *Op de doot van Willem den derden* (1702)[15] which is at once openly republican, anti-English, and anti-French. Dutch disappointment with the alliance with England continued to find expression sporadically in the pamphlets throughout the War of the Spanish Succession (1702–13), as in *De Eerste Fransche Harlequin*[16] where a Frenchman boasts of his country's new-found friendship with Britain and a Dutchman bemoans English duplicity in the negotiations over the Barrier Treaty. Yet, while the number of critical tracts gradually increases, especially (as one might expect) after 1711, the general tone, until well into the 1720s, remains remarkably conciliatory towards Britain and even optimistic.

The first major general history of the Netherlands written by a Dutchman

[12] For this and the following pamphlets, I refer to W. P. C. Knuttel, *Catalogus van de pamflettenverzameling berustende in de Koninklijke Bibliotheek* (9 vols., The Hague, 1889–1920). This pamphlet is Knuttel no. 14,398.

[13] Knuttel no. 13,291.

[14] Knuttel no. 14,800.

[15] Knuttel no. 14,696.

[16] Knuttel no. 16,084.

since Lieuwe van Aitzema's *Saecken van Staet en Oorlogh*, a large-scale multi-volume chronicle of Dutch history and politics of the early and mid-seventeenth century, was published only in the fourth and fifth decades of the eighteenth century. This was Jan Wagenaar's twenty-one volume *Vaderlandsche Historie*, which takes the history of the Netherlands from the earliest times up to his own day.[17] Although Wagenaar endeavoured to achieve a high degree of objectivity, and avoided obvious bias, it cannot be denied that his great work consistently reflects the views and opinions of the Dutch regent class. Specifically, Wagenaar's history sought to buttress and justify the views held by the Amsterdam regents about the structure of Dutch domestic politics and about foreign policy, as well as their own role in these spheres and their ideas about the policies best suited to ensure the continuance of Dutch prosperity. Wagenaar's account of Dutch history remained in the ascendant down to the end of the Republic and even beyond. Though his own writing carried the story only to 1752, his work was continued by a series of scholars albeit mostly in a less coherent, annalistic fashion, down to the early years of the nineteenth century.

If we analyse what Wagenaar wrote about the Glorious Revolution and the onset of the Anglo-Dutch alliance,[18] one is struck first of all by the prominence which he gives to the observations in manuscript left by Nicolaas Witsen, the most influential of the then Amsterdam burgomasters and a man who was by no means an uncritical accomplice of the Stadholder-king.[19] According to Wagenaar, Witsen realized that William had asked the States General to send him as one of their ambassadors extraordinary to England in 1689 chiefly so as to emphasize and reinforce Amsterdam's (not always firm) support for his English policy. Wagenaar makes no attempt to play down the serious problems with the English which became evident almost as soon as the detailed negotiations over Anglo-Dutch military and naval co-operation began. Wagenaar shows that William made no attempt to counteract English demands that English admirals should have precedence and superiority in decision-making in the combined Anglo-Dutch war fleet which the Dutch (already irritated by Parliament's reluctance to repay the Republic the whole of the 7.5m guilders expenses incurred in fitting out the expedition to England, requested by the States General) took as a serious affront. When the English also refused to pay their full share of expenditure on troops which, according to the Dutch ambassadors extraordinary ought to be appreciably larger than the Dutch share, tempers really started to flare. The treaty of alliance which was finally concluded in September 1689, also included a clause allowing the English to seize Dutch as well as other ships

[17] J. Wagenaar, *Vaderlandsche Historie vervattende de geschiedenissen der nu Vereenigde Nederlanden* (21 vols., Amsterdam, 1749–59), see vol. XVI.

[18] Ibid., XVI, pp. 20–102 *passim*.

[19] Ibid., XVI, p. 41 *et seq*. On Witsen's political role during the reign of William III see also J. Gebhard, *Het leven van Mr Nicolaas Cornelisz Witsen (1641–1717)* (2 vols., Utrecht, 1881–2).

seeking to evade the Anglo-Dutch embargo on trade with France, though Witsen and Amsterdam had tenaciously opposed this as a measure which could only harm the Republic's position in international trade and, therefore, in international politics as well. Wagenaar exposes the underlying divergence of priorities of William and Amsterdam with particular clarity when he describes Witsen's unsuccessful attempts to have the detested English Navigation Act rescinded. Citing Witsen, the historian relates how the Stadholder-king merely laughed at the proposal. Wagenaar gives considerable emphasis to what he sees as the pernicious policy of the English to destroy the economic position of the Dutch. His anti-Orangism and lack of sympathy for the Anglo-Dutch alliance emerge also from the many pages of the history devoted to those incidents in Dutch internal politics which arose from William's undiminished determination to manage the Dutch provinces, and the Dutch decision-making process, after 1688, and the efforts of the regents to counter the Stadholder-king's growing influence.

It was only logical that with the establishment of the House of Orange as the hereditary dynasty of the new-founded kingdom of the Netherlands in 1813, the tone of official historiography, both in general terms and with respect to the Glorious Revolution, should change markedly. When the great figure of early nineteenth-century Dutch romantic literature, Willem Bilderdijk, published his popular *Geschiedenis des Vaderlands*,[20] he showed much more appreciation than had Wagenaar both of the dynastic background of William III's English policy and of its role in the Prince's European schemes as a whole. Bilderdijk went out of his way to denigrate the propensities of Wagenaar's great work and generally sought to discredit the policies of the regents as selfish and petty. Though no lover of the English as such, Bilderdijk was a fervent admirer of the Stadholder-king and therefore could not but depict the Prince's English policy as something advantageous to the Dutch, or, at least, necessary. The aspects of the Glorious Revolution highlighted by Wagenaar are, in Bilderdijk, either omitted entirely or else belittled. Even so, in the end Bilderdijk could not deny that the Anglo-Dutch alliance had quickly resulted in a situation which was far from altogether favourable to Dutch maritime and commercial interests. Even though unappreciative of the regents' political role, he was certainly not unaware of the national importance of the priorities they favoured. Bilderdijk too realized that William III's linkage of the Republic's fortunes to England, however heroic and advantageous to begin with, eventually set the United Provinces on a downhill path.

Still more partisan in a pro-Orange sense was the general history written by the prominent Dutch statesman Guillaume Groen van Prinsterer. Significantly, Groen called his work, the *Handboek der Geschiedenis van het Vaderland*, a

[20] W. Bilderdijk, *Geschiedenis des Vaderlands*, ed. H. W. Tydeman (13 vols., Amsterdam, 1832–53), X, pp. 73–84, 130–204.

'handbook'.[21] It was the outcome of a state-sponsored competition for the writing of a new Dutch history that would teach the population the virtues of patriotism and citizenship within the framework of the newly established kingdom. Groen, therefore, continually stressed the God-given mission of the Princes of Orange as the champions of Protestantism and presented what was now the Dutch ruling house as the foundation of Dutch liberty through the ages. These inspiring tendencies culminated, in his view, in the figure of William III. According to Groen, William, even if he was not a monarch in the United Provinces, should have been given the power to direct the Republic as he saw fit. Being constitutionally a many-headed monster, the Dutch Republic, without such firm direction from above, simply lacked the cohesion and strength to pursue the grandiose policies which were needed. The odd feature of Groen's analysis is that he thought that what was needed above all was a strong naval policy, the one thing that the regents always stressed whilst William had put more emphasis on the army, deliberately allowing the English to play the leading role at sea. But while Groen insists on the rightness and necessity of William's strategy at home and abroad, and therefore approves of his hero's English policy, he nevertheless always presents William III as the fulfilment of Dutch national destiny. Describing developments from the Glorious Revolution down to the Treaty of Utrecht, of 1713, Groen cannot but lament the unmistakable decline of Dutch power and, in doing so, has to blame England, a power which looked only to her own needs, first exploiting Dutch money and troops to restore her internal stability and then going on to establish her international position at the expense of the Dutch. He deplores the fact that England could not, nay would not, see the vital importance to the Dutch of their 'barrier' in the southern Netherlands. He blames England which settled matters with France as soon as she had attained her own goals. Here we may ask whether the fact that in the 1830s, when Groen was writing, Belgian independence, sponsored by Britain, was being negotiated at the expense of the concept of a United Netherlands did not serve as a painful reminder of English treatment of the Dutch in the years preceding the Peace of Utrecht? In the end, Groen saw only a state – the Dutch Republic – which had given its best for the good of others and, in particular, of Britain and had received little or nothing in return. By a strange turn of mind, he castigated the regents for opposing William's policies and power whilst he lived, and failing to accept a strong, or, indeed, any successor to the Stadholderate after his death, whilst at the same time seeing the tying of the Republic to an ungrateful England as the root of Dutch humiliation and decline.

Not all nineteenth-century Dutch history writing adopted such an openly pro-Orangist stance. In the same years that Groen wrote his *Handboek*, N. G. van

[21] G. Groen van Prinsterer, *Handboek der Geschiedenis van het Vaderland* (2 vols., Leiden, 1846), I, pp. 78–206.

Kampen, who had also competed for the status of state historiographer, completed his two-volume *Geschiedenis der Nederlanden.*[22] Van Kampen was decidedly critical of the policies of William III, largely sharing Wagenaar's opinions on this subject. He also took the view that the Anglo-Dutch alliance forged by William had, from the outset, been seriously detrimental to the commercial and maritime interests of the Dutch, even implying that William sided with his new subjects against his countrymen. Van Kampen does praise the Stadholder-king's European policy while at the same time showing a preference for the situation after his death when his European policy, upheld by Heinsius and Marlborough, continued to dominate but now under a republican regime.

During the late nineteenth century, the prevailing outlook on Dutch history in the Netherlands was moderately Orangist but with a marked lack of enthusiasm for the Anglo-Dutch connection arising from the Glorious Revolution. Especially prominent were the weighty volumes produced by J. P. Arend in the 1850s as his *Algemene Geschiedenis des Vaderlands*,[23] and continued by three well-known historians till the fifteen-volume series was completed in the early 1890s. Arend's history, buttressed by long excerpts from original documents, pamphlets, and letters, cannot be said to be as strongly Orangist as most preceding nineteenth-century general works. On the other hand, it cannot be said to adopt a pro-regent stance either. The overall impression conveyed by the several hundred pages devoted to the period of William III and the Glorious Revolution is one of cool detachment coloured by a certain anti-English attitude, fed by the depicting in vivid prose of such unedifying episodes as the defeat by the French of the combined Anglo-Dutch fleet off Beachy Head in 1690, a humiliation roundly blamed by the Dutch (not without justification) on the English.

The early years of the twentieth century saw the publication of no less than three multi-volume general histories of the Netherlands. The first of these, the *Geschiedenis van het Nederlandse Volk*,[24] written at the turn of the century by the Leiden professor P. J. Blok, is often considered to be of monumental dullness. My own view, however, is that it is still eminently readable. Blok is an obvious Orangist and a warm admirer of William III who, in his eyes, was one of the greatest personalities of the Dutch seventeenth century. He accepts that for the Stadholder-king war was not an end in itself but the only means to arrive at a secure and lasting peace and that, in consequence, everything else had to be subordinated to the needs of his war policy. Thus Blok, when discussing what William failed to do, such as attempting to restructure the Dutch

[22] N. G. van Kampen, *Verkorte Geschiedenis der Nederlanden* (3 vols., Haarlem, 1837), esp. II.
[23] J. P. Arend, *Algemene Geschiedenis des Vaderlands* (15 vols., Amsterdam, 1840–82), IV, part 2.
[24] P. J. Blok, *Geschiedenis van het Nederlandsche Volk* (2nd edn, 4 vols., Leiden, 1912–15), III, pp. 193–340.

political system and the (in Dutch eyes) less laudable things that he did do – such as his going too far in humouring English sensibilities in the drawing up of the 1689 treaty of alliance – tends always to explain and justify these actions in terms of William's overriding European aims. While Blok does see the makings of decline in the Dutch situation of the late seventeenth century, it is noticeable that for him decline only really begins after William's death when the Republic lacked a firm hand to guide the Dutch through the dangers and intricacies of the opening years of the new century. The alliance with England was a dangerous venture. The Dutch and English being at once allies and great economic and maritime rivals in the Mediterranean, East Indies, the Spanish colonies, and the Spanish Netherlands, the outcome of the War of the Spanish Succession (1702–13) had inevitably to be a bitter disappointment for one or the other maritime power. In the end, the English, playing a double game, betrayed their Dutch allies and pocketed the gains.

The second Dutch general history of our century and, probably, the most famous of all the Dutch general histories – though it is certainly not the most readable – is, of course, Pieter Geyl's *Geschiedenis van de Nederlandsche Stam*,[25] the only one of these works, as far as I know, to be translated, and into several languages at that! Geyl has rightly become renowned for his attempt to compose a history of all the Netherlands, the original seventeen provinces rather than just the area that formed the Republic. He postulates an underlying cultural unity for the whole region of the Netherlands but a unity which was fractured and finally broken for all practical purposes by the vicissitudes of politics and the self-interest of power groups. In Geyl's vision, the House of Orange had a national mission, viz, to unite the seventeen Netherlands, but continually failed to fulfil it. With regard to William III, Geyl takes the view that the Prince looked on the Republic essentially as a pawn in his relentless, Europe-wide chess contest with Louis XIV. For the Dutch, William's Grand Design was full of danger. The English alliance in effect brought about what three preceding Anglo-Dutch wars had failed to do: the alliance forced the Dutch to abandon their maritime supremacy and acquiesce in inferiority. Therefore Geyl cites with approval the strong criticism which many Dutchmen, from the 1690s onwards voiced against William III's policies. In the end the Dutch felt duped because more and more they had to play second fiddle to the English whilst paying for a costly war which brought them fewer rewards than they had reckoned on gaining.

The eight-volume *Geschiedenis van Nederland*,[26] published in the late 1930s, reveals the profound preoccupation with economic history of its general editor, the Amsterdam historian H. Brugmans. He himself wrote the volumes dealing with the early modern period. It is remarkable that in his treatment of William

[25] Pieter Geyl, *Geschiedenis van de Nederlandsche Stam* (4 vols., Amsterdam, 1930–7), III, pp. 13–120.
[26] H. Brugmans (ed.), *Geschiedenis van Nederland* (8 vols., Amsterdam, 1935–8), V, 193–217, 341–47.

37 *The Verdict of the Scales (August 1692).*
This political print is a reply to the French success in capturing Namur (in Dutch, Namen) in June 1692, a week after the battle at La Hougue. This setback to the Anglo-Dutch cause was due to William III's difficulties in assembling in time the allied field army in the southern Netherlands. The print depicts a huge pair of scales suspended from a world globe. To the left is weighed the Anglo-Dutch naval victory at La Hougue which is shown to be convincingly the weightier triumph, with Admirals Russell and (seated in the foreground) Almonde looking on. Behind the right-hand scale, with the sun shining mockingly over the Anglo-Dutch fleet behind him, stands Louis XIV flanked by a group including Madame de Maintenon and (in the foreground) the maréchal de Luxembourg, commander of the French army in the Spanish Netherlands. Louis places the arms of Namur together with an infant prince (presumably James, Prince of Wales) in the scale but, despite the energetic efforts of the Devil to assist, the contents of this scale remain obstinately less weighty than those of the scale opposite. Assuming that the prince is the Prince of Wales, the younger lady standing next to Madame de Maintenon, holding the infant, would then be Mary of Modena and the gentleman standing next to Louis, King James II.

III and the Glorious Revolution most of the considerations which had loomed large in the interpretations put forward by his predecessors are given scant attention. Brugmans tends to concentrate on different issues. He is highly critical of the Prince's failure to establish a better form of government in the Netherlands and of his consistent use of corrupt and immoral favourites in provincial politics.

Surprisingly, he scarcely mentions the making of the Anglo-Dutch alliance and special relationship and fails to remark on its many negative consequences for the Dutch economy. Consequently, Brugmans' work does not leave one with any impression of the impact of the Glorious Revolution on the Dutch, positive or negative.

In recent decades Dutch historiography shows both the persistence of old points of view and the variability of new fashions even if sometimes adopted with much of the passion which infused the old faiths. Reading the twelve-volume *Algemene Geschiedenis der Nederlanden*, publication of which began in the 1950s,[27] one notices how the chapters devoted to the period of William III are pervaded by a strong conviction of the importance of the economic factor, a belief rooted perhaps in contemporary preoccupations since for the Netherlands, as for much of the rest of Europe, the years following the Second World War were a period of economic reconstruction. Kramer, the author of these chapters, sees the Glorious Revolution in England as the victory of a class which, at least in part, was identified with commercial interests. It was not to be expected that such a victory would produce policies in any way accommodating to the needs and aspirations of England's greatest commercial rival. Consequently, there were no feelings of gratitude in Parliament. All the advantages of the 1689 treaty accrued to the English who secured the primary role at sea whilst the Dutch, losing their former pre-eminence in this vital sphere, were saddled with a costly and unrewarding war on land. The Glorious Revolution, in his view, was glorious only for the English. For the northern Netherlands it meant giving up everything that had given them their strength and precipitated a process of steep decline. In Kramer's view William himself was partly to blame for he not only tolerated what happened but, for political and strategic reasons, actually encouraged the growth of the English fleet, of English power, and of English penetration of overseas markets. The two great wars with France down to the Treaty of Utrecht, in 1713, allegedly brought enormous profits to the English while at the same time crippling Dutch public finance. Even the southern Netherlands 'barrier' which was finally realized turned out to be more profitable to the English than the Dutch as it gave England a free hand in the Flemish ports.

In another general history of the Netherlands, that by A. and H. Algra, the Christian faith and related ideological preoccupations obtrude even in the title: *Dispereert niet.*[28] A staunch adherent of the Dutch Reformed Church and fervent romantic, Algra writes in the nineteenth-century tradition established by Groen, depicting the House of Orange as the bulwark of Protestantism and the Stadholders as the guarantors of liberty. But, as with Groen, the final touchstone

[27] J. A. van Houtte, J. F. Niermeyer and J. Presser *et al.* (eds.), *Algemene Geschiedenis der Nederlanden* (12 vols., Utrecht, 1949–58), VII, pp. 153–61, 321–38 (chapters by J. Kramer).
[28] A. and H. Algra, *Dispereert Niet* (5 vols., Franeker, 1973), II, pp. 416–30.

for Algra is the fate of the Dutch nation and here William III fails on two accounts with respect to both his domestic and his international policy. After the Glorious Revolution William did not utilize his expanded power to establish a proper – read monarchical – system of government in the Netherlands. His rule was marred by his selection of favourites and the way he used them to manipulate the politics of faction to achieve his ends. This left the Republic a rudderless ship on the event of his death. Once again we are told in no uncertain terms that the Anglo-Dutch alliance served only English interests. Algra cites approvingly a Dutch doggerel that went around after the battle of Beachy Head where the English left the Dutch to face the French broadsides on their own and take the losses, resulting in an ignominious defeat for the supposedly combined fleet. Algra notes that the perfidious English admiral responsible was not even properly punished.

In the *Winkler Prins Geschiedenis der Nederlanden*, published in four volumes in the late 1970s, we find a tendency to depersonalize the historical picture.[29] As a result of William III's policies the Republic incurred heavy new international commitments. At the same time, during his Stadholderate the former independence, the economic superiority, even the cultural identity of the Dutch Republic began to fade. Yet, according to Schöffer, one of the authors, it would not do to blame the Stadholder-king but rather the international situation as a whole. William did, through his vigorous leadership, prevent the untimely demise of the Republic in 1672. He then went on to make the Republic the key nexus of the international balance of power system. However, the costs of performing this role proved too high. The inevitable result was crisis at home and loss of power and prestige abroad. The Republic lapsed into decline.

In the new (and for several decades probably the last) 'General History of the Netherlands', a heavily criticized fifteen-volume compilation published in the late 1970s and early 1980s,[30] the chapters dealing with the period of William III were written by the late D. J. Roorda. Roorda was the Dutch historian who seemed most obviously destined to write a modern scholarly biography of the Stadholder-king,[31] the first Dutchman to attempt a major treatment since the authoritative historical biographies of Japikse and Oudendijk.[32] However,

[29] J. A. Bornewasser, R. C. van Caenegem, H. P. H. Jansen, I. Schöffer and H. van der Wee (eds.), *Winkler Prins Geschiedenis der Nederlanden* (3 vols., Amsterdam and Brussels, 1977), II, pp. 199 *et seq.* (chapter by I. Schöffer), and p. 204 *et seq.* (chapter by G. J. Schutte).

[30] D. P. Blok, W. Prevenier, D. J. Roorda *et al.* (eds.), *Algemene Geschiedenis der Nederlanden* (15 vols., Haarlem, 1977–83), VIII, pp. 292, *et seq.* (chapter by D. J. Roorda), and IX, pp. 16 *et seq.* (chapter by A. J. Veenendaal).

[31] D. J. Roorda, 'Prins Willem III, de Stadhouder-koning', in C. Tamse (ed.), *Nassau en Oranje in de Nederlandse Geschiedenis* (Alphen aan de Rijn, 1979), pp. 155–86.

[32] N. Japikse, *Prins Willem III, de Stadhouder-koning* (2 vols., Amsterdam, 1930–3), and J. Oudendijk, *Willem III* (Amsterdam, 1954); further on these two works, see Murk van der Bijl, 'Prins Willem III, King William III. Een historiografische verkenning', *Groniek. Gronings Historisch Tijdschrift*, 101 (1988), pp. 122–4.

Roorda's vision is in some respects a somewhat odd one precisely because, as it seems to me at least, his view of how the Glorious Revolution has appeared in the Dutch historiographical tradition is a distorted one. He writes as if Dutch historiography generally presents William III's expedition to England, and the events of the Glorious Revolution, as a happy conclusion to a preceding period of Anglo-Dutch tension and ill-feeling. Yet, clearly, this is not at all the impression which one gains from a reading of the general histories cited in this essay. Most Dutch historians since the eighteenth century have agreed in depicting the last decade of the seventeenth century as the beginning of the decline of the Dutch Republic, a decline which was definitely hastened if not caused by the new special relationship and alliance with England.

By concentrating on a structure-of-politics analysis that reflects both a fashion in Dutch historiography and the Namierite origins of his approach, first manifested in his highly influential thesis on Dutch 'party and faction' in the 1670s, Roorda does indeed illuminate many aspects of William III's management of affairs in the Dutch Republic. His main concern is to explain how William succeeded in so effectively managing the political scene in the Dutch provinces and at The Hague both before and after the Glorious Revolution, uncovering the network of the Prince's favourites and clients at home and his methods of manipulating the political factions in the town councils and among the landed gentry, and therefore also in the provincial assemblies. In doing so, Roorda, whether or not consciously, tends to leave other questions aside. He prefers not to write in terms of a loss of Dutch primacy at sea because, according to him, the English were already in any case the stronger maritime power. Likewise, he plays down the anti-Orangist and anti-English sentiment to be found both amongst the political elite and the common people, arguing that these emotions could, and did, not exert any great influence on (let alone alter) the Prince's political course. How far Roorda's views about William III and the Glorious Revolution will prove influential in the future is especially hard to judge in that, contrary to what might have been expected, the tercentenary celebrations of 1988–9 did not produce any new scholarly biography of the Stadholder-king.

By way of conclusion, two observations seem appropriate. In the first place, it is clear that in the twentieth century a fundamental change has come about in Dutch history writing in general as reflected in accounts of the era of William III and the Glorious Revolution. The grand narrative sweep, the emotion-laden story, the penchant for the attractive anecdote and colourful detail largely disappear from the general histories compiled in the Netherlands. This may well coincide with a change in the function of these products. Quite probably, unlike their nineteenth-century predecessors, they are no longer intended to be part of the culture of the home and household, full of fascinating tales to be studied at home, possibly even read aloud, in the evening, to edify and amuse young and old alike, to instil in all a sense of patriotism, and to inculcate reverence for national values. A parallel development is, of course, the diminishing importance accorded to the role of the individual in history, apparent even in the treatment of so central a figure as William III. Even so, it has to be admitted that none of the historians discussed here actually denies his importance. On the contrary, it is obvious that his role continues to be considered integral to any interpretation of the politics of the period.

In the second place we may conclude that nearly three hundred years of Dutch history writing have produced nothing like a consensus on the period of William III and the Glorious Revolution. The eighteenth-century prevalence of the regents' point of view gave way in the nineteenth century to an emphasis on the profound links between the House of Orange, the national Church and the destiny of the nation. In the twentieth century, by contrast, faith in all the old causes and factions, Orangist and regent, largely evaporated to be replaced by a new sort of fervour, viz., for the quickly passing fashions of contemporary historiography. But through all the changes in the way the era of the Glorious Revolution is presented in Dutch historiography one element remains constant: a strong sense of disillusionment with English behaviour, indeed a feeling of betrayal even. Instead of being grateful to the Dutch whose help was decisive in changing their political destiny by gaining them their liberty, the English took advantage of the situation to strengthen themselves at the expense of the Dutch. No sooner had the fateful Anglo-Dutch alliance of 1689 been forged than the English began ousting the Dutch from what was seen as their rightful position in world trade and navigation. Should one perhaps conclude that what holds true for politics holds true for historiography as well: if it is based on faith, it is bound to meet with this kind of profound disappointment?

Chapter 16

Epilogue: the Glorious Revolution

HUGH TREVOR-ROPER

The Glorious Revolution of 1688–9 in England was made by an alliance of three parties, or at least three political or ideological groups: Whigs, who provided its necessary motive force; Tories, who provided its necessary parliamentary majority; and radicals, who sought to provide its philosophy. Without the Whigs it would never have got up the necessary steam; without the Tories it would never have been carried through; without the radicals it would have lacked a continuing philosophical appeal. These three parties, united against James II, preserved their uneasy unity so long as there was a possibility that he, or his male descendants, being Roman Catholic, might be restored to the throne. They continued to preserve it long afterwards on ritual occasions. And yet on each such occasion their internal differences would break through, adding a nice flavour of controversy – a sign of its continuing significance – to the interpretation of the Revolution.

After 1715, when the Revolution had been secured by the Hanoverian succession, the Whigs, being settled in power, imposed their own interpretation on it. It became their revolution, almost their monopoly. It was they who trumpeted its glory; and although, in their practice, they conveniently modified some of its original aims, in their public utterances they presented their ancestors as its true authors and themselves as its rightful heirs. Meanwhile they took over some old Tory practices and adapted – some would say exenterated – some old radical ideas. Having thus adjusted it to their taste, they placed it at the centre of English history and saw to it that it was properly celebrated. Every year it would be 'thankfully remembered in the public services of the restored Church', and societies with appropriate names – the London Revolution Society, the Constitutional Society, the Society for the Defence of the Bill of Rights – would meet to commemorate it with sermons and dinners. The chosen day of commemoration was 4 November, the birthday of the Great Deliverer, William of Orange, the eve of his landing in Torbay. That was no doubt very proper response to the annual sermons and celebrations on 30 January, when Tories remembered the royal martyr, Charles I.[1]

[1] *An Abstract of the History and Proceedings of the Revolution Society in London* (London, 1789); cf., in general, E. C. Black, *The Association: Extraparliamentary Political Organisations, 1769–93* (Harvard, 1963), pp. 11, 14, 30, 214–16; H. T. Dickinson, 'The Eighteenth-Century Debate on the "Glorious Revolution"', *History*, 61 (1976), pp. 28–45.

However, these ritual exercises could not altogether submerge the original passions which had concurred in making the Revolution. All through the years of the Whig Ascendancy the voice of 'real Whigs' could be heard, often from the provinces – from Scotland, Ireland, America – protesting that the original 'Revolution Principles' had been betrayed by the political establishment. In the 1770s the American Revolution gave a new, disquieting power to these voices, but there was even worse to come. How unfortunate that the first centenary of our Glorious Revolution should be followed so closely by a much less respectable, indeed in the end a terrifying revolution in France! The consolidating fears which had held the various parties together had, by now, dissolved. The Jacobite threat had been extinguished in 1746; the Stuart dynasty, reduced to one elderly bachelor in Rome, was all but extinct; and without this necessary cement the old internal divisions were re-inflamed and exposed.[2]

They were exposed – and how splendidly they were exposed! – in the famous controversy between Edmund Burke and Tom Paine: a controversy fired initially by the commemorative sermon of the Rev. Richard Price to the London Revolution Society at Old Jewry on 4 November 1789. It was Price's sermon ending in a dithyrambic exaltation of the American and French Revolutions with their rational new constitutions,[3] which provoked Burke to launch his famous tirade, defending the ancient, organic, elastic constitution of England, which the pragmatic Revolution of 1688 had preserved, against the 'geometrical and arithmetical constitution' of the French National Assembly; and it was Burke's tirade which, in its turn, would provoke Paine to write his equally famous rejoinder the *Rights of Man*. In that controversy two revolutions faced each other, the historical and the philosophical. Burke was able to prophesy the capture of the French Revolution by a Bonaparte and to supply a gospel of European resistance to French imperialism. To Paine all this was 'spouting rant', 'a chivalric rhapsody', a 'pantomime'. As for the Glorious Revolution of England, so cried up by Burke, that, he exclaimed, in another century would be altogether forgotten: 'mankind will then scarcely believe that a country calling itself free would send to Holland for a man, and clothe him with power, on purpose to put themselves in fear of him, and give him almost a million sterling a year for leave to submit themselves and their posterity, like bondmen and bondwomen, for ever'.[4]

Paine would be proved wrong. A century later the Glorious Revolution was not forgotten. How could it be, when Macaulay had put it back so firmly and so magisterially in the centre of our history – and indeed had given it a new

[2] For the 'real Whigs', see Caroline Robbins, *The Eighteenth-Century Commonwealthman* (Cambridge, Mass., 1959).
[3] Richard Price, *A Discourse on the love of Our Country . . . 4 Nov. 1789* (London, 1789).
[4] E. Burke, *Reflexions on the French Revolution*, in *Works* (6 vols., London, 1815), V, pp. 287, 328–30; T. Paine, *The Rights of Man* (London, 1791), pp. 13, 24, 44, 82.

significance as the motor of economic progress? Just as Burke, in his *Reflexions on the French Revolution* had trounced the 'geometrical' constitutions of the French assembly, so Macaulay, in his essays on Mill and Mackintosh, trounced the 'geometrical' constitutions offered by the English radicals and utilitarians of his day. Politics, he insisted, was an empirical, not a logical science, and the glory of the English Revolution lay not in its ideas but in its lack of ideas, its pragmatism. It was a compromise indeed, but a compromise which, because it rested on organic strength, could be the basis of later progress, whereas any more systematic and coherent revolution, running ahead of its time, would ultimately have foundered, like the French Revolution after it or the English Puritan Revolution before it, in the reaction it would have provoked.

Macaulay's interpretation was classical for the rest of the nineteenth century, and indeed beyond. So in 1888, when the second centenary came round, the Glorious Revolution still held its place in our public history, or mythology. It is true, the commemorations of that year were somewhat muted. Queen Victoria's Jubilee had just taken place and it would have been tactless to cap that royal apotheosis with too public a celebration of an event of which she did not like to hear. Perhaps also it was a bad time at which to boast of the victory of the Boyne. But Whigs were still around, active and powerful. A committee was formed to do justice to the occasion; a statue of the Great Deliverer was set up at Torquay, to commemorate his landing; and in Derbyshire the duke of Devonshire, as lord lieutenant, organized a church service, a gigantic procession, formed or witnessed (we are told) by 40,000 persons, and a great banquet.[5] The Cavendish family had done very well out of the Revolution, and were very conscious of their ancestor's part in it, as the pompous Latin inscription in the new hall of Chatsworth showed.

Today Whig mythology, even the Whig history of Macaulay, is out of fashion: out with the Whig party, whose relics were destroyed by Lloyd George, out with the death of Macaulay's intellectual heir and continuator, G. M. Trevelyan. Into the vacuum thus created moved the heirs of the other parties. First the allies whom the Whigs, in their days of triumph, had eclipsed: the radicals, the Marxists, who now saw the Revolution as the triumph of the capitalist bourgeoisie, and the Tories, disciples of Sir Lewis Namier, who saw it as an episode in 'high politics', with no deep social or economic content. These, of course, were still 'Revolution Tories', the heirs of Halifax and Nottingham, of those Tories who had been parties to the consensus of 1688. Then, in 1980, when English Toryism cut itself free from consensus, there emerged another historical party, the self-styled 'revisionists', the new Jacobites, who rejected

[5] The celebrations of 1888 are recorded in *The Times* (4 Dec. and 19 Dec. 1888). I am grateful to Mr J. F. A. Mason and Mr Colin Matthew for their observations on this subject.

the Revolution altogether, dismissing it as a mere 'petulant outburst',[6] insignificant except as a bold, bad act of treachery to an anointed king. With them we are back in 1688: Locke, Burke, Paine are outdated; Filmer and Brady live again.

Not regarding myself as an adherent of any of these parties, but aware of their flickering knives, I wish to start from the safety of undisputed ground. Whatever their differences, all the historians of the Revolution agree that, whether treacherous or glorious, superficial or profound, it was a decisive act. Men did not blunder into it unwillingly, as they had blundered into the civil war of 1642. They took firm decisions, knowing full well the probable consequences. They knew that their action demanded great political skill, careful planning, strong nerves, and that it entailed enormous risks: risks through disunity, delay, mere ill luck. How could they not know? Their whole lives had been spent in the shadow of the civil wars, the republic, the usurpation. All those disasters had stemmed from a well-prepared programme of reform which had gone wrong. And then there were their own fierce internal divisions only a few years ago. Nevertheless, laying aside these divisions, they were now drawn together in a perilous adventure by a conviction of overwhelming imminent danger. In their secret 'invitation' to William of Orange they urged him to come without delay, to save the liberties of England 'before it be too late'.

William did indeed come speedily. But he came for his own reasons, not theirs, to save the liberty not of England but of his own country, which, he believed, was in similar peril, and whose peril meant much more to him than any threat to the liberties or privileges of Englishmen. He too took an enormous risk. He left the Netherlands exposed to foreign attack and sailed, with his invading force, the whole length of the Channel, past that strong English fleet on which James II had bestowed such care. There was no comforting precedent for success either in such an invasion or in such a rebellion. Monmouth had failed, Argyll had failed. He was attempting what Philip II of Spain had attempted exactly a hundred years ago; and Philip II had failed too. Even if his army, unlike that of Philip, should succeed in landing, what guarantee had he of success? James II's standing army – it was one of the charges against him – was very different from the militia of Elizabeth. And how could he rely on the cohesion of his English allies? He knew, only too well, the fickleness, the treachery of the English, including, especially, the English Whigs. He too was well aware that the last aristocratic rebellion against the Stuarts had led to a decade of 'blood and confusion'. Short of quick and complete success (and how could he, or anyone, be sure of that?), he might well, as Louis XIV hoped and indeed expected, be entangled for years in that incalculable island.

[6] J. C. D. Clark, *Revolution and Rebellion: State and Society in England in the Seventeenth and Eighteenth Centuries* (Cambridge, 1986), p. 130.

We know that in fact this did not happen. But who could have predicted the accidents which prevented it: the winds which bottled James' fleet in port and carried William's to land; the nervous collapse of James, who had always hitherto shown such resolution; his 'flight' from London, which enabled his Whig and Tory opponents to sink their ideological differences in the imperatives of the hour? And if we cannot assume this, then we have to ask, what force, what conviction, impelled the conspirators to take this fearful risk? Why did they believe – both the Englishmen for their reasons and the Dutchman for his – that they all stood on the razor's edge, that they must act decisively together, that it was now or never? I do not believe that the answer to such a question is to be sough in 'high politics', in personal 'petulance' or 'treachery', or in economic interest. Such slender motives cannot carry men through so huge a risk. The only force which can unite men of different, even opposite interests in desperate common action is overriding common fear. The men who acted together in 1688 believed that they were facing a fearful threat: that they were threatened – to use their own words – with 'popery and slavery'.

Popery and slavery are abstract terms. What, in 1688, did they mean? If we are to answer this question, we must, I believe, look at the Revolution, as they did, in a large context, in both time and space: in time, because men do not live in one moment only, their philosophy is formed by the accumulated experience of their lives, and those of their generation; in space, because England was not, except in a geographical sense, an island. It was, is, always has been, part of Europe.

Most of the Englishmen who took an active part in the Revolution of 1688 were, at that time, middle-aged. Their minds had been formed in the middle years of the century: troubled years in Europe as in England. They were conscious that, throughout Europe, royal power was becoming 'absolute' – not absolute in a literal sense, not arbitrary, tyrannical (though they sometimes used these adjectives), but centralized, authoritarian, its authority buttressed by a subservient law. This process they ascribed not to the objective momentum of politics but to the machiavellian policy of power-hungry rulers. They also observed that those rulers who were most successful in building up and preserving such power were Roman Catholics: indeed, that Counter-Reformation Catholicism was a kind of magic ointment, warranted to preserve such a monarchy, once established, against disintegration or reform. This view was held by monarchs too. It was indeed a truism of the time.

One of those who held it was the Catholic Queen of Charles I, Henrietta Maria. She considered that her husband had made a great mistake in seeking to base an authoritarian monarchy on the fragile basis of the Anglican Church, which, not being a true Church, lacked the essential preservative ingredients and, in consequence, had both failed him and itself dissolved in ruin. Why could he not have learned the lesson that her father, Henri IV, had so usefully learned? These views she pressed, in her widowed exile in the 1650s, on her two sons, who found them plausible, and who both, after the Restoration, in their different ways – the one indolent and astute, the other a conscientious bigot – sought to realize them. The opportunity to do so came after 1667, with the fall of Clarendon, who had made the Restoration on the old Anglican base. It was then that the courtier Bab May 'ketched the King about the legs and joyed him, and said that this was the first time that ever he could call him King of England, being freed this great man'.[7] Being really king, he could embark on a personal policy, and in his astute, indolent way, he did.

The crucial years were 1670–2. In 1670, by the secret Treaty of Dover, Charles II promised Louis XIV, against payment of £200,000 to be made at a convenient time, to declare himself a Roman Catholic and to import a French army to assist in the conversion of England. In 1672 he prepared the way by publishing, on his own authority, a 'Declaration of Indulgence', i.e. a general toleration for Dissenters from the established Church. Such a toleration would have many practical advantages. It would weaken the established Church and engage the support of the Protestant Dissenters. It would also remove the disabilities of the Roman Catholic Dissenters and enable them, with the help of royal patronage and the 6,000 French troops, to play their part in the great design.

This personal policy of 1670–2 had its foreign dimension, for by the same Treaty of Dover Charles II also committed himself to a war against the Netherlands in collusion with Louis XIV. Such a war would not necessarily be unpopular in England. If successful, it would be profitable to English mercantile interests, which would thus be won over, and their increased profits would in turn, through the increased revenue from customs, improve the finances, and therefore the independence, of the Crown. Meanwhile the French subsidy would help. So a coherent policy was devised: toleration of Dissent, Catholic as well as Protestant; mercantile support; royal affluence. This much was avowed. The other element in the plan, the catholicization of England, was secret.

This coherent personal policy of Charles II soon foundered, and it foundered first of all in the Netherlands. When the French armies invaded the Netherlands, a popular revolt swept the old 'appeasing' rulers aside and brought the young William of Orange to the power from which he had hitherto been carefully excluded. Thanks to him, the invasion was halted. In that great national crisis, when the Dutch Republic was nearly extinguished by French power, William's life acquired its purpose. The Republic, he resolved, must never again be exposed to such peril. European coalitions must be organized to protect its independence, not now from Spain – that danger was over – but from France. Above all,

[7] Samuel Pepys, *Diary*, entry for 11 Nov. 1667.

England must not fall into dependence on France. That combination could be fatal to the Netherlands – as it would have been, had the policy of Louis XIV and Charles II succeeded. In fact, on this occasion, thanks to the Orangist coup d'état of 1672, it had not succeeded. The Netherlands had been saved. With the failure of the French attack, and the prolongation of the war, Charles II's coherent policy began to crumble. England pulled out of an expensive and indecisive war. The policy of religious toleration failed too. Charles II found himself obliged to withdraw the Declaration of Indulgence. Finally, his secret treaty became less secret. Instead of granting toleration to Roman Catholics, he was forced to accept a Test Act excluding them from office, and his cabinet – half accomplices, half dupes – disintegrated in disarray. He did not declare himself a Catholic. He never would.

Thus already in 1670–2 we see, as it were, a dress-rehearsal for the drama of 1687–8. Some of the actors would change in the interim, but one, William of Orange, would not. Nor would the plot of the play. Weaving his coalitions from The Hague, William, himself half-English, and from 1677 married to the heiress presumptive to the English Crown, watched it progress. Charles II had indeed been forced to draw back from his great design; but was that design abandoned, or merely suspended? In particular, would it be revived if or when the King's Catholic brother should succeed him? In the later 1670s the men who would be called Whigs were convinced that it would, and so they mounted a determined attempt to exclude that brother from the succession, unscrupulously exploiting for their purpose the *canard* of the Popish Plot. That attempt ultimately failed, broken on the resistance of the 'Tories' who, whatever their apprehensions, clung to that lifeline of the monarchy, divine hereditary right. When it had failed, Charles II, exploiting its failure, resumed his old policy. But after those traumatic experiences he resumed it more cautiously. Whatever his own religious preferences, he would not now meddle with popery. That was too dangerous a subject for public policy: a powder-keg which had nearly blown him up. Instead, he would build up his power with the aid of the new Tory party which had proved its worth and strength in the days of crisis, and he would rest it, ideologically, at least for the time being, as his father had done, on the Anglican Church, now greatly strengthened, since Laudian times, by lay support. Half a loaf was better than no bread. Louis XIV would understand, and pay. Perhaps, when royal power had been secured, it could be used to complete the policy which, in 1672, he had been forced to suspend.

Perhaps, perhaps not: or at least not yet. In his last years, when he had dismissed his last Parliament, broken the organization of his enemies, and remodelled the institutions which they had used against him, Charles II felt that he was as absolute a king as any of his predecessors. He had also learned an important lesson. Popery might be the preservative of monarchy, but only if carefully and correctly applied by a qualified physician. The dose had to be adjusted to the patient, for it could encounter dangerous allergies or cause dangerous side-effects. England, he knew, was a difficult patient. He also knew that his brother was not a careful physician. Might he, if he were put in charge, apply it too rashly and risk disaster? In his last days, when he realized that his brother would in fact be put in charge, Charles II seems to have had doubts and to have contemplated a complete reversal of recent policy, or at least tactics. He would declare his own Protestant son, the duke of Monmouth, legitimate and thus disinherit his Catholic brother. But death forestalled him. 'Ah, cruel Fate!' Monmouth wrote in his diary on hearing that his hopes, so recently raised, had been so suddenly dashed.[8] If the report was true, it means that Charles II believed that the time for an open Catholic policy had not yet come; that the monarchy needed to be still further strengthened on its present Anglican base before the perilous leap could be risked; that meanwhile it was essential to move slowly; and that his brother could not be trusted to go slow. If so, he was dead right.

Here we must leave historical detail and face two more general but important questions. First, could royal 'absolutism' have been built up by a continuation of Charles II's methods, on a Protestant base? Secondly, what was the real significance of the violent, even paranoid hatred of popery in England: a hatred which had been unscrupulously mobilized in the attempt to exclude James from the succession in the 1670s and which, in the end, would bring him down?

To these questions, in this brief space, I can only offer tentative answers. To the first I would simply say that a radical transformation of government – a change from the co-operation of monarch and estates to institutionalized, centralised monarchical rule – was not impossible, even in England. It had happened in several countries in contemporary Europe, and history had shown that it could happen, and the process be completed, within a very short time. Power, once established, is a magnet and soon exercises its attractive force. How easily the princes of Italy had taken over the old communes! Particular interests soon adjust themselves to new realities. Merchants are not necessarily hostile to central power, which is also patronage, especially in a mercantilist age. By 1685, in England, many old Whigs had made their peace with the government; those who were obstinate were in exile, and had resorted – sure sign of despair – to attempted assassination. If Charles II had lived longer, or if James II had continued his methods, as indeed he did until 1687, it is difficult to argue that those policies would necessarily have failed. The crux was finance; but that

8 Historians have never been able to agree on this alleged episode. The evidence is conflicting and irreconcilable. See James Welwood, *Memoirs of the most material Transactions in England* (7th edn, London, 1736), pp. 319–23; H. C. Foxcroft, *The Life and Letters of George Savile, Bart., first Marquis of Halifax* (2 vols, London, 1898), I, pp. 423–6; Ronald Hutton, *Charles II, King of England, Scotland and Ireland* (Oxford, 1989), p. 441.

problem now seemed soluble: increase of trade and of customs on trade could meet foreseeable peacetime needs. War indeed made a difference: Charles I might have succeeded but for the cost of the Scottish war, so skilfully forced upon him; but Charles II had secured himself against that danger. No latterday Pym or Hampden was capable of mobilizing an invasion, or a parliament, against him. Even when James II had succeeded to the throne, but while he was still continuing his brother's methods, his Parliament supported him and the invasions mounted by his exiled enemies were easily repelled. We do an injustice to the men of 1688, and indeed to their precursors, if we suggest that the threat which faced them was unreal, either then or half a century before.

That the threat was independent of religion, that slavery could have been imposed without popery – indeed could even have been introduced more smoothly without it, although popery might be added when it was secure, as its final fixative – was recognized by contemporaries. In 1694, Robert Molesworth, who had been ambassador in Denmark, published *An Account of Denmark*, in which he described how, in 1660, that kingdom had 'in four days' time been changed from an estate little different from aristocracy to as absolute a monarchy as any is at present in the world'; and he argued that Charles II, in his last years, had almost achieved this in England, and that James II could have achieved it, 'had he left the business of religion untouched'.[9] For it was the change of policy in 1687, the precipitate attempt to substitute a Roman Catholic for an Anglican base, which, by alienating the Tory party and the established Church, had begun the ruin of James II.

So we come to the second general question: what was the real significance of the paranoid anti-popery which the opponents of James II were able to mobilize against him? The answer, I believe, lies at two levels, one rational, the other irrational. On a rational level, the politicians who opposed the Stuart kings were convinced that Roman Catholicism, though allowable as a personal religion, was, in politics, inseparable from the absolutism which they feared. Therefore it could be tolerated only in private. This view was held by most literate Protestant Englishman. Milton, who advocated universal toleration of all forms of Christianity, excepted Roman Catholics – although he had good personal relations with his own Catholic kinsmen – on the ground that Catholicism was not Christian at all.[10] Archbishop Ussher, Oliver Cromwell, Andrew Marvell were equally ambivalent. John Locke, who wrote explicitly in favour of the natural right to toleration of all religions, equally explicitly denied that right to Catholics, on the same grounds. For this rational and limited political anti-popery of the educated classes there was ample justification in contemporary Europe. It did

[9] Robert Molesworth, *An Account of Denmark as it was in the year 1692* (London, 1694), pp. 43, 73, 259. On Molesworth, see Robbins, *The Eighteenth-Century Commonwealthman*, pp. 88–133.

[10] D. M. Wolfe (ed.), *The Complete Prose Works of John Milton* (8 vols., New Haven, Conn., 1953–82), VII, p. 256.

not provide a reason for persecuting papists, only for excluding them from political activity.

The irrational anti-popery of the common people was quite different. It was, I suggest, a form of popular hysteria comparable with the persecution of supposed witches at that time or with anti-semitism at all times. Like them, it had a rationalized justification, but it was essentially irrational, an expression of popular psychology, of a *grande peur*. Moreover, having once been formulated and used for public purposes, it had acquired a momentum of its own: a dangerous momentum which was both increased and prolonged by periodic deliberate mobilization for in certain circumstances it was a means, perhaps the only means, of mobilizing popular violence, if that were judged necessary, against a government which had a monopoly of legitimate, organized force. In 1641 it had been mobilized against Charles I and Archbishop Laud. Since both men were firm Anglicans, it was then rationally indefensible, but it was used unscrupulously and defended cynically as a political necessity. Its use during the Exclusion Crisis, in the exploitation of the 'Popish Plot', was rationally more defensible in that there were some shreds of evidence for such a plot and the heir to the throne who was to be excluded was an avowed Catholic. In 1688 it needed no justification.[11]

Of course the high Tories, the Jacobites, the Nonjurors denied this. They persuaded themselves that James II, when he offered toleration to Roman Catholics, intended no more than he said: that he was simply seeking equal rights for all his subjects. He would be a Catholic king of a Protestant country, just as the Elector of Brandenburg was a Calvinist ruler of a Lutheran country. No doubt this would bring some incidental advantage to his fellow Catholics, but it would not alter the constitution of Church or State. This argument was of course necessary to Protestant Jacobites, as the only solution of the dilemma in which they found themselves: how else could they defend their double loyalty, to the Church and king? It is amusing to hear it advanced today by their modern successors, who thus find themselves commending, in James II, a design to dismantle 'the confessional state' and replace it by 'a plural society' – precisely the policy which they condemn so severely in the Liberals of the 1820s and 1830s, when Catholicism was really ceasing to be committed to a particular political form. But let that pass. The more politically minded Tories of the time did not entertain such views. Forced to decide whether to be consistent with their own past actions – their resolute and successful championship of James' inalienable right to succeed – or to face the unmistakable implications of his present policy, their minds were marvellously concentrated. They swallowed their pride and, with some face-saving formulae, joined their former adversaries and kicked him out.

Indeed, it was their kick which was decisive. Without Tory support in the

[11] I have developed this argument in my *Catholics, Anglicans and Puritans* (London, 1987), pp. 103–6.

country and in Parliament, neither the Revolution nor the subsequent settlement would have been achieved, at least in its actual form, and some respect is due to the men who were prepared, in effect, to admit that their hard-fought battle had been a mistake and their hard-won victory vain, for their opponents had been right. It cannot have been an easy admission. Naturally enough, they did what they could to save their faces, and their former adversaries helped them to do so. Thus the abuses of power which were cited to justify William's invasion, and which would be set out in the Bill of Rights, did not include those practised in the last years of Charles II, when the victorious Tories had been in power. The whole burden of guilt was laid upon James II. This concentration of blame narrowed the context and abridged the pedigree of the Revolution. Historically it was inexact, but it served its immediate practical purpose: it enabled the Tories to make common front with the Whigs rather than be caught in the dilemma, or resort to the weak arguments, of the Nonjurors and Protestant Jacobites.

It is difficult to argue that they were wrong. William Penn, the Quaker, like some other Dissenters, swallowed the bait of the Declaration of Indulgence. From an opponent of Charles II he became an election agent of James II, an active supporter of his policies. He evidently believed that, thanks to his personal influence with the king, the Quakers would be safe; and he preferred the promise of Catholic protection to the reality of Anglican persecution. But what if that personal link were snapped, as ultimately it must be? Could Quakers, or their continental equivalents – Mennonites, Bohemian Brethren, Moravians – be found flourishing under any Catholic monarchy? And what of the Huguenots of France, granted legal toleration in 1598 and now, after their legal immunities had been withdrawn, their aristocratic protectors seduced by the court, and their numbers diminished by constant harassment, summarily ordered to conform or to be expelled from their country? This example of the king of France was quickly followed by his satellite, the duke of Savoy. No doubt, once Roman Catholicism had become firmly entrenched in the English court, and the assets and the patronage of the established Church had been taken over (for that, clearly, was the end of the process of which the attack on the universities was the beginning), the same pressure and the same seduction would have been applied in England; and perhaps, in the end, the same force. So long as James II had no male heir, that argument could be countered, for the heir presumptive was his Protestant daughter, the wife of William of Orange himself. But the birth of the Prince of Wales changed all that. No wonder his adversaries decided that the time had come for desperate measures: to play the anti-popish card. The myth of the warming-pan was the new version of the Popish Plot: factually false, unscrupulously used, but, in a desperate situation, judged to be politically necessary.

The warning example of the French Huguenots must have been particularly obvious to the subjects of James II. Once again it is necessary to recall the context, in time and space, in which the men of 1688 had lived, the memories they had inherited. The fortunes of the French Huguenots had been closely followed in England ever since the reign of Elizabeth. English governments, until the personal rule of Charles I, had supported successive Huguenot enterprises, even *prises d'armes*, in France. A great Huguenot leader, the duc de Rohan, had been godfather to Charles I, and English aristocrats – an earl of Southampton, an earl of Derby – had married into great Huguenot houses. But as the French monarchy became more 'absolute', the Huguenot nobility had been reduced to impotence, and in 1685, the very year in which James II succeeded to the English throne, their last rights were withdrawn. As the exiled Huguenots, including some inconvertible noblemen, sought refuge in England, English Protestant noblemen could see what might well be the fate of their descendants under the 'absolute' rule of a Catholic House of Stuart. The process which had now ended in France was about to begin in England.

The same process could be observed, even more closely, from the Netherlands. The original Revolt of the Netherlands had been sustained, on the spot, by *émigré* French Huguenots. The daughters of the House of Orange were married to great Huguenot leaders. Huguenot noblemen and gentry served as officers in the army of the Prince of Orange. After 1685 their numbers were greatly increased. Holland was then, in the phrase of Pierre Bayle, the great Ark of the refugees. The Prince welcomed them, for he needed their help. The 1680s, the years of apparent creeping absolutism in England, were also the years when Louis XIV's power was being extended most aggressively: the years of the Chambres de Réunion, the invasions and annexations and interventions in Flanders and Germany: Strasburg, Luxemburg, Cologne, the Palatinate. With the Crown of England apparently a paid satellite of France, the situation, seen from the Netherlands, was ominously reminiscent of that of 1672. Once again William was seeking to organize resistance, to persuade the States General and the city of Amsterdam of the danger. The arrival of the Huguenot refugees turned the scale. It weakened the voice of dissent, and strengthened the Orangist party throughout the country. On their side, the Huguenots hailed William as their Joshua, the man chosen by God to restore their fortunes.[12] So the army which he would bring to England and which would fight in Ireland was swollen with Huguenot volunteers. Louis XIV did nothing to hinder the expedition to England. He reckoned that his most formidable enemy was being removed from Europe. Instead, in a few years, he would become its arbiter.

But what of the consequences in England? The astonishing speed and completeness of the Revolution, which constituted part of its 'glory', ensured that, socially, its effects were limited. The great risk, once William had safely landed and

[12] Cf. Erich Haase, *Einführung in der Literatur des Refuge* (Berlin, 1959), p. 119.

thus survived the first hazard, was of civil war. If James II had not lost his nerve and fled, if he had stood firm until the cracks in the alliance had opened up, who can say that civil war would not have broken out? That, after all, was what had happened in the reign of his father, in the great crisis of 1641–2 which was ever present in men's minds. At that time future royalists, like Hyde and Falkland, and future parliamentarians, like Pym and Hampden, had worked together, just as Whigs and Tories would do in 1688–9: it was Charles I's refusal to yield, his conviction that God was on his side and that there were men who would fight his battles – if not in England, then in Scotland and Ireland – which broke up the parliamentary coalition and led to the long struggle for sovereignty. In the course of that struggle, which no one had wanted, radical ideas and radical social forces had emerged. In 1688–9 all these possibilities existed; but the collapse of James II and the presence of an agreed heir enabled a still undivided political nation to settle for a quick compromise. That compromise, in the circumstances, was bound to be conservative. Civil war was confined to Ireland and Scotland, and there isolated. The radicals, the heirs of the Levellers, the Republicans, the Commonwealth-men of the 1640s and 1650s, were given no chance to emerge. The Revolution was therefore, in their eyes, incomplete.

One of those who discovered this was the old republican, Edmund Ludlow. For twenty-nine years he had lived in exile in Switzerland, a centre of conspiracy against the hated House of Stuart. In 1689 he boldly returned to London, in order, as he said, to strengthen the hands of the English Gideon. At the request of the House of Commons the English Gideon promptly ordered his arrest on the old charge of high treason, and he hurried back to Switzerland. Another was John Locke, whom now, with Richard Ashcraft, we must see as a radical. In 1690 Locke would publish his *Two Treatises of Government* (originally written against the rule of Charles II), in order, as he said, 'to establish the throne of our great restorer, our present King William'. That was very sound Whig language: William was presented as the restorer of the ancient English 'mixed' constitution. But privately Locke deplored the compromises of 1689. Why, he asked, did a revolutionary convention concern itself with 'small matters', as if it were an ordinary, traditional parliament when it had a priceless but brief opportunity to mend 'the great frame of the government' and set up a new and lasting constitution 'for the security of civil rights and the liberty and property of all the subjects of the nation'? Like the Levellers forty years before, Locke wished not to amend the government but to 'melt it down and make all new'.[13] Though he would be captured by the eighteenth-century Whigs and made into their philosopher, he looks forward not to Burke and Macaulay but to Tom

[13] Richard Ashcraft, *Revolutionary Politics and Locke's Two Treatises of Government* (Princeton, 1986), pp. 592–600.

Paine and the nineteenth-century Utilitarians. Whether his new model of government, if established, would have lasted is another matter, and is open to question.

The political system – if it can be so called – established by the Revolution did last. That indeed is its great merit. Some of it is with us still. Since it was essentially defensive, the product of determined resistance to innovation, it too was necessarily conservative. The framers of the Bill of Rights insisted that they were defending an ancient constitution: the institution of Parliament, the regularity of parliaments, the parliamentary control of finance, the independence of the judges, the rights of the established national Church. But even a conservative revolution can incidentally liberate new forces and many of the consequences of the Revolution of 1688 were incidental, not intended. For revolutions must be defended against counter-revolution. The Revolution of 1688 was quickly over in England, but its defence involved it, as it had involved the more protracted and bloody revolution of the 1640s, in war in Scotland and Ireland, ending in an oppressive reconquest of Ireland and a parliamentary union with Scotland: here, as in other respects, the completion of the Cromwellian settlement, at less cost, and more durably, but without its social content. It also led to a foreign war, which in turn entailed a Financial Revolution: the founding of the Bank of England, the creation of the National Debt. At the same time it brought continued discrimination against Roman Catholic and indeed – in theory at least – Protestant Dissenters for another 150 years. William III, who has become the tribal hero of the most intolerant sectarianism in the British Isles, would have relieved both Catholics and Protestants, but was prevented. The disastrous attempt of James II to impose both 'popery and slavery' on his country, and even, after his failure, to set up a separate kingdom of Ireland under French protection, rebounded terribly on those whom he had claimed to serve. But what, we must ask, would have been the consequences of his victory: if William's fleet had been destroyed at sea or if his enterprise had foundered in civil war? At once we are lost in vain speculation. One thing we can perhaps venture to say. If James had succeeded in his plans, the English Parliament would not have survived in a recognizably continuous form and thus a vital organ of peaceful change would have been reduced to impotence. Whatever modifications we may make to the classical Whig interpretation, in the end it is difficult to contest Macaulay's thesis, that the English Revolution of 1688 saved England from a different kind of revolution a century later.

Index